THE ROYAL SOCIETY OF LONDON
YEAR BOOK

Supplement to the Year Book for 1976

THE ROYAL SOCIETY
ELECTIONS 1976

Date of Election

1976 ALLEN, GEOFFREY. Professor of Polymer Science at the Imperial College of Science and Technology in the University of London. *Department of Chemical Engineering and Chemical Technology, Imperial College, Prince Consort Road, London, SW7 2BY. (Telephone:* 01-589 5111, *extension* 1900); and 40 *Pine Grove, Lake Road, Wimbledon, London, SW19 7HE. (Telephone:* 01-947 7459); also *Athenaeum.*

1976 ANDREW, SYDNEY PERCY SMITH. Research and Development Group Manager of the Agricultural Division of Imperial Chemical Industries Limited. *Agricultural Division, I.C.I. Limited, Billingham, Cleveland. (Telephone:* Stockton 553601); and *Holland Fen*, 83 *Hutton Avenue, Hartlepool, Cleveland, TS26 9PR. (Telephone:* Hartlepool 5329).

1976 BAKER, PETER FREDERICK. Halliburton Professor of Physiology at King's College in the University of London. *Department of Physiology, King's College, Strand, London, WC2R 2LS. (Telephone:* 01-836 5454, *extension* 2475); and *Meadow Cottage, Bourn, Cambridge. (Telephone:* Caxton 212).

1976 BIGGS, PETER MARTIN, D.Sc. Director of the Houghton Poultry Research Station, Huntingdon. *Houghton Poultry Research Station, Houghton, Huntingdon, Cambridgeshire, PE17 2DA. (Telephone:* St Ives 64101); and *The Willows, London Road, St Ives, Huntingdon, Cambridgeshire, PE17 4ES. (Telephone:* St Ives 63471).

1976 BLACK, JAMES WHYTE. Professor and Head of the Department of Pharmacology at University College in the University of London. *Department of Pharmacology, University College London, Gower Street, London, WC1E 6BT. (Telephone:* 01-387 7050, *extension* 352); and 53 *Wrensfield, Hemel Hempstead, Hertfordshire, HP1 1RP. (Telephone:* Hemel Hempstead 2087).

1976 BLIN-STOYLE, ROGER JOHN. Professor of Theoretical Physics in the University of Sussex. *School of Mathematical and Physical Sciences, University of Sussex, Falmer, Brighton, BN1 9QH. (Telephone:* Brighton 66755); and 14 *Hill Road, Lewes, East Sussex, BN7 1DB. (Telephone:* Lewes 3640).

1976 BRADLEY, DANIEL JOSEPH. Professor of Applied Optics at the Imperial College of Science and Technology in the University of London. *Optics Section, Department of Physics, The Blackett Laboratory, Imperial College, Prince Consort Road, London, SW7 2BZ. (Telephone:* 01-589 5111); also *Athenaeum.*

1976 CADOGAN, JOHN IVAN GEORGE. Forbes Professor of Organic Chemistry in the University of Edinburgh. *Department of Chemistry, University of Edinburgh, West Mains Road, Edinburgh, EH9 3JJ. (Telephone:* 031-667 1081); and 30 *Cluny Drive, Edinburgh* 10. *(Telephone:* 031-447 3363); also *Athenaeum.*

Date of Election

1976 CHALONER, WILLIAM GILBERT. Professor and Head of the Department of Botany at Birkbeck College in the University of London. *Department of Botany, Birkbeck College, Malet Street, London, WC1E 7HX.* (*Telephone:* 01-580 6622); and 20 *Parke Road, London, S.W.*13. (*Telephone:* 01-748 4702).

1976 CHARNOCK, HENRY. Director of the Institute of Oceanographic Sciences and Visiting Professor of Physical Oceanography in the University of Southampton. *Institute of Oceanographic Sciences, Wormley, Godalming, Surrey, GU8 5UB.* (*Telephone: Wormley* 2122); and *Wildcroft, Gasden Lane, Witley, Godalming, Surrey, GU8 5RJ.* (*Telephone: Wormley* 2813).

1976 CLARKE, PATRICIA HANNAH. Professor of Microbial Biochemistry at University College in the University of London. *Department of Biochemistry, University College London, Gower Street, London, WC1E 6BT.* (*Telephone:* 01-387 7050, extension 297); and 11 *Selwyn House, Lansdowne Terrace, London, WC1N 1DJ.* (*Telephone:* 01-278 3918).

1976 EGLINTON, GEOFFREY. Professor of Organic Geochemistry in the University of Bristol. *School of Chemistry, The University, Bristol, BS8 1TS.* (*Telephone: Bristol* 24161, extension 623); and 7 *Red House Lane, Bristol, BS9 3RY.* (*Telephone: Bristol* 683833).

1976 ELLIOTT, ROGER JAMES. Wykeham Professor of Theoretical Physics in the University of Oxford. *Department of Theoretical Physics,* 12 *Parks Road, Oxford, OX1 3PQ.* (*Telephone: Oxford* 53281); and 11 *Crick Road, Oxford.* (*Telephone: Oxford* 58369).

1976 EVANS, LLOYD THOMAS, D.Sc. Chief of the Division of Plant Industry, Commonwealth Scientific and Industrial Research Organization. *Division of Plant Industry, C.S.I.R.O., P.O. Box* 1600, *Canberra City, A.C.T.* 2601, *Australia.* (*Telephone:* 46-5250); and 3 *Elliott Street, Campbell, A.C.T.* 2601, *Australia.* (*Telephone:* 47-7815).

1976 FRÖHLICH, ALBRECHT. Professor of Pure Mathematics at King's College in the University of London. *Department of Mathematics, King's College, Strand, London, WC2R 2LS.* (*Telephone:* 01-836 5454); and 63 *Drax Avenue, London, S.W.*20. (*Telephone:* 01-946 6550).

1976 GIBSON, FRANK WILLIAM ERNEST. Professor of Biochemistry in the Australian National University. *John Curtin School of Medical Research, Australian National University, P.O. Box* 334, *Canberra City, A.C.T.* 2601, *Australia.* (*Telephone:* 49-2499); and 7 *Waller Crescent, Campbell, A.C.T.* 2601, *Australia.* (*Telephone:* 49-8463).

1976 GOODWIN, LEONARD GEORGE, M.B., B.S. Director of Science, The Zoological Society of London. *The Zoological Society of London, Regent's Park, London, NW1 4RY.* (*Telephone:* 01-722 3333); and *Shepperlands Farm, Park Lane, Finchampstead, Berkshire, RG11 4QF.*

1976 GRAY, EDWARD GEORGE. Professor of Anatomy (Cytology) at University College in the University of London. *Department of Anatomy and Embryology, University College London, Gower Street, London, WC1E 6BT.* (*Telephone:* 01-387 7050, extension 306); and 58 *New Park Road, Newgate Street, Hertford, SG13 8RF.*

Date of Election

1976 WATT, WILLIAM, O.B.E. Senior Research Fellow at the Department of Metallurgy and Materials Science in the University of Surrey, and Consultant to the Materials Department of the Royal Aircraft Establishment. *Department of Metallurgy and Materials Science, University of Surrey, Guildford, Surrey, GU2 5XH. (Telephone: Guildford 71281); and Eilean Donan, 28 Avenue Road, Farnborough, Hampshire. (Telephone: Farnborough 42560).*

1976 WHELAN, MICHAEL JOHN, D.Phil. Reader in the Physical Examination of Materials in the University of Oxford. *Department of Metallurgy and Science of Materials, Parks Road, Oxford, OX1 3PH. (Telephone: Oxford 59981); and 18 Salford Road, Old Marston, Oxford, OX3 0RX. (Telephone: Oxford 44556).*

1976 WIDDOWSON, ELSIE MAY, D.Sc. Formerly Head of the Infant Nutrition Division of the Dunn Nutritional Laboratory, Cambridge. *Department of Medicine, Level 5, New Addenbrooke's Hospital, Hills Road, Cambridge. (Telephone: Cambridge 44014, extension 235); and Orchard House, Barrington, Cambridge. (Telephone: Cambridge 870219).*

1976 WOOD, RONALD KARSLAKE STARR. Professor of Plant Pathology at the Imperial College of Science and Technology in the University of London. *Department of Botany, Imperial College, Prince Consort Road, London, S.W.7. (Telephone: 01-589 5111); and Pyrford Woods, Pyrford, near Woking, Surrey. (Telephone: Byfleet 43827).*

FOREIGN MEMBERS

Date of Election

1976 BENZER, PROFESSOR SEYMOUR. *Division of Biology, California Institute of Technology, Pasadena, California 91125, U.S.A.*

1976 MUNK, PROFESSOR WALTER HEINRICH. *Institute of Geophysics and Planetary Physics, Mail Code A-025, Scripps Institution of Oceanography, University of California, San Diego, La Jolla, California 92093, U.S.A.*

1976 SPERRY, PROFESSOR ROGER WOLCOTT. *Division of Biology, California Institute of Technology, Pasadena, California 91125, U.S.A.*

1976 TOWNES, PROFESSOR CHARLES HARD. Nobel Laureate, Physics, 1964. *Department of Physics, University of California, Berkeley, California 94720, U.S.A.*

THE YEAR BOOK

OF THE

ROYAL SOCIETY OF LONDON

1977

LONDON
THE ROYAL SOCIETY

Published by the Royal Society
6 Carlton House Terrace,
London, SW1Y 5AG

No. 81   ISBN 0 85403 084 0

Information in this *Year Book* is corrected to 31 December 1976;
New Year Honours are included

PRINTED IN GREAT BRITAIN FOR THE ROYAL SOCIETY OF LONDON BY
STAPLES PRINTERS LIMITED AT THE STANHOPE PRESS, ROCHESTER, KENT.

CONTENTS

	PAGE
Past Officers of the Royal Society	7
The Foundation of the Royal Society	9
Memorandum on Benefactions	10
Calendar	11
Council and Office Staff	12
The Fellowship—	
List of Fellows	13
List of Foreign Members	100
Fellows and Foreign Members deceased in 1976	105
Fellows and Foreign Members elected in 1976	106
Associate Editors	107
Committees and Boards—	
Regulations	108
Sectional Committees	110
Standing Committees	114
Joint Committees	122
Government Grant Boards	129
Scientific Publications Board	130
Committees on International Relations—	
International Non-Governmental Organizations	131
National Committee for I.C.S.U.	136
British National Committees	137
Public and other responsibilities	156
Statutes of the Royal Society	164
Standing Orders and Procedure—	
Standing Orders of the Royal Society	186
Council Procedure—	
In the nomination of Council	198
In the award of Medals	200
In the appointment of Lecturers	201
In the administration of certain elements of the Parliamentary Grant-in-aid	202
The Society's Medals	207
The Society's Lectures	213
The Society's Library	217
The Society's Publications	219
The Society's Funds	221

	PAGE
Paul Instrument Fund	251
Grants for Travelling Expenses and Organizing Expenses of International Conferences	252
The European Science Exchange Programme	254
Agreements on cooperation between the Royal Society and Scientific Academies and Research Councils of other countries	256
Royal Society Commonwealth Bursaries Scheme	257
Overseas Visiting Professorships	259
Royal Society—Israel Academy Visiting Research Professorships Scheme	260
Royal Society Leverhulme Studentships	261
Royal Society Research Professorships	262
Royal Society Scientific Information Research Fellowships	262
General Regulations governing Royal Society Research Professorships and Appointments	263, 265
Royal Society Research Appointments	267
Report of Council for 1976	270
Organization of Royal Society Office	385
Accounts for 1976 and Treasurer's statement	391
Index	403

RECENT PAST OFFICERS OF THE ROYAL SOCIETY

(In continuation of the lists in *The Record*, pp. 334–44)

Presidents	Tenure of Office
†Sir HENRY DALE, O.M., G.B.E.	30 Nov. 1940–30 Nov. 1945
†Sir ROBERT ROBINSON, O.M.	30 Nov. 1945–30 Nov. 1950
Lord ADRIAN, O.M.	30 Nov. 1950–30 Nov. 1955
†Sir CYRIL HINSHELWOOD, O.M.	30 Nov. 1955–30 Nov. 1960
†Lord FLOREY, O.M.	30 Nov. 1960–30 Nov. 1965
†Lord BLACKETT, O.M., C.H.	30 Nov. 1965–30 Nov. 1970
Sir ALAN HODGKIN, O.M., K.B.E.	30 Nov. 1970– 1 Dec. 1975

Treasurers	
†Sir THOMAS MERTON, K.B.E.	30 Nov. 1939–30 Nov. 1956
Lord PENNEY, K.B.E.	30 Nov. 1956–30 Nov. 1960
†Lord FLECK, K.B.E.	30 Nov. 1960– 6 Aug. 1968
†Sir FREDERICK BAWDEN	30 Nov. 1968– 8 Feb. 1972
Sir JAMES MENTER	18 May 1972–30 Nov. 1976

Biological Secretaries	
Professor A. V. HILL, C.H., O.B.E.	30 Nov. 1935–30 Nov. 1945
Sir EDWARD SALISBURY, C.B.E.	30 Nov. 1945–30 Nov. 1955
†Sir LINDOR BROWN, C.B.E.	30 Nov. 1955–30 Nov. 1963
Sir ASHLEY MILES, C.B.E.	30 Nov. 1963–30 Nov. 1968
Sir BERNARD KATZ	30 Nov. 1968–30 Nov. 1976

Physical Secretaries	
†Sir ALFRED EGERTON	30 Nov. 1938–30 Nov. 1948
†Sir DAVID BRUNT, K.B.E.	30 Nov. 1948–30 Nov. 1957
†Sir WILLIAM HODGE	30 Nov. 1957–30 Nov. 1965
Sir JAMES LIGHTHILL	30 Nov. 1965– 1 Dec. 1969

Foreign Secretaries	
†Sir HENRY TIZARD, G.C.B., A.F.C.	30 Nov. 1940–30 Nov. 1945
Professor A. V. HILL, C.H., O.B.E.	30 Nov. 1945–30 Nov. 1946
Lord ADRIAN, O.M.	30 Nov. 1946–30 Nov. 1950
†Sir CYRIL HINSHELWOOD, O.M.	30 Nov. 1950–30 Nov. 1955
Sir GERARD THORNTON	30 Nov. 1955–30 Nov. 1960
†Sir PATRICK LINSTEAD, C.B.E.	30 Nov. 1960–30 Nov. 1965
Sir HAROLD THOMPSON, C.B.E.	30 Nov. 1965–30 Nov. 1971
Sir KINGSLEY DUNHAM	30 Nov. 1971–30 Nov. 1976

Postal address

The Royal Society, 6 Carlton House Terrace, London, SW1Y 5AG

Telegrams: Inland—Lonroysoc London SW1Y 5AG
Overseas—Lonroysoc London SW1Y 5AG England

Telephone: 01-839 5561
Telex: 917876 (ROYSOC)

THE FOUNDATION OF THE ROYAL SOCIETY

The origins of the Royal Society date back to the middle of the seventeenth century when a group of scholars made a habit of meeting together in London from about 1645 to discuss the, then, new or experimental philosophy. The Civil War and the Protectorate interrupted these meetings. Some of the group went to Oxford, in particular Robert Boyle and John Wilkins, where these meetings were continued in the rooms of the latter in Wadham College; others remained in or near London. After the Restoration the meetings were resumed in London. At one of them, on 28 November 1660, after hearing Mr Wren's lecture at Gresham College the company present withdrew into Mr Rooke's apartments 'for mutuall converse. Where amongst other matters that were discoursed of, Something was offered about a designe of founding a Colledge for the Promoting of Physico-Mathematicall, Experimentall Learning.' Those present at that meeting, which is the first to be recorded in the *Journal Book*, were 'The Lord Brouncker, Mr Boyle, Mr Bruce, Sr Robert Moray, Sr Paul Neile, Dr Wilkins, Dr Goddard, Dr Petty, Mr Ball, Mr Rooke, Mr Wren, Mr Hill'. These twelve can be taken as being the Original Founder Fellows.

Charles II became interested in the Society through Sir Robert Moray and two years after its foundation the King granted the Society its first Charter on 15 July 1662. In this the Society is 'called and named The Royal Society'. It is not known who first named the infant society 'The Royal Society' but the first time this appears in print is in John Evelyn's preface to his translation of Gabriel Naudé's *Instructions Concerning Erecting of a Library* published in November 1661.

A second Charter, granted on 22 April 1663, extended the Society's privileges and at the same time made the grant of the Arms. The motto chosen by the Society, *Nullius in verba*, was an expression of determination to withstand dogma and to verify all statements by an appeal to facts. In this second Charter the Society is referred to as 'The Royal Society of London for Improving Natural Knowledge', which is its full title.

MEMORANDUM AS TO THE WISHES OF THE COUNCIL IN RESPECT OF BENEFACTIONS TO THE SOCIETY

The Royal Society has, from time to time since its foundation, through the generosity of benefactors, received funds now amounting to a very considerable sum. In the majority of the benefactions the terms of gift have limited the application of the money to certain definite purposes, and, in particular, to the award of medals or other prizes for scientific discoveries or other contributions to the advancement of Natural Knowledge.

The President and Council desire to make it known that the funds belonging absolutely to the Society, tied down by no special directions as to their applications and which the Society are free to use for general purposes, are very few indeed. It has often been the experience of the President and Council that the usefulness of the Society for the advancement of Natural Knowledge has been greatly hampered by the lack of funds of which they could freely make use according to their own judgment.

The President and Council are confident that it would not be difficult, whenever desirable, to associate in some conspicuous manner the name of the benefactor with any gift to the Society, and indeed they would wish to do so. It is desired to make it generally known that, while they will willingly receive gifts to be applied to special objects or for the benefit of particular sciences indicated by the donors, they consider that, in view of the varying necessities of Science, the most useful benefactions are those which are given to the Society in general terms for the advancement of Natural Knowledge.

CALENDAR
1977

13 January	MEETING OF COUNCIL
20 January	MEETING OF CHAIRMEN OF SECTIONAL COMMITTEES WITH COUNCIL
1 February	MEETING OF GOVERNMENT GRANT BOARDS
3 February	MEETING OF COUNCIL AS COMMITTEE
10 February	MEETING OF COUNCIL
3 March	MEETING OF COUNCIL
17 March	MEETING OF SOCIETY FOR ELECTION OF FELLOWS
25 March	ANNUAL CONTRIBUTIONS DUE
31 March	MEETING OF COUNCIL
21 April	MEETING OF SOCIETY FOR ELECTION OF FOREIGN MEMBERS
5 May	MEETING OF COUNCIL
12 May	CONVERSAZIONE
17 May	MEETING OF GOVERNMENT GRANT BOARDS
16 June	MEETING OF COUNCIL
23 June	CONVERSAZIONE
4 July	MEETING OF SCIENTIFIC PUBLICATIONS BOARD
21 July	MEETING OF COUNCIL
31 July	LAST DAY FOR RECEIVING CERTIFICATES OF CANDIDATES
13 October	MEETING OF COUNCIL
1 November	MEETING OF GOVERNMENT GRANT BOARDS
10 November	MEETING OF COUNCIL
17 November	SPECIAL GENERAL MEETING TO CONSIDER THE ANNUAL REPORT OF COUNCIL
30 November	MEETING OF COUNCIL AT 12 NOON ANNIVERSARY MEETING IN THE AFTERNOON
5 December	MEETING OF SCIENTIFIC PUBLICATIONS BOARD
15 December	MEETING OF COUNCIL

THE COUNCIL 1977

Lord TODD, President
Dr B. J. MASON, Treasurer and Vice-President
Sir HARRIE MASSEY, Secretary and Vice-President
Professor D. C. PHILLIPS, Secretary and Vice-President
Dr M. G. P. STOKER, Foreign Secretary and Vice-President
Dr G. D. H. BELL, Vice-President
Professor B. B. BOYCOTT
Dr S. BRENNER
Professor J. CHATT
Sir ALAN COTTRELL, Vice-President
Professor G. S. DAWES, Vice-President
Professor H. L. KORNBERG
Sir ANGUS PATON, Vice-President
Professor C. G. PHILLIPS
Professor R. A. RAPHAEL
Professor J. SUTTON, Vice-President
Sir PETER SWINNERTON-DYER
Professor W. F. VINEN
Dr R. WECK
Dr J. H. WILKINSON
Dr D. T. N. WILLIAMSON

This Council will continue until 30 November 1977

Editors of *Notes and Records*—Professor R. V. JONES and
Professor W. D. M. PATON

SENIOR OFFICE STAFF

*R. W. J. KEAY, O.B.E., B.Sc., M.A., D.Phil., F.I.Biol., Executive Secretary
C. R. ARGENT, B.Sc.
J. H. BOREHAM, O.B.E.
RATTI Z. BULSARA
BRENDA M. de VERE
J. J. P. DEVERILL
W. G. EVANS, B.Sc., Assistant Editor
D. J. H. GRIFFIN, B.Sc., A.R.C.S.
D. W. HARLOW
G. E. HEMMEN
N. A. W. LE GRAND, F.C.I.S.
W. M. MALCOLM, B.Sc., B.L.
URSULA M. A. MAUNSELL, M.A.
N. H. ROBINSON, Librarian
NADIA SLOW
P. WIGLEY, D.F.C.

*Appointed Executive Secretary on 13 January 1977 in succession to Sir David Martin who died on 16 December 1976.

A description of the organization of the Royal Society office and subjects dealt with by the senior office staff is given between pages 385 and 389.

THE FELLOWSHIP 1977
PATRON: HER SACRED MAJESTY QUEEN ELIZABETH II

Date of
Election   ROYAL FELLOWS
1951   H.R.H. THE PRINCE PHILIP, DUKE OF EDINBURGH, K.G., K.T., O.M.
1956   HER MAJESTY QUEEN ELIZABETH THE QUEEN MOTHER

1971   HIS MAJESTY EMPEROR HIROHITO OF JAPAN, K.G.

Service on
Council

(Telephone numbers are included in the entries of those Fellows who have indicated their agreement to these being shown.)

1958   ABERCROMBIE, MICHAEL. Director of the Strangeways Research   1967-69
Laboratory. *Strangeways Research Laboratory, Wort's Causeway, Cambridge CB1 4RN. (Telephone: Cambridge 43231); and East Lodge, Little Shelford, Cambridge, CB2 5HE. (Telephone: Shelford 3366).*

1958   ABRAHAM, EDWARD PENLEY, C.B.E. Professor of Chemical Pathology, University of Oxford. MEDAL: ROYAL (1973). *Sir William Dunn School of Pathology, South Parks Road, Oxford, OX1 3RE. (Telephone: Oxford 57321); and Badgers Wood, Bedwell Heath, Boars Hill, Oxford. (Telephone: Oxford 735395); also Athenaeum.*

1939   ADAIR, GILBERT SMITHSON. Formerly Reader in Biophysics at the Physiological Laboratory, Cambridge. *92 Grantchester Meadows, Cambridge.*

1963   ADAMS. JOHN BERTRAM, C.M.G., Hon.D.Sc. Director-General, European Organization for Nuclear Research (Cern). MEDAL: LEVERHULME (1972). *European Organization for Nuclear Research (Cern), 1211 Geneva 23, Switzerland. (Telephone: Geneva 41 98 11).*

1964   ADAMS, JOHN FRANK. Lowndean Professor of Astronomy and   1969-70
Geometry in the University of Cambridge. *Department of Pure Mathematics and Mathematical Statistics, 16 Mill Lane, Cambridge, CB2 1SB (Telephone: Cambridge 65621).*

1970   ADDISON, CYRIL CLIFFORD. Professor of Inorganic Chemistry in the University of Nottingham. *Department of Chemistry, The University, Nottingham, NG7 2RD. (Telephone: Nottingham 56101, extension 2366); and 5 Wortley Hall Close, University Park, Nottingham. (Telephone: Nottingham 77410).*

1923   ADRIAN, OF CAMBRIDGE, EDGAR DOUGLAS, BARON, O.M.   1927-28
PAST-PRESIDENT. Emeritus Professor of Physiology in the   1934-36
University of Cambridge. LECTURES: CROONIAN (1931),   For. Sec.
FERRIER (1938). MEDALS: ROYAL (1934), COPLEY (1946).   1946-50
Nobel Laureate, Physiology and Medicine, 1932. *Trinity*   Pres.
College, Cambridge, CB2 1TQ; also Athenaeum.   1950-55

Date of Election		Service on Council

1976 ALLEN, GEOFFREY. Professor of Chemical Technology at the Imperial College of Science and Technology in the University of London. *Department of Chemical Engineering and Chemical Technology, Imperial College, Prince Consort Road, London, SW7 2BY.* (*Telephone:* 01-589 5111, *extension* 1900); and *40 Pine Grove, Lake Road, Wimbledon, London, SW19 7HE.* (*Telephone:* 01-947 7459); also *Athenaeum.*

1949 ALLEN, JOHN FRANK. Professor of Natural Philosophy in the School of Physical Sciences, University of St Andrews. *North Haugh, St Andrews, KY16 9SS, Scotland.* (*Telephone: St Andrews* 4381); and *2 Shorehead, St Andrews, KY16 9RG, Scotland.* (*Telephone: St Andrews* 2717).

1973 ALLEN, PERCIVAL. Professor of Geology, Head of the Department of Geology and Director of the Sedimentology Research Laboratory in the University of Reading. *Department of Geology, The University, Whiteknights, Reading, RG6 2AB.* (*Telephone: Reading* 85123, *extension* 7864); and *6 St Barnabas Road, Emmer Green, Reading, RG4 8RA.* (*Telephone: Reading* 472407).

1948 ALLIBONE, THOMAS EDWARD, C.B.E., D.Sc. External Professor of Electrical Engineering, University of Leeds, and Visiting Professor of Physics, City University. Formerly Chief Scientist, Central Electricity Generating Board. LECTURE: RUTHERFORD MEMORIAL (1963). *York Cottage, Lovel Road, Winkfield, Windsor, Berkshire.* (*Telephone: Winkfield Row* 4501).

1957 AMOROSO, EMMANUEL CIPRIANO, C.B.E. Emeritus Professor of Veterinary Physiology in the University of London. *Agricultural Research Council, Institute of Animal Physiology, Babraham, Cambridge, CB2 4AT.* (*Telephone: Cambridge* 832312, *extension* 209); and *29 Derwent Close, Cherry Hinton Road, Cambridge, CB1 4DY.* (*Telephone: Cambridge* 47825); also *Athenaeum.*

1968 ANDERSON, EPHRAIM SAUL, C.B.E. Director of the Enteric Reference Laboratory of the Public Health Laboratory Service. Visiting Professor in Applied Biology, School of Biological Sciences, Brunel University. *Enteric Reference Laboratory, Public Health Laboratory Service, Colindale Avenue, London, N.W.9.* (*Telephone:* 01-205 7041).

1953 ANDERSON, JOHN STUART. Emeritus Professor of Inorganic Chemistry at the University of Oxford. MEDAL; DAVY (1973). *Edward Davies Chemical Laboratories, University College of Wales, Aberystwyth, Dyfed, SY23 1NE.* (*Telephone: Aberystwyth* 7645); and *The Cottage, Abermagwr, near Aberystwyth, Dyfed, SY23 4AR.*

1976 ANDREW, SYDNEY PERCY SMITH. Research and Development Group Manager of the Agricultural Division of Imperial Chemical Industries Limited. *Agricultural Division, I.C.I. Limited, Billingham, Cleveland.* (*Telephone: Stockton* 553601); and *Holland Fen, 83 Hutton Avenue, Hartlepool, Cleveland, TS26 9PR.* (*Telephone: Hartlepool* 5329).

THE FELLOWSHIP 1977

Date of Election		Service on Council
1939	ANDREWES, SIR CHRISTOPHER (HOWARD). Formerly Deputy Director, National Institute for Medical Research. LECTURE: LEEUWENHOEK (1951). *Overchalke, Coombe Bissett, Salisbury, Wiltshire.*	1945-47
1963	ASHBY, OF BRANDON, ERIC, BARON. Formerly Master of Clare College, Cambridge. LECTURE: BERNAL (1971). *Norman Cottage, Manor Road, Brandon, Suffolk, IP27 0LG. (Telephone: Thetford 810695);* and 22 *Eltisley Avenue, Cambridge, CB3 9JG. (Telephone: Cambridge 56216).*	1964-65
1971	ASHTON, NORMAN HENRY, C.B.E. Professor of Pathology and Director of the Department of Pathology at the Institute of Ophthalmology in the University of London. *Department of Pathology, Institute of Ophthalmology, Judd Street, London, WC1H 9QS. (Telephone: 01-387 9621, extension 35);* and 2 *The Cloisters, Westminster Abbey, London, S.W.1. (Telephone: 01-222 4982);* also *Athenaeum.*	
1973	ASKONAS, BRIGITTE ALICE, Ph.D. Member of the Scientific Staff of the Medical Research Council. *National Institute for Medical Research, Mill Hill, London NW7 1AA. (Telephone: 01-959 3666);* and 23 *Hillside Gardens, London, N.6. (Telephone: 01-348 6792).*	
1962	ATIYAH, MICHAEL FRANCIS. Royal Society Research Professor at the University of Oxford. LECTURE: BAKERIAN (1975). MEDAL: ROYAL (1968). *Mathematical Institute, 24-29 St Giles, Oxford, OX1 3LB. (Telephone: Oxford 54295);* and *Shotover Mound, Headington, Oxford, OX3 8LG. (Telephone: Oxford 62359).*	1972-74
1957	AUERBACH, CHARLOTTE. Emeritus Professor of Animal Genetics in the University of Edinburgh. MEDAL: DARWIN (1976). *Institute of Animal Genetics, The University, West Mains Road, Edinburgh, 9.*	
1973	BACON, FRANCIS THOMAS, O.B.E. Formerly Consultant to Fuel Cells Limited (London). *Westfield, High Street, Little Shelford, Cambridge, CB2 5ES. (Telephone: Shelford 2244);* also *Athenaeum.*	
1961	BADDILEY, SIR JAMES. Professor and Director of the Microbiological Chemistry Research Laboratory in the University of Newcastle upon Tyne. LECTURE: LEEUWENHOEK (1967). MEDAL: DAVY (1974). *The Microbiological Chemistry Research Laboratory, The University, Newcastle upon Tyne, NE1 7RU. (Telephone: Newcastle upon Tyne 28511);* and 26 *Woolsington Park South, Woolsington, Newcastle upon Tyne, NE13 8BJ. (Telephone: Newcastle upon Tyne 860229).*	
1944	BAGNOLD, RALPH ALGER, O.B.E. Brigadier (retired). *Rickwoods, Mark Beech, near Edenbridge, Kent;* also *Athenaeum.*	1949-50
1973	BAKER, ALAN. Professor of Pure Mathematics in the University of Cambridge. *Trinity College, Cambridge, CB2 1TQ. (Telephone: Cambridge 58201).*	

Date of Election		Service on Council
1976	BAKER, PETER FREDERICK. Halliburton Professor of Physiology at King's College in the University of London. *Department of Physiology, King's College, Strand, London, WC2R 2LS. (Telephone:* 01-836 5454, *extension* 2475); and *Meadow Cottage, Bourn, Cambridge. (Telephone: Caxton* 212).	
1956	BAKER, JOHN FLEETWOOD, BARON, O.B.E. Formerly Head of the Department of Engineering and Professor of Mechanical Sciences in the University of Cambridge. MEDAL: ROYAL (1970). 100 *Long Road, Cambridge. (Telephone: Trumpington* 2152); also *Athenaeum.*	1959–61
1958	BAKER, JOHN RANDAL, D.Sc. Emeritus Reader in Cytology, University of Oxford. *The Mill,* 26 *Mill End, Kidlington, Oxford, OX5 2EG.*	
1946	BAKER, WILSON. Emeritus Professor of Organic Chemistry in the University of Bristol. *Department of Organic Chemistry, The University, Bristol,* 2; and *Lane's End, Church Road, Winscombe, Avon. (Telephone: Winscombe* 3112).	1954–55
1964	BAMFORD, CLEMENT HENRY. Campbell Brown Professor of Industrial Chemistry in the University of Liverpool. *Department of Inorganic, Physical and Industrial Chemistry, The Donnan Laboratories, Grove Street, P.O. Box* 147, *Liverpool, L69* 3*BX. (Telephone:* 051-709 6022, *extension* 2550); and *Broom Bank, Tower Road, Prenton, Birkenhead, Merseyside, L42 8LH. (Telephone:* 051-608 3979).	
1953	BARCROFT, HENRY. Emeritus Professor of Physiology at St Thomas's Hospital Medical School in the University of London. 44 *Wood Lane, Highgate, London, N6 5UB. (Telephone:* 01-340 2338); also *Athenaeum.*	
1961	BARLOW, HAROLD EVERARD MONTEAGLE. Emeritus Professor of Electrical Engineering in the University of London. *University College, Gower Street, London, W.C.*1. *(Telephone:* 01-387 7050); and 13 *Hookfield, Epsom, Surrey. (Telephone: Epsom* 21586); also *Athenaeum.*	
1969	BARLOW, HORACE BASIL. Royal Society Research Professor at the University of Cambridge. *Physiological Laboratory, Downing Street, Cambridge, CB2 3EG. (Telephone: (Psychological Laboratory) Cambridge* 51386); *Trinity College, Cambridge, CB2 2TQ. (Telephone: Cambridge* 58201); and 10 *Green Street, Cambridge, CB2 3JU. (Telephone: Cambridge* 66618).	
1972	BARR, MURRAY LLEWELLYN. Professor of Anatomy in the University of Western Ontario. *Department of Anatomy, Health Sciences Centre, University of Western Ontario, London* 72, *Ontario, Canada. (Telephone:* (519) 679-3745); and 452 *Wonderland Road, London* 62, *Ontario, Canada. (Telephone:* (519) 471-5618).	
1956	BARRER, RICHARD MALING. Professor of Physical Chemistry at the Imperial College of Science and Technology in the University of London. *Imperial College of Science and Technology, London, SW7 2AY. (Telephone:* 01-589 5111, *extension* 1200).	

Date of Election		Service on Council
1967	BARRINGTON, ERNEST JAMES WILLIAM. Emeritus Professor of Zoology in the University of Nottingham. *Cornerways, 2 St Margaret's Drive, Alderton, Tewkesbury, Gloucestershire, GL20 8NY. (Telephone: Alderton 375).*	1970–72 V.P. 1971–72
1961	BARTLETT, MAURICE STEVENSON. Emeritus Professor of Biomathematics at the University of Oxford. *117 Littlehampton Road, Worthing, West Sussex, BN13 1QU.*	1965–67
1973	BARTLETT, NEIL. Professor of Chemistry in the University of California, Berkeley, and Principal Investigator in the Inorganic Materials Division at the Lawrence Berkeley Laboratory. *Department of Chemistry, University of California, Berkeley, California 94720, U.S.A. (Telephone:* (415) 642-7259); *and 6 Oak Drive, Orinda, California 94563, U.S.A. (Telephone:* (415) 254-5322).	
1954	BARTON, SIR DEREK (HAROLD RICHARD). Hofmann Professor of Organic Chemistry at the Imperial College of Science and Technology in the University of London. LECTURE: BAKERIAN (1970). MEDALS: DAVY (1961), ROYAL (1972). Nobel Laureate, Chemistry, 1969. *Imperial College of Science and Technology, Imperial Institute Road, London, SW7 2AY;* also *Athenaeum.*	1964–66
1957	BATCHELOR, GEORGE KEITH. Professor of Applied Mathematics and Head of Department of Applied Mathematics and Theoretical Physics in the University of Cambridge. *Department of Applied Mathematics and Theoretical Physics, Silver Street, Cambridge, CB3 9EW. (Telephone: Cambridge 51645);* and *Cobbers, Conduit Head Road, Cambridge, CB3 0EY. (Telephone: Cambridge 56387).*	
1968	BATEMAN, LESLIE CLIFFORD, C.M.G., D.Sc. Secretary-General, International Rubber Study Group. *International Rubber Study Group, Brettenham House, 5–6 Lancaster Place, London, WC2E 7ET. (Telephone:* 01-836 6811); *and 3 Palmerston Close, Welwyn Garden City, Hertfordshire. (Telephone: Welwyn Garden 22391).*	
1955	BATES, DAVID ROBERT. Professor of Theoretical Physics in the Queen's University of Belfast. MEDAL: HUGHES (1970). *Queen's University, Belfast, Northern Ireland, BT7 1NN. (Telephone: Belfast 45133);* and *6 Deramore Park, Belfast, Northern Ireland, BT9 5JT. (Telephone: Belfast 665640).*	
1950	BATES, LESLIE FLEETWOOD, C.B.E. Emeritus Professor of Physics in the University of Nottingham. *Flat 2, Castlethorpe, Newcastle Circus, The Park, Nottingham NG7 1BJ. (Telephone: Nottingham 42135);* also *Athenaeum.*	
1966	BATTERSBY, ALAN RUSHTON. Professor of Organic Chemistry in the University of Cambridge. *University Chemical Laboratory, Lensfield Road, Cambridge, CB2 1EW. (Telephone: Cambridge 66499).*	1973–75

Date of Election		Service on Council
1952	BAWN, CECIL EDWIN HENRY, C.B.E. Emeritus Professor of Physical Chemistry in the University of Liverpool. *Springfields, Stoodleigh, Tiverton, Devon.* (*Telephone: Oakford* 220).	1956–57
1959	BEALE, GEOFFREY HERBERT, M.B.E. Royal Society Research Professor at the University of Edinburgh. LECTURE: LEEUWENHOEK (1976). *Institute of Animal Genetics, West Mains Road, Edinburgh, EH9 3JN.* (*Telephone:* 031-667 1081, *extension* 3503); and 23 *Royal Terrace, Edinburgh, EH7 5AH.* (*Telephone:* 031-557 1329).	
1951	BEALS, CARLYLE SMITH, D.Sc. Consultant, Celestial and Earth Sciences. Formerly Dominion Astronomer. *Manotick, Ontario, Canada.* (*Telephone:* (613) 692-3247).	
1964	BEAMENT, JAMES WILLIAM LONGMAN. Drapers Professor of Agriculture and Head of the Department of Applied Biology in the University of Cambridge. *Department of Applied Biology, Pembroke Street, Cambridge, CB2 3DX.* (*Telephone: Cambridge* 58381); *Queens' College, Cambridge, CB3 9ET.* (*Telephone: Cambridge* 65511); and 19 *Sedley Taylor Road, Cambridge, CB2 2PW.* (*Telephone: Cambridge* 46045).	
1965	BELL, GEORGE DOUGLAS HUTTON, C.B.E., Ph.D. Formerly Director, Plant Breeding Institute, Cambridge. MEDAL: MULLARD (1967). 6 *Worts Causeway, Cambridge, CB1 4RL.* (*Telephone: Cambridge* 47449); and *Selwyn College, Cambridge.*	1976– V.P. 1976–
1972	BELL, JOHN STEWART, Ph.D. Senior Physicist, European Organization for Nuclear Research (Cern). *Theoretical Physics Division, Cern,* 1211 *Geneva* 23, *Switzerland.*	
1965	BELL, ROBERT EDWARD. Rutherford Professor of Physics and Principal and Vice-Chancellor in McGill University. *Principal's Office, McGill University, P.O. Box* 6070, *Station 'A', Montreal, Quebec, H3C 3G1, Canada.* (*Telephone:* (514) 392-5347); and 363 *Olivier Avenue, Westmount, Montreal, Quebec, H3Z 2C8, Canada.* (*Telephone:* (514) 935-3769).	
1944	BELL, RONALD PERCY. Honorary Research Professor of Chemistry in the University of Leeds. *School of Chemistry, The University, Leeds, LS2 9JT;* and 28 *Ayresome Terrace, Roundhay, Leeds, LS8 1BH.* (*Telephone: Leeds* 664236).	1960–61
1966	BENJAMIN, THOMAS BROOKE. Professor of Mathematics and Director of the Fluid Mechanics Research Institute in the University of Essex. *Fluid Mechanics Research Institute, University of Essex, Wivenhoe Park, Colchester, Essex.* (*Telephone: Colchester* 44144); and *Clifton House, Chapel Road, Wivenhoe, Colchester, Essex.* (*Telephone: Wivenhoe* 4780).	
1959	BERGEL, FRANZ. Emeritus Professor of Chemistry in the University of London. *Magnolia Cottage, Bel Royal, Jersey, Channel Islands.* (*Telephone: Jersey Central* 33688); also *Athenaeum.*	
1952	BERRILL, NORMAN JOHN, D.Sc. Formerly Strathcona Professor of Zoology, McGill University. 410 *Swarthmore Avenue, Swarthmore, Pa* 19081, *U.S.A.*	

Date of Election		Service on Council

1938 BEST, CHARLES HERBERT, C.H., C.B.E. Emeritus Professor of Physiology, formerly Director of the Banting and Best Department of Medical Research in the University of Toronto. LECTURE: CROONIAN (1955). 105 *Woodlawn Avenue West, Toronto, Canada;* also *Athenaeum.*

1975 BEVERTON, RAYMOND JOHN HEAPHY, C.B.E. Secretary of the Natural Environment Research Council, London. *Natural Environment Research Council, 27–33 Charing Cross Road, London, WC2H 0AX. (Telephone:* 01-930 9232); *and 54 Priest's Lane, Shenfield, Essex, CM15 8BY (Telephone: Brentwood* 213920); also *Athenaeum.*

1971 BEYNON, JOHN HERBERT. Royal Society Research Professor at the University College of Swansea in the University of Wales. *Department of Chemistry, University College of Swansea, Singleton Park, Swansea, SA2 8PP. (Telephone:* Swansea 25678, *extension* 297); and 17 *Coltshill Drive, Mumbles, Swansea, SA3 4SN. (Telephone: Swansea* 68718); also *Athenaeum.*

1973 BEYNON, SIR (WILLIAM JOHN) GRANVILLE, C.B.E. Professor of Physics and Head of the Department of Physics in the University College of Wales, Aberystwyth. *Department of Physics, University College of Wales, Penglais, Aberystwyth, SY23 3BZ, Dyfed. (Telephone: Aberystwyth* 3111).

1976 BIGGS, PETER MARTIN, D.Sc. Director of the Houghton Poultry Research Station, Huntingdon. *Houghton Poultry Research Station, Houghton, Huntingdon, Cambridgeshire, PE17 2DA. (Telephone: St Ives* 64101); and *The Willows, London Road, St Ives, Huntingdon, Cambridgeshire, PE17 4ES. (Telephone: St Ives* 63471).

1961 BILLINGHAM, RUPERT EVERETT. Professor and Chairman, Department of Cell Biology, University of Texas. *Department of Cell Biology, University of Texas, Southwestern Medical School at Dallas, 5323 Harry Hines Boulevard, Dallas, Texas* 75235, *U.S.A. (Telephone:* (214) 688-2224); *and* 6181 *Preston Haven Drive, Dallas, Texas* 75230, *U.S.A. (Telephone:* (214) 661-9895).

1960 BINNIE, ALFRED MAURICE. Emeritus Reader in Engineering in the University of Cambridge. *Trinity College, Cambridge. (Telephone: Cambridge* 58201).

1975 BINNIE, GEOFFREY MORSE. Consultant to Binnie and Partners, Chartered Civil Engineers, London. *Binnie and Partners, Artillery House, Artillery Row, London, SW1P 1RX. (Telephone:* 01- 222 7755); and *St Michael's Lodge, Benenden, Cranbrook, Kent, TN17 4EZ. (Telephone: Benenden* 498); also *Athenaeum.*

1958 BIRCH, ARTHUR JOHN. Professor of Organic Chemistry in the Research School of Chemistry, Institute of Advanced Studies, Australian National University. MEDAL: DAVY (1972). *The Research School of Chemistry, The Australian National University, P.O. Box* 4, *Canberra, A.C.T., Australia;* and 3 *Arkana Street, Yarralumla, A.C.T.* 2600, *Australia. (Telephone:* 81-3618).

Date of Election		Service on Council
1972	BIRCH, BRYAN JOHN, Ph.D. Reader in Mathematics in the University of Oxford. *Mathematical Institute, 24–29 St Giles, Oxford, OX1 3LB. (Telephone: Oxford 54295);* and *Green Cottage, Boars Hill, Oxford. (Telephone: Oxford 735367).*	
1959	BISHOP, ANN, Sc.D. Formerly Director of the Medical Research Council Chemotherapy Research Unit, Cambridge. 47 *Sherlock Close, Cambridge, CB3 0HP. (Telephone: Cambridge 54915).*	
1976	BLACK, JAMES WHYTE. Professor and Head of the Department of Pharmacology at University College in the University of London. *Department of Pharmacology, University College London, Gower Street, London, WC1E 6BT (Telephone: 01-387 7050, extension 352);* and 53 *Wrensfield, Hemel Hempstead, Hertfordshire, HP1 1RP. (Telephone: Hemel Hempstead 2087).*	
1959	BLACKMAN, GEOFFREY EMETT. Emeritus Professor of Rural Economy at the University of Oxford. *Department of Forestry, South Parks Road, Oxford, OX1 3RB. (Telephone: Oxford 511431);* and *Woodcroft, Foxcombe Lane, Boars Hill, Oxford, OX1 5DH. (Telephone: Oxford 735148);* also *Athenaeum.*	1966–68 V.P. 1966–68
1962	BLACKMAN, MOSES. Emeritus Professor of Physics and Senior Research Fellow at the Imperial College of Science and Technology in the University of London. *Department of Physics, Imperial College, Prince Consort Road, London, S.W.7. (Telephone:* 01-589 5111); and 48 *Garden Royal, Kersfield Road, London, S.W.15. (Telephone:* 01-789 1706).	
1962	BLASCHKO, HERMANN KARL FELIX, Ph.D. Emeritus Reader in Biochemical Pharmacology at the University of Oxford. *Department of Pharmacology, South Parks Road, Oxford, OX1 3QT. (Telephone: Oxford 57062);* and 24 *Park Town, Oxford, OX2 6SH. (Telephone: Oxford 55005).*	
1967	BLAXTER, KENNETH LYON, D.Sc. Director, Rowett Research Institute. *Rowett Research Institute, Bucksburn, Aberdeen, AB2 9SB. (Telephone: Bucksburn 2751);* and *Wardenhill, Bucksburn, Aberdeen, AB2 9SB. (Telephone: Bucksburn 2623).*	
1950	BLEANEY, BREBIS, C.B.E. Dr Lee's Professor of Experimental Philosophy and Head of the Clarendon Laboratory, Oxford. MEDAL: HUGHES (1962). *Clarendon Laboratory, Parks Road, Oxford, OX1 3PU. (Telephone: Oxford 59291).*	1955–56
1976	BLIN-STOYLE, ROGER JOHN. Professor of Theoretical Physics in the University of Sussex. *School of Mathematical and Physical Sciences, University of Sussex, Falmer, Brighton, BN1 9QH. (Telephone: Brighton 66755);* and 14 *Hill Road, Lewes, East Sussex, BN7 1DB. (Telephone: Lewes 3640).*	
1972	BLOW, DAVID MERVYN, Ph.D. Member of the Scientific Staff of the Medical Research Council. *M.R.C. Laboratory of Molecular Biology, Hills Road, Cambridge. (Telephone: Cambridge 48011); Trinity College, Cambridge;* and *Plough Meadow, Little Eversden, Cambridge. (Telephone: Comberton 2219).*	

THE FELLOWSHIP 1977 21

Date of   Service on
Election   Council

1974   BODMER, WALTER FRED. Professor of Genetics in the University
       of Oxford. *Genetics Laboratory, Department of Biochemistry,
       South Parks Road, Oxford, OX1 3QU. (Telephone: Oxford
       511267); and Manor House, 15 Mill Lane, Old Marston, Oxford.
       (Telephone: Oxford 43904).*

1973   BOLTON, JOHN GATENBY. Chief Research Scientist in the Commonwealth Scientific and Industrial Research Organization.
       *C.S.I.R.O. Division of Radiophysics, Box 276, Parkes, N.S.W.
       2870, Australia. (Telephone: Parkes 63-3133); and 67 East Street,
       Parkes, N.S.W., Australia. (Telephone: Parkes 62-2665).*

1972   BOND, GEORGE. Emeritus Professor of Botany in the University of
       Glasgow. *Department of Botany, The University, Glasgow,
       G12 8QQ. (Telephone: 041-339 8855).*

1959   BONDI, SIR HERMANN, K.C.B. Chief Scientific Adviser, Ministry of
       Defence. Professor of Applied Mathematics at King's College
       in the University of London. *Ministry of Defence, Main Building, Whitehall, London, SW1A 2HB. (Telephone: 01-218 6588);
       and East House, Buckland Corner, Reigate Heath, Surrey.*

1970   BONSALL, FRANK FEATHERSTONE. McLaurin Professor of Mathematics in the University of Edinburgh. *Department of Mathematics, James Clerk Maxwell Building, The King's Buildings,
       Mayfield Road, Edinburgh, EH9 3JZ. (Telephone: 031-667 1081,
       extension 2998); and 4 Craiglockhart Park, Edinburgh, EH14
       1ER. (Telephone: 031-443 3511).*

1974   BOON, WILLIAM ROBERT, Ph.D. Formerly Managing Director of
       Plant Protection Limited, Imperial Chemical Industries. MEDAL:
       MULLARD (1972). *The Gables, Sid Road, Sidmouth, Devon,
       EX10 9AQ. (Telephone: Sidmouth 4069).*

1967   BOOTH, ERIC STUART, C.B.E. Chairman of the Yorkshire Electricity
       Board. *Yorkshire Electricity Board, Scarcroft, Leeds, LS14
       3HS. (Telephone: Leeds 892123).*

1972   BORN, GUSTAV VICTOR RUDOLF. Sheild Professor of Pharmacology
       in the University of Cambridge. *Department of Pharmacology,
       Medical School, Hills Road, Cambridge, CB2 2QD. (Telephone:
       Cambridge 45171); Gonville and Caius College, Cambridge.
       (Telephone: Cambridge 312211); and 58B Redington Road, London,
       N.W.3. (Telephone: 01-435 7202).*

1935   BOWEN, EDMUND JOHN, D.Sc. Formerly Aldrichian Praelector in   1943–45
       Chemistry at the University of Oxford. MEDAL: DAVY (1963).
       *Physical Chemistry Laboratory, South Parks Road, Oxford; and
       10 Park Town, Oxford. (Telephone: Oxford 57631).*

1975   BOWEN, EDWARD GEORGE, C.B.E., Ph.D. Formerly Counsellor
       (Scientific) at the Embassy of Australia in Washington, D.C.,
       U.S.A. *5010 Maxwell Avenue, West River, Md 20881, U.S.A.
       (Telephone: (301) 261-5715); also Athenaeum.*

Date of Election		Service on Council
1975	BOWIE, STANLEY HAY UMPHRAY, D.Sc. Assistant Director and Chief Geochemist of the Institute of Geological Sciences, London. *Geochemical Division, Institute of Geological Sciences, 64/78 Gray's Inn Road, London, WC1X 8NG. (Telephone: 01-405 4932 and 01-242 4531, extension 145); and 18 Spencer Road, North Wembley, Middlesex, HA0 3SF. (Telephone: 01-904 1561).*	
1971	BOYCOTT, BRIAN BLUNDELL. Professor of Biology at King's College in the University of London. *M.R.C. Cell Biophysics Unit, Department of Biophysics, King's College, 26–29 Drury Lane, London, W.C.2. (Telephone: 01-836 8851); and 84 Baldry Gardens, Streatham, London, S.W.16. (Telephone: 01-764 2793).*	1976–
1951	BOYD, SIR JOHN (SMITH KNOX), O.B.E., Brigadier (retired). Late Director, Wellcome Laboratories of Tropical Medicine. *Mossbank, 6 The Covert, Northwood, Middlesex. (Telephone: Northwood 22437); also Athenaeum.*	1956-58
1969	BOYD, ROBERT LEWIS FULLARTON, C.B.E. Professor of Physics in the University of London and Director of the Mullard Space Science Laboratory of the Department of Physics and Astronomy at University College London. *Mullard Space Science Laboratory, Holmbury St Mary, Dorking, Surrey. (Telephone: Forest Green 292); Department of Physics and Astronomy, University College, Gower Street, London, WC1E 6BT. (Telephone: 01-387 7050, extension 374); and Ariel House, Holmbury St Mary, Dorking, Surrey. (Telephone: Ewhurst 478).*	
1976	BRADLEY, DANIEL JOSEPH. Professor of Optics and Head of the Department of Physics at the Imperial College of Science and Technology in the University of London. *Department of Physics, The Blackett Laboratory, Imperial College, Prince Consort Road, London, SW7 2BZ. (Telephone: 01-589 5111); also Athenaeum.*	
1965	BRENNER, SYDNEY, D.Phil. Member of the Scientific Staff of the Medical Research Council. MEDAL: ROYAL (1974). *M.R.C. Laboratory of Molecular Biology, Hills Road, Cambridge.*	1975–
1958	BRIAN, PERCY WRAGG, C.B.E. Professor of Botany in the University of Cambridge. LECTURE: LEEUWENHOEK (1966). *Botany School, Downing Street, Cambridge, CB2 3EA. (Telephone: Cambridge 61414); and Walkers Field, Kingston, Cambridge, CB3 7NG. (Telephone: Comberton 2200).*	1968–70
1935	BRIGGS, GEORGE EDWARD. Emeritus Professor of Botany in the University of Cambridge. *10 Luard Road, Cambridge, CB2 2PJ. (Telephone: Cambridge 47181).*	
1965	BRINDLEY, GILES SKEY. Professor of Physiology at the Institute of Psychiatry, University of London. *Institute of Psychiatry, de Crespigny Park, Denmark Hill, London, S.E.5. (Telephone: 01-703 5411, extension 341); and 102 Ferndene Road, London, S.E.24. (Telephone: 01-274 2598).*	

Date of Election		Service on Council
	THE FELLOWSHIP 1977	

1968 BROADBENT, DONALD ERIC, C.B.E., Sc.D. Member of the External Staff of the Medical Research Council. *Department of Experimental Psychology, South Parks Road, Oxford, OX1 3UD. (Telephone: Oxford 56789).*

1965 BROCKHOUSE, BERTRAM NEVILLE. Professor of Physics at McMaster University. *Department of Physics, McMaster University, Hamilton, Ontario, Canada.*

1975 BROWN, GEORGE MALCOLM. Professor of Geology in the University of Durham. *Department of Geological Sciences, The University, South Road, Durham, DH1 3LE. (Telephone: Durham 64971, extension 392 and 302); and 26 High Wood View, Durham, DH1 3DT. (Telephone: Durham 2910).*

1956 BROWN, ROBERT. Regius Professor of Botany in the University of Edinburgh. *Department of Botany, The King's Buildings, Mayfield Road, Edinburgh, EH9 3JH; and 15A Corrennie Drive, Edinburgh, EH10 6EG.*

1960 BROWN, ROBERT HANBURY. Professor of Physics (Astronomy) in the University of Sydney. MEDAL: HUGHES (1971). *Chatterton Astronomy Department, School of Physics, The University of Sydney, Sydney, N.S.W. 2006, Australia. (Telephone: Sydney 692-1122, extension 2934).*

1975 BUCKINGHAM, AMYAND DAVID. Professor of Chemistry in the University of Cambridge. *University Chemical Laboratory, Lensfield Road, Cambridge, CB2 1EW. (Telephone: Cambridge 66499); and 37 Millington Road, Cambridge, CB3 9HW. (Telephone: Cambridge 50012).*

1966 BUDDEN, KENNETH GEORGE, Ph.D. Reader in Physics in the University of Cambridge. *Cavendish Laboratory, Madingley Road, Cambridge, CB3 0HE. (Telephone: Cambridge 66477); and 15 Adams Road, Cambridge. (Telephone: Cambridge 54752).*

1958 BÜLBRING, EDITH. Emeritus Professor of Pharmacology, University of Oxford. *University Laboratory of Physiology, Parks Road, Oxford, OX1 3PT. (Telephone: Oxford 57765); and 15 Northmoor Road, Oxford. (Telephone: Oxford 57270).*

1941 BULLARD, SIR EDWARD (CRISP). Professor of Geophysics in the University of California at San Diego. LECTURE: BAKERIAN (1967). MEDALS: HUGHES (1953), ROYAL (1975). I.G.P.P. A025, *University of California, La Jolla, California 92093, U.S.A. (Telephone: (714) 452-2159); and 2491 Horizon Way, La Jolla, California 92037, U.S.A. (Telephone: (714) 453-7395); also Athenaeum.*
1945–47 V.P.
1946–47

1972 BULLERWELL, WILLIAM, Ph.D. Deputy Director of the Institute of Geological Sciences. *Institute of Geological Sciences, Exhibition Road, London, SW7 2DE. (Telephone: 01-589 3444, extension 295); and 84 Kenilworth Court, Lower Richmond Road, London, SW15 1HA. (Telephone: 01-788 9892).*
1974–75

Date of Election		Service on Council
1967	BUNN, CHARLES WILLIAM, D.Sc. Formerly Dewar Research Fellow, The Royal Institution of Great Britain. 6 *Pentley Park, Welwyn Garden City, Hertfordshire.* (*Telephone: Welwyn Garden* 23581).	
1964	BURBIDGE, ELEANOR MARGARET. Professor of Astronomy in the University of California. *Department of Physics, C-011, University of California at San Diego, La Jolla, California 92093, U.S.A.* (*Telephone:* (714) 452-4479).	
1968	BURBIDGE, GEOFFREY RONALD. Professor of Physics in the University of California. *Department of Physics, C-011, University of California at San Diego, La Jolla, California 92093, U.S.A.* (*Telephone:* (714) 452-4479).	
1944	BURCH, CECIL REGINALD, C.B.E., D.Sc. Formerly Warren Research Fellow. MEDAL: RUMFORD (1954). *H. H. Wills Physics Laboratory, Royal Fort, Bristol,* 8. (*Telephone: Bristol* 24161); and 2 *Holmes Grove, Westbury-on-Trym, Bristol, BS9 4EE.* (*Telephone: Bristol* 627322).	
1957	BURCHAM, WILLIAM ERNEST. Oliver Lodge Professor of Physics in the University of Birmingham. *Department of Physics, The University of Birmingham, Edgbaston, Birmingham,* 15. (*Telephone:* 021-472 1301); and 95 *Witherford Way, Birmingham, B29 4AN.* (*Telephone:* 021-472 1226).	
1964	BURGEN, SIR ARNOLD (STANLEY VINCENT). Director, National Institute for Medical Research. *National Institute for Medical Research, The Ridgeway, Mill Hill, London, NW7 1AA.* (*Telephone:* 01-959 3666); and *Penshurst, Hill Crescent, Totteridge, London, N.20.* (*Telephone:* 01-445 6848).	1972–73
1963	BURHOP, ERIC HENRY STONELEY. Professor of Physics at University College in the University of London. *Department of Physics and Astronomy, University College London, Gower Street, London, WC1E 6BT.* (*Telephone:* 01-387 7050); and 206 *Gilbert House, Barbican, London, EC2Y 8BD.* (*Telephone:* 01-638 8816).	
1953	BURKILL, JOHN CHARLES, Sc.D. Formerly Master of Peterhouse and Emeritus Reader in Mathematical Analysis in the University of Cambridge. 2 *Archway Court, Barton Road, Cambridge, CB3 9LW.*	1959–61
1972	BURKITT, DENIS PARSONS, C.M.G. Honorary Senior Research Fellow at St Thomas's Hospital Medical School. *Department of Morbid Anatomy, St Thomas's Hospital Medical School, London, SE1 7EH.* (*Telephone:* 01-928 9292); and *The Knoll, Shiplake, Oxon.* (*Telephone: Wargrave* 2186).	
1942	BURN, JOSHUA HAROLD. Emeritus Professor of Pharmacology in the University of Oxford. 3 *Squitchey Lane, Oxford.* (*Telephone: Oxford* 58209).	1944–45

Date of Election

Service on Council

1942 BURNET, SIR (FRANK) MACFARLANE, O.M., K.B.E. Formerly Director, Walter and Eliza Hall Institute. Emeritus Professor of Experimental Medicine, University of Melbourne. LECTURE: CROONIAN (1950). MEDALS: ROYAL (1947), COPLEY (1959). Nobel Laureate, Physiology or Medicine, 1960. *Department of Microbiology, University of Melbourne, Parkville, 3052, Victoria, Australia. (Telephone: 3451844, extension 5712); and* 48 *Monomeath Avenue, Canterbury,* 3126, *Victoria, Australia. (Telephone:* 834526).

1968 BURNS, BENEDICT DELISLE, M.R.C.S., L.R.C.P. Member of the External Staff of the Medical Research Council. *Department of Anatomy, The Medical School, University Walk, Bristol, BS8 1TD. (Telephone: Bristol* 24161).

1974 BURTON, KENNETH. Professor of Biochemistry in the University of Newcastle upon Tyne. *Department of Biochemistry, Ridley Building, University of Newcastle upon Tyne, Newcastle upon Tyne, NE1 7RU. (Telephone: Newcastle* 28511, *extension* 3437); *and* 87 *Errington Road, Ponteland, Newcastle upon Tyne, NE20 9LA. (Telephone: Ponteland* 23492).

1961 BUTLER, CLIFFORD CHARLES, Ph.D. Vice-Chancellor of Loughborough University of Technology. *Loughborough University of Technology, Loughborough, Leicestershire, LE11 3TU. (Telephone: Loughborough* 63171).

1970 BUTLER, COLIN GASKING, O.B.E., Ph.D. Formerly Head of the Entomology Department, Rothamsted Experimental Station. *Silver Birches, Porthpean, St Austell, Cornwall, PL26 6RU. (Telephone: St Austell* 2480).

1956 BUTLER, JOHN ALFRED VALENTINE. Emeritus Professor of Physical Chemistry in the University of London. *Nightingale Corner, Rickmansworth, Hertfordshire. (Telephone: Rickmansworth* 72938).

1976 CADOGAN, JOHN IVAN GEORGE. Forbes Professor of Organic Chemistry in the University of Edinburgh. *Department of Chemistry, University of Edinburgh, West Mains Road, Edinburgh, EH9 3JJ. (Telephone:* 031-667 1081); *and* 30 *Cluny Drive, Edinburgh* 10. *(Telephone:* 031-447 3363); *also Athenaeum.*

1974 CAIRNS, HUGH JOHN FORSTER, D.M. Head of the Imperial Cancer Research Fund Mill Hill Laboratories. *Imperial Cancer Research Fund, Mill Hill Laboratories, Burtonhole Lane, London, NW7 1AD. (Telephone:* 01-959 3236); *and Manor End, Partingdale Lane, London, N.W.7. (Telephone:* 01-346 8180).

1975 CALDWELL, PETER CHRISTOPHER, D.Phil. Reader in Zoology in the University of Bristol. *Department of Zoology, The University of Bristol, BS8 1UG. (Telephone: Bristol* 24161, *extension* 800); *and White Oak House, Youngwood Lane, Nailsea, Bristol, BS19 2NS. (Telephone: Nailsea* 2436).

Date of Election		Service on Council
1963	CALLAN, HAROLD GARNET. Professor of Natural History, St Salvator's College, University of St Andrews. *Department of Zoology, Bute Buildings, The University, St Andrews, Fife, KY16 9TS. (Telephone: St Andrews 2823);* and 2 *St Mary's Street, St Andrews, Fife. (Telephone: St Andrews 2311).*	1974–76
1958	CALLOW, ROBERT KENNETH, D.Phil. Lately Member of Staff of Rothamsted Experimental Station. Formerly Member of Staff of the Medical Research Council. 39 *Hendon Wood Lane, London, NW7 4HT. (Telephone:* 01-959 2572).	
1974	CALNE, ROY YORKE. Professor of Surgery in the University of Cambridge. *Department of Surgery, University of Cambridge, Addenbrooke's Hospital, Cambridge. (Telephone: Cambridge 42708);* and 22 *Barrow Road, Cambridge. (Telephone: Cambridge 59831).*	
1971	CARRINGTON, ALAN. Professor of Chemistry in the University of Southampton. *Department of Chemistry, The University, Southampton, SO9 5NH, Hampshire. (Telephone: Southampton 559122;* and 46 *Lakewood Road, Chandler's Ford, Eastleigh, Hampshire, SO5 1EX. (Telephone: Chandler's Ford 5092).*	
1947	CARTWRIGHT, DAME MARY (LUCY), D.B.E. Emeritus Reader in the Theory of Functions in the University of Cambridge. MEDAL: SYLVESTER (1964). 38 *Sherlock Close, Cambridge, CB3 0HP. (Telephone: Cambridge* 52574).	1955–57
1970	CASEY, RAYMOND, D.Sc. Senior Principal Scientific Officer at the Institute of Geological Sciences. *Institute of Geological Sciences, Exhibition Road, London, S.W.7. (Telephone:* 01-589 3444); *and* 38 *Reed Avenue, Orpington, Kent. (Telephone: Farnborough (Kent)* 51728).	
1959	CASSELS, JAMES MACDONALD. Lyon Jones Professor of Physics in the University of Liverpool. *Oliver Lodge Laboratory, The University of Liverpool, P.O. Box* 147, *Liverpool, L69* 3*BX. (Telephone:* 051-709 6022).	1968–69
1963	CASSELS, JOHN WILLIAM SCOTT. Sadleirian Professor of Pure Mathematics in the University of Cambridge. MEDAL: SYLVESTER (1973). *Department of Pure Mathematics and Mathematical Statistics,* 16 *Mill Lane, Cambridge, CB2* 1*SB. (Telephone: Cambridge* 65621); and 3 *Luard Close, Cambridge CB2 2PL. (Telephone: Cambridge* 46108).	1970–72
1951	CATCHESIDE, DAVID GUTHRIE, D.Sc. Formerly Director and Professor of Genetics, Research School of Biological Sciences in the Australian National University. *University of Adelaide, Waite Agricultural Institute, Glen Osmond, South Australia* 5064, *Australia. (Telephone:* 79.7901); *and* 16 *Rodger Avenue, Leabrook, South Australia* 5068, *Australia. (Telephone:* 332.3915).	1959–61

Date of Election		Service on Council
1949	CHAIN, SIR ERNST (BORIS). Senior Research Fellow and Emeritus Professor of Biochemistry at the Imperial College of Science and Technology in the University of London. Nobel Laureate, Physiology and Medicine, 1945. *Department of Biochemistry, Imperial College, London, S.W.7. (Telephone: 01-589 5111, extension* 1140); also *Athenaeum.*	
1976	CHALONER, WILLIAM GILBERT. Professor and Head of the Department of Botany at Birkbeck College in the University of London. *Department of Botany, Birkbeck College, Malet Street, London, WC1E 7HX. (Telephone:* 01-580 6622); and 20 *Parke Road, London, S.W.*13. *(Telephone:* 01-748 4702).	
1944	CHANDRASEKHAR, SUBRAHMANYAN. Morton D. Hull Distinguished Service Professor in the University of Chicago. MEDAL: ROYAL (1962). *Laboratory for Astrophysics and Space Research,* 933 *East 56th Street, Chicago, Illinois* 60637, *U.S.A. (Telephone:* (312) 753-8562).	
1975	CHARNLEY, SIR JOHN, C.B.E. Consultant Orthopaedic Surgeon and Director of the Centre for Hip Surgery, Wrightington Hospital, Lancashire. Professor of Orthopaedic Surgery in the University of Manchester. *Wrightington Hospital, Appley Bridge, Wigan, Lancashire;* and *Birchwood, Moss Lane, Mere, Knutsford, Cheshire. (Telephone: Knutsford* 2267).	
1976	CHARNOCK, HENRY. Director of the Institute of Oceanographic Sciences and Visiting Professor of Physical Oceanography in the University of Southampton. *Institute of Oceanographic Sciences, Wormley, Godalming, Surrey, GU8 5UB. (Telephone: Wormley* 2122); and *Wildcroft, Gasden Lane, Witley, Godalming, Surrey, GU8 5RJ. (Telephone: Wormley* 2813).	
1961	CHATT, JOSEPH. Professor of Chemistry in the University of Sussex. Director, Unit of Nitrogen Fixation, Agricultural Research Council. *School of Molecular Sciences, The University of Sussex, Falmer, Brighton, BN1 9QJ. (Telephone: Brighton* 63446); and *High Norton,* 28 *Tongdean Avenue, Hove, East Sussex, BN3 6TN. (Telephone: Brighton* 554377).	1975-
1969	CHESTERS, JOHN HUGH, O.B.E., D.Sc.Tech. Formerly Director, The Corporate Laboratories of the British Steel Corporation (Bisra). 21 *Slayleigh Lane, Sheffield, S*10 3*RF. (Telephone: Sheffield* 301257).	
1937	CHIBNALL, ALBERT CHARLES. Emeritus Professor of Biochemistry at the Imperial College of Science and Technology in the University of London. LECTURE: BAKERIAN (1942). 6 *Millington Road, Cambridge. (Telephone: Cambridge* 53923); also *Athenaeum.*	1946–48
1975	CHRISTIAN, JOHN WYRILL. Professor of Physical Metallurgy in the University of Oxford. *Department of Metallurgy and Science of Materials, Parks Road, Oxford, OX*1 3*PH. (Telephone: Oxford* 59981); and 27 *Linton Road, Oxford. (Telephone: Oxford* 58569).	

Date of Election		Service on Council
1926	CHRISTOPHERS, SIR (SAMUEL) RICKARD, C.I.E., O.B.E., Colonel I.M.S. (retired). MEDAL: BUCHANAN (1952). *Cluanie House, 18 Ridgeway, Broadstone, Dorset.*	
1960	CHRISTOPHERSON, SIR DERMAN (GUY), O.B.E. Vice-Chancellor and Warden of the University of Durham. *Old Shire Hall, Durham, DH1 3HP, Co. Durham. (Telephone: Durham 64466);* also *Athenaeum.*	1974-75
1959	CLAPHAM, ARTHUR ROY, C.B.E. Emeritus Professor of Botany in the University of Sheffield. *The Parrock, Arkholme, Carnforth, Lancashire, LA6 1AU. (Telephone: Hornby 21206).*	1963-64
1970	CLARKE, SIR CYRIL (ASTLEY), K.B.E. Honorary Nuffield Research Fellow in the Department of Genetics and Emeritus Professor of Medicine in the University of Liverpool. *Royal College of Physicians, 11 St Andrew's Place, Regent's Park, London, NW1 4LE. (Telephone: 01-935 1174); Nuffield Unit of Medical Genetics, The University, Crown Street, P.O. Box 147, Liverpool, L69 3BX. (Telephone: 051-709 6022, extension 596);* and *High Close, Thorsway, Caldy, The Wirral, Merseyside, L48 2JJ. (Telephone: 051-625 8811);* also *Athenaeum.*	
1976	CLARKE, PATRICIA HANNAH. Professor of Microbial Biochemistry at University College in the University of London. *Department of Biochemistry, University College London, Gower Street, London, WC1E 6BT. (Telephone: 01-387 7050, extension 297);* and 11 *Selwyn House, Lansdowne Terrace, London, WC1N 1DJ. (Telephone: 01-278 3918).*	
1937	CLEMO, GEORGE ROGER. Emeritus Professor of Organic Chemistry and lately Director of the Chemistry Department at King's College in the University of Durham. *Cherryburn, Mickley-on-Tyne, Northumberland. (Telephone: Stocksfield 3285).*	
1970	COALES, JOHN FLAVELL, C.B.E. Emeritus Professor of Engineering in the University of Cambridge. *Department of Engineering, Management and Control Engineering Division, Mill Lane, Cambridge, CB2 1SF. (Telephone: Cambridge 66466);* and 4 *Latham Road, Cambridge, CB2 2EQ. (Telephone: Cambridge 63596);* also *Athenaeum.*	
1962	COCHRAN, WILLIAM. Professor of Natural Philosophy in the University of Edinburgh. *Department of Physics, The University, James Clerk Maxwell Building, The King's Buildings, Mayfield Road, Edinburgh, EH9 3JZ. (Telephone: 031-667 1081, extension 2800);* and 71 *Clermiston Road, Edinburgh.*	
1967	COCKERELL, SIR CHRISTOPHER (SYDNEY), C.B.E. Chairman of Ripplecraft Company Limited. Consultant to the British Hovercraft Corporation and formerly Director and Consultant of Hovercraft Development Limited. MEDAL: ROYAL (1966). 16 *Prospect Place, Hythe, Southampton, Hampshire, SO4 6AU. (Telephone: Southampton 842931).*	
1965	COLLAR, ARTHUR RODERICK, C.B.E. Emeritus Professor of Aeronautical Engineering in the University of Bristol. 12 *Rockleaze, Bristol, BS9 1NE. (Telephone: Bristol 681491).*	1971-73

Date of Election		Service on Council
1969	COOK, ALAN HUGH. Jacksonian Professor of Natural Philosophy in the University of Cambridge. *Cavendish Laboratory, Madingley Road, Cambridge, CB3 0HE. (Telephone: Cambridge 66477); King's College, Cambridge, CB2 1ST. (Telephone: Cambridge 50411); and 8 Wootton Way, Cambridge, CB3 9LX. (Telephone: Cambridge 56887).*	1972-73
1951	COOK, ARTHUR HERBERT, D.Sc. Formerly Director, Brewing Industry Research Foundation. *Merrylands, Lympstone, Devon. (Telephone: Exmouth 71426);* also *Athenaeum.*	
1962	COOK, SIR WILLIAM (RICHARD JOSEPH), K.C.B. Formerly Chief Adviser (Projects and Research), Ministry of Defence. *Adbury Springs, Newbury, Berkshire. (Telephone: Newbury 40409);* also *Athenaeum.*	1964-65
1969	COOKE, GEORGE WILLIAM, C.B.E., Ph.D. Chief Scientific Officer to the Agricultural Research Council. *Agricultural Research Council, 160 Great Portland Street, London, W1N 6DT. (Telephone: 01-580 6655, extension 275);* and *33 Topstreet Way, Harpenden, Hertfordshire. (Telephone: Harpenden 2899).*	
1968	COOKSON, RICHARD CLIVE. Professor of Chemistry in the University of Southampton. *Department of Chemistry, The University, Southampton, SO9 5NH. (Telephone: Southampton 559122).*	
1965	COOMBS, ROBERT ROYSTON AMOS. Quick Professor of Biology in the University of Cambridge. *Immunology Division, Department of Pathology, Laboratories' Block, Addenbrooke's Hospital, Hills Road, Cambridge, CB2 2QQ. (Telephone: Cambridge 45171, extension 336);* and *6 Selwyn Gardens, Cambridge. (Telephone: Cambridge 52681).*	
1964	COOPER, LESLIE HUGH NORMAN, O.B.E., D.Sc. Formerly Chemist, Marine Biological Association of the United Kingdom. *2 Queens Gate Villas, Lipson, Plymouth, PL4 7PN. (Telephone: Plymouth 61174).*	
1971	COPP, DOUGLAS HAROLD. Professor of Physiology in the University of British Columbia. *Department of Physiology, University of British Columbia, Vancouver, 8, B.C., Canada. (Telephone: (604)-228-2671);* and *4755 Belmont Avenue, Vancouver, Canada. (Telephone: (604)-224-3793).*	
1955	CORNER, EDRED JOHN HENRY, C.B.E. Emeritus Professor of Tropical Botany in the University of Cambridge. MEDAL: DARWIN (1960). *91 Hinton Way, Great Shelford, Cambridgeshire, CB2 5AH. (Telephone: Shelford 2167).*	1961-62
1953	CORNFORTH, SIR JOHN (WARCUP), C.B.E. Royal Society Research Professor in the University of Sussex. MEDALS: DAVY (1968), ROYAL (1976). Nobel Laureate, Chemistry, 1975. *School of Molecular Sciences, University of Sussex, Falmer, Brighton, BN1 9QJ. (Telephone: Brighton 66755, extension 260);* and *Saxon Down, Cuilfail, Lewes, East Sussex, BN7 2BE. (Telephone: Lewes 4729).*	

Date of Election		Service on Council
1972	COSSLETT, VERNON ELLIS, Sc.D. Emeritus Reader in Electron Physics in the University of Cambridge and Fellow of Corpus Christi College, Cambridge. *Corpus Christi College, Cambridge; and Cavendish Laboratory, Free School Lane, Cambridge.* (*Telephone: Cambridge* 58381, *extension* 321).	
1955	COTTRELL, SIR ALAN (HOWARD). Master of Jesus College, Cambridge. LECTURE: BAKERIAN (1963). MEDALS: HUGHES (1961), RUMFORD (1974). *The Master's Lodge, Jesus College, Cambridge, CB5 8BL.* (*Telephone: Cambridge* 53310); also *Athenaeum*.	1963–65 1975– V.P. 1964–65 1975–
1947	COWLING, THOMAS GEORGE. Emeritus Professor of Applied Mathematics in the University of Leeds. *19 Hollin Gardens, Headingley, Leeds, LS16 5NL.* (*Telephone: Leeds* 785342).	
1973	COX, DAVID ROXBEE. Professor of Statistics at the Imperial College of Science and Technology in the University of London. *Department of Mathematics, Imperial College, Queen's Gate, London, SW7 5HH.* (*Telephone:* 01-589 5111, *extension* 2600); *and* 16 *Morford Way, Eastcote, Ruislip, Middlesex.* (*Telephone:* 01-868 8669).	
1954	COX, SIR (ERNEST) GORDON, K.B.E., T.D. Formerly Secretary, Agricultural Research Council. *117 Hampstead Way, London, NW11 7JN.* (*Telephone:* 01-455 2618); also *Athenaeum*.	
1950	COXETER, HAROLD SCOTT MACDONALD. Professor of Mathematics, University of Toronto. *67 Roxborough Drive, Toronto M4W 1X2, Ontario, Canada.* (*Telephone:* (416) 962-5665).	
1968	CRAIG, DAVID PARKER. Professor of Physical and Theoretical Chemistry at the Institute of Advanced Studies in the Australian National University. *Research School of Chemistry, Australian National University, P.O. Box 4, Canberra, A.C.T. 2600, Australia.* (*Telephone:* 49.3578); *and* 199 *Dryandra Street, O'Connor, A.C.T. 2601, Australia.* (*Telephone:* 49.1976).	
1947	CRAIGIE, JAMES, O.B.E., Ph.D. *24 Inveralmond Drive, Cramond, Edinburgh, EH4 6JX.*	
1952	CRAIGIE, JOHN HUBERT, Ph.D. *479 Kensington Avenue, Ottawa, 3, Canada.*	
1947	CRANE, MORLEY BENJAMIN. Formerly Deputy Director and Head of the Department of Pomology in the John Innes Horticultural Institution. *Fishponds Way, Haughley, near Stowmarket, Suffolk.*	
1959	CRICK, FRANCIS HARRY COMPTON, Ph.D. Research Worker for the Medical Research Council. LECTURE: CROONIAN (1966). MEDALS: ROYAL (1972), COPLEY (1975). Nobel Laureate, Physiology or Medicine, 1962. *M.R.C. Laboratory of Molecular Biology, Hills Road, Cambridge, CB2 2QH.* (*Telephone: Cambridge* 48011); *and The Golden Helix,* 19 *Portugal Place, Cambridge.*	

Date of Election		Service on Council

1968 CRISP, DENNIS JOHN. Professor of Marine Biology at the University College of North Wales in the University of Wales. Honorary Director of the Natural Environment Research Council's Unit of Marine Invertebrate Biology. *Marine Science Laboratories, Menai Bridge, Gwynedd. (Telephone: Menai Bridge* 712641); and *Craig y Pin, Llandegfan, Menai Bridge, Gwynedd. (Telephone: Menai Bridge* 712775).

1973 CROMBIE, LESLIE. Sir Jesse Boot Professor of Organic Chemistry in the University of Nottingham. *Department of Chemistry, The University, Nottingham, NG7 2RD. (Telephone: Nottingham* 56101, *extension* 2401); also *Athenaeum.*

1975 CROSS, BARRY ALBERT, Sc.D. Director of the Agricultural Research Council Institute of Animal Physiology, Babraham, Cambridge. *A.R.C. Institute of Animal Physiology, Babraham, Cambridge, CB2 4AT. (Telephone: Sawston* 2312); and 6 *Babraham Road, Cambridge, CB2 2RA. (Telephone: Cambridge* 48368).

1953 CURRAN, SIR SAMUEL (CROWE). Principal and Vice-Chancellor, The University of Strathclyde, Glasgow. *The University of Strathclyde, Royal College,* 204 *George Street, Glasgow, G1 1XW. (Telephone:* 041-552 4400); and 5 *Camstradden Drive East, Bearsden, Glasgow, G61 4AH. (Telephone:* 041-942 3936).

1974 CURTIS, DAVID RODERICK. Professor of Pharmacology at the John Curtin School of Medical Research, Australian National University. *Department of Pharmacology, Australian National University, P.O. Box* 334, *Canberra City, A.C.T.* 2601, *Australia. (Telephone: Canberra* 49 2757); and 7 *Patey Street, Campbell, Canberra City, A.C.T.* 2601, *Australia. (Telephone: Canberra* 48 5664).

1967 DACIE, SIR JOHN (VIVIAN). Professor of Haematology at the Royal Postgraduate Medical School in the University of London. *Royal Postgraduate Medical School, Ducane Road, London, W.*12; *(Telephone:* 01-743 2030); and 10 *Alan Road, Wimbledon, London, S.W.*19. *(Telephone:* 01-946 6086).

1957 DAINTON, SIR FREDERICK (SYDNEY). Chairman of the University Grants Committee. MEDAL: DAVY (1969). *University Grants Committee,* 14 *Park Crescent, London, W1N 4DH. (Telephone:* 01-636 7799); and *Fieldside, Water Eaton Lane, Oxford, OX5 2PR. (Telephone: Kidlington* 5132); also *Athenaeum.* 1964-66

1972 DALGARNO, ALEXANDER. Professor of Astronomy at Harvard University and Associate Director of the Center for Astrophysics. 60 *Garden Street, Cambridge, Massachusetts* 02138, *U.S.A. (Telephone:* (617) 495-4403).

Date of Election		*Service on Council*

1960 DALITZ, RICHARD HENRY. Royal Society Research Professor at the University of Oxford. LECTURE: BAKERIAN (1969). MEDAL: HUGHES (1975). *Department of Theoretical Physics, 12 Parks Road, Oxford, OX1 3PQ. (Telephone: Oxford 53281, extension 352); and All Souls College, Oxford.*

1975 DALZIEL, KEITH, Ph.D. Lecturer in Biochemistry in the University of Oxford. *Department of Biochemistry, South Parks Road, Oxford, OX1 3QU. (Telephone: Oxford 59214); Wolfson College, Oxford;* and *25 Hampden Drive, Kidlington, Oxford. (Telephone: Kidlington 2623).*

1969 DANCKWERTS, PETER VICTOR, G.C., M.B.E. Shell Professor of Chemical Engineering in the University of Cambridge. *Department of Chemical Engineering, Pembroke Street, Cambridge. CB2 3RA. (Telephone: Cambridge 58231);* and *The Abbey House, Abbey Road, Cambridge. (Telephone: Cambridge 57275).*

1957 DANIELLI, JAMES FREDERIC, D.Sc. Head of the Department of Life Sciences at Worcester Polytechnic Institute, U.S.A. *Department of Life Sciences, Worcester Polytechnic Institute, Worcester, Massachusetts 01609, U.S.A. (Telephone: (617) 753-1411);* and *Tangnefedd, Dinas Cross, Dyfed.*

1941 DARLINGTON, CYRIL DEAN. Emeritus Professor of Botany in the University of Oxford and Honorary Fellow of Magdalen College, Oxford. LECTURE: TERCENTENARY (1960). MEDAL: ROYAL (1946). *Botany School, South Parks Road, Oxford. (Telephone: Oxford 53391); Magdalen College, Oxford;* and *Pin Farm Cottage, South Hinksey, Oxford, OX1 5BB. (Telephone: Oxford 735288).*   1944-45

1974 DAVIDSON, JOHN FRANK. Professor of Chemical Engineering in the University of Cambridge. *Department of Chemical Engineering, Pembroke Street, Cambridge, CB2 3RA. (Telephone: Cambridge 58231);* and *5 Luard Close, Cambridge, CB2 2PL. (Telephone: Cambridge 46104).*

1966 DAVIES, ROBERT ERNEST. Benjamin Franklin Professor of Molecular Biology in the University of Pennsylvania. *Department of Animal Biology, School of Veterinary Medicine, Philadelphia, Pennsylvania 19104, U.S.A. (Telephone: 215-243-7861).*

1971 DAWES, GEOFFREY SHARMAN. Professor in the University of Oxford and Director of the Nuffield Institute for Medical Research, University of Oxford, *Nuffield Institute for Medical Research, Headley Way, Headington, Oxford, OX3 9DS. (Telephone: Oxford 65855);* and *8 Belbroughton Road, Oxford. (Telephone: Oxford 58131).*   1975– V.P 1975–

1944 DEACON, SIR GEORGE (EDWARD RAVEN), C.B.E. Formerly Director, National Institute of Oceanography. MEDAL: ROYAL (1969). *Institute of Oceanographic Sciences, Wormley, near Godalming, Surrey, GU8 5UB. (Telephone: Wormley 2122);* and *Flitwick House, Milford, Surrey, GU8 5DS. (Telephone: Godalming 5929).*   1957–59

Date of Election		Service on Council
1967	DE BRUYNE, NORMAN ADRIAN, Ph.D. Chairman, Techne Inc. 3700 *Brunswick Pike, Princeton, New Jersey* 08540, *U.S.A.* (*Telephone:* (609)-452-9275).	
1941	DEE, PHILIP IVOR, C.B.E. Emeritus Professor of Natural Philosophy in the University of Glasgow. LECTURE: RUTHERFORD MEMORIAL (1965). MEDAL: HUGHES (1952). *Speedwell, Buchanan Castle Estate, Drymen, Stirlingshire.* (*Telephone: Drymen* 283).	1952-53
1962	DEER, WILLIAM ALEXANDER. Professor of Mineralogy and Petrology in the University of Cambridge. *Department of Mineralogy and Petrology, Downing Place, Cambridge, CB2 3EW.* (*Telephone: Cambridge* 64131); and *Steading, Church Street, Great Shelford, Cambridgeshire.* (*Telephone: Shelford* 3671).	1966-67
1975	DE MAYO, PAUL. Professor of Chemistry in the University of Western Ontario, Canada. *Photochemistry Laboratory, Department of Chemistry, University of Western Ontario, London, N6A 5B7, Ontario, Canada.* (*Telephone:* (519) 679-2473); and 436 *St George Street, London, Ontario, Canada.* (*Telephone:* (519) 679-9026).	
1965	DENBIGH, KENNETH GEORGE, D.Sc. Principal of Queen Elizabeth College, University of London. *Queen Elizabeth College, Campden Hill Road, London, W.8.* (*Telephone:* 01-937 5078); and 19 *Sheridan Road, Merton Park, London, S.W.19.*	
1964	DENTON, ERIC JAMES, C.B.E. Secretary of the Marine Biological Association of the United Kingdom and Director of the Plymouth Laboratory. Honorary Professor at the University of Bristol. LECTURE: CROONIAN (1973). *The Laboratory, Citadel Hill, Plymouth, PL1 2PB.* (*Telephone: Plymouth* 21761); and *Fairfield House, St Germans, Saltash, Cornwall, PL12 5LS.* (*Telephone: St Germans (Cornwall)* 204).	1969-71
1955	DEVONS, SAMUEL. Professor of Physics, Columbia University and Director of the History of Physics Laboratory, Barnard College, Columbia University. *Pupin Laboratory, Columbia University, New York, N.Y.* 10027, *U.S.A.* (*Telephone:* (212) 280-5102 *and* 4124); and *Lewis Road, Irvington-on-Hudson, N.Y.* 10533, *U.S.A.* (*Telephone:* (914) *L Y*-1-7681).	
1960	DEWAR, MICHAEL JAMES STEUART. Robert A. Welch Professor of Chemistry in the University of Texas. *Department of Chemistry, University of Texas, Austin, Texas* 78712, *U.S.A.* (*Telephone:* (512) 471-5053).	
1946	DICKENS, FRANK. Emeritus Professor of Biochemistry at Middlesex Hospital Medical School in the University of London. 9 *Doone End, Ferring, West Sussex, BN12 5PT.* (*Telephone: Worthing* 43627).	1953-55

Date of Election		Service on Council
1930	DIRAC, PAUL ADRIEN MAURICE, O.M. Emeritus Professor of Mathematics in the University of Cambridge. Professor of Physics at Florida State University. LECTURE: BAKERIAN (1941). MEDALS: ROYAL (1939), COPLEY (1952). Nobel Laureate, Physics, 1933. *St John's College, Cambridge; and Department of Physics, Florida State University, Tallahassee, Florida 32306, U.S.A.*	
1962	DITCHBURN, ROBERT WILLIAM. Emeritus Professor of Physics in the University of Reading. *New Applied Science Building, Whiteknights Park, Reading, RG6 2AY. (Telephone: Reading 85123);* and 9 *Summerfield Rise, Goring, Reading, RG8 0DS. (Telephone: Goring 3470).*	
1958	DIXEY, SIR FRANK, K.C.M.G., O.B.E., D.Sc. Formerly Geological Adviser to the Secretary of State for the Colonies, and Director of Overseas Geological Surveys. *Woodpecker Cottage, Bramber, near Steyning, West Sussex. (Telephone: Steyning 812313); also Athenaeum.*	
1942	DIXON, MALCOLM. Emeritus Professor of Enzyme Biochemistry in the University of Cambridge. *Department of Biochemistry, Tennis Court Road, Cambridge. (Telephone: Cambridge 51781);* and 27 *Parkside, Cambridge, CB1 1JE. (Telephone: Cambridge 50340); also Athenaeum.*	
1975	DODD, JAMES MUNRO. Lloyd-Roberts Professor of Zoology and Head of the Department of Zoology at the University College of North Wales in the University of Wales. *Department of Zoology, University College of North Wales, Bangor, Gwynedd, LL57 2UW. (Telephone: Bangor 51151, extension 500);* and *Weirglodd Wen, Bulkeley Road, Bangor, Gwynedd, LL57 2BP. (Telephone: Bangor 2236).*	
1966	DOLL, SIR (WILLIAM) RICHARD (SHABOE), O.B.E. Regius Professor of Medicine in the University of Oxford. MEDAL: BUCHANAN (1972). 13 *Norham Gardens, Oxford. (Telephone: Oxford 55207).*	1970–71 V.P. 1970–71
1970	DOUGLAS, ALEXANDER EDGAR, Ph.D. Principal Research Officer, National Research Council of Canada. *Herzberg Institute of Astrophysics, National Research Council, Ottawa, K1A 0R6, Canada. (Telephone: 996-1688);* and 150 *Blenheim Drive, Ottawa, Canada. (Telephone: 746-1453).*	
1955	DOWNIE, ALLAN WATT. Emeritus Professor of Bacteriology in the University of Liverpool. *Canna, College Close, Southport, Merseyside. (Telephone: Southport 67269).*	
1937	DRURY, SIR ALAN (NIGEL), C.B.E. Formerly Member of Staff of the Agricultural Research Council. 36 *Gretton Court, High Street, Girton, Cambridge, CB3 0QN (Telephone: Cambridge 77181).*	1940–41 1954–56 V.P. 1955–56

THE FELLOWSHIP 1977 35

Date of Election		Service on Council

1960 DUKE-ELDER, Sir (William) Stewart, G.C.V.O. President, Institute of Ophthalmology, University of London. 28 *Elm Tree Road, London, N.W.8.* (*Telephone:* 01-286 9491); also *Athenaeum.*

1955 DUNHAM, Sir Kingsley (Charles). Formerly Director of the Institute of Geological Sciences, and Emeritus Professor of Geology in the University of Durham. Medal: ROYAL (1970). *Charleycroft, Quarryheads Lane, Durham, DH1 3DY.* (*Telephone: Durham* 3977); also *Athenaeum.*
   1964–66
   1971–76
   For. Sec.
   1971–76
   V.P.
   1971–76

1974 DUNITZ, Jack David. Professor of Chemical Crystallography at the Swiss Federal Institute of Technology (E.T.H.), Zurich. *Laboratorium für organische Chemie der ETH-Z, Universitätstrasse 16, CH-8092 Zürich, Switzerland.* (*Telephone:* (01) 326211, *extension* 2892); and *Obere Heslibachstrasse 77, CH-8700 Küsnacht, Switzerland.* (*Telephone:* (01) 901723).

1952 DYSON, Freeman John. Professor of Physics at the Institute for Advanced Study, Princeton. Medal: HUGHES (1968). *Institute for Advanced Study, Princeton, New Jersey, U.S.A.*

1968 DYSON, James, Sc.D. Formerly Deputy Chief Scientific Officer, Division of Mechanical and Optical Metrology, National Physical Laboratory. 19 *Hansler Grove, East Molesey, Surrey, KT8 9JN.* (*Telephone:* 01-979 6403).

1970 EABORN, Colin. Professor of Chemistry in the University of Sussex. *School of Molecular Sciences, University of Sussex, Brighton, BN1 9QJ.* (*Telephone: Brighton* 66755); and 3 *Ridgway Paddock, Kingston, Lewes, East Sussex, BN7 3LA.* (*Telephone: Lewes* 3680).

1968 EASTWOOD, Sir Eric, C.B.E. Consultant, GEC-Marconi Electronics Limited. Lecture: CLIFFORD PATERSON (1976). *Marconi Research Laboratories, GEC-Marconi Electronics Limited, West Hanningfield Road, Great Baddow, Chelmsford, CM2 8HN.* (*Telephone: Chelmsford* 73331, *extension* 296); and *Greenlanes, Little Baddow, Chelmsford, Essex.* (*Telephone: Danbury* 3240).

1941 ECCLES, Sir John (Carew). Distinguished Professor Emeritus at the State University of New York at Buffalo. Lecture: FERRIER (1959). Medal: ROYAL (1962). Nobel Laureate, Physiology or Medicine, 1963. *Ca' a la Gra', CH 6611, Contra (Locarno; Ticino), Switzerland.* (*Telephone:* 093-67 29 31).

1974 EDMAN, Pehr Victor, M.D. Director of Department in the Max-Planck Institute of Biochemistry, Munich. *Max-Planck Institut für Biochemie, 8033 Martinsried bei München, Federal Republic of Germany.* (*Telephone:* 8585-475); and *Pasteurstrasse 7, 8033 Martinsried bei München, Federal Republic of Germany.*

Date of Election		Service on Council
1968	EDWARDS, SIR GEORGE (ROBERT), O.M., C.B.E. Formerly Chairman, British Aircraft Corporation Limited. MEDAL: ROYAL (1974). *Albury Heights, White Lane, Guildford, Surrey. (Telephone: Guildford 4488); also Athenaeum.*	
1966	EDWARDS, SIR SAM (SAMUEL FREDERICK). Chairman of the Science Research Council and John Humphrey Plummer Professor of Physics in the University of Cambridge. *Science Research Council, State House, High Holborn, WC1R 4TA. (Telephone: 01-242 1262, extension 1); and 7 Penarth Place, Cambridge, CB3 9LU. (Telephone: Cambridge 66610); also Athenaeum.*	
1976	EGLINTON, GEOFFREY. Professor of Organic Geochemistry in the University of Bristol. *School of Chemistry, The University, Bristol, BS8 1TS. (Telephone: Bristol 24161, extension 623); and 7 Red House Lane, Bristol, BS9 3RY. (Telephone: Bristol 683833).*	
1964	ELEY, DANIEL DOUGLAS, O.B.E. Professor of Physical Chemistry in the University of Nottingham. *Department of Chemistry, The University, University Park, Nottingham, NG7 2RD. (Telephone: Nottingham 56101); and Brooklands, 35 Brookland Drive, Chilwell, Beeston, Nottingham, NG9 4BD. (Telephone: Nottingham 255701).*	
1973	ELLIOT, HARRY, C.B.E. Professor of Physics at the Imperial College of Science and Technology in the University of London. *Department of Physics, Imperial College, London, SW7 2AZ. (Telephone: 01-589 5111, extension 2301).*	
1976	ELLIOTT, ROGER JAMES. Wykeham Professor of Theoretical Physics in the University of Oxford. *Department of Theoretical Physics, 12 Parks Road, Oxford, OX1 3PQ. (Telephone: Oxford 53281); and 11 Crick Road, Oxford. (Telephone: Oxford 58369).*	
1929	ELLIS, SIR CHARLES (DRUMMOND). Scientific Adviser, Gas Council, British American Tobacco Co. Ltd, and Battelle Memorial Institute. *Seawards, Cookham Dean, Berkshire. (Telephone: Marlow 3166); also Athenaeum.*	
1953	ELTON, CHARLES SUTHERLAND. MEDAL: DARWIN (1970). Formerly Reader in Animal Ecology and Director of the Bureau of Animal Population, Oxford. *61 Park Town, Oxford, OX2 6SL.*	
1946	EMELÉUS, HARRY JULIUS, C.B.E. Emeritus Professor of Inorganic Chemistry in the University of Cambridge. MEDAL: DAVY (1962). *University Chemical Laboratory, Lensfield Road, Cambridge, CB2 1EW. (Telephone: Cambridge 56491); and 149 Shelford Road, Trumpington, Cambridge, CB2 2ND. (Telephone: Trumpington 2374).*	1952–54
1946	ENGLEDOW, SIR FRANK (LEONARD), C.M.G. Emeritus Professor of Agriculture in the University of Cambridge. *Hadleigh, Huntingdon Road, Girton, Cambridge, CB3 0LH. (Telephone: Cambridge 76138).*	1948–49

Date of Election		Service on Council
1975	ERDÉLYI, ARTHUR. Professor of Mathematics in the University of Edinburgh. *Department of Mathematics, James Clerk Maxwell Building, The King's Buildings, Mayfield Road, Edinburgh, EH9 3JZ.* (*Telephone:* 031-667 1081, *extension* 2999); and 26 *Gilmour Road, Edinburgh, EH16 5NT.* (*Telephone:* 031-667 3238).	
1974	ESHELBY, JOHN DOUGLAS. Professor of the Theory of Materials in the University of Sheffield. *Department of the Theory of Materials, University of Sheffield, St George's Square, Mappin Street, Sheffield, S1 3JD.* (*Telephone:* Sheffield 78555, *extension* 245); and *Flat 9, Beech Court, Beech Hill Road, Sheffield, S10 2SA.*	
1960	ESSEN, LOUIS, O.B.E., D.Sc. Formerly Deputy Chief Scientific Officer, National Physical Laboratory. *High Hallgarth,* 41 *Durleston Park Drive, Great Bookham, Surrey.* (*Telephone: Bookham* 54103).	
1960	EVANS, SIR DAVID (GWYNNE), C.B.E. Formerly Director of the National Institute for Biological Standards and Control. Emeritus Professor of Bacteriology and Immunology in the University of London. *National Institute for Biological Standards and Control, Holly Hill, London, NW3 6RB.* (*Telephone:* 01-435 2232); and 33 *Elmtree Green, Great Missenden, Buckinghamshire, HP16 9AF.* (*Telephone: Great Missenden* 3278); also *Athenaeum.*	1966–67
1976	EVANS, LLOYD THOMAS, D.Sc. Chief of the Division of Plant Industry, Commonwealth Scientific and Industrial Research Organization. *Division of Plant Industry, C.S.I.R.O., P.O. Box 1600, Canberra City, A.C.T. 2601, Australia.* (*Telephone:* 46-5250); and 3 *Elliott Street, Campbell, A.C.T. 2601, Australia.* (*Telephone:* 47-7815).	
1949	EVANS, ULICK RICHARDSON, C.B.E., Sc.D. Honorary Fellow of King's College, Cambridge. Emeritus Reader in the Science of Metallic Corrosion in the University of Cambridge. 19 *Manor Court, Grange Road, Cambridge.* (*Telephone:* Cambridge 55005).	
1958	EWALD, PAUL PETER. Emeritus Professor of Physics at the Polytechnic Institute of Brooklyn, U.S.A. 108 *Sheldon Road, Ithaca, N.Y. 14850, U.S.A.*	
1942	FAGE, ARTHUR, C.B.E. Formerly Superintendent of the Aerodynamics Division of the National Physical Laboratory. 65 *High Point, Richmond Hill Road, Edgbaston, Birmingham, B15 3RS.* (*Telephone:* 021-454 3205).	
1960	FALCON, NORMAN LESLIE. Formerly Chief Geologist, British Petroleum Company Limited. *The Downs, Chiddingfold, Surrey.* (*Telephone: Wormley* 3101).	
1973	FALCONER, DOUGLAS SCOTT. Professor of Genetics in the University of Edinburgh and Director of the Agricultural Research Council Unit of Animal Genetics. *Institute of Animal Genetics, West Mains Road, Edinburgh, EH9 3JN.* (*Telephone:* 031-667 1081, *extension* 3508).	

Date of Election		Service on Council
1972	FARLEY, FRANCIS JAMES MACDONALD, Sc.D. Dean of the Royal Military College of Science, Shrivenham. *Royal Military College of Science, Shrivenham, Swindon, Wiltshire, SN6 8LA. (Telephone: Shrivenham 782551, extension 204); and Brandon, Buckland, Faringdon, Oxfordshire, SN7 8QW. (Telephone: Buckland 676);* also *Athenaeum.*	
1969	FATT, PAUL. Professor of Biophysics at University College in the University of London. *Department of Biophysics, University College, Gower Street, London, WC1E 6BT.*	
1945	FEATHER, NORMAN. Emeritus Professor of Natural Philosophy in the University of Edinburgh. *Department of Physics, James Clerk Maxwell Building, Mayfield Road, Edinburgh, EH9 3JZ. (Telephone:* 031-667 1081, *extension* 2798); *and* 9 *Priestfield Road, Edinburgh, EH*16 5*HJ. (Telephone:* 031-667 2631).	1956–58
1959	FEILDEN, GEOFFREY BERTRAM ROBERT, C.B.E., D.Sc.(Hon.). Director-General, British Standards Institution. *British Standards Institution,* 2 *Park Street, London, W1A* 2*BS. (Telephone:* 01-629 9000); *and Greys End, Rotherfield Greys, Henley-on-Thames, Oxfordshire. (Telephone: Rotherfield Greys* 211); also *Athenaeum.*	1962–63 1966–69 V.P. 1967–69
1947	FELDBERG, WILHELM SIEGMUND, C.B.E. Emeritus Professor. Attached worker, Division of Neurophysiology and Neuropharmacology, National Institute for Medical Research. LECTURE: FERRIER (1974). *National Institute for Medical Research, Mill Hill, London, NW*7 1*AA. (Telephone:* 01-959 3666); and *Lavenham,* 74 *Marsh Lane, Mill Hill, London, NW*7 4*NT. (Telephone:* 01-959 5545).	
1952	FELL, DAME HONOR (BRIDGET), D.B.E. Formerly Director of the Strangeways Research Laboratory. *Department of Pathology, Division of Immunology, Laboratories' Block, Addenbrooke's Hospital, Hills Road, Cambridge, CB*2 2*QQ. (Telephone: Cambridge* 45171, *extension* 339); *and* 42*b Queen Edith's Way, Cambridge. (Telephone: Cambridge* 47022).	
1958	FENNER, FRANK JOHN, C.M.G., M.B.E. Professor of Environmental Studies and Director, Centre for Resource and Environmental Studies, Australian National University. LECTURE: LEEUWENHOEK (1961). *Centre for Resource and Environmental Studies, Australian National University, Canberra, A.C.T., Australia. (Telephone:* 49-4588).	
1969	FINCHAM, JOHN ROBERT STANLEY. Professor of Genetics in the University of Edinburgh. *Department of Genetics, University of Edinburgh, King's Buildings, West Mains Road, Edinburgh, EH*9 3*JN;* and 93A *Mayfield Road, Edinburgh, EH*9 3*AQ.*	1974–76
1955	FINNEY, DAVID JOHN. Professor of Statistics in the University of Edinburgh, and Director of the Agricultural Research Council's Unit of Statistics. *Department of Statistics, University of Edinburgh, James Clerk Maxwell Building, The King's Buildings, Mayfield Road, Edinburgh, EH*9 3*JZ. (Telephone:* 031-667 1081); *and* 43 *Cluny Drive, Edinburgh, EH*10 6*DU. (Telephone:* 031-447 2332).	

Date of Election		Service on Council
1969	FINNISTON, SIR (HAROLD) MONTAGUE. Chairman of Sears Engineering Ltd. *Sears Holdings Ltd*, 40 *Duke Street, London, W1M 6AN*. (*Telephone:* 01-408 1180); and *Flat No. 72, 33 Prince Albert Road, St John's Wood, London, N.W.8*. (*Telephone:* 01-722 8197); also *Athenaeum*.	1971–72 V.P. 1971–72

1971 FISHER, MICHAEL ELLIS. Horace White Professor of Chemistry, Physics and Mathematics at Cornell University and Chairman of the Department of Chemistry. *Baker Laboratory, Cornell University, Ithaca, New York* 14850, *U.S.A.* (*Telephone:* (607) 256-4174).

1967 FLEMING, SIR CHARLES (ALEXANDER), K.B.E. Formerly Chief Palaeontologist, New Zealand Geological Survey. Honorary Lecturer in Geology in the Victoria University of Wellington. 42 *Wadestown Road, Wellington,* 1, *New Zealand*. (*Telephone:* Wellington 737.288).

1961 FLOWERS, SIR BRIAN (HILTON). Rector of the Imperial College of Science and Technology, University of London. *Imperial College of Science and Technology, London, SW7 2AZ*. (*Telephone:* 01-589 5111); also *Athenaeum*.

1965 FOGG, GORDON ELLIOTT. Professor of Marine Biology in the University College of North Wales. LECTURE: LEEUWENHOEK (1968). *Department of Marine Biology, Marine Science Laboratories, Menai Bridge, Gwynedd, LL59 5EH*. (*Telephone:* Menai Bridge 712641, *extension* 27); and *Bodolben, Llandegfan, Menai Bridge, Gwynedd*. (*Telephone: Menai Bridge* 712916); also *Athenaeum*.

1965 FORD, CHARLES EDMUND, D.Sc. Member, External Staff, Medical Research Council. *Sir William Dunn School of Pathology, South Parks Road, Oxford, OX1 3RE*. (*Telephone: Oxford* 57321); and 156 *Oxford Road, Abingdon, Oxfordshire*. (*Telephone:* Abingdon 20001).

1946 FORD, EDMUND BRISCO. Emeritus Professor of Ecological Genetics in the University of Oxford. MEDAL: DARWIN (1954). *The Genetics Laboratory, Department of Zoology, South Parks Road, Oxford, OX1 3PS*. (*Telephone: Oxford* 56789); 5 *Apsley Road, Oxford*. (*Telephone: Oxford* 58147); and *All Souls College, Oxford*. (*Telephone: Oxford* 22251).

1967 FORD, SIR HUGH. Professor of Mechanical Engineering and Head of the Department of Mechanical Engineering at the Imperial College of Science and Technology in the University of London. *Department of Mechanical Engineering, Imperial College, Exhibition Road, London, S.W.*7. (*Telephone:* 01-589 5111); 18 *Shrewsbury House, Cheyne Walk, London, S.W.*3. (*Telephone:* 01-352 3804); and *Shamley Cottage, Shamley Green, Surrey*. (*Telephone: Bramley* 2366); also *Athenaeum*. 1973–74

Date of Election		Service on Council
1966	FORREST, JOHN SAMUEL. Visiting Professor of Electrical Engineering at the University of Strathclyde. Formerly Director of the Central Electricity Research Laboratories. *Arbores, Portsmouth Road, Thames Ditton, Surrey, KT7 0EG.* (*Telephone:* 01-398 4389).	1972–75 V.P. 1972–75
1964	FOWDEN, LESLIE, Ph.D. Director of Rothamsted Experimental Station. *Rothamsted Experimental Station, Harpenden, Hertfordshire, AL5 2JQ.* (*Telephone: Harpenden* 63133); *7 Ferncroft, 15 Basire Street, London, N.1.* (*Telephone:* 01-226 7043); and *1 West Common, Harpenden, Hertfordshire.* (*Telephone: Harpenden* 64628).	1970–72
1964	FOWLER, PETER HOWARD. Royal Society Research Professor at the University of Bristol. LECTURE: RUTHERFORD MEMORIAL (1971). MEDAL: HUGHES (1974). *The H. H. Wills Physics Laboratory, Royal Fort, Bristol, BS8 1TL.* (*Telephone: Bristol* 24161, *extension* 113); *and 320 Canford Lane, Westbury-on-Trym, Bristol.* (*Telephone: Bristol* 681142).	
1954	FRANK, FREDERICK CHARLES, O.B.E. Emeritus Professor of Physics in the University of Bristol. LECTURE: BAKERIAN (1973). *The H. H. Wills Physics Laboratory, Royal Fort, Bristol, BS8 1TL.* (*Telephone: Bristol* 24161); *and Orchard Cottage, Grove Road, Coombe Dingle, Bristol, BS9 2RL.* (*Telephone: Bristol* 681708); also *Athenaeum.*	1967–69 V.P. 1967–69
1953	FRANKEL, SIR OTTO (HERZBERG). Senior Research Fellow, Commonwealth Scientific and Industrial Research Organization, Division of Plant Industry. *C.S.I.R.O., Box* 1600, *Canberra City, A.C.T.* 2601, *Australia.*	
1966	FRASER, FRANCIS CHARLES, C.B.E., D.Sc. Formerly Keeper of Zoology, British Museum (Natural History). *78 Hayes Road, Bromley, Kent, BR2 9AB.* (*Telephone:* 01-460 3668); also *Athenaeum.*	
1948	FRISCH, OTTO ROBERT, O.B.E. Emeritus Professor of Natural Philosophy in the University of Cambridge. *Trinity College, Cambridge, CB2 1TQ.*	
1976	FRÖHLICH, ALBRECHT. Professor of Pure Mathematics at King's College in the University of London. *Department of Mathematics, King's College, Strand, London, WC2R 2LS.* (*Telephone:* 01-836 5454); *and 63 Drax Avenue, London, S.W.20.* (*Telephone:* 01-946 6550).	
1951	FRÖHLICH, HERBERT. Emeritus Professor of Theoretical Physics in the University of Liverpool. Visiting Fellow at the Department of Electrical Engineering, University of Salford. *Department of Physics, Oliver Lodge Laboratory, The University, Oxford Street, P.O. Box* 147, *Liverpool, L69 3BX.* (*Telephone:* 051-709 6022, *extension* 2259 *and* 2260).	

Date of Election		Service on Council
1972	FRYER, GEOFFREY, D.Sc. Senior Principal Scientific Officer, Freshwater Biological Association. *Freshwater Biological Association, Windermere Laboratory, The Ferry House, Far Sawrey, Ambleside, Cumbria, LA22 0LP. (Telephone: Windermere 2468);* and *Elleray Cottage, Windermere, Cumbria, LA23 1AW.*	
1974	FUCHS, SIR VIVIAN (ERNEST). Formerly Director of the British Antarctic Survey. *78 Barton Road, Cambridge, CB3 9LH. (Telephone: Cambridge 59238);* also *Athenaeum.*	
1969	FYFE, WILLIAM SEFTON. Chairman of the Department of Geology and Professor of Geology in the University of Western Ontario. *Department of Geology, University of Western Ontario, London 72, Ontario, Canada.*	
1956	GABOR, DENNIS, C.B.E. Emeritus Professor of Applied Electron Physics in the University of London. Staff Scientist, C.B.S. Laboratories, Stamford, Connecticut, U.S.A. MEDAL: RUMFORD (1968). Nobel Laureate, Physics, 1971. *Department of Electrical Engineering, Imperial College, Exhibition Road, London, SW7 2BT;* and (Summer residence) *La Margioretta, Anzio, Lavinio, Viale dei Gigli, Italy;* also *Athenaeum.*	
1953	GALE, ERNEST FREDERICK. Professor of Chemical Microbiology in the University of Cambridge. LECTURE: LEEUWENHOEK (1956). *Department of Biochemistry, Tennis Court Road, Cambridge. (Telephone: Cambridge 51781).*	1962–64
1964	GARNHAM, PERCY CYRIL CLAUDE, C.M.G. Emeritus Professor of Medical Protozoology in the University of London. Senior Research Fellow, Imperial College of Science and Technology, London. *Imperial College Field Station, Ashurst Lodge, Ascot, Berkshire;* and *Southernwood, Farnham Common, Buckinghamshire. (Telephone: Farnham Common 3863).*	
1967	GARRETT, STEPHEN DENIS. Emeritus Professor of Mycology in the University of Cambridge. *Botany School, Downing Street, Cambridge, CB2 3EA. (Telephone: Cambridge 61414);* and *179 Hills Road, Cambridge, CB2 2RN. (Telephone: Cambridge 47865).*	
1969	GARTON, WILLIAM REGINALD STEPHEN. Professor of Spectroscopy at the Imperial College of Science and Technology in the University of London. *Department of Physics, Imperial College, Prince Consort Road, London, S.W.7. (Telephone: 01-589 5111, extension 2338);* and *1 Broomhouse Road, London, S.W.6. (Telephone: 01-736 3454).*	
1953	GAYDON, ALFRED GORDON. Emeritus Professor of Molecular Spectroscopy in the University of London and Senior Research Fellow at the Imperial College of Science and Technology. Formerly Warren Research Fellow. MEDAL: RUMFORD (1960). *Department of Chemical Engineering and Chemical Technology, Imperial College, London, SW7 2BY. (Telephone: 01-589 5111);* and *Dale Cottage, Shellbridge Road, Slindon Common, near Arundel, West Sussex. (Telephone: Slindon 277).*	

YEAR BOOK OF THE ROYAL SOCIETY

Date of Election / *Service on Council*

1972 GAZE, RAYMOND MICHAEL, D.Phil. Head of the Division of Developmental Biology, National Institute for Medical Research. *National Institute for Medical Research, The Ridgeway, Mill Hill, London, N.W.*7. *(Telephone:* 01-959 3666, *extension* 379); *and* 65 *Talbot Road, London, N*6 4*QX*. *(Telephone:* 01-340 3870).

1951 GEE, GEOFFREY, C.B.E. Pro-Vice-Chancellor and Honorary Professor of Chemistry in the University of Manchester. *The University, Manchester, M*13 9*PL*. *(Telephone:* 061-273 3333); *and* 8 *Holmfield Drive, Cheadle Hulme, Cheshire*. *(Telephone:* 061-485 3713). 1957–59

1969 GELL, PHILIP GEORGE HOUTHEM. Professor of Experimental Pathology in the University of Birmingham. *Department of Experimental Pathology, The Medical School, Vincent Drive, Birmingham, B*15 2*TJ*. *(Telephone:* 021-472 1301, *extension* 3344); *and Chadwich Manor, Bromsgrove, Worcestershire*. *(Telephone:* 021-453 3521).

1963 GEORGE, THOMAS NEVILLE. Emeritus Professor of Geology in the University of Glasgow. *Department of Geology, University of Glasgow, Glasgow, W*.2. *(Telephone:* 041-339 8855, *extension* 224).

1976 GIBSON, FRANK WILLIAM ERNEST. Howard Florey Professor of Medical Research and Director of the John Curtin School of Medical Research in the Australian National University. *John Curtin School of Medical Research, Australian National University, P.O. Box* 334, *Canberra City, A.C.T.* 2601, *Australia*. *(Telephone:* 49-2597); *and* 7 *Waller Crescent, Campbell, A.C.T.* 2601, *Australia*. *(Telephone:* 49-8463).

1969 GIBSON, QUENTIN HOWIESON. Professor of Biochemistry and Molecular Biology in Cornell University. *Department of Biochemistry and Molecular Biology, Wing Hall, Cornell University, Ithaca, N.Y.* 14850, *U.S.A.* *(Telephone:* (607) 256-2203).

1973 GILBERT, GEOFFREY ALAN. Professor of Biochemistry in the University of Birmingham. *Department of Biochemistry, The University, P.O. Box* 363, *Birmingham, B*15 2*TT*. *(Telephone:* 021-472 1301, *extension* 2018); *and* 194 *Selly Park Road, Birmingham, B*29 7*H Y*. *(Telephone:* 021-472 0755).

1971 GLASS, DAVID VICTOR. Martin White Professor of Sociology at the London School of Economics and Political Science in the University of London. *London School of Economics, Houghton Street, London, WC*2*A* 2*AE*. *(Telephone:* 01-405 7686).

1969 GLUECKAUF, EUGEN, D.Sc. Formerly Deputy Chief Scientist and Head of the Physical and Radio-Chemistry Branch, now Consultant, A.E.R.E., Harwell, Oxfordshire. *Bankside, Chilton, Oxfordshire, OX*11 0*RZ*. *(Telephone:* Rowstock 296).

1970 GLYNN, IAN MICHAEL. Professor of Membrane Physiology in the University of Cambridge. *Physiological Laboratory, Downing Street, Cambridge, CB*2 3*EG*. *(Telephone:* Cambridge 64131); *Trinity College, Cambridge; and Daylesford, Conduit Head Road, Cambridge, CB*3 0*EY*. *(Telephone:* Cambridge 53079).

Date of Election		Service on Council
1945	GODWIN, SIR HARRY. Emeritus Professor of Botany in the University of Cambridge. LECTURE: CROONIAN (1960). *The Botany School, Cambridge, CB2 3EA. (Telephone: Cambridge 61414); and 30 Barton Road, Cambridge, CB3 9LF. (Telephone: Cambridge 50883).*	1957-59
1964	GOLD, THOMAS. Director of the Center for Radiophysics and Space Research and John L. Wetherill Professor of Astronomy at Cornell University. *Center for Radiophysics and Space Research, Space Science Building, Cornell University, Ithaca, New York, 14853, U.S.A. (Telephone: (607) 256-5284).*	
1972	GOLD, VICTOR. Professor and Head of the Department of Chemistry at King's College in the University of London. *Department of Chemistry, King's College, Strand, London, WC2R 2LS. (Telephone: 01-836 5454); also Athenaeum.*	
1937	GOLDSTEIN, SYDNEY. Emeritus Professor of Applied Mathematics at Harvard University. *28 Elizabeth Road, Belmont, Mass. 02178, U.S.A.*	1945-47
1940	GOODEVE, SIR CHARLES (FREDERICK), O.B.E. Commander, R.N.V.R. (retired). Formerly Director of the British Iron and Steel Research Association. *38 Middleway, London, N.W.11. (Telephone: 01-455 7308); also Athenaeum.*	1968-70 V.P. 1968-70
1976	GOODWIN, LEONARD GEORGE, C.M.G., M.B., B.S. Director of Science, The Zoological Society of London. *The Zoological Society of London, Regent's Park, London, NW1 4RY. (Telephone: 01-722 3333); and Shepperlands Farm, Park Lane, Finchampstead, Berkshire, RG11 4QF. (Telephone: Eversley (Hants) 732153).*	
1968	GOODWIN, TREVOR WALWORTH, C.B.E. Johnston Professor of Biochemistry in the University of Liverpool. *Department of Biochemistry, The University, P.O. Box 147, Liverpool, L69 3BX. (Telephone: 051-709 6022); and The Beeches, Storeton Road, Prenton, Birkenhead, Merseyside. (Telephone: 051-608 2021).*	1972-73 1974-75
1963	GOWANS, JAMES LEARMONTH, C.B.E. Henry Dale Research Professor of the Royal Society. Honorary Director, Medical Research Council Cellular Immunology Unit. MEDAL: ROYAL (1976). *Sir William Dunn School of Pathology, South Parks Road, Oxford, OX1 3RE. (Telephone: Oxford 57321); St Catherine's College, Oxford; and 75 Cumnor Hill, Oxford, OX2 9HX. (Telephone: Cumnor 2304).*	1973-75 V.P. 1973-75
1967	GRACE, MICHAEL ANTHONY, D.Phil. Reader in Nuclear Physics in the University of Oxford and Student of Christ Church. *Nuclear Physics Laboratory, Oxford. (Telephone: Oxford 59911); and 13 Blandford Avenue, Oxford. (Telephone: Oxford 58464); also Athenaeum.*	
1934	GRANT, RONALD THOMSON, O.B.E., M.D. *Farley Green Cottage, Winterfold Lane, Albury, Guildford, Surrey, GU5 9EQ. (Telephone: Shere 2164).*	

Date of Election		Service on Council

1976 GRAY, EDWARD GEORGE. Professor of Anatomy (Cytology) at University College in the University of London. *Department of Anatomy and Embryology, University College London, Gower Street, London, WC1E 6BT.* (*Telephone:* 01-387 7050, *extension* 306); and 58 *New Park Road, Newgate Street, Hertford, SG13 8RF.*

1972 GRAY, SIR JOHN (ARCHIBALD BROWNE). Secretary of the Medical Research Council. *Medical Research Council, 20 Park Crescent, London, W1N 4AL.* (*Telephone:* 01-636 5422, *extension* 2); and 75 *Cholmeley Crescent, Highgate, London, N6 5EX.* (*Telephone:* 01-340 1387); also *Athenaeum.*

1958 GREEN, ALBERT EDWARD. Sedleian Professor of Natural Philosophy at the University of Oxford. *The Mathematical Institute, 24–29 St Giles, Oxford, OX1 3LB.* (*Telephone: Oxford* 54295); and 20 *Lakeside, Oxford.* (*Telephone: Oxford* 52116).

1962 GREGORY, PHILIP HERRIES, D.Sc. Formerly Head of the Plant Pathology Department, Rothamsted Experimental Station. LECTURE: LEEUWENHOEK (1970). *Rothamsted Experimental Station, Harpenden, Hertfordshire, AL5 2JQ.* (*Telephone: Harpenden* 63133); and 11 *Topstreet Way, Harpenden, Hertfordshire, AL5 5TU.* (*Telephone: Harpenden* 5612).

1965 GREGORY, RODERIC ALFRED, C.B.E. George Holt Professor of Physiology in the University of Liverpool. *The Physiological Laboratory, The University, P.O. Box* 147, *Liverpool, L69 3BX.* (*Telephone:* 051-709 6022, *extension* 37).   1971–73 V.P. 1971–73

1956 GRÜNEBERG, HANS. Emeritus Professor of Genetics in the University of London *University College, Wolfson House,* 4 *Stephenson Way, London, N.W.1.* (*Telephone:* 01-387 7050); and 66A *Belsize Park Gardens, London, N.W.3.* (*Telephone:* 01-722 1069).

1971 GURDON, JOHN BERTRAND, D.Phil. Member of the Scientific Staff of the Medical Research Council. LECTURE: CROONIAN (1976). *M.R.C. Laboratory of Molecular Biology, Hills Road, Cambridge, CB2 2QH.* (*Telephone: Cambridge* 48011); and 4 *The Cenacle, Newnham, Cambridge, CB3 9JS.*

1976 GUTTMANN, SIR LUDWIG, C.B.E. Professor Emeritus of the University of Cologne, and Emeritus Consultant to the Stoke Mandeville Hospital. *The Stoke Mandeville Sports Stadium for the Paralysed and other Disabled, Harvey Road, Aylesbury, Buckinghamshire.* (*Telephone: Aylesbury* 84848); and *Menorah,* 26 *Northumberland Avenue, Aylesbury, Buckinghamshire.* (*Telephone: Aylesbury* 4901); also *Athenaeum.*

1972 HADDOW, ALEXANDER JOHN, C.M.G. Professor of Administrative Medicine and Administrative Dean of the Faculty of Medicine, University of Glasgow. *Office of the Faculty of Medicine, University of Glasgow, Glasgow, G12 8QQ.* (*Telephone:* 041-339 8855, *extension* 249); and 16 *Hamilton Drive, Glasgow, G12 8DR.* (*Telephone:* 041-339 7187).

Date of Election		Service on Council
1973	HAILSHAM OF ST MARYLEBONE, QUINTIN MCGAREL HOGG, BARON, C.H., P.C. *House of Lords, London, SW1A 0PW.*	
1953	HALL, SIR ARNOLD (ALEXANDER). Chairman and Managing Director, Hawker Siddeley Group Limited. LECTURE: TERCENTENARY (1960). *Hawker Siddeley Group Limited, 18 St James's Square, London, S.W.1. (Telephone:* 01-930 6177); and *Wakehams, Dorney, Buckinghamshire;* also *Athenaeum.*	
1942	HALL, PHILIP. Emeritus Professor of Pure Mathematics in the University of Cambridge. MEDAL: SYLVESTER (1961). *50 Impington Lane, Histon, Cambridgeshire.*	1950-52
1956	HALLPIKE, CHARLES SKINNER, C.B.E. Honorary Aural Physician to the National Hospital for Nervous Diseases, Queen Square, London. *Fern Lodge, West Moors, Wimborne, Dorset, BH22 0LS. (Telephone: Ferndown* 874418).	
1974	HALPERN, JACK. Louis Block Professor of Chemistry in the University of Chicago. *Department of Chemistry, University of Chicago, Illinois 60637, U.S.A. (Telephone:* (312) 753-8271); and *5630 Dorchester Avenue, Chicago, Illinois 60637, U.S.A. (Telephone:* (312) 643-6837).	
1969	HALSBURY, JOHN ANTHONY HARDINGE, EARL OF. Consultant Director of the Distillers Company Limited and Head Wrightson and Company Limited. *Flat 4, Campden House, 29 Sheffield Terrace, London, W.8. (Telephone:* 01-727 3125 *(office))* and 01-727 3035 *(private));* also *Athenaeum.*	
1976	HAMMERSLEY, JOHN MICHAEL, D.Sc. Reader in Mathematical Statistics in the University of Oxford. *Institute of Economics and Statistics, St Cross Building, Manor Road, Oxford, OX1 3UL. (Telephone: Oxford* 49631); and *Willow Cottage,* 11 *Eynsham Road, Oxford, OX2 9BS. (Telephone: Cumnor* 2181).	
1942	HANES, CHARLES SAMUEL. Emeritus Professor of Biochemistry in the University of Toronto. *60 Beech Avenue, Apt 4, Toronto, Ontario, M4E 3H4, Canada.*	1950-51
1940	HARDY, SIR ALISTER (CLAVERING). Emeritus Professor of Zoology in the University of Oxford. *7 Capel Close, Oxford, OX2 7LA. (Telephone: Oxford* 54381).	1947-49 V.P. 1948 49
1973	HARISH-CHANDRA. Professor of Mathematics at the Institute for Advanced Study, Princeton, U.S.A. *Institute for Advanced Study, Princeton, N.J.* 08540, *U.S.A. (Telephone:* (609) 924-4400, *extension* 314).	
1943	HARLAND, SYDNEY CROSS. Emeritus Professor of Botany in the University of Manchester. *Cliff Grange, Snainton, Scarborough, North Yorkshire. (Telephone: Snainton* 549); also *Athenaeum.*	
1964	HARLEY, JOHN LAKER. Professor of Forest Science in the University of Oxford. *Commonwealth Forestry Institute, South Parks Road, Oxford. (Telephone: Oxford* 511431); and *The Orchard, Old Marston, Oxford. (Telephone: Oxford* 49068).	1973- 75

Date of Election		Service on Council
1966	HARRIS, HARRY. Harnwell Professor of Human Genetics in the University of Pennsylvania. *Department of Human Genetics, Richards Building/G4, School of Medicine, University of Pennsylvania, Philadelphia, Pennsylvania* 19174, *U.S.A. (Telephone:* (215) 243-6891); and *Apartment G-610, Garden Court Apartments,* 4631 *Pine Street, Philadelphia, Pennsylvania* 19143, *U.S.A. (Telephone:* (215) 476-6443).	
1968	HARRIS, HENRY. Professor of Pathology at the University of Oxford. LECTURE: CROONIAN (1971). *Sir William Dunn School of Pathology, South Parks Road, Oxford, OX1 3RE. (Telephone: Oxford* 57321); and 73 *Cumnor Hill, Oxford. (Telephone: Cumnor* 2511).	1971–72
1948	HARRIS, THOMAS MAXWELL. Emeritus Professor of Botany in the University of Reading. *Department of Geology, The University, Reading, Berkshire, RG6* 2*AB. (Telephone: Reading* 85123); and *Chusan, Farley Court, Farley Hill, near Reading, Berkshire. (Telephone: Reading* 732046).	1959–61 V.P. 1960–61
1973	HARRISON, RICHARD JOHN. Professor of Anatomy in the University of Cambridge. *Anatomy School, Downing Street, Cambridge. (Telephone: Cambridge* 58761); and *The Beeches,* 8 *Woodlands Road, Great Shelford, Cambridgeshire. (Telephone: Shelford* 3287).	
1971	HARTLEY, BRIAN SELBY. Professor and Head of the Department of Biochemistry at the Imperial College of Science and Technology in the University of London. *Department of Biochemistry, Imperial College of Science and Technology, London, SW7* 2*AZ. (Telephone:* 01-589 5111).	
1968	HASZELDINE, ROBERT NEVILLE. Principal of the University of Manchester Institute of Science and Technology, and Professor of Chemistry. *University of Manchester Institute of Science and Technology, Sackville Street, Manchester, M60* 1*QD. (Telephone:* 061-236 3311); and *Windyridge, Lyme Road, Disley, Cheshire. (Telephone: Disley* 2223).	
1961	HAUGHTON, SIDNEY HENRY, D.Sc. Formerly Director, Geological Survey of South Africa. *Bernard Price Institute for Palaeontological Research, University of the Witwatersrand, Johannesburg, South Africa.*	
1952	HAWKES, LEONARD. Emeritus Professor of Geology, Bedford College, University of London. 26 *Moor Lane, Rickmansworth, Hertfordshire. (Telephone: Rickmansworth* 72955).	1958–60
1974	HAWKING, STEPHEN WILLIAM, Ph.D. Reader in Gravitational Physics at the Department of Applied Mathematics and Theoretical Physics in the University of Cambridge. MEDAL: HUGHES (1976). *Department of Applied Mathematics and Theoretical Physics, Silver Street, Cambridge, CB3 9EW. (Telephone: Cambridge* 51645); *Institute of Astronomy, Madingley Road, Cambridge, CB3 0HA. (Telephone: Cambridge* 62204); and 5 *West Road, Cambridge. (Telephone: Cambridge* 51905).	

Date of Election		Service on Council
1971	HAWORTH, LIONEL, O.B.E. Director of Design, Rolls-Royce (1971) Ltd. *Rolls-Royce (1971) Ltd, Bristol Engine Division, P.O. Box 3, Filton, Bristol. (Telephone: Bristol 693871, extension 653); and 10 Hazelwood Road, Sneyd Park, Bristol, 9. (Telephone: Bristol 683032).*	
1944	HAWORTH, ROBERT DOWNS. Emeritus Professor of Chemistry in the University of Sheffield. MEDAL: DAVY (1956). *Department of Chemistry, The University, Sheffield, S3 7HF. (Telephone: Sheffield 78555, extension 445); and 67 Tom Lane, Sheffield, S10 3PA. (Telephone: Sheffield 302595).*	1957–59
1955	HAWTHORNE, SIR WILLIAM (REDE), C.B.E. Master of Churchill College, Cambridge, and Professor of Applied Thermodynamics in the University of Cambridge. *University Engineering Laboratory, Trumpington Street, Cambridge. (Telephone: Cambridge 66466); and Churchill College, Cambridge. (Telephone: Cambridge 61200); also Athenaeum.*	1968–70 V.P. 1969–70
1975	HAYDON, DENIS ARTHUR, Ph.D. Reader in Surface and Membrane Biophysics in the University of Cambridge. *Physiological Laboratory, Downing Street, Cambridge, CB2 3EG. (Telephone: Cambridge 64131); Trinity Hall, Cambridge. (Telephone: Cambridge 51401); and 23 Porson Road, Cambridge. (Telephone: (Cambridge 59826).*	
1964	HAYES, WILLIAM. Professor and Head of the Department of Genetics, Research School of Biological Sciences, The Australian National University. LECTURE: LEEUWENHOEK (1965). *Department of Genetics, Research School of Biological Sciences, The Australian National University, Box 475, P.O., Canberra City, A.C.T. 2601, Australia. (Telephone: 49-4011); and 25 Canning Street, Ainslie, A.C.T. 2602, Australia. (Telephone: 47-5401).*	
1956	HAYMAN, WALTER KURT. Professor of Pure Mathematics at the Imperial College of Science and Technology in the University of London. *Imperial College, London, SW7 1BZ. (Telephone: 01-589 5111, extension 2601); and Morden House, 9 Westmead, London, SW15 5BH. (Telephone: 01-788 2400).*	1962–63
1960	HEATH, OSCAR VICTOR SAYER. Formerly Director of the Agricultural Research Council Unit of Flower Crop Physiology. Emeritus Professor of Horticulture in the University of Reading. *10 St Peter's Grove, London, W6 9AZ. (Telephone: 01-748 0471).*	
1966	HEBB, DONALD OLDING. Emeritus Professor of Psychology, McGill University. *Department of Psychology, McGill University, 1205 McGregor Avenue, Montreal, Quebec, H3A 1B1, Canada. (Telephone: 392-4609).*	
1974	HEINE, VOLKER. Professor of Theoretical Physics in the University of Cambridge. *Cavendish Laboratory, Madingley Road, Cambridge, CB3 0HE. (Telephone: Cambridge 66477); and 7 Impington Lane, Histon, Cambridge, CB4 4LT. (Telephone: Histon 2083).*	

Date of Election		Service on Council
1948	HEITLER, WALTER HEINRICH. Professor of Theoretical Physics in the University of Zürich. *Institut für Theoretische Physik. University of Zürich, Switzerland;* and *Am Guggenberg* 5, *CH-8053 Zürich, Switzerland.*	
1969	HEMS, BENJAMIN ARTHUR, D.Sc. Formerly Managing Director, Glaxo Research Limited. 18 *Milton Court, Ickenham, Uxbridge, Middlesex.* (*Telephone: Ruislip* 39254).	
1976	HENDERSON, SIR WILLIAM (MACGREGOR). Secretary to the Agricultural Research Council, London. *Agricultural Research Council,* 160 *Great Portland Street, London, W*1*N* 6*DT.* (*Telephone:* 01-580 6655); and 8 *Hobart Court, Roxborough Avenue, Harrow Hill, Middlesex, HA*1 3*DW.* (*Telephone:* 01-864 7093); also *Athenaeum.*	
1951	HERZBERG, GERHARD, D.Sc. Distinguished Research Scientist, National Research Council of Canada. LECTURE: BAKERIAN (1960). MEDAL: ROYAL (1971). Nobel Laureate, Chemistry, 1971. *National Research Council, Ottawa, Ontario, K*1*A* 0*R*6, *Canada.* (*Telephone:* 992-2350); and 190 *Lakeway Drive, Ottawa, Ontario, K*1*L* 5*B*3, *Canada.* (*Telephone:* 746-4126).	
1970	HESLOP-HARRISON, JOHN. Royal Society Research Professor at the University College of Wales, Aberystwyth, in the University of Wales (*from* 1 *March* 1977). LECTURE: CROONIAN (1974). *Welsh Plant Breeding Station, Plas Gogerddan, Aberystwyth, SY*23 3*EB.* (*Telephone: Aberystwyth* 87255); and *Old Post, Hatfield, near Leominster, Herefordshire.*	1975–76
1968	HEWISH, ANTONY. Professor of Radioastronomy in the University of Cambridge. Nobel Laureate, Physics, 1974. *Cavendish Laboratory, Madingley Road, Cambridge, CB*3 0*HE.* (*Telephone: Cambridge* 66477); and *Pryor's Cottage, Field Road, Kingston, Cambridge.* (*Telephone: Comberton* 2657).	
1955	HEY, DONALD HOLROYDE. Emeritus Professor of Chemistry in the University of London. 5 *Wrayfield Avenue, Reigate, Surrey, RH*2 0*NF.* (*Telephone: Reigate* 47053).	
1971	HIDE, RAYMOND. Chief Scientific Officer, Meteorological Office. Visiting Professor in the Department of Mathematics, University College London, and the Department of Geophysics, University of Reading. *Geophysical Fluid Dynamics Laboratory* (*Met. O*.21), *Meteorological Office, Bracknell, Berkshire.* (*Telephone: Bracknell* 20242, *extension* 2592); and 11 *Clare Avenue, Wokingham, Berkshire.* (*Telephone: Wokingham* 785852).	
1958	HIGMAN, GRAHAM. Waynflete Professor of Pure Mathematics, University of Oxford. *Mathematical Institute,* 24–29 *St Giles, Oxford, OX*1 3*LB.* (*Telephone: Oxford* 54295); and 64 *Sandfield Road, Headington, Oxford.* (*Telephone: Oxford* 62974).	

Date of Election		Service on Council
1918	HILL, ARCHIBALD VIVIAN, C.H., O.B.E.(Mil.). Emeritus Professor of Physiology in the University of London and Honorary Fellow of University College London. LECTURE: CROONIAN (1926). MEDALS: ROYAL (1926), COPLEY (1948). Nobel Laureate, Physiology and Medicine, 1922. 11A *Chaucer Road, Cambridge, CB2 2EB*. (*Telephone: Cambridge* 54551).	1932–34 Sec. 1935–45 V P. 1943–44 1945–46 For. Sec. 1945–46

1954 HILL, SIR AUSTIN BRADFORD, C.B.E. Emeritus Professor of Medical Statistics in the University of London. Past Honorary Director of the Statistical Research Unit of the Medical Research Council. *Green Acres, Little Kingshill, Great Missenden, Buckinghamshire*. (*Telephone: Great Missenden* 2380).

1972 HILL, DAVID KEYNES. Professor of Biophysics at the Royal Postgraduate Medical School in the University of London. *Royal Postgraduate Medical School, Ducane Road, London, W12 0HS*. (*Telephone:* 01-743 2030, *extension* 402); and *Castlett Farm, Guiting Power, Cheltenham, Gloucestershire, GL54 5UZ*. (*Telephone: Guiting Power* 275).

1965 HILL, DOROTHY, C.B.E. Emeritus Professor of Geology in the University of Queensland. *The University of Queensland, St Lucia, Brisbane, Australia*. (*Telephone: Brisbane* 703433).

1946 HILL, ROBERT, Sc.D. Formerly Member of Staff of the Agricultural Research Council. MEDAL: ROYAL (1963). *Department of Biochemistry, Tennis Court Road, Cambridge, CB2 1QW*. (*Telephone: Cambridge* 51781); and 1 *Comberton Road, Barton, Cambridge, CB3 7BA*.

1961 HILL, RODNEY. Professor of the Mechanics of Solids in the University of Cambridge. *Department of Applied Mathematics and Theoretical Physics, Silver Street, Cambridge, CB3 9EW*.

1954 HILLS, EDWIN SHERBON, C.B.E. Emeritus Professor of Geology and formerly Deputy Vice-Chancellor in the University of Melbourne. *Department of Geology, University of Melbourne, Parkville, Victoria, 3052, Australia*. (*Telephone:* 3451844); and 25 *Barry Street, Kew, Victoria, 3101, Australia*. (*Telephone:* 868572).

1955 HIMSWORTH, SIR HAROLD (PERCIVAL), K.C.B. Formerly Deputy Chairman and Secretary, Medical Research Council; Consulting Physician to University College Hospital, London. 13 *Hamilton Terrace, London, NW8 9RE*. (*Telephone:* 01-286 6996); also *Athenaeum*. 1961–62

1974 HINDE, ROBERT AUBREY. Royal Society Research Professor in the University of Cambridge and Honorary Director of the Medical Research Council Unit on Development and Integration of Behaviour. *M.R.C. Unit on the Development and Integration of Behaviour, Madingley, Cambridge, CB3 8AA*. (*Telephone: Madingley* 301); and *Park Lane, Madingley, Cambridge*. (*Telephone: Madingley* 430).

Date of Election		Service on Council

1954 HINTON OF BANKSIDE, CHRISTOPHER, BARON, O.M., K.B.E. Deputy Chairman, Electricity Supply Research Council. LECTURE: TERCENTENARY (1960). MEDAL: RUMFORD (1970). *Tiverton Lodge, Dulwich Common, London, SE21 7EW. (Telephone:* 01-693 6447). — 1958-59

1961 HINTON, HOWARD EVEREST. Professor of Zoology and Head of the Department of Zoology in the University of Bristol. *Department of Zoology, The University, Bristol, BS8 1UG;* and 16 *Victoria Walk, Bristol,* 6. *(Telephone: Bristol* 41433).

1963 HIRSCH, SIR PETER (BERNHARD). Isaac Wolfson Professor of Metallurgy at the University of Oxford. MEDAL: HUGHES (1973). *Department of Metallurgy and Science of Materials, Parks Road, Oxford, OX1 3PH. (Telephone: Oxford* 59981); and 8 *Lakeside, Oxford. (Telephone: Oxford* 59523).

1970 HIRST, JOHN MALCOLM, D.S.C. Director of Long Ashton Research Station and Professor of Agricultural and Horticultural Science in the University of Bristol. *Long Ashton Research Station, Long Ashton, Bristol, BS18 9AF. (Telephone: Long Ashton* 2181); and *The Cottage, Butcombe, Bristol, BS18 6XQ. (Telephone: Lulsgate* 2880).

1950 HOARE, CECIL ARTHUR, D.Sc. Formerly Head, Protozoological Department, Wellcome Laboratories of Tropical Medicine. *Wellcome Museum of Medical Science,* 183 *Euston Road, London, NW1 2BP. (Telephone:* 01-387 4477); and 77 *Sutton Court Road, London, W4 3EQ. (Telephone:* 01-994 4838).

1948 HODGKIN, SIR ALAN (LLOYD), O.M., K.B.E. PAST-PRESIDENT. John Humphrey Plummer Professor of Biophysics in the University of Cambridge. LECTURES: CROONIAN (1957), TERCENTENARY (1960). MEDALS: ROYAL (1958), COPLEY (1965). Nobel Laureate, Physiology or Medicine, 1963. *Physiological Laboratory, Cambridge, CB2 3EG. (Telephone: Cambridge* 64131); and 25 *Newton Road, Cambridge. (Telephone: Cambridge* 59284). — 1958-60 Pres. 1970-75

1947 HODGKIN, DOROTHY MARY CROWFOOT, O.M. Wolfson Research Professor of the Royal Society. LECTURES: TERCENTENARY (1960), BAKERIAN (1972). MEDALS: ROYAL (1956), COPLEY (1976). Nobel Laureate, Chemistry, 1964. *Laboratory of Molecular Biophysics, Department of Zoology, South Parks Road, Oxford, OX1 3PS. (Telephone: Oxford* 56789, extension 234); and 20c *Bradmore Road, Oxford. (Telephone: Oxford* 57125).

1962 HOLDER, DOUGLAS WILLIAM. Professor of Engineering Science, University of Oxford. *Engineering Laboratory, Parks Road, Oxford, OX1 3PJ. (Telephone: Oxford* 56120); and *Woods End, Hamels Lane, Boars Hill, Oxford. (Telephone: Oxford* 735171). — 1969-71

1976 HOLLIDAY, ROBIN, Ph.D. Head of the Division of Genetics at the National Institute for Medical Research. *National Institute for Medical Research, Mill Hill, London, NW7 1AA. (Telephone:* 01-959 3666); and *Brick Kiln Cottage, Ashridge Road, Berkhamsted, Hertfordshire. (Telephone: Little Gaddesden* 2483).

Date of Election		Service on Council
1964	HOLT, JOHN RILEY. Professor of Experimental Physics in the University of Liverpool. *Oliver Lodge Laboratory, The University of Liverpool, P.O. Box 147, Liverpool, L69 3BX.* (*Telephone: 051-709 6022*); and *Rydalmere, Stanley Avenue, Bebington, Wirral, Merseyside, L63 5QE.* (*Telephone: 051-608 2041*).	
1962	HOOKER, SIR STANLEY (GEORGE), C.B.E. Technical Director of Rolls-Royce (1971) Limited. *Rolls-Royce (1971) Limited, P.O. Box 31, Derby, DE2 8BJ.* (*Telephone: Derby 42424, extension 1385*); *P.O. Box 3, Filton, Bristol.* (*Telephone: Bristol 693871*); and *Orchard Hill, Milbury Heath, Wotton-under-Edge, Gloucestershire.* (*Telephone: Thornbury 412078*); also *Athenaeum.*	1965–67 V.P. 1965–67
1973	HOPKINS, HAROLD HORACE. Professor of Applied Optics in the University of Reading. *Department of Physics, The University, Whiteknights, Reading, RG6 2AH.* (*Telephone: Reading 85123*), extension 381); and 26 *Cintra Avenue, Reading, Berkshire, RG2 7AU.* (*Telephone: Reading 81913*).	
1976	HORLOCK, JOHN HAROLD. Vice-Chancellor of the University of Salford and Professor of Engineering. *The University, Salford, M5 4WT.* (*Telephone: 061-736 5843*); and 247 *Hale Road, Hale, Altrincham, WA15 8RE.* (*Telephone: 061-980 6944*); also *Athenaeum.*	
1969	HORRIDGE, GEORGE ADRIAN. Professor, Research School of Biology, Australian National University, Canberra. *Department of Neurobiology, Research School of Biological Sciences, The Australian National University, P.O. Box 475, Canberra, A.C.T. 2601, Australia.* (*Telephone: 49-4532*).	
1972	HOUGHTON, JOHN THEODORE. Professor of Atmospheric Physics in the University of Oxford and Fellow of Jesus College, Oxford. *Department of Atmospheric Physics, Clarendon Laboratory, Oxford, OX1 3PU.* (*Telephone: Oxford 53344*); and 1 *Begbroke Lane, Begbroke, Oxford.* (*Telephone: Kidlington 3344*).	
1975	HOUNSFIELD, GODFREY NEWBOLD, C.B.E. Chief Staff Scientist, E.M.I. Central Research Laboratories, Middlesex. *E.M.I. Central Research Laboratories, Blyth Road, Hayes, Middlesex.* (*Telephone: 01-573 3888, extension 2872*); and *South Airfield Farm, Winthorpe, near Newark, Nottinghamshire.* (*Telephone: Newark 3637*).	
1950	HOWARTH, LESLIE, O.B.E. Emeritus Professor of Mathematics in the University of Bristol. *School of Mathematics, University Walk, Bristol, BS8 1TW;* and 10 *The Crescent, Henleaze, Bristol, BS9 4RW.* (*Telephone: Bristol 626346*).	1956–56
1957	HOYLE, SIR FRED. Formerly Plumian Professor of Astronomy in the University of Cambridge and formerly Director of the Institute of Theoretical Astronomy. LECTURE: BAKERIAN (1968). MEDAL: ROYAL (1974). *Cockley Moor, Dockray, Penrith, Cumbria, CA11 0LG.*	1969–71 V.P. 1969–71

Date of Election		Service on Council
1964	HUDSON, SIR WILLIAM, K.B.E. Formerly Commissioner of the Snowy Mountains Hydro-Electric Authority, Australia. 39 *Flanagan Street, Garran, A.C.T.* 2605, *Australia.*	
1963	HUMPHREY, JOHN HERBERT, C.B.E. Professor of Immunology in the University of London. *Royal Postgraduate Medical School, Hammersmith Hospital, Ducane Road, London, W12 0HS.* (*Telephone:* 01-743 2030); and 17 *Mortimer Crescent, London, NW6 5NP.* (*Telephone:* 01-624 9376).	1967–69
1951	HUTCHINSON, SIR JOSEPH (BURTT), C.M.G. Emeritus Professor of Agriculture in the University of Cambridge. MEDAL: ROYAL (1967). *St John's College, Cambridge.* (*Telephone: Cambridge* 61621); and *Huntingfield, Huntingdon Road, Cambridge.* (*Telephone: Cambridge* 76272).	
1966	HUTCHISON, SIR (WILLIAM) KENNETH, C.B.E. Consultant. Formerly Deputy Chairman, The Gas Council. 2 *Arlington Road, Twickenham Park, Middlesex, TW*1 2*BG.* (*Telephone:* 01-892 1685); also *Athenaeum.*	
1955	HUXLEY, SIR ANDREW (FIELDING). Royal Society Research Professor at University College in the University of London. LECTURE: CROONIAN (1967). MEDAL: COPLEY (1973). Nobel Laureate, Physiology or Medicine, 1963. *Department of Physiology, University College, Gower Street, London, WC1E 6BT.* (*Telephone:* 01-387 7050); and *Manor Field, Grantchester, Cambridge.* (*Telephone: Trumpington* 2207).	1960–62
1960	HUXLEY, HUGH ESMOR, M.B.E., Sc.D. Research Worker for the Medical Research Council. LECTURE: CROONIAN (1970). *M.R.C. Laboratory of Molecular Biology, Hills Road, Cambridge, CB*2 2*QH.* (*Telephone: Cambridge* 48011); *Churchill College, Cambridge;* and *Binsted, Herschel Road, Cambridge.* (*Telephone: Cambridge* 56117).	1973–75
1970	INGRAM, VERNON MARTIN. Professor of Biochemistry in the Massachusetts Institute of Technology. *Department of Biology, Massachusetts Institute of Technology,* 77 *Massachusetts Avenue, Cambridge, Massachusetts* 02139, *U.S.A.* (*Telephone:* (617) 253-3706.	
1967	ISSIGONIS, SIR ALEC (ARNOLD CONSTANTINE), C.B.E. Advanced Design Consultant, British Leyland (Austin-Morris) Limited. MEDAL: LEVERHULME (1966). *British Leyland (Austin-Morris) Limited, Longbridge, Birmingham.* (*Telephone:* 021-475 2101); *and* 12 *Westbourne Gardens, Westbourne Road, Edgbaston, Birmingham,* 15. (*Telephone:* 021-454 5514).	
1947	JACKSON, DEREK AINSLIE, O.B.E., D.F.C., A.F.C., D.Sc. Formerly Professor of Spectroscopy at the University of Oxford. *Laboratoire Aimé Cotton, Centre National de la Recherche Scientifique, Faculté des Sciences,* 91405- *Orsay, France;* and 20 *Avenue des Figuiers,* 1007 *Lausanne, Switzerland.*	

THE FELLOWSHIP 1977   53

Date of *Service on*
Election *Council*

1970 JAEGER, JOHN CONRAD. Emeritus Professor of Geophysics in the Australian National University. *Private Bag, 5, P.O. Sorell 7172, Tasmania, Australia.*

1968 JAMES, IOAN MACKENZIE. Savilian Professor of Geometry, University of Oxford. *Mathematical Institute, 24-29 St Giles, Oxford, OX1 3LB.*

1952 JAMES, WILLIAM OWEN. Emeritus Professor of Botany in the University of London. *Imperial College, Prince Consort Road, London, S.W.7;* and 14 *Roedean Crescent, London, SW15 5JU. (Telephone:* 01-876 3785). 1964–66

1969 JAMISON, ROBIN RALPH, Ph.D. Formerly Chief Technical Executive (Research), Rolls-Royce (1971) Limited, Bristol Engine Division. 2 *The Crescent, Henleaze, Bristol, BS9 4RN. (Telephone: Bristol* 627083).

1925 JEFFREYS, SIR HAROLD. Emeritus Professor of Astronomy in the University of Cambridge. LECTURE: BAKERIAN (1952). MEDALS: ROYAL (1948), COPLEY (1960). 160 *Huntingdon Road, Cambridge, CB3 0LB. (Telephone: Cambridge* 56153); and *St John's College, Cambridge.*

1970 JINKS, JOHN LEONARD. Professor of Genetics in the University of Birmingham. *Department of Genetics, The University, P.O. Box 363, Edgbaston, Birmingham, B15 2TT. (Telephone:* 021-472 1301, extension 2030); and 81 *Witherford Way, Selly Oak, Birmingham,* 29. *(Telephone:* 021-472 2008).

1965 JOHNSON, ALAN WOODWORTH. Professor of Chemistry in the University of Sussex. *School of Molecular Sciences, University of Sussex, Falmer, Brighton, BN1 9QJ. (Telephone: Brighton* 66755); and *Mays Corner, Selmeston, East Sussex. (Telephone: Ripe* 261). 1966–67
1971–73

1968 JONES, DOUGLAS SAMUEL, M.B.E. Ivory Professor of Mathematics in the University of Dundee. *Department of Mathematics, The University, Dundee, DD1 4HN. (Telephone: Dundee* 23181). 1973–74

1950 JONES, SIR EWART (RAY HERBERT). Waynflete Professor of Chemistry at the University of Oxford. MEDAL: DAVY (1966). *Dyson Perrins Laboratory, South Parks Road, Oxford, OX1 3QY. (Telephone: Oxford* 57809); and 6 *Sandy Lane, Yarnton, Oxford, OX5 1PB. (Telephone: Kidlington* 2581); also *Athenaeum.* 1969–71

1967 JONES, FRANCIS EDGAR, M.B.E., Ph.D. Formerly Chairman and Managing Director of Mullard Ltd. *Wendacre, Burtons Way, Chalfont St Giles, Buckinghamshire. (Telephone: Little Chalfont* 2228); also *Athenaeum.*

1952 JONES, HARRY. Emeritus Professor of Mathematics and Senior Research Fellow at the Imperial College of Science and Technology in the University of London. *Department of Mathematics, Imperial College, Exhibition Road, London, S.W.7. (Telephone:* 01-589 5111); and 41 *Berwyn Road, Richmond, Surrey. (Telephone:* 01-876 1931).

Date of Election		Service on Council
1957	JONES, JOHN KENYON NETHERTON. Chown Research Professor in Chemistry at Queen's University, Kingston, Ontario, Canada. *Department of Chemistry, Queen's University, Kingston, Ontario, Canada. (Telephone:* (613) 547 6278); and *Treasure Island, R.R.1, Kingston, Ontario, Canada. (Telephone:* (613) 548-4340).	
1965	JONES, REGINALD VICTOR, C.B., C.B.E. Professor of Natural Philosophy in the University of Aberdeen. LECTURE: WILKINS (1969). *Department of Natural Philosophy, The University, Aberdeen, AB9 2UE. (Telephone: Aberdeen* 40241); and 8 *Queens Terrace, Aberdeen, AB1 1XL. (Telephone: Aberdeen* 28184); also *Athenaeum.*	1970–72 V.P. 1971–72
1970	JOSEPHSON, BRIAN DAVID. Professor of Physics in the University of Cambridge. MEDAL: HUGHES (1972). Nobel Laureate, Physics, 1973. *Cavendish Laboratory, Madingley Road, Cambridge, CB3 0HE. (Telephone: Cambridge* 66477).	
1929	KAPITZA, Peter LEONIDOVICH, Ph.D. LECTURES: RUTHERFORD MEMORIAL (1969), BERNAL (1976). *Institute for Physical Problems, Vorobyevskoye Shosse* 2, *Moscow* 117334, *U.S.S.R. (Telephone:* 1373247).	
1966	KASSANIS, BASIL, D.Sc. Senior Principal Scientific Officer in the Department of Plant Pathology, Rothamsted Experimental Station. *Rothamsted Experimental Station, Harpenden, Hertfordshire, AL5 2JQ;* and 3 *Rosebery Avenue, Harpenden, Hertfordshire.*	
1952	KATZ, SIR BERNARD. Professor of Biophysics at University College in the University of London. LECTURE: CROONIAN (1961). MEDAL: COPLEY (1967). Nobel Laureate, Physiology or Medicine, 1970. *Department of Biophysics, University College, Gower Street, London, W.C.1;* and 28 *Kenton Gardens, Kenton, Middlesex.*	1963–65 V.P. 1964–65, 1968–76 Sec. 1968–76
1961	KEARTON, CHRISTOPHER FRANK, BARON, O.B.E. Chairman of the British National Oil Corporation. *Stornoway House,* 13 *Cleveland Row, St James's, London, SW1A 1DH. (Telephone:* 01-839 7080); and *The Old House, Whitchurch, near Aylesbury, Buckinghamshire. (Telephone: Whitchurch (Buckinghamshire)* 232); also *Athenaeum.*	1970–71
1935	KEEN, SIR BERNARD (AUGUSTUS). Formerly Director, East African Agriculture and Forestry Research Organization. *Suite* 5, *Hotel Bristowe, Grange Road, Southbourne, Bournemouth, BH6 3NY. (Telephone: Bournemouth* 422650); also *Athenaeum.*	
1966	KEKWICK, RALPH AMBROSE. Emeritus Professor of Biophysics in the University of London and formerly Head of the Division of Biophysics at the Lister Institute. 31 *Woodside Road, Woodford Wells, Essex. (Telephone:* 01-504 4264).	

Date of Election		Service on Council

1972 KELLER, ANDREW. Research Professor in Polymer Science in the University of Bristol. *H. H. Wills Physics Laboratory, University of Bristol, Royal Fort, Tyndall Avenue, Bristol, BS8 1TL. (Telephone: Bristol 24161, extension 773);* and 41 *Westbury Road, Bristol, BS9 3AU. (Telephone: Bristol 628526).*

1973 KELLY, ANTHONY, Sc.D. Vice-Chancellor of the University of Surrey. *The University, Guildford, Surrey, GU2 5XH. (Telephone: Guildford 71281);* and *Headley Cottage, Weston Green, Thames Ditton, Surrey. (Telephone:* 01-398 0506); also *Athenaeum.*

1965 KEMBALL, CHARLES. Professor of Chemistry in the University of Edinburgh. *Department of Chemistry, University of Edinburgh, West Mains Road, Edinburgh, EH9 3JJ. (Telephone:* 031-667 1081, *extension* 3408); and 5 *Hermitage Drive, Edinburgh, EH10 6DE. (Telephone:* 031-447 2315); also *Athenaeum.*

1956 KEMMER, NICHOLAS. Tait Professor of Mathematical Physics in the University of Edinburgh. MEDAL: HUGHES (1966). *Department of Physics, The University, James Clerk Maxwell Building, Mayfield Road, Edinburgh, EH9 3JZ. (Telephone:* 031-667 1081); and 35 *Salisbury Road, Edinburgh, EH16 5AA. (Telephone:* 031-667 2893).   1958–59

1964 KENDALL, DAVID GEORGE. Professor of Mathematical Statistics in the University of Cambridge. MEDAL: SYLVESTER (1976). *Statistical Laboratory, Department of Pure Mathematics and Mathematical Statistics,* 16 *Mill Lane, Cambridge, CB2 1SB. (Telephone: Cambridge* 65621); and 37 *Barrow Road, Cambridge, CB2 2AR. (Telephone: Cambridge* 53991).   1967–69

1927 KENDALL, JAMES. Emeritus Professor of Chemistry in the University of Edinburgh. 26 *Lasswade Road, Eskbank, Midlothian, EH22 3EE. (Telephone:* 031-663 2146).

1960 KENDREW, SIR JOHN (COWDERY), C.B.E. Director-General of the European Molecular Biology Laboratory, Heidelberg. MEDAL: ROYAL (1965). Nobel Laureate, Chemistry, 1962. *European Molecular Biology Laboratory,* 69 *Heidelberg, Postfach* 10.2209, *Federal Republic of Germany. (Telephone:* (6221) 27355); and *The Guildhall,* 4 *Church Lane, Linton, Cambridge, CB1 6JX. (Telephone: Cambridge* 891545); also *Athenaeum.*   1965–67

1965 KENNEDY, JOHN STODART. Deputy Chief Scientific Officer, Agricultural Research Council, and Professor of Animal Behaviour at the Imperial College of Science and Technology in the University of London. *Imperial College Field Station, Silwood Park, Ascot, Berkshire. (Telephone: Ascot* 23911); and 3 *The Glade, Woodend Drive, South Ascot, Berkshire. (Telephone: Ascot* 20633).

1949 KENNEDY, WILLIAM QUARRIER. Emeritus Professor of Geology in the University of Leeds. *Loseberry, Kirkpark Road, Elie, Fife, Scotland. (Telephone: Elie* 343).

Date of Election		Service on Council
1964	KENNER, GEORGE WALLACE. Royal Society Research Professor at the University of Liverpool. LECTURE: BAKERIAN (1976). *The Robert Robinson Laboratories, The University, Oxford Street, Liverpool, L69 3BX. (Telephone: 051-709 6022 and 6589).*	
1966	KENT, SIR PETER (PERCY EDWARD). Chairman of the Natural Environment Research Council. MEDAL: ROYAL (1971). *Natural Environment Research Council, Alhambra House, Charing Cross Road, London, WC2H 0AX. (Telephone: 01-930 9232); and 38 Rodney Road, West Bridgford, Nottingham, NG2 6JH. (Telephone: Nottingham 231355).*	1967–69
1970	KERENSKY, OLEG ALEXANDER, C.B.E., D.Sc. Consultant, Freeman, Fox and Partners, Consulting Engineers. *Abford House, Wilton Road, London, S.W.1. (Telephone: 01-834 2121); and 27 Pont Street, London, S.W.1. (Telephone: 01-235 7173); also Athenaeum.*	
1959	KEYNES, RICHARD DARWIN. Professor of Physiology in the University of Cambridge. *Physiological Laboratory, Downing Street, Cambridge, CB2 3EG. (Telephone: Cambridge 64131); and 3 Herschel Road, Cambridge. (Telephone: Cambridge 53107).*	1965–68 V.P. 1965–68
1965	KILBURN, TOM, C.B.E. Professor of Computer Science in the University of Manchester. *Department of Computer Science, The University, Manchester, M13 9PL. (Telephone: 061-273 5466).*	
1954	KING, FREDERICK ERNEST, D.Sc. Formerly Scientific Adviser, British Petroleum Company Limited. *360 The Water Gardens, London, W.2; and Glyde's Farm, Ashburnham, Battle, East Sussex; also Athenaeum.*	
1966	KING-HELE, DESMOND GEORGE. Deputy Chief Scientific Officer, Space Department, Royal Aircraft Establishment. LECTURE: BAKERIAN (1974). *Royal Aircraft Establishment, Farnborough, Hampshire. (Telephone: Aldershot 24461); and 3 Tor Road, Farnham, Surrey. (Telephone: Farnham 4755).*	
1971	KINGMAN, JOHN FRANK CHARLES. Professor of Mathematics in the University of Oxford. *Mathematical Institute, 24–29 St Giles, Oxford, OX1 3LB. (Telephone: Oxford 54295); and 8 Montpelier Villas, Brighton, BN1 3DH. (Telephone: Brighton 26981).*	
1960	KITCHING, JOHN ALWYNE, O.B.E. Emeritus Professor of Biology in the School of Biological Sciences in the University of East Anglia, Norwich. *School of Biological Sciences, University of East Anglia, University Plain, Norwich, NR4 7TJ. (Telephone: Norwich 56161); and 29 Newfound Drive, Cringleford, Norwich, NR4 7RY. (Telephone: Norwich 52886).*	
1969	KLUG, AARON, Ph.D. Member of Staff of the Medical Research Council. LECTURE: LEEUWENHOEK (1973). *M.R.C. Laboratory of Molecular Biology, Hills Road, Cambridge. (Telephone: Cambridge 48011); Peterhouse, Cambridge; and 70 Cavendish Avenue, Cambridge. (Telephone: Cambridge 48959).*	

THE FELLOWSHIP 1977

Date of Election		Service on Council

1973 KODICEK, EGON HYNEK, C.B.E., M.D. Formerly Director of the Dunn Nutritional Laboratory, University of Cambridge and Medical Research Council. *Strangeways Research Laboratory, Wort's Causeway, Cambridge, CB1 4RN. (Telephone: Cambridge 43231);* 11 *Bulstrode Gardens, Cambridge, CB3 0EN. (Telephone: Cambridge 57321).*

1965 KORNBERG, HANS LEO. Sir William Dunn Professor of Biochemistry in the University of Cambridge. LECTURE: LEEUWENHOEK (1972). *Department of Biochemistry, Tennis Court Road, Cambridge, CB2 1QW. (Telephone: Cambridge 51781);* and *Pine Trees,* 111 *Glebe Road, Cambridge, CB1 4TE. (Telephone: Cambridge 49483).* 1975–

1947 KREBS, SIR HANS (ADOLF). Emeritus Professor of Biochemistry at the University of Oxford. LECTURE: CROONIAN (1963). MEDALS: ROYAL (1954), COPLEY (1961). Nobel Laureate, Physiology and Medicine, 1953. *Metabolic Research Laboratory, Nuffield Department of Clinical Medicine, Radcliffe Infirmary, Oxford, OX2 6HE. (Telephone: Oxford* 49891)*;* and 27 *Abberbury Road, Iffley, Oxford. (Telephone: Oxford* 777534). 1964–66 V.P. 1965–66

1966 KREISEL, GEORG. Professor of Logic and the Foundations of Mathematics, Stanford University. *Department of Philosophy, Stanford University, Stanford, California* 94305, *U.S.A.*

1963 KROHN, PETER LESLIE. Formerly Professor of Endocrinology in the University of Birmingham. *La Forêt, St Mary, Jersey, Channel Islands. (Telephone: Jersey Central* 62158).

1954 KUHN, HEINRICH GERHARD, Dr Phil. Emeritus Reader in Physics at the University of Oxford. *Department of Astrophysics, University Observatory, South Parks Road, Oxford, OX1 3RQ;* and 25 *Victoria Road, Oxford. (Telephone: Oxford* 55308).

1956 KURTI, NICHOLAS, C.B.E. Emeritus Professor of Physics in the University of Oxford. MEDAL: HUGHES (1969). *Department of Engineering Science, Parks Road, Oxford, OX1 3PJ. (Telephone: Oxford* 59988, *extension* 350)*;* and 38 *Blandford Avenue, Oxford, OX2 8DZ. (Telephone: Oxford* 56176)*;* also *Athenaeum.* 1964–67 V.P. 1965–67

1970 LA COUR, LEONARD FRANCIS, O.B.E. Professor of the University, University of East Anglia and formerly Senior Principal Scientific Officer, John Innes Institute. *School of Biological Sciences, University of East Anglia, Norwich, NR4 7TJ. (Telephone: Norwich* 56161)*;* and 24 *Cranleigh Rise, Eaton, Norwich, NR4 6PQ.*

1975 LANE, ANTHONY MILNER, Ph.D. Deputy Chief Scientific Officer at the Atomic Energy Research Establishment, Harwell. *Theoretical Physics Division, Atomic Energy Research Establishment, Harwell, Didcot, Oxfordshire, OX11 0RA. (Telephone: Abingdon* 24141, *extension* 3247)*;* and *Nayles Bridge Cottage, Church Road, Blewbury, Didcot, Oxfordshire, OX11 9PY. (Telephone: Blewbury* 850416).

Date of Election		Service on Council
1975	LANG, ANDREW RICHARD, Ph.D. Reader in Physics in the University of Bristol. *The H. H. Wills Physics Laboratory, Royal Fort, Bristol, BS8 1TL.* (*Telephone: Bristol* 24161); *and 1B Elton Road, Bristol, BS8 1SJ.* (*Telephone: Bristol* 39784).	
1965	LEBLOND, CHARLES PHILIPPE. Professor of Anatomy, McGill University. *Department of Anatomy, McGill University, P.O. Box* 6070, *Montreal, P.Q., H3C* 3G1, *Canada.* (*Telephone:* 514-392-4931); *and* 68 *Chesterfield Avenue, Westmount, P.Q., H3Y 2M5, Canada.* (*Telephone:* 514-486-4837).	
1968	LEES, ANTHONY DAVID. Deputy Chief Scientific Officer, Agricultural Research Council. Professor of Insect Physiology at the Imperial College of Science and Technology in the University of London. *Imperial College Field Station, Silwood Park, Ascot, Berkshire.* (*Telephone: Ascot* 22204); *and Wells Lane Corner, Sunninghill, Ascot, Berkshire.* (*Telephone: Ascot* 20732).	
1959	LE FEVRE, RAYMOND JAMES WOOD. Emeritus Professor of Chemistry and formerly Head of the School of Chemistry in the University of Sydney. *School of Chemistry, Macquarie University, North Ryde, N.S.W.* 2113, *Australia; and* 6 *Aubrey Road, Northbridge, N.S.W.* 2063, *Australia.* (*Telephone:* 95-1018).	
1972	LEHMANN, HERMANN. Professor of Clinical Biochemistry in the University of Cambridge. University Biochemist to the Cambridge United Hospitals (Addenbrooke's Hospital). *Department of Clinical Biochemistry, Addenbrooke's Hospital, Hills Road, Cambridge, CB2 2QR.* (*Telephone: Cambridge* 45171 (*University*) *and* 45151 (*Hospital Laboratory*))*; and* 22 *Newton Road, Cambridge, CB2 2AL.* (*Telephone: Cambridge* 50866); *also Athenaeum.*	
1967	LEMIEUX, RAYMOND URGEL. Professor of Organic Chemistry in the University of Alberta, Canada. *Department of Chemistry, University of Alberta, Edmonton, Alberta, Canada.*	
1955	LEWIS, DAN. Quain Professor of Botany at University College in the University of London. *Department of Botany and Microbiology, University College London, Gower Street, London, WC1E 6BT.* (*Telephone:* 01-387 7050, *extension* 340); *and* 50 *Canonbury Park North, London, N1 2JT.* (*Telephone:* 01-226 9136).	1962-64
1973	LEWIS, JACK. Professor of Inorganic Chemistry in the University of Cambridge. *University Chemical Laboratory, Lensfield Road, Cambridge, CB2 1EW.* (*Telephone: Cambridge* 66499, *extension* 236); *and* 5 *Bentley Road, Cambridge.* (*Telephone: Cambridge* 50935).	
1945	LEWIS, WILFRID BENNETT, C.B.E., Ph.D. Formerly Senior Vice-President, Science, Atomic Energy of Canada Limited. MEDAL: ROYAL (1972). *Box* 189, 13 *Beach Avenue, Deep River, Ontario, K0J 1P0, Canada.* (*Telephone:* (613) 584-3561); *and Department of Physics, Queen's University, Kingston, Ontario, K7L 3N6, Canada.* (*Telephone:* (613) 547-2869).	

Date of Election		Service on Council
1939	LIDDELL, EDWARD GEORGE TANDY. Emeritus Professor of Physiology at the University of Oxford. 69 *Old High Street, Headington, Oxford, OX3 9HT. (Telephone: Oxford* 62839).	1952-54
1953	LIGHTHILL, SIR (MICHAEL) JAMES. Lucasian Professor of Mathematics in the University of Cambridge. LECTURE: BAKERIAN (1961). MEDAL: ROYAL (1964). *Department of Applied Mathematics and Theoretical Physics, Silver Street, Cambridge, CB3 9EW. (Telephone: Cambridge* 51645); also *Athenaeum.*	1958-59 Sec. 1965-69 V.P. 1965-69
1957	LIPSON, HENRY SOLOMON, C.B.E. Professor of Physics in the Faculty of Technology of the University of Manchester. *The University of Manchester Institute of Science and Technology, Sackville Street, Manchester, M60 1QD. (Telephone:* 061-236 3311); and 22 *Cranmer Road, Manchester, M20 0AW. (Telephone:* 061-445 4517).	
1954	LISSMANN, HANS WERNER, Dr Rer.Nat. Reader in Experimental Zoology in the University of Cambridge. Director of the Sub-Department of Animal Behaviour in the Department of Zoology. *Sub-Department of Animal Behaviour, High Street, Madingley, Cambridge; Trinity College, Cambridge;* and 9 *Bulstrode Gardens, Cambridge.*	
1974	LITHERLAND, ALBERT EDWARD. Professor of Physics in the University of Toronto. *Department of Physics, University of Toronto, Toronto, Ontario, Canada, M5S 1A7. (Telephone:* (416)-928-3785); and 3 *Hawthorn Gardens, Toronto, Ontario, Canada, M4W 1P4. (Telephone:* (416)-923-5616).	
1916	LITTLEWOOD, JOHN EDENSOR. Lately Rouse Ball Professor of Mathematics in the University of Cambridge. MEDALS: ROYAL (1929), SYLVESTER (1943), COPLEY (1958). *Trinity College, Cambridge. (Telephone: Cambridge* 58201).	1927-28 1932-33
1949	LOCKSPEISER, SIR BEN, K.C.B. Formerly Secretary of the Department of Scientific and Industrial Research. *Birchway,* 15 *Waverley Road, Farnborough, Hampshire. (Telephone: Farnborough* 43021); also *Athenaeum.*	
1958	LONGUET-HIGGINS, HUGH CHRISTOPHER. Royal Society Research Professor at the University of Sussex. *Centre for Research in Perception and Cognition, Laboratory of Experimental Psychology, University of Sussex, Falmer, Brighton, BN1 9QY. (Telephone: Brighton* 66755, extension 71); and 2 *Hanover Crescent, Brighton, BN2 2SB. (Telephone: Brighton* 685349); also *Athenaeum.*	
1963	LONGUET-HIGGINS, MICHAEL SELWYN. Royal Society Research Professor at the University of Cambridge. *Department of Applied Mathematics and Theoretical Physics, Silver Street, Cambridge, CB3 9EW. (Telephone: Cambridge* 51645); *Institute of Oceanographic Sciences, Wormley, near Godalming, Surrey, GU8 5UB. (Telephone: Wormley* 2122); and *Wayside,* 1 *Long Road, Cambridge. (Telephone: Cambridge* 47430).	

Date of Election		Service on Council

1963 LOUTIT, JOHN FREEMAN, C.B.E., D.M. Formerly Member of the Scientific Staff of the Medical Research Council. *M.R.C. Radiobiology Unit, Harwell, Didcot, Oxfordshire, OX11 0RD.* (*Telephone: Rowstock* 393); and *Green Farm, Steventon, Oxfordshire, OX13 6SA*). (*Telephone: Steventon* 279).

1955 LOVELL, SIR (ALFRED CHARLES) BERNARD, O.B.E. Professor of Radio Astronomy in the University of Manchester and Director of the Nuffield Radio Astronomy Laboratories, Jodrell Bank. LECTURE: TERCENTENARY (1960). MEDAL: ROYAL (1960). *Nuffield Radio Astronomy Laboratories, Jodrell Bank, Macclesfield, Cheshire, SK11 9DN.* (*Telephone: Lower Withington* 321); and *The Quinta, Swettenham, near Congleton, Cheshire;* also *Athenaeum.*   1963-65

1974 LOVELOCK, JAMES EPHRAIM. Visiting Professor at the Department of Engineering and Cybernetics in the University of Reading. *Bowerchalke, Salisbury, Wiltshire.* (*Telephone: Salisbury* 78387).

1955 LOWENSTEIN, OTTO EGON. Emeritus Professor of Zoology and Comparative Physiology in the University of Birmingham. *Neurocommunications Research Unit, Medical School, The University, P.O. Box* 363, *Edgbaston, Birmingham, B*15 2*TT.* (*Telephone:* 021-472 1301, *extension* 2581); and 22 *Estria Road, Birmingham, B*15 2*LQ.* (*Telephone:* 021-440 2526).   1967-68

1966 LUCAS, SIR CYRIL (EDWARD), C.M.G. Formerly Director of Fisheries Research for Scotland and Director of the Marine Laboratory, Aberdeen. *c/o Marine Laboratory, Department of Agriculture and Fisheries for Scotland, Victoria Road, Aberdeen, AB*9 8*DB.* (*Telephone: Aberdeen* 29944); and 16 *Albert Terrace, Aberdeen, AB*1 1*XY.* (*Telephone: Aberdeen* 25568).

1963 LUND, JOHN WALTER GUERRIER, C.B.E., D.Sc. Deputy Chief Scientific Officer, Freshwater Biological Association. *The Freshwater Biological Association, The Ferry House, Far Sawrey, Ambleside, Cumbria, LA*22 0*LP.* (*Telephone: Windermere* 2468); and *Ellerbeck, Ellerigg Road, Ambleside, Cumbria, LA*22 9*EU.* (*Telephone: Ambleside* 2369).

1973 LYON, MARY FRANCES, Sc.D. Member of the Scientific Staff of the Medical Research Council. *M.R.C. Radiobiology Unit, Harwell, Oxfordshire, OX*11 0*RD.* (*Telephone: Rowstock* 393, *extension* 241).

1958 LYTHGOE, Basil. Professor of Organic Chemistry in the University of Leeds. *School of Chemistry, The University, Leeds,* 2.

1955 LYTTLETON, RAYMOND ARTHUR. Professor of Theoretical Astronomy in the University of Cambridge and Member of the Institute of Astronomy. MEDAL: ROYAL (1965). *St John's College, Cambridge.* (*Telephone: Cambridge* 61621); *Institute of Astronomy, Madingley Road, Cambridge.* (*Telephone: Cambridge* 62204); and 165 *Huntingdon Road, Cambridge.* (*Telephone: Cambridge* 54910).   1959-61

Date of Election		Service on Council
1943	McCANCE, SIR ANDREW. Formerly Chairman, Colvilles Limited. 27 *Broom Cliff, Newton Mearns, Glasgow.* (*Telephone:* 041-639 5115).	
1948	McCANCE, ROBERT ALEXANDER, C.B.E. Emeritus Professor of Experimental Medicine in the University of Cambridge. 4 *Kent House, Sussex Street, Cambridge, CB1 1PH.* (*Telephone: Cambridge* 54082).	1952–54
1952	McCREA, WILLIAM HUNTER. Emeritus Professor of Astronomy in the University of Sussex. *Astronomy Centre, University of Sussex, Falmer, Brighton, BN1 9QH.* (*Telephone: Brighton* 66755); and 87 *Houndean Rise, Lewes, BN7 1EJ, East Sussex.* (*Telephone: Lewes* 3296); also *Athenaeum.*	1954–55
1956	MACFARLANE, ROBERT GWYN, C.B.E. Emeritus Professor of Clinical Pathology, University of Oxford. *Park Cottage, Ramsden, Oxford.*	1960–61
1966	McGEE, JAMES DWYER, O.B.E. Emeritus Professor of Applied Physics in the University of London. Senior Research Fellow, Imperial College of Science and Technology in the University of London. *The Blackett Laboratory, Imperial College, London, SW7 2BZ.* (*Telephone:* 01-589 5111); and 56 *Corringway, London, W.5.* (*Telephone:* 01-997 7160); also *Athenaeum.*	
1954	MACINTOSH, FRANK CAMPBELL. Joseph Morley Drake Professor of Physiology, McGill University, Montreal. *Department of Physiology, McGill University, McIntyre Medical Sciences Building, Montreal, H3G 1Y6, Canada.* (*Telephone:* 514-392-4347); and 145 *Wolseley Avenue, Montreal West, H4X 1V8, Canada.* (*Telephone:* 514-481-7939).	
1976	MACKANESS, GEORGE BELLAMY, D.Phil. President of the Squibb Institute for Medical Research, Princeton, U.S.A. *Squibb Institute for Medical Research, P.O. Box* 4000*, Princeton, N.J.* 08540*, U.S.A.* (*Telephone:* (609) 921-4487); and 313 *Cherry Valley Road, Princeton, N.J.* 08540*, U.S.A.*	
1946	MACKENZIE, CHALMERS JACK, C.M.G., M.C., D.Sc. Formerly President, National Research Council of Canada. 210 *Buena Vista Road, Rockcliffe Park, Ottawa, Ontario, K1N 0V7, Canada.*	
1976	McKENZIE, DAN PETER, Ph.D. Assistant Director of Research at the Department of Geodesy and Geophysics in the University of Cambridge. *Department of Geodesy and Geophysics, Madingley Rise, Madingley Road, Cambridge, CB3 0EZ.* (*Telephone: Cambridge* 51686); and 14 *Humberstone Road, Cambridge, CB4 1JE.* (*Telephone: Cambridge* 59790).	
1975	McLAREN, ANNE LAURA, D.Phil. Director of the Medical Research Council Mammalian Development Unit at University College in the University of London. *M.R.C. Mammalian Development Unit, Wolfson House, University College London,* 4 *Stephenson Way, London, NW1 2HE.* (*Telephone:* 01-387 7171); and 9 *Steele's Road, London, N.W.3.* (*Telephone:* 01-722 3193).	

Date of Election		Service on Council
1933	McLEOD, JAMES WALTER, O.B.E. (Mil.). Emeritus Professor of Bacteriology in the University of Leeds. Research worker in the Laboratory of General Microbiology, Western General Hospital, Edinburgh. 30 *Ravelston Garden, Edinburgh,* 4. *(Telephone:* 031-337 1524).	
1957	McMICHAEL, SIR JOHN. Emeritus Professor of Medicine in the University of London. 2 *North Square, London, NW*11 *7AA.* *(Telephone:* 01-455 8731); also *Athenaeum.*	1968–70 V.P. 1968–70
1962	MACMILLAN, MAURICE HAROLD, O.M., P.C. *Birch Grove House, Chelwood Gate, Haywards Heath, West Sussex.*	
1967	MADDOCK, SIR IEUAN, C.B., O.B.E. Chief Scientist, Department of Industry. *Department of Industry, Abell House, John Islip Street, London, SW*1*P 4LN. (Telephone:* 01-211 3000, *extension* 7363); and 13 *Darell Road, Caversham, Reading, Berkshire. (Telephone: Reading* 474096).	1974–76
1948	MAHLER, KURT. Emeritus Professor of Mathematics at the Institute of Advanced Studies, Australian National University, Canberra, Australia. *Department of Mathematics, Institute of Advanced Studies, Australian National University, P.O. Box* 4, *Canberra, A.C.T.* 2600, *Australia.*	
1971	MANDELSTAM, JOEL. Iveagh Professor of Microbiology in the University of Oxford. LECTURE: LEEUWENHOEK (1975). *Microbiology Unit, Department of Biochemistry, South Parks Road, Oxford. (Telephone: Oxford* 55740).	
1962	MANDELSTAM, STANLEY. Professor of Physics in the University of California. *Department of Physics, University of California, Berkeley* 4, *California, U.S.A.*	
1947	MANN, FREDERICK GEORGE, Sc.D. Fellow of Trinity College. Emeritus Reader in Organic Chemistry in the University of Cambridge. *University Chemical Laboratory, Lensfield Road, Cambridge, CB*2 1*EW. (Telephone: Cambridge* 66499); and 24 *Porson Road, Cambridge, CB*2 2*EU. (Telephone: Cambridge* 52704).	
1951	MANN, THADDEUS ROBERT RUDOLPH, C.B.E. Emeritus Professor of Physiology of Reproduction in the University of Cambridge. 1 *Courtney Way, Cambridge, CB*4 2*EE. (Telephone: Cambridge* 55891).	
1971	MANSFIELD, ERIC HAROLD, Sc.D. Deputy Chief Scientific Officer, Royal Aircraft Establishment. *Structures Department, Royal Aircraft Establishment, Farnborough, Hampshire. (Telephone: Aldershot* 24461, *extension* 2403); and *Evergreens,* 53 *Tudor Way, Church Crookham, Hampshire.*	
1961	MANTON, IRENE. Emeritus Professor of Botany in the University of Leeds. 15 *Harrowby Crescent, West Park, Leeds,* 6.	

Date of Election		Service on Council
1948	MANTON, SIDNIE MILANA (MRS J. P. HARDING), Sc.D. Honorary Research Fellow, Queen Mary College, London. *88 Ennerdale Road, Richmond, Surrey. (Telephone:* 01-940 2908).	

1961 MARION, LEO, M.B.E. Honorary Professor and formerly Dean of the Faculty of Pure and Applied Science, University of Ottawa. *National Research Council of Canada, Ottawa 7, Canada;* and *211 Wurtemburg Street, Apartment 1413, Ottawa, Canada, K1N 8R4. (Telephone:* 236-0076).

1956 MARKHAM, ROY. John Innes Professor of Cell Biology and Director, John Innes Institute, University of East Anglia, Norwich. *John Innes Institute, Colney Lane, Norwich, NR4 7UH. (Telephone: Norwich* 52571); and *10 Daniels Road, Norwich, NR4 6QZ. (Telephone: Norwich* 53429).

1944 MARRIAN, GUY FREDERIC, C.B.E., D.Sc. Formerly Director of Research, The Imperial Cancer Research Fund. *School Cottage, Ickham, Canterbury, Kent. (Telephone: Littlebourne* 317); also *Athenaeum.*   1948–50

1970 MARSHALL, NORMAN BERTRAM. Professor and Head of the Department of Zoology and Comparative Physiology at Queen Mary College in the University of London. *Department of Zoology and Comparative Physiology, Queen Mary College, Mile End Road, London, E1 4NS. (Telephone:* 01-980 4811, extension 360); and *6 Park Lane, Saffron Walden, Essex. (Telephone: Saffron Walden* 22528).

1963 MARSHALL, SHEINA MACALISTER, O.B.E., D.Sc. Formerly Senior Principal Scientific Officer, The Marine Station, Millport. *University Marine Station, Millport, Isle of Cumbrae, Scotland, KA28 0EG. (Telephone: Millport* 581); and *Bellevue, Millport, Isle of Cumbrae, Buteshire. (Telephone: Millport* 406).

1971 MARSHALL, WALTER CHARLES, C.B.E., Ph.D. Deputy Chairman of the United Kingdom Atomic Energy Authority. Chief Scientist, Department of Energy. *Atomic Energy Research Establishment, Harwell, Didcot, Oxfordshire, OX11 0RA. (Telephone: Abingdon* 24141, extension 2620); and *Bridleway House, Goring-on-Thames, near Reading, Berkshire. (Telephone: Goring-on-Thames* 2890).

1950 MARTIN, ARCHER JOHN PORTER, C.B.E. Professorial Fellow in the University of Sussex. Robert A. Welch Professor in the University of Houston. Director, Abbotsbury Laboratories Limited. MEDAL: LEVERHULME (1963). Nobel Laureate, Chemistry, 1952. *Abbotsbury, Barnet Lane, Elstree, Hertfordshire. (Telephone:* 01-953 1031).

1957 MARTIN, SIR LESLIE (HAROLD), C.B.E. Emeritus Professor, University of Melbourne. *46 Getting Crescent, P.O. Box 71, Campbell, A.C.T. 2601, Australia.*

Date of Election		Service on Council
1965	MASON, BASIL JOHN, C.B., D.Sc. TREASURER. Director-General of the Meteorological Office. LECTURE: BAKERIAN (1971). MEDAL: RUMFORD (1972). *Meteorological Office, London Road, Bracknell, Berkshire, RG12 2SZ. (Telephone: Bracknell 20242, extension 2389);* and 64 *Christchurch Road, East Sheen, S.W.*14. *(Telephone:* 01-876 2557); also *Athenaeum.*	1976– V.P. 1976– Treas. 1976–
1975	MASON, RONALD. Professor of Chemistry in the University of Sussex. *School of Molecular Sciences, University of Sussex, Brighton, BN*1 9*QJ. (Telephone: Brighton* 66755); and 14 *Roedean Crescent, Brighton, BN*2 5*RH. (Telephone: Brighton* 682077); also *Athenaeum.*	
1940	MASSEY, SIR HARRIE (STEWART WILSON) SECRETARY. Emeritus Professor of Physics in the University of London and Honorary Research Fellow in the Department of Physics and Astronomy at University College London. LECTURE: RUTHERFORD MEMORIAL (1967). MEDALS: HUGHES (1955), ROYAL (1958). *Department of Physics and Astronomy, University College, Gower Street, London, WC*1*E* 6*BT. (Telephone:* 01-387 7050); and *Kalamunda, Pelhams Walk, Esher, Surrey;* also *Athenaeum.*	1949–51 1959–60 Sec. 1969– V.P. 1969–
1949	MATHER, KENNETH, C.B.E. Honorary Professor of Genetics at the University of Birmingham. MEDAL: DARWIN (1964). *Department of Genetics, University of Birmingham, P.O. Box* 363, *Birmingham, B*15 2*TT. (Telephone:* 021-472 1301); and *The White House,* 296 *Bristol Road, Edgbaston, Birmingham, B*5 7*SN. (Telephone:* 021-472 2093); also *Athenaeum.*	1954–56 1964–66
1940	MATTHEWS, SIR BRYAN (HAROLD CABOT), C.B.E. Emeritus Professor of Physiology in the University of Cambridge and Fellow of King's College, Cambridge. *King's College, Cambridge, CB*2 1*ST. (Telephone: Cambridge* 50411); and *Priest's House, Swaffham Bulbeck, Cambridge. (Telephone: Cambridge* 811227).	1954–56 V.P. 1956–58
1974	MATTHEWS, DRUMMOND HOYLE, Ph.D. Reader in Marine Geology in the University of Cambridge. *Department of Geodesy and Geophysics, Madingley Rise, Madingley Road, Cambridge, CB*3 0*EZ. (Telephone: Cambridge* 51686); and 34 *Fulbrooke Road, Cambridge. (Telephone: Cambridge* 69103).	
1954	MATTHEWS, LEONARD HARRISON, Sc.D. Formerly Scientific Director, The Zoological Society of London. *The Old Rectory, Stansfield, Sudbury, Suffolk.*	
1973	MATTHEWS, PETER BRYAN CONRAD, D.Sc. Lecturer in the University of Oxford and Student of Christ Church. *University Laboratory of Physiology, Parks Road, Oxford, OX*1 3*PT. (Telephone: Oxford* 57451); and 3 *Dean Court Road, Cumnor Hill, Oxford, OX*2 9*JL. (Telephone: Cumnor* 2326).	
1963	MATTHEWS, PAUL TAUNTON, C.B.E., Ph.D. Vice-Chancellor of the University of Bath. *The University, Claverton Down, Bath, BA*2 7*AY. (Telephone: Bath* 6941); and *The Lodge, North Road, Claverton Down, Bath.*	1956–66

Date of Election		Service on Council
1974	MATTHEWS, RICHARD ELLIS FORD. Professor of Microbiology at the Department of Cell Biology in the University of Auckland. *Department of Cell Biology, University of Auckland, Private Bag, Auckland 1, New Zealand. (Telephone: Auckland 74740, extension 9697);* and 3 *Sadgrove Terrace, Mount Albert, Auckland 3, New Zealand. (Telephone: Auckland 866005).*	
1965	MAYNEORD, WILLIAM VALENTINE, C.B.E. Emeritus Professor of Physics as Applied to Medicine in the University of London. Formerly Director of the Physics Department, Institute of Cancer Research: Royal Cancer Hospital. 7 *Downs Way Close, Tadworth, Surrey. (Telephone: Tadworth 2297);* also *Athenaeum.*	
1949	MEDAWAR, SIR PETER (BRIAN), C.H., C.B.E. Member of the Scientific Staff of the Medical Research Council. LECTURES: CROONIAN (1958), TERCENTENARY (1960). MEDALS: ROYAL (1959), COPLEY (1969). Nobel Laureate, Physiology or Medicine, 1960. *Clinical Research Centre, Watford Road, Harrow, Middlesex, HA1 3UJ. (Telephone: 01-864 5311);* and 25 *Downshire Hill, Hampstead, London, NW3 1NT. (Telephone: 01-435 0822).*	1953–54 1962–64
1941	MELVILLE, SIR HARRY (WORK), K.C.B. Formerly Principal, Queen Mary College, University of London. LECTURE: BAKERIAN (1956). MEDAL: DAVY (1955). *Norwood, Dodds Lane, Chalfont St Giles, Buckinghamshire, HP8 4EL. (Telephone: Chalfont St Giles 2222);* also *Athenaeum.*	1945–47
1951	MENDELSSOHN, KURT ALFRED GEORG, D.Phil. Emeritus Reader in Physics at the University of Oxford. Emeritus Professorial Fellow of Wolfson College. MEDAL: HUGHES (1967). *Wolfson College, Oxford. (Telephone: Oxford 56711 and 58991);* and 235 *Iffley Road, Oxford. (Telephone: Oxford 43747);* also *Athenaeum.*	
1970	MENON, MAMBILLIKALATHIL GOVIND KUMAR, Ph.D. Scientific Adviser to the Minister for Defence; Secretary to the Government of India, Ministry of Defence for Defence Research; and Director General, Defence Research and Development Organization. Chairman, Electronics Commission and Secretary to the Government of India, Department of Electronics. *Vigyan Bhavan Annexe, Moulana Azad Road, New Delhi 110011, India. (Telephone: 381310);* and 81 *Lodi Estate, New Delhi 110003, India. (Telephone: 611533).*	
1966	MENTER, SIR JAMES (WOODHAM). Principal, Queen Mary College, University of London. *Queen Mary College, Mile End Road, London, E1 4NS. (Telephone: 01-980 4811);* and 1 *The Pierhead, Wapping High Street, London, E1 9PN. (Telephone: 01-488 3393).*	1969–71 May 1972-76 Treas. May 1972-76 V.P. 1970–71 May 1972-76

Date of Election		Service on Council
1965	MENZIES, Sir Robert (Gordon), K.T., C.H., P.C., Q.C. 95 Collins Street, Melbourne C.1, Victoria, Australia. (Telephone: Melbourne 63 9463).	
1969	MERRISON, Sir Alexander (Walter). Vice-Chancellor of the University of Bristol. Senate House, Tyndall Avenue, Bristol, BS8 1TH. (Telephone: Bristol 24161, extension 84); also Athenaeum.	
1970	MILEDI, Ricardo. Foulerton Research Professor of the Royal Society. Department of Biophysics, University College, Gower Street, London, WC1E 6BT. (Telephone: 01-387 7050, extension 286); and 5 Park Crescent Mews East, London, W1N 5HB. (Telephone: 01-636 3240).	
1961	MILES, Sir (Arnold) Ashley, C.B.E. Emeritus Professor of Experimental Pathology in the University of London. Department of Medical Microbiology, London Hospital Medical College, Turner Street, London, E1 2AD. (Telephone: 01-247 0644, extension 121); also Athenaeum.	1962–68 Sec. 1963–68 V.P. 1963–68
1970	MILLER, Jacques Francis Albert Pierre, D.Sc. Head, Experimental Pathology Unit, Walter and Eliza Hall Institute of Medical Research. Walter and Eliza Hall Institute of Medical Research, R.M.H. Post Office, Victoria, 3050, Australia. (Telephone: 347-1511); and 32 Burke Road North, East Ivanhoe, Victoria, 3079, Australia. (Telephone: 49-3481).	
1963	MILLS, Bernard Yarnton. Professor of Physics (Astrophysics) in the University of Sydney. School of Physics, University of Sydney, Sydney, N.S.W., Australia.	
1975	MILSTEIN, César, Ph.D. Member of staff of the Medical Research Council. M.R.C. Laboratory of Molecular Biology, Hills Road, Cambridge, CB2 2QH. (Telephone: Cambridge 48011); and 292A Hills Road, Cambridge. (Telephone: Cambridge 45677).	
1973	MITCHELL, George Francis. Professor of Quaternary Studies in the University of Dublin. Trinity College, Dublin 2, Republic of Ireland. (Telephone: Dublin 772941); and Townley Hall, near Drogheda, Co. Louth, Republic of Ireland. (Telephone: Drogheda 8218).	
1956	MITCHELL, John Wesley. William Barton Rogers Professor of Physics, University of Virginia. Department of Physics, University of Virginia, McCormick Road, Charlottesville, Virginia 22901, U.S.A.; also Athenaeum.	
1952	MITCHELL, Joseph Stanley, C.B.E. Emeritus Regius Professor of Physic and formerly Professor of Radiotherapeutics in the University of Cambridge. The Radiotherapeutic Centre, Addenbrooke's Hospital, Hills Road, Cambridge, CB2 2QQ. (Telephone: Cambridge 43619 and 45151); and Thorndyke, Huntingdon Road, Cambridge, CB3 0LG. (Telephone: Cambridge 76102).	1955–57

Date of Election		Service on Council
1974	MITCHELL, PETER DENNIS, Ph.D. Director of Research at the Glynn Research Laboratories, Bodmin, Cornwall. *Glynn Research Limited, Bodmin, Cornwall, PL30 4AU. (Telephone: Cardinham* 273); and *Glynn House, Bodmin, Cornwall, PL30 4AU. (Telephone: Cardinham* 381).	
1967	MITCHISON, NICHOLAS AVRION. Jodrell Professor of Zoology and Comparative Anatomy at University College in the University of London. *Department of Zoology, University College London, Gower Street, London, WC1E 6BT. (Telephone:* 01-388 0905).	
1968	MOLLISON, PATRICK LOUDON. Professor of Haematology in the University of London. Director (part-time), Medical Research Council Experimental Haematology Unit. *Department of Haematology, St Mary's Hospital Medical School, London, W2 1PG. (Telephone:* 01-723 1252, extension 206); and 60 *King Henry's Road, London, NW3 3RR. (Telephone:* 01-722 1947).	
1971	MONTEITH, JOHN LENNOX. Professor of Environmental Physics in the University of Nottingham School of Agriculture. *University of Nottingham School of Agriculture, Sutton Bonington, Loughborough, Leicestershire, LE12 5RD. (Telephone: Kegworth* 2386); and *Hillcroft, College Road, Sutton Bonington, Loughborough, Leicestershire. (Telephone: Kegworth* 2522).	
1947	MOON, PHILIP BURTON. Emeritus Professor of Physics in the University of Birmingham. LECTURE: RUTHERFORD (1975). 42 *Serpentine Road, Selly Park, Birmingham, B29 7HU. (Telephone:* 021-472 5615).	1953–55
1975	MORAN, PATRICK ALFRED PIERCE. Professor of Statistics and Head of the Department of Statistics in the Australian National University, Canberra. *Department of Statistics, Institute of Advanced Studies, Australian National University, P.O. Box* 4, *Canberra, A.C.T.* 2600, *Australia. (Telephone: Canberra* 493697); and 17 *Tennyson Crescent, Forrest, Canberra, A.C.T.* 2603, *Australia. (Telephone: Canberra* 731140).	
1972	MORGAN, SIR MORIEN (BEDFORD), C.B. Master of Downing College, Cambridge. *The Master's Lodge, Downing College, Cambridge. (Telephone: Cambridge* 56338); also *Athenaeum.*	
1949	MORGAN, WALTER THOMAS JAMES, C.B.E. Emeritus Professor of Biochemistry in the University of London. LECTURE: CROONIAN (1959). MEDAL: ROYAL (1968). 57 *Woodbury Drive, Sutton, Surrey, SM2 5RA. (Telephone:* 01-642 2319); also *Athenaeum.*	1956–58 1961–64 V.P. 1961–64
1964	MORROGH, HENTON, C.B.E., D.Sc. (Hon.). Director, British Cast Iron Research Association. *British Cast Iron Research Association, Alvechurch, Birmingham, B94 5HH. (Telephone: Redditch* 66414); and *Cedarwood, Penn Lane, Tanworth-in-Arden, Warwickshire. (Telephone: Tanworth-in-Arden* 2414).	

Date of Election		Service on Council
1958	MORTIMER, CLIFFORD HILEY, D.Sc. Formerly Secretary of the Scottish Marine Biological Association and Director of the Marine Station, Millport. *Center for Great Lakes Studies, The University of Wisconsin-Milwaukee, Milwaukee* 53201, *U.S.A.* (*Telephone:* (414) 963-4196).	
1950	MORTON, RICHARD ALAN. Emeritus Professor of Biochemistry in the University of Liverpool. *c/o Department of Zoology, The University, P.O. Box* 147, *Liverpool*. (*Telephone:* 051-709 6022, *extension* 191); and 39 *Greenhill Road, Liverpool,* L18 6JJ. (*Telephone:* 051-724 1331).	1959-61 1970-72
1936	MOTT, SIR NEVILL (FRANCIS). Emeritus Professor of Physics in the University of Cambridge. LECTURES: BAKERIAN (1953), RUTHERFORD MEMORIAL (1962). MEDALS: HUGHES (1941), ROYAL (1953), COPLEY (1972). *Cavendish Laboratory, Madingley Road, Cambridge, CB3 0HE.* (*Telephone: Cambridge* 66477); also *Athenaeum*.	1955-57
1966	MOUNTBATTEN OF BURMA, Admiral of the Fleet, EARL, K.G., G.C.B., O.M., G.C.S.I., G.C.I.E., G.C.V.O., D.S.O., P.C. Chairman of the National Electronics Council. *Broadlands, Romsey, Hampshire, SO5 9ZD.* (*Telephone: Romsey* 3333).	
1966	MOURANT, ARTHUR ERNEST, D.Phil., D.M. Honorary Senior Lecturer in Haematology at St Bartholomew's Hospital Medical College and formerly Director of the Medical Research Council Serological Population Genetics Laboratory. *St Bartholomew's Hospital, West Smithfield, London, E.C.*1. (*Telephone:* 01-606 4673); and 5 *Mercier Road, Putney, London, S.W.*15. (*Telephone:* 01-788 1496); also *Athenaeum*.	
1971	NABARRO, FRANK REGINALD NUNES, M.B.E. City of Johannesburg Professor of Physics in the University of the Witwatersrand. *Department of Physics, University of the Witwatersrand, Johannesburg, South Africa.* (*Telephone: Johannesburg* 724-1311, *extension* 219); and 32 *Cookham Road, Auckland Park, Johannesburg, South Africa.* (*Telephone: Johannesburg* 31-3833).	
1948	NEEDHAM, MRS DOROTHY MARY MOYLE, Sc.D. Biochemist, Biochemical Laboratory, University of Cambridge. 42 *Grange Road, Cambridge, CB3 9DG.* (*Telephone: Cambridge* 52183).	
1941	NEEDHAM, JOSEPH, Sc.D. Fellow of Gonville and Caius College. Emeritus Sir William Dunn Reader in Biochemistry in the University of Cambridge. LECTURE: WILKINS (1958). *East Asian History of Science Library,* 8 *Shaftesbury Road, Cambridge, CB2 2BW.* (*Telephone: Cambridge* 311545); *Gonville and Caius College, Cambridge.* (*Telephone: Cambridge* 312211, *extension* 347); and 42 *Grange Road, Cambridge, CB3 9DG.* (*Telephone: Cambridge* 52183).	

THE FELLOWSHIP 1977

Date of Election		Service on Council
1951	NEUBERGER, ALBERT, C.B.E. Emeritus Professor of Chemical Pathology in the University of London. *Department of Biochemistry, Charing Cross Hospital Medical School, Fulham Palace Road, London, W6 8RF. (Telephone:* 01-748 2050, extension 2607); *and* 22 *West Heath Avenue, London, NW*11 7*QL. (Telephone:* 01-455 2217); also *Athenaeum.*	1966-68
1959	NEUMANN, BERNHARD HERMANN, D.Sc. Senior Research Fellow, Commonwealth Scientific and Industrial Research Organization, Division of Mathematics and Statistics, and Honorary Fellow, Department of Mathematics, Institute of Advanced Studies, Australian National University. *Australian National University, Box* 4, *P.O., Canberra, A.C.T.* 2600, *Australia. (Telephone:* (062) *Canberra* 494504); *C.S.I.R.O., Box* 1965, *P.O., Canberra City, A.C.T.* 2601, *Australia. (Telephone:* (062) *Canberra* 822011); *and* 20 *Talbot Street, Forrest, A.C.T.* 2603, *Australia. (Telephone:* (062) *Canberra* 733447).	
1942	NEWITT, DUDLEY MAURICE, M.C. Emeritus Professor of Chemical Engineering in the University of London. MEDAL: RUMFORD (1962). *Hollycot, Runfold, near Farnham, Surrey;* also *Athenaeum.*	1957-59
1939	NEWMAN, MAXWELL HERMAN ALEXANDER. Emeritus Professor of Mathematics in the University of Manchester. MEDAL: SYLVESTER (1958). *Cross Farm, Comberton, Cambridge. (Telephone: Comberton* 2276).	1946-47
1967	NICOL, JOSEPH ARTHUR COLIN. Professor of Zoology, The University of Texas at Austin, Marine Science Institute. *Port Aransas, Texas* 78373, *U.S.A. (Telephone:* (512) 749-6741); *and P.O. Box* 1153, *Port Aransas, Texas* 78373, *U.S.A.*	
1959	NOCKOLDS, STEPHEN ROBERT, Ph.D. Formerly Reader in Geochemistry in the University of Cambridge. *Department of Mineralogy and Petrology, Downing Place, Cambridge; Trinity College, Cambridge; and The Bell House, Castle Street, Saffron Walden, Essex.*	
1936	NORRISH, RONALD GEORGE WREYFORD. Emeritus Professor of Physical Chemistry in the University of Cambridge. LECTURE: BAKERIAN (1966). MEDAL: DAVY (1958). Nobel Laureate, Chemistry, 1967. *University Physical Chemistry Laboratories, Lensfield Road, Cambridge. (Telephone: Cambridge* 66499); 7 *Park Terrace, Cambridge. (Telephone: Cambridge* 55147); *and Emmanuel College, Cambridge. (Telephone: Cambridge* 65411).	
1968	NORTHCOTE, DONALD HENRY. Master of Sidney Sussex College and Professor of Plant Biochemistry in the University of Cambridge. *Department of Biochemistry, Tennis Court Road, Cambridge. (Telephone: Cambridge* 51781); *and The Master's Lodge, Sidney Sussex College, Cambridge. (Telephone: Cambridge* 55860).	
1961	NORTHCOTT, DOUGLAS GEOFFREY. Town Trust Professor of Mathematics in the University of Sheffield. *The University, Sheffield,* 10; *and* 25 *Parkhead Road, Ecclesall, Sheffield, S*11 9*RA.*	

Date of Election		Service on Council
1970	NORTHUMBERLAND, HUGH ALGERNON PERCY, DUKE OF, K.G., T.D., P.C. *Alnwick Castle, Northumberland.*	
1968	NUTMAN, PHILLIP SADLER, Ph.D. Head of the Soil Microbiology Department, Rothamsted Experimental Station. *Rothamsted Experimental Station, Harpenden, Hertfordshire, AL5 2JQ.* (*Telephone: Harpenden* 63133); and 2 *Lyndhurst Drive, Harpenden, Hertfordshire.* (*Telephone: Harpenden* 4249).	
1976	NYE, JOHN FREDERICK. Professor of Physics in the University of Bristol. *The H. H. Wills Physics Laboratory, Tyndall Avenue, Bristol, BS8 1TL.* (*Telephone: Bristol* 24161); and 45 *Canynge Road, Bristol, BS8 3LH.* (*Telephone: Bristol* 33769).	
1969	OATLEY, SIR CHARLES (WILLIAM), O.B.E. Emeritus Professor of Electrical Engineering in the University of Cambridge. MEDAL: ROYAL (1969), MULLARD (1973). *Department of Engineering, Trumpington Street, Cambridge, CB2 1PZ.* (*Telephone: Cambridge* 66466); and 16 *Porson Road, Cambridge, CB2 2EU.* (*Telephone: Cambridge* 56194); also *Athenaeum*.	1970–72
1952	OFFORD, ALBERT CYRIL. Senior Research Fellow, Imperial College of Science and Technology, London, and Emeritus Professor of Mathematics in the University of London. *Department of Mathematics, Imperial College, London, SW7 2BZ.* (*Telephone:* 01-589 5111); and 70 *Elms Road, Harrow, Middlesex, HA3 6BS.* (*Telephone:* 01-954 2684).	1957–58
1955	OGSTON, ALEXANDER GEORGE, D.Sc. President of Trinity College, Oxford. *The President's Lodging, Trinity College, Oxford, OX1 3BH.* (*Telephone: Oxford* 41801).	
1937	OLIPHANT, SIR MARK (MARCUS LAURENCE ELWIN), K.B.E. Formerly Governor of South Australia and formerly Director of the Research School of Physical Sciences, Australian National University. LECTURES: BAKERIAN (1955), RUTHERFORD MEMORIAL (1955). MEDAL: HUGHES (1943). 37 *Colvin Street, Hughes, Canberra, A.C.T., Australia;* also *Athenaeum*.	1946–48
1972	OLLIS, WILLIAM DAVID. Professor of Organic Chemistry in the University of Sheffield. *Department of Chemistry, The University, Sheffield, S3 7HF.* (*Telephone: Sheffield* 78555, *extension* 462); also *Athenaeum*.	
1962	ORGEL, LESLIE ELEAZER. Adjunct Professor, Department of Chemistry, University of California, San Diego. Resident Fellow, The Salk Institute for Biological Studies. *The Salk Institute, P.O. Box* 1809, *San Diego, California,* 92112, *U.S.A.* (*Telephone:* (714) 453-4100, *extension* 321).	
1947	OROWAN, EGON. Professor Emeritus, Massachusetts Institute of Technology. 44 *Payson Terrace, Belmont, Mass.* 02178, *U.S.A.* (*Telephone:* (617) 484-8334).	

Date of Election		Service on Council
1971	OWEN, PAUL ROBERT, C.B.E. Zaharoff Professor of Aviation and Head of the Department of Aeronautics at the Imperial College of Science and Technology in the University of London. *Department of Aeronautics, Imperial College, London, S.W.7. (Telephone: 01-589 5111), 1 Horbury Crescent, London, W.11. (Telephone: 01-229 5111);* and *Strangmoor, Pentridge, Dorset. (Telephone: Handley 327);* also *Athenaeum.*	
1972	PAL, BENJAMIN PEARY, Ph.D. Formerly Director General of the Indian Council of Agricultural Research. *P.11, Hauz Khas Enclave, New Delhi 16, India. (Telephone: Delhi 626145).*	
1972	PARKE, MARY, D.Sc. Senior Principal Scientific Officer, Marine Biological Association of the United Kingdom. *The Laboratory, Citadel Hill, Plymouth, PL1 2PB. (Telephone: Plymouth 21761);* and *6 Alfred Street, Plymouth, PL1 2RP. (Telephone: Plymouth 68609).*	
1933	PARKES, SIR ALAN (STERLING), C.B.E. Emeritus Professor of the Physiology of Reproduction in the University of Cambridge. *The Galton Foundation, 7 Downing Place, Cambridge, CB2 3EL. (Telephone: Cambridge 59729).*	
1962	PARRINGTON, FRANCIS REX, Sc.D. Emeritus Reader in Vertebrate Zoology and formerly Director of the Museum of Zoology in the University of Cambridge. *24 Birch Trees Road, Great Shelford, Cambridge, CB2 5AW. (Telephone: Shelford 3893).*	
1970	PARTRIDGE, STANLEY MILES. Deputy Chief Scientific Officer at the Meat Research Institute, Agricultural Research Council, and Professor of Biochemistry in the University of Bristol. *A.R.C. Meat Research Institute, Langford, near Bristol. (Telephone: Churchill 852661);* and *Millstream House, St Andrew's Road, Cheddar, Somerset. (Telephone: Cheddar 742130).*	
1968	PASHLEY, DONALD WILLIAM, Ph.D. Director of Research, Tube Investments Limited, and Director of Tube Investments Research Laboratories. *Tube Investments Research Laboratories, Hinxton Hall, near Saffron Walden, Essex. (Telephone: Cambridge 832381);* and *32 Beeches Close, Saffron Walden, Essex. (Telephone: Saffron Walden 23509).*	
1969	PATON, SIR (THOMAS) ANGUS (LYALL), C.M.G. Senior Partner, Sir Alexander Gibb and Partners, Consulting Engineers. *Earley House, 427 London Road, Earley, Reading, RG6 1BL. (Telephone: Reading 61061);* also *Athenaeum.*	1976– V.P. 1976–
1956	PATON, WILLIAM DRUMMOND MACDONALD, C.B.E. Professor of Pharmacology at the University of Oxford. *Department of Pharmacology, South Parks Road, Oxford, OX1 3QT. (Telephone: Oxford 57062);* and *13 Staverton Road, Oxford. (Telephone: Oxford 58355);* also *Athenaeum.*	1967–69

Date of Election		Service on Council
1966	PEARSON, EGON SHARPE, C.B.E. Emeritus Professor of Statistics in the University of London. *Department of Statistics, University College, Gower Street, London, W.C.*1; *and Pendean Home, West Lavington, Midhurst, West Sussex, GU29 0ER. (Telephone: Midhurst 4304).*	
1969	PEART, WILLIAM STANLEY. Professor of Medicine at St Mary's Hospital Medical School in the University of London. *Medical Unit, St Mary's Hospital, London, W2 1NY. (Telephone:* 01-262 1280, *extension* 18); *and* 5 *Fordington Road, London, N.*6. *(Telephone:* 01-883 9346).	1973–74
1945	PEIERLS, SIR RUDOLF (ERNST), C.B.E. Emeritus Professor of Theoretical Physics at the University of Oxford. MEDAL: ROYAL (1959). *Department of Theoretical Physics,* 12 *Parks Road, Oxford, OX*1 3*PQ; also Athenaeum.*	1957–58
1962	PENMAN, HOWARD LATIMER, O.B.E., Ph.D. Formerly Head of the Physics Department, Rothamsted Experimental Station. 31 *Dalkeith Road, Harpenden, Hertfordshire, AL5 5PP. (Telephone: Harpenden 3366).*	
1946	PENNEY, OF EAST HENDRED, WILLIAM GEORGE, BARON, O.M., K.B.E. Formerly Rector of the Imperial College of Science and Technology, London. MEDAL: RUMFORD (1966). *Orchard House, East Hendred, Wantage, Oxfordshire, OX*12 8*JT. (Telephone: East Hendred* 206); *also Athenaeum.*	1950–52 Treas. 1956–60 V.P. 1957–60
1972	PENROSE, ROGER. Rouse Ball Professor of Mathematics in the University of Oxford. *Mathematical Institute,* 24-29 *St Giles, Oxford, OX*1 3*LB. (Telephone: Oxford* 54295.)	
1973	PEREIRA, HELIO GELLI, M.D. Head of the Department of Epidemiology and World Reference Centre for Foot and Mouth Disease, Animal Virus Research Institute. *Department of Epidemiology, Animal Virus Research Institute, Pirbright, Woking, Surrey. (Telephone: Worplesdon* 2441); *and* 3 *Ducks Walk, Twickenham, TW*1 2*DD. (Telephone:* 01-892 4511).	
1969	PEREIRA, SIR (HERBERT) CHARLES. Chief Scientist, Ministry of Agriculture, Fisheries and Food. *Ministry of Agriculture, Fisheries and Food, Whitehall Place, London, S.W.*1. *(Telephone:* 01-839 7711); *and Great East, East Malling Research Station, Maidstone, Kent. (Telephone: West Malling* 840195).	
1966	PERKINS, DONALD HILL. Professor of Elementary Particle Physics at the University of Oxford. *Department of Nuclear Physics, The University, Keble Road, Oxford, OX*1 3*RH. (Telephone: Oxford* 59911).	
1974	PERRY, SAMUEL VICTOR. Professor and Chairman of the Department of Biochemistry in the University of Birmingham. *Department of Biochemistry, University of Birmingham, P.O. Box* 363, *Birmingham, B*15 2*TT. (Telephone:* 021-472 1301, *extension* 3123); *and* 64 *Meadowhill Road, King's Norton, Birmingham. (Telephone:* 021-458 1511).	

Date of Election		Service on Council
1954	PERUTZ, MAX FERDINAND, C.H., C.B.E., Ph.D. Chairman of the Medical Research Council Laboratory of Molecular Biology. LECTURE: CROONIAN (1968). MEDAL: ROYAL (1971). Nobel Laureate, Chemistry, 1962. *M.R.C. Laboratory of Molecular Biology, Hills Road, Cambridge. (Telephone: Cambridge* 48011); and 42 *Sedley Taylor Road, Cambridge. (Telephone: Cambridge* 46041).	
1974	PETCH, NORMAN JAMES. Professor of Metallurgy in the University of Strathclyde. *Department of Metallurgy, Colville Building, University of Strathclyde,* 48 *North Portland Street, Glasgow,* G1 1*XN. (Telephone:* 041-552 4400); and *Abbotsford, Printers Row, Balfron, By Glasgow,* G63 0*RH. (Telephone: Balfron* 249).	
1935	PETERS, SIR RUDOLPH (ALBERT), M.C. (with Bar). Professor Emeritus of Biochemistry at the University of Oxford. LECTURE: CROONIAN (1951). MEDAL: ROYAL (1949). *Department of Biochemistry, Tennis Court Road, Cambridge;* and 3 *Newnham Walk, Cambridge. (Telephone: Cambridge* 50819).	1944–46 1955–56 V.P. 1945–46 1955–56
1974	PHILIP, JOHN ROBERT, D.Sc. Chief of Division of Environmental Mechanics, Commonwealth Scientific and Industrial Research Organization. *C.S.I.R.O. Division of Environmental Mechanics, P.O. Box* 821, *Canberra, A.C.T.* 2601, *Australia. (Telephone:* (062) 46-5645); and 42 *Vasey Crescent, Campbell, A.C.T.* 2601, *Australia. (Telephone:* (062) 47-8958).	
1963	PHILLIPS, CHARLES GARRETT. Dr Lee's Professor of Anatomy in the University of Oxford. LECTURE: FERRIER (1968). *Department of Human Anatomy, South Parks Road, Oxford, OX*1 3*QX. (Telephone: Oxford* 58686); and *Aubrey House, Horton-cum-Studley, Oxford, OX*9 1*BU.*	1966–67 1976–
1967	PHILLIPS, DAVID CHILTON. SECRETARY. Professor of Molecular Biophysics at the University of Oxford. MEDAL: ROYAL (1975). *Laboratory of Molecular Biophysics, Department of Zoology, South Parks Road, Oxford, OX*1 3*PS. (Telephone: Oxford* 56789); *Corpus Christi College, Oxford;* and 3 *Fairlawn End, Upper Wolvercote, Oxford, OX*2 8*AR. (Telephone: Oxford* 55828).	1969–70 1971–73 1976– V.P. 1972–73 1976– Sec. 1976–
1968	PHILLIPS, OWEN MARTIN. Professor of Geophysics, The Johns Hopkins University. *Department of Earth and Planetary Sciences, The Johns Hopkins University, Baltimore, Maryland* 21218, *U.S.A. (Telephone:* (301) 338-7036).	
1976	PICKAVANCE, THOMAS GERALD, C.B.E., Ph.D. Formerly Director of Nuclear Physics, Science Research Council. 3 *Kingston Close, Abingdon, Oxfordshire, OX*14 1*ES. (Telephone: Abingdon* 23934).	
1960	PICKERING, SIR GEORGE (WHITE). Formerly Master of Pembroke College, Oxford. 5 *Horwood Close, Headington, Oxford. (Telephone: Oxford* 64260); also *Athenaeum.*	

Date of Election		Service on Council
1966	PICKFORD, LILLIAN MARY. Emeritus Professor in the Department of Physiology in the University of Edinburgh. Part-time Professor of Endocrinology in the University of Nottingham. *The Hall, King Sterndale, near Buxton, Derbyshire.* (*Telephone: Buxton* 3822).	
1969	PILKINGTON, SIR ALASTAIR (LIONEL ALEXANDER BETHUNE). Chairman, Pilkington Brothers Limited. MEDAL: MULLARD (1968). *Pilkington Brothers Limited, St Helens, Merseyside.* (*Telephone: St Helens* 28882); and *The Crossways, View Road, Rainhill, Prescot, Merseyside, L35 0LS.* (*Telephone:* 051-426 4228).	
1956	PIPPARD, SIR (ALFRED) BRIAN. Cavendish Professor of Physics in the University of Cambridge. MEDAL: HUGHES (1959). *Cavendish Laboratory, Madingley Road, Cambridge, CB3 0HE.* (*Telephone: Cambridge* 66477); and 30 *Porson Road, Cambridge.* (*Telephone: Cambridge* 58713).	1963-64
1949	PIRIE, NORMAN WINGATE. Formerly Head of the Biochemistry Department, Rothamsted Experimental Station. Visiting Professor at the University of Reading and in the Indian Statistical Institute, Calcutta. LECTURE: LEEUWENHOEK (1963). MEDAL: COPLEY (1971). *Rothamsted Experimental Station, Harpenden, Hertfordshire, AL5 2JQ.* (*Telephone: Harpenden* 63133).	
1957	PITT, HARRY RAYMOND, Ph.D. Vice-Chancellor of the University of Reading. *The University, Reading, Berkshire.*	
1954	PITT-RIVERS, ROSALIND VENETIA, Ph.D. Formerly Head of the Chemistry Division of the National Institute for Medical Research. *Department of Pharmacology, University College London, Gower Street, London, WC1E 6BT.* (*Telephone:* 01-387 7050, *extension* 359).	
1936	PLASKETT, HARRY HEMLEY. Emeritus Professor of Astronomy at the University of Oxford. 48 *Blenheim Drive, Oxford.* (*Telephone: Oxford* 58109).	1951-53
1973	POLANI, PAUL EMANUEL. Prince Philip Professor of Paediatric Research in the University of London and Director of the Paediatric Research Unit at Guy's Hospital Medical School. *Paediatric Research Unit, Prince Philip Research Laboratories, Guy's Hospital Medical School, London, SE1 9RT.* (*Telephone:* 01-407 7600, *extension* 2330); and *Little Meadow, West Clandon, near Guildford, Surrey, GU4 7TL.* (*Telephone: Guildford* 222436); also *Athenaeum.*	
1971	POLANYI, JOHN CHARLES. University Professor and Professor of Chemistry in the University of Toronto. *Department of Chemistry, University of Toronto,* 80 *St George Street, Toronto 5, Ontario, Canada.* (*Telephone:* (416) 978-3580); and 3 *Rosedale Road, Toronto 5, Ontario, Canada.* (*Telephone:* (416) 961-6545).	

Date of Election		Service on Council
1974	POLKINGHORNE, JOHN CHARLTON. Professor of Mathematical Physics in the University of Cambridge. *Department of Applied Mathematics and Theoretical Physics, Silver Street, Cambridge, CB3 9EW.* (*Telephone: Cambridge* 51645); and *22 Rutherford Road, Cambridge, CB2 2HH.* (*Telephone: Trumpington* 3321).	
1962	POLLOCK, MARTIN RIVERS. Emeritus Professor of Biology in the University of Edinburgh. *Marsh Farm House, Margaret Marsh, Shaftesbury, Dorset, SP7 0AZ.* (*Telephone: Marnhull* 479).	
1955	PONTECORVO, GUIDO, Ph.D. Formerly Professor of Genetics in the University of Glasgow, and Honorary Consultant Geneticist, Imperial Cancer Research Fund. LECTURE: LEEUWENHOEK (1962). *Flat 25, Cranfield House, 97 Southampton Row, London, WC1B 4HH.* (*Telephone:* 01-636 9441).	1958–59
1961	POPJÁK, GEORGE JOSEPH. Professor of Biochemistry at the Medical School of the University of California, Los Angeles. MEDAL: DAVY (1968). *Departments of Psychiatry and Biological Chemistry, University of California, Los Angeles, Center for the Health Sciences, Los Angeles, California 90024, U.S.A.*	
1961	POPLE, JOHN ANTHONY. John Christian Warner University Professor of Natural Sciences at the Carnegie-Mellon University. *Department of Chemistry, Carnegie-Mellon University, Pittsburgh, Pennsylvania 15213, U.S.A.*	
1976	POPPER, SIR KARL (RAIMUND). Emeritus Professor of Logic and Scientific Method in the University of London. *Fallowfield, Manor Road, Penn, Buckinghamshire, HP10 8HZ.* (*Telephone: Penn* 2126).	
1960	PORTER, SIR GEORGE. Fullerian Professor of Chemistry and Director of the Royal Institution. MEDAL: DAVY (1971). Nobel Laureate, Chemistry, 1967. *The Royal Institution, 21 Albemarle Street, London, W1X 4BS.* (*Telephone:* 01-493 2710); also *Athenaeum.*	1966–67
1956	PORTER, HELEN KEMP (*née* ARCHBOLD). Emeritus Professor of Plant Physiology in the University of London. *49E Beaumont Street, London, W1N 1RE.* (*Telephone:* 01-935 5862).	
1964	PORTER, RODNEY ROBERT. Whitley Professor of Biochemistry at the University of Oxford. MEDAL: ROYAL (1973). Nobel Laureate, Physiology or Medicine, 1972. *Department of Biochemistry, South Parks Road, Oxford, OX1 3QU.* (*Telephone: Oxford* 59214); and *Downhill Farm, Witney, Oxfordshire.* (*Telephone: Witney* 3831).	1973–74
1971	POSNETTE, ADRIAN FRANK, C.B.E. Director of the East Malling Research Station. Visiting Professor in Plant Sciences, Wye College. *East Malling Research Station, Maidstone, Kent.* (*Telephone: West Malling* 843833); and *Walnut Tree Cottage, East Sutton, Maidstone, Kent.* (*Telephone: Sutton Valence* 3282).	

Date of Election		Service on Council
1953	POWELL, HERBERT MARCUS. Emeritus Professor of Chemical Crystallography in the University of Oxford. Emeritus Fellow of Hertford College, Oxford. 46 *Davenant Road, Oxford;* and *Hertford College, Oxford.*	
1951	PRESCOTT, JAMES ARTHUR, C.B.E. Emeritus Professor of Agricultural Chemistry in the University of Adelaide. 6 *Kinross Lodge,* 2 *Netherby Avenue, Netherby, South Australia* 5062, *Australia.*	
1954	PRESTON, REGINALD DAWSON. Emeritus Professor of Plant Biophysics in the University of Leeds. Visiting Professor in the Department of Botany, Imperial College of Science and Technology, London. *Room* 6-23, *Department of Physics, Physics/Administration Building, The University, Leeds, LS2 9JT. (Telephone:* Leeds 31751); and 117 *St Anne's Road, Leeds,* 6. *(Telephone:* Leeds 785248).	
1959	PRICE, WILLIAM CHARLES. Emeritus Professor of Physics at King's College in the University of London. *Department of Physics, King's College, Strand, London, W.C.2. (Telephone:* 01-836 5454); *and* 38 *Cross Way, Petts Wood, Kent. (Telephone: Orpington* 28815).	
1967	PRIESTLEY, CHARLES HENRY BRIAN, Sc.D. Chairman for Environmental Physics Research, Commonwealth Scientific and Industrial Research Organization, Australia. *C.S.I.R.O. Division of Atmospheric Physics, Aspendale, Victoria* 3195, *Australia;* and 11 *Coonil Crescent, Malvern, Victoria* 3144, *Australia.*	
1954	PRINGLE, JOHN WILLIAM SUTTON, M.B.E. Linacre Professor of Zoology at the University of Oxford. *Department of Zoology, South Parks Road, Oxford, OX*1 3*PS. (Telephone: Oxford* 56789); *Merton College, Oxford;* and 437 *Banbury Road, Oxford, OX*2 8*ED. (Telephone: Oxford* 58470).	1963–65
1951	PRYCE, MAURICE HENRY LECORNEY. Professor of Physics in the University of British Columbia. *Department of Physics, University of British Columbia, Vancouver* 8, *B.C., Canada. (Telephone:* 228-3771); *and* 4754 *West 6th Avenue, Vancouver* 8, *B.C., Canada. (Telephone:* 224-1596); also *Athenaeum.*	
1952	PUGSLEY, SIR ALFRED (GRENVILE), O.B.E. Emeritus Professor of Civil Engineering in the University of Bristol. 4 *Harley Court, Clifton Down, Bristol, BS*8 3*JU. (Telephone: Bristol* 39400); also *Athenaeum.*	1959–61
1940	QUASTEL, JUDA HIRSCH. Professor of Neurochemistry in the University of British Columbia. LECTURE: LEEUWENHOEK (1954). *Neurochemistry Section, Kinsmen Laboratories, University of British Columbia, Vancouver, B.C., V*6*T* 1*W*5, *Canada. (Telephone:* 228-2203); *and* 4585 *Langara Avenue, Vancouver, B.C., V*6*R* 1*C*9, *Canada. (Telephone:* 224-4755).	

Date of Election		Service on Council

1952 RACE, ROBERT RUSSELL, C.B.E., Ph.D. Formerly Director, Medical Research Council Blood Group Unit. *Wolfson House, 4 Stephenson Way, London, NW1 2HE. (Telephone: 01-388 7752); and 22 Vicarage Road, London, SW14 8RU. (Telephone: 01-876 1508).*

1975 RAINEY, REGINALD CHARLES, D.Sc. Senior Principal Scientific Officer at the Centre for Overseas Pest Research of the Ministry of Overseas Development, London. *Centre for Overseas Pest Research, College House, Wrights Lane, London, W8 5SJ. (Telephone: 01-937 8191, extension 207); and Elmslea, Old Risborough Road, Stoke Mandeville, Buckinghamshire. (Telephone: Stoke Mandeville 2493).*

1955 RAMSAY, JAMES ARTHUR, M.B.E. Emeritus Professor of Comparative Physiology in the University of Cambridge. *The Boxer's Croft, Abriachan, Inverness-shire. (Telephone: Dochgarroch 269).*

1973 RAMSAY, JOHN GRAHAM. Professor of Geology in the Eidgenössische Technische Hochschule, Zürich. *ETH-Z, Sonnegstrasse 5, CH-8006 Zürich, Switzerland.*

1946 RANDALL, SIR JOHN (TURTON). Emeritus Professor of Biophysics in the University of London and formerly Director of the Medical Research Council Biophysics Unit. Honorary Professor in the University of Edinburgh. MEDAL: HUGHES (1946). *Department of Zoology, University of Edinburgh, West Mains Road, Edinburgh, EH9 3JT. (Telephone: 031-667 1081, extension 3203); and 16 Kevock Road, Lasswade, Lothian Region, EH18 1HT. (Telephone: 031-663 8019); also Athenaeum.*

1967 RAO, CALYAMPUDI RADHAKRISHNA, Sc.D. Jawaharlal Nehru Professor, Indian Statistical Institute. *Indian Statistical Institute, 7 S.J.S. Sansanwal Marg, New Delhi 110029, India. (Telephone: 678247).*

1962 RAPHAEL, RALPH ALEXANDER. Professor of Organic Chemistry in the University of Cambridge. *University Chemical Laboratory, Lensfield Road, Cambridge, CB2 1EW. (Telephone: Cambridge 66499); also Athenaeum.* 1975–

1951 RATCLIFFE, JOHN ASHWORTH, C.B., C.B.E. Formerly Director of the Science Research Council's Radio and Space Research Station. LECTURE: RUTHERFORD MEMORIAL (1966). MEDAL: ROYAL (1966). *193 Huntingdon Road, Cambridge, CB3 0DL. (Telephone: Cambridge 76328).* 1954–55

1972 RAWCLIFFE, GORDON HINDLE. Emeritus Professor of Electrical Engineering in the University of Bristol. *28 Upper Belgrave Road, Clifton, Bristol, BS8 2XL. (Telephone: Bristol 37940); also Athenaeum.*

Date of Election		Service on Council

1959 RAYNOR, GEOFFREY VINCENT. Professor of Physical Metallurgy in the University of Birmingham. *Department of Physical Metallurgy and Science of Materials, The University, P.O. Box 363, Edgbaston, Birmingham, B15 2TT. (Telephone:* 021-472 1301, *extension* 3230); and 94 *Gillhurst Road, Harborne, Birmingham, B17 8PA. (Telephone:* 021-429 3176).

1971 REASON, RICHARD EDMUND, O.B.E., Hon.D.Sc. Consultant, Metrology Division, Rank Precision Industries Limited. Visiting Research Fellow, University of Manchester Institute of Science and Technology. 5 *Manor Road, Great Bowden, Leicestershire. (Telephone: Market Harborough* 3219).

1974 REES, CHARLES WAYNE. Professor of Organic Chemistry in the University of Liverpool. *Department of Organic Chemistry, The University of Liverpool, P.O. Box 147, Liverpool, L69 3BX. (Telephone:* 051-709 6022); and *High Close, Wetstone Lane, West Kirby, Wirral, Merseyside, L48 7HG. (Telephone:* 051-625 6005).

1968 REES, DAVID. Professor of Pure Mathematics in the University of Exeter. *Department of Mathematics, The University, North Park Road, Exeter, EX4 4QE, Devon. (Telephone: Exeter* 77911, *extension* 460); and 6 *Hillcrest Park, Exeter, EX4 4SH, Devon. (Telephone: Exeter* 59398).

1971 REES, FLORENCE GWENDOLEN. Emeritus Professor of Zoology in the University of Wales. *Department of Zoology, University College of Wales, Aberystwyth. (Telephone: Aberystwyth* 3111); and *Grey Mist, North Road, Aberystwyth, Dyfed. (Telephone: Aberystwyth* 2389).

1976 REES, HUBERT, D.F.C. Professor of Agricultural Botany in the University College of Wales, Aberystwyth. *Department of Agricultural Botany, University College of Wales, Penglais, Aberystwyth, Dyfed. (Telephone: Aberystwyth* 3111); and *Irfon, Llanbadarn Road, Aberystwyth, Dyfed. (Telephone: Aberystwyth* 3668).

1959 RICHARDS, OWAIN WESTMACOTT. Emeritus Professor of Zoology and Applied Entomology in the University of London. 89 *St Stephens Road, Ealing, W13 8JA. (Telephone:* 01-997 3562).

1959 RICHARDS, REX EDWARD, D.Sc. Warden of Merton College, University of Oxford. MEDAL: DAVY (1976). *Merton College, Oxford. (Telephone: Oxford* 49651); and *Biochemistry Laboratory, South Parks Road, Oxford. (Telephone: Oxford* 59214).   1973-75

1968 RICHARDSON, FREDERICK DENYS. Professor of Extraction Metallurgy at the Imperial College of Science and Technology in the University of London. *Department of Metallurgy, Imperial College, Prince Consort Road, London, S.W.7. (Telephone:* 01-589 5111, *extension* 1703); and 4 *College Avenue, Epsom, Surrey.*

Date of Election		Service on Council
1967	RILEY, RALPH. Director of the Plant Breeding Institute, Cambridge. Special Professor of Botany in the University of Nottingham. *Plant Breeding Institute, Maris Lane, Trumpington, Cambridge, CB2 2LQ. (Telephone: Trumpington 2411); and 2 High Street, Little Shelford, Cambridge. (Telephone: Shelford 3845).*	1972–74
1954	RIMINGTON, CLAUDE. Emeritus Professor of Chemical Pathology, University College Hospital Medical School, London. *c/o Department of Chemical Pathology, University College Hospital Medical School, University Street, London, W.C.1.*	
1972	RINGWOOD, ALFRED EDWARD. Professor of Geochemistry in the Australian National University. *Research School of Earth Sciences, Australian National University, Canberra, A.C.T. 2600, Australia. (Telephone: Canberra 493420); and 3 Vancouver Street, Red Hill, Canberra, A.C.T. 2603, Australia. (Telephone: Canberra 959929).*	
1974	RISHBETH, JOHN, Sc.D. Reader in Plant Pathology in the University of Cambridge. *Botany School, Downing Street, Cambridge, CB2 3EA. (Telephone: Cambridge 61414); and 36 Wingate Way, Cambridge, CB2 2HD. (Telephone: Trumpington 3298).*	
1976	RITCHIE, JOSEPH MURDOCH. Professor of Pharmacology in Yale University. *Department of Pharmacology, Yale University Medical School, New Haven, Connecticut 06510, U.S.A. (Telephone: (203) 436-3617); and 47 Deepwood Drive, Hamden, Connecticut 06157, U.S.A. (Telephone: (203) 777-0420).*	
1965	ROBERTS, SIR GILBERT. Partner, Freeman, Fox and Partners, Consulting Engineers. MEDAL: ROYAL (1968). *Freeman, Fox and Partners, Alliance House, Caxton Street, London, S.W.1. (Telephone: 01-799 1883); and 42 Wynnstay Gardens, Allen Street, London, W.8. (Telephone: 01-937 5714); also Athenaeum.*	
1963	ROBERTS, JOHN ALEXANDER FRASER, C.B.E., M.D. Geneticist, Paediatric Research Unit, Guy's Hospital Medical School. *Paediatric Research Unit, Guy's Hospital Medical School, London, S.E.1. (Telephone: 01-407 7600); and 10 Aspley Road, Wandsworth, London, SW18 2DB. (Telephone: 01-874 4826); also Athenaeum.*	
1964	ROBERTSON, ALAN, O.B.E. Honorary Professor in the University of Edinburgh. Deputy Chief Scientific Officer, Agricultural Research Council Unit of Animal Genetics. *Institute of Animal Genetics, West Mains Road, Edinburgh, 9. (Telephone: 031-667 1081); and 47 Braid Road, Edinburgh, 10. (Telephone: 031-447 4239).*	
1940	ROBERTSON, ANDREW. Emeritus Professor of Mechanical Engineering in the University of Bristol. *New Cote, Cote House Lane, Westbury-on-Trym, Bristol.*	1941–42
1945	ROBERTSON, JOHN MONTEATH, C.B.E. Emeritus Professor of Chemistry and formerly Director of the Chemical Laboratories in the University of Glasgow. MEDAL: DAVY (1960). *42 Bailie Drive, Bearsden, Glasgow, G61 3AH. (Telephone: 041-942 2640); also Athenaeum.*	1954–56

Date of Election		Service on Council

1961 ROBERTSON, SIR RUTHERFORD (NESS), C.M.G. Emeritus Professor of Botany in the University of Adelaide. Director, Research School of Biological Sciences in the Australian National University. *Research School of Biological Sciences, Australian National University, Box 475, P.O., Canberra City, A.C.T. 2601, Australia. (Telephone: 49-2469).*

1976 ROBINSON, STEPHEN JOSEPH, O.B.E. Product Director of the M.E.L. Equipment Company Ltd. *The M.E.L. Equipment Company Ltd, Manor Royal, Crawley, West Sussex, RH10 2PZ. (Telephone: Crawley 28787);* and *Greenfields, Carlton Road, South Godstone, Surrey. (Telephone: South Godstone 3310).*

1958 ROCHESTER, GEORGE DIXON. Emeritus Professor of Physics in the University of Durham. *Department of Physics, University of Durham, South Road, Durham. (Telephone: Durham 64971);* and *18 Dryburn Road, Durham. (Telephone: Durham 64796).*   1972–74

1959 ROGERS, CLAUDE AMBROSE. Astor Professor of Mathematics at University College in tne University of London. *Department of Mathematics, University College, Gower Street, London, WC1E 6BT. (Telephone: 01-387 7050);* and *8 Grey Close, London, NW11 6QG. (Telephone: 01-455 8027).*   1966–68

1941 ROOM, THOMAS GERALD. Emeritus Professor of Mathematics in the University of Sydney. *100 Rosedale Road, St Ives, N.S.W. 2075, Australia.*

1957 ROSE, FRANCIS LESLIE, O.B.E., D.Sc. Consultant, Imperial Chemical Industries Limited. MEDAL: LEVERHULME (1975). *I.C.I. Ltd, Alderley Park, Macclesfield, Cheshire, SK10 4TG. (Telephone: Alderley Edge 582828);* and *26 Queensway, Heald Green, Cheadle, Cheshire. (Telephone: 061-437 2876):* also *Athenaeum.*

1976 ROSENBROCK, HOWARD HARRY. Professor of Control Engineering in the University of Manchester Institute of Science and Technology. *Control Systems Centre, University of Manchester Institute of Science and Technology, P.O. Box 88, Manchester, M60 1QD. (Telephone: 061-236 3311);* and *Manor Lodge, Mill Lane, Cheadle, Cheshire. (Telephone: 061-428 7482).*

1946 ROSENHEAD, LOUIS, C.B.E. Emeritus Professor of Applied Mathematics in the University of Liverpool. *30 Wheatcroft Road, Liverpool, L18 9UF. (Telephone: 051-427 6033).*   1956–58

1960 ROTH, KLAUS FRIEDRICH. Professor of Pure Mathematics at the Imperial College of Science and Technology in the University of London. *Department of Mathematics, Imperial College, Exhibition Road, London, S.W.7;* and *24 Burnsall Street, London, S.W.3.*

1963 ROTHERHAM, LEONARD, C.B.E., D.Sc. Formerly Vice-Chancellor of the University of Bath. *Westhanger, Horningsham, nr Warminster, Wiltshire, BA12 7LH. (Telephone: Maiden Bradley 315);* also *Athenaeum.*   1965–66

Date of Election		Service on Council
1953	ROTHSCHILD, NATHANIEL MAYER VICTOR, LORD, G.B.E., G.M. Formerly Director General, Central Policy Review Staff, Cabinet Office. 11 *Herschel Road, Cambridge, CB*3 9*AG*. (*Telephone: Cambridge* 50488).	1957–58

1970 ROWLINSON, JOHN SHIPLEY. Dr Lee's Professor of Chemistry in the University of Oxford. *Physical Chemistry Laboratory, South Parks Road, Oxford, OX*1 3*QZ*. (*Telephone: Oxford* 53324); and 12 *Pullen's Field, Headington, Oxford, OX*3 0*BU*. (*Telephone: Oxford* 67507).

1973 ROWSON, LIONEL EDWARD ASTON, O.B.E. Director of the Artificial Insemination Centre, Officer-in-charge of the Agricultural Research Council Animal Research Station and Fellow of Wolfson College, Cambridge. *Animal Research Station, 307 Huntingdon Road, Cambridge, CB*3 0*JQ*. (*Telephone: Cambridge* 77222); and *The Grove, 22 Water Lane, Histon, Cambridge, CB*4 4*LR*. (*Telephone: Histon* 2534).

1965 RUNCORN, STANLEY KEITH. Professor of Physics and Head of the School of Physics in the University of Newcastle upon Tyne. LECTURE: RUTHERFORD MEMORIAL (1970). *School of Physics, The University, Newcastle upon Tyne, NE*1 7*RU*. (*Telephone: Newcastle upon Tyne* 28511, *extension* 3362).

1948 RUSHTON, WILLIAM ALBERT HUGH. Distinguished Research Professor in Psychobiology at Florida State University. LECTURE: FERRIER (1962). MEDAL: ROYAL (1970). *Trinity College, Cambridge; Institute of Molecular Biophysics, The Florida State University, Tallahassee, Florida* 32306, *U.S.A.*; and *Shawms, Conduit Head Road, Cambridge*. (*Telephone: Cambridge* 54742).

1970 RUSSELL, SIR ARCHIBALD (EDWARD), C.B.E. Formerly Chairman and Managing Director of the Filton Division of the British Aircraft Corporation. *Glendower House, Clifton Park, Bristol*, 8. (*Telephone: Bristol* 39208).

1938 RUSSELL, SIR FREDERICK (STRATTEN), C.B.E., D.S.C., D.F.C. Formerly Secretary of the Marine Biological Association of the United Kingdom and Director of the Plymouth Laboratory. *Wardour, 295 Tavistock Road, Plymouth, PL*6 8*AA*. (*Telephone: Plymouth* 772887).

1952 RYLE, SIR MARTIN. Astronomer Royal, and Professor of Radio Astronomy in the University of Cambridge. LECTURE: BAKERIAN (1958). MEDAL: HUGHES (1954), ROYAL (1973). Nobel Laureate, Physics, 1974. *The Cavendish Laboratory, Cambridge*. (*Telephone: Cambridge* 66477); and 5A *Herschel Road, Cambridge*.

1959 SALAM, ABDUS. Professor of Theoretical Physics at the Imperial College of Science and Technology in the University of London. MEDAL: HUGHES (1964). *Department of Physics, Imperial College, London, S.W.*7; also *Athenaeum*.

Date of Election		Service on Council
1933	SALISBURY, SIR EDWARD (JAMES), C.B.E. Formerly Director, Royal Botanic Gardens, Kew. MEDAL: ROYAL (1945). *Croindene, Strandway, Felpham, Bognor Regis, West Sussex.*	1937-38 1942–44 V.P. 1942-43 1946-55 Sec. 1945-55
1956	SALT, GEORGE, Sc.D. Emeritus Reader in Animal Ecology in the University of Cambridge. *King's College, Cambridge. (Telephone: Cambridge* 50411); and 21 *Barton Road, Cambridge.*	
1954	SANGER, FREDERICK, C.B.E., Ph.D. Member of Staff of the Medical Research Council. LECTURE: CROONIAN (1975). MEDAL: ROYAL (1969). Nobel Laureate, Chemistry, 1958. *M.R.C. Laboratory of Molecular Biology, Hills Road, Cambridge, CB2 2QH. (Telephone: Cambridge* 48011).	
1972	SANGER, RUTH ANN (Mrs R. R. RACE), Ph.D. Director of the Medical Research Council Blood Group Unit. *M.R.C. Blood Group Unit, Wolfson House,* 4 *Stephenson Way, London, NW*1 2*HE. (Telephone:* 01-388 7752); and 22 *Vicarage Road, London, SW*14 8*RU. (Telephone:* 01-876 1508).	
1958	SAUNDERS, SIR OWEN (ALFRED). Emeritus Professor of Mechanical Engineering at the Imperial College of Science and Technology. *Imperial College of Science and Technology, Prince Consort Road, London, S.W.*7. *(Telephone:* 01-589 5111); and *Oakbank, Sea Lane, Middleton-on-Sea, West Sussex. (Telephone: Middleton-on-Sea* 2966); also *Athenaeum.*	1961-62
1962	SAWYER, JOHN STANLEY. Formerly Director of Research in the Meteorological Office. *Ivy Corner, Corfe, Taunton, Somerset, TA*3 7*AN. (Telephone: Blagdon Hill* 612).	
1966	SCHILD, HEINZ OTTO. Emeritus Professor of Pharmacology in the University of London. *Department of Pharmacology, University College, Gower Street, London, W.C.*1. *(Telephone:* 01-387 7050); and *Moleridge, St Mary's Road, Leatherhead, Surrey. (Telephone: Leatherhead* 73773).	
1962	SCHNEIDER, WILLIAM GEORGE, Ph.D. President, National Research Council of Canada. *National Research Council, Montreal Road, Ottawa, K*1*A* 0*R*6, *Canada. (Telephone:* (613) 993-2024); and 133 *Blenheim Drive, Ottawa, K*1*L* 5*B*7, *Canada.*	
1967	SEATON, MICHAEL JOHN. Professor of Physics at University College in the University of London. *Department of Physics and Astronomy, University College, Gower Street, London, WC*1*E* 6*BT. (Telephone:* 01-387 7050); and 51 *Hall Drive, Sydenham, London, SE*26 6*XL. (Telephone:* 01-778 7121).	1974-76
1971	SERIES, GEORGE WILLIAM. Professor of Physics in the University of Reading. *J. J. Thomson Physical Laboratory, Whiteknights, Reading, RG*6 2*AF. (Telephone: Reading* 85123, *extension* 385); and 4 *Sandfield Road, Headington, Oxford. (Telephone: Oxford* 62260).	

Date of Election		Service on Council
1971	SHACKLETON, ROBERT MILLNER. Emeritus Professor of Geology in the University of Leeds. *Department of Earth Sciences, The University, Leeds, LS2 9JT.* (*Telephone: Leeds* 31751, *extension* 6474); and *Flat 9, Grove House Court, North Lane, Leeds, LS8 2NQ.* (*Telephone: Leeds* 650979).	
1950	SHENSTONE, ALLEN GOODRICH, O.B.E., M.C. Emeritus Professor of Physics, Princeton University. *Department of Physics, Princeton University, Princeton, N.J.* 08540, *U.S.A.;* also *Athenaeum.*	
1967	SHEPPARD, NORMAN. Professor of Chemistry in the University of East Anglia. *School of Chemical Sciences, University of East Anglia, University Plain, Norwich, NR4 7TJ.* (*Telephone: Norwich* 56161); and 5 *Hornor Close, Norwich, NR2 2LY.* (*Telephone: Norwich* 53052).	
1964	SHEPPARD, PERCIVAL ALBERT, C.B.E. Emeritus Professor of Meteorology in the University of London. *Blackett Laboratory, Department of Physics, Imperial College, Prince Consort Road, London, SW7 2BZ.* (*Telephone:* 01-589 5111, *extension* 2341); and *Weathering, Longbottom, Seer Green, Buckinghamshire, HP9 2UL.* (*Telephone: Beaconsfield* 71297).	1970-72
1953	SHOENBERG, DAVID, M.B.E. Professor of Physics in the University of Cambridge. *The Cavendish Laboratory, Madingley Road, Cambridge, CB3 0HE.* (*Telephone: Cambridge* 66477); *Gonville and Caius College, Cambridge;* and 2 *Long Road, Cambridge.* (*Telephone: Cambridge* 47995).	
1956	SHOPPEE, CHARLES WILLIAM. Emeritus Professor of Chemistry in the University of Sydney, Australia. 41 *Kenthurst Road, St Ives, Sydney* 2075, *Australia.* (*Telephone:* 449-7603).	
1974	SHORT, ROGER VALENTINE. Honorary Professor. Director of the Medical Research Council Unit of Reproductive Biology in the University of Edinburgh. *M.R.C. Unit of Reproductive Biology,* 2 *Forrest Road, Edinburgh, EH1 2QW.* (*Telephone:* 031-225 3186); and *Bonnyton House, Craigluscar Road, By Dunfermline, Fife.* (*Telephone: Dunfermline* 23687).	
1950	SHORTT, COLONEL HENRY EDWARD, C.I.E. Formerly Professor of Medical Protozoology in the University of London. *Rivenhall, Lenten Street, Alton, Hampshire.* (*Telephone: Alton* 83252).	
1956	SHOTTON, FREDERICK WILLIAM, M.B.E. Emeritus Professor of Geology in the University of Birmingham. *The University, P.O. Box* 363, *Birmingham, B15 2TT.* (*Telephone:* 021-472 1301, *extension* 2634); and 111 *Dorridge Road, Dorridge, Solihull, B93 8BP, West Midlands.* (*Telephone: Knowle* 2820).	1962-63
1961	SIDDIQUI, SALIMUZZAMAN, M.B.E. President, Pakistan Academy of Sciences 1968. Professor of Chemistry in the University of Karachi. *The University of Karachi, Karachi, Pakistan.* (*Telephone:* 413414).	

Date of Election		Service on Council
1961	SKEMPTON, ALEC WESTLEY. Professor of Civil Engineering at Imperial College in the University of London. *Department of Civil Engineering, Imperial College of Science and Technology, London, S.W.7;* and *16 The Boltons, London, S.W.10. (Telephone:* 01-370 3457); also *Athenaeum.*	
1975	SLATER, EDWARD CHARLES. Professor of Physiological Chemistry in the University of Amsterdam, The Netherlands. *Laboratory of Biochemistry, B. C. P. Jansen Institute, Plantage Muidergracht 12, Amsterdam*—1004, *The Netherlands. (Telephone:* 020-5222150); and *Elger 9, Monnickendam, The Netherlands. (Telephone:* 02995-1450).	
1975	SLATYER, RALPH OWEN. Professor of Environmental Biology at the Research School of Biological Sciences, Australian National University. *Department of Environmental Biology, Research School of Biological Sciences, Australian National University, P.O. Box 475, Canberra City, A.C.T.* 2601, *Australia. (Telephone:* (062)-49-3743); and 10 *Tennyson Crescent, Forrest, A.C.T.* 2603, *Australia. (Telephone:* (062)-73-2875).	
1975	SMITH, DAVID CECIL. Melville Wills Professor of Botany in the University of Bristol. *Department of Botany, The University, Woodland Road, Bristol, BS8 1UG. (Telephone: Bristol* 24161, extension 832); and *Hilbre, 1 Grove Road, Coombe Dingle, Bristol, BS9 2RQ. (Telephone: Bristol* 683828).	
1952	SMITH, DAVID MACLEISH, D.Sc. Formerly Consulting Mechanical Engineer, Associated Electrical Industries Limited. *Flowermead, 4 Winton Road, Bowdon, Cheshire, WA14 2PG. (Telephone:* 061-928 1053).	
1957	SMITH, ERNEST LESTER, D.Sc. Formerly Senior Biochemist, Glaxo Laboratories Limited. *Amberheath, Three Oaks, Guestling, Hastings, East Sussex. (Telephone: Hastings* 751062).	
1970	SMITH, FRANCIS GRAHAM. Director, Royal Greenwich Observatory. Visiting Professor at the University of Sussex. *The Royal Greenwich Observatory, Herstmonceux Castle, near Hailsham, East Sussex, BN27 1RP. (Telephone: Herstmonceux* 3171); and *Rock's Farm, Herstmonceux, Hailsham, East Sussex. (Telephone: Herstmonceux* 3412).	
1957	SMITH, SIR (FRANK) EWART. Formerly a Deputy Chairman of Imperial Chemical Industries Limited. *Manesty, Weydown Road, Haslemere, Surrey. (Telephone: Haslemere* 2167); also *Athenaeum.*	1963-64
1958	SMITH, (JAMES) SIR ERIC, C.B.E. Formerly Secretary of the Marine Biological Association of the United Kingdom and Director of the Plymouth Laboratory. *The Laboratory, Citadel Hill, Plymouth, PL1 2PB;* and *Wellesley House, 7 Coombe Road, Saltash, Cornwall, PL12 4ZR;* also *Athenaeum.*	1962-63 1972-74 V.P. 1973-74

Date of Election		Service on Council
1976	SMITH, JOHN DEREK, Ph.D. Member of the Scientific Staff of the Medical Research Council. *M.R.C. Laboratory of Molecular Biology, Hills Road, Cambridge, CB2 2QH. (Telephone: Cambridge* 48011); *and* 12 *Stansgate Avenue, Cambridge. (Telephone: Cambridge* 47841).	
1938	SMITH, KENNETH MANLEY, C.B.E., D.Sc. Lately Visiting Professor in the Department of Botany, University of Texas in Austin. Formerly Director of the Agricultural Research Council Virus Research Unit, Cambridge. LECTURE: LEEUWENHOEK (1953). *Hedingham House,* 3 *Sedley Taylor Road, Cambridge. (Telephone: Cambridge* 47238).	1956–58
1962	SMITH, ROBERT ALLAN, C.B.E. Honorary Professor, and formerly Principal and Vice-Chancellor, of Heriot-Watt University. 2/18 *Succoth Court, Succoth Park, Edinburgh, EH*12 6*BZ. (Telephone:* 031-337 4840).	
1976	SMITH, STANLEY DESMOND. Professor and Head of the Department of Physics in Heriot-Watt University, Edinburgh. *Department of Physics, Heriot-Watt University, Riccarton, Edinburgh, EH*14 4*AS. (Telephone:* 031-449 5111, *extension* 2333 *and* 031-449 5542); *and* 4 *Cherry Tree View, Balerno, Edinburgh, EH*14 5*AP. (Telephone:* 031-449 4520).	
1967	SMYTH, DAVID HENRY. Emeritus Professor of Physiology in the University of Sheffield. *M.R.C. Unit, Middlewood Hospital, Sheffield, S*6 1*TP. (Telephone: Sheffield* 349491, *extension* 409); *and The Swevic, Foolow, Derbyshire. (Telephone: Tideswell* 871330).	
1967	SONDHEIMER, FRANZ. Royal Society Research Professor at University College in the University of London. *Department of Chemistry, University College,* 20 *Gordon Street, London, WC*1*H* 0*AJ. (Telephone:* 01-387 7050); *and* 43 *Green Street, London, W*1*Y* 3*FJ. (Telephone:* 01-629 2816).	
1952	SPRING, FRANK STUART, D.Sc. Formerly Director of Research, Laporte Industries Limited. *Flat* 26, 1 *Hyde Park Square, London, W.*2. *(Telephone.* 01-262 8174).	
1950	STACEY, MAURICE, C.B.E. Emeritus Professor of Chemistry in the University of Birmingham. *The University, Edgbaston, Birmingham,* 15. *(Telephone:* 021-472 1301, *extension* 3100); *and* 12 *Bryony Road, Weoley Hill, Birmingham,* 29. *(Telephone:* 021-475 2065); *also Athenaeum.*	1955–57
1966	STANLEY, HERBERT MUGGLETON, Ph.D. Formerly Chemicals Adviser to B.P. Chemicals International Limited. *West Halse, Bow, Crediton, Devon.*	1967–68
1963	STEVENS, THOMAS STEVENS. Emeritus Professor of Chemistry in the University of Sheffield. 313 *Albert Drive, Glasgow, G*41 5*RP. (Telephone:* 041-423 6928).	

Date of Election		Service on Council
1957	STEWARD, FREDERICK CAMPION. Emeritus Professor of Biological Sciences in Cornell University and Research Professor at the State University of New York, Stony Brook. LECTURE: CROONIAN (1969). *State University of New York, Stony Brook, New York, N.Y.* 11790, *U.S.A.;* and 1612 *Inglewood Drive, Charlottesville, Virginia* 22901, *U.S.A.*	
1964	STEWART, SIR FREDERICK (HENRY). Regius Professor of Geology in the University of Edinburgh. *Department of Geology, West Mains Road, Edinburgh,* 9. (*Telephone:* 031-667 1081); and 79 *Morningside Park, Edinburgh,* 10. (*Telephone:* 031-447 2620); also *Athenaeum.*	1969–71
1970	STEWART, ROBERT WILLIAM, Ph.D. Director-General, Ocean and Aquatic Sciences, Pacific Region. *Environment Canada,* 512 *Federal Building, Victoria, B.C., Canada.* (*Telephone:* (604) 388-3383).	
1965	STEWARTSON, KEITH. Goldsmid Professor of Mathematics at University College in the University of London. *Department of Mathematics, University College, Gower Street, London, W.C.*1; (*Telephone:* 01-387 7050); and 51 *Dunstan Road, London, N.W.*11. (*Telephone:* 01-455 1702).	1971–73
1957	STILES, WALTER STANLEY, O.B.E., D.Sc. Formerly Deputy Chief Scientific Officer, National Physical Laboratory. 89 *Richmond Hill Court, Richmond, Surrey, TW*10 6*BG.* (*Telephone:* 01-940 4334).	
1966	STOCKER, BRUCE ARNOLD DUNBAR. Professor of Medical Microbiology in Stanford University. *Department of Medical Microbiology, Stanford University, Stanford, California* 94305, *U.S.A.* (*Telephone:* (415) 497-2004).	
1975	STOICHEFF, BORIS PETER. Professor of Physics and Chairman of the Division of Engineering Science in the University of Toronto, Canada. *Department of Physics, University of Toronto, Ontario, Canada, M*5*S* 1*A*7. (*Telephone:* (416) 978-2948); and 66 *Collier Street, Suite* 6*B, Toronto, Ontario, Canada, M*4*W* 1*L*9. (*Telephone:* (416) 923-9622).	
1968	STOKER, MICHAEL GEORGE PARKE, C.B.E., M.D. FOREIGN SECRETARY. Director, Imperial Cancer Research Fund Laboratories. LECTURE: LEEUWENHOEK (1971). *Imperial Cancer Research Fund Laboratories, Lincoln's Inn Fields, London, WC*2*A* 3*PX.* (*Telephone:* 01-242 0200); and *Oxley House, Lenham, near Maidstone, Kent.* (*Telephone:* Lenham 251); also *Athenaeum.*	1976– V.P. 1976– For. Sec. 1976–
1976	STONE, FRANCIS GORDON ALBERT. Professor of Inorganic Chemistry in the University of Bristol. *Department of Inorganic Chemistry, The University, Bristol, BS*8 1*TS.* (*Telephone:* Bristol 24161, *extension* 640); and 6 *Rylestone Grove, Bristol, BS*9 3*UT.* (*Telephone:* Bristol 627408).	

Date of Election		Service on Council
1974	STUART, JOHN TREVOR. Professor of Theoretical Fluid Mechanics and Head of the Department of Mathematics at the Imperial College of Science and Technology in the University of London. *Department of Mathematics, Imperial College, London, SW7 2DZ*. (*Telephone:* 01-589 5111, extension 2602); and *3 Steeple Close, Church Road, Wimbledon, London, SW19 5AD*. (*Telephone:* 01-946 7019).	
1944	STUBBLEFIELD, SIR (CYRIL) JAMES. Formerly Director of the Geological Survey of Great Britain and the Museum of Practical Geology. *35 Kent Avenue, Ealing, London, W13 8BE*. (*Telephone:* 01-997 5051).	1960–62
1940	SUCKSMITH, WILLIE. Emeritus Professor of Physics in the University of Sheffield. *27 Endcliffe Grove Avenue, Sheffield, 10*.	
1963	SUGDEN, THEODORE MORRIS, C.B.E., Sc.D. Master of Trinity Hall, Cambridge. MEDAL: DAVY (1975). *The Master's Lodge, Trinity Hall, Cambridge, CB2 1TJ*. (*Telephone: Cambridge 51401*).	1972–74 V.P. 1973–74
1957	SUTCLIFFE, REGINALD COCKCROFT, C.B., O.B.E. Professor Emeritus of Meteorology in the University of Reading. *Green Side, Winslow Road, Nash, Milton Keynes, Buckinghamshire, MK17 0EJ*. (*Telephone: Whaddon (Buckinghamshire)* 343).	1968–70
1949	SUTHERLAND, SIR GORDON (BRIMS BLACK McIVOR). Master of Emmanuel College, Cambridge. *The Master's Lodge, Emmanuel College, Cambridge*. (*Telephone: Cambridge* 65411).	1960–63 V.P. 1961–63
1966	SUTTON, JOHN. Professor of Geology at the Imperial College of Science and Technology in the University of London. *Department of Geology, Imperial College, Prince Consort Road, London, S.W.7*. (*Telephone:* 01-589 5111); and *Hartfield, Sandy Drive, Cobham, Surrey*. (*Telephone: Oxshott* 3129).	1975– V.P. 1975–
1950	SUTTON, LESLIE ERNEST, D.Phil. Formerly Reader in Physical Chemistry at the University of Oxford. *Chemical Crystallography Laboratory, 9 Parks Road, Oxford, OX1 3PD*. (*Telephone: Oxford* 57387); and *62 Osler Road, Oxford, OX3 9BN*. (*Telephone: Oxford* 66456).	
1949	SUTTON, SIR (OLIVER) GRAHAM, C.B.E. Formerly Chairman of the Natural Environment Research Council. *Hafod, 4 The Bryn, Sketty Green, Swansea, SA2 8DD*. (*Telephone: Swansea* 21005).	1961–63
1968	SWALLOW, JOHN CROSSLEY, Ph.D. Deputy Chief Scientific Officer, Institute of Oceanographic Sciences. *Institute of Oceanographic Sciences, Wormley, near Godalming, Surrey*. (*Telephone: Wormley* 2122); and *Crossways, Witley, Surrey*. (*Telephone: Wormley* 2819).	
1973	SWAMINATHAN, MONKOMBU SAMBASIVAN, Ph.D. Director General of the Indian Council of Agricultural Research. *Indian Council of Agricultural Research, Krishi Bhavan, New Delhi-1, India*. (*Telephone: New Delhi* 382629).	

Date of Election		Service on Council
1962	SWANN, SIR MICHAEL (MEREDITH). Chairman of the British Broadcasting Corporation. *Broadcasting House, London, W.*1. *(Telephone:* 01-580 4468); *and Ormsacre, Barnton Avenue, Edinburgh,* 4. *(Telephone:* 031-336 1325); *also Athenaeum.*	
1967	SWINNERTON-DYER, SIR (HENRY) PETER (FRANCIS), Bt. Master of St Catharine's College, Cambridge, and Professor of Mathematics in the University of Cambridge. *The Master's Lodge, St Catharine's College, Cambridge, CB*2 1*RL. (Telephone: Cambridge* 59445).	1976–
1943	SYKES, SIR CHARLES, C.B.E. Formerly Group Managing Director of Thos Firth and John Brown Limited. *Upholme, Blackamoor Crescent, Dore, Sheffield. (Telephone: Sheffield* 360339).	1953–55
1943	SYNGE, JOHN LIGHTON. Emeritus Professor in the School of Theoretical Physics, Dublin Institute for Advanced Studies. 10 *Burlington Road, Dublin* 4, *Republic of Ireland;* and 8 *Stillorgan Park, Blackrock, Co. Dublin, Republic of Ireland. (Telephone:* 881251).	
1950	SYNGE, RICHARD LAURENCE MILLINGTON. Formerly Biochemist, Agricultural Research Council's Food Research Institute. Honorary Professor of Biology, University of East Anglia. Nobel Laureate, Chemistry, 1952. *Food Research Institute, Colney Lane, Norwich, NR*4 7*UA. (Telephone: Norwich* 56122); and 19 *Meadow Rise Road, Norwich, NR*2 2*QE. (Telephone: Norwich* 53503).	
1966	SZWARC, MICHAEL. Distinguished Professor of Chemistry and Director of Polymer Research Institute at State University College of Environmental Science and Forestry, Syracuse, New York. *Department of Chemistry, State University College of Environmental Science and Forestry, Syracuse, N.Y.* 13210, *U.S.A.;* and 406 *Hillsboro Parkway, Syracuse, N.Y.* 13214, *U.S.A. (Telephone:* (315) 446-2448).	
1963	TABOR, DAVID. Professor of Physics in the University of Cambridge. *Cavendish Laboratory, Madingley Road, Cambridge, CB*3 0*HE. (Telephone: Cambridge* 66477); *Gonville and Caius College, Cambridge;* and 8 *Rutherford Road, Cambridge, CB*2 2*HH. (Telephone: Trumpington* 3336).	
1959	TAIT, JAMES FRANCIS. Joel Professor of Physics as Applied to Medicine at the Middlesex Hospital Medical School in the University of London. *Department of Physics as Applied to Medicine, The Middlesex Hospital Medical School, London, W*1*P* 6*DB. (Telephone:* 01-636 8333, *extension* 642); *and* 110 *Gilbert House, Barbican, London, E.C.*2. *(Telephone:* 01-628 7925).	
1959	TAIT, SYLVIA AGNES SOPHIA, MRS. Endocrinologist. *Department of Physics Applied to Medicine, The Middlesex Hospital Medical School, London, W*1*P* 6*DB. (Telephone:* 01-636 8333, *extension* 7162); *and* 110 *Gilbert House, Barbican, London, E.C.*2. *(Telephone:* 01-628 7925).	

Date of
Election

Service on
Council

1973 TATA, JAMSHED RUSTOM, D.ès Sc. Head of the Laboratory of Developmental Biochemistry, National Institute for Medical Research. *National Institute for Medical Research, Mill Hill, London, NW7 1AA.* (*Telephone:* 01-959 3666, *extension* 269); and 15 *Bittacy Park Avenue, Mill Hill, London, NW7 2HA.* (*Telephone:* 01-346 6291).

1952 TAYLOR, EDWARD WILFRED, C.B.E., Hon.D.Sc. Formerly Director of Messrs Cooke Troughton and Simms Ltd. 7 *St Peter's Grove, York, YO3 6AQ.* (*Telephone:* York 22621).

1968 TAYLOR, SIR GEORGE. Director of the Stanley Smith Horticultural Trust. Formerly Director, Royal Botanic Gardens, Kew. *Belhaven House, Dunbar, East Lothian, Scotland.* (*Telephone:* Dunbar 62392 or 63546); also *Athenaeum.*

1970 TAYLOR, JOHN BRYAN, Ph.D. Head of Theoretical Physics Division, United Kingdom Atomic Energy Authority Culham Laboratory. *Culham Laboratory, Abingdon, Oxfordshire.* (*Telephone:* Abingdon 21840, *extension* 344).

1943 TEMPLE, GEORGE FREDERICK JAMES, C.B.E. Emeritus Professor of Natural Philosophy at the University of Oxford. MEDAL: SYLVESTER (1970). 341 *Woodstock Road, Oxford.* (*Telephone:* Oxford 57334); also *Athenaeum.*

1952–54

1965 THODAY, JOHN MARION. Arthur Balfour Professor of Genetics in the University of Cambridge. *Department of Genetics, Downing Street, Cambridge, CB2 3EH.* (*Telephone:* Cambridge 69551); and 7 *Clarkson Road, Cambridge.*

1954 THODE, HENRY GEORGE, M.B.E. Professor of Chemistry, McMaster University. *Department of Chemistry, Nuclear Research Building, McMaster University, 1280 Main Street W., Hamilton, Ontario, Canada, L8S 4K1.* (*Telephone:* (416) 525-9140 *and* (416) 522-7428).

1949 THOMAS, MEIRION. Emeritus Professor of Botany in the University of Newcastle upon Tyne. *Glannant, Bryn Crug, Tywyn, Gwynedd, LL36 9PH.*

1946 THOMPSON, SIR HAROLD (WARRIS), C.B.E. Emeritus Professor of Chemistry in the University of Oxford. MEDAL: DAVY (1965). *St John's College, Oxford.* (*Telephone:* Oxford 47671); and 33 *Linton Road, Oxford.* (*Telephone:* Oxford 58925).

1959–60
1961–64
V.P.
1963–64
1965–71
For. Sec.
1965–71

1974 THOMPSON, ROBERT HENRY STEWART, C.B.E. Emeritus Professor of Biochemistry in the University of London. *The Wellcome Trust, 1 Park Square West, London, NW1 4LJ.* (*Telephone:* 01-486 4902); and *The Spinney, 27 Wheeler Avenue, Oxted, Surrey.* (*Telephone:* Oxted 3526); also *Athenaeum.*

Date of Election		Services on Council
1941	THORNTON, SIR (HENRY) GERARD. Formerly Head of the Department of Soil Microbiology at Rothamsted Experimental Station, Harpenden. LECTURE: LEEUWENHOEK (1955). 3 *Romeland Cottage, St Albans, Hertfordshire.* (*Telephone: St Albans* 51333); also *Athenaeum.*	1948–50 For. Sec 1955–60 V.P. 1959–60
1951	THORPE, WILLIAM HOMAN. Emeritus Professor of Animal Ethology in the University of Cambridge. *Sub-Department of Animal Behaviour, High Street, Madingley, Cambridge.* (*Telephone: Madingley* 301); *Jesus College, Cambridge;* and 9 *Wilberforce Road, Cambridge.* (*Telephone: Cambridge* 50943).	1956–57
1976	THRUSH, BRIAN ARTHUR, Sc.D. Reader in Physical Chemistry in the University of Cambridge. *Department of Physical Chemistry, Lensfield Road, Cambridge, CB2 1EP.* (*Telephone: Cambridge* 66499); and *Brook Cottage, Pemberton Terrace, Cambridge, CB2 1JA.* (*Telephone: Cambridge* 57637).	
1962	TINBERGEN, NIKOLAAS, Ph.D. Formerly Professor of Animal Behaviour, University of Oxford. LECTURE: CROONIAN (1972). Nobel Laureate, Physiology or Medicine, 1973. *Department of Zoology, South Parks Road, Oxford, OX1 3PS.* (*Telephone: Oxford* 56789); *Wolfson College, Oxford;* and 88 *Lonsdale Road, Oxford, OX2 7ER.* (*Telephone: Oxford* 58662).	
1942	TODD, OF TRUMPINGTON, ALEXANDER ROBERTUS, BARON. PRESIDENT. Master of Christ's College and Emeritus Professor of Chemistry in the University of Cambridge. LECTURES: BAKERIAN (1954), TERCENTENARY (1960). MEDALS: DAVY (1949), ROYAL (1955), COPLEY (1970). Nobel Laureate, Chemistry, 1957. *The Master's Lodge, Christ's College, Cambridge, CB2 3BU.* (*Telephone: Cambridge* 56688 (*private*), 67641 (*office*); also *Athenaeum.*	1950–52 1967–69 Pres. 1975–
1948	TODD, JOHN ARTHUR, Ph.D. Emeritus Reader in Geometry in the University of Cambridge. 30 *Glebe Hyrst, Sanderstead, South Croydon, Surrey, CR2 9JE.* (*Telephone:* 01-657 4994).	
1955	TOMPKINS, FREDERICK CLIFFORD. Professor of Physical Chemistry in the University of London. *Department of Chemistry, Imperial College, Imperial Institute Road, London, S.W.7.* (*Telephone:* 01-589 5111); and 32 *Grosvenor Street, London, W.1.* (*Telephone:* 01-493 9575).	
1960	TOWNSEND, ALBERT ALAN, Ph.D. Reader in Physics in the University of Cambridge. *Emmanuel College, Cambridge.*	
1973	TURNER, DAVID WARREN, Ph.D. Fellow and Tutor of Balliol College, Oxford, and University Lecturer in Physical Chemistry. *Balliol College, Oxford, OX1 3BJ.* (*Telephone: Oxford* 49601).	
1970	TYRRELL, DAVID ARTHUR JOHN, M.D. Deputy Director and Head of the Division of Communicable Diseases, Clinical Research Centre, Medical Research Council. *M.R.C. Clinical Research Centre, Watford Road, Harrow, Middlesex, HA1 3UJ.* (*Telephone:* 01-864 5311); and 29 *The Ridgeway, Stanmore, Middlesex, HA7 4BE.* (*Telephone:* 01-954 4422).	1974–76

Date of Election		Service on Council

1951 UBBELOHDE, ALFRED RENE JOHN PAUL, C.B.E. Emeritus Professor of Thermodynamics and Senior Research Fellow, Imperial College of Science and Technology, London. *Department of Chemical Engineering and Chemical Technology, Imperial College, London, S.W.7;* 48 *Cottesmore Court, Stanford Road, London, W.8. (Telephone:* 01-937 0616)*;* and *Platts Farm, Burwash, East Sussex. (Telephone: Burwash* 882393)*;* also *Athenaeum.*

1970 UNDERWOOD, ERIC JOHN, C.B.E. Emeritus Professor of Agriculture and formerly Director of the Institute of Agriculture of the University of Western Australia. Honorary Research Fellow in the University of Western Australia. *Department of Animal Science, Institute of Agriculture, University of Western Australia, Nedlands, Western Australia,* 6009, *Australia. (Telephone: Perth* 80.2521).

1972 URSELL, FRITZ JOSEPH. Beyer Professor of Applied Mathematics in the University of Manchester. *Department of Mathematics, The University, Manchester, M*13 9*PL. (Telephone:* 061-273 7121)*;* and 28 *Old Broadway, Manchester, M*20 9*DF. (Telephone:* 061-445 5791).

1974 VANE, JOHN ROBERT, D.Sc. Group Research and Development Director, The Wellcome Foundation Limited. *Wellcome Research Laboratories, Langley Court, Beckenham, Kent, BR*3 3*BS. (Telephone:* 01-658 2211)*;* and *White Angles,* 7 *Beech Dell, Keston Park, Kent, BR*2 6*EP. (Telephone: Farnborough* 53128)*;* also *Athenaeum.*

1974 VINE, FREDERICK JOHN. Professor of Environmental Sciences in the University of East Anglia. *School of Environmental Sciences, University of East Anglia, Norwich, NR*4 7*TJ. (Telephone: Norwich* 56161, *extension* 2646)*;* and 144 *Christchurch Road, Norwich, NR*2 3*PG. (Telephone: Norwich* 53875).

1973 VINEN, WILLIAM FRANK. Poynting Professor of Physics in the University of Birmingham. *Department of Physics, The University, Birmingham, B*15 2*TT. (Telephone:* 021-472 1301)*;* and 52 *Middle Park Road, Birmingham, B*29 4*BJ. (Telephone:* 021-475 1328).   1976–

1952 VOGT, MARTHE LOUISE, M.D. Formerly Head of the Pharmacology Unit, Agricultural Research Council Institute of Animal Physiology, Babraham, Cambridge   *A.R.C. Institute of Animal Physiology, Babraham, Cambridge. (Telephone: Cambridge* 832312)*;* and 5 *Marion Close, Cambridge.*   1969–71

1960 WAIN, RALPH LOUIS, C.B.E. Professor of Agricultural Chemistry at Wye College in the University of London and Director of the Agricultural Research Council Plant Growth Substance and Systemic Fungicides Unit. *Wye College, near Ashford, Kent. (Telephone: Wye* 812401)*;* and *Staple Farm, Hastingleigh, near Ashford, Kent. (Telephone: Elmsted* 248).

Date of Election		Service on Council
1955	WALKER, ARTHUR GEOFFREY. Emeritus Professor of Pure Mathematics in the University of Liverpool. *Beechcroft, Roundabout Lane, West Chiltington, Pulborough, West Sussex, RH20 2RL.* (*Telephone: West Chiltington* 2412).	1961-62
1975	WALKER, GEORGE PATRICK LEONARD, Ph.D. Reader in Geology at the Imperial College of Science and Technology in the University of London. *Department of Geology, Imperial College of Science and Technology, Prince Consort Road, London, S.W.7.* (*Telephone:* 01-589 5111); and 209 *Tolworth Rise North, Surbiton, Surrey, KT5 9ET.*	
1969	WALL, CHARLES TERENCE CLEGG. Professor of Pure Mathematics in the University of Liverpool. *Department of Pure Mathematics, University of Liverpool, Liverpool, L69 3BX.* (*Telephone:* 051-709 6022, *extension* 3080).	1974-76
1945	WALLIS, SIR BARNES (NEVILLE), C.B.E. Formerly Chief of Aeronautical Research and Development, British Aircraft Corporation Limited, Weybridge Division. MEDAL: ROYAL (1975). *White Hill House, Effingham, Surrey.* (*Telephone: Bookham* 52027); also *Athenaeum*.	1947-48
1969	WALSH, ALAN, D.Sc. Assistant Chief, Division of Chemical Physics, Commonwealth Scientific and Industrial Research Organization. MEDAL: ROYAL (1976). *C.S.I.R.O. Division of Chemical Physics, P.O. Box* 160, *Clayton, Victoria* 3168, *Australia.* (*Telephone: Melbourne* 544 0633); *and* 11 *Dendy Street, Brighton, Victoria* 3186, *Australia.* (*Telephone: Melbourne* 92 4897).	
1964	WALSH, ARTHUR DONALD. Baxter Professor of Chemistry in the University of Dundee. *Department of Chemistry, The University, Dundee.* (*Telephone: Dundee* 23181); *and* 26 *Glamis Drive, Dundee.* (*Telephone: Dundee* 65843).	
1965	WARD, JOHN CLIVE. Professor of Physics in the Macquarie University, Sydney, Australia. *School of Mathematics and Physics, Macquarie University, N. Ryde, Sydney, N.S.W., Australia.*	
1969	WAREING, PHILIP FRANK. Professor of Botany in the University of Wales. *Department of Botany and Microbiology, University College of Wales, Aberystwyth.* (*Telephone: Aberystwyth* 3111); *and Brynrhedyn, Cae Melyn, Aberystwyth, SY23 3DA, Dyfed.* (*Telephone: Aberystwyth* 3910).	1972-73
1976	WARNER, SIR FREDERICK (EDWARD). Senior Partner, Cremer and Warner, Consulting Engineers, and Visiting Professor in Chemical Engineering at the Imperial College of Science and Technology in the University of London. *Messrs Cremer and Warner,* 140 *Buckingham Palace Road, London, SW1W 9SQ.* (*Telephone:* 01-730 0777); also *Athenaeum*.	
1967	WATERHOUSE, DOUGLAS FREW, C.M.G., D.Sc. Chief, Division of Entomology, Commonwealth Scientific and Industrial Research Organization. *P.O. Box* 1700, *Canberra, A.C.T.* 2601, *Australia.* (*Telephone: Canberra* 46-4911); *and* 60 *National Circuit, Deakin, A.C.T., Australia.* (*Telephone: Canberra* 731722).	

THE FELLOWSHIP 1977   93

Date of
Election

Service on
Council

1954 WATERS, WILLIAM ALEXANDER. Emeritus Professor of Chemistry in the University of Oxford. 5 *Field House Drive, Oxford, OX2 7NT.* (*Telephone: Oxford* 55234).

1969 WATKINS, WINIFRED MAY, D.Sc. Head of Division of Immunochemical Genetics, Clinical Research Centre, Medical Research Council. *M.R.C. Clinical Research Centre, Watford Road, Harrow, Middlesex, HA1 3UJ.* (*Telephone:* 01-864 5311).

1957 WATT, ALEXANDER STUART, Ph.D. Formerly Lecturer in Forest Botany in the University of Cambridge. 38 *Chesterton Hall Crescent, Cambridge, CB4 1AP.* (*Telephone: Cambridge* 59371).

1976 WATT, WILLIAM, O.B.E. Senior Research Fellow at the Department of Metallurgy and Materials Science in the University of Surrey, and Consultant to the Materials Department of the Royal Aircraft Establishment. *Department of Metallurgy and Materials Science, University of Surrey, Guildford, Surrey, GU2 5XH.* (*Telephone: Guildford* 71281); and *Eilean Donan,* 28 *Avenue Road, Farnborough, Hampshire.* (*Telephone: Farnborough* 42560).

1973 WEATHERLEY, PAUL EGERTON. Regius Professor of Botany in the University of Aberdeen. *Department of Botany, St Machar Drive, Aberdeen, AB9 2UD.* (*Telephone: Aberdeen* 40241, *extension* 334); and 8 *The Chanonry, Aberdeen, AB2 1RN.* (*Telephone: Aberdeen* 43751).

1975 WECK, RICHARD, C.B.E., Ph.D. Director-General of the Welding Institute, Cambridge. *The Welding Institute, Abington Hall, Abington, Cambridge, CB1 6AL.*(*Telephone: Cambridge* 891162); *The Welding Institute,* 54 *Prince's Gate, Exhibition Road, London, SW7 2PG.* (*Telephone:* 01-584 8556); and *Abington Hall, Cambridge, CB1 6AH.* (*Telephone: Cambridge* 891339); also *Athenaeum.* 1975-

1971 WEEDON, BASIL CHARLES LEICESTER, C.B.E., D.Sc. Vice-Chancellor of the University of Nottingham. *University of Nottingham, University Park, Nottingham, NG7 2RD.* (*Telephone: Nottingham* 56101).

1955 WELLS, GEORGE PHILIP. Emeritus Professor of Zoology at University College in the University of London. *Department of Zoology, University College, Gower Street, London, WC1E 6BT.*

1962 WELSH, HARRY LAMBERT. Professor of Physics in the University of Toronto. *Department of Physics, University of Toronto, Toronto, Ontario, M5S 1A7, Canada.* (*Telephone:* (415) 978-2939); and 8 *Tally Lane, Willowdale, Ontario, M2K 1V4, Canada.* (*Telephone:* (416) 225-7175).

1968 WEST, RICHARD GILBERT. Professor of Palaeoecology in the University of Cambridge and Director of the Sub-Department of Quaternary Research. *The Botany School, Cambridge.* (*Telephone: Cambridge* 61414); and 3A *Woollards Lane, Great Shelford, Cambridge.* (*Telephone: Shelford* 2578).

Date of Election		Service on Council
1952	WESTOLL, THOMAS STANLEY. J. B. Simpson Professor and Head of Department of Geology in the University of Newcastle upon Tyne. *The University, Newcastle upon Tyne, NE1 7RU. (Telephone: Newcastle upon Tyne* 28511); and 21 *Osborne Avenue, Newcastle upon Tyne, NE2 1JQ. (Telephone: Newcastle upon Tyne* 811622).	1966-68
1971	WETHERELL, ALAN MARMADUKE, Ph.D. Senior Physicist, European Organization for Nuclear Research (Cern). *Nuclear Physics Division, European Organization for Nuclear Research (Cern),* 1211 *Geneva* 23, *Switzerland. (Telephone: Geneva* 41 98 11, *extension* 3020).	
1975	WHATLEY, FREDERICK ROBERT. Sherardian Professor of Botany in the University of Oxford. *Botany School, South Parks Road, Oxford. OX1 3RA. (Telephone: Oxford* 53391); and 50 *Church Road, Sandford-on-Thames, Oxford. (Telephone: Oxford* 771602).	
1976	WHELAN, MICHAEL JOHN, D.Phil. Reader in the Physical Examination of Materials in the University of Oxford. *Department of Metallurgy and Science of Materials, Parks Road, Oxford, OX1 3PH. (Telephone: Oxford* 59981); and 18 *Salford Road, Old Marston, Oxford, OX3 0RX. (Telephone: Oxford* 44556).	
1966	WHIFFEN, DAVID HARDY. Professor of Physical Chemistry in the University of Newcastle upon Tyne. *Department of Physical Chemistry, The University, Newcastle upon Tyne, NE1 7RU (Telephone: Newcastle upon Tyne* 28511, *extension* 3055).	1971-73
1956	WHITE, ERROL IVOR, C.B.E., D.Sc. Formerly Keeper of the Department of Palaeontoiogy, British Museum (Natural History). *Prospect House, North Stoke, near Benson, Oxfordshire, OX9 6BL. (Telephone: Wallingford* 37342).	
1966	WHITE, SIR FREDERICK (WILLIAM GEORGE), K.B.E. Formerly Chairman of the Commonwealth Scientific and Industrial Research Organization. 57 *Investigator Street, Red Hill, Canberra, A.C.T.* 2603, *Australia. (Telephone:* 957424).	
1961	WHITE, MICHAEL JAMES DENHAM, D.Sc. Visiting Fellow at the Australian National University. *Department of Population Biology, Research School of Biological Sciences, Australian National University, P.O. Box* 475, *Canberra City, A.C.T.* 2601, *Australia;* and 20 *Blackbutt Street, O'Connor, A.C.T.* 2601, *Australia.*	
1965	WHITHAM, GERALD BERESFORD. Professor of Applied Mathematics in the California Institute of Technology. *California Institute of Technology, Pasadena, California* 91125, *U.S.A. (Telephone:* (213) 795-6811).	
1949	WHITTAKER, JOHN MACNAGHTEN, D.Sc. Formerly Vice-Chancellor of the University of Sheffield. 11B *Endcliffe Crescent, Sheffield, S*10 3*EB. (Telephone: Sheffield* 663712).	

Date of Election		Service on Council
1973	WHITTAM, RONALD. Professor of Physiology in the University of Leicester. *Department of Physiology, The University, Leicester, LE1 7RH. (Telephone: Leicester 50000, extension 150).*	
1953	WHITTERIDGE, DAVID. Professor of Physiology at the University of Oxford. *University Laboratory of Physiology, Parks Road, Oxford, OX1 3PT. (Telephone: Oxford 59804);* and *Winterslow, Lincombe Lane, Boars Hill, Oxford, OX1 5DZ. (Telephone: Oxford 735211).*	
1971	WHITTINGTON, HARRY BLACKMORE. Woodwardian Professor of Geology in the University of Cambridge. *Department of Geology, Sedgwick Museum, Downing Street, Cambridge, CB2 3EQ. (Telephone: Cambridge 51585, extension 27);* and *20 Rutherford Road, Cambridge, CB2 2HH. (Telephone: Trumpington 2350).*	
1947	WHITTLE, SIR FRANK, K.B.E., C.B., Air Commodore. Consulting Engineer. MEDAL: RUMFORD (1950). *Walland Hill, Chagford, Devon.*	
1976	WIDDOWSON, ELSIE MAY, D.Sc. Formerly Head of the Infant Nutrition Division of the Dunn Nutritional Laboratory, Cambridge. *Department of Medicine, Level 5, New Addenbrooke's Hospital, Hills Road, Cambridge. (Telephone: Cambridge 44014, extension 235);* and *Orchard House, Barrington, Cambridge. (Telephone: Cambridge 870219).*	
1969	WIESNER, KAREL FRANTIŠEK. Research Professor at the University of New Brunswick. *814 Burden Street, Fredericton, New Brunswick, Canada. (Telephone: 506 454-4007).*	
1939	WIGGLESWORTH, SIR VINCENT (BRIAN), C.B.E. Formerly Quick Professor of Biology in the University of Cambridge and Director of Agricultural Research Council Unit of Insect Physiology. LECTURES: CROONIAN (1948), TERCENTENARY (1960). MEDAL: ROYAL (1955). *Department of Zoology, Downing Street, Cambridge. (Telephone: Cambridge 58717);* and *14 Shilling Street, Lavenham, Suffolk. (Telephone: Lavenham 293).*	1943-44 1949-51
1970	WILD, JOHN PAUL, Sc.D. Chief, Division of Radiophysics, Commonwealth Scientific and Industrial Research Organization. *Division of Radiophysics, C.S.I.R.O., P.O. Box 76, Epping, N.S.W. 2121, Australia. (Telephone: (612) 869-1111).*	
1956	WILKES, MAURICE VINCENT. Head of the Computer Laboratory and Professor of Computer Technology, Cambridge. *The Computer Laboratory, Corn Exchange Street, Cambridge, CB2 3QG. (Telephone: Cambridge 52435).*	
1971	WILKIE, DOUGLAS ROBERT. Jodrell Professor of Physiology at University College in the University of London and Head of the Department of Physiology. *Department of Physiology, University College, Gower Street, London, W.C.1. (Telephone: 01-387 7050, extension 321);* and *4 Grange Road, Highgate, London, N6 4AP. (Telephone: 01-348 0145).*	

Date of Election		Service on Council

1959 WILKINS, MAURICE HUGH FREDERICK, C.B.E. Professor of Biophysics and Head of Department of Biophysics at King's College in the University of London. Director of the Medical Research Council Cell Biophysics Unit. Nobel Laureate, Physiology or Medicine, 1962. *Department of Biophysics, King's College, 26–29 Drury Lane, London, WC2B 5RL. (Telephone: 01-836 8851).*

1956 WILKINSON, SIR DENYS (HAIGH). Vice-Chancellor of the University of Sussex. MEDAL: HUGHES (1965). *University of Sussex, Sussex House, Falmer, Brighton, BN1 9RH. (Telephone: Brighton 66755).*

1965 WILKINSON, SIR GEOFFREY. Professor of Inorganic Chemistry at Imperial College in the University of London. Nobel Laureate, Chemistry, 1973. *Department of Chemistry, Imperial College, London, SW7 2AY. (Telephone: 01-589 5111, extension 1203).*

1969 WILKINSON, JAMES HARDY, Sc.D. Chief Scientific Officer, National Physical Laboratory. *Division of Numerical Analysis and Computing, National Physical Laboratory, Teddington, Middlesex. (Telephone: 01-977 3222);* and *40 Atbara Road, Teddington, Middlesex. (Telephone: 01-977 1207).*   1974–

1967 WILLIAMS, ALWYN, D.Sc. Principal and Vice-Chancellor of the University of Glasgow. *The University of Glasgow, Glasgow, G12 8QQ. (Telephone: 041-339 8855, extension 250);* and *The Principal's Lodgings, The University of Glasgow, Glasgow, G12 8QG. (Telephone: 041-339 0383).*   1973–74

1954 WILLIAMS, CARRINGTON BONSOR, Sc.D. Formerly Head of the Department of Entomology, Rothamsted Experimental Station. *8 The Crofts, Kirkcudbright, Scotland. (Telephone: Kirkcudbright 30015).*

1950 WILLIAMS, SIR FREDERIC (CALLAND), C.B.E. Professor of Electrical Engineering in the University of Manchester. LECTURE: BAKERIAN (1964). MEDAL: HUGHES (1963). *Electrical Engineering Department, The University, Manchester, 13. (Telephone: 061-273 3333);* and *Spinney End, The Village, Prestbury, Cheshire. (Telephone: Prestbury 48154).*   1961–62

1967 WILLIAMS, RICHARD TECWYN. Emeritus Professor of Biochemistry in the University of London. *95 Vernon Drive, Stanmore, Middlesex. (Telephone: 01-427 5554).*

1972 WILLIAMS, ROBERT JOSEPH PATON. Napier Research Professor of the Royal Society. *Wadham College, Oxford, OX1 3PN. (Telephone: Oxford 42564); Inorganic Chemistry Laboratory, South Parks Road, Oxford, OX1 3PN. (Telephone: Oxford 57387);* and *115 Victoria Road, Oxford, OX2 7QG. (Telephone: Oxford 58926).*

1968 WILLIAMSON, DAVID THEODORE NELSON, D.Sc.(Hon.). Formerly Group Director—Engineering, Rank Xerox Limited. *Home Farm House, Mentmore Road, Leighton Buzzard, Bedfordshire. (Telephone: Leighton Buzzard 71305).*   1976–

Date of Election		Service on Council

1960 WILLMER, EDWARD NEVILL. Emeritus Professor of Histology in the University of Cambridge. *Clare College, Cambridge;* and *Yew Garth, 41 Mill Way, Grantchester, Cambridge, CB3 9ND. (Telephone: Trumpington 2360).*

1942 WILSON, SIR ALAN (HERRIES). Formerly Chairman, Glaxo Group Limited. *65 Oakleigh Park South, Whetstone, London, N20 9JL;* also *Athenaeum.*

1963 WILSON, ARTHUR JAMES COCHRAN. Professor of Crystallography in the University of Birmingham. *Department of Physics, The University of Birmingham, Birmingham, B15 2TT. (Telephone: 021-472 1301).*

1969 WILSON, SIR (JAMES) HAROLD, K.G., O.B.E., P.C., M.P. *House of Commons, Westminster, London, SW1A 0AA.*

1968 WILSON, JOHN TUZO, O.B.E., Sc.D. Director General of the Ontario Science Centre and Distinguished Lecturer in the University of Toronto. *Ontario Science Centre, 770 Don Mills Road, Don Mills, Ontario, M3C 1T3, Canada. (Telephone: (416) 429-4100);* and *27 Pricefield Road, Toronto, Ontario, M4W 1Z8, Canada. (Telephone: (416) 923-4244).*

1975 WILSON, ROBERT. Perren Professor of Astronomy and Director of the Observatories at University College in the University of London. *Department of Physics and Astronomy, University College London, Gower Street, London, WC1E 6BT. (Telephone: 01-387 7050);* and *3 Fitzharrys Road, Abingdon, Oxfordshire. (Telephone: Abingdon 20677).*

1963 WOLFSON, SIR ISAAC, Bt. Chairman, The Great Universal Stores Limited. Founder and President, Wolfson Foundation. *74 Portland Place, London, W.1.*

1976 WOOD, RONALD KARSLAKE STARR. Professor of Plant Pathology at the Imperial College of Science and Technology in the University of London. *Department of Botany, Imperial College, Prince Consort Road, London, S.W.7. (Telephone: 01-589 5111);* and *Pyrford Woods, Pyrford, near Woking, Surrey. (Telephone: Byfleet 43827).*

1968 WOODRUFF, SIR MICHAEL (FRANCIS ADDISON). Formerly Professor of Surgery in the University of Edinburgh. *The Bield, 506 Lanark Road, Midlothian, EH14 5DH. (Telephone: 031-441 1253);* also *Athenaeum.*

1974 WOODS, STEPHEN ESSLEMONT, D.Phil. Senior Scientist, Rio Tinto Zinc Services Limited. *York House, Bond Street, Bristol 1. (Telephone: Bristol 421191);* and *27 Roman Way, Bristol, BS9 1SQ. (Telephone: Bristol 683279).*

1953 WOOLLEY, SIR RICHARD (VAN DER RIET), O.B.E. Director of the South African Astronomical Observatory. *P.O. Box 9, Observatory, Cape, South Africa;* also *Athenaeum.*

Date of Election		Service on Council
1970	WYNNE, CHARLES GORRIE. Professor of Optical Design at the Imperial College of Science and Technology in the University of London. *Royal Greenwich Observatory, Herstmonceux Castle, near Hailsham, East Sussex, BN27 1RP. (Telephone: Herstmonceux 3171); Department of Physics, Imperial College of Science and Technology, Prince Consort Road, London, S.W.7;* and *Morar, Boreham Street, near Hailsham, East Sussex. (Telephone: Herstmonceux 2234).*	
1970	WYNNE-EDWARDS, VERO COPNER, C.B.E. Emeritus Professor of Natural History in the University of Aberdeen. *Ravelston, William Street, Torphins, Via Banchory, Aberdeenshire, AB3 4JR. (Telephone: Torphins 434).*	
1948	YATES, FRANK, C.B.E., Sc.D. Formerly Deputy Director and Head of the Department of Statistics and Agricultural Research Statistical Service at Rothamsted Experimental Station. MEDAL: ROYAL (1966). *Rothamsted Experimental Station, Harpenden, Hertfordshire, AL5 2JQ. (Telephone: Harpenden 62271);* and *Stackyard, Rothamsted, Harpenden, Hertfordshire, AL5 2BQ. (Telephone: Harpenden 2732);* also *Athenaeum.*	
1946	YONGE, SIR (CHARLES) MAURICE, C.B.E. Honorary Fellow in Zoology, University of Edinburgh. MEDAL: DARWIN (1968). *Department of Zoology, West Mains Road, Edinburgh, EH9 3JT;* and 13 *Cumin Place, Edinburgh, EH9 2JX. (Telephone: 031-667 3678).*	1952-54 1968-70
1973	YOUNG, ALEC DAVID, O.B.E. Professor and Head of the Department of Aeronautical Engineering at Queen Mary College in the University of London. *Department of Aeronautical Engineering, Queen Mary College, Mile End Road, London, E1 4NS. (Telephone:* 01-980 4811, *extension* 364); and 17 *Regent Square, Bruce Road, Bow, London, .E3 3HQ. (Telephone:* 01-980 9355).	
1972	YOUNG, CHRISTOPHER ALWYNE JACK, D.Tech.(Hon.). Formerly Technical Director, Corporate Laboratory, Imperial Chemical Industries Limited. *Concord House, White Cross, Zeals, Warminster, Wiltshire, BA12 6PH. (Telephone: Bourton (Dorset) 482).*	
1949	YOUNG, SIR FRANK (GEORGE). Formerly Master of Darwin College, Cambridge. Emeritus Professor of Biochemistry in the University of Cambridge. LECTURE: CROONIAN (1962). 11 *Bentley Road, Cambridge, CB2 2AW. (Telephone: Cambridge 52650);* also *Athenaeum.*	1950-51
1945	YOUNG, JOHN ZACHARY. Emeritus Professor of Anatomy in the University of London. LECTURES: FERRIER (1950), CROONIAN (1965). MEDAL: ROYAL (1967). *The Wellcome Institute for the History of Medicine,* 183 *Euston Road, London, NW1 2BP. (Telephone:* 01-387 4477, *extension* 38); and 166 *Camden Road, London, N.W.1. (Telephone:* 01-485 0498).	1950-52 1958-60

Date of Election		Service on Council
1974	YOUNG, PIERRE HENRY JOHN. Director of Advanced Engineering, Rolls-Royce (1971) Limited, *P.O. Box* 3, *Filton, Bristol*. *(Telephone: Bristol* 693871); and 5 *Rockleaze Avenue, Bristol* 9. *(Telephone: Bristol* 682379).	
1975	ZEEMAN, ERIK CHRISTOPHER. Professor of Mathematics and Director of the Mathematics Research Centre in the University of Warwick. *Mathematics Institute, University of Warwick, Coventry, CV4 7AL (Telephone: Coventry* 24011); and 40 *Warwick New Road, Leamington Spa, Warwickshire. (Telephone: Leamington Spa* 26997).	
1967	ZIMAN, JOHN MICHAEL. Henry Overton Wills Professor of Physics in the University of Bristol. LECTURE: RUTHERFORD MEMORIAL (1968). *H. H. Wills Physics Laboratory, Tyndall Avenue, Bristol, BS8 1TL. (Telephone: Bristol* 24161); and *Eastfield Lodge,* 20 *Eastfield, Bristol, BS9 4BE. (Telephone: Bristol* 625551).	
1943	ZUCKERMAN, OF BURNHAM THORPE, SOLLY, BARON, O.M., K.C.B. Professor Emeritus, University of Birmingham and University of East Anglia. Honorary Secretary of The Zoological Society of London. *The Zoological Society of London, Regent's Park, London, N.W.*1. *(Telephone:* 01-722 3333).	1945–46 1948–50 1965–67

FOREIGN MEMBERS 1977

Date of
Election

1968 AMALDI, PROFESSOR EDOARDO. *Istituto di Fisica, Citta Universitaria, Rome, Italy;* and *Viale Parioli 50, 00197 Rome, Italy.*

1969 AMBARTSUMIAN, ACADEMICIAN VIKTOR AMAZASPOVITCH. *Academy of Sciences of Armenian S.S.R., Barekamatjan 24, Erevan, Armenia, U.S.S.R.*

1973 BARDEEN, PROFESSOR JOHN. Nobel Laureate, Physics, 1956 *and* 1972. *Department of Physics, University of Illinois at Urbana-Champaign, Urbana, Illinois 61801, U.S.A.*

1960 BEADLE, DR GEORGE WELLS. Nobel Laureate, Physiology or Medicine, 1958. *5533 Dorchester Avenue, Chicago, Illinois, 60637, U.S.A.*

1976 BENZER, PROFESSOR SEYMOUR. *Division of Biology, California Institute of Technology, Pasadena, California 91125, U.S.A.*

1957 BETHE, PROFESSOR HANS ALBRECHT. Nobel Laureate, Physics, 1967. *Nuclear Studies Laboratory, Cornell University, Ithaca, N.Y., U.S.A.*

1972 BIJVOET, PROFESSOR JOHANNES MARTIN. *Meddo 27, Winterswyk, The Netherlands.*

1962 BOVET, PROFESSOR DANIEL. Nobel Laureate, Physiology or Medicine, 1957. *Laboratorio di Psicobiologia, Via Reno 1, 00198 Roma, Italy.*

1966 BRACHET, PROFESSOR JEAN LOUIS. *Université libre de Bruxelles, 67 rue des Chevaux, Rhode St Genèse, Belgium;* and *avenue des Lilas 11, 1410 Waterloo, Belgium.*

1953 BROGLIE, PRINCE LOUIS VICTOR PIERRE RAYMOND DE. Nobel Laureate, Physics, 1929. *94 rue Perronet, Neuilly-sur-Seine, France.*

1968 BUTENANDT, PROFESSOR ADOLF FRIEDRICH JOHANN. Nobel Laureate, Chemistry, 1939. *Marsopstrasse 5, D-8 München 60, Federal Republic of Germany.*

1959 CALVIN, PROFESSOR MELVIN. LECTURE: BAKERIAN (1965). MEDAL: DAVY (1964). Nobel Laureate, Chemistry, 1961. *Laboratory of Chemical Biodynamics, University of California, Berkeley, California 94720, U.S.A.*

1971 CARTAN, PROFESSOR HENRI. *95 Boulevard Jourdan, 75014 Paris, France.*

1970 CASIMIR, DR HENDRIK BRUGT GERHARD. *Philips Research Laboratories, Eindhoven, The Netherlands.*

1972 COLE, DR KENNETH STEWART. *National Institutes of Health, Building 36, Room 2A29, Bethesda, Maryland 20014, U.S.A.*

1941 CONANT, DR JAMES BRYANT. *200 East 66th Street, New York, N.Y. 10021, U.S.A.*

1950 CORI, PROFESSOR CARL FERDINAND. Nobel Laureate, Physiology and Medicine, 1947. *Massachusetts General Hospital, Enzyme Research Laboratory, Fruit Street, Boston, Mass. 02114, U.S.A.*

1955 CORNER, DR GEORGE WASHINGTON. *American Philosophical Society, 104 South Fifth Street, Philadelphia, Pennsylvania 19106, U.S.A.*

FOREIGN MEMBERS 1977

Date of Election

1953 COURRIER, PROFESSOR MARIE JULES CONSTANT ROBERT. *College de France, Place M. Berthelot, Paris V, France.*

1967 DELBRÜCK, PROFESSOR MAX. Nobel Laureate, Physiology or Medicine, 1969. *California Institute of Technology, Pasadena, California, U.S.A.;* and *1510 Oakdale Street, Pasadena, California 91106, U.S.A.*

1974 DULBECCO, DR RENATO. LECTURE: LEEUWENHOEK (1974). Nobel Laureate, Physiology or Medicine, 1975. *Imperial Cancer Research Fund Laboratories, Lincoln's Inn Fields, London, WC2A 3PX;* and *Hedgerows, Wilderness Road, Chislehurst, Kent.*

1973 EIGEN, PROFESSOR MANFRED. Nobel Laureate, Chemistry, 1967. *Max-Planck-Institut für Biophysikalische Chemie, Karl-Friedrich-Bonhoeffer-Institut, D-3400 Göttingen-Nikolausberg, Postfach 968, Federal Republic of Germany.*

1967 ENDERS, PROFESSOR JOHN FRANKLIN. Nobel Laureate, Physiology and Medicine, 1954. *The Children's Hospital Medical Center, Boston, Massachusetts 02115, U.S.A.;* and *64 Colbourne Crescent, Brookline, Massachusetts 02146, U.S.A.*

1973 VON EULER, PROFESSOR ULF SVANTE. Nobel Laureate, Physiology or Medicine, 1970. *Department of Physiology, Karolinska Institute, S-10401 Stockholm 60, Sweden.*

1965 FEYNMAN, PROFESSOR RICHARD PHILLIPS. Nobel Laureate, Physics, 1965. *California Institute of Technology, Pasadena, California, U.S.A.*

1963 FREUDENBERG, PROFESSOR KARL JOHANN. *Wilckensstrasse 34, 69 Heidelberg Federal Republic of Germany.*

1957 FREY-WYSSLING, PROFESSOR ALBERT. *Institut für Allgemeine Botanik, Eidgenössische Technische Hochschule, Universitätstrasse 2, 8006 Zürich, Switzerland.*

1954 VON FRISCH, PROFESSOR KARL. Nobel Laureate, Physiology or Medicine, 1973. *Uber der Klause 10, München 90, Federal Republic of Germany.*

1975 GILMAN, PROFESSOR HENRY. *Department of Chemistry, Iowa State University, Ames, Iowa 50010, U.S.A.*

1968 GÖDEL, PROFESSOR KURT. *Institute for Advanced Study, Princeton, N.J., U.S.A.*

1960 GRANIT, PROFESSOR RAGNAR ARTHUR. Nobel Laureate, Physiology or Medicine, 1967. *Medicinska Nobelinstitutet, Neurofysiologiska avdelningen, Karolinska Institutet, S-104 01, Stockholm 60, Sweden.*

1970 HÄMMERLING, PROFESSOR JOACHIM. *Max-Planck-Institut für Zellbiologie, Anton Dohrn Weg 59, 294 Wilhelmshaven, Federal Republic of Germany;* and *Schopenhauerstrasse 27, 294 Wilhelmshaven, Federal Republic of Germany.*

1966 HARTLINE, PROFESSOR HALDAN KEFFER. Nobel Laureate, Physiology or Medicine, 1967. *The Rockefeller University, New York, N.Y. 10021, U.S.A.*

1975 HEIDELBERGER, PROFESSOR MICHAEL. *Department of Pathology, New York University School of Medicine, 550 First Avenue, New York, N.Y. 10016, U.S.A.*

1974 HITCHINGS, DR GEORGE HERBERT. MEDAL: MULLARD (1976). *Wellcome Research Laboratories, Research Triangle Park, North Carolina, U.S.A.;* and *4022 Bristol Road, Durham, North Carolina 27707, U.S.A.*

Date of
Election

1952 HORSTADIUS, Professor Sven Otto. *Zoologiska Institutionen, Box 561, 751 22 Uppsala, Sweden.*

1973 JACOB, Professor Francois. Nobel Laureate, Physiology or Medicine, 1965. *Département de Biologie Moléculaire, Institut Pasteur, 25 rue du Dr Roux, 75015 Paris, France.*

1960 KISTIAKOWSKY, Professor George Bogdan. *Department of Chemistry, Harvard University, 12 Oxford Street, Cambridge 38, Massachusetts, U.S.A.*

1964 KOLMOGOROV, Academician Andrei Nikolaevich. *Moscow M.V. Lomonosov State University, Leninskie Gory, Moscow 5, U.S.S.R.*

1970 KORNBERG, Professor Arthur. Nobel Laureate, Physiology or Medicine, 1959. *Stanford University, Stanford, California 94305, U.S.A.*

1971 KUFFLER, Professor Stephen William. Lecture: FERRIER (1965). *Department of Neurobiology, Harvard Medical School, 25 Shattuck Street, Boston, Massachusetts 02115, U.S.A.*

1969 LEHMANN, Dr Inge. *Kastelsvej 26, 2100 Copenhagen, Denmark.*

1972 LELOIR, Dr Luis Federico. Nobel Laureate, Chemistry, 1970. *Instituto de Investigaciones Bioquímicas, Fundación Campomar, Obligado 2490, Buenos Aires 28, Argentina.*

1962 LIPMANN, Professor Fritz Albert. Nobel Laureate, Physiology and Medicine, 1953. *The Rockefeller University, New York, N.Y. 10021, U.S.A.*

1964 LORENZ, Professor Konrad Zacharias. Nobel Laureate, Physiology or Medicine, 1973. *Institut für vergleichende Verhaltensforschung, Abteilung 4 Tiersoziologie, 3422 Altenberg, Austria.*

1958 LWOFF, Dr André Michel. Lecture: LEEUWENHOEK (1960). Nobel Laureate, Physiology or Medicine, 1965. *Institut Pasteur, 25 rue du Docteur Roux, 75 Paris XVe, France.*

1975 LYNEN, Professor Feodor. Nobel Laureate, Physiology or Medicine, 1964. *Max-Planck Institut für Biochemie, 8033 Martinsried bei München, Federal Republic of Germany.*

1971 MOTHES, Professor Kurt Albin. *401 Halle/Saale, Hoher Weg 23, German Democratic Republic.*

1967 MULLIKEN, Professor Robert Sanderson. Nobel Laureate, Chemistry, 1966. *Department of Chemistry, University of Chicago, 5735 South Ellis Avenue, Chicago, Illinois 60637, U.S.A.*

1976 MUNK, Professor Walter Heinrich. *Institute of Geophysics and Planetary Physics, Mail Code A-025, Scripps Institution of Oceanography, University of California, San Diego, La Jolla, California 92093, U.S.A.*

1966 NÉEL, Professor Louis Eugène Félix. Nobel Laureate, Physics, 1970. *15 rue Marcel Allégot, 92190, Meudon-Bellevue, France.*

1961 NESMEYANOV, Academician Aleksandr Nikolaevich. *Academy of Sciences of the U.S.S.R., Lenin Prospekt Moscow, U.S.S.R.*

1938 NÖRLUND, Professor Niels Erik. *Malmøgade 6, Copenhagen, Denmark.*

1974 OCCHIALINI, Professor Giuseppe Paolo Stanislao. *Istituto di Fisica dell' Università, Via Celoria 16, 20133 Milano, Italy.*

Date of Election

1965 OCHOA, PROFESSOR SEVERO. Nobel Laureate, Physiology or Medicine, 1959. *Roche Institute of Molecular Biology, Nutley, New Jersey 07110, U.S.A.;* and *530 East 72nd Street, New York, N.Y. 10021, U.S.A.*

1959 OORT, PROFESSOR JAN HENDRIK. *President Kennedylaan 169, Oegstgeest, The Netherlands.*

1948 PAULING, PROFESSOR LINUS CARL. MEDAL: DAVY (1947). Nobel Laureate, Chemistry, 1954, Peace, 1962. *Big Sur, California, U.S.A.*

1962 PRELOG, PROFESSOR VLADIMIR. MEDAL: DAVY (1967). Nobel Laureate Chemistry, 1975. *Laboratorium für organische Chemie der ETH-Z, Universitätstrasse 16, CH-8006 Zürich, Switzerland.*

1952 REICHSTEIN, PROFESSOR TADEUS. MEDAL: COPLEY (1968). Nobel Laureate, Physiology and Medicine, 1950. *Institut für Organische Chemie der Universität, St Johanns-Ring 19, CH-4056 Basel, Switzerland.*

1958 SEMENOV, ACADEMICIAN NIKOLAI NIKOLAEVICH. Nobel Laureate, Chemistry 1956. *Institute of Chemical Physics, Vorobyevskoye Shosse 2-B, Moscow 117334, U.S.S.R.*

1974 SERRE, PROFESSOR JEAN-PIERRE. *Collège de France, 75231 Paris, France;* and *6 avenue de Montespan, 75116 Paris, France.*

1954 SIEGBAHN, PROFESSOR KARL MANNE GEORG. MEDALS: HUGHES (1934), RUMFORD (1940). Nobel Laureate, Physics, 1924. *Nobel Institutet för Fysik,* 104 05 *Stockholm 50, Sweden.*

1958 SIMPSON, PROFESSOR GEORGE GAYLORD. MEDAL: DARWIN (1962). *The Simroe Foundation, 5151 East Holmes Street, Tucson, Arizona 85711, U.S.A.;* and *Department of Geosciences, University of Arizona, Tucson, Arizona 85721, U.S.A.*

1964 SONNEBORN, PROFESSOR TRACY MORTON. *Department of Zoology, Jordan Hall 220, Indiana University, Bloomington, Indiana, U.S.A.;* and *319 S. Mitchell Street, Bloomington, Indiana, U.S.A.*

1976 SPERRY, PROFESSOR ROGER WOLCOTT. *Division of Biology, California Institute of Technology, Pasadena, California 91125, U.S.A.*

1946 STENSIÖ, PROFESSOR ERIK ANDERSSON. *Naturhistoriska Riksmuseum, Stockholm 50, Sweden.*

1959 THEORELL, PROFESSOR AXEL HUGO TEODOR. Nobel Laureate, Physiology and Medicine, 1955. *Medicinska Nobel Institutet, Biokemiska avd., Solnavägen 1, Stockholm 60, Sweden.*

1969 THIMANN, PROFESSOR KENNETH VIVIAN. *Thimann Laboratories, University of California, Santa Cruz, California 95064, U.S.A.*

1976 TOWNES, PROFESSOR CHARLES HARD. Nobel Laureate, Physics, 1964. *Department of Physics, University of California, Berkeley, California 94720, U.S.A.*

1947 UREY, PROFESSOR HAROLD CLAYTON. MEDAL: DAVY (1940). Nobel Laureate, Chemistry, 1934. *University of California, P.O. Box 109, La Jolla, California 92037, U.S.A.*

1967 VAN VLECK, PROFESSOR JOHN HASBROUCK. *Lyman Laboratory of Physics, Harvard University, Cambridge, Massachusetts 02138, U.S.A.*

Date of Election

1942 VINOGRADOV, ACADEMICIAN IVAN MATVEEVICH. *Matematicheskii Institut Akademii Nauk SSSR, Bolshaya Kaluzhskaya 14, Moscow, U.S.S.R.*

1966 WEIL, PROFESSOR ANDRE. *School of Mathematics, The Institute for Advanced Study, Princeton, New Jersey 08540, U.S.A.*

1970 WIGNER, PROFESSOR EUGENE PAUL. Nobel Laureate, Physics, 1963. *Joseph Henry Laboratories, Jadwin Hall, Princeton University, Princeton, N.J. 08540, U.S.A.*

1956 WOODWARD, PROFESSOR ROBERT BURNS. MEDAL: DAVY (1959). *Nobel Laureate, Chemistry, 1965. Department of Chemistry, Harvard University, 12 Oxford Street, Cambridge 02138, Massachusetts, U.S.A.*

1963 WRIGHT, PROFESSOR SEWALL. *Department of Genetics, University of Wisconsin. Madison 6, Wisconsin, U.S.A.;* and *3905 Council Crest, Madison 11, Wisconsin, U.S.A.*

1951 WYCKOFF, PROFESSOR RALPH WALTER GRAYSTONE. *Department of Physics, University of Arizona, Tucson, Arizona 85721, U.S.A.*

1963 YUKAWA, PROFESSOR HIDEKI. Nobel Laureate, Physics, 1949. *Research Institute for Fundamental Physics, Kyoto University, Kyoto, Japan.*

FELLOWS AND FOREIGN MEMBERS DECEASED IN 1976

23 Sept.	BULLEN, Keith Edward	b. 29 June 1906
19 Sept.	DENT, Charles Enrique	b. 25 Aug. 1911
11 Mar.	DOBSON, Gordon Miller Bourne	b. 25 Feb. 1889
30 June	GLANVILLE, William Henry	b. 1 Feb. 1900
30 Jan.	GOLD, Ernest	b. 24 July 1881
21 Jan.	HADDOW, Alexander	b. 18 Jan. 1907
13 Jan.	HARTRIDGE, Hamilton	b. 7 May 1886
1 Feb.	HEISENBERG, Werner	b. 5 Dec. 1901
24 Nov.	KAY, Herbert Davenport	b. 9 Sept. 1893
23 Feb.	KÜCHEMANN, Dietrich	b. 11 Sept. 1911
10 Feb.	MAIZELS, Montague	b. 30 Sept. 1899
11 Mar.	MITCHELL, George Hoole	b. 31 Dec. 1902
31 May	MONOD, Jacques Lucien	b. 9 Feb. 1910
5 Oct.	ONSAGER, Lars	b. 27 Nov. 1903
5 Apr.	PENFIELD, Wilder Graves	b. 26 Jan. 1891
22 Feb.	POLANYI, Michael	b. 12 Mar. 1891
14 Oct.	ROSE, John Donald	b. 2 Jan. 1911
26 Sept.	RUZICKA, Leopold	b. 13 Sept. 1887
17 Oct.	SHEPPARD, Philip MacDonald	b. 27 July 1921
10 Mar.	SPENCE, Robert	b. 7 Oct. 1905
2 Feb.	STONELEY, Robert	b. 14 May 1894
22 July	WHEELER, Robert Eric Mortimer	b. 10 Sept. 1890

FOREIGN MEMBER DECEASED IN 1975

18 Dec.	DOBZHANSKY, Theodosius	b. 25 Jan. 1900

FELLOWS ELECTED IN 1976

ALLEN, Geoffrey
ANDREW, Sydney Percy Smith
BAKER, Peter Frederick
BIGGS, Peter Martin
BLACK, James Whyte
BLIN-STOYLE, Roger John
BRADLEY, Daniel Joseph
CADOGAN, John Ivan George
CHALONER, William Gilbert
CHARNOCK, Henry
CLARKE, Patricia Hannah
EGLINTON, Geoffrey
ELLIOTT, Roger James
EVANS, Lloyd Thomas
FRÖHLICH, Albrecht
GIBSON, Frank William Ernest
GOODWIN, Leonard George
GRAY, Edward George
GUTTMANN, Ludwig
HAMMERSLEY, John Michael
HENDERSON, William MacGregor
HOLLIDAY, Robin
HORLOCK, John Harold
MACKANESS, George Bellamy
McKENZIE, Dan Peter
NYE, John Frederick
PICKAVANCE, Thomas Gerald
POPPER, Karl Raimund
REES, Hubert
RITCHIE, Joseph Murdoch
ROBINSON, Stephen Joseph
ROSENBROCK, Howard Harry
SMITH, John Derek
SMITH, Stanley Desmond
STONE, Francis Gordon Albert
THRUSH, Brian Arthur
WARNER, Frederick Edward
WATT, William
WHELAN, Michael John
WIDDOWSON, Elsie May
WOOD, Ronald Karslake Starr

FOREIGN MEMBERS ELECTED IN 1976

BENZER, Seymour
MUNK, Walter Heinrich
SPERRY, Roger Wolcott
TOWNES, Charles Hard

Table Showing the Number of Fellows and Foreign Members of the Society

	Patron and Royal	Foreign Members	Fellows
31 December 1976 . . .	4	78	790
Elected 1976 . . .	0	4	41
Deceased 1976 . . .	0	4	18
31 December 1976 . . .	4†	78	813

† Includes 2 Fellows elected under Statute 12.
* Includes 10 Fellows elected under Statute 12.

ASSOCIATE EDITORS

(For Standing Orders see pp. 192–196)

A. *Mathematical and Physical Sciences*

PROFESSOR R. J. ELLIOTT (1976)
PROFESSOR F. C. FRANK (1972)
PROFESSOR W. R. S. GARTON (1972)
DR M. A. GRACE (1973)
PROFESSOR R. HIDE (1976)
PROFESSOR D. W. HOLDER (1975)
PROFESSOR R. PENROSE (1976)
PROFESSOR W. C. PRICE (1972)
PROFESSOR J. S. ROWLINSON (1975)
PROFESSOR F. G. SMITH (1972)
PROFESSOR K. STEWARTSON (1973)
PROFESSOR F. C. TOMPKINS (1973)

B. *Biological Sciences*

PROFESSOR B. B. BOYCOTT (1973)
SIR JOHN DACIE (1976)
PROFESSOR T. N. GEORGE (1972)
PROFESSOR I. M. GLYNN (1973)
DR J. B. GURDON (1976)
PROFESSOR D. LEWIS (1975)
PROFESSOR H. C. LONGUET-HIGGINS (1975)
PROFESSOR O. E. LOWENSTEIN (1973)
PROFESSOR A. NEUBERGER (1972)
DR A. G. OGSTON (1973)
PROFESSOR W. S. PEART (1973)
PROFESSOR D. WHITTERIDGE (1974)

COMMITTEES

Ex Officio Membership by Officers

1. The President, by statute, presides over all committees which he attends. The chairmen of committees named below are appointed to act as chairmen in the President's absence.

2. The Treasurer is Chairman of the Finance and Investment Advisory Committees and is a member of all Standing Committees (except the Bruno Mendel Fellowship Committee), of the Warren Research Fund Committee and of the National Committee for the International Institute for Applied Systems Analysis.

3. The Secretaries are members of the following committees: Education, Expeditions, Finance, Hooke, Industrial Activities, International Relations, Library, Royal Society Esso Award, Royal Mullard Award, Scientific Relief, Soirée.

4. One of the Secretaries shall be appointed a member of (i) standing committees and (ii) joint committees, as follows, and also of the National Committees:

   (i) Aldabra Research, Browne, Hill and Murray, Gassiot, Medical Sciences Research, Bruno Mendel Fellowship, Newton Letters, Ordnance Survey, Royal Society Leverhulme Studentships, Rutherford Memorial, Scientific Information, Southern Zone Research, Space Ranging Research.

   (ii) Armourers and Brasiers' Company Research Fellowship, Naples Zoological Station, Scientific Research in Schools, Smithson Research Fund, Sorby Research Fund, Symbols, Tyndall Mining Bequest, Warren Research Fund.

5. The Foreign Secretary is Chairman of the British National Committee for I.C.S.U. and of the International Relations Committee. He is a member of the Scientific Relief Committee and of all the National Committees.

Retirement from Committees

1. The retirement of members of the Sectional Committees is laid down in Standing Orders.

2. In all other committees, excepting the Scientific Relief Committee, the Volcanological and Seismological Research Committee and those mentioned below, a number not less than one-sixth of the total number of each committee shall retire each December, and the names for retirement shall be selected, so far as practicable, in the following order (exceptions being made of Officers of the Society serving in their official capacity and of members whose continuance on the committee is desired for special reasons): (i) members who have expressed their wish to retire; (ii) members whose record of attendance has been meagre; and (iii) members whose service on the committee has been longest. Members selected for retirement shall not be eligible for immediate reappointment.

(For retirement from the Bruno Mendel Fellowship, Smithson, Sorby and Warren Research Fund Committees, see pp. 228, 234, 236, 240.)

Cooption by Committees

Each committee, except the Sectional Committees, the Scientific Relief Committee and any committees composed of representatives of the Royal Society and other bodies jointly, has power to suggest to Council names of additional members for appointment on such committee; the names not being necessarily those of Fellows of the Society.

Duration of Service

The date of constitution is printed at the head of each committee. The date of appointment of each member of a committee is given after his name in the case of the Standing Committees and in that of most of the Joint Committees. In the case of the Sectional Committees, the Paul Instrument Fund Committee, the British National Committees corresponding with Unions and the Government Grant Boards, the dates of retirement are indicated.

Government Grant Boards

Membership of the Boards is intended to cover representation, as far as possible, of Scotland and Northern Ireland, and is not confined to Fellows of the Royal Society.

SECTIONAL COMMITTEES

(For Standing Orders, etc., see pp. 188–191)

Sectional Committee 1 [1963]

Pure mathematics, theoretical and applied mechanics, mathematical astronomy, statistics (theory), theoretical fluid mechanics, mathematics applied to physical theory, operational research.

CHAIRMAN: † PROFESSOR J. F. ADAMS

* PROFESSOR D. R. COX
* PROFESSOR W. K. HAYMAN
* PROFESSOR F. J. URSELL
† PROFESSOR D. R. BATES

† PROFESSOR T. B. BENJAMIN
§ DR B. J. BIRCH
§ PROFESSOR R. H. DALITZ
§ PROFESSOR D. J. FINNEY

Sectional Committee 2 [1963]

Experimental physics (including atomic, nuclear, low temperature and solid state physics, acoustics, spectroscopy, magnetism, heat, optics), crystallography, optical and radio astronomy, ionospheric physics, applied physics, theoretical physics relating to these subjects.

CHAIRMAN: † PROFESSOR F. G. SMITH

* SIR SAM EDWARDS
* DR D. W. PASHLEY
* PROFESSOR D. H. WHIFFEN
† PROFESSOR H. ELLIOT

† DR W. C. MARSHALL
§ PROFESSOR D. J. BRADLEY
§ DR A. R. LANG
§ PROFESSOR J. C. POLKINGHORNE

Sectional Committee 3 [1963]

Chemistry, applied chemistry, theoretical chemistry.

CHAIRMAN: † PROFESSOR G. W. KENNER

* PROFESSOR G. GEE
* PROFESSOR J. LEWIS
* PROFESSOR F. SONDHEIMER
† DR F. L. ROSE

† PROFESSOR F. C. TOMPKINS
§ PROFESSOR A. CARRINGTON
§ PROFESSOR V. GOLD
§ PROFESSOR R. MASON

* To retire 31 July 1977
† To retire 31 July 1978
§ To retire 31 July 1979

Sectional Committee 4(i) [1963]

Engineering (civil and structural, mechanical, computer, control, aeronautical, turbo machinery), experimental fluid dynamics.

CHAIRMAN: * SIR GILBERT ROBERTS

* SIR WILLIAM HAWTHORNE
* SIR MORIEN MORGAN
† PROFESSOR T. KILBURN
† DR E. H. MANSFIELD

† PROFESSOR A. D. YOUNG
§ MR G. M. BINNIE
§ PROFESSOR H. H. ROSENBROCK
§ MR P. H. J. YOUNG

Sectional Committee 4(ii) [1963]

Engineering (electric power, electronics, nuclear, chemical), metallurgy, instrumentation.

CHAIRMAN: * DR F. E. JONES

* DR J. H. CHESTERS
* DR A. KELLY
† PROFESSOR J. F. DAVIDSON
† DR J. DYSON

† PROFESSOR N. J. PETCH
§ PROFESSOR H. E. M. BARLOW
§ SIR ERIC EASTWOOD
§ MR S. J. ROBINSON

Sectional Committee 5 [1963]

Meteorology, hydrology, oceanography (excluding marine biology), geology, geodesy, geophysics, soil physics, geochemistry, mineralogy, physical geography, archaeology, theoretical physics relating to these subjects.

CHAIRMAN: * DR D. H. MATTHEWS

* MR D. G. KING-HELE
* DR A. WILLIAMS
† PROFESSOR G. M. BROWN
† PROFESSOR G. F. MITCHELL

† MR J. S. SAWYER
§ DR S. H. U. BOWIE
§ PROFESSOR H. CHARNOCK
§ DR G. P. L. WALKER

Sectional Committee 6 [1963]

Plant anatomy and physiology; plant taxonomy, mycology, plant pathology (including infective diseases of plants), applied plant sciences, plant breeding, plant ecology, palaeobotany.

CHAIRMAN: * PROFESSOR G. E. FOGG

* PROFESSOR O. V. S. HEATH
* PROFESSOR A. F. POSNETTE
† PROFESSOR J. L. MONTEITH
† DR J. RISHBETH

† PROFESSOR D. C. SMITH
§ DR J. W. G. LUND
§ DR P. S. NUTMAN
§ PROFESSOR R. K. S. WOOD

* To retire 31 July 1977
† To retire 31 July 1978
§ To retire 31 July 1979

Sectional Committee 7 [1963]

Vertebrate and invertebrate zoology and palaeozoology, human and comparative anatomy, taxonomy and systematics, entomology, parasitology, protozoology, marine and freshwater biology, animal ecology and population dynamics, animal behaviour, physical anthropology.

CHAIRMAN: * PROFESSOR R. J. HARRISON

* PROFESSOR E. J. DENTON
* PROFESSOR O. W. RICHARDS
† DR R. M. GAZE
† PROFESSOR A. D. LEES

† PROFESSOR J. Z. YOUNG
§ PROFESSOR J. M. DODD
§ DR SIDNIE M. MANTON
§ PROFESSOR H. B. WHITTINGTON

Sectional Committee 8 [1963]

Biochemistry, molecular biophysics, chemical microbiology.

CHAIRMAN: * SIR JAMES BADDILEY

* PROFESSOR S. V. PERRY
* PROFESSOR R. WHITTAM
† PROFESSOR K. BURTON
† PROFESSOR G. A. GILBERT

† PROFESSOR F. R. WHATLEY
§ DR D. M. BLOW
§ DR K. DALZIEL
§ PROFESSOR E. C. SLATER

Sectional Committee 9 [1963]

Animal and human physiology (including nutrition), biophysics, pharmacology, endocrinology (including applied and comparative aspects), reproduction, psychology.

CHAIRMAN: * DR P. B. C. MATTHEWS

* PROFESSOR R. MILEDI
* PROFESSOR R. V. SHORT
† PROFESSOR H. B. BARLOW
† DR B. A. CROSS

† PROFESSOR R. A. HINDE
§ DR K. L. BLAXTER
§ DR D. A. HAYDON
§ DR J. R. VANE

Sectional Committee 10 [1963]

Medical sciences, bacteriology, virology and general microbiology, epidemiology, immunology, pathology, radiobiology, medical statistics and demography.

CHAIRMAN: * SIR DAVID EVANS

* DR BRIGITTE A. ASKONAS
* PROFESSOR R. H. S. THOMPSON
† PROFESSOR R. R. A. COOMBS
† SIR RICHARD DOLL

† PROFESSOR P. E. POLANI
† DR P. M. BIGGS
§ SIR JOHN DACIE
§ DR L. G. GOODWIN

* To retire 31 July 1977
† To retire 31 July 1978
§ To retire 31 July 1979

Sectional Committee 11 [1973]

Genetics (including molecular, microbial and population genetics), experimental cytology, cell biology, differentiation and development.

CHAIRMAN: † PROFESSOR W. F. BODMER

* PROFESSOR D. S. FALCONER
* DR MARY F. LYON
* PROFESSOR J. MANDELSTAM
† DR H. J. F. CAIRNS

† PROFESSOR J. M. THODAY
§ DR R. HOLLIDAY
§ DR ANNE L. McLAREN
§ PROFESSOR D. H. NORTHCOTE

Committee on General Candidates [1962]

The Committee on General Candidates assists Council in the consideration of the claims of candidates for election into the Fellowship who are not explicitly covered by the terms of Standing Order 10 or by Statute 12.

CHAIRMAN: * SIR FREDERICK STEWART

* SIR PETER MEDAWAR
* SIR HAROLD THOMPSON
† SIR HERMANN BONDI
† SIR FREDERICK DAINTON

† SIR JOHN GRAY
§ SIR MONTAGUE FINNISTON
§ SIR BRIAN FLOWERS
§ SIR WILLIAM HENDERSON

Ad hoc Committee on Applied Sciences Candidates [1964]

Council on 18 June 1964 appointed an *ad hoc* Committee on Applied Sciences Candidates to assist Council in the consideration of the claims of such candidates for election into the Fellowship and to operate under the rules for Sectional Committees in a somewhat similar way to the Committee on General Candidates. On 18 May 1972 Council resolved that the Committee be continued on an *ad hoc* basis.

CHAIRMAN: § SIR IEUAN MADDOCK

* SIR CYRIL CLARKE
* PROFESSOR R. RILEY
* DR T. M. SUGDEN
† MR G. N. HOUNSFIELD

† SIR PETER KENT
† PROFESSOR J. E. LOVELOCK
§ PROFESSOR J. H. HORLOCK
§ DR D. A. J. TYRRELL

* To retire 31 July 1977
† To retire 31 July 1978
§ To retire 31 July 1979

STANDING COMMITTEES

ALDABRA RESEARCH COMMITTEE [1967]

To co-ordinate and extend the existing proposals for research work and conservation on the island of Aldabra.

CHAIRMAN: PROFESSOR T. S. WESTOLL (1967)

THE TREASURER
THE BIOLOGICAL SECRETARY
DR M. J. COE (1977)
PROFESSOR G. M. DUNNET (1976)
PROFESSOR D. LEWIS (1972)
DR M. G. MORRIS (1976)
MR J. F. PEAKE (1973)

PROFESSOR T. R. E. SOUTHWOOD (1977)
DR D. R. STODDART (1968)
PROFESSOR W. H. THORPE (1967)
DR C. A. WRIGHT (1971)
NATURAL ENVIRONMENT RESEARCH COUNCIL REPRESENTATIVE

STATION MANAGEMENT SUBCOMMITTEE

Dr D. R. Stoddart (*chairman*), The Biological Secretary, Dr M. J. Coe, Professor D. Lewis, Mr J. F. Peake, Professor W. H. Thorpe, Mr F. W. Topliffe, Professor T. S. Westoll, Dr C. A. Wright.

WORKING GROUPS

Herpetology: Professor G. M. Dunnet (*chairman*), Professor P. Armitage, Professor A. d'A. Bellairs, Dr M. J. Coe, Mr J. F. Peake, Dr D. R. Stoddart.

Ornithology: Professor W. H. Thorpe (*chairman*), Dr J. B. Nelson, Mr J. F. Peake, Dr D. W. Snow, Dr D. R. Stoddart.

Botany: Professor D. Lewis (*chairman*), Mr J. P. M. Brenan, Mr J. F. Peake, Dr D. R. Stoddart, Dr S. R. J. Woodell.

Terrestrial Invertebrates: Dr C. A. Wright (*chairman*), Dr B. H. Cogan, Mr J. F. Peake, Dr D. R. Stoddart, Dr Nadia Waloff.

Marine Sciences Working Group: Professor N. B. Marshall (*chairman*), Professor D. J. Crisp, Dr R. N. Hughes, Mr N. R. Merrett, Mr J. F. Peake, Dr G. W. Potts, Dr D. R. Stoddart, Dr J. D. Taylor.

Earth Sciences: Professor T. S. Westoll (*chairman*), Dr C. J. R. Braithwaite, Mr J. F Peake, Dr D. R. Stoddart, Dr J. D. Taylor.

ALDABRA DATA UNIT STEERING GROUP

Dr D. R. Stoddart (*chairman*), Mr C. C. Leamy, Mr J. F. Peake, Mr G. L. Radford, Dr M. G. Schultz, Dr D. B. Williams, Dr C. A. Wright.

ALDABRA LIAISON GROUP

Dr D. R. Stoddart (*chairman*), Dr M. J. Coe, Professor D. Lewis, Dr J. B. Nelson, Mr J. F. Peake, Dr G. W. Potts, Dr D. W. Snow, Dr J. D. Taylor, Dr C. A. Wright.

BROWNE, HILL AND MURRAY COMMITTEE [1974]

To advise on the use of the Browne Research, John Murray Travelling Studentship and Maurice Hill Research Funds.

CHAIRMAN: PROFESSOR E. J. DENTON (1974)

THE TREASURER
THE BIOLOGICAL SECRETARY
PROFESSOR H. CHARNOCK (1977)
PROFESSOR J. M. DODD (1977)

PROFESSOR G. E. FOGG (1974)
DR G. FRYER (1974)
PROFESSOR F. J. VINE (1977)

STANDING COMMITTEES 115

EDUCATION COMMITTEE (1969)
To advise Council on matters relating to education at all levels.

CHAIRMAN: DR C. C. BUTLER (1969)

THE TREASURER
THE BIOLOGICAL SECRETARY
THE PHYSICAL SECRETARY
CHAIRMAN, BIOLOGICAL EDUCATION
  COMMITTEE
CHAIRMAN, CHEMICAL EDUCATION
  COMMITTEE
CHAIRMAN, ENGINEERING
  EDUCATION COMMITTEE
CHAIRMAN, MATHEMATICAL
  EDUCATION COMMITTEE
CHAIRMAN, PHYSICS EDUCATION
  COMMITTEE
PROFESSOR C. C. ADDISON (1974)

PROFESSOR C. EABORN (1977)
PROFESSOR J. S. FORREST (1974)
PROFESSOR D. W. HOLDER (1977)
SIR NEVILL MOTT (1972)
PROFESSOR P. R. OWEN (1976)
PROFESSOR P. F. WAREING (1975)
PROFESSOR D. H. WHIFFEN (1976)
PROFESSOR E. C. ZEEMAN (1976)
MR A. R. HALL (1970) (*representing the Association for Science Education*)
MR G. A. DUMMETT (1975) (*representing the Council of Engineering Institutions*)

EXPEDITIONS COMMITTEE [1936]
To advise on proposals for, or applications for financial support to, expeditions, whether biological or otherwise.

CHAIRMAN: PROFESSOR F. W. SHOTTON (1971)

THE TREASURER
THE BIOLOGICAL SECRETARY
THE PHYSICAL SECRETARY
PROFESSOR P. ALLEN (1974)
MR G. P. ASKEW (1975)
MR J. P. M. BRENAN (1977)
DR F. C. FRASER (1972)

SIR VIVIAN FUCHS (1976)
PROFESSOR J. GREEN (1974)
MR W. B. HARLAND (1977)
PROFESSOR J. G. HAWKES (1976)
DR R. H. HEDLEY (1974)
DR C. A. WRIGHT (1975)
SIR MAURICE YONGE (1967)

FINANCE COMMITTEE [1785]
To advise on financial and other related matters.

CHAIRMAN: THE TREASURER

THE BIOLOGICAL SECRETARY
THE PHYSICAL SECRETARY
SIR ARNOLD BURGEN (1974)
SIR HUGH FORD (1976)
SIR HARRY MELVILLE (1973)

SIR JAMES MENTER (1977)
SIR ANGUS PATON (1975)
SIR ALASTAIR PILKINGTON
  (1977)
DR L. ROTHERHAM (1969)

GASSIOT COMMITTEE [1871]
To stimulate meteorological research with special reference to the physical and chemical processes of the atmosphere.

CHAIRMAN: PROFESSOR W. R. S. GARTON (1966)

THE TREASURER
THE PHYSICAL SECRETARY
DR B. BATES (1972)
DR A. E. J. EGGLETON (1968)
DR H. A. GEBBIE (1976)
PROFESSOR J. B. HASTED (1969)
PROFESSOR T. R. KAISER (1971)

DR G. V. MARR (1968)
PROFESSOR W. C. PRICE (1960)
PROFESSOR P. A. SHEPPARD (1949)
DR A. C. H. SMITH (1972)
DR B. A. THRUSH (1968)
THE DIRECTOR-GENERAL,
  Meteorological Office

HEAD BEQUEST COMMITTEE [1942]
To administer the Head Bequest.

CHAIRMAN: PROFESSOR C. G. PHILLIPS (1977)

THE TREASURER
PROFESSOR H. B. BARLOW (1977)

PROFESSOR W. D. M. PATON (1964)
PROFESSOR W. S. PEART (1975)

HOOKE COMMITTEE [1962]
To make suggestions to the Secretaries for the programme of the Society's Ordinary Meetings.

CHAIRMAN: DR R. E. RICHARDS (1973)

THE TREASURER
THE BIOLOGICAL SECRETARY
THE PHYSICAL SECRETARY
DR S. BRENNER (1974)
DR W. BULLERWELL (1973)
SIR HUGH FORD (1975)
PROFESSOR I. M. GLYNN (1977)

PROFESSOR G. W. KENNER (1975)
PROFESSOR H. C. LONGUET-HIGGINS (1976)
PROFESSOR W. S. PEART (1977)
PROFESSOR R. RILEY (1973)
SIR DENYS WILKINSON (1976)
DR R. WECK (1977)

INDUSTRIAL ACTIVITIES COMMITTEE [1969]
To advise Council on any matters related to scientific, engineering and technological work in industry.

CHAIRMAN: SIR ANGUS PATON (1969)

THE TREASURER
THE BIOLOGICAL SECRETARY
THE PHYSICAL SECRETARY
DR G. D. H. BELL (1969)
SIR ERNST CHAIN (1969)
SIR ALAN COTTRELL (1976)
SIR ERIC EASTWOOD (1969)
DR G. B. R. FEILDEN (1969)
SIR MONTAGUE FINNISTON (1969)
EARL OF HALSBURY (1969)
PROFESSOR D. W. HOLDER (1969)
MR G. N. HOUNSFIELD (1976)

SIR KENNETH HUTCHISON (1969)
DR F. E. JONES (1969)
LORD KEARTON (1969)
SIR PETER KENT (1969)
SIR IEUAN MADDOCK (1976)
SIR MORIEN MORGAN (1976)
SIR ALASTAIR PILKINGTON (1969)
DR F. L. ROSE (1972)
DR J. R. VANE (1976)
DR R. WECK (1976)
DR D. T. N. WILLIAMSON (1969)
CHAIRMAN, HOOKE COMMITTEE

INTERNATIONAL RELATIONS COMMITTEE [1966]
To advise Council on general policy in international relations.

CHAIRMAN: THE FOREIGN SECRETARY

THE TREASURER
THE BIOLOGICAL SECRETARY
THE PHYSICAL SECRETARY
PROFESSOR ALAN H. COOK (1974)
SIR ALAN COTTRELL (1968)
SIR KINGSLEY DUNHAM (1976)
SIR BRIAN FLOWERS (1973)
DR L. FOWDEN (1972)
PROFESSOR HENRY HARRIS (1972)
SIR WILLIAM HENDERSON (1977)

PROFESSOR J. HESLOP-HARRISON (1973)
SIR HAROLD HIMSWORTH (1970)
SIR JOHN KENDREW (1966)
PROFESSOR R. D. KEYNES (1975)
SIR GEORGE PORTER (1972)
MR J. S. SAWYER (1975)
PROFESSOR R. M. SHACKLETON (1973)
SIR HAROLD THOMPSON (1972)

FELLOWSHIPS SELECTION SUBCOMMITTEE

To recommend to Council, on behalf of the International Relations Committee, the names of persons to be awarded fellowships in the European Science Exchange Programme and Royal Society-Israel Academy Programme.

The Foreign Secretary (*chairman*), The Biological Secretary (*ex officio*), The Physical Secretary (*ex officio*), Professor T. Brooke Benjamin, Professor W. E. Burcham, Sir Kingsley Dunham, Professor T. W. Goodwin, Professor R. A. Gregory, Professor A. W. Johnson, Professor N. Kurti, Professor D. Lewis, Professor J. Lewis, Professor I. G. MacDonald, Dr G. K. Radda, Dr L. Rotherham, Professor S. K. Runcorn, Sir Harold Thompson.

OVERSEAS VISITING PROFESSORSHIPS SUBCOMMITTEE

To recommend to Council, on behalf of the International Relations Committee, the countries and institutions to be offered Overseas Visiting Professorships and their incumbents and to advise Council on matters relating to the International Council of Scientific Unions' Committee on Science and Technology in Developing Countries (Costed).

The Foreign Secretary (*chairman*), Dr L. Fowden, Sir Joseph Hutchinson, Sir Ewart Jones, Sir Nevill Mott, Sir Charles Pereira, Professor N. W. Pirie, Dr G. Pontecorvo, Sir Owen Saunders and observers from the Association of Commonwealth Universities (Sir Hugh Springer), The British Council (Dr F. H. Taylor), the Inter-University Council for Higher Education Overseas (Mr I. C. M. Maxwell) and the Leverhulme Trust Fund (The Director).

INVESTMENT ADVISORY COMMITTEE [1952]

To advise on the investment of funds managed by Robert Fleming and Company Limited.

CHAIRMAN: THE TREASURER

MR G. F. B. GRANT (1974)
MR C. K. R. NUNNELEY (1971)

LORD REMNANT (1974)
DR L. ROTHERHAM (1969)

LIBRARY COMMITTEE [1782]

To advise on questions connected with the maintenance and administration of the Library, including applications for exchange or presentation of publications.

CHAIRMAN: PROFESSOR E. J. DENTON (1971)

THE TREASURER
THE BIOLOGICAL SECRETARY
THE PHYSICAL SECRETARY
PROFESSOR A. R. CLAPHAM (1977)
MR N. L. FALCON (1976)
PROFESSOR J. S. FORREST (1974)
PROFESSOR V. GOLD (1975)

PROFESSOR HENRY HARRIS (1973)
PROFESSOR J. D. McGEE (1975)
PROFESSOR N. B. MARSHALL (1975)
PROFESSOR W. V. MAYNEORD (1976)
PROFESSOR A. W. SKEMPTON (1973)
PROFESSOR G. F. J. TEMPLE (1974)
PROFESSOR D. WHITTERIDGE (1974)

MEDICAL SCIENCES RESEARCH COMMITTEE [1936]

To recommend as to research appointments in medicine and medical science; to advise, when desired, on matters connected with medicine and the use of the medical funds; and to report from time to time on the regulations governing the use of these funds, namely, the Beringer, Florey, Forsyth, Foulerton, Foulerton Gift, E. Alan Johnston, Lawrence, Horace Le Marquand and Dudley Bigg, Locke, Moseley and Stothert Funds.

CHAIRMAN: PROFESSOR W. S. PEART (1972)

THE TREASURER
THE BIOLOGICAL SECRETARY
PROFESSOR H. B. BARLOW (1976)
PROFESSOR W. F. BODMER (1977)
DR S. BRENNER (1971)
DR D. E. BROADBENT (1973)
PROFESSOR G. S. DAWES (1977)

PROFESSOR I. M. GLYNN (1973)
PROFESSOR D. K. HILL (1975)
PROFESSOR J. H. HUMPHREY (1972)
PROFESSOR S. V. PERRY (1977)
DR RUTH A. SANGER (1974)
DR J. R. VANE (1976)

BRUNO MENDEL FELLOWSHIP COMMITTEE [1964]

To recommend annually a suitable candidate for the award of the Bruno Mendel Fellowship.

CHAIRMAN: THE BIOLOGICAL SECRETARY

SIR HANS KREBS (1964), PROFESSOR P. L. MOLLISON (1977) (United Kingdom)
PROFESSOR F. DEKKING (1974), PROFESSOR E. C. SLATER (1964) (The Netherlands)
PROFESSOR B. SHAPIRO (1972), PROFESSOR N. SHARON (1977) (Israel)

NEWTON LETTERS COMMITTEE [1938]

To advise on matters concerned with the publication now in progress of Isaac Newton's correspondence.

CHAIRMAN: SIR JAMES LIGHTHILL (1971)

THE TREASURER
THE PHYSICAL SECRETARY
PROFESSOR A. R. HALL (1972)
MR J. W. J. HERIVEL (1972)
DR M. A. HOSKIN (1972)
DR J. NEEDHAM (1972)
DR R. SCHLAPP (1961)

PROFESSOR W. H. SEMPLE (1962)
MR H. G. STRIDE (1964)
PROFESSOR J. L. SYNGE (1968)
PROFESSOR G. J. WHITROW (1968)
THE LIBRARIAN OF TRINITY
  COLLEGE, CAMBRIDGE

ORDNANCE SURVEY COMMITTEE [1974]

To advise Council (i) on the requirements of the scientific community in relation to the services of the Ordnance Survey and (ii) on the recommendations to be made to the Ordnance Survey concerning such requirements and concerning other activities of a purely scientific nature which might be carried out by the Ordnance Survey.

CHAIRMAN: SIR HARRIE MASSEY (1974)

THE TREASURER
THE PHYSICAL SECRETARY
DR W. BULLERWELL (1974)
PROFESSOR ALAN H. COOK (1974)
PROFESSOR J. T. COPPOCK (1974)
PROFESSOR H. C. DARBY (1974)

SIR KINGSLEY DUNHAM (1974)
PROFESSOR J. L. HARLEY (1974)
MR G. W. LENNON (1974)
MAJOR GENERAL B. ST G. IRWIN (1974) (*representing the Ordnance Survey*)

ROYAL SOCIETY ESSO AWARD COMMITTEE [1974]
To advise on suitable candidates for the Royal Society Esso Award for the conservation of energy.

CHAIRMAN: DR T. M. SUGDEN (1974)

THE TREASURER
THE BIOLOGICAL SECRETARY
THE PHYSICAL SECRETARY
DR P. J. AGIUS (1974)
SIR WILLIAM HAWTHORNE (1974)
PROFESSOR J. HESLOP-HARRISON (1974)
SIR GEORGE PORTER (1974)

DR F. A. ROBINSON (1974) (representing the Council of Science and Technology Institutes)
DR L. ROTHERHAM (1977)
DR F. H. M. TAYLOR (1974) (representing the Council of Engineering Institutions)
PROFESSOR A. R. J. P. UBBELOHDE (1977)

ROYAL SOCIETY LEVERHULME STUDENTSHIPS COMMITTEE [1963]
To recommend to Council arrangements for the operation of the Studentships scheme and to recommend suitable candidates.

CHAIRMAN: SIR GEORGE TAYLOR (1969)

THE TREASURER
THE BIOLOGICAL SECRETARY
MR J. P. M. BRENAN (1976)
SIR MILES CLIFFORD (1963)
PROFESSOR E. J. DENTON (1975)
MR N. L. FALCON (1973)
DR L. G. GOODWIN (1977)
PROFESSOR J. S. KENNEDY (1977)
PROFESSOR P. W. RICHARDS (1974)

PROFESSOR R. RILEY (1975)
PROFESSOR R. M. SHACKLETON (1974)
PROFESSOR R. V. SHORT (1976)
PROFESSOR T. R. E. SOUTHWOOD (1975)
DR D. R. STODDART (1974)
PROFESSOR W. H. THORPE (1977)

ROYAL SOCIETY MULLARD AWARD COMMITTEE [1967]
To advise on suitable candidates for the Royal Society Mullard Award.

CHAIRMAN: SIR IEUAN MADDOCK (1973)

THE TREASURER
THE BIOLOGICAL SECRETARY
THE PHYSICAL SECRETARY
* MR G. A. DUMMETT (1974)
* SIR RALPH FREEMAN (1969)
* DR D. F. GALLOWAY (1974)
SIR ASHLEY MILES (1972)

SIR CHARLES OATLEY (1977)
PROFESSOR P. R. OWEN (1977)
SIR ALASTAIR PILKINGTON (1972)
DR F. L. ROSE (1971)
DR J. R. VANE (1976)
SIR FREDERICK WARNER (1977)
DR D. T. N. WILLIAMSON (1976)

* Nominated by the Council of Engineering Institutions

RUTHERFORD MEMORIAL COMMITTEE [1938]
To commemorate the services to science of the late Lord Rutherford.

CHAIRMAN: PROFESSOR W. E. BURCHAM (1960)

THE TREASURER
THE PHYSICAL SECRETARY
PROFESSOR E. H. S. BURHOP (1965)
PROFESSOR R. H. DALITZ (1975)
PROFESSOR H. ELLIOT (1977)

Corresponding Members:
SIR CHARLES FLEMING (1971)
DR W. B. LEWIS (1963)

PROFESSOR P. H. FOWLER (1975)
PROFESSOR G. W. SERIES (1974)
PROFESSOR F. R. WHATLEY (1977)
PROFESSOR D. H. WHIFFEN (1976)
PROFESSOR R. J. P. WILLIAMS (1976)

SIR MARK OLIPHANT (1954)

SCIENTIFIC INFORMATION COMMITTEE [1959]

To keep under review developments in scientific information services, and to recommend appointments to scientific information research fellowships.

CHAIRMAN: PROFESSOR J. HESLOP-HARRISON (1977)

THE TREASURER
THE PHYSICAL SECRETARY
PROFESSOR G. BLACK (1967)
DR K. L. BLAXTER (1972)
PROFESSOR E. C. COCKING (1975)
DR G. B. R. FEILDEN (1969)
MR J. C. GRAY (1972)
PROFESSOR H. L. KORNBERG (1969)

PROFESSOR N. KURTI (1965)
PROFESSOR A. J. MEADOWS (1977)
MR A. C. NICHOLAS (1977)
DR F. L. ROSE (1973)
PROFESSOR J. S. ROWLINSON (1973)
DR G. D. SIMS (1972)
MISS M. F. WEBB (1968)
PROFESSOR A. J. C. WILSON (1977)

SCIENTIFIC RELIEF COMMITTEE [1859]

To administer the Scientific Relief Fund.

CHAIRMAN: PROFESSOR J. S. FORREST (1977)

THE PRESIDENT
THE TREASURER
THE BIOLOGICAL SECRETARY
THE PHYSICAL SECRETARY
THE FOREIGN SECRETARY
SIR HAROLD HIMSWORTH (1971)

PROFESSOR W. H. McCREA (1975)
PROFESSOR HELEN K. PORTER (1968)
MR J. A. RATCLIFFE (1975)
PROFESSOR R. A. SMITH (1975)

SOIRÉE COMMITTEE [1873]

To make arrangements for the Soirées and Anniversary Dinner, including invitations, exhibits, etc.

CHAIRMAN: PROFESSOR E. J. DENTON (1972)

THE TREASURER
THE BIOLOGICAL SECRETARY
THE PHYSICAL SECRETARY
PROFESSOR H. B. BARLOW (1974)
PROFESSOR G. V. R. BORN (1973)
PROFESSOR G. S. BRINDLEY (1974)
DR G. W. COOKE (1976)
SIR SAM EDWARDS (1975)
PROFESSOR D. D. ELEY (1977)
SIR HUGH FORD (1976)
PROFESSOR J. S. FORREST (1968)
DR L. FOWDEN (1977)

PROFESSOR V. GOLD (1976)
DR L. G. GOODWIN (1977)
PROFESSOR R. A. HINDE (1975)
MR G. N. HOUNSFIELD (1976)
PROFESSOR R. V. JONES (1975)
DR A. KELLY (1974)
PROFESSOR J. S. KENNEDY (1974)
SIR PETER KENT (1975)
SIR IEUAN MADDOCK (1968)
PROFESSOR W. S. PEART (1973)
PROFESSOR A. F. POSNETTE (1974)

SOUTHERN ZONE RESEARCH COMMITTEE [1956]

To promote the study of the southern zone and to advise on matters connected with the Pacific Science Association.

CHAIRMAN: SIR MAURICE YONGE (1966)

THE TREASURER
THE BIOLOGICAL SECRETARY
MR J. P. M. BRENAN (1977)
SIR FRANK CLARINGBULL (1973)
SIR GEORGE DEACON (1971)
MR N. L. FALCON (1974)
DR G. FRYER (1975)
PROFESSOR A. J. HADDOW (1973)

DR R. H. HEDLEY (1976)
DR R. M. LAWS (1974)
LT-CDR T. McANDREW (1972)
PROFESSOR P. W. RICHARDS (1977)
DR D. R. STODDART (1976)
DR H. G. VEVERS (1973)
PROFESSOR P. E. WEATHERLEY (1976)

STANDING COMMITTEES

SPACE RANGING RESEARCH COMMITTEE [1973]

To advise Council on the encouragement and promotion of geophysical, geometric, geodetic and celestial mechanical studies by laser ranging and radio-astronomical techniques.

CHAIRMAN: PROFESSOR ALAN H. COOK (1973)

THE TREASURER
THE PHYSICAL SECRETARY
DR H. H. ATKINSON (1977)
DR D. E. CARTWRIGHT (1977)
DR P. A. CROSS (1977)
MR B. ELSMORE (1973)
DR F. HORNER (1973)
MAJOR-GENERAL B.St G. IRWIN (1973)
MAJOR-GENERAL J. KELSEY (1973)

MR D. G. KING-HELE (1973)
SIR BERNARD LOVELL (1973)
PROFESSOR A. J. MEADOWS (1976)
MR C. A. MURRAY (1973)
PROFESSOR S. A. RAMSDEN (1973)
DR A. R. ROBBINS (1973)
PROFESSOR S. K. RUNCORN (1973)
DR G. A. WILKINS (1973)

TRAVELLING EXPENSES COMMITTEE [1963]

To consider applications for grants for travelling expenses and to make recommendations on them to Council.

CHAIRMAN: THE TREASURER

DR G. D. H. BELL
PROFESSOR C. G. PHILLIPS
PROFESSOR R. A. RAPHAEL

DR M. G. P. STOKER
PROFESSOR J. SUTTON

VOLCANOLOGICAL AND SEISMOLOGICAL RESEARCH COMMITTEE [1963]

To advise on the promotion of research in volcanology and short-lived geological phenomena.

CHAIRMAN: SIR KINGSLEY DUNHAM (1972)

ex officio
  The TREASURER
  CHAIRMAN, Seismology and Physics of the Earth's Interior Subcommittee of the British National Committee for Geodesy and Geophysics
  CHAIRMAN, Volcanology and Chemistry of the Earth's Interior Subcommittee of the British National Committee for Geodesy and Geophysics
  CHAIRMAN of the Etna Research Subcommittee
  ROYAL SOCIETY REPRESENTATIVE on Governing Council of the International Seismological Centre.

ETNA RESEARCH SUBCOMMITTEE

Professor E. A. Vincent (*chairman*), Professor D. K. Bailey, Dr M. S. Beck, Dr J. E. Guest, Dr A. T. Huntingdon, Professor R. G. Mason, Dr G. P. L. Walker, Dr M. K. Wells, Dr P. L. Willmore, Professor R. L. Wilson.

JOINT COMMITTEES

(Composed of representatives of The Royal Society and other bodies jointly.)

ARMOURERS AND BRASIERS' COMPANY RESEARCH FELLOWSHIP COMMITTEE [1923]

To make appointments to the Fellowship. (See p. 269.)

CHAIRMAN: MR H. H. WAGSTAFF

The Royal Society
THE PHYSICAL SECRETARY
SIR ALAN COTTRELL (1958)
PROFESSOR F. C. FRANK (1959)
SIR PETER HIRSCH (1968)

The Armourers and Brasiers' Company
MR A. F. R. HATFIELD (1972)
MR H. H. WAGSTAFF (1974)
DR J. M. WALKER (1974)

BIOLOGICAL EDUCATION COMMITTEE [1962]

Under the joint sponsorship of The Royal Society and The Institute of Biology, to promote improvement in the teaching of biology.

CHAIRMAN: PROFESSOR R. WHITTAM

Association for Science Education (3)
† MR D. W. G. BACON
§ MISS G. MONGER
* DR E. E. ZUILL

Biological Council (1)
* PROFESSOR D. E. HUGHES

Department of Education and Science
(1 *observer*)
MR A. G. CLEGG

Institute of Biology (3)
* DR R. COOPER
† PROFESSOR W. H. DOWDESWELL
§ MR B. M. JONES

National Association of Teachers in Further and Higher Education (1)
† DR G. D. WATTS

Royal Society (3)
† PROFESSOR F. R. WHATLEY
* PROFESSOR R. WHITTAM
§ PROFESSOR D. R. WILKIE

Scottish Education Department
(1 *observer*)
MR S. T. S. SKILLEN

Schools Council (1)
* MR J. H. GRAY

University Biological Education Tutors (1)
§ MISS D. E. MANUEL

Other Member
DR R. A. KILLE

Secretary: MR B. GREGSON-ALLCOTT, The Institute of Biology

* To retire 31 December 1977
† To retire 31 December 1978
§ To retire 31 December 1979

CHEMICAL EDUCATION COMMITTEE [1962]

Under the joint sponsorship of The Royal Society and the Chemical Society, to promote improvement in the teaching of chemistry.

CHAIRMAN: PROFESSOR V. GOLD

Association for Science Education (3)
  § MR R. C. BAILEY
  † MR T. P. BORROWS
  * DR D. G. NEWMAN
Association of University Chemical Education Tutors (1)
  † MR M. VOKINS
Biochemical Society (1)
  † PROFESSOR G. A. D. HASLEWOOD
Chemical Society (3)
  § DR B. R. CURRELL
  † DR M. DAVIS
  † PROFESSOR K. S. W. SING
Department of Education and Science (1)
  * MR I. G. E. WILDING
Institution of Chemical Engineers (1)
  † DR J. A. BARNARD

Ministry of Education, N. Ireland (1)
  § MR I. H. N. WALLACE
Open University (1)
  † PROFESSOR L. J. HAYNES
Royal Institute of Chemistry (1)
  † DR R. J. ELLIS
Royal Society (3)
  § PROFESSOR G. EGLINTON
  † PROFESSOR V. GOLD
  * DR F. L. ROSE
Schools Council (1)
  † MR D. BLACK
Scottish Education Department (1)
  § MR A. W. JEFFREY
Society of Chemical Industry (1)
  § DR G. A. GAMLEN

Other Member
MR D. G. CHISMAN

Secretary: DR M. D. ROBINSON, The Chemical Society

MATHEMATICAL EDUCATION COMMITTEE [1969]

Under the joint sponsorship of The Royal Society and The Institute of Mathematics and its Applications, to promote improvement in the teaching of mathematics.

CHAIRMAN: PROFESSOR M. F. ATIYAH

Association of Teachers of Mathematics (1)
  § MR A. J. McINTOSH
British Computer Society (1)
  § MR M. BRIDGER
Department of Education and Science (1 observer)
  MR T. J. FLETCHER
Institute of Mathematics and its Applications (3)
  † MR R. H. DAVIES
  § PROFESSOR A. C. OFFORD
  * MR A. R. TAMMADGE
Joint Mathematical Council (1)
  † MR H. NEILL
London Mathematical Society (1)
  § PROFESSOR H. HALBERSTAM
Mathematical Association (1)
  * DR A. G. HOWSON

Ministry of Education of Northern Ireland (1 observer)
  MR A. WEAR
National Association of Teachers in Further and Higher Education (1)
  * MR K. L. GARDNER
Royal Society (3)
  † PROFESSOR M. F. ATIYAH
  § DR H. R. PITT
  * PROFESSOR C. T. C. WALL
Royal Statistical Society (1)
  † PROFESSOR V. BARNETT
Schools Council (1 observer)
  MR P. M. DINES
University Departments of Education Mathematical Study Group (1)
  † MR M. BARBER

Secretary: MR N. CLARKE, The Institute of Mathematics and its Applications

* To retire 31 December 1977
† To retire 31 December 1978
§ To retire 31 December 1979

NAPLES ZOOLOGICAL STATION COMMITTEE [1960]

To advise Council on the provision of facilities at the Stazione Zoologica, Naples, for investigations sponsored by institutions in the United Kingdom.

CHAIRMAN: THE BIOLOGICAL SECRETARY

DR P. J. S. BOADEN, *Queen's University of Belfast*
PROFESSOR H. G. CALLAN, *University of St Andrews*
DR E. T. B. FRANCIS, *University of Sheffield*
DR C. B. GOODHART, *University of Cambridge*
PROFESSOR H. E. HINTON, *University of Bristol*
DR E. J. ILES, *University of Manchester*
PROFESSOR B. M. JONES, *University of Wales*
SIR BERNARD KATZ, *Physiological Society*
PROFESSOR E. NAYLOR, *University of Liverpool*
PROFESSOR J. G. PHILLIPS, *University of Hull*
PROFESSOR J. D. ROBERTSON, *University of Glasgow*
PROFESSOR P. N. R. USHERWOOD, *University of Nottingham*
PROFESSOR J. E. WEBB, *University of London*
PROFESSOR J. Z. YOUNG, *The Royal Society*

PAUL INSTRUMENT FUND COMMITTEE [1945]

(See p. 251.)

To administer the income from the R. W. Paul Instrument Fund.

CHAIRMAN: PROFESSOR R. V. JONES

The Royal Society
† PROFESSOR ALAN H. COOK (1970)
* PROFESSOR A. G. GAYDON (1957)
§ SIR ANDREW HUXLEY (1962)

Institute of Physics
§ PROFESSOR O. S. HEAVENS (1972)
† PROFESSOR R. V. JONES (1952)

Institution of Electrical Engineers
* SIR CHARLES OATLEY (1972)

* To retire in 1977
† To retire in 1978
§ To retire in 1979

PHYSICS EDUCATION COMMITTEE [1965]

Under the joint sponsorship of The Royal Society and The Institute of Physics to promote improvement in the teaching of physics.

CHAIRMAN: PROFESSOR J. R. HOLT

Association of Departments of Education Physics Tutors (1)
† MR B. R. CHAPMAN

Association for Science Education (3)
* MR E. N. BONSALL
§ MR A. M. KAVANAGH
† MR L. T. ROGERS

Department of Education and Science (1 observer)
MR J. B. WHINNERAH

Institute of Physics (3)
§ MR J. L. LEWIS
† PROFESSOR C. A. TAYLOR
VICE-PRESIDENT FOR EDUCATION, INSTITUTE OF PHYSICS

Ministry of Education of Northern Ireland (1 observer)
MR A. J. BERKIN

National Association of Teachers in Further and Higher Education (1)
* MR S. W. SMITH

Nuffield Science Project (1)
† MRS B. SCHOFIELD

Open University (1)
* DR P. CLARK

Royal Institution (1)
§ PROFESSOR R. KING

Royal Society (3)
* DR F. J. M. FARLEY
* PROFESSOR J. R. HOLT
§ PROFESSOR W. F. VINEN

Schools Council (1)

Scottish Education Department (1 observer)
MR D. G. CARTER

Other Member
* MR J. B. WILLIAMS

Secretary: MR M. G. EBISON, The Institute of Physics

* To retire 31 December 1977
† To retire 31 December 1978
§ To retire 31 December 1979

ROYAL SOCIETY COMMONWEALTH BURSARIES COMMITTEE [1953]
(See p. 257.)

To administer the Royal Society Commonwealth Bursaries Scheme and to report to the Council of the Royal Society, the Trustees of the Nuffield Foundation and the Trustees of the Commonwealth Foundation.

CHAIRMAN: PROFESSOR A. W. JOHNSON

The Royal Society (4)
DR K. L. BLAXTER (1970)
PROFESSOR D. J. BRADLEY (1977)
PROFESSOR W. E. BURCHAM (1974)
PROFESSOR J. SUTTON (1976)

The Nuffield Foundation (4)
PROFESSOR G. S. DAWES (1974)
PROFESSOR A. W. JOHNSON (1968)
PROFESSOR H. L. KORNBERG (1974)
MR J. R. MADDOX (1975)

The Commonwealth Foundation (3)
DR G. D. H. BELL (1970)
MR J. CHADWICK (1970)
PROFESSOR J. L. HARLEY (1973)

ROYAL SOCIETY/COUNCIL OF ENGINEERING INSTITUTIONS EDUCATION COMMITTEE [1974]

To promote the teaching of science and mathematics related to the needs of engineering and industry.

CHAIRMAN: PROFESSOR J. F. COALES
VICE-CHAIRMAN: PROFESSOR D. W. HOLDER

Royal Society
PROFESSOR J. S. FORREST
PROFESSOR D. W. HOLDER
PROFESSOR J. T. STUART

Council of Engineering Institutions
PROFESSOR J. F. COALES
MR H. W. FRENCH

Other Members

MR A. J. W. ADDIS
MR R. A. ARCULUS
PROFESSOR A. C. BAJPAI
MR J. F. LING
MR D. R. MATHEWS

MR S. L. PARSONSON
MISS H. B. SHUARD
DR W. TAGG
MR K. WIBBERLEY

Department of Education and Science
DR T. A. BURDETT

Secretary: MR J. RAYSON, Council of Engineering Institutions

ROYAL SOCIETY UNESCO COMMITTEE [1947]

This Committee, which is appointed by the Minister for Overseas Development, is the Science Advisory Committee of the British National Commission for Unesco.

CHAIRMAN: SIR JOHN KENDREW
VICE-CHAIRMAN: SIR KINGSLEY DUNHAM

The Royal Society
SIR GRANVILLE BEYNON
PROFESSOR H. CHARNOCK
PROFESSOR J. S. FORREST
PROFESSOR R. D. KEYNES
DR H. L. PENMAN
PROFESSOR R. RILEY

Department of Education and Science
MR A. S. GANN

Department of the Environment
DR A. F. E. WISE

Ministry of Overseas Development
MR A. R. MELVILLE
MR K. J. WINDSOR

The British Council
DR F. H. TAYLOR

Additional Member
DR L. ROTHERHAM

Joint Secretaries: MR D. A. BELL (Ministry of Overseas Development)
Dr R. W. J. KEAY (Royal Society)

SCIENTIFIC RESEARCH IN SCHOOLS COMMITTEE [1957]
(See p. 249.)

To assist school science teachers who wish to pursue research.

CHAIRMAN: PROFESSOR H. L. KORNBERG

The Royal Society
A SECRETARY (SIR HARRIE MASSEY)
SIR GORDON COX (1969)
PROFESSOR H. L. KORNBERG (1971)
DR RUTH A. SANGER (1974)
PROFESSOR W. F. VINEN (1976)

Association for Science Education
DR D. J. DANIELS (1974)
MR J. B. DAVIES (1974)
MR C. P. ELLIOTT (1977)
MRS J. GLOVER (1969)

JOINT COMMITTEES

SMITHSON RESEARCH FUND COMMITTEE [1929]
(See p. 234.)
To administer the Smithson Research Fund.

CHAIRMAN: PROFESSOR W. H. THORPE

The Royal Society
A SECRETARY (PROFESSOR D. C. PHILLIPS)
SIR ALAN COTTRELL (1975)
PROFESSOR J. W. S. PRINGLE (1972)
PROFESSOR W. H. THORPE (1968)

University of Cambridge
PROFESSOR P. W. BRIAN (1971)
PROFESSOR ALAN H. COOK (1977)
PROFESSOR J. LEWIS (1973)

SORBY RESEARCH FUND COMMITTEE [1909]
To administer the Sorby Research Fund. (See p. 236.)

CHAIRMAN: PROFESSOR E. J. W. BARRINGTON

The Royal Society
A SECRETARY (SIR HARRIE MASSEY)
PROFESSOR E. J. W. BARRINGTON (1974)
DR J. H. CHESTERS (1974)
PROFESSOR E. F. GALE (1966)

University of Sheffield
PROFESSOR W. GALBRAITH (1974)
PROFESSOR R. McWEENY (1971)
PROFESSOR J. A. ROPER (1970)

SYMBOLS COMMITTEE [1939]
To review from time to time scientific symbols, abbreviations and nomenclature, and to recommend such alterations and additions as may become desirable.

CHAIRMAN: PROFESSOR L. F. BATES

The Royal Society
A SECRETARY (SIR HARRIE MASSEY)
PROFESSOR L. F. BATES (1960)
SIR JOHN RANDALL (1969)

The Chemical Society
PROFESSOR M. L. McGLASHAN (1964)
PROFESSOR F. C. TOMPKINS (1948)
Institute of Physics
DR R. J. BELL (1976)
DR P. DEAN (1970)

Additional Members

DR J. V. DUNWORTH (1969)
DR G. B. R. FEILDEN (1969)
DR L. FOWDEN (1971)
PROFESSOR F. C. FRANK (1975)
DR H. M. GLASS (1971)

SIR ANDREW HUXLEY (1974)
PROFESSOR E. J. LE FEVRE (1969)
PROFESSOR P. R. OWEN (1975)
PROFESSOR G. W. SERIES (1975)
PROFESSOR D. H. WHIFFEN (1969)

TYNDALL MINING BEQUEST COMMITTEE [1910]
To administer the Tyndall Mining Research Fund. (See p. 239.)

CHAIRMAN: SIR KINGSLEY DUNHAM

The Royal Society
THE PHYSICAL SECRETARY
DR S. H. U. BOWIE (1976)
SIR KINGSLEY DUNHAM (1963)
PROFFESSOR D. M. NEWITT (1959)

Institution of Mining Engineers
SIR ANDREW BRYAN (1959)
PROFESSOR F. B. HINSLEY (1963)
DR H. L. WILLETT (1972)
THE SECRETARY

The Institution of Mining and Metallurgy
MR M. J. CAHALAN (1972)
PROFESSOR M. G. FLEMING (1972)
PROFESSOR R. N. PRYOR (1972)
MR J. T. M. TAYLOR (1972)

WARREN RESEARCH FUND COMMITTEE [1936]
To direct, control and administer the Warren Research Fund. (See p. 240.)

CHAIRMAN: SIR ALAN COTTRELL

The Royal Society
THE TREASURER
THE PHYSICAL SECRETARY
SIR ALAN COTTRELL (1959)
SIR HUGH FORD (1974)
SIR PETER HIRSCH (1974)
SIR JAMES MENTER (1977)

PROFESSOR A. KELLER (1977)
DR H. MORROGH (1971)
PROFESSOR R. A. SMITH (1971)
PROFESSOR D. TABOR (1968)
Williams & Glyn's Bank Limited
SIR JOHN HOGG
MR G. P. PIRIE-GORDON

WARREN RESEARCH FUND INVESTMENT SUBCOMMITTEE (1956)
The Chairman, The Treasurer, Sir John Hogg, Mr G. P. Pirie-Gordon, Professor R. A. Smith.

GOVERNMENT GRANT BOARDS

Constituted in their present form in 1888 with the
exception of Board D added in 1945

(For Regulations, see pp. 202-204)

Ex officio members of all Boards and of the Scientific Publications Board:

THE PRESIDENT THE BIOLOGICAL SECRETARY
THE TREASURER THE PHYSICAL SECRETARY

BOARD A (Mathematics, computing science, astronomy, meteorology, statistics, geodesy and geophysics)

CHAIRMAN: ‡ PROFESSOR T. B. BENJAMIN

* PROFESSOR J. T. HOUGHTON § DR D. H. MATTHEWS
* PROFESSOR R. WILSON § PROFESSOR S. MICHAELSON
† DR H. RISHBETH ‡ PROFESSOR D. R. COX
† PROFESSOR R. S. SCORER

BOARD B (Experimental physics and crystallography)

CHAIRMAN: † PROFESSOR E. H. S. BURHOP

* DR A. H. COOKE § PROFESSOR D. TABOR
* DR C. HILSUM ‡ PROFESSOR A. KELLER
† PROFESSOR C. A. TAYLOR ‡ PROFESSOR W. F. VINEN
§ DR P. F. CHESTER

BOARD C (Chemistry)

CHAIRMAN: § PROFESSOR L. CROMBIE

* PROFESSOR G. ALLEN § PROFESSOR E. A. V. EBSWORTH
* PROFESSOR G. W. KIRBY ‡ PROFESSOR M. F. LAPPERT
† PROFESSOR R. O. C. NORMAN ‡ DR B. A. THRUSH
† PROFESSOR J. M. THOMAS

BOARD D (Engineering science and metallurgy)

CHAIRMAN: § DR R. WECK

* DR K. G. DENBIGH § PROFESSOR F. D. RICHARDSON
* SIR ALFRED PUGSLEY ‡ PROFESSOR J. F. DAVIDSON
† PROFESSOR H. E. M. BARLOW ‡ DR E. H. MANSFIELD
† DR R. R. JAMISON

BOARD E (Geological sciences and geography)

CHAIRMAN: † PROFESSOR E. H. BROWN

* DR A. S. LAUGHTON § DR MARJORIE M. SWEETING
* DR D. J. SHEARMAN ‡ PROFESSOR F. J. VINE
† DR H. W. BALL ‡ DR G. P. L. WALKER
§ DR P. E. BAKER

* To retire 15 November 1977
† To retire 15 November 1978
§ To retire 15 November 1979
‡ To retire 15 November 1980

BOARD F (Botany and agriculture)

CHAIRMAN: * PROFESSOR P. E. WEATHERLEY

* PROFESSOR D. H. NORTHCOTE
† PROFESSOR J. G. HAWKES
† PROFESSOR A. J. WILLIS
§ PROFESSOR A. J. RUTTER

§ PROFESSOR D. C. SMITH
‡ PROFESSOR W. G. CHALONER
‡ PROFESSOR F. R. WHATLEY

BOARD G (Zoology, comparative anatomy and physical anthropology)

CHAIRMAN: § PROFESSOR T. R. E. SOUTHWOOD

* PROFESSOR A. D'A. BELLAIRS
* PROFESSOR J. S. WEINER
† PROFESSOR J. D. CURREY
† PROFESSOR K. SIMKISS

§ DR P. WARD
‡ PROFESSOR J. M. DODD
‡ DR G. FRYER

BOARD H (Animal physiology, biochemistry and medical subjects)

CHAIRMAN: † PROFESSOR G. S. DAWES

* PROFESSOR H. R. V. ARNSTEIN
* PROFESSOR N. A. MITCHISON
† PROFESSOR C. G. PHILLIPS
§ PROFESSOR E. F. GALE

§ DR D. A. HAYDON
‡ PROFESSOR J. W. BLACK
‡ PROFESSOR R. WHITTAM

* To retire 15 November 1977
† To retire 15 November 1978
§ To retire 15 November 1979
‡ To retire 15 November 1980

SCIENTIFIC PUBLICATIONS BOARD

Constituted 1945

(For Regulations, see pp. 204-205)

CHAIRMAN: † PROFESSOR H. B. WHITTINGTON

* PROFESSOR R. J. HARRISON
* PROFESSOR G. W. SERIES
* DR G. P. L. WALKER
† PROFESSOR A. R. CLAPHAM
† PROFESSOR R. V. SHORT
§ PROFESSOR B. B. BOYCOTT

§ PROFESSOR H. ELLIOT
§ PROFESSOR D. C. SMITH
‡ PROFESSOR PATRICIA H. CLARKE
‡ PROFESSOR N. B. MARSHALL
‡ DR R. C. RAINEY

* To retire 31 December 1977
† To retire 31 December 1978
§ To retire 31 December 1979
‡ To retire 31 December 1980

COMMITTEES CONCERNED WITH INTERNATIONAL NON-GOVERNMENTAL ORGANIZATIONS

INTERNATIONAL COUNCIL OF SCIENTIFIC UNIONS

As the result of an International Conference held in the rooms of the Royal Society in October 1918, and of subsequent conferences held in Paris in November 1918, and in Brussels in July 1919, an International Research Council was formed for the purpose of facilitating international cooperation in scientific work, and promoting the formation of International Unions in different branches of science. In 1931 the International Research Council became the International Council of Scientific Unions. The affairs of the International Council are managed by a General Committee consisting of the Officers, representatives of the Scientific Unions and representatives of the National Members.

The Royal Society, as the national academy of science for the United Kingdom of Great Britain and Northern Ireland, is the adhering organization for the United Kingdom and appoints the United Kingdom delegates to the meetings of the International Council and of its International Unions and Committees.

The Royal Society adheres to seventeen Unions, namely those for Astronomy, Biochemistry, Biology, Biophysics, Chemistry, Crystallography, Geodesy and Geophysics, Geography, Geological Sciences, History of Science, Mathematics, Nutritional Sciences, Pharmacology, Physics, Physiological Sciences, Radio Science, and Theoretical and Applied Mechanics.

The International Council of Scientific Unions in 1952 set up a Special Committee for the International Geophysical Year to organize a programme of observations during the period July 1957 to December 1958. This special committee gave rise to a series of scientific committees, on Antarctic Research, on Oceanic Research and on Space Research, which were set up in 1958 by the International Council of Scientific Unions, and in January 1966, to the Inter-Union Commission (reconstituted in 1972 as a Special Committee) on Solar-Terrestrial Physics. A Committee on Data for

Science and Technology was set up in 1966. In 1968 the International Council for Scientific Unions and the World Meteorological Organization established a Joint Organizing Committee for the Global Atmospheric Research Programme. An Inter-Union Commission on Geodynamics was established in 1969 and a Scientific Committee on Problems of the Environment in 1970.

Under the statutes of each International Union an adhering academy, society, research council or government should appoint a committee to maintain contact with the Bureau of each Union to which it has adhered with the object of facilitating international cooperation in the branch of science with which it is concerned, to recommend to the adhering organization such changes of statute, proposals for scientific action or matters for discussion as may be desirable to bring before the General Assembly of the Union and also to select delegates to represent the adhering organization at the General Assembly of the Union.

British National Committee for I.C.S.U.

The chairmen of the National Committees corresponding with Unions and Committees of the International Council of Scientific Unions, together with United Kingdom members of the General Committee of I.C.S.U. form the National Committee for I.C.S.U., which is under the chairmanship of the FOREIGN SECRETARY. This committee is particularly concerned with United Kingdom relations with the International Council.

British National Committees corresponding with Unions

For each of the seventeen Unions mentioned above a committee for the United Kingdom has been formed; the functions of such committees are defined in the statutes of the various Unions. In general, they are the promotion of the branches of sciences with which they are concerned, more especially as regards international requirements, the nomination of delegates to represent the United Kingdom at meetings of the Unions, and the initiation of proposals or questions for discussion at such meetings.

These Committees for Astronomy, Biochemistry, Biology, Biophysics, Chemistry, Crystallography, Geodesy and Geophysics, Geography, Geology, History of Science, Medicine and Technology, Mathematics, Nutritional Sciences, Pharmacology, Physics, Physiological Sciences, Radio Science, and Theoretical and Applied Mechanics have been constituted by the Council of the Royal Society, their appointment being governed by the following rules (*Council Minutes*, 26 *May* 1921, 18 *January* 1923, 12 *December* 1963):

The members nominated to a committee by any body shall in no case serve as nominees of that same body for a period exceeding six years consecutively. No ordinary member of a committee shall serve as chairman for more than six years consecutively and when an *ex officio* member of a committee is appointed to act as chairman his tenure of office as chairman shall in no case exceed six consecutive years. All United Kingdom members of the executive bodies of the International Unions are *ex officio* members of the relevant National Committees.

Each committee has power to recommend to the Council of the Royal Society the appointment of 'Additional Members' to the Committee, the number of such additional members not to exceed three at any time, and their appointment in no case to extend beyond the end of the then current three-year period.

Membership of subcommittees, panels, etc. of National Committees is on a personal basis and appointments are made by the appropriate National Committee. There are no general rules governing retirement from subcommittees, panels, etc., but these bodies are encouraged nevertheless to review their membership from time to time in order to ensure the inclusion of scientists active in the science concerned without unduly increasing the number of members.

British National Committees corresponding with Special and Scientific Committees

The Council of the Royal Society has also appointed National Committees on Antarctic Research, on Data for Science and Technology, on Oceanic Research, for Problems of the Environment, for Solar-Terrestrial Physics and on Space Research to correspond with the special and scientific committees set up by the International Council of Scientific Unions. In general, these National Committees have the additional duty of coordinating the United Kingdom scientific programme in relation to the international programmes.

A National Committee for Geodynamics has been formed to correspond with the Inter-Union Commission.

The membership of these National Committees is governed by the following rules (*Council Minutes*, 7 *November* 1963): The chairman of each committee shall review its membership, in consultation with half of the nominating bodies, every three years and make recommendations to Council. All United Kingdom members of the executive bodies of the International Special or Scientific Committees are *ex officio* members of the relevant National Committee.

Membership of subcommittees, panels, etc. of National Committees corresponding with special or scientific committees follows the same practice as for the subordinate bodies of National Committees corresponding with Unions (see above).

British National Committees Corresponding with Other International Organizations

In 1970 Council appointed a representative on the International Committee of the International Centre of Insect Physiology and Ecology, Nairobi. At the same time it appointed a National Committee to advise its representative.

Council in 1972 appointed a National Committee for the International Institute for Applied Systems Analysis, as the Royal Society was one of the twelve founding members of this non-governmental Institute, at Laxenburg, near Vienna.

In 1972, Council established a British National Committee for the Global Atmospheric Research Programme to act as a link to the Joint Organizing Committee set up by I.C.S.U. and the World Meterorological Organization for this international governmental/non-governmental cooperative programme. In 1976 Council reconstituted the British National Committee for the International Geological Correlation Programme, which previously had consisted of members of the National Committee for Geology supplemented by representatives of Government departments.

In 1974, Council appointed—for an initial period of three years—a National Committee for Hydrological Sciences, principally to provide scientific advice to H.M. Government on United Kingdom participation in the Unesco International Hydrological Programme, but also to coordinate United Kingdom activities in relation to other international activities in hydrology and particularly those concerning the I.C.S.U. Committee on Water Research (Cowar).

. . . . . .

The following pages show the membership of the various committees:

(i) British National Committee for I.C.S.U. (p. 136)

(ii) British National Committees corresponding with Unions (see p. 137)

(iii) British National Committees corresponding with Special and Scientific Committees (see p. 150)

(iv) British National Committees corresponding with other international organizations (see p. 154)

NATIONAL COMMITTEE FOR I.C.S.U. [1966]

To advise Council on policy with regard to I.C.S.U., on the appointment of delegates to the General Assembly of I.C.S.U., and to coordinate the work of the British National Committees corresponding with Unions and Committees of I.C.S.U.

CHAIRMAN: THE FOREIGN SECRETARY

ex officio

SIR ARNOLD BURGEN (Member of the General Committee of I.C.S.U.)
DR C. C. BUTLER (Member of the General Committee of I.C.S.U.)
MR L. J. COHEN (Member of the General Committee of I.C.S.U.)
PROFESSOR DOROTHY M. C. HODGKIN (Member of the General Committee of I.C.S.U.)
SIR JOHN KENDREW (Secretary-General of I.C.S.U.)
PROFESSOR R. D. KEYNES (Member of the General Committee of I.C.S.U.)
DR M. G. P. STOKER (Member of the General Committee of I.C.S.U.)

The chairmen of the British National Committees corresponding with Unions and Committees of I.C.S.U.

PROFESSOR M. J. SEATON (Astronomy)
PROFESSOR T. W. GOODWIN (Biochemistry)
PROFESSOR J. M. DODD (Biology)
PROFESSOR D. C. PHILLIPS (Biophysics)
DR T. M. SUGDEN (Chemistry)
PROFESSOR A. J. C. WILSON (Crystallography)
PROFESSOR ALAN H. COOK (Geodesy and Geophysics)
PROFESSOR H. C. DARBY (Geography)
SIR PETER KENT (Geology)
PROFESSOR R. V. JONES (History of Science, Medicine and Technology)
PROFESSOR J. W. S. CASSELS (Mathematics)
PROFESSOR N. W. PIRIE (Nutritional Sciences)
SIR ARNOLD BURGEN (Pharmacology)
PROFESSOR P. H. FOWLER (Physics)
PROFESSOR D. H. SMYTH (Physiological Sciences)
DR J. A. SAXTON (Radio Science)
PROFESSOR P. R. OWEN (Theoretical and Applied Mechanics)
SIR MILES CLIFFORD (Antarctic Research)
PROFESSOR N. KURTI (Data for Science and Technology)
PROFESSOR J. SUTTON (Geodynamics)
SIR GEORGE DEACON (Oceanic Research)
SIR FREDERICK WARNER (Problems of the Environment)
SIR GRANVILLE BEYNON (Solar-Terrestrial Physics)
SIR HARRIE MASSEY (Space Research)
PROFESSOR J. T. HOUGHTON (Global Atmospheric Research Programme)
SIR CHARLES PEREIRA (Hydrological Sciences)
SIR KINGSLEY DUNHAM (International Geological Correlation Programme)

NATIONAL COMMITTEE FOR ASTRONOMY [1919]
CHAIRMAN: PROFESSOR M. J. SEATON

ex officio
PHYSICAL SECRETARY, Royal Society
FOREIGN SECRETARY, Royal Society
ASTRONOMER ROYAL
ASTRONOMER ROYAL for Scotland
DIRECTOR of the Royal Greenwich Observatory
SUPERINTENDENT of the Nautical Almanac Office
PRESIDENT, Royal Astronomical Society
PRESIDENT, British Astronomical Association

Royal Society (6)
§ PROFESSOR D. E. BLACKWELL
* DR R. G. CONWAY
* PROFESSOR B. E. J. PAGEL
* PROFESSOR J. RING
§ PROFESSOR M. J. SEATON
§ DR C. G. WYNN-WILLIAMS

British Astronomical Association (2)
§ DR V. BAROCAS
§ MR G. E. TAYLOR

Royal Astronomical Society (6)
§ DR J. L. CULHANE
* PROFESSOR R. D. DAVIES
§ DR V. P. MYERSCOUGH
* PROFESSOR M. J. REES
§ DR J. R. SHAKESHAFT
* PROFESSOR R. WILSON

Royal Society of Edinburgh (2)
* DR M. J. SMYTH
§ PROFESSOR P. A. SWEET

Science Research Council (1)
* MR M. O. ROBINS

NATIONAL COMMITTEE FOR BIOCHEMISTRY [1955]
CHAIRMAN: PROFESSOR T. W. GOODWIN

ex officio
BIOLOGICAL SECRETARY, Royal Society
FOREIGN SECRETARY, Royal Society
CHAIRMAN, Committee of the Biochemical Society
PROFESSOR P. N. CAMPBELL (Member of the Council of the Union)

Royal Society (7)
* PROFESSOR P. N. CAMPBELL
* PROFESSOR PATRICIA H. CLARKE
§ PROFESSOR T. W. GOODWIN
* PROFESSOR B. S. HARTLEY
* PROFESSOR D. H. NORTHCOTE
§ PROFESSOR R. R. PORTER
* DR WINIFRED M. WATKINS

Association of Clinical Biochemists (1)
* PROFESSOR A. L. LATNER

Biochemical Society (3)
§ PROFESSOR K. BURTON
* PROFESSOR A. N. DAVISON
§ PROFESSOR M. G. HARRINGTON

British Biophysical Society (1)
§ PROFESSOR R. H. PAIN

Chemical Society (3)
§ PROFESSOR G. R. BARKER
§ PROFESSOR W. G. OVEREND
* DR F. A. ROBINSON

Nutrition Society (1)
§ DR D. J. MILLWARD

Physiological Society (1)
* DR D. S. PARSONS

Society of Chemical Industry (1)
§ DR K. SARGEANT

Society for Experimental Biology (1)
* PROFESSOR D. D. DAVIES

Society for General Microbiology (1)
* DR H. J. ROGERS

* To retire 31 December 1978
§ To retire 31 December 1981

NATIONAL COMMITTEE FOR BIOLOGY [1930]

ex officio   CHAIRMAN: PROFESSOR J. M. DODD
BIOLOGICAL SECRETARY, Royal Society
FOREIGN SECRETARY, Royal Society
PROFESSOR A. MACFADYEN (Member of the Executive Committee of the Union)
The CHAIRMEN of the Subcommittees listed below

Royal Society (3)
* PROFESSOR D. J. CRISP
* PROFESSOR N. W. PIRIE
§ PROFESSOR R. RILEY

Royal Society of Edinburgh (1)
§ PROFESSOR M. B. WILKINS

Institute of Biology (1)
* DR T. G. ONIONS

Additional Member
* PROFESSOR J. M. DODD

BIOLOGICAL CONTROL SUBCOMMITTEE

Professor J. S. Kennedy (*chairman*), Mr D. Bevan, Mr T. H. Coaker, Mr D. C. M. Corbett, Dr C. A. Edwards, Dr J. F. D. Frazer, Dr P. T. Haskell, Dr N. W. Hussey, Professor F. G. W. Jones, Mr H. J. Killick, Dr F. G. H. Lupton, Dr R. K. Murton, Dr D. Price Jones, Dr F. J. Simmonds, Dr T. W. Tinsley, Professor M. J. Way, Dr R. J. Wood.

BOTANY SUBCOMMITTEE

ex officio   CHAIRMAN: Professor J. Heslop-Harrison
Professor R. K. S. Wood (Past-President, IUBS Section of Plant Pathology)

To retire 31 December 1978
Dr J. K. A. Bleasdale (*Association of Applied Biologists*), Mr C. D. Brickell (*Royal Horticultural Society*), Dr M. J. Carlile (*Society for General Microbiology*), Professor W. G. Chaloner (*Palaeontological Association*), Dr I. K. Ferguson (*Botanical Society of the British Isles*), Dr D. Gareth Jones (*Federation of British Plant Pathologists*), Professor V. H. Heywood (*Linnean Society*), Mr J. R. Laundon (*British Lichen Society*), Mr H. T. Powell (*British Phycological Society*), Professor R. Riley (*Genetical Society*), Dr J. G. Vaughan (*Phytochemical Society*), Professor R. G. West (*Quaternary Research Association*), Professor F. R. Whatley (*British Photobiology Society*).

To retire 31 December 1981
Dr J. E. Dale (*Society for Experimental Biology*), Dr D. L. Hawksworth (*Systematics Association*), Mr D. M. Henderson (*British Mycological Society*).

ENVIRONMENTAL BIOLOGY SUBCOMMITTEE

ex officio   CHAIRMAN: Professor J. L. Harley
Professor A. Macfadyen (President, IUBS Section of Ecology)
Professor J. S. Weiner (President, IUBS Section of Human Biology)

To retire 31 December 1978
Dr G. R. Coope (*Quaternary Research Association*), Mr R. I. Currie (*Scottish Marine Biological Association*), Professor J. Green (*Zoological Society*), Dr D. L. Gunn (*Association of Applied Biologists*), Mr D. W. Jolly (*Fisheries Society of the British Isles*), Dr Amicia Melland (*British Ornithologists' Union*), Dr M. G. Morris (*Royal Entomological Society*), Mr R. S. Tayler (*British Grassland Society*), Professor J. S. Weiner (*Society for the Study of Human Biology*), Professor R. Whittenbury (*Society for General Microbiology*).

To retire 31 December 1981
Dr G. Boalch (*Marine Biological Association*), Dr P. E. Brandham (*Botanical Society of the British Isles*), Dr D. V. Crawford, Dr G. Fryer (*Freshwater Biological Association*), Mr G. D. Holmes, Dr H. Kruuk (*Association for the Study of Animal Behaviour*), Professor T. R. E. Southwood (*British Ecological Society*), Dr P. Spencer Davies (*Society for Experimental Biology*).

* To retire 31 December 1978
§ To retire 31 December 1981

COMMITTEES ON INTERNATIONAL RELATIONS 139

FUNCTIONAL AND ANALYTICAL BIOLOGY SUBCOMMITTEE
CHAIRMAN: Professor E. J. W. Barrington

ex officio
Dr L. M. Franks (General Secretary, IUBS Section of Cell Biology)
Professor R. Riley (Secretary, IUBS Section of Genetics)

To retire 31 December 1978
Professor E. J. W. Barrington (*Zoological Society*), Professor P. L. Broadhurst (*British Psychological Society*), Dr D. A. Ede (*British Society for Developmental Biology*), Professor J. R. S. Fincham (*Genetical Society*), Dr E. L. Leafe (*Association of Applied Biologists*), Dr W. A. Marshall (*Society for the Study of Human Biology*), Professor A. G. E. Pearse (*Royal Microscopical Society*), Dr B. M. Richards (*British Society for Cell Biology*), Professor M. H. Richmond (*Society for General Microbiology*), Dr P. J. B. Slater (*Association for the Study of Animal Behaviour*), Professor M. A. Sleigh (*Society for Experimental Biology*), Professor J. F. Tait (*Society for Endocrinology*), Dr Angela E. R. Taylor (*British Society for Parasitology*).

MICROBIOLOGY SUBCOMMITTEE
CHAIRMAN: Professor M. H. Richmond

ex officio
Sir Ashley Miles (President, International Association of Microbiological Societies)
Professor P. Wildy (Chairman of the International Association of Microbiological Societies Section of Virology)

To retire 31 December 1978
Professor E. A. Bevan (*Society for Experimental Biology*), Dr D. Gareth Jones (*Federation of British Plant Pathologists*), Dr B. D. Harrison (*Association of Applied Biologists*), Professor D. A. Hopwood (*Genetical Society*), Dr S. P. Lapage (*United Kingdom Federation for Culture Collections*), Dr B. A. Newton (*British Section of the Society of Protozoologists*), Professor S. J. Pirt (*Society of Chemical Industry, Microbiology Fermentation and Enzyme Technology Group*)), Dr M. Richards (*British Society for Mycopathology*), Professor M. H. Richmond (*Society for General Microbiology*), Dr Angela E. R. Taylor (*British Society for Parasitology*).

To retire 31 December 1981
Dr F. Brown (*Society for General Microbiology, virology group*), Dr N. E. Gillies (*British Photobiology Society*), Professor A. A. Glynn (*Pathological Society*), Professor D. H. Jennings (*British Mycological Society*), Professor J. R. Norris (*Society for Applied Bacteriology*), Professor P. A. Sneath (*Society for General Microbiology*).

ZOOLOGY SUBCOMMITTEE
CHAIRMAN: Dr C. A. Wright

ex officio
Dr L. A. Mound (Secretary-Treasurer, IUBS Section of Entomology)
Mr R. V. Melville (Secretary, IUBS Section of Zoological Nomenclature)
Dr B. T. Pickering (Secretary-Treasurer, IUBS Section of Comparative Endocrinology)

To retire 31 December 1978
Professor Ruth E. M. Bowden (*Anatomical Society of Great Britain and Ireland*), Dr C. K. Catchpole (*British Ornithologists' Union*), Professor J. M. Dodd (*Society for Experimental Biology*), Dr B. G. Gardiner (*Linnean Society*), Dr P. E. Gibbs (*Marine Biological Association*), Professor A. Graham (*Malacological Society*), Professor M. R. House (*Palaeontological Association*), Mr F. H. Jacob (*Association of Applied Biologists*), Dr R. Killick-Kendrick (*British Section of the Society of Protozoologists*), Dr Mary F. Lyon (*Genetical Society*), Dr G. Sheals (*Zoological Society*), Dr Angela E. R. Taylor (*British Society for Parasitology*).

To retire 31 December 1981
Dr D. L. Gunn (*Royal Entomological Society*), Dr D. L. Hawksworth (*Systematics Association*).

NATIONAL COMMITTEE FOR BIOPHYSICS [1962]
ex officio CHAIRMAN: PROFESSOR D. C. PHILLIPS
BIOLOGICAL SECRETARY, Royal Society
PHYSICAL SECRETARY, Royal Society
FOREIGN SECRETARY, Royal Society
SECRETARY of the British Biophysical Society
PROFESSOR R. D. KEYNES (Secretary-General of the Union)
PROFESSOR D. C. PHILLIPS (Member of the Council of the Union)

Royal Society (4)
* PROFESSOR P. FATT
§ DR A. KLUG
* PROFESSOR C. G. PHILLIPS
§ PROFESSOR N. D. SYMONDS

Association for Radiation Research (1)
* PROFESSOR J. W. BOAG

Biochemical Society (1)
§ DR J. C. METCALFE

British Biophysical Society (3)
* DR E. M. BRADBURY
§ PROFESSOR W. FULLER
§ DR H. C. WATSON

British Institute of Radiology (1)
*PROFESSOR F. T. FARMER

British Photobiology Society (1)
§ DR J. BARBER

Genetical Society (1)
§ DR C. E. FORD

Hospital Physicists Association (1)
§ PROFESSOR J. R. MALLARD

Physiological Society (1)
* DR R. H. ADRIAN

Society for Experimental Biology (1)
* PROFESSOR J. W. S. PRINGLE

NATIONAL COMMITTEE FOR CHEMISTRY [1935]
ex officio CHAIRMAN: DR T. M. SUGDEN
PHYSICAL SECRETARY, Royal Society
FOREIGN SECRETARY, Royal Society
THE GOVERNMENT CHEMIST
PRESIDENT, Chemical Society
PRESIDENT, Society of Chemical Industry
SIR HAROLD THOMPSON (Past-President of the Union)
SIR DEREK BARTON (Member of the Bureau of the Union)

Royal Society (6)
* PROFESSOR G. ALLEN
§ PROFESSOR C. H. BAMFORD
* PROFESSOR A. R. BATTERSBY
§ PROFESSOR V. GOLD
§ PROFESSOR R. N. HASZELDINE
§ DR F. L. ROSE

Association of Clinical Biochemists (1)
* PROFESSOR J. H. WILKINSON

Biochemical Society (2)
* DR D. F. ELLIOTT
§ PROFESSOR R. J. P. WILLIAMS

Chemical Society (9)
* MR M. P. BERRY
§ MR K. C. BRYANT
* PROFESSOR J. CHATT
* SIR EWART JONES
§ PROFESSOR C. KEMBALL
§ PROFESSOR J. E. SALMON

* PROFESSOR W. G. OVEREND
* MR C. WHALLEY
§ PROFESSOR D. H. WHIFFEN

Institute of Fuel and Institution of Gas Engineers (1)
* DR J. A. GRAY

Institute of Petroleum (1)
§ MR A. L. MILLS

Institution of Chemical Engineers (1)
§ PROFESSOR W. J. THOMAS

Oil and Colour Chemists' Association (1)
§ DR R. C. DENNEY

Society of Chemical Industry (2)
§ DR A. L. SMITH
§ PROFESSOR A. R. J. P. UBBELOHDE

Society of Dyers and Colourists and Society of Leather Technologists and Chemists (1)
* MR J. BOULTON

THE CHAIRMAN of the Analytical Chemistry Subcommittee
THE CHAIRMAN of the Applied Chemistry Subcommittee

Additional Members
* Dr T. M. SUGDEN   * PROFESSOR J. W. BARRETT

* To retire 31 December 1978
§ To retire 31 December 1981

ANALYTICAL CHEMISTRY SUBCOMMITTEE

Professor T. S. West (*chairman*), Professor R. Belcher, Mr K. M. Bills, Professor E. Bishop, Dr A. C. Docherty, Dr H. Egan, Mr R. W. Fennell, Professor H. M. N. H. Irving, Dr M. Kapel, Professor A. J. B. Robertson, Dr F. J. C. Rossotti, Dr R. O. Scott, Dr A. A. Smales, Dr G. Svehla, Dr A. Townshend, Mr C. Whalley, Dr K. A. Williams, the Honorary Secretary of the Analytical Division of the Chemical Society, the Chairman of the Applied Chemistry Subcommittee of the National Committee for Chemistry.

APPLIED CHEMISTRY SUBCOMMITTEE

Dr P. J. Agius (*chairman*), Professor G. Allen, Professor C. H. Bamford, Dr K. A. Barbour, Professor J. W. Barrett, Dr C. B. C. Boyce, Dr J. F. Cavalla, Dr P. L. Clegg, Dr J. D. Cox, Dr H. Egan, Professor N. N. Greenwood, Mr S. G. Luxon, Professor M. L. McGlashan, Professor M. J. Perkins, Professor S. J. Pirt, Mr C. N. Thompson, Mr C. Whalley, the Chairman of the Analytical Chemistry Subcommittee of the National Committee for Chemistry.

NATIONAL COMMITTEE FOR CRYSTALLOGRAPHY [1947]

CHAIRMAN: PROFESSOR A. J. C. WILSON

ex officio
    PHYSICAL SECRETARY, Royal Society
    FOREIGN SECRETARY, Royal Society
    PROFESSOR DOROTHY M. C. HODGKIN (Past-President of the Union)
    CHAIRMAN, Crystallography Group, Institute of Physics
    CHAIRMAN, Chemical Crystallography Group, Chemical Society

Royal Society (7)
  * DR D. M. BLOW
  * PROFESSOR W. COCHRAN
  * PROFESSOR D. W. J. CRUICKSHANK
  § PROFESSOR C. A. TAYLOR
  § DR D. G. WATSON
  * PROFESSOR A. J. C. WILSON
  § PROFESSOR M. M. WOOLFSON

Chemical Society (1)
  § DR P. G. OWSTON

Institute of Physics (1)
  * PROFESSOR M. HART

Metals Society (1)
  § PROFESSOR G. V. RAYNOR

Mineralogical Society (1)
  * PROFESSOR H. F. W. TAYLOR

* To retire 31 December 1978
§ To retire 31 December 1981

NATIONAL COMMITTEE FOR GEODESY AND GEOPHYSICS [1919]

CHAIRMAN: PROFESSOR ALAN H. COOK

ex officio
PHYSICAL SECRETARY, Royal Society
FOREIGN SECRETARY, Royal Society
ASTRONOMER ROYAL
CHAIRMAN, Natural Environment Research Council
DIRECTOR-GENERAL of the Meteorological Office
DIRECTOR of Overseas Surveys
DIRECTOR of the Institute of Geological Sciences
DIRECTOR of Military Survey
DIRECTOR-GENERAL of the Ordnance Survey
HYDROGRAPHER of the Navy
DIRECTOR of the Institute of Oceanographic Sciences
PROFESSOR H. CHARNOCK (Past-President of the Union)
DR P. E. BAKER (Secretary-General, International Association of Volcanology and Chemistry of the Earth's Interior)
CHAIRMAN, British National Committee for Geodynamics
CHAIRMAN, British National Committee for Hydrological Sciences
THE CHAIRMEN of the Subcommittees listed below

Royal Society (11)
§ PROFESSOR N. N. AMBRASEYS
* DR S. BUCHAN
* PROFESSOR I. G. GASS
§ DR P. C. HEDGECOCK
* PROFESSOR R. HIDE
§ PROFESSOR J. A. JACOBS
* MR D. G. KING-HELE
* MR B. R. LEATON
§ DR J. RODDA
* DR J. C. SWALLOW
§ DR H. I. S. THIRLAWAY

British Association (1)
* DR A. W. WOODLAND

Geological Society (2)
* PROFESSOR D. H. GRIFFITHS
* PROFESSOR W. S. PITCHER

Royal Astronomical Society (2)
§ PROFESSOR ALAN H. COOK
* DR J. A. HUDSON

Royal Geographical Society (2)
* SIR EDMUND IRVING

Royal Meteorological Society (2)
* PROFESSOR R. P. PEARCE
§ DR S. A. THORPE

Royal Society of Edinburgh (2)
* PROFESSOR K. M. CREER
§ DR M. GADSDEN

* To retire 31 December 1978
§ To retire 31 December 1981

GEODESY SUBCOMMITTEE

Dr A. R. Robbins (*chairman*), Dr V. Ashkenazi, Brigadier G. Bomford, Major-General R. Ll. Brown, Dr W. Bullerwell, Mr P. J. Carmody, Professor Alan H. Cook, Major-General R. C. A. Edge, Major-General B. St G. Irwin, Mr J. E. Jackson, Sir Harold Jeffreys, Major-General J. Kelsey, Mr D. G. King-Hele, Mr G. W. Lennon, Dr A. C. McLean, Professor R. G. Mason, Mr D. T. F. Munsey, Lt-Col M. R. Richards, Mr H. M. Smith, Mr D. E. Warren, Mr J. A. Weightman.

SATELLITE GEODESY WORKING GROUP

Major-General J. Kelsey (*chairman*), Mr A. L. Allan, Mr C. R. Argent, Dr V. Ashkenazi, Dr D. E. Cartwright, Major J. Eady, Mr D. G. King-Hele, Mr N. A. G. Leppard, Mr B. McInnes, Mrs E. M. Morgan, Lt-Col M. R. Richards, Dr A. R. Robbins, Mr J. A. Weightman.

COMMITTEES ON INTERNATIONAL RELATIONS 143

SEISMOLOGY AND PHYSICS OF THE EARTH'S INTERIOR SUBCOMMITTEE

Dr W. Bullerwell (*chairman*), Professor N. N. Ambraseys, Mr E. F. Baxter, Professor Alan H. Cook, Dr S. Crampin, Dr A. T. J. Dollar, Mr A. Douglas, Dr T. F. Gaskell, Professor D. H. Griffiths, Dr J. A. Hudson, Professor J. A. Jacobs, Sir Harold Jeffreys, Sir Peter Kent, Mr G. W. Lennon, Dr R. E. Long, Professor S. K. Runcorn, Dr H. I. S. Thirlaway, Mr E. Tillotson, Dr P. L. Willmore.

EAST AFRICAN RIFT WORKING GROUP

Professor S. K. Runcorn (*chairman*), Dr W. Bullerwell, Dr J. B. Dawson, Professor I. G. Gass, Dr R. W. Girdler, Professor D. H. Griffiths, Professor A. N. Hunter, Dr M. A. Khan, Professor B. C. King, Dr R. E. Long, Professor R. G. Mason, Mr A. Mayer, Dr H. I. S. Thirlaway.

EARTH STRAIN STUDIES WORKING GROUP

Professor Alan H. Cook (*chairman*), Professor N. N. Ambraseys, Professor M. H. P. Bott, Dr W. Bullerwell, Dr S. Crampin, Dr R. W. Girdler, Professor R. V. Jones, Dr G. C. P. King, Mr G. W. Lennon, Professor R. G. Mason, Dr S. A. F. Murrell, Lt-Col M. R. Richards, Dr W. H. Ward.

HEAT FLOW STUDIES WORKING GROUP

Professor S. K. Runcorn (*chairman*), Dr W. Bullerwell, Professor J. W. Elder Dr T. F. Gaskell, Dr R. W. Girdler, Dr E. R. Oxburgh, Dr D. C. Tozer, Mr J Wheildon.

VOLCANOLOGY AND CHEMISTRY OF THE EARTH'S INTERIOR SUBCOMMITTEE

Professor I. G. Gass (*chairman*), Professor D. K. Bailey, Dr P. E. Baker, Dr J. D. Bell, Professor G. M. Brown, Dr P. E. Brown, Dr W. Bullerwell, Professor J. R. Cann, Professor J. B. Dawson, Dr E. H. Francis, Dr J. E. Guest, Dr D. L. Hamilton, Dr M. M. J. W. Herath, Dr M. J. Le Bas, Professor M. J. O'Hara, Dr J. D. A. Piper, Dr B. G. J. Upton, Professor E. A. Vincent, Dr G. P. L. Walker.

GEOMAGNETISM AND AERONOMY SUBCOMMITTEE

Mr B. R. Leaton (*chairman*), Dr W. Bullerwell, Professor K. M. Creer, Professor J. W. Dungey, Dr M. Gadsden, Dr J. K. Hargreaves, Dr P. C. Hedgecock, Professor J. A. Jacobs, Professor T. R. Kaiser, Professor P. C. Kendall, Dr J. W. King, Dr F. J. Lowes, Dr S. R. C. Malin, Mr G. E. Murt, Dr D. Orr, Dr H. Rishbeth, Dr W. G. V. Rosser, Professor S. K. Runcorn.

METEOROLOGY AND ATMOSPHERIC PHYSICS SUBCOMMITTEE

Professor D. R. Davies (*chairman*), Professor H. Charnock, Sir George Deacon, Mr P. Goldsmith, Dr J. S. A. Green, Professor J. T. Houghton, Professor H. H. Lamb, Professor J. Latham, Dr D. H. McIntosh, Dr R. J. Murgatroyd, Professor R. P. Pearce, Professor R. S. Scorer, Professor P. A. Sheppard.

HYDROLOGY SUBCOMMITTEE

Dr S. Buchan (*chairman*), Mr A. Bleasdale, Dr W. M. Edmunds, Dr J. W. Glen, Dr D. A. Gray, Mr M. Mansell-Moullin, Dr J. S. G. McCulloch, Professor J. L. Monteith, Professor J. F. Nye, Professor T. O'Donnell, Dr H. L. Penman, Sir Charles Pereira, Mr H. J. Richards, Dr J. C. Rodda, Dr D. E. Walling, Dr W. H. Ward, Professor P. O. Wolf.

PHYSICAL SCIENCES OF THE OCEANS SUBCOMMITTEE

Professor K. F. Bowden (*chairman*), Captain R. K. Alcock, Professor T. B. Benjamin, Professor H. Charnock, Mr R. L. Cloet, Dr L. H. N. Cooper, Sir George Deacon, Dr A. E. Gill, Commander N. C. Glen, Sir Edmund Irving, Mr A. J. Lee, Mr G. W. Lennon, Professor M. S. Longuet-Higgins, Dr D. H. Matthews, Dr R. T. Pollard, Dr J. H. Steele, Dr J. C. Swallow.

NATIONAL COMMITTEE FOR GEOGRAPHY [1920]

ex officio   CHAIRMAN: PROFESSOR H. C. DARBY
A SECRETARY, Royal Society (SIR HARRIE MASSEY)
FOREIGN SECRETARY, Royal Society
HYDROGRAPHER of the Navy
DIRECTOR-GENERAL of the Ordnance Survey
DIRECTOR of Military Survey
DIRECTOR of Overseas Surveys
SECRETARY, British Academy
PROFESSOR M. J. WISE (President of the Union)
CHAIRMAN, Cartography Subcommittee
GROUP CAPTAIN, Deputy-Director of Operations (Electronic Warfare and Reconnaissance) (Royal Air Force)

Royal Society (3)
* * PROFESSOR D. V. GLASS
* * DR D. R. STODDART
* * PROFESSOR R. G. WEST

British Academy (3)
* § PROFESSOR J. T. COPPOCK
* * PROFESSOR W. L. D. RAVENHILL
* * PROFESSOR H. R. WILKINSON

British Association (Section E) (1)
* § PROFESSOR W. G. V. BALCHIN

Department of the Environment (1)
* § MR A. BUCHANAN

Geographical Association (3)
* * MR R. A. BEDDIS
* § PROFESSOR S. GREGORY
* * MR J. E. OLD

Institute of British Geographers (3)
* * PROFESSOR E. H. BROWN
* * PROFESSOR R. LAWTON
* § PROFESSOR D. THOMAS

Royal Geographical Society (3)
* * PROFESSOR EILA M. J. CAMPBELL
* § PROFESSOR J. I. CLARKE
* § PROFESSOR J. GOTTMANN

Royal Scottish Geographical Society (2)
* § PROFESSOR G. M. HOWE
* * PROFESSOR R. MILLER

Royal Society of Edinburgh (1)
* * PROFESSOR J. WREFORD WATSON

Scottish Development Department (1)
* § DR C. P. A. LEVEIN

Additional Members
* * PROFESSOR H. C. DARBY
* * PROFESSOR W. R. MEAD

CARTOGRAPHY SUBCOMMITTEE

Brigadier R. A. Gardiner (*chairman*) (*Royal Geographical Society*), Mr K. B. Atkinson (*Photogrammetric Society*), Professor W. G. V. Balchin (*Geographical Association*), Mr J. C. Bartholomew (*Royal Scottish Geographical Society*), Mr D. P. Bickmore (*NERC Experimental Cartography Unit*), Professor G. E. Blackman (*Royal Society*), Dr C. Board (*Institute of British Geographers*), Mr A. Buchanan (*Department of the Environment*), Professor Eila M. J. Campbell, Mr P. K. Clark (*Directorate of Military Survey*), Mr A. G. Dalgliesh (*Ordnance Survey*), Mr H. Fullard, Mr J. S. Keates, Dr D. H. Maling, Mr I. Mumford (*British Cartographic Society*), Mr D. Newson, Mr C. I. M. O'Brien (*Directorate of Overseas Surveys*), Professor A. L. F. Rivet, Mr D. Russom (*Hydrographic Department*), Mr L. Scott (*Royal Institution of Chartered Surveyors*), Dr Helen Wallis (*British Library Map Room*), Dr E. C. Willatts, Brigadier E. P. J. Williams, Dr A. W. Woodland (*Institute of Geological Sciences*).

STANDING SUBCOMMITTEE

Professor H. C. Darby (*chairman*), Colonel R. G. Atkey (*survey organizations*), Mr A. Buchanan (*Department of the Environment/Scottish Development Department*), Professor J. T. Coppock (*Scottish interests*), Professor S. Gregory (*Geographical Association*), Professor J. H. Johnston (*Heads of Geography Departments Conference*), Professor R. Lawton (*Institute of British Geographers*), Professor W. R. Mead (*Royal Geographical Society*), Dr D. R. Stoddart (*Royal Society*), Professor H. R. Wilkinson (*British Academy*).

20TH INTERNATIONAL GEOGRAPHICAL CONGRESS FUND SUBCOMMITTEE

Professor H. C. Darby (*chairman*), Professor E. H. Brown, Professor Eila M. J. Campbell, Professor J. T. Coppock, Professor W. R. Mead, Professor M. J. Wise.

* To retire 31 December 1978
§ To retire 31 December 1981

NATIONAL COMMITTEE FOR GEOLOGY [1959]

CHAIRMAN: SIR PETER KENT

ex officio
PHYSICAL SECRETARY, Royal Society
FOREIGN SECRETARY, Royal Society
DIRECTOR of the Institute of Geological Sciences
FOREIGN SECRETARY, Geological Society
CHAIRMAN, British National Committee for Geodynamics
The CHAIRMEN of the Subcommittees listed below

Royal Society (3)
* * PROFESSOR M. H. P. BOTT
* § DR S. H. U. BOWIE
* § SIR PETER KENT

Geological Society (2)
* * PROFESSOR W. W. BISHOP
* § MR P. F. F. LANCASTER-JONES

Geologists' Association (1)
* § PROFESSOR D. V. AGER

Glasgow Geological Society (1)
* § DR W. D. I. ROLFE

Institute of Oceanographic Sciences
* * DR A. S. LAUGHTON

Institute of Petroleum (1)
* * DR C. A. FOTHERGILL

Institution of Civil Engineers (1)
* § DR A. C. MEIGH

Institution of Mining and Metallurgy (1)
* * MR J. W. PALLISTER

Institution of Mining Engineers (1)
* * PROFESSOR G. HIBBERD

Mineralogical Society (1)
* § MR J. E. T. HORNE

Palaeontological Association (1)
* § PROFESSOR C. H. HOLLAND

Royal Astronomical Society (1)
* * DR T. F. GASKELL

Royal Geographical Society (1)
* § DR D. J. SHEARMAN

Royal Society of Edinburgh (1)
* * MR R. A. EDEN

Yorkshire Geological Society (1)
* * SIR FREDERICK STEWART

Additional Member
* SIR KINGSLEY DUNHAM

ENGINEERING GEOLOGY SUBCOMMITTEE

Professor W. R. Dearman (*chairman*), Mr A. M. Clarke, Mr D. Eastaff, Dr P. G. Fookes, Dr A. B. Hawkins, Professor J. L. Knill, Dr. J. D. Mather, Mr P. F. F. Lancaster-Jones, Professor J. K. T. L. Nash.

GEOCHEMISTRY AND COSMOCHEMISTRY SUBCOMMITTEE

Professor E. A. Vincent (*chairman*), Dr J. R. Butler, Dr A. A. Moss, Professor D. G. Murchison, Dr P. A. Sabine, Dr A. A. Smales, Dr N. J. Snelling, Sir Frederick Stewart, Professor J. S. Webb.

HISTORY OF GEOLOGICAL SCIENCES SUBCOMMITTEE

Dr D. A. Bassett (*chairman*), Professor G. Y. Craig, Professor D. T. Donovan, Dr V. A. Eyles, Dr T. D. Ford, Dr M. J. S. Rudwick, Mr J. C. Thackray.

HYDROGEOLOGY SUBCOMMITTEE

Mr J. B. W. Day (*chairman*), Dr T. C. Atkinson, Mr A. Hunter Blair, Dr S. Buchan, Mr R. A. Downing, Dr W. H. Edmunds, Sir Angus Paton, Professor D. H. Griffiths, Mr B. J. Hardcastle, Dr J. W. Lloyd, Mr H. Piper, Dr W. B. Wilkinson.

QUATERNARY RESEARCH (INQUA) SUBCOMMITTEE

Professor F. W. Shotton (*chairman*), Professor W. W. Bishop, Dr D. Q. Bowen, Mr W. B. Evans, Mr E. A. Francis, Sir Harry Godwin, Dr W. G. Jardine, Dr P. A. Mellars, Dr L. F. Penny, Professor R. G. West.

* To retire 31 December 1978
§ To retire 31 December 1981

NATIONAL COMMITTEE FOR THE HISTORY OF SCIENCE, MEDICINE AND TECHNOLOGY [1960]

CHAIRMAN: PROFESSOR R. V. JONES

ex officio
A SECRETARY, Royal Society (PROFESSOR D. C. PHILLIPS)
FOREIGN SECRETARY, Royal Society
DIRECTOR of the Science Museum
PRESIDENT, British Society for the History of Science
DR J. NEEDHAM (Past-President of the History Division of the Union)
DR F. GREENAWAY (Secretary-General of the History Division of the Union)

Royal Society (7)
§ SIR GEORGE DEACON
§ DR E. G. FORBES
* PROFESSOR F. C. FRANK
§ PROFESSOR R. V. JONES
* PROFESSOR W. D. M. PATON
* PROFESSOR J. S. ROWLINSON
* PROFESSOR F. SONDHEIMER

British Academy (1)
§ PROFESSOR MARY HESSE

British Society for the History of Science (2)
§ DR R. H. FOX
§ PROFESSOR A. R. HALL

Newcomen Society (1)
* MR R. J. LAW

Worshipful Society of Apothecaries (1)
* DR T. D. WHITTET

Additional Member
* PROFESSOR D. S. L. CARDWELL

CONTEMPORARY SCIENTIFIC ARCHIVES SUBCOMMITTEE

Professor N. Kurti (*chairman*), Professor Margaret M. Gowing, Lord Hinton of Bankside, Professor R. V. Jones, Mr M. W. Leonard, Professor W. D. M. Paton, Professor J. S. Rowlinson.

NATIONAL COMMITTEE FOR MATHEMATICS [1949]

CHAIRMAN: PROFESSOR J. W. S. CASSELS

ex officio
PHYSICAL SECRETARY, Royal Society
FOREIGN SECRETARY, Royal Society
PROFESSOR J. W. S. CASSELS (Vice-President of the Union)

Royal Society (3)
§ PROFESSOR M. F. ATIYAH
* PROFESSOR F. F. BONSALL
* PROFESSOR I. M. JAMES

Edinburgh Mathematical Society (1)
* PROFESSOR A. G. MACKIE

Institute of Mathematics and its Applications (1)
* DR J. H. WILKINSON

London Mathematical Society (3)
§ DR W. H. COCKCROFT
* PROFESSOR H. HALBERSTAM
* PROFESSOR C. T. C. WALL

Mathematical Association (1)
* MR J. W. HERSEE

Royal Society of Edinburgh (1)
* PROFESSOR W. N. EVERITT

Royal Statistical Society (1)
*PROFESSOR R. L. PLACKETT

THE CHAIRMAN of the Mathematical Instruction Subcommittee

MATHEMATICAL INSTRUCTION SUBCOMMITTEE

Professor J. V. Armitage (*chairman*), Mr M. Bridger, Professor H. Halberstam, Professor J. Hunter, Mr R. Jeffrey, Mr A. J. McIntosh, Mr A. Penfold, Miss H. B. Shuard, Dr J. H. Wilkinson, Mrs E. M. Williams.

* To retire 31 December 1978
§ To retire 31 December 1981

COMMITTEES ON INTERNATIONAL RELATIONS 147

NATIONAL COMMITTEE FOR NUTRITIONAL SCIENCES [1964]
CHAIRMAN: PROFESSOR N. W. PIRIE
ex officio
BIOLOGICAL SECRETARY, Royal Society
FOREIGN SECRETARY, Royal Society
PRESIDENT of the Nutrition Society
MISS D. F. HOLLINGSWORTH (Member of the Council of the Union)

Royal Society (4)
* PROFESSOR R. A. McCANCE
* PROFESSOR A. NEUBERGER
§ PROFESSOR N. W. PIRIE
§ DR ELSIE M. WIDDOWSON

Biochemical Society (1)
*PROFESSOR D. ROBINSON

British Nutrition Foundation (1)
§ DR R. G. WHITEHEAD

Nutrition Society (4)
§ DR D. J. NAISMITH
* DR G. L. S. PAWAN
§ DR J. D. SUTTON
* PROFESSOR A. S. TRUSWELL

Physiological Society (1)
§ DR J. V. G. A. DURNIN

Society of Chemical Industry (Food Group) (1)
§ PROFESSOR J. B. M. COPPOCK

Society for General Microbiology (1)
§ DR ELLA M. BARNES

U.K. Council for Food Science and Technology (4)
§ PROFESSOR A. E. BENDER
* DR W. F. J. CUTHBERTSON
* PROFESSOR J. HAWTHORN

NATIONAL COMMITTEE FOR PHARMACOLOGY [1972]
CHAIRMAN: SIR ARNOLD BURGEN
ex officio
BIOLOGICAL SECRETARY, Royal Society
FOREIGN SECRETARY, Royal Society
FOREIGN SECRETARY, British Pharmacological Society
SIR ARNOLD BURGEN (Past-President of the Union)
PROFESSOR C. T. DOLLERY (Member of the Council of the Union)

Royal Society (4)
* SIR ARNOLD BURGEN
* PROFESSOR G. S. DAWES
§ PROFESSOR D. V. PARKE
§ PROFESSOR R. H. S. THOMPSON

Biochemical Society (1)
§ DR R. J. B. KING

Chemical Society (1)
* SIR FRANK HARTLEY

Medical Research Society (1)
* PROFESSOR D. G. GRAHAME-SMITH

Pharmaceutical Society of Great Britain (1)
§ PROFESSOR P. S. J. SPENCER

Pharmacological Society (4)
§ PROFESSOR E. W. HORTON
* PROFESSOR G. P. LEWIS
§ DR A. J. SMITH
* DR J. R. VANE

Physiological Society (1)
§ PROFESSOR C. B. FERRY

Society for Drug Research (1)
* DR D. JACK

Society for Endocrinology (1)
§ PROFESSOR M. GINSBURG

Society for General Microbiology (1)
* PROFESSOR M. R. W. BROWN

NATIONAL COMMITTEE FOR PHYSICS [1921]
CHAIRMAN: PROFESSOR P. H. FOWLER
ex officio
PHYSICAL SECRETARY, Royal Society
FOREIGN SECRETARY, Royal Society
DIRECTOR of the National Physical Laboratory
CONTROLLER of Establishment and Research, Ministry of Defence
DR C. C. BUTLER (President of the Union)
PROFESSOR A. SALAM (a Vice-President of the Union)

* To retire 31 December 1978 § To retire 31 December 1981

148   YEAR BOOK OF THE ROYAL SOCIETY

Royal Society (4)
* Professor M. BLACKMAN
§ Professor D. J. BRADLEY
§ Professor F. C. FRANK
* Dr H. G. KUHN

British Institute of Radiology (1)
§ Dr J. F. FOWLER

Institute of Physics (3)
§ Professor R. G. CHAMBERS
§ Professor E. R. DOBBS
* Professor DAPHNE F. JACKSON

Institution of Electrical Engineers (1)
* Dr G. D. SIMS

Royal Meteorological Society (1)
* Dr F. PASQUILL

Royal Society of Edinburgh (1)
§ Professor S. D. SMITH

The CHAIRMAN of the Optical Subcommittee

Additional Member
* Professor P. H. FOWLER

OPTICAL SUBCOMMITTEE

To act through the National Committee for Physics in matters connected with the International Commission for Optics.

Professor W. R. S. Garton (chairman), Dr K. G. Birch, Professor D. J. Bradley, Professor Alan H. Cook, Mr J. N. Davidson, Mr D. Day, Dr H. A. Gebbie, Professor H. H. Hopkins, Dr E. R. Pike, Professor W. C. Price, Mr F. H. Smith, Mr W. N. Sproson, Mr G. L'E. Turner, Professor W. T. Welford.

NATIONAL COMMITTEE FOR PHYSIOLOGICAL SCIENCES [1955]

Chairman: Professor D. H. SMYTH

ex officio
BIOLOGICAL SECRETARY, Royal Society
FOREIGN SECRETARY, Royal Society
Professor E. NEIL (President of the Union)

Royal Society (4)
§ Professor H. B. BARLOW
* Professor R. J. FITZPATRICK
§ Dr J. T. FITZSIMONS
§ Dr D. NOBLE

Biochemical Society (1)
* Dr D. C. WATTS

Pharmacological Society (2)
§ Professor J. W. BLACK
* Professor G. V. R. BORN

Physiological Society (4)
§ Dr R. S. COMLINE
* Professor S. M. HILTON
* Professor D. H. SMYTH
* Professor R. WHITTAM

Society for Experimental Biology (1)
§ Professor W. T. W. POTTS

Additional Member
* Professor C. G. PHILLIPS

NATIONAL COMMITTEE FOR RADIO SCIENCE [1920]

ex officio   Chairman: Dr J. A. SAXTON
PHYSICAL SECRETARY, Royal Society
FOREIGN SECRETARY, Royal Society
DIRECTOR of the Appleton Laboratory (S.R.C.)
Sir GRANVILLE BEYNON (Past-President of the Union)
Dr J. W. KING (Chairman, U.R.S.I. Commission G)

* To retire 31 December 1978
§ To retire 31 December 1981

COMMITTEES ON INTERNATIONAL RELATIONS

Royal Society (8)
* PROFESSOR H. E. M. BARLOW
§ PROFESSOR K. W. CATTERMOLE
* PROFESSOR A. L. CULLEN
§ PROFESSOR J. G. DAVIES
* DR L. ESSEN
* SIR MARTIN RYLE
§ DR J. O. THOMAS
§ DR P. A. WATSON

British Broadcasting Corporation (1)
* MR G. D. MONTEATH

Directorate of Radio Technology (Home Office) (1)
§ MR W. H. BELLCHAMBERS

Institute of Physics (2)
§ DR R. S. BOOTH
* DR T. B. JONES

Institution of Electrical Engineers (2)
§ PROFESSOR E. A. ASH
* DR F. HORNER

Meteorological Office (1)
§ MR J. CRABTREE

Ministry of Defence (Procurement Executive) (1)
§ DR G. N. TAYLOR

Ministry of Defence (1)
§AIR VICE-MARSHAL S. M. DAVIDSON

National Physical Laboratory (1)
* MR A. E. BAILEY

Post Office (1)
§ DR J. THIRLWELL

Royal Society of Edinburgh (2)
* PROFESSOR G. R. NICOLL
§ MR A. C. WESLEY

NATIONAL COMMITTEE FOR THEORETICAL AND APPLIED MECHANICS [1947]

ex officio CHAIRMAN: PROFESSOR P. R. OWEN
PHYSICAL SECRETARY, Royal Society
FOREIGN SECRETARY, Royal Society
SIR JAMES LIGHTHILL (Member of the Bureau of the Union)
PROFESSOR G. K. BATCHELOR (Chairman, Euromech Committee)
PROFESSOR L. MAUNDER (President of the International Federation for the Theory of Machines and Mechanisms)

Royal Society (6)
§ PROFESSOR R. HIDE
* PROFESSOR D. W. HOLDER
* DR E. H. MANSFIELD
§ DR H. K. MOFFATT
* PROFESSOR D. C. PACK
§ DR D. A. SPENCE

British Society of Rheology (1)
*PROFESSOR K. WALTERS

Council of Engineering Institutions (1)
*PROFESSOR R. E. D. BISHOP

Institute of Acoustics (1)
* PROFESSOR P. E. DOAK

Institute of Mathematics and its Applications (1)
§ PROFESSOR T. B. BENJAMIN

Institute of Physics (1)
*PROFESSOR J. F. RAFFLE

Institution of Chemical Engineers (1)
* MR S. P. S. ANDREW

Institution of Civil Engineers (1)
§ DR B. RICHMOND

Institution of Mechanical Engineers (2)
§ PROFESSOR D. E. NEWLAND
* DR J. M. PRENTIS

London Mathematical Society (1)
* DR A. B. TAYLER

Royal Aeronautical Society (1)
§ PROFESSOR R. D. MILNE

Royal Institution of Naval Architects (1)
§ PROFESSOR G. J. GOODRICH

Royal Meteorological Society (1)
* DR P. G. DRAZIN

Additional Member
* PROFESSOR P. R. OWEN

MACHINES AND MECHANISMS SUBCOMMITTEE

To advise the National Committee on matters concerning the International Federation for the Theory of Machines and Mechanisms.

Dr J. M. Prentis (*chairman*), Professor R. E. D. Bishop, Dr J. N. Fawcett, Mr J. R. Jones, Professor L. Maunder, Professor D. E. Newland.

* To retire 31 December 1978
§ To retire 31 December 1981

NATIONAL COMMITTEE ON ANTARCTIC RESEARCH [1958]
CHAIRMAN: SIR MILES CLIFFORD

ex officio
BIOLOGICAL SECRETARY, Royal Society
PHYSICAL SECRETARY, Royal Society
FOREIGN SECRETARY, Royal Society
DIRECTOR of the British Antarctic Survey
DIRECTOR OF RESEARCH, Meteorological Office
DIRECTOR of Overseas Surveys
HYDROGRAPHER of the Navy
DIRECTOR of the Institute of Oceanographic Sciences
SECRETARY, Natural Environment Research Council
DR G. DE Q. ROBIN (U.K. delegate to S.C.A.R.)

Royal Society (10)
DR R. J. ADIE
SIR MILES CLIFFORD
DR F. C. FRASER
SIR VIVIAN FUCHS
DR D. H. MATTHEWS
DR M. W. HOLDGATE
MR W. R. PIGGOTT
MR A. H. SHEFFIELD
PROFESSOR F. W. SHOTTON
DR P. L. WILLMORE

Royal Geographical Society (2)
SIR GEORGE DEACON
REAR-ADMIRAL SIR EDMUND IRVING

Medical Research Council (1)
DR O. G. EDHOLM

Royal Meteorological Society (1)
PROFESSOR H. H. LAMB

Royal Society of Edinburgh (1)
DR W. L. S. FLEMING

Scott Polar Research Institute (1)
DR D. J. DREWRY

NATIONAL COMMITTEE ON DATA FOR SCIENCE AND TECHNOLOGY [1966]
CHAIRMAN: PROFESSOR N. KURTI

ex officio
PHYSICAL SECRETARY, Royal Society
FOREIGN SECRETARY, Royal Society
PROFESSOR H. GUTFREUND (Member of the Executive Committee of Codata)
PROFESSOR N. KURTI (Treasurer of Codata)

Royal Society (10)
DR S. ANGUS
MR C. F. BEATON
PROFESSOR G. BLACK
PROFESSOR G. Y. CRAIG
PROFESSOR H. GUTFREUND
DR OLGA KENNARD
MR R. W. McINTYRE
PROFESSOR J. S. ROWLINSON
SIR GORDON SUTHERLAND
PROFESSOR A. J. C. WILSON

British Library (1)
MR D. H. MAY

Department of Industry (3)
DR H. EGAN
DR D. A. EVEREST
DR J. SUTTON

Science Research Council (1)
PROFESSOR R. MASON

COMMITTEES ON INTERNATIONAL RELATIONS 151

NATIONAL COMMITTEE FOR GEODYNAMICS [1971]
CHAIRMAN: PROFESSOR J. SUTTON
ex officio
PHYSICAL SECRETARY, Royal Society
FOREIGN SECRETARY, Royal Society
CHAIRMAN, British National Committee for Geodesy and Geophysics
CHAIRMAN, British National Committee for Geology

PROFESSOR M. H. P. BOTT
PROFESSOR J. C. BRIDEN
PROFESSOR ALAN H. COOK
DR T. F. GASKELL
PROFESSOR I. G. GASS
PROFESSOR J. A. JACOBS
DR A. S. LAUGHTON
DR D. H. MATTHEWS

PROFESSOR M. J. O'HARA
DR E. R. OXBURGH
PROFESSOR S. K. RUNCORN
PROFESSOR R. M. SHACKLETON
PROFESSOR J. SUTTON
DR H. I. S. THIRLAWAY
PROFESSOR F. J. VINE

NATIONAL COMMITTEE ON OCEANIC RESEARCH [1959]
CHAIRMAN: SIR GEORGE DEACON
ex officio
PHYSICAL SECRETARY, Royal Society
FOREIGN SECRETARY, Royal Society
DIRECTOR of Fishery Research, Ministry of Agriculture, Fisheries and Food
DIRECTOR of Fisheries Research, Department of Agriculture and Fisheries for Scotland
DIRECTOR of the British Antarctic Survey
DIRECTOR of Research, Meteorological Office
DIRECTOR of the Institute of Oceanographic Sciences
DIRECTOR of Underwater Research, Ministry of Defence
CHAIRMAN, Preparatory Group C, Natural Environment Research Council
CHAIRMAN, Preparatory Group D, Natural Environment Research Council
CHAIRMAN, Advisory Committee on International Oceanographic Affairs, Natural Environment Research Council
SECRETARY, Natural Environment Research Council
HYDROGRAPHER of the Navy
CHAIRMAN, Subcommittee, Physical Sciences of the Oceans, National Committee for Geodesy and Geophysics

Royal Society (9)
PROFESSOR K. F. BOWDEN
DR H. A. COLE
MR P. M. DAVID
PROFESSOR E. J. DENTON
DR F. C. FRASER
DR T. F. GASKELL
DR A. S. LAUGHTON
PROFESSOR J. E. G. RAYMONT
DR J. C. SWALLOW
British Museum (Natural History) (1)
DR J. G. SHEALS
Challenger Society (1)
MR A. J. LEE
Council of Engineering Institutions (1)
MR J. M. WRIGHT
Geological Society (1)
PROFESSOR D. CURRY

Linnean Society (1)
DR Q. BONE

Marine Biological Association (1)
DR M. R. CLARKE

Royal Astronomical Society (1)
DR D. H. MATTHEWS

Royal Geographical Society (1)
SIR GEORGE DEACON

Royal Meteorological Society (1)
DR S. A. THORPE

Royal Society of Edinburgh (1)
DR J. H. STEELE

Scottish Marine Biological Association (1)
MR R. I. CURRIE

NATIONAL COMMITTEE FOR PROBLEMS OF THE ENVIRONMENT [1971]

CHAIRMAN: SIR FREDERICK WARNER

ex officio
PHYSICAL SECRETARY, Royal Society
FOREIGN SECRETARY, Royal Society
DR R. W. J. KEAY (Treasurer of S.C.O.P.E.)

PROFESSOR J. H. BIRD
DR T. A. CONNORS
DR G. W. COOKE
SIR RICHARD DOLL
DR H. EGAN
MR P. GOLDSMITH
PROFESSOR G. T. GOODMAN
PROFESSOR J. L. HARLEY
DR M. W. HOLDGATE

PROFESSOR T. R. LEE
SIR CYRIL LUCAS
PROFESSOR A. NEUBERGER
PROFESSOR D. D. REID
DR T. M. SUGDEN
SIR FREDERICK WARNER
PROFESSOR V. C. WYNNE-EDWARDS

Department of the Environment (1)
MR A. J. FAIRCLOUGH

Natural Environment Research Council (1)
MR R. J. H. BEVERTON

NATIONAL COMMITTEE FOR SOLAR-TERRESTRIAL PHYSICS [1968]

CHAIRMAN: SIR GRANVILLE BEYNON

ex officio
PHYSICAL SECRETARY, Royal Society
FOREIGN SECRETARY, Royal Society
DR J. W. KING (Vice-President of S.C.O.S.T.P.)

SIR GRANVILLE BEYNON
DR G. M. BROWN
DR D. L. CROOM
DR P. C. HEDGECOCK
PROFESSOR T. R. KAISER
MR B. R. LEATON
MR W. R. PIGGOTT
DR D. REES

DR H. RISHBETH
MISS P. ROTHWELL
DR J. A. SAXTON
DR D. J. SOUTHWOOD
DR K. H. STEWART
DR L. THOMAS
DR G. L. WRENN

NATIONAL COMMITTEE ON SPACE RESEARCH [1959]

CHAIRMAN: SIR HARRIE MASSEY

ex officio
BIOLOGICAL SECRETARY, Royal Society
PHYSICAL SECRETARY, Royal Society
FOREIGN SECRETARY, Royal Society
CHAIRMAN, Astronomy, Space and Radio Board, Science Research Council
DIRECTOR of the Appleton Laboratory
U.K. delegate to Cospar

Royal Society (12)
PROFESSOR R. L. F. BOYD
PROFESSOR P. H. FOWLER
PROFESSOR G. V. GROVES
PROFESSOR R. HIDE
MR D. G. KING-HELE
SIR IEUAN MADDOCK
MR G. K. C. PARDOE
PROFESSOR N. W. PIRIE
MR M. O. ROBINS
PROFESSOR A. P. WILLMORE
PROFESSOR R. WILSON
MR H. S. WOLFF

Institution of Electrical Engineers (1)
MR R. DALZIEL

Institute of Physics (1)
SIR GRANVILLE BEYNON

Meteorological Office (1)
DR K. H. STEWART

Ministry of Defence (Procurement Executive) (1)
MR H. G. R. ROBINSON

United Kingdom Industrial Space Committee (4)
MR G. DAWSON
MR D. O. FRASER
DR J. W. HEATON
MR W. R. THOMAS

Physiological Society (1)
GROUP CAPTAIN P. HOWARD

Royal Aeronautical Society (1)
MR J. L. CROWDER

Royal Astronomical Society (1)
PROFESSOR K. A. POUNDS

Royal Meteorological Society (1)
PROFESSOR P. A. SHEPPARD

Science Research Council (1)
DR H. H. ATKINSON

Additional Members
DR DAPHNE J. OSBORNE
DR M. J. RYCROFT

SUBCOMMITTEE ON BIOLOGICAL EXPERIMENTS

Professor N. W. Pirie (*chairman*), Professor P. Alexander, Professor G. Eglinton, Group Captain P. Howard, Professor J. R. Postgate, Professor P. H. A. Sneath, Professor F. R. Whatley, Mr H. S. Wolff.

SUBCOMMITTEE ON OPTICAL TRACKING

Mr D. G. King-Hele (*chairman*), Mr D. M. Brierley, Dr C. J. Brookes, Major J. Eady, Mr R. D. Eberst, Mr H. G. Miles, Mrs E. M. Morgan, Mr D. A. Richards, Mr G. E. Taylor, Mrs D. C. Walker, Mr M. D. Waterman.

SUBCOMMITTEE ON PLANETARY SCIENCES

Professor R. Hide (*chairman*), Dr M. Bowthorpe, Professor G. Eglinton, Dr A. H. Gabriel, Dr J. E. Guest, Dr P. C. Hedgecock, Dr G. E. Hunt, Professor W. H. McCrea, Professor A. J. Meadows, Dr A. I. Rees, Dr H. Rishbeth, Professor S. K. Runcorn, Professor P. A. Sweet, Professor M. M. Woolfson.

NATIONAL COMMITTEE FOR THE GLOBAL ATMOSPHERIC RESEARCH PROGRAMME [1972]

CHAIRMAN: PROFESSOR J. T. HOUGHTON

ex officio
PHYSICAL SECRETARY, Royal Society
FOREIGN SECRETARY, Royal Society
DIRECTOR-GENERAL, Meteorological Office
DIRECTOR, Institute of Oceanographic Sciences
DIRECTOR of Naval Oceanography and Meteorology, Ministry of Defence

Royal Society (5)
PROFESSOR R. HIDE
PROFESSOR J. T. HOUGHTON
SIR JAMES LIGHTHILL
PROFESSOR P. A. SHEPPARD
DR J. C. SWALLOW

Meteorological Office (3)
MR G. A. CORBY
MR A. GILCHRIST
DR K. H. STEWART

Natural Environment Research Council (1)
MR J. S. SAWYER

Royal Meteorological Society (1)
PROFESSOR R. P. PEARCE

Science Research Council (1)
DR H. H. ATKINSON

AIR-SEA INTERACTION SUBCOMMITTEE

Professor H. Charnock (*chairman*), Captain R. K. Alcock, Mr C. J. Bridger, Dr D. J. Carson, Mr J. Crease, Mr H. D. Dooley, Dr D. J. Ellett, Mr A. E. Fisher, Mr P. Goldsmith, Mr A. J. Lee, Mr P. H. Lindop, Lt-Cmdr T. McAndrew, Dr R. T. Pollard, Professor P. A. Sheppard, Dr J. C. Swallow, Dr N. Thompson.

NATIONAL COMMITTEE FOR HYDROLOGICAL SCIENCES [1975]

CHAIRMAN: SIR CHARLES PEREIRA
VICE-CHAIRMAN: MR J. S. SAWYER

ex officio
PHYSICAL SECRETARY, Royal Society
FOREIGN SECRETARY, Royal Society
CHAIRMAN, Inter-departmental Committee on International Hydrology
CHAIRMAN, Hydrology Subcommittee, British National Committee for Geodesy and Geophysics
CHAIRMAN, Hydrogeology Subcommittee, British National Committee for Geology

MR V. K. COLLINGE
PROFESSOR G. E. FOGG
PROFESSOR M. J. HAMLIN

DR J. S. G. McCULLOCH
SIR NORMAN ROWNTREE
PROFESSOR A. W. SKEMPTON

NATIONAL COMMITTEE FOR THE INTERNATIONAL CENTRE OF INSECT PHYSIOLOGY AND ECOLOGY [1970]

CHAIRMAN: PROFESSOR J. W. S. PRINGLE

ex officio
BIOLOGICAL SECRETARY, Royal Society
FOREIGN SECRETARY, Royal Society

DR J. N. BRADY
DR C. G. BUTLER
DR P. T. HASKELL
SIR ALAN HODGKIN
PROFESSOR A. W. JOHNSON
DR C. G. JOHNSON

PROFESSOR J. S. KENNEDY
PROFESSOR J. W. S. PRINGLE
DR R. C. RAINEY
PROFESSOR T. R. E. SOUTHWOOD
SIR VINCENT WIGGLESWORTH

NATIONAL COMMITTEE FOR THE INTERNATIONAL GEOLOGICAL CORRELATION PROGRAMME [1973]

CHAIRMAN: SIR KINGSLEY DUNHAM

ex officio
PHYSICAL SECRETARY, Royal Society
FOREIGN SECRETARY, Royal Society
FOREIGN SECRETARY, Geological Society
CHAIRMAN, National Committee for Geology
CHAIRMAN, National Committee for Geodynamics
DIRECTOR, Institute of Geological Sciences

PROFESSOR D. V. AGER
PROFESSOR W. W. BISHOP
DR J. W. COWIE
PROFESSOR K. M. CREER
SIR KINGSLEY DUNHAM
PROFESSOR I. G. GASS
DR J. M. HANCOCK
MR W. B. HARLAND
PROFESSOR C. H. HOLLAND

MR N. F. HUGHES
PROFESSOR B. C. KING
DR A. S. LAUGHTON
DR J. D. LAWSON
PROFESSOR W. S. PITCHER
DR D. J. SHEARMAN
PROFESSOR F. W. SHOTTON
PROFESSOR R. G. WEST
DR B. F. WINDLEY

Department of the Environment (1)
MR W. G. B. PHILLIPS

Natural Environment Research Council (1)
MR A. E. S. MAYER

Ministry of Overseas Development (1)
MR D. A. BELL

NATIONAL COMMITTEE FOR THE INTERNATIONAL INSTITUTE FOR APPLIED SYSTEMS ANALYSIS [1972]

CHAIRMAN: SIR KINGSLEY DUNHAM

ex officio
TREASURER, Royal Society
PHYSICAL SECRETARY, Royal Society
FOREIGN SECRETARY, Royal Society
SIR KINGSLEY DUNHAM (Member of the Council of I.I.A.S.A.)

Royal Society (8)
PROFESSOR D. R. COX
PROFESSOR A. S. DOUGLAS
PROFESSOR J. F. C. KINGMAN
SIR JAMES LIGHTHILL
PROFESSOR D. D. REID
MR R. C. TOMLINSON
DR J. H. WILKINSON
LORD ZUCKERMAN

Centre for Environmental Studies (1)
DR T. A. BROADBENT

Council of Engineering Institutions (2)
PROFESSOR J. F. COALES
SIR ANGUS PATON

Department of the Environment (2)
DR M. W. HOLDGATE
MR P. C. ROBERTS

Department of Energy (1)
MR T. A. KENNEDY

Department of Industry (1)
MR D. HARRISON

Operational Research Society (1)
MR A. M. LEE

Science Research Council (1)
PROFESSOR H. H. ROSENBROCK

Social Science Research Council (1)
PROFESSOR P. D. HENDERSON

PUBLIC AND OTHER RESPONSIBILITIES

CUSTODIANS: STANDARD WEIGHTS AND MEASURES
(WEIGHTS AND MEASURES ACT, 1878)
The imperial standard yard and pound are at the Standards Office of the Board of Trade. Of the four copies of each of them, deposited in other places in case of injury to or loss of the standards, one set is in the custody of the Royal Society.

PARLIAMENTARY GRANT-IN-AID
Since 1849 the Royal Society has administered a Parliamentary Grant-in-aid. Until 1964 such Parliamentary Grants-in-aid were negotiated with H.M. Treasury and came in a specified series of grants for particular purposes. Since 1964 one comprehensive Parliamentary Grant-in-aid has been made annually to the Society to be used for a variety of purposes negotiated with the Department of Education and Science. The history of these Parliamentary Grants-in-aid is to be found in *The Record*, pp. 185–193, and in the Society's *Year Books* 1940–1976.

The table below indicates the growth in recent years and principal uses of the Parliamentary Grant-in-aid:

	1964/65 £	1968/69 £	1972/73 £	1976/77 £
Research professorships	45 600	100 200	146 440	263 220
Exchange fellowships, etc.		115 000	868 800	561 970
Travel grants, etc.	34 917	88 720	100 100	206 580
Scientific investigations	100 000	127 930	218 440	313 480
Scientific publications and libraries assistance	10 000	10 000	11 700	14 210
Rating assistance		35 000	43 500	50 280
History of science			1 300	21 860
Science/technology relations and education			14 000	29 510
Subscriptions to unions etc.	26 878	46 330	66 000	128 430
International Biological Programme scientific projects		88 800	51 240	
Aldabra research station		40 070	33 500	66 550

The Parliamentary Grant-in-aid is administered by Council which has authority to alter the amount from one category to another except for a few specially earmarked grants. The arrangements made by Council for the administration of the principal sections of the Parliamentary Grant-in-aid and related information are set out elsewhere in the *Year Book*, e.g., research professorships (p. 262), exchange fellowships (mainly directed to the European Science Exchange Programme (p. 254), travel grants (p. 252), scientific investigations (pp. 129, 202), scientific publications and libraries assistance (pp. 130, 204), history of science (p. 205), subscriptions to unions, etc. (p. 206). For allocations and awards, see pp. 267, 367, 378, 383, 384).

PUBLIC AND OTHER RESPONSIBILITIES

In addition, the Royal Society appoints or nominates representatives to the institutions and other bodies in the following list.

City and Guilds of London Institute (Governor)	Appointed
THE PRESIDENT	*ex officio*
Conway Evans Trust	
THE PRESIDENT	*ex officio*
Goodall Lecture Committee Society of Apothecaries (Nomination to)	
THE PRESIDENT	*ex officio*
Hunterian Museum (Trustee)	
THE PRESIDENT	*ex officio*
Victor Horsley Memorial Fund	
THE PRESIDENT	*ex officio*
Agricultural Research Council (Assessor)	
DR G. D. H. BELL	16 Dec. 1976
Algae and Protozoa Culture Centre Steering Committee	
DR J. W. G. LUND	12 Dec. 1968
Aslib: Council	
PROFESSOR J. M. ZIMAN	10 Feb. 1972
Aslib: International Relations Committee	
PROFESSOR N. SHEPPARD	1 Sept. 1975
Aston University: Convocation	
PROFESSOR G. V. RAYNOR	5 May 1966
Bath University Court	
PROFESSOR A. R. COLLAR	1 Aug. 1972
Biological Council (Observer)	
PROFESSOR R. WHITTAM	1 Jan. 1976
Biological Council's Co-ordinating Committee for Symposia on Drug Action	
PROFESSOR W. S. FELDBERG	16 June 1960
Biological Information: Joint Institute of Biology/Biological Council/Aslib Committee	
PROFESSOR E. J. W. BARRINGTON	11 Nov. 1971
Birmingham University Court	
DR D. W. PASHLEY	1 Jan. 1976
Bradford University Court	
DR J. H. CHESTERS	1 Dec. 1969
Bragg Lecture Fund Committee	
DR C. W. BUNN	11 Nov. 1971
Bristol University Court	
SIR STANLEY HOOKER	16 July 1970
British Academy: Committee for the Study of the Conservation of Medieval Stained Glass	
PROFESSOR N. KURTI	13 May 1976
DR D. S. OLIVER	13 May 1976
SIR GORDON SUTHERLAND	13 May 1976

British Academy: Committee on cheaper methods of book production   Appointed
SIR GORDON SUTHERLAND . . . . . 17 May 1973
British Academy: National Committee for the Philosophy of Science
PROFESSOR W. H. MCCREA . . . . . 12 July 1973
SIR PETER MEDAWAR . . . . . 12 Apr. 1973
British Association: General Committee
PROFESSOR J. S. FORREST . . . . . 14 June 1973

British Broadcasting Corporation (consultative group of scientists)

British Council: Science Advisory Panel
PROFESSOR J. HESLOP-HARRISON . . . . 17 June 1976
PROFESSOR A. W. JOHNSON. . . . . 17 June 1976
British Council: Agricultural Advisory Panel
DR L. FOWDEN . . . . . . 17 June 1976
British Heart Foundation: Science Committee
PROFESSOR H. O. SCHILD . . . . . 6 Mar. 1969
British Library Board: Advisory Council
PROFESSOR B. B. BOYCOTT . . . . . 17 Apr. 1975
DR A. WILLIAMS . . . . . . 17 Apr. 1975
British Museum (Trustee)
SIR JOHN KENDREW . . . . . 1 May 1974
British Museum: National Reference Library for Science and Invention Committee
DR R. K. CALLOW . . . . . . 12 Nov. 1964
British Museum (Natural History) (Trustee)
PROFESSOR J. SUTTON . . . . . 6 Nov. 1975
British National Bibliography Research Fund Committee
PROFESSOR E. J. W. BARRINGTON . . . 9 Oct. 1975
British Nutrition Foundation (Scientific Governors)
DR K. L. BLAXTER . . . . . . 12 July 1973
PROFESSOR R. L. M. SYNGE . . . . 12 July 1973
British Standards Institution: Quantities, Units and Symbols Committee
CHAIRMAN, SYMBOLS COMMITTEE (PROFESSOR
L. F. BATES) . . . . 17 July 1969
Bureau of Hygiene and Tropical Diseases
PROFESSOR P. C. C. GARNHAM . . . . 11 Oct. 1973
Cambridge University Committee for Geodesy and Geophysics
PROFESSOR F. C. FRANK . . . . . 1 Jan. 1975
Cancer Research Campaign: Grand Council
DR D. A. J. TYRRELL . . . . . 3 July 1975
Cancer Research Campaign: Scientific Advisory Committee (joint nomination with Medical Research Council)
DR T. A. CONNORS . . . . . . 15 May 1975
PROFESSOR A. R. CURRIE . . . . . 15 May 1969
DR J. B. GURDON . . . . . . 15 June 1972
PROFESSOR HENRY HARRIS . . . . 15 June 1972
DR L. KINLEN . . . . 17 June 1976

PUBLIC AND OTHER RESPONSIBILITIES

Charities Aid Foundation: Council — *Appointed*

Charles Darwin Foundation for the Galapagos Isles (Executive Council)
Professor R. D. KEYNES . . . . . . 17 Apr. 1975

Charterhouse (School)—Board of Governors
Sir GEORGE DEACON . . . . . . 16 July 1959

Chelsea Physic Garden
Professor D. LEWIS . . . . 14 Oct. 1971

Christ's Hospital (Governor)
Professor D. G. NORTHCOTT . . . . . Jan. 1976

City and Guilds of London Institute
Professor D. M. NEWITT . . . . . . 15 Jan. 1959

City and Guilds of London Institute: Advisory Committee for the Communication of Technical Information
Mr W. G. EVANS . . . . 19 Dec. 1972

City University: Court
Sir OWEN SAUNDERS . . . . . . 5 Mar. 1970

Council of Engineering Institutions: British National Committee on Ocean Engineering
Sir GEORGE DEACON . . . . . . 13 May 1971

Cranfield Institute of Technology: Court
Professor D. W. HOLDER . . . . . . 16 Apr. 1970

Cruelty to Animals Act: Advisory Committee
Sir FRANCIS AVERY JONES . . . . . 30 Nov. 1972
Sir JOHN McMICHAEL . . . . . . 10 Oct. 1968
Sir VINCENT WIGGLESWORTH . . . . 10 Feb. 1972

Department of Education and Science: British National Committee on Unisist
Dr R. W. J. KEAY . . . . 9 Nov. 1972
Sir HAROLD THOMPSON . . . . . 9 Nov. 1972

Department of Education and Science: United Kingdom National Committee for Man and the Biosphere Programme (Unesco)
Professor A. R. CLAPHAM . . . . . 12 Oct. 1972
Dr R. W. J. KEAY . . . . 12 Oct. 1972

Department of Trade and Industry: Fundamental Standards Requirements Board
Professor ALAN H. COOK . . . . . 12 Apr. 1973

Dulwich College (Governor)
Professor R. V. JONES . . . . . . 1 Jan. 1966

East Malling Research Station (Governor)
Dr G. D. H. BELL . . . . June 1975

Eddington Memorial Lectureship Fund (Trustee)
Sir MARTIN RYLE . . . . 8 Oct. 1970

Essex University: Court
Professor N. B. MARSHALL . . . . . 12 Oct. 1972

Eton College (Governor) — *Appointed*
PROFESSOR R. D. KEYNES . . . . . . 10 Oct. 1963
Exeter University: Court
SIR FREDERICK RUSSELL . . . . . 11 May 1967
Field Studies Council
PROFESSOR J. L. HARLEY . . . . . . 11 Nov. 1965
Fisher, Sir Ronald, Memorial Committee of Great Britain
PROFESSOR W. F. BODMER . . . . . . 16 Jan. 1975
Freshwater Biological Association
PROFESSOR E. J. W. BARRINGTON . . . . 5 July 1974
Great Britain/China Committee

Harrow School (Governor)
DR M. A. GRACE . . . . 17 July 1969
Sir Harold Hartley Lecture Committee
PROFESSOR R. V. JONES . . . . . . 15 June 1972
THE EXECUTIVE SECRETARY . . . . . 15 June 1972
Hatfield Memorial Lectureship Committee
SIR ALAN COTTRELL . . . . . . 12 Nov. 1964
DR L. ROTHERHAM . . . . 18 May 1972
Heriot-Watt University: General Convocation
SIR FREDERICK STEWART . . . . 1 July 1972
Hull University: Court
PROFESSOR B. LYTHGOE . . . . . . 1 Oct. 1976
Imperial Cancer Research Fund
PROFESSOR HENRY HARRIS (Governor) . . . 26 Mar. 1976
DR S. BRENNER (Member of Council) . . . 23 Mar. 1973
PROFESSOR R. MARKHAM (Member of Council) . . 26 Mar. 1976
Imperial College of Science and Technology
SIR EWART JONES . . . . 17 Apr. 1975
Institute of Cancer Research: Royal Cancer Hospital (Committee of Management)
PROFESSOR A. NEUBERGER . . . . . 8 Nov. 1973
International Centre of Insect Physiology and Ecology (International Committee)
SIR VINCENT WIGGLESWORTH . . . . . 12 Feb. 1970
International Council for Bird Preservation (British Section)
PROFESSOR R. A. HINDE . . . . . . 12 Nov. 1964
SIR DENYS WILKINSON . . . . . . 13 May 1976
International Institute for Applied Systems Analysis (Council)
SIR KINGSLEY DUNHAM . . . . . 12 Oct. 1972
International Seismological Centre (Governing Council)
DR H. I. S. THIRLAWAY . . . . . . 5 Nov. 1970
International Wildfowl Research Institute: Finance Board
PROFESSOR W. H. THORPE . . . . . 6 Nov. 1958

PUBLIC AND OTHER RESPONSIBILITIES 161

Jenner Museum Trust *Appointed*
   Sir DAVID EVANS . . . . . . 13 Oct. 1966

Joint Mathematical Council of the United Kingdom
   Professor C. A. ROGERS . . . . . 17 Dec. 1970

Jungfraujoch and Gornergrat International Foundation Governing Board
   Professor C. G. PHILLIPS . . . . . 7 Nov. 1963
   Sir GORDON SUTHERLAND . . . . . 16 June 1960

King's School, Grantham (Governor)
   Sir JAMES LIGHTHILL . . . . . . 16 July 1970

Lanchester Polytechnic (Board of Governors)
   Professor W. E. BURCHAM . . . . . 8 Oct. 1970

Lawes Agricultural Trust (Trustees)
   The DUKE OF NORTHUMBERLAND . . . 18 May 1972
   Sir EDWARD SALISBURY . . . . . 15 May 1947
   Sir RICHARD VERDIN . . . . . . 16 Jan. 1969

Lawes Agricultural Trust Committee (Rothamsted)
   Professor T. W. GOODWIN . . . . . 1 Jan. 1977
   Professor J. L. HARLEY . . . . . 17 June 1976
   Professor K. MATHER . . . . . . 16 Apr. 1970
   Sir GORDON SUTHERLAND . . . . . 11 Nov. 1965

Learned and Professional Society Publishers, Association of
   Mr J. H. BOREHAM . . . . . . 12 Oct. 1972

Lindemann Fellowships Selection Committee
   Professor ALAN H. COOK . . . . . 13 May 1976
   Professor F. G. SMITH . . . . . . 12 Oct. 1972

Lister Institute
   Sir DAVID EVANS (Council) . . . . 17 June 1965
   Professor J. H. HUMPHREY (Governing Body) . . 7 Oct. 1976

Liverpool University Court
   Sir ALASTAIR PILKINGTON . . . . . 1 Jan. 1975

London School of Hygiene and Tropical Medicine
   Sir BERNARD KATZ (Governor) . . . . 12 Dec. 1974
   Dr D. A. J. TYRRELL (Board of Management) . . 1 Jan. 1977

Loughborough University of Technology: Court
   Professor D. D. ELEY . . . . . . 7 Nov. 1968

MacRobert Award: Selection Committee
   Dr F. E. JONES . . . . 4 Apr. 1974
   Sir PETER KENT . . . . 15 May 1975
   Sir IEUAN MADDOCK . . . . . . 13 May 1976

Marine Biological Association
   Sir BERNARD KATZ . . . . . . 11 Nov. 1965

Medical Research Council (Assessor)
   Professor G. S. DAWES . . . . . . 18 Dec. 1975

National Committee for Photogrammetry
   Mr N. L. FALCON . . . . 8 Oct. 1970

National Electronics Council: Committee   *Appointed*
PROFESSOR H. E. M. BARLOW . . . . . 1 Dec. 1969
National Physical Laboratory: Advisory Board
    SIR JAMES LIGHTHILL . . . . . 16 Jan. 1969
         (representing THE PRESIDENT)
    PROFESSOR G. GEE . . . . . . 16 Jan. 1969
    DR F. E. JONES . . . . 16 Jan. 1969
National Vegetable Research Station (Governing Body)
    PROFESSOR D. C. SMITH . . . . . 29 Sept. 1976
Natural Environment Research Council (Assessor)
    PROFESSOR J. SUTTON . . . . . 18 Dec. 1975
Open University: Advisory Committee on Studies in Education
    PROFESSOR A. C. OFFORD . . . . . 15 July 1976
Open University: Council
    PROFESSOR B. B. BOYCOTT . . . . . 1 Aug. 1975
Percy Sladen Memorial Fund (Trustee)
    PROFESSOR G. E. FOGG . . . . . 1 July 1976
Primary Communications Research Centre, University of Leicester
    (Project Committee)
    PROFESSOR A. J. C. WILSON. . . . . 7 Oct. 1976
Royal Anthropological Institute: Blood Group Committee
    DR J. F. LOUTIT . . . . . . 11 Nov. 1965
Royal Geographical Society: Expeditions Committee
    DR F. C. FRASER . . . . . . 15 May 1969
Royal Veterinary College
    MR L. E. A. ROWSON . . . . . 1 Jan. 1976
Rugby School (Governor)
    PROFESSOR W. F. VINEN . . . . . 12 June 1975
Salford University: Court
    PROFESSOR C. H. BAMFORD . . . . 18 Dec. 1975
Science Research Council (Assessor)
    SIR HARRIE MASSEY . . . . . 1 Oct. 1972
Science Research Council: Astronomy, Space and Radio Board (Assessor)
    SIR HARRIE MASSEY . . . . . 1 Oct. 1974
Science Research Council: Astronomy, Space and Radio Board:
    Royal Greenwich Observatory Advisory Committee
    PROFESSOR M. J. SEATON . . . . . 17 Dec. 1970
        Astronomy I Committee (Assessor)
    PROFESSOR G. D. ROCHESTER . . . . 1 Oct. 1974
        Astronomy II Committee (Assessor)
    SIR HARRIE MASSEY . . . . . 1 Oct. 1974
        Solar Systems Committee (Assessor)
    SIR HARRIE MASSEY . . . . . 1 Oct. 1974
Science Research Council: Committee to coordinate support for
    science-based archaeology
    SIR KINGSLEY DUNHAM . . . . . 17 June 1976
Scott Polar Research Institute Committee
    PROFESSOR F. W. SHOTTON . . . . 30 Nov. 1965

PUBLIC AND OTHER RESPONSIBILITIES 163

	Appointed
Shrewsbury School (Governor)	
Sir HAROLD THOMPSON	17 Jan. 1963
Sir John Soane's Museum (Trustee)	
Dr M. G. P. STOKER	18 Dec. 1969
Social Science Research Council (Assessor)	
Dr D. E. BROADBENT	17 Jan. 1974
Standing Conference on Schools' Science and Technology	
Dr C. C. BUTLER	16 July 1970
Education Officer (Royal Society)	13 May 1971
Strathclyde University: General Convocation	
Professor G. BOND	1 Jan. 1977
Professor A. J. HADDOW	7 Mar. 1974
Surrey, University of: Court	
Dr E. H. MANSFIELD	4 Mar. 1976
Trans-Antarctic Association: U.K. Advisory Committee	
Sir MILES CLIFFORD	9 Feb. 1961
United Kingdom Committee for International Nature Conservation	
Dr R. W. J. KEAY	6 Nov. 1975
Professor W. H. THORPE	6 Nov. 1975
United Kingdom Coordinating Committee for the International Phase of Ocean Drilling	
Dr D. H. MATTHEWS	1 Dec. 1975
Uppingham School (Trustee)	
Professor A. W. JOHNSON	11 June 1970
Walcott Fund: Board of Trustees	
Dr A. WILLIAMS	7 Mar. 1974
Wales, University of: Court	
Professor P. F. WAREING	6 Mar. 1969
Professor R. T. WILLIAMS	16 July 1970
Warwick University: Court	
Professor A. J. C. WILSON	1 Aug. 1974
Westminster School (Governor)	
Sir RICHARD DOLL	1 Jan. 1967
Winchester College (Governor)	
Professor J. H. HUMPHREY	12 Oct. 1967
Wolfson Research Professorship Fund (Trustees)	
Sir JAMES MENTER	15 June 1972
Lord TODD	1 Dec. 1975
Woolsthorpe Manor (Committee of Management)	
The PRESIDENT	*ex officio*
Lord ADRIAN	7 Nov. 1957
Sir RICHARD WOOLLEY	30 Nov. 1960
World Energy Conference (British National Committee)	
Professor J. S. FORREST	7 Oct. 1976
York University (Court)	
Dr J. H. CHESTERS	1 Aug. 1972

STATUTES OF THE ROYAL SOCIETY

CONTENTS

CHAP.	PAGE
I. OF THE ELECTION AND ADMISSION OF FELLOWS	164
II. OF THE OBLIGATION TO BE SUBSCRIBED	169
III. OF THE PAYMENTS TO BE MADE BY THE FELLOWS TO THE SOCIETY .	170
IV. OF THE DEATH OR RECESS OF FELLOWS	171
V. OF THE CAUSES AND FORM OF EJECTION	171
VI. OF THE ELECTION OF THE COUNCIL AND OFFICERS . . .	172
VII. OF THE PRESIDENT	173
VIII. OF THE TREASURER AND HIS ACCOUNTS	174
IX. OF THE TWO SECRETARIES	175
X. OF THE FOREIGN SECRETARY	176
XI. OF THE EXECUTIVE SECRETARY	176
XII. OF THE ORDINARY MEETINGS OF THE SOCIETY	177
XIII. OF SPECIAL GENERAL MEETINGS OF THE SOCIETY . . .	178
XIV. OF THE PUBLICATION OF PAPERS	179
XV. OF THE BOOKS AND PAPERS OF THE SOCIETY	181
XVI. OF THE ARCHIVES OF THE SOCIETY	182
XVII. OF THE LIBRARY	182
XVIII. OF THE COMMON SEAL AND DEEDS	182
XIX. OF THE RESTRAINT OF DIVIDENDS TO FELLOWS	183
XX. OF THE STANDING ORDERS OF THE SOCIETY	183
XXI. OF THE MAKING, AMENDING, AND REPEALING OF LAWS . .	183
XXII. OF THE INTERPRETATION OF THE STATUTES	184

CHAPTER I

Of the Election and Admission of Fellows

Certificate of Candidature

1. EVERY candidate, who must be a British subject or Commonwealth citizen or citizen of the Irish Republic, shall be proposed and recommended by a certificate in writing signed by six or more Fellows, of whom three at least shall certify their recommendation from personal knowledge, but either of the two Secretaries shall have power to sign a certificate on behalf of a Fellow on receiving a written request from him, if the Fellow so requesting is not resident at a place within a radius of 100 miles from the Society's apartments, or, being so resident is, in the opinion of the Council, physically incapacitated from attending at the Society's apartments and there signing the certificate. The certificate shall specify the name, rank, profession, qualifications, nationality, date of birth and usual place of residence of the candidate; and being delivered to the Executive

Secretary, shall be registered, with the date of delivery, in a book to be kept for the purpose, and read at the next Ordinary Meeting; and, unless otherwise ordered, shall be suspended in some convenient place in the Society's apartments until the day of election. Nothing herein contained shall render women ineligible as candidates.

2. Of the Fellows who sign a certificate from personal knowledge of the candidate, two shall undertake the responsibility of acting as proposer and seconder respectively, in so far that all communications on the subject of the candidature shall take place with one of these. The proposer shall be responsible for informing the candidate of the Obligation to be subscribed and of the payments to be made to the Society before he can be admitted a Fellow.

3. In November, a list of all candidates proposed prior to the first day of the month of August immediately preceding, and also a list of those candidates whose certificates have been resuspended as hereinafter provided, shall be arranged in alphabetical order, without reference to the dates of the certificates of the candidates. These certificates shall remain suspended until the day of election. *Names of Candidates to be listed in November*

4. In November, a list shall be printed containing the names of all the candidates, arranged in alphabetical order, together with the names of the Fellows by whom each candidate is proposed and recommended; and a copy of such list shall immediately thereafter be sent to every Fellow. *List of Candidates to be printed*

5. The Council shall select by ballot from such printed list of candidates a number not exceeding forty, to be recommended to the Society for election; but no such selection by the Council shall be valid unless eleven Members at least be present and vote, a majority deciding, or in the event of equality the President having a second or casting vote. *Selection by Council*

6. At the first Ordinary Meeting of the Society after the Meeting of the Council at which the selection has been made, the President shall read from the Chair the names of the candidates whom the Council have selected as most eligible, arranged in alphabetical order; and after such meeting, a circular letter shall be forthwith sent to every Fellow, naming the day and hour of election, and *Selected Names communicated to Fellows*

enclosing a printed list of the selected candidates, with space for such alterations as any Fellow may determine to make in pursuance of Statute 8.

Date of Election

7. The election of Fellows not included in the classes referred to in Statutes 11 and 12 of this Chapter, shall take place on the third Thursday of March; unless the Council shall alter the day of Election to any other day in the month of March, in which case due notice of such alteration shall be given to every Fellow.

Election Procedure

8. On the day of election two scrutators shall be nominated by the President, with the approbation of the Society, to assist the Secretaries in examining the lists; and each Fellow present and voting, shall deliver to one of the Secretaries or scrutators one of the printed lists mentioned in Statute 6, having erased the name of any candidate or candidates for whom he does not vote, and, if he shall have thought fit, having substituted the name of any other candidate or candidates contained in the printed list sent in pursuance of Statute 4. One of the Secretaries shall take down the names of the Fellows who vote. No list shall be valid which contains more than forty names.

9. The scrutators, after examining the lists with the Secretaries, shall report to the President the names of the candidates who shall have been duly elected in compliance with the Charters, and the President shall announce those names from the Chair.

Renewal of Candidature

10. Any candidate whose name shall have been printed in a previous list of candidates, but who shall not have been elected, shall, unless his proposer or seconder withdraw his name before 31 July immediately preceding an election, be a candidate at such election; his name shall be placed in alphabetical order with those of the new candidates, and his certificate shall be suspended along with those of the new candidates. Provided always that the same certificate shall not be valid for more than seven successive elections and provided further that a new certificate in respect of a previous candidate shall not be accepted for suspension except after three annual elections shall have taken place; such new certificate shall not be valid for more than three successive elections and renewals of candidature thereafter shall always be after three annual elections shall have taken place and in each instance shall not be valid for more than three

successive elections. Any separate paper attached to the certificate, if intended to be printed for circulation to the Fellows, shall bear the signatures of six of the signatories to the certificate. Corrections of fact may be made upon the certificate after it has been sent in, if initialled by the proposer or seconder, and marked unmistakably as new matter. However, changes in the candidate's occupation, post held or address, but no other amendment, may be communicated in writing by the proposer or seconder to one of the Secretaries for insertion and initialling by proxy on the proposer's or seconder's behalf.

11. Any one of Her Majesty's subjects who is a Prince of the Blood Royal may be proposed at one of the Ordinary Meetings of the Society by any Fellow, and may be put to the vote for election on the same day, provided public notice of such proposal shall have been given by the proposer at the preceding Meeting of the Society. _{Royal Family}

12. In cases in which the Council is of opinion that, in the interests of the advancement of Natural Knowledge, it is desirable that persons be elected Fellows of the Society otherwise than as provided by Statutes 1 to 11 of this Chapter, they may recommend to the Society for election persons, who, in their opinion, either have rendered conspicuous service to the cause of science, or are such that their election would be of signal benefit to the Society. Not more than one person shall be so elected in any one calendar year, except that in the event of no election being made in any year the Council shall be at liberty in the following year to nominate, for election, two persons under this Statute. The persons so to be recommended shall be selected by the Council by ballot. Provided always that no person shall be so recommended unless he obtains two-thirds of the votes of the members of Council present and voting, the total number of votes registered in his favour being not less than eleven. _{Special Elections}

At the Ordinary Meeting of the Society next following the meeting of Council at which such selection is made, the person or persons nominated shall be proposed for election by means of a certificate prepared in accordance with Statute 1, no distinction, however, being made between personal and general knowledge. Such certificate, on being allowed by the Society, shall be suspended in some convenient place in the Society's apartments until the day on which a ballot is taken upon it. The date for the ballot, which shall not be earlier than the third Ordinary Meeting after that at which the certificate is read shall be announced at the head of the certificate.

Admission

13. Every person who is elected a Fellow shall appear for his admission on or before the fourth Ordinary Meeting of the Society after the day of his election, or within such further time as shall, for some sufficient cause, be granted by the Council; otherwise his election shall be void. Provided that no person shall be admitted a Fellow of the Society on the day of the Anniversary Meeting for electing the Council and Officers.

14. The admission of any Fellow into the Society shall be in manner and form following, he having first made the payments required by the Statutes. He shall subscribe the Obligation in the Charter Book, and be introduced to the President, who, taking him by the hand, shall say these words:

I do, by the authority and in the name of the Royal Society of London for Improving Natural Knowledge, admit you a Fellow thereof.

Admission &c., to be recorded

15. The election, the payments made previous to admission, and the admission of every person into the Society, with the time thereof, shall be recorded in the Journal Book.

16. No person shall be deemed a Fellow of the Society until he has made the payments required by the Statutes: nor shall he be entitled to vote at any election or meeting of the Society until he shall have been admitted in the manner and form above specified.

Foreign Members

17. Persons may be elected into the Society, under the title of Foreign Members, who are not British subjects or Commonwealth citizens or citizens of the Irish Republic, and shall be exempted from the operation of Chapters II and III of these Statutes; they shall be selected from among persons of the greatest eminence for their scientific discoveries and attainments.

Procedure for Election of Foreign Members

18. The Council shall from time to time, as they shall see fit, put in nomination persons for election as Foreign Members, but not more than four persons shall be elected as Foreign Members in any one year.

19. A book shall be kept in which Fellows of the Society may enter the names of those men of science whom they suggest as Foreign Members; each entry shall be signed by the proposer and

be accompanied by a statement of the principal grounds on which the suggestion is made, and shall be valid for three years only.

20. When vacancies in the list of Foreign Members are to be filled up, a list of the persons so entered up to and on 31 July immediately preceding shall be sent to each member of the Council, together with notice of the meeting at which the list will be considered. At the meeting thus appointed the claims of those men of science whose names have been duly entered in the book shall be considered, and a selection of names shall be made, from among which the Council, at a subsequent meeting to be then appointed, may make nominations to the Society.

21. At the second meeting the selection of candidates to be so nominated for Foreign Membership shall be by ballot; when, if two-thirds of the members of the Council present be in favour of the nomination of any candidate, his name shall be proposed at the next Ordinary Meeting of the Society, and shall be put to the vote by ballot at the following Ordinary Meeting.

CHAPTER II

Of the Obligation to be Subscribed

22. EVERY person elected a Fellow of the Society shall, before his admission, subscribe the Obligation in the following words: [Obligation to be subscribed by every Fellow]

We who have hereunto subscribed, do hereby promise each for himself, that we will endeavour to promote the good of the Royal Society of London, for Improving Natural Knowledge, and to pursue the ends for which the same was founded; that we will be present at the meeting of the Society, as often as conveniently we can, especially at the Anniversary elections, and upon extraordinary occasions; and that we will observe the Statutes and Orders of the said Society. Provided, that whensoever any of us shall signify to the President under his hand, that he desireth to withdraw from the Society, he shall be free from this Obligation for the future.

And if any person elected shall refuse to subscribe the said Obligation, the election of that person shall be void.

CHAPTER III

Of the Payments to be made by the Fellows to the Society

Annual Contributions

23. EVERY person elected a Fellow of the Society under Statutes 1 to 9, shall, before he is admitted, pay the sum of *twenty pounds* for admission money, the sum of *twenty pounds* for the year of his election, and the same sum annually in advance so long as he shall continue a Fellow of the Society, except that any Fellow on attaining the age of 67 years may pay the sum of *ten pounds*. And if any such person shall fail to pay the said sums, he shall not be admitted, and his election shall be void: except the said sums be remitted in whole, or in part, by special order of the Council.

A Fellow elected under Statute 12 shall pay no admission money; he shall pay a subscription of *twenty pounds* for the year in which he was elected and annually so long as he remains a Fellow of the Society, except that any Fellow on attaining the age of 67 years may pay the sum of *ten pounds*, provided that the Council may by special order remit the fees payable.

Princes of the Blood Royal elected under Statute 11 shall not be required to pay an admission fee or annual subscription.

Life Compositions

24. All who have or may become Fellows of the Society may, between 25 March and 31 August, compound for their annual payments, by paying such sum as Council may from time to time determine.

Annual Contributions due 25 March

25. All annual contributions shall be considered to be due on the twenty-fifth day of March in each year. Every Fellow of the Society liable to an annual payment shall, previously to the twenty-fifth day of March in every year, bring or send the same to the Treasurer or the Executive Secretary. And if any such Fellow, after notice sent by post to his usual address, in May, and again in August, shall fail to pay the same before the first day of September in each year, his name shall be suspended in the public Meeting

Consequences of Nonpayment

Room of the Society as being in arrear, and shall continue so suspended until the sum due be paid. And if any such Fellow shall fail to pay his subscription on or before the first day of October in each year, no satisfactory reason having been assigned to the President and Council for such non-payment, he shall cease to be a Fellow of the Society. Provided, nevertheless, that on a solicitation for

STATUTES OF THE ROYAL SOCIETY 171

readmission being addressed to the President and Council by an individual so circumstanced, within the space of one year following St Andrew's Day, the case of the individual so soliciting shall be stated by the President from the Chair, at one of the Ordinary Meetings of the Society, and the question of his readmission to be put to the vote at the next Ordinary Meeting of the Society.

CHAPTER IV

Of the Death or Recess of Fellows

26. THE death or recess of any Fellow of the Society shall be forthwith recorded in the Register of Fellows, and the names thus recorded shall be announced from the Chair at the Anniversary Meeting for electing the Council and Officers. Record of Deaths, &c.

CHAPTER V

Of the Causes and Form of Ejection

27. IF any Fellow of the Society shall contemptuously or contumaciously disobey the Statutes or Orders of the Society or Council; or shall, by speaking, writing, or printing, publicly defame the Society; or advisedly, maliciously, or dishonestly do anything to the damage, detriment, or dishonour thereof, he shall be ejected out of the Society. Grounds for Ejection of Fellows

28. Whensoever there shall appear to be cause for the ejection of any Fellow out of the Society, the subject shall be laid before the Council; and if a majority of the Council shall, after due deliberation, determine by ballot to propose to the Society the ejection of the said Fellow, the President shall in that case, at some Ordinary Meeting of the Society, announce from the Chair such determination of the Council; and at the Ordinary Meeting next after that at which the said announcement has been made, the Society shall proceed to determine the question; and on its appearing that two-thirds of the Members present have voted for the ejection of the said Fellow, the President shall proceed to cancel his name in the Register, and at the same time pronounce him ejected in these words: Procedure in Ejection of Fellows

> *I do, by the authority and in the name of the Royal Society of London, for Improving Natural Knowledge, declare A. B. to be now ejected and no longer a Fellow thereof.*

And the ejection of every such person shall be then recorded in the Journal Book of the Society; and his name, as ejected, be also read at the next Anniversary Meeting for elections.

CHAPTER VI

Of the Election of the Council and Officers

Notice of Election of Council and Officers

29. At the two Ordinary Meetings of the Society next preceding the day of the Anniversary election, the President shall give notice of the said election; and declare how much it imports the good of the Society, that such persons may be chosen into the Council, as are most likely to attend the Meetings and business of the Council, out of whom there may be made the best choice of a President and other Officers.

Summons to Anniversary Meeting

30. Every Fellow of the Society resident in the United Kingdom shall have notice of the Anniversary Meeting for electing the Council and Officers for the year ensuing, by particular summons, which summons shall be sent to the address of such Fellow, a week at the least before the day of meeting, and shall be to this effect:

> *These are to give notice, that on   the   day of the Council and Officers of the Royal Society are to be elected for the year ensuing; at which Election your presence is expected, at   of the clock in the   precisely.*

Nomination of the Council and Officers

31. The Council for the ensuing year, out of which shall be chosen the President, Treasurer, two Secretaries, and Foreign Secretary, shall consist of eleven members of the existing Council, and of ten Fellows who are not members of the existing Council.

32. The President and Council shall, previous to the Anniversary Meeting, nominate, by ballot, eleven members of the existing Council, and also ten Fellows, not members of the existing Council, whom they recommend to the Society for election into the Council for the ensuing year. The President and Council shall also, in like manner, nominate by ballot, out of the proposed Council, the persons whom they recommend to the Society for election to the offices of President, Treasurer, two Secretaries, and Foreign Secretary for the ensuing year.

33. At the Ordinary Meeting of the Society preceding the Anniversary Meeting the names of such persons so recommended for election as Council and Officers for the ensuing year shall be announced from the Chair.

34. Lists, with the names of the Fellows recommended by the President and Council and having a blank column opposite for such alterations as any Fellow may wish to make, shall be prepared for the use of the Fellows one week before the day of election. *Balloting Papers*

35. Two scrutators shall be nominated by the President, with the approbation of the Society, to examine the lists. *Scrutators*

36. Each Fellow voting shall deliver his list to one of the Secretaries or scrutators; and the name of each Fellow who shall so deliver in his list shall be noted by one of the Secretaries. *Mode of Voting*

37. The scrutators, after examining the lists, shall report to the Society the names of those having the majority of votes for composing the Council, and filling the offices of President, Treasurer, the two Secretaries and Foreign Secretary.

38. For electing any member of the Council, or any officer to be elected by the Society, upon such vacancies as shall happen in the intervals of the Anniversary elections, the summons for such election, and the proceedings in it, shall be after the same manner as is directed for the Anniversary election. *Elections to fill Casual Vacancies*

39. Upon any vacancy of the President's place, occurring in the intervals of the Anniversary elections, the Treasurer, or, in his absence, one of the Secretaries, shall cause the Council to be summoned for the election of a new President: and the Council, meeting thereupon in the usual place, or any eleven or more of them, shall proceed to the said Election, and not separate until the major part of them shall have agreed upon a new President..

CHAPTER VII

Of the President

40. THE business of the President shall be to preside at all the meetings, and regulate all the debates, of the Society, Council, and Committees; to state and put questions both in the affirmative and *Business of the President*

negative, according to the sense and intention of the meetings to call for reports and accounts from Committees, and others; to check irregularities, and to keep all persons to order; to summon all meetings of the Council, and Committee of Papers; and to execute, or see to the execution of, the Statutes of the Society.

Precedence of the President

41. The President shall take precedence of every Fellow of the Society, at their ordinary place of meeting; and also in all other places, where any number of the Fellows meet as a Society, Council, or Committee.

Vice-Presidents

42. The President shall annually appoint two or more members of Council to be Vice-Presidents. In the absence of the President, one of the Vice-Presidents shall act as his deputy, and may do the same acts as the President himself could do if present; provided always that the Council may appoint any Fellow to be Chairman of any Committee other than the Committee of Papers, and in the absence of the President, such Fellow shall act as Chairman of such Committee.

CHAPTER VIII

Of the Treasurer and his Accounts

Duties of the Treasurer

43. THE Treasurer, or some person appointed by him, with the approval of the Council, shall receive for the use of the Society all sums of money due or payable to the Society; and shall pay and disburse all sums due from or payable by the Society; and shall keep particular Accounts of all such receipts and payments.

Power to make Payments

44. Every sum of money, payable on account of the Society, exceeding Two Hundred Pounds, shall be paid only by order of the Council; but payments for rates or taxes, to any amount, may be made by the Treasurer, without any specific order of the Council for that purpose.

Investment of Moneys

45. All sums of money, which there shall not be present occasion for expending or otherwise disposing of to the use of the Society, shall be laid out in such Government or other securities as shall be approved of and directed by the Council.

Audit of Accounts

46. The accounts of the Treasurer shall be audited annually a short time preceding the Anniversary elections, by a Committee consisting

of three Members of the Council, of whom the President or one of the Secretaries to be one; and of three Fellows of the Society not members of the Council, who are to be nominated by the President, with the consent of the major part of the Fellows present, given by ballot at one of the three next preceding weekly meetings; any one or more of the said three members of the Council, together with any one or more of the said three Fellows, shall be a Quorum of the said Committee: the members of the said Committee who are of the Council shall make their report to the Council held next after such audit, on or before the Anniversary election; and the members of the said Committee who are not of the Council shall make their report to the Society, upon the Meeting next before the Anniversary election, or on the day of the said election.

47. As soon after the audit as may be, and before the Anniversary Meeting, the Treasurer shall cause an abstract of the Society's accounts of the preceding year to be printed for the use of the Fellows. *Accounts to be printed*

48. The Treasurer shall have the charge of the title deeds of the Society's estates, the policies of insurance, and securities, and shall have the general care of the Society's property. *Charge of Title Deeds*

CHAPTER IX

Of the Two Secretaries

49. THE two Secretaries shall be responsible to the Council for the general conduct of the Society's correspondence, publications, and all other business, excepting that which relates to finance. *Duties of the Secretaries*

50. The Secretaries, or one of them, shall attend all meetings of the Society, Council, and Committee of Papers; where, when the President has taken the Chair, one of the Secretaries shall read the minutes, orders, and entries of the preceding meeting; and shall be responsible for the accuracy of the minutes of the business and orders of the present meeting, to be entered by the Executive Secretary in the respective books to which they relate.

CHAPTER X

Of the Foreign Secretary

Duties of the Foreign Secretary

51. THE duty of the Secretary for Foreign Correspondence shall be to conduct correspondence with foreign parts, relating to the business of the Society, to return thanks for presents from foreigners made to the Society, and to forward to persons elected Foreign Members the Diplomas certifying their election into the Society.

CHAPTER XI

Of the Executive Secretary

Appointment of the Executive Secretary

52. THE appointment of a person to the office of Executive Secretary shall be by the Council, to whom the Officer so appointed shall give security, at the discretion of the Council; and he shall hold office during the pleasure of the Council.

Executive Secretary not a Fellow

53. The person who shall be chosen to the office of Executive Secretary, shall either not be a Fellow of the Society, or, if a Fellow, shall cease to be so upon his appointment to, and acceptance of, that office.

Payment of the Executive Secretary

54. The Executive Secretary shall be paid for his services according to the determination of the Council. He shall be subject to such Standing Orders as shall be made, and shall follow such directions as may be given by the President and Council. He shall give all his time to the work of the Society, and shall attend in the office of the Society as prescribed by such Standing Orders.

55. The Executive Secretary shall act under the general direction of the Secretaries, and in their absence shall represent them.

He shall also act on the directions which may be given him from time to time by the Treasurer in that part of his duties which relates to the finances of the Society.

Duties of the Executive Secretary

56. Subject to such Standing Orders and directions as aforesaid, the Executive Secretary shall be charged with (1) the general administrative business of the Society; (2) the control of the offices and library and of all persons therein employed, and the arrangement of the office work; (3) the conduct of the general correspondence.

It shall be his duty, except on such special occasions as may be specified by Standing Orders, or as may be determined by the President, to attend all meetings of the Council and Committees and take the minutes thereof, which minutes he shall submit to the Secretaries for their revision or approval.

57. He shall, subject as aforesaid, have the charge and custody of the Charter Book, Statute Book, Journal Books of the Society and Council, Register Books, Manuscripts, and Archives belonging to the Society; all which shall, except in such cases as the Council shall otherwise order, be kept in the Society's apartments, that they may be in readiness to be produced at any meetings of the Society or Council, as the case may require, or as shall be ordered by the Society, Council, or President.

58. He shall also, subject as aforesaid, have the charge and custody of the papers and writings relating to the business of the Society, and shall not suffer them to be removed from the Society's apartments without the sanction of the Officers.

CHAPTER XII

Of the Ordinary Meetings of the Society

59. THE Session of the Society shall commence on the first Thursday in November, and end on the last Thursday in June. *Duration of Session*

60. The Ordinary Meetings of the Society shall be on Thursdays weekly (excepting Christmas, Passion, and Easter weeks, and such other weeks at Christmas and Easter, in each year, as the Council may in the preceding year determine) and shall begin at half-past Four o'clock in the afternoon precisely. *Days of Meeting*

61. No stranger shall be permitted to be present during the meeting, unless by invitation of the President, or by his leave or order upon the recommendation of some Fellow. *Admission of Strangers*

62. The business of the Society in their Ordinary Meetings shall be to order, take account, consider, and discourse of philosophical experiments and observations; to read, hear, and discourse upon letters, reports, and other papers containing philosophical matters; as also to view, and discourse upon, rarities of nature and art; and thereupon to consider, what may be deduced from them, or any of *Business of Ordinary Meetings*

them; and how far they, or any of them, may be improved for use or discovery.*

Procedure at Meetings

63. At the meetings of the Society, lists of the presents made from time to time to the Society shall be laid on the table, by one of the Secretaries, for the inspection of the Fellows; and the thanks of the Society to the donors shall be proposed from the Chair previously to the reading of the first paper. One of the Secretaries shall give notice of any candidate who stands proposed for election into the Society at that meeting; and the Secretaries shall read letters and papers presented to the Society, in such manner as the President shall direct.

Communication of Papers

64. No letter, report, or other paper shall be read at any Ordinary Meeting unless it be communicated by a Fellow or Foreign Member; and it shall be the duty of each Fellow or Foreign Member to satisfy himself that any letter, report, or other paper which he may communicate, is suitable to be read before the Society.

Conduct of Meetings

65. The conduct of the Ordinary Meetings shall be in accordance with the Standing Orders determined from time to time by the President and Council, provided always that at the Ordinary Meetings nothing relating to Statutes or management of the Society shall be brought forward or discussed.

CHAPTER XIII

Of Special General Meetings of the Society

Anniversary Meeting

66. THE Anniversary Meeting for the election of the Council and Officers, and the Annual Meeting for the election of Fellows, shall take place at an hour to be determined by the Council.

Special General Meetings

67. The President or Council may at any time call a Special General Meeting of the Society when it may appear to them to be necessary.

68. Any six Fellows may, by notice in writing, signed by them, and delivered to one of the Secretaries at an Ordinary Meeting of the Society, require a Special General Meeting of the Society to be convened, for the purpose of considering and determining on the matters specified in such requisition, and the President shall, within

* This is the wording of the Statute as given in the Statutes of 1663.

one week after such requisition shall have been so delivered, appoint a day for a Special General Meeting accordingly.

69. One week's notice of any Special General Meeting shall be given to each Fellow resident in the United Kingdom, and such notice shall state the object of such Meeting.

70. At such meeting no business shall be brought forward except what shall have been so notified

71. A Special General Meeting of the Society shall be held before the Annual Meeting on the Thursday preceding the Annual Meeting. At such Special Meeting the Report of the Council, having been previously circulated, shall be presented, and Fellows shall be invited to comment thereon. Matters not arising out of the Report shall not be discussed except by permission of the President. The Report shall be finally presented to the Society at the Anniversary Meeting, but no change shall be introduced after its first presentation other than such as the Council may think fit to adopt on consideration of the comments made at the Special General Meeting.

CHAPTER XIV

Of the Publication of Papers

72. THE members of the Council for the time being shall constitute and be a standing committee, to be called the Committee of Papers, to whom the consideration of the acceptance, reading, and publication of all papers communicated to the Society shall be referred, and who shall execute their powers in accordance with Standing Orders determined from time to time by the President and Council. The Committee of Papers shall meet at such times as shall be appointed by the President; due and sufficient notice of such meeting having been previously sent to every member of the Committee. *Committee of Papers*

73. At a meeting of the said Committee no less number than seven of the members (of which number the President, or, in his absence, a Vice-President, shall always be one) shall be a quorum. *Quorum*

74. The decisions of the Committee of Papers shall be determined by the majority of votes of those present and voting, and the voting shall be open, unless the President shall direct that the voting shall *Voting*

be by ballot. In case of an equality of votes, the President shall have a second or casting vote.

The decisions of the Committee shall be duly entered in the Minute Book of the Committee.

Form of Publication

75. The publication of papers communicated to the Society, and of such other matters as the President and Council may judge fit to publish, shall take place under Standing Orders determined from time to time by the President and Council, but always in such a way that a proper portion of them shall from time to time be printed and published under the title of the *Philosophical Transactions of the Royal Society of London*, and another proper portion under the title of the *Proceedings of the Royal Society of London* provided always that the President and Council shall have power to publish either papers or other matters in such form and under such conditions as they may from time to time determine.

Papers communicated

76. The original copy of every Paper received at the Society shall be considered the property of the Society, if there be no previous engagement with its author to the contrary.

Fellows entitled to Publications

77. The *Philosophical Transactions* and the *Proceedings* shall be printed at the sole charge, and for the use and benefit, of the Society and of the Fellows thereof; to the intent that each of the present Fellows, who actually contributes and pays towards the support of the Society, or who has compounded for such contribution, according to the rules and orders established in relation thereto, or who has for other particular reasons been exonerated and discharged from such contribution by order of the Council, may receive in accordance with Standing Orders determined by the President and Council copies of such of the *Philosophical Transactions*, and of the *Proceedings* as shall be printed as aforesaid; and that all persons who shall hereafter be admitted Fellows shall, under the same conditions, be entitled to the like benefit and advantage.

Delivery of Transactions

78. The Executive Secretary shall deliver in accordance with the Standing Orders copies of the *Transactions* to every Fellow of the Society (except as hereinafter excepted) who shall demand the same, either in person or by letter.

Provided always, that no Fellow whatsoever of the Society shall be entitled to demand or receive any such copy of the *Transactions*, whose election and payment of admission fees and regular contributions shall not have preceded the date of the time appointed for the delivery of the said *Transactions*; neither shall the executor of any deceased Fellow receive a copy of the *Transactions* published after the death of such Fellow.

Provided also, that no Fellow of the Society shall receive, or be entitled to receive, any copy or copies of the *Transactions*, so printed as aforesaid, after five years shall have elapsed from the time of the Executive Secretary's having begun to deliver out such copies respectively; but his neglecting to demand them for so long a time shall be deemed a forfeiture and dereliction of his right thereto; unless the Council for the time being, upon being made acquainted with the reason of such delay, and having regard to the circumstances of the application, and the amount of stock in hand, shall *order* such copies as they may think fit to be so delivered. *Limitation Time for ordering Transactions*

79. The Executive Secretary shall further cause to be distributed to the Fellows of the Society, in accordance with the Standing Orders, copies of the *Proceedings* as soon as may be convenient after their appearance. *Delivery of Proceedings*

CHAPTER XV

Of the Books and Papers of the Society

80. THERE shall be had and kept a book, called the *Charter Book*, wherein shall be fairly written the copy of the Charters, all the Royal Grants on the behalf of the Society, and the Obligation to be subscribed by the Fellows of the Society in their own handwriting. *Charter Book*

81. There shall be kept a book, called the *Statute Book*, wherein shall be fairly written, or printed, all the Laws, Statutes, and Constitutions made, or to be made, concerning the government and regulating of the Society or Council; and also a Register of the Fellows of the Society, with the times of their election and admission. *Statute Book Register of Fellows*

82. There shall be kept *Journal Books* of the Society, and also of the Council wherein shall be entered all the minutes, orders, and business of the Society and Council at their respective meetings; to which Journal Books any Fellow may have access at such times as the Library is open. *Journal Books*

83. A book shall be kept, in which the title of each communication received, the date of its reception at the Society's apartments, and *Register of Papers*

the name of the Fellow or Foreign Member who communicates it, shall be duly entered in the order of its reception.

CHAPTER XVI

Of the Archives of the Society

Manuscripts 84. THE scientific and historical manuscript collections of the Society, including the collections of engravings, and also confidential reports relating to papers submitted to the Society, shall be preserved in the Archives, and catalogued so as to be available to duly authorized persons for consultation and study. The manuscripts of all papers read before the Society, of which the publication has been deferred, shall be preserved in the Archives.

Catalogue 85. A catalogue of the manuscripts in the Archives shall be available for reference at the Society's apartments; and permission may be granted by the Council or Officers of the Society to Fellows or to any person duly introduced by a Fellow, to consult and examine specified manuscripts not of a confidential character.

Manuscripts not to be removed 86. No manuscript deposited in the Archives shall be removed from the rooms of the Society without permission of the Council, on security given for its safe custody and return.

CHAPTER XVII

Of the Library

Library Regulations 87. THE Library shall be open to the Fellows on such days, and at such hours, and subject to such regulations, as the Council may from time to time determine by Standing Orders.

CHAPTER XVIII

Of the Common Seal and Deeds

Care of the Seal 88. IT shall be the duty of the Executive Secretary to be responsible for the safe custody of the Common Seal of the Society.

Sealing Deeds 89. Every instrument to which the Common Seal is to be affixed shall normally be passed and sealed in Council, but by order of the President or a Vice-President when urgency demands the instrument may be passed and sealed in the intervals between the meetings of Council. Every instrument to which the Common Seal of the Society is affixed shall be signed by two persons approved by the Council for such purpose.

CHAPTER XIX

Of the Restraint of Dividends to Fellows

90. THE Society shall not, and by its laws may not, make any dividend, gift, division, or bonus in money unto or between any of its members. *(Restraint of Dividends to Fellows)*

CHAPTER XX

Of the Standing Orders of the Society

91. THE Council may from time to time make Standing Orders for the regulation of the affairs of the Society, provided that such Standing Orders be not contrary to anything contained in the Charters or Statutes of the Society. Such Standing Orders may be made, amended or repealed at any meeting of the Council, provided that notice of any proposed new Standing Order, amendment or repeal has been given at the preceding Council. Such notice shall specify the proposed new Standing Order, amendment or repeal. *(Power to make and alter Standing Orders)*

CHAPTER XXI

Of the Making, Amending, and Repealing of Laws

92. FOR the making of any new Statute of the Society, or for the amendment or repeal of any Statute or any part thereof, notice of the proposed new Statute, amendment or repeal shall be given in writing at a meeting of the Council, and such notice shall specify the proposed new Statute, amendment or repeal. The Council shall thereupon appoint a day for the consideration of the proposal. On such day the proposal shall be discussed and the question to be resolved at this or any subsequent meeting of Council to which the discussion may be adjourned shall be to this effect, viz.: Whether the proposed new Statute, amendment or repeal, with such alterations *(Procedure in making or altering Statutes)*

as the Council may have seen fit to introduce, shall be provisionally agreed upon. If this be decided in the affirmative, the President shall summon a special General Meeting of the Society for the discussion of the proposal provisionally agreed upon by Council. Not less than three weeks shall elapse between the date at which the proposed alteration of Statute is communicated to the Fellows and the date of the General Meeting. At the General Meeting the new Statute, amendment or repeal shall be submitted to the meeting for discussion, and it shall be in order for any Fellow to move a resolution requesting the Council to reconsider the proposal as a whole or in part. Such resolution or resolutions having been duly seconded shall be discussed and put to the vote by the President.

At the next meeting of Council following this meeting the Council shall take these resolutions into consideration before approving or amending the proposal provisionally agreed upon. At this, or a subsequent meeting of Council, the question to be decided shall be to this effect, viz.: Whether the new Statute, amendment or repeal as finally approved of, shall be entered into the Statute Book of the Society. If this be decided in the affirmative it shall be so recorded and passed into law.

CHAPTER XXII

Of the Interpretation of the Statutes

93. IN the foregoing Statutes and in any Standing Order of the Council and in any Rules or Regulations adopted by the Royal Society or by any Joint Committee for the administration of Trusts to which the Royal Society is a party, words importing the male sex shall include the female unless the context requires a contrary construction.

The foregoing Statutes are those adopted by Council in March 1915 *and subsequently amended in October* 1916; *October* 1918; *November* 1920; *January* 1921; *December* 1930; *May* 1933; *June* 1934; *February* 1937; *July* 1937; *May* 1939; *October* 1944; *October* 1945; *February* 1946; *December* 1947; *March* 1948; *May* 1949; *June* 1951; *May* 1954; *June* 1958; *April* 1962; *June* 1962; *March* 1963; *June* 1964; *December* 1965; *December* 1966; *June* 1968; *July* 1973; *May* 1975.

Note

By the Charter and Statutes, the quorum required is as follows:

Meetings of the Society

Ordinary Meeting	9
Anniversary Meeting for election of Council . . .	31
Meeting to elect to casual vacancies on Council . . .	21
Meeting for election of Fellows	21

Meetings of Council

As Council	9
As Committee of Papers . . .	7

STANDING ORDERS OF COUNCIL

RELATING TO MEETINGS OF THE SOCIETY, SECTIONAL COMMITTEES, PUBLICATIONS AND REPRESENTATION ON OUTSIDE BODIES

Note

By Statutes, Chapter XIV, Statute 72, the consideration of the acceptance, reading and publication of all papers communicated to the Society is referred to the Council sitting as Committee of Papers; and in the following Standing Orders the word 'Council', when used in connexion with the acceptance, reading, or publication of papers, is to be understood to mean the Council sitting as Committee of Papers.

(A) RELATING TO THE CONDUCT OF ORDINARY MEETINGS

1. At each Ordinary Meeting, any formal business of the Society which may be necessary, such as the reading of certificates, balloting for candidates under Statutes, Chapter I, announcements, returning thanks for presents, etc., shall, unless the President direct otherwise, be the first business of the meeting.

2. At each Ordinary Meeting, not being a Meeting for Discussion, as hereinafter provided, or for the Croonian, Bakerian, Ferrier, Wilkins or Leeuwenhoek Lecture, or other special lectures, the President shall determine what papers are to be read, and the order in which they shall be taken. He may also, whenever he sees fit, direct the author of a paper or one of the Secretaries to read an abstract of the paper or the paper itself, if it be sufficiently brief, or may invite the author to make an oral statement of the nature of its contents, and may also invite remarks upon the paper. When an oral statement is desired, the author shall, so far as possible, be previously informed of the fact.

3. At any Ordinary Meeting, not being a Meeting for Discussion, any Fellow of the Society may, with the approval of the President, and at such period of the meeting as the President may determine, make a communication not of the nature of a 'paper', or exhibit objects having relation to the advancement of Natural Knowledge.

4. The president shall further have power at any Ordinary meeting, and at any period of that meeting which he may think proper, to make such announcements or statements, as he may think desirable, relating to the advancement of Natural Knowledge.

5. The Secretaries may cancel an Ordinary Meeting of the Society, if, in their opinion, sufficient papers of a suitable nature are not available, or if the President in any emergency so order. Due notice shall be given of such cancellation.

6. In each year certain meetings shall be devoted each to the hearing and consideration of some one important communication or to the discussion of some important topic; these meetings shall be termed 'Meetings for Discussion'. The Secretaries may arrange for such meetings to take place at other times than those appointed for Ordinary Meetings.

The Council shall from time to time give due notice of the dates at which Meetings for Discussion will be held.

7. The Council, of its own motion, or upon the recommendation of a Sectional Committee, may select some communication made to the Society in the ordinary way, as the subject for such a Meeting for Discussion, or it may select for that purpose some question, the discussion of which would, in their judgment, be likely to advance Natural Knowledge. In the latter case, the Council shall appoint some person to open the discussion by means of a communication made by him for that purpose.

8. When a Meeting for Discussion has been arranged, the Council, or the Officers, shall direct printed copies of the communication which has been approved of for the said meeting (or of an adequate abstract of it) to be sent not later than one week before the date of the Meeting, to each Fellow, or to certain Fellows of the Society, and to such other persons as the President may direct. And the Council shall take such other steps as may seem to it desirable to render the discussion useful towards the advancement of Natural Knowledge.

9. At each Meeting for Discussion, the conduct of the discussion shall be under the direction of the President, who shall arrange for the Fellows present and desiring to speak, and who shall have the power to invite, if he think fit, persons present, not Fellows of the Society, to take part in the discussion. Any Fellow shall be at liberty

to send to the Secretaries, previous to the meeting, written remarks on the communication which is the subject of the meeting, and the President shall, if he see fit, direct one or other of the Secretaries to read these remarks at the meeting.

The Council will, from time to time, lay down such regulations as they think fit with regard to communications to the Press of papers read, discussions, or other matters transacted at the Ordinary Meetings of the Society. All proceedings at the Special General Meetings are to be considered as confidential, and no communication to the Press with regard to any business transacted at these meetings shall be made without the authority of the Council.

(B) Relating to Sectional Committees

10. The Council shall appoint, from among the Fellows of the Society, Committees representing the several branches of Natural Knowledge, and called 'Sectional Committees'. The members of each Committee shall be chosen with a view to secure, so far as is possible, a representation of the several subdivisions of each branch of Natural Knowledge, and to obtain the assistance of Fellows who, from their connexion with other societies, and otherwise, are specially qualified to advise the Council in respect to particular parts of Natural Knowledge.

11. Each Sectional Committee shall advise the Council or any of the Officers upon matters referred to it by the Council or by any of the Officers, and otherwise shall make to the Council such suggestions as it may think desirable touching the branch or branches of Natural Knowledge which it represents and touching the Society's scientific meetings and journals.

12. The Council shall each year appoint a member of each Committee to serve as Chairman of that Committee, and to be the channel of communication between the Committee and the Council or Officers. He is authorized to appoint one of the Committee his Deputy when necessary.

13. The Sectional Committees shall be a number greater than *ten* and referred to by number and not by name. The allocation of subjects by Committees shall be as follows:

Sectional Committee 1
Pure mathematics, theoretical and applied mechanics, mathematical astronomy, statistics (theory), theoretical fluid mechanics, mathematics applied to physical theory, operational research.

Sectional Committee 2
Experimental physics (including atomic, nuclear, low temperature and solid state physics, acoustics, spectroscopy, magnetism, heat, optics), crystallography, optical and radio astronomy, ionospheric physics, applied physics, theoretical physics relating to these subjects.

Sectional Committee 3
Chemistry, applied chemistry, theoretical chemistry.

Sectional Committee 4 (i)
Engineering (civil and structural, mechanical, computer, control, aeronautical, turbo machinery), experimental fluid dynamics.

Sectional Committee 4 (ii)
Engineering (electric power, electronics, nuclear, chemical), metallurgy, instrumentation.

Sectional Committee 5
Meteorology, hydrology, oceanography (excluding marine biology), geology, geodesy, geophysics, soil physics, geochemistry, mineralogy, physical geography, archaeology, theoretical physics relating to these subjects.

Sectional Committee 6
Plant anatomy and physiology; plant taxonomy, mycology, plant pathology (including infective diseases of plants), applied plant sciences, plant breeding, plant ecology, palaeobotany.

Sectional Committee 7
Vertebrate and invertebrate zoology and palaeozoology, human and comparative anatomy, taxonomy and systematics, entomology, parasitology, protozoology, marine and freshwater biology, animal ecology and population dynamics, animal behaviour, physical anthropology.

Sectional Committee 8
Biochemistry, molecular biophysics, chemical microbiology.

Sectional Committee 9

Animal and human physiology (including nutrition), biophysics, pharmacology, endocrinology (including applied and comparative aspects), reproduction, psychology.

Sectional Committee 10

Medical sciences, bacteriology, virology and general microbiology, epidemiology, immunology, pathology, radiobiology, medical statistics and demography.

Sectional Committee 11

Genetics (including molecular, microbial and population genetics), experimental cytology, cell biology, differentiation and development.

There shall also be a Committee, to be known as the Committee on General Candidates, to assist Council in the consideration of the claims of candidates for election into the Fellowship who are not explicitly covered by the terms of Standing Order 10 or by Statute 12. The Standing Orders for this Committee shall be as for the Sectional Committees where appropriate, including that providing for the attendance of members of Council at the meetings.*

14. Each Sectional Committee shall consist of nine members of whom three shall retire each year; four members shall form a quorum.

15. Any member of Council who desires to attend the meetings of any Sectional Committee, of which he is not a member, shall be entitled to do so and to take part in the deliberations of the Committee, but he shall not have the power to vote. Each member of Council shall be invited to state the Sectional Committee or Committees the meetings of which he wishes to attend: the summons and agenda for every meeting of each committee concerned shall then be sent to him as to an ordinary member of each committee during his tenure of office as a member of Council. The Chairman shall be expected to correspond with him as with an ordinary member of the Committee.

*Council on 18 June 1964 appointed an *ad hoc* Committee on Applied Sciences Candidates to assist Council in the consideration of the claims of such candidates for election into the Fellowship and to operate under the rules for Sectional Committees in a somewhat similar way to the Committee on General Candidates. On 18 May 1972 Council resolved that the Committee be continued on an *ad hoc* basis.

STANDING ORDERS OF COUNCIL

16. The retirement of members shall be determined by seniority of appointment to the Committee.

17. The retiring members of the Committee shall each year vacate office on 31 July, and shall not be eligible for election for the ensuing year.

18. Should, by reason of death or otherwise, a vacancy occur at any intermediate time, the Council shall appoint a person to fill the vacancy. The retirement of the person so appointed shall be according to the rules which would have applied to the member whose place he fills. If, however, at the date of retirement of the person appointed to fill the vacancy, he has not served more than one year, he shall be eligible for immediate re-appointment.

19. The appointment of the Fellows to serve as new members of Committee shall be made by the Council in June, and the members so appointed shall enter office upon 1 August ensuing.

20. Each Committee shall hold a meeting in January every year.

21. The decisions arrived at by a meeting of the Committee at which the members present do not form a quorum shall be valid, if subsequently agreed to in writing by not less than two-thirds of the whole Committee.

22. Voting shall be open unless any member of the Committee demands a ballot.

23. The Minutes of the Committee shall be duly recorded in a book kept for that purpose, and preserved in the Society's apartments, together with such correspondence and documents relating to the business of the Committee as the Committee may think it desirable to preserve.

24. The Chairmen of Sectional Committees, together with the Officers of the Society, shall be a Standing Committee with powers to make such recommendations to the Council as they think fit concerning questions affecting the Sectional Committees jointly, or on any matters affecting the Society and not specifically excluded from their purview by resolution of Council. They shall meet at least once a year.

(C) Relating to 'Proceedings', 'Philosophical Transactions' and other Publications of the Society

25. The *Proceedings* shall be the medium for publication of papers of approved merit not normally exceeding twenty-four printed pages in length, and not containing numerous or elaborate illustrations: the Council may, however, on a report from one of the Secretaries order papers of greater length to be printed in the *Proceedings*. The *Proceedings* shall also include such other matters as the Council may judge desirable to insert.

26. The *Philosophical Transactions* shall be the medium for publication (*a*) of papers of approved merit which contain numerous or elaborate illustrations, or which cannot without detriment to their scientific value be condensed into the space reserved for papers in the *Proceedings;* (*b*) of such reports or investigations carried out by a Committee of the Society as the Council may order to be printed in the *Transactions;* (*c*) of reports of Discussion Meetings of a length exceeding the normal size of an issue of *Proceedings*.

27. The *Proceedings* shall be issued in two series, namely series A containing papers relating to the physical sciences, and series B, papers relating to the biological sciences.

28. Subject to the powers given to the Secretaries and Associate Editors in Standing Orders 39 and 43, it shall rest with the Council, after a report of the appropriate Secretary whether *Proceedings* or *Philosophical Transactions* is the more suitable medium for publication. The Communicator of a paper shall, however, be at liberty to indicate his preference for one or other of the two forms of publication.

29. The *Proceedings* shall be published in numbers issued at as short intervals as may be found suitable.

30. Each paper ordered by the Council for publication in the *Philosophical Transactions* shall be published separately (except that two or more allied papers may constitute one issue) in paper covers, the date on which it is issued being marked on the cover. The papers shall be issued in two series, namely series A containing papers relating to the physical sciences and series B papers relating to the

biological sciences. At suitable intervals the papers in each series shall be collected into a volume.

31. There shall be published annually (1) a *Year Book* of the Society, containing a list of Fellows of the Society and their addresses, together with such other matters as the Council may order to be inserted, (2) *Biographical Memoirs of Fellows of the Royal Society*, (3) *Notes and Records*, and such other compilations as Council may decide.

(D) Relating to Acceptance, Reading and Publication of Papers

32. A Fellow or Foreign Member communicating a paper shall satisfy himself that the paper is a fit and proper one to be communicated to the Society, and has not been previously published elsewhere (Statute 64). Once the receipt of a paper has been acknowledged to the communicator, future correspondence relating to it shall be with the author but the communicator shall also be informed of the decision regarding its acceptance. The communicator shall inform the Executive Secretary of the address of the author, or of one of the authors if there are several.

33. Each paper must be accompanied by an abstract (in triplicate) not exceeding 5 per cent of the length of the paper, showing the general scope of the investigation and the main conclusions.

34. The Executive Secretary shall ensure that every communicated paper received: (*a*) shall have marked upon it the date of its receipt; (*b*) shall be recorded in the register of papers (Statute 83); and (*c*) shall be brought to the attention of the appropriate Secretary and the appropriate Associate Editor.

35. The two Secretaries, who are responsible to the Council for the conduct of the Society's publications (Statute 49), shall each be assisted by a number of Associate Editors covering different scientific disciplines.

36. Associate Editors, who shall be Fellows, shall be appointed by the Council after consultation with the appropriate Sectional Committees. The appointments shall be made in November and shall be for a period of one year from 1 December. An Associate Editor shall be eligible for reappointment annually for four further consecutive years.

37. The Associate Editors for papers relating to the physical and biological sciences respectively, with the appropriate Secretary in the chair, shall meet once a year to discuss editorial policy.

38. Each Associate Editor shall advise on the suitability for publication of papers that fall within the subject category for which he is responsible.

39. After consulting the appropriate Associate Editor, a Secretary may, if he thinks fit, proceed to publication with any paper received that does not exceed twenty-four pages of either the *Proceedings* or the *Philosophical Transactions*. The Secretary and the Associate Editor shall give due weight to the opinion of the communicator if the subject of the paper falls within his competence.

40. When a referee or referees are necessary they shall be nominated by the appropriate Associate Editor. The choice of referees need not be restricted to Fellows or to persons resident in the United Kingdom. The choice should be aimed at promoting the publication of papers of high standard as expeditiously as possible.

41. When a paper is submitted to a referee, his opinion in writing shall be asked as follows:

(i) Does it contain contributions to knowledge of sufficient scientific interest for the space required?

(ii) Does the abstract give an adequate indication of the content of the paper, including any important results?

(iii) Are any portions of the paper, or any illustrations redundant?

(iv) Should the paper be published by the Society? (See Standing Order 42 below.)

(v) If so, in the *Philosophical Transactions* or the *Proceedings*?

(vi) Comments or criticisms which might enable the author to improve or correct his statement.

(vii) If the amendments are of a relatively minor kind, do you wish to see the revised version?

42. The attention of referees shall be drawn to the fact that the publications of the Society are not the proper medium for the mere accumulation of data, or the elaboration of minor details. In reporting on papers they should have regard, *inter alia*, to the following considerations: (i) whether the paper submitted contains results or

methods of critical importance; (ii) whether, disregarding considerations of cost, it could more appropriately be published by some other body; (iii) whether it is likely to be of value to others than specialists in the particular subject. A paper should not be recommended for rejection merely because a referee disagrees with opinions, theories, or conclusions put forward by the author, unless in the course of the exposition logical fallacy or experimental error is made evident.

43. In the event of the report(s) on a paper being favourable and the Associate Editor recommending publication, such a recommendation shall be submitted to the Council (sitting as the Committee of Papers) by the appropriate Secretary who shall also in anticipation of the paper's acceptance authorize its printing. The communicator and the author shall be informed of the favourable recommendation.

44. In the event of the report(s) on a paper being unfavourable and the Associate Editor not recommending publication, the Secretary shall after considering the report(s) of one or more referees and the advice of the Associate Editor be authorized to reject the paper.

45. If the opinions of two referees disagree, a Secretary or an Associate Editor shall normally submit the paper to a third referee, and they shall have power to communicate to him the grounds on which the original referees have expressed their respective opinions.

46. The anonymity of a referee shall be strictly preserved by all concerned. Exceptionally, when a referee wishes to discuss a paper with the author or to obtain the confidential opinion of a colleague he may do so only after he has obtained the express permission of the appropriate Secretary.

47. When the appropriate Associate Editor is the author of a paper the Secretaries shall consult some other suitably qualified Fellow.

48. A summary or abstract (see Standing Order 33) shall be printed at the head of each full paper when this is published and shall also be circulated with the programme of the meeting if the paper is read before the Society, unless the author wishes to provide a different version for that purpose.

49. The Secretaries are responsible, if necessary in consultation with the appropriate Associate Editors, for selecting papers to be read before the Society.

50. Each paper published by the Society shall bear the date on which it was received by the Society. No addition or change other than minor corrections shall be made subsequently either in the manuscript or in correcting the proofs for press without indication of the date of such addition or change.

51. If after a decision to recommend a paper for publication, the Secretaries shall, from any discussion that may take place at the meeting at which the paper is read, or otherwise, have good reason to think that the decision should be reconsidered, they shall after consultation with the Associate Editor, have power to postpone the publication of the paper, or after reconsideration by the Council to reject it.

52. The Council shall, at some convenient time during each of its meetings, sit as a Committee of Papers (Statute 72), and the summons to the meeting of the Council shall be considered sufficient notice for such meeting of the Committee of Papers.

53. At each meeting of the Committee of Papers a full statement shall be laid on the table giving lists of the authors and titles of all papers which, since the previous meeting, have been (*a*) received, and (*b*) recommended by the Secretaries for publication, and the Committee of Papers shall confirm, or otherwise, the recommendations.

54. The Council, sitting as a Committee of Papers, at each meeting shall formally record its decisions.

(E) Relating to Distribution of Publications to Fellows

55. The publications available *gratis* to each Fellow shall be (*a*) one copy of each issue of (1) *Year Book*, (2) *Biographical Memoirs*, (3) *Notes and Records* and (4) *Proceedings* Series A or *Philosophical Transactions* Series A or *Proceedings* Series B or *Philosophical Transactions* Series B; and (*b*), under the procedure set out in Standing Order 58, one offprint each of a limited number of papers in the journals listed in (4) other than the journal chosen to be received *gratis*. In each instance the binding shall be as decided by Council.

STATUTES OF THE ROYAL SOCIETY 197

56. Any Fellow wishing to purchase *Philosophical Transactions* and *Proceedings* not receivable under Standing Order 55 may do so on payment of fifty per cent of the price to the public either by way of a subscription (payable in advance of publication) or by payment for individual issues.

57. On election each Fellow shall be invited to make a choice (which may be varied subsequently on three months' notice being given) as to which publications, if any, he wishes to receive, how he wishes to order them, whether he wishes to use the offprints service (Standing Order 58) and how he wishes to pay for those publications not supplied *gratis*.

58. The procedure for ordering offprints of papers in *Philosophical Transactions* and *Proceedings* shall be as follows: they shall be selected from the advance lists of papers accepted for publication and circulated normally monthly to those Fellows who have intimated that they wish to use this service; notification of the papers selected from a list must be received by the Executive Secretary not later than one month after the date of circulation of that list.

59. The Standing Orders in this Section shall apply also to Foreign Members elected after 1973.

60. Although Council has power under Statute 91 to make and alter Standing Orders, Council may call a Special General Meeting (in accordance with the Statutes, Chapter XIII) before altering the Standing Orders in this Section relating to the availability of publications to Fellows.

(F) RELATING TO REPRESENTATION ON OUTSIDE BODIES

61. Service by representatives of the Society on outside bodies shall not in general exceed ten consecutive years, unless specifically authorized by Council for a longer period and they shall ordinarily be replaced on attaining the age of 75 years.

COUNCIL PROCEDURE

I. IN THE NOMINATION OF THE COUNCIL*

1. The subject of the new Council shall be taken into consideration at the first meeting of Council to be held in October; and with the summons for that meeting there shall be transmitted a list of the members of the existing Council, with the number of their attendances at meetings up to that date; also a list of the Fellows of the Society, with an indication of those who have at any time served on the Council, and the dates of their service; also a further list containing the name of any Fellow which has been forwarded to the Secretaries before the first day of October in that year, with a statement, signed by at least six other Fellows, that they regard him as suitable for consideration for membership of the Council.

A list of members of Council, with those retiring separately marked, shall be sent to members of Council three weeks before the October meeting. Members of Council may then fill in on the list the names of any whom they wish to propose for service on Council in place of retiring members. These names, together with any proposals received from Fellows in accordance with this Standing Order, will then be placed before the meeting of Council at which consideration is given to the selection of members of Council for the ensuing year. All names duly proposed and seconded at the meeting will be considered in deciding on the list of the new Council recommended for election by the Society at the Anniversary Meeting.

2. At the first meeting of Council held in October the names of those members of the existing Council who retire at the ensuing Anniversary shall be determined.

The retirement of members of Council will be determined upon in the following order; with the proviso that every member of Council retains the right to exercise his vote according to his discretion, subject only to the terms of the Charter, which ordains that ten members of Council, and no more, shall be changed at each Anniversary:

* From Minutes of Council, 20 June 1872, 21 May 1914, 7 March 1935, 20 February 1941, 15 June 1944, 30 November 1955, 17 May 1956, 21 January 1960, 11 November 1976.

COUNCIL PROCEDURE

(i) Members who have expressed their wish to retire; and those who will have served for two years by the ensuing Anniversary, excepting the Officers for the time being.

(ii) Former Officers of the Society who have continued to serve after vacating office and who will have served for one more year by the ensuing Anniversary.

(iii) Members who have been absent from more than two meetings since the last Anniversary, in the order of least attendance.

(iv) Members who have served on the Council for the first time during the current session.

Provided that if the number of members who would vacate under the preceding four categories be greater than ten the necessary adjustment shall be made by re-nominating a sufficient number of members who are serving for the first time, in the order of their seniority as Fellows or, if there is an insufficient number of such members, by re-nominating a sufficient number of members in categories (i) and (ii).

(v) If the number of members who vacate under the above categories should be less than ten, the required vacancies shall be made up by the retirement of members who have served on a previous Council, excepting Officers for the time being; such retirement to take place in the order of least seniority as Fellows.

(Seniority shall be counted by the date of election into the Society, and, in the case of Fellows elected during the same year, by the order of their admission into the Society.)

(vi) In cases where any member of the Council considers that the re-nomination of a member is—for special reasons—desirable, although such member would not be re-nominated according to the above rules, a ballot shall be taken on a motion to re-nominate such member, notice having been given at a previous meeting, and the question of re-nomination shall be determined by the vote of the majority of the members of the Council present and voting.

Thereafter each member present shall hand to one of the Secretaries a List of not exceeding ten Fellows whom he proposes for the new Council, *of whom five shall not have already served on the Council.* Members not able to be present may send in similar lists previous to the meeting. The several lists of names so proposed shall then be read out by the Secretaries.

3. Before the next following meeting, the President and other Officers shall prepare a list of twenty-one names for consideration by the Council, which list shall include ten names selected from those proposed at the previous meeting, or other names, if required to make up that number. The list so prepared, together with a statement of the names proposed, and the number of votes given for each, shall be sent out confidentially with the summons for the ensuing meeting, at which meeting the names to be finally recommended shall be balloted for. In taking the ballot, a copy of the list, prepared by the Officers, shall, with such alterations as he may see fit to make therein, be delivered by each member of the Council present and voting, and the names found to have the majority of votes shall form the list to be recommended to the Society.

4. The President and Council shall then nominate by ballot, out of the proposed Council, the persons whom they recommend to the Society for election to the offices of President, Treasurer, Principal Secretaries and Foreign Secretary, for the ensuing year.

No person shall be nominated for further re-election to the office of President after he has held that office for five years, to the office of Treasurer after he has held that office for ten years, or to the office of Foreign Secretary after he has held that office for five years. When a person has been five times elected to the office of Treasurer or of a Principal Secretary, Council shall decide during the fifth year of his tenure of that office, by a resolution taken in his absence, whether he shall be eligible for further annual nominations for election, and if so for what additional number of such annual nominations, not exceeding five to the office of Treasurer and three to the office of a Principal Secretary.

II. IN THE AWARD OF THE MEDALS

1. At the first meeting on the subject of the Medals, the members of Council are invited to *suggest* a name, or names, which they may deem worthy of consideration in the adjudication of each of the several Medals. The list of suggested names then formed to be entered on the Minutes, with power to members of Council to add to it afterwards, if they see fit.

COUNCIL PROCEDURE

2. At a subsequent meeting (or meetings), to be held before the Midsummer Recess (at which additions may be made to the List of Suggestions), every member of the Council present is at liberty to propose for each Medal the name of a person whom he recommends to be selected to receive it, specifying the particular work or works which form the ground of his recommendation; and these proposals, being seconded, shall be entered on the Minutes. After this meeting the proposer is expected to prepare and forward to one of the Secretaries a detailed statement of the claims of the person recommended by him, for consultation by members of the Council, should they so desire.

3. The Council is to be summoned in October, for the purpose of discussing the merits, as regards the award of the Medals, of the persons severally proposed. Additional proposals may be made at this meeting, if assented to by two-thirds of the members present.

4. The Council is to meet for final consideration of the proposals at an early date thereafter, but before the Anniversary Meeting.

The medals to be awarded are:
>The Copley Medal [1731]: annually.
>The Rumford Medal [1800]: biennially.
>The Royal Medals [1825 and 1965]: annually.
>The Davy Medal [1877]: annually.
>The Darwin Medal [1890]: biennially.
>The Buchanan Medal [1897]: quinquennially
>The Sylvester Medal [1901]: triennially.
>The Hughes Medal [1902]: annually.
>The Leverhulme Medal [1960]: triennially.
>The Mullard Medal [1967]: annually (but with a different procedure for consideration of nominations).
>The Esso Medal [1974:] annually (but with a different procedure for consideration of nominations).

For the conditions governing the awards, see pp. 207–212.

III. IN THE APPOINTMENT OF THE LECTURERS

1. The Croonian, Bakerian and Clifford Paterson Lectures are delivered annually, the Ferrier, Wilkins and Bernal Lectures triennially, and the Leeuwenhoek Lecture annually or at such intervals as Council may decide.

2. Members of Council at the meeting in December are invited to propose candidates for the lectureships to be filled in the following year. A statement of approximately 500 words setting forth the claims of each candidate so proposed should be sent to the Secretaries not later than 31 December.

3. These statements are circulated to members of Council prior to the January meeting, at which the lecturers for the year are duly appointed.

IV. IN THE ADMINISTRATION OF CERTAIN ELEMENTS OF THE PARLIAMENTARY GRANT-IN-AID*

The following regulations for the administration of certain elements of the Parliamentary Grant-in-aid have been adopted by the Council:

(1) SCIENTIFIC INVESTIGATIONS

(i) The grant for scientific investigations is provided to promote and support research in science and to assist scientific expeditions and collections; it is not intended for personal maintenance, payment of stipends or to aid scientific publications. It is administered by the President and Council of the Royal Society. (Council considers it undesirable, in general, that applications should be made for (*a*) recurrent grants towards the expense of established research, when such expense could naturally be regarded as having become a proper charge upon the university or other establishment where the work is being carried out or (*b*) grants for items of equipment which the Council would expect might be provided by ordinary departmental funds.)

(ii) To assist in the review of applications and obtain expert advice on them, the President and Council of the Royal Society shall set up eight Boards, namely:

Board A. Mathematics, computing science, astronomy, meteorology, statistics, geodesy and geophysics.
Board B. Experimental physics and crystallography.
Board C. Chemistry.
Board D. Engineering science and metallurgy.
Board E. Geological sciences and geography.
Board F. Botany and agriculture.
Board G. Zoology, comparative anatomy and physical anthropology.
Board H. Animal physiology, biochemistry and medical subjects.

* From Minutes of Council, 12 July 1945, 3 March 1955, 13 December 1962, 6 November 1969, 11 July 1974, 10 July 1975, 6 November 1975, 18 December 1975, 17 June 1976, 15 July 1976.

(iii) Each Board shall consist of eight members, who shall not necessarily be Fellows of the Royal Society. The President and Council shall appoint the members of the Boards. When practicable, arrangements will be made in constituting the Boards to ensure that the interests of Northern Ireland, Scotland and Wales are represented.

(iv) Service on, and retirement from, the Boards shall be governed by the following rules:

- (a) Each member shall serve for four years, and shall not be eligible for re-appointment until after the lapse of one year.
- (b) Two of the eight members shall retire annually, the rotation of retirement being determined by the date of appointment.
- (c) In the event of a vacancy occurring, by death or otherwise, the President and Council of the Royal Society shall appoint a person to fill the vacancy. The person so appointed shall be regarded as having served for the same period as the member whose place he has taken; but in the event of the latter having served for more than two years the substituted member shall be eligible immediately on completing his appointment for re-appointment for a full term.

(v) The President and Council of the Royal Society shall appoint a member of each Board to act as chairman of the Board. He shall manage the business of the Board, and shall have a second or casting vote. When unable to attend to the business before the Board or to be present at meetings, he shall have authority to nominate to the Society a member of the Board to act as his deputy, who shall exercise all the powers of the chairman.

(vi) Three members of a Board shall be regarded as a quorum; but decisions reached at a meeting at which less than three members are present shall be deemed valid if subsequently agreed to in writing by five or more members of the Board.

(vii) The function of the Boards shall be:

- (a) To review applications for grants and make recommendations on them to the President and Council of the Royal Society.
- (b) To review the reports from those to whom grants have been made and report on them to the President and Council of the Royal Society, with such recommendations as to the continuance or withdrawal of the grants as they think proper.
- (c) To review the list of apparatus purchased by grants, whether in use by recipients of grants or returned to the Royal Society.
- (d) When desired, to initiate an inquiry and to recommend a grant for the purpose.

(viii) The President and Council of the Royal Society shall advertise in the press that applications will be received three times annually, namely, before 15 March, 15 July, and 15 November.

(ix) Applicants, who must be British subjects, domiciled in the United Kingdom, shall furnish in their applications, on forms obtainable from the Executive Secretary, information under the following heads (certain additional information is required from applicants for expeditions):

    (a) Proposed research and expected scientific results.
    (b) Appointment held and relevant publications during the past five years.
    (c) Amount asked for (with details of the cost of the various items and provision for V.A.T., if required) and whether any part of the grant is intended to meet personal expenses connected with the research. (N.B. By agreement with the Department of Education and Science, no application exceeding £12 500 can be considered.)
    (d) Other grants for the proposed or related research obtained or sought within the preceding three years.
    (e) Where the proposed research is to be done and whether the application has been approved by the head of the applicant's department.

(x) The conditions governing the allocation of grants shall be determined by the President and Council of the Royal Society, and shall be revised triennially. The Department of Education and Science shall be informed of these conditions, or of any modification of them.

(xi) The chairman of a Board may recommend to the President and Council of the Royal Society the transfer of any apparatus or material obtained by means of a grant and no longer needed. When apparatus is no longer required the Treasurer of the Royal Society shall be authorized to dispose of it by sale for the credit of the fund. When the recipient of a grant has collected, by means of that grant, specimens or material of permanent value, the President and Council of the Royal Society shall determine, after consultation with the appropriate Board, as to their final disposal.

(2) SCIENTIFIC PUBLICATIONS AND LIBRARIES ASSISTANCE

(i) The element for scientific publications is provided for the assistance of scientific publications in the United Kingdom, particularly, but not exclusively, those of scientific societies and institutions. An element is also provided for the assistance of the libraries of scientific societies in the United Kingdom. They shall be administered by the President and Council of the Royal Society.

(ii) To assist in the review of applications and obtain expert advice on them, the President and Council of the Royal Society shall set up a *Scientific Publications Board*.

(iii) This Board shall consist of twelve members, who shall not necessarily be Fellows of the Royal Society.

(iv) Service on, and retirement from, the Board shall be governed by rules similar to those for the Boards dealing with the grant for scientific investigations.

(v) The President and Council of the Royal Society shall appoint the chairman of the Board. He shall manage the business of the Board, and shall have a second or casting vote. When unable to attend to the business before the Board or be present at meetings he shall have authority to nominate to the Society a member of the Board to act as his deputy, who shall exercise all the powers of the chairman.

(vi) Three members of the Board shall be regarded as a quorum; but decisions reached at a meeting of the Board, at which less than three members are present, shall be deemed valid if subsequently agreed to in writing by not less than five members of the Board in all.

(vii) The President and Council of the Royal Society shall advertise in the Press that applications, on forms obtainable from the Executive Secretary, will be received twice annually, namely, before 8 June and 8 November.

(viii) The Department of Education and Science shall be informed of any modifications made in these regulations.

(3) History of Science

(i) The element for history of science is provided for purposes in connexion with the promotion and support of research in the history of science (including mathematics), medicine and technology; but not to meet the cost of publishing results. It is administered by the President and Council of the Royal Society.

(ii) The President and Council of the Royal Society may obtain expert advice from, and be assisted in the review of applications by, the British National Committee for the History of Science, Medicine and Technology.

(iii) The President and Council of the Royal Society shall advertise that applications, on forms obtainable from the Executive Secretary, will be received once each year, normally before 31 October.

(iv) Applicants, who must be domiciled in the United Kingdom, shall furnish in their applications, on forms obtainable from the Executive Secretary, information under the following heads:

(*a*) The nature of the research to be followed.
(*b*) The amount of money required and details of the cost of the various items.
(*c*) Whether any application has been made to other grant-giving bodies, and with what result.
(*d*) The place of research and whether the programme of research has been approved by the head of the department in which it will be carried out.

(4) INTERNATIONAL RELATIONS

(i) The element for international relations includes provision for (*a*) the payment of subscriptions to international unions and other international bodies to which the Royal Society (as the national academy for the United Kingdom, see p. 131) adheres or supports, (*b*) expenses of delegates attending meetings of international scientific organizations and (*c*) assisting with travel expenses of scientists to scientific meetings or visiting laboratories overseas.

(ii) The grant shall be administered by the President and Council of the Royal Society who shall, if deemed necessary, seek the advice of the Travelling Expenses Committee, the National Committee for I.C.S.U. of the Royal Society or the appropriate National Committee.

GENERAL

The President, Treasurer and Secretaries of the Royal Society shall be *ex officio* members of the Boards set up to advise on allocations for scientific investigations and for scientific publications.

THE SOCIETY'S MEDALS

Copley Medal (1731)

The medal is of silver gilt, and is awarded annually to the living author of such philosophical research, either published or communicated to the Society, as may appear to the Council to be deserving of that honour. The subject or subjects of research, on account of which the medal is awarded, must be specified in making the award.

No limitation is imposed either as to the period of time within which that research was made, or to the particular country to which its author may belong. The medal may not be awarded to any person who is a member of Council at the time when the award is made; it may be given more than once to the same person if the Council deem it expedient. (See *Record*, p. 112.)

A gift of £100 accompanies the medal. Since 1957 a Mr and Mrs John Jaffé Prize of £1 000 has accompanied the Copley Medal and Gift and, if the medallist as a Nobel Laureate has been precluded from receiving a Jaffé Prize, £1 000 has been provided from another source.

Rumford Medal (1800)

A silver gilt medal is awarded once every second year 'to the author of the most important discovery or useful improvement which shall be made and published by printing or in any way made known to the public in any part of Europe during the preceding two years on Heat or on Light, the preference always being given to such discoveries as, in the opinion of the President and Council of the Royal Society, tend most to promote the good of mankind.' (See *Record*, p. 115.)

'If during any term of years from the last award no new discovery or improvement shall have been made in any part of Europe relative to Light or Heat, in the opinion of the President and Council of sufficient importance to deserve the award, it may not be given, but the value of it may be reserved, and being laid out in the purchase of additional stock may augment the capital; and the interest of the same, by which the capital may from time to time be so augmented, may be given in money' at a subsequent award with the medal.

A gift of £200 accompanies the medal.

The Royal Medals (1825 and 1965)

Three Royal Medals, known also as The Queen's Gold Medals, are awarded annually by the Sovereign upon the recommendation of the Council, two for the most important contributions to the advancement of Natural Knowledge (one to each of the two great divisions) and the other for distinguished contributions in the applied sciences, published originally in Her Majesty's Dominions within a period of not more than ten years, and of not less than one year of the date of the award. (See *Record*, p. 116.)

Davy Medal (1877)

The medal is of bronze, and is awarded annually for the most important discovery in Chemistry made in Europe or in Anglo-America. (See *Record*, p. 114.)

A gift of £200 accompanies the medal.

The Darwin Medal (1890)

A silver medal is given biennially in reward of work of acknowledged distinction (especially in Biology) in the field in which Charles Darwin himself laboured. The award may be made either to a British subject or a foreigner, and without distinction of sex. (See *Record*, p. 114.)

A gift of £200 accompanies the medal.

Buchanan Medal (1897)

A silver gilt medal is awarded every five years in respect of distinguished services to Hygienic Science or Practice in the direction either of original research or of professional, administrative, or constructive work, without limit of nationality or sex. (See *Record*, p. 113.)

A gift of £200 accompanies the medal.

Sylvester Medal (1901)

A bronze medal is awarded triennially for the encouragement of Mathematical Research, irrespective of nationality. (See *Record*, p. 115.)

A gift of £200 accompanies the medal.

Hughes Medal (1902)

A silver gilt medal, bearing a bust of the late Professor D. E. Hughes, is awarded annually to such person as the President and Council may consider the most worthy recipient, without restriction of sex or nationality, as the reward of original discovery in the Physical Sciences, particularly electricity and magnetism or their applications, such discovery or applications having been published not less than one year before the award. If in any year the Council do not see fit to award the medal, owing to no one being deemed sufficiently worthy of it, the income for that year is invested and added to the principal of the Fund. (See *Record*, p. 114.)

A gift of £200 accompanies the medal.

Leverhulme Medal to commemorate the Society's Tercentenary (1960).

The Trustees of the Leverhulme Trust Fund expressed a desire to mark the occasion of the Tercentenary of the Royal Society by the award of a gold medal. The medal is to be awarded by the Society, every three years, to the individual who, in the opinion of its Council, shall have made the most significant contribution in the field of pure or applied chemistry or engineering, including chemical engineering. The medal is accompanied by a monetary award of £500.

Mullard Medal (1967)

The Royal Society Mullard Award, which consists of a gold medal and a prize of £1000, was provided by a gift to the Society by the Board of Directors of Mullard Limited.

Scheme (adopted by Council on 10 November 1966 and amended 15 July 1971):

1. The Award shall consist of a gold medal and a prize of £1000.

2. The Award shall be made annually by the Council of the Royal Society to an individual or individuals who, in the opinion of Council, had made an outstanding contribution or contributions to the advancement of science or engineering or technology leading directly to national prosperity in the United Kingdom of Great Britain and Northern Ireland.

3. Council shall be advised on suitable candidates for the Award by a special Committee appointed by Council.

4. Nominations for the Award shall be invited from all Fellows of the Society and from such other sources as the Committee may decide.

5. The nominations shall consist of:
   (*a*) Full name, age and address of candidate.
   (*b*) Academic or professional qualifications.
   (*c*) An appropriate description of not less than 500 words of his achievements in relation to the purpose of the Award supported by any published or other relevant evidence.
   (*d*) The names of at least two referees from whom further supporting statements could be sought.
   (*e*) Name of proposer.

6. The Committee, after adjudication, shall submit to Council for its July meeting each year a report containing recommendations of three candidates for the Award in order of preference with reasons for the order and supporting statements.

7. The Award shall be presented at the Society's Anniversary Meeting.

8. The Award may not be made to any person who is a member of the Council at the time when Council decides who shall be the recipient.

Esso Award (1974)

The Royal Society Esso Award for the Conservation of Energy, which consists of a gold medal and a prize of £1000, was instituted following agreement reached between the Royal Society and Esso Petroleum Company Ltd for a special award for outstanding contributions to the advancement of science or engineering or technology leading to the more efficient conversion or use of energy.

Scheme (adopted by Council on 14 February 1974):

1. The Award shall consist of a gold medal and a prize of £1000. In the event of an award being shared by two or more individuals, each shall receive a gold medal and an equal share of the prize.

2. The Award shall be made by the Council of the Royal Society to an individual or individuals who, in the opinion of Council, had made an outstanding contribution or contributions to the advancement of science or engineering or technology leading to the more efficient conversion or use of energy.

3. Ordinarily the Award shall be made annually, but if in the opinion of Council there is no worthy candidate in any year, it shall not be made in that year.

4. Council shall be advised on suitable candidates for the Award by a Committee appointed by Council.

5. Nominations for the Award shall be invited from all Fellows of the Society and from such other sources as the Committee may decide.

6. The nominations shall consist of:
   (*a*) Full name, age and address of candidate.
   (*b*) Academic or professional qualifications and position.
   (*c*) An appropriate description of about 500 words of the candidate's achievements in relation to the purpose of the Award supported by any published or other relevant evidence.
   (*d*) The names of at least two referees from whom further supporting statements could be sought.
   (*e*) Name of proposer.

7. The Committee, after adjudication, shall submit to Council for its July meeting each year a report containing recommendations of three candidates for the Award in order of preference with reasons for the order and supporting statements.

8. The Award shall be presented at the Society's Anniversary Meeting.

9. The Award may not be made to any person who is a member of the Council at the time when Council decides who shall be the recipient.

AWARD OF MEDALS 1976

THE COPLEY MEDAL to PROFESSOR DOROTHY MARY CROWFOOT HODGKIN in recognition of her outstanding work on the structures of complex molecules, particularly penicillin, vitamin B_{12} and insulin.

A ROYAL MEDAL to PROFESSOR JOHN WARCUP CORNFORTH in recognition of his fundamental contribution to our knowledge of the biosynthesis of steroids.

A ROYAL MEDAL to PROFESSOR JAMES LEARMONTH GOWANS in recognition of his distinguished research in the field of immunology, especially as regards the recirculation and immunological role of lymphocytes.

A ROYAL MEDAL to DR ALAN WALSH in recognition of his distinguished contributions to emission and infra-red spectroscopy and his origination of the atomic absorption method of quantitative analysis.

THE RUMFORD MEDAL to PROFESSOR ILYA PRIGOGINE in recognition of his distinguished contributions to the theory of irreversible thermodynamics.

THE DAVY MEDAL to DR REX EDWARD RICHARDS in recognition of his outstanding contributions to nuclear magnetic resonance spectroscopy and its application to chemical and biological problems.

THE DARWIN MEDAL to PROFESSOR CHARLOTTE AUERBACH in recognition of her discovery of and continuing work on chemical mutagenesis.

THE SYLVESTER MEDAL to PROFESSOR DAVID GEORGE KENDALL in recognition of his many distinguished contributions to probability theory and its applications.

THE HUGHES MEDAL to DR STEPHEN WILLIAM HAWKING in recognition of his distinguished contributions to the application of general relativity to astrophysics, especially to the behaviour of highly condensed matter.

THE MULLARD MEDAL to DR GEORGE HERBERT HITCHINGS in recognition of his distinguished contributions to chemotherapy.

THE ESSO MEDAL to THOMAS BRUCE JACKSON in recognition of his development of an electronic optimum control for building heating systems.

(Medal Lists for the years until 1939 are printed in *The Record*, pp. 345–355, and lists for the years 1940–1974 inclusive in the *Year Book* for 1975, pp. 209–211.)

THE SOCIETY'S LECTURES

Croonian Lecture

Dr Croone, one of the original members of the Society, left on his death in 1684 a scheme for two lectureships, one at the Royal Society and the other at the Royal College of Physicians. His widow, in 1701, provided the means for carrying out this scheme and indicated that the bequest was 'for the support of a lecture and illustrative experiment for the advancement of natural knowledge on local motion, or (conditionally) of such other subjects as, in the opinion of the President for the time being, should be most useful in promoting the objects for which the Royal Society was instituted'.

The income of the fund is received from the Charity Commissioners and the gift paid to the lecturer is approximately £45. Since 1957 an additional Mr and Mrs John Jaffé Prize of £200 has been awarded and, if the lecturer as a Nobel Laureate has been precluded from receiving a Jaffé Prize, £200 has been provided from another source.

Bakerian Lecture

This lecture originated in 1775 through a bequest by Mr Henry Baker, F.R.S., of £100 for an oration or discourse which was to be spoken or read yearly by one of the Fellows of the Society on such part of natural history or experimental philosophy, at such time and in such manner as the President and Council of the Society for the time being shall please to order and appoint.

The gift for the lecturer is now £25. Since 1957 an additional Mr and Mrs John Jaffé Prize of £200 has been awarded and, if the lecturer as a Nobel Laureate has been precluded from receiving a Jaffé Prize, £200 has been provided from another source.

Ferrier Lecture

At the request of the contributors to a Fund to perpetuate the memory of Sir David Ferrier and his pioneer work on the functions of the brain, the Society in 1928 accepted the sum of £1 000 in trust for the institution of a David Ferrier lecture which is given triennially on a subject related to the advancement of natural knowledge on the structure and function of the nervous system.

The lecturer's gift at the present time is £150.

Wilkins Lecture

The Wilkins Lecture Fund was established in 1947 by means of an endowment of £1 000 by Mr J. D. Griffith Davies, Assistant Secretary of the Society from 1937 to 1946.

The purpose of the fund is to found a lectureship in the history of science, to be called the Wilkins Lecture after John Wilkins, first Secretary of the Society.

In accordance with the wishes of the donor, his gift is associated with the names of Margaret Ann Davies and Elizabeth Kellogg Chase, in whose memory it was made.

The administration of the fund is in the hands of the Council of the Royal Society, by whom the Wilkins lecturer will be appointed triennially or at such intervals as may be thought fit. A gift of £100 is payable to the lecturers.

Leeuwenhoek Lecture

The George Gabb Fund was founded in 1948 by a bequest of £1000 from Mr George Gabb for an annual lecture in the field of microbiology to be called the Leeuwenhoek lecture after Antony van Leeuwenhoek, F.R.S. The fee paid to the lecturer is £100.

Rutherford Memorial Lecture

The Rutherford Memorial Lecture was established in 1952 as part of the Rutherford Memorial Scheme. The Lecture is to be delivered at selected university centres in the British Commonwealth overseas, at least one in three to be given in New Zealand.

Tercentenary Lectures

On the occasion of the Tercentenary Celebrations in July 1960 it was decided that a number of lectures should be given on scientific subjects illustrating recent research in the United Kingdom. A synopsis of each lecture is printed in *Notes and Records*, volume 16, part 1. The full texts have not been printed in the Society's publications but might have appeared elsewhere at the lecturer's discretion.

Bernal Lecture

The Bernal Lecture Fund was established in 1969 by means of an endowment of £2000 by Professor J. D. Bernal, F.R.S. The purpose of the fund is to found a lectureship on some aspect of the social function of science.

The lecture is given triennially, and the first lecture was delivered in 1971. A gift of £200 is payable to the lecturer.

Clifford Paterson Lecture

The General Electric Company Limited covenanted in 1975 to provide £2500 a year over seven years to endow the Clifford Paterson Lecture on electrical science and technology, inclusive of the science and technology of electronic materials, components and systems. The lecture is to be given annually. The lecturer's gift is £200.

LECTURERS 1976

THE CROONIAN LECTURE was given by DR JOHN BERTRAND GURDON on: Egg cytoplasm and gene control in development.

THE BAKERIAN LECTURE was given by PROFESSOR GEORGE WALLACE KENNER on: Towards synthesis of proteins.

THE LEEUWENHOEK LECTURE was given by PROFESSOR GEOFFREY HERBERT BEALE on: The varied contributions of protozoa to genetical knowledge.

THE BERNAL LECTURE was given by DR PETER LEONIDOVICH KAPITZA on: Scientific and social approaches for the solution of global problems.

THE WILKINS LECTURE was given by PROFESSOR MARGARET MARY GOWING on: Science, technology and education: England in 1870.

THE CLIFFORD PATERSON LECTURE was given by SIR ERIC EASTWOOD on: Radar: new techniques and applications.

(Lectures up to 1940 are listed in the *Record*, pp. 355–375; lectures between 1940 and 1974 are listed in the *Year Book* for 1975, pp. 215–222.)

THE LIBRARY OF THE ROYAL SOCIETY

1. The Library is open on Mondays to Fridays from 10 a.m. to 5 p.m.

2. Any Fellow may have the loan of any of the printed books or journals of the Society, excepting such as the Council may order not to be taken out of the Library.

3. Dictionaries, cyclopaedias and works of general reference are not available for loan.

4. Books or pamphlets must not be removed from the Library until a receipt has been signed and left with the Librarian. When a borrower returns a book his receipt shall be returned to him.

5. Persons desiring a book or books to be sent to them must send to the Librarian a written order and pay the whole cost of carriage. The borrower shall be responsible for the safe custody of books issued to him by the Librarian until they are returned. Volumes returned through the post must be securely packed in a box, or otherwise protected to prevent injury. Whenever practicable a Fellow wishing to borrow any volume published before 1800 should make arrangements to do so personally or to send a messenger.

6. In no circumstances may books be taken or sent out of the United Kingdom.

7. Borrowers shall be at liberty to retain a book or a bound volume of a journal until 1 August next ensuing as laid down in paragraph 10 below, unless, at any time after the expiration of a fortnight, notice is received that the book is required by another reader, in which circumstances it must be returned at once. Single parts of journals may not be retained longer than one month.

8. Borrowers retaining books longer than the time specified, or neglecting to return them when requested, shall forfeit the right to borrow books from the Library until the volume or volumes so retained be returned.

9. Borrowers to whom books have been issued shall be held responsible for their preservation from injury; and if any book when returned is found to have been damaged, the Council may order that it be repaired or replaced at the expense of the borrower. In the event of any book being lost or being detained after application has been made for its return, the Council may replace, at the cost of the

borrower, the volume or volumes so lost or detained. This rule shall also apply to single parts of current periodicals.

10. All books shall be returned to the Library not later than 1 August, but books borrowed during the month of July immediately preceding need not be returned until 1 August twelve months later unless recalled as provided in paragraph 7 above.

11. Fellows may recommend other persons for the privilege of the use of the Library for reference purposes or to borrow books. Such recommendations must be made in writing to the Librarian and must state whether the person so introduced is recommended to use the Library for reference purposes only or to borrow books and periodicals as well. Unless the Fellow specifically sets a term to his recommendation it will be deemed to remain in force until the Fellow cancels the recommendation in writing or the privilege is withdrawn by Council. Except in exceptional circumstances persons recommended by Fellows will not be allowed to borrow books published before 1800. Persons so introduced by Fellows must comply with the regulations set out in the preceding paragraphs. Fellows will be responsible for any damage or loss sustained through the issue of books to persons recommended by them.

12. Persons holding Royal Society research appointments and members of the Society's staff may, at the discretion of the Librarian, use the Library and borrow books during the term of their appointment or service. Such persons must comply with the regulations set out in the preceding paragraphs.

13. Permission to borrow manuscripts or any other documents, and records preserved in the Society's Archives must be specially given by the President and Council.

Adopted by Council, June 1961

The Library is closed on Saturdays and all Public Holidays.

THE SOCIETY'S PUBLICATIONS

Philosophical Transactions of the Royal Society
   Series A (Mathematical and Physical Sciences)
   Series B (Biological Sciences)
   First issued in March 1664/5.
   Papers are published separately and are priced individually according to length.

Proceedings of the Royal Society
   Series A (Mathematical and Physical Sciences)
   Series B (Biological Sciences)
   First issued in 1832 when abstracts of papers appearing in *Philosophical Transactions* from 1800 onwards were printed.

Biographical Memoirs of Fellows of the Royal Society
   First issued 1955 in continuation of Obituary Notices. One cloth bound volume published annually.
   Ten-year indexes to the above publications are available from 1931.

Year Book of the Royal Society
   First issued in 1898 and published annually.

Notes and Records of the Royal Society
   First issued in 1938. Published irregularly, normally one volume per annum. Two parts complete a volume.

The Royal Society: Its Origins and Founders
   Edited by Sir Harold Hartley, F.R.S.
   Published 1960.

A Brief History of the Royal Society
   By E. N. da C. Andrade, F.R.S.
   Published 1960.

The Record of the Royal Society
   First edition 1898, second edition 1901, third edition 1912, fourth edition 1940.

General notes on the preparation of scientific papers
   Issued 1950, reprinted May 1950, August 1950, October 1950, February 1957. Revised edition August 1974, price £0.45.

Quantities, units, and symbols
   New edition July 1975, price £1.00.

Mathematical Tables

The following volumes have been published in the Royal Society series of *Mathematical Tables*: (1) *The Farey Series of Order 1025* (1950); (2) *Rectangular-Polar Conversion Tables* (1956); (3) *Table of Binomial Coefficients* (1954); (4) *Tables of Partitions* (1956); (5) *Representations of Primes by Quadratic Forms* (1960); (6) *The Riemann Zeta Function* (1960); (7) *Bessel Functions, part III—Zeros and Associated Functions* (1960); (8) *Natural and Common Logarithms* (1964); (9) *Tables of Indices and Primitive Roots* (1968); (10) *Bessel Functions, part IV—Kelvin Functions* (1964); (11) *Coulomb Wave Functions* (1964). The following *Shorter Mathematical Tables* have been issued: No. 1, *Bessel Functions of half-odd-integer orders* (1952); No. 2, *Bessel Functions and Formulae* (1953); No. 3, *Bessel Functions of integer orders and large arguments* (1954).

The British Association series of mathematical tables is also published by the Royal Society.

The Correspondence of Isaac Newton

The first three volumes of *The Correspondence of Isaac Newton* edited by H. W. Turnbull, F.R.S., the fourth volume edited by J. F. Scott and the fifth and sixth volumes edited by A. R. Hall and Laura Tilling have been published for the Royal Society by the Cambridge University Press. The seventh, and last, volume is in the course of preparation.

The Correspondence of Isaac Newton may be obtained from booksellers.

. . . .

All orders, subscriptions and inquiries for all these publications (with the exception of *The Correspondence of Isaac Newton*) should be addressed to the Publications Department at the Royal Society.

THE SOCIETY'S FUNDS

In addition to the Medal and Lecture funds already described and the Parliamentary grants mentioned elsewhere, the Society administers a number of funds most of which have their origin in gifts or bequests from Fellows or benefactors of the Society. The history of those funds established before 1940 is given in *The Record* on pp. 107–138.

RESEARCH FUNDS

The Research Funds are those which are to be employed in scientific research or in other ways which appear to Council conducive to the interests of science in general or of the Society in particular, within any limits which may have been laid down by the donor or testator. Where there are special regulations governing the use of the funds for research appointments the regulations are given.

The following Research Funds are administered by the Royal Society:

Beringer

Dr F. J. A. Beringer, who died on 25 April 1930, bequeathed to the Society his residuary estate, subject to a life interest to his widow who died on 26 August 1952. The income of the fund is to be applied in research work tending towards the discovery of the nature, cause and cure of disease in man. Council decided in 1953 that the income should be allowed to accumulate and the Medical Sciences Research Committee invited to advise as to its use, and in November 1966 Council accepted a recommendation from the Committee that a Beringer Research Fellowship be established for research in the aforementioned field, preferably to be carried out at the London Hospital or the London Hospital Medical College. (See p. 394.)

Browne

In December 1937 E. T. Browne bequeathed to the Society the residue of his estate to aid marine expeditions and marine biological research. A standing committee advises on the use of the fund, together with the Maurice Hill and John Murray funds. (See p. 394.)

Conway

Under the will of Philip Conway, the Society received in 1967 the proceeds of the sale of small parcels of land in Wales, the income from which to be used for such purposes of national character with regard to increased food production in the British Isles as the Society may determine. During the first ten years the income is to be given to the Welsh Plant-Breeding Station near Aberystwyth for the collection and study of exotic plant material which through breeding could lead to the development of improved varieties or possibly the introduction of new crops for British agriculture. (See p. 394.)

Cook

Since 1973 the Trustees of the Ernest Cook Trust have made grants to support research fellowships in environmental studies, including research in pollution control. (See p. 394.)

Courtauld's

Council accepted in 1972 a gift of £20000 from the trustees of Courtauld's Educational Trust Fund to be used in providing facilities of benefit to the United Kingdom in those branches of science and technology with which the Courtauld group of companies is concerned. (See p. 394.)

Cumulative (Anon.)

In 1968 an anonymous donor transferred securities valued at £45000 for a new research fund, the income of which is to be added annually to the capital until the donor's death, when the income will be used to provide three-year research appointments in chemistry, physics, biology and medicine. (See p. 394.)

Darwin

In 1885 the Committee of the International Darwin Memorial Fund transferred to the Society the balance of the fund in trust that the proceeds should be devoted to the promotion of biological studies and research. After providing for the biennial award of a silver medal and gift (see p. 208) the surplus income is available to aid biological research in the Darwinian field. (See p. 394.)

Dewrance, Donation and Jodrell

In 1914 Sir John Dewrance made a donation of £2000 to the Society in order that the income should be expended in accordance with the terms of the trust of the Donation Fund, which see below.

By order of Council on 1 April 1954, the Dewrance Fund was amalgamated with the Donation and Jodrell Fund.

The Donation Fund, the earliest research fund of the Society, was established in 1828 by W. H. Wollaston (P.R.S. 1820), who gave the sum of £2000 3 per cent Consols to be called the Donation Fund, the dividends to be applied from time to time in promoting experimental researches or in rewarding those by whom such researches have been made, or in such other manner as shall appear to the President and Council for the time being most conducive to the interests of the Society in particular, or of science in general. The application of the income extends to individuals of all countries, but not to members of the Council of the Royal Society. The capital of the fund was added to by gifts from Dr Davies Gilbert (P.R.S. 1827–1830) and other Fellows, and by legacies from Sir Francis Ronalds, F.R.S., and Sir Charles Wheatstone, F.R.S.

The Jodrell Fund originated as a gift of £6000 from T. J. Phillips Jodrell in 1876 to be applied in any manner 'most conducive to the encouragement, among our countrymen, of original research in the Physical Sciences'. Subsequently, the donor expressed the wish that the proceeds should be treated as part of the ordinary revenues of the Society. In 1879 £1000 was transferred to the Fee Reduction Fund and in 1889 the remainder was, in accordance with the donor's wishes, incorporated with the Donation Fund. (See p. 394.)

FLECK

Lord Fleck bequeathed to the Society in 1970 12% of the residuary income of his estate after payment of certain annuities, to be used as Council may think fit, either for the Society's general purposes or specific charitable purposes. (See p. 394.)

FLOREY

This fund was raised by subscription in 1969 to commemorate Lord Florey, O.M., F.R.S., and a similar fund was established at the same time by the Australian National University. The income is to be used for Florey Fellowships to enable promising young scientists under the age of 30 in the United Kingdom and Australia to pursue research in the biomedical sciences by making two-year visits to the United Kingdom or Australia. (See p. 394.)

Folley

On the death of his widow in 1975, the residuary estate of the late Professor S. J. Folley, F.R.S., was received by the Society; it was the wish of the donor that the fund be used for the advancement of research into experimental endocrinology. (See p. 394.)

Forsyth

Professor A. R. Forsyth, F.R.S., who died in 1942, bequeathed to the Society his residuary estate, without imposing any trust or obligation. He suggested that the income from the fund be applied in aid of medical research, especially in relation to cancer and like diseases. By order of Council the income can be used in conjunction with the Foulerton fund. There is a life interest in the estate which is represented by the Forsyth Annuity Fund. (See p. 394.)

Foulerton

In July 1919 Miss Lucy A. Foulerton bequeathed to the Society the residue of her estate to be used as the Council may think best for grants for original research in medicine for the discovery of disease, the causes of it, and the relief therefrom of human suffering. Since 1923 the fund has been used for the endowment of Foulerton Professorships and in otherwise endowing scientific research by men of proved ability for independent research in the field of medicine, with a break from 1969 to 1974, during which time income has accumulated to finance a professorial appointment. (See pp. 263, 394.)

Foulerton Gift

In February 1919, in accordance with the wish of the late Dr John Foulerton, his executrix and sole legatee, Miss Lucy Foulerton, transferred to the Society £20000 of 5 per cent National War Loan Stock, the income of which is to be expended in making awards to students, especially younger ones, of sufficient amount to enable them to devote themselves, under the supervision and control of the President and Council, to original research in medicine, to the improvement of the treatment of disease, and the relief of human suffering. It is a condition that a candidate for a Foulerton Fellowship must show, if called upon to do so, that he or she is, and that his or her father and paternal grandfather are, or were at the date of their respective deaths, of British nationality. (See p. 394.)

Gassiot

This fund was established by John P. Gassiot, F.R.S., in 1871 to assist in carrying on and continuing magnetic and meteorological observations with self-recording instruments, and any other physical investigations that may be practicable and desirable at Kew Observatory. The income is now paid over to the Ministry of Defence (Air) for the use of the Meteorological Office which is responsible for the operation of Kew Observatory. (See p. 394.)

General Research

In 1879 Sir William Trevelyan bequeathed to the Society the sum of £1500, 'the interest to be applied to the promotion of scientific research'. In 1925 M. le Bel, Foreign Member, made a gift to the Society of a sum of £206 for encouraging and furthering scientific research. In 1930 the sum of £500 was bequeathed to the Society by Colonel G. H. Leatham. In 1937 the sum of £5000 was bequeathed to the Society by the Duchess of Bedford. These four funds were amalgamated as the General Research Fund in 1938. To them was added a bequest from Sir Robert Hadfield, F.R.S., in 1940, and another from William Rushton received in December 1950. Further sums have been added from time to time. (See p. 394.)

George

The late Dr W. H. George in 1973 bequested the residue of his estate absolutely to the Society. Without imposing any legal trust, he expressed a wish that the money be applied to the encouragement of scientific study of scientific method as distinct from philosophical study of the scientific method. (See p. 394.)

Gore

George Gore, F.R.S., bequeathed to the Society £2436 in 1908 for the purpose of assisting original scientific discovery. (See p. 394.)

Gunning

In 1891 R. H. Gunning gave to the Society £1000, the income to be applied triennially to the promotion of physical science and biology. (See p. 394.)

Handley

Under the will of E. H. Handley, dated 1840, the reversion of his property was bequeathed to the Society, the income to be applied as a reward for important inventions in art or discoveries in science, physical and metaphysical, or for assistance in the prosecution of any such invention or discovery, but with power to the President and Council to apply the income as they deem best for the advancement of science. (See p. 394.)

Head

In 1940 Sir Henry Head, F.R.S., bequeathed to the Society his residuary estate for the purpose of the advancement in England of the science of medicine in the widest sense. The fund is administered by a committee of not less than three and not more than five Fellows of the Society appointed by Council. (See p. 395.)

Maurice Hill

£36000 has been donated in memory of M. N. Hill, F.R.S., for the encouragement of research in physical oceanography and marine geophysics. A standing committee advises on the use of the fund, together with the Browne and John Murray funds. (See p. 395.)

Jaffé

The fund is governed by the following regulations:

1. The fund may be used for the endowment of original research in the practical sciences (e.g. chemistry, physics and medicine) and the application of scientific discoveries to industry by providing pecuniary assistance to persons pursuing investigations in such sciences, including the granting of prizes and awards.

2. One half of the fund may also be used for the education of the growing generation by providing pecuniary assistance for scientific or technical students of limited means.

3. All gifts under the bequest are open to persons of any nationality or religious persuasion. They must all be called the 'Mr and Mrs John Jaffé donations', except that, by special wish of the testator, the grants made under the terms of paragraph 1 may be described as 'Mr and Mrs John Jaffé Prizes'.

4. No gift may be made to a Nobel Prize winner.

5. The capital as well as the income of the fund may be spent.

6. The investment of Jaffé Fund securities may be made in any manner authorized by the investment clause contained in the will. (See p. 395.)

E Alan Johnston

In 1935 the trustees of Mr William Johnston, of Liverpool, at the instance of Professor P. E. Newberry and Mrs Newberry, made a gift of £10000 to be used for the furtherance of scientific research directed to the increase of knowledge concerning the causes of disease and the conditions of healthy life, development and inheritance, with a view to the prevention and relief of human suffering and the promotion of racial health. The donors gave instructions that the income of the fund should be used for the payment of the E. Alan Johnston Research Fellow or Student but agreed that it might also be used from time to time for a special grant in support of expenses, including material or equipment, of an investigation already in progress. By order of Council this fund is now administered in conjunction with the Lawrence and Moseley funds, which see below. (See p. 395.)

Joule

In 1890 the Joule Memorial Committee transferred to the Society the balance remaining in their hands, in order that the proceeds should be applied for the encouragement of research, both in England and abroad, especially amongst younger men, in those branches of physical science more immediately connected with Joule's work. By order of Council this fund is now used in conjunction with the Mackinnon Fund, which see below. (See p. 395.)

Lawrence

In 1914 Miss L. E. Lawrence and Miss M. W. Lawrence presented to the Society the sum of £4000 in trust, the interest arising therefrom to be devoted to the furtherance of research into the cause and cure of disease in man and animals, in such manner as the Council may from time to time determine, the donors desiring to associate the gift with the names of their father, Sir William Lawrence, Bt., F.R.S., and their brother, Sir Trevor Lawrence, Bt. The fund is now used in conjunction with the Johnston and Moseley funds. (See p. 395.)

Horace Le Marquand and Dudley Bigg Trust

Dr H. S. Le Marquand, who died on 13 May 1962, bequeathed certain securities, the income from which is to be used to establish a Fellowship to promote research to further the application of physiological principles to medicine, such definitions to be interpreted in the widest sense, or such other research of a biological nature in relation to the problems of health or disease in the widest sense as the Society may decide. In 1974 Mrs D. Bigg donated £26000 for addition to the capital. (See p. 395.)

Locke

In 1949 F. S. Locke bequeathed to the Society one-half of his residuary estate, establishing no trust or obligation, but expressing the wish that the money should be used for the endowment of Locke Researchships in experimental physiology and pharmacology. (See p. 395.)

Mackinnon

In 1897 Sir William Mackinnon bequeathed to the Society the residue of his estate upon trust for the foundation and endowment of prizes and scholarships called after Sir William Mackinnon for the purpose of furthering natural and physical science and of furthering original research and investigation in pathology. By order of Council this fund is now used in conjunction with the Joule Fund to form a single fund to aid research in the physical sciences. Whilst the fund has been used to endow the Mackinnon Research Studentship, the income is now insufficient for this purpose. (See p. 395).

Medical Research

In 1924 the Society received an anonymous legacy of £10000 and in 1925, £28108, being part of the residue of an estate, for the prosecution of original research in medicine for the prevention of disease and relief of suffering, with special reference to tropical diseases in British Possessions and to cancer and tuberculosis. By order of Council the income can be used in conjunction with the Foulerton fund. (See p. 395.)

Bruno Mendel Fellowship Fund

In August 1964 the Society received from Mrs Hertha Mendel, widow of the late Professor Bruno Mendel, F.R.S., securities to the value of £64480 for the purpose of establishing a fund, the income of which might be applied by Council in its absolute discretion for the promotion of learning and education in the field of science.

In accordance with the wishes of Mrs Mendel, the income was used from 1965 to 1975 for travelling fellowships tenable either in the United Kingdom, The Netherlands or Israel by candidates from one of the other two countries. In May 1976 Council decided, with the approval of Mrs Mendel, to widen the scheme by removing the travelling requirement, and the income is now applied as follows:

1. The Bruno Mendel Fellowship shall be awarded to a postgraduate candidate desiring to carry out research in medicine or the biomedical sciences at a university, medical research centre or medical school for a period of one year, renewable for one year and exceptionally for two years, on such terms and conditions as the Council of the Royal Society may in each appointment from time to time prescribe.

2. The fellowship is intended for a candidate normally resident in the United Kingdom, The Netherlands or Israel.

3. Any question whether a person is eligible as a candidate shall be determined by the Biological Secretary of the Royal Society, whose determination shall be final and binding.

4. If in the judgment of the Council in any year there is no candidate of sufficient merit the Council may make no appointment.

5. (i) A Committee may be appointed by the Council for the purpose of recommending annually a suitable candidate to the Council.

(ii) Any Committee shall be composed of two residents of each of the said three countries holding scientific degrees together with the Biological Secretary *ex officio* who shall be Chairman of the Committee.

(iii) The Members of the Committee other than the Biological Secretary shall be appointed for six years and one member from each country shall retire from office in the year 1967 and every third year thereafter. The member to retire shall be the member who has been longest in office since his last appointment and as between persons who become members on the same day those to retire shall (unless they otherwise agree) be determined by lot. A member retiring shall be eligible for reappointment. A member may resign from the Committee at any time by notice in writing to the Royal Society.

(iv) A casual vacancy occurring among the members other than the Biological Secretary may be filled by the Council but a person appointed to fill a casual vacancy shall only hold office for the remainder of the period for which the person in whose place he is appointed would have held office.

(v) The proceedings of the Committee shall not be invalidated by any vacancy among its members.

(vi) The members shall have power from time to time to fix their own quorum and to settle their own procedure except that every question which comes before the Committee shall be decided by the vote of the majority of the members voting. In case of an equality of votes the Chairman shall have a casting vote in addition to his vote as a member of the Committee.

(vii) The Committee may vote on any resolution by letters written by the Biological Secretary to the other members of the Committee and by the other members of the Committee to the Biological Secretary and any of the powers and authorities given to or vested in the members may be exercised in this manner by the majority of the members voting if one or more members fail for a period of twenty-one days to reply to a letter from the Biological Secretary asking for their votes on any resolution provided that at least three members vote in favour of the resolution.

(viii) The travelling expenses of members attending meetings of the Committee and other necessary expenses of the Committee may be charged to the Trust Fund.

(ix) The Council may for any reason as shall in its opinion be sufficient remove any member other than the Biological Secretary from office before the expiration of his period of office notwithstanding anything in the foregoing provisions of this Clause. (See p. 395.)

Messel

In 1920 Rudolf Messel, F.R.S., left four-fifths of his residuary estate to the Society without imposing any legal trust or obligation. He wished the income to be applied to aid the furtherance of scientific research and such other scientific objects as the Council may determine. The testator's wish was that the capital of the fund be kept intact and no part of the income applied for such charitable objects as the granting of pensions or the like. (See p. 394.)

Mond

In 1923 the Society received a legacy of £50000 from Dr Ludwig Mond, F.R.S., the income to be employed in the endowment of research in natural science more particularly but not exclusively in chemistry and physics, by providing rewards for new discoveries and pecuniary assistance (including scholarships) to persons pursuing scientific investigations and in supplying apparatus and appliances for laboratories and observatories, and in improving existing or erecting new laboratories and observatories and in such other manner as the Royal Society shall decide to be best calculated to promote scientific research. The income may also be used to provide for the publication and circulation of the reports and papers communicated to the Society and for the preparation and publication of catalogues and indexes of scientific literature which the Royal Society may have undertaken or may in the future undertake. In 1930 the fund was used for the building and equipping of the Royal Society Mond Laboratory which was completed in 1933, for special physical investigations in the University of Cambridge, to be used in the first instance for magnetic and cryogenic research. (See p. 395.)

Moseley

Lieutenant H. G. J. Moseley, killed in action in 1915, bequeathed to the Society the whole of his estate to be applied to 'the furtherance of experimental research in pathology, physics, physiology, chemistry, or other branches of science, but not in pure mathematics, astronomy, or any branch of science which aims merely at describing, cataloguing or systematizing'. In 1928 Mrs Amabel N. Sollas left a sum of, approximately, £10000 to be added to this bequest. The fund, together with the Johnston and Lawrence funds, is at present used to endow the Johnston, Lawrence and Moseley Fellowship, governed by the following regulations:

1. An Alan Johnston, Lawrence and Moseley Research Fellowship for research directed to increase knowledge of the causes of disease in men and animals and conditions of healthy life, development and inheritance, with a view to the prevention and relief of human suffering and promotion of racial health, shall be tenable at any place approved by the Council of the Royal Society.

2. The stipend attached to the Fellowship shall not be less than £500 per annum together with superannuation allowance.

3. Appointments to the Fellowship shall be made by the President and Council of the Royal Society, acting, if they think fit, upon the recommendation of an advisory committee.

4. Appointments to the Fellowship shall usually be for two years in the first instance, but may be renewed for such periods as Council may determine. The total length of tenure of each appointment shall not normally exceed five years, but may in exceptional circumstances be extended.

5. Every applicant for a Fellowship shall be required to state the general nature and scope of the research which he proposes to undertake, and to forward with his application the names of not more than two referees.

6. A Fellow shall normally devote his whole time to research, and shall not undertake any paid work, or hold any paid office, apart from his Fellowship, without the written consent of the Council.

7. A Fellow shall annually, or more often if required, present to Council a report on the progress of his work.

8. If any Alan Johnston, Lawrence and Moseley Research Fellow shall commit a breach of any terms or conditions of his appointment, or shall become, in the opinion of the Council, unfit or unable to pursue the research work for which he is appointed, Council may determine the tenure of the Fellowship by not less than one month's notice in writing.

9. Grants to meet research expenses, or for any other purpose consistent with the terms of the three trusts, may be authorized by Council. (See p. 395.)

John Murray

In 1949 the trustees of the John Murray Scientific Trust invited the Society to administer this fund for the encouragement of travel and work in oceanography or limnology. The income is devoted to a travelling studentship in oceanography and limnology, open to

British postgraduate students under the age of thirty-five, awarded for a period of one year or less, but the tenure may be extended to two years. Although it is not a condition of the award, since this is also available for limnological work, it is hoped that students who benefit from the Studentship will take advantage of all facilities for gaining practical experience, especially in the field of deep-sea oceanography as initiated by the Challenger Expedition, and that they can be assisted to take any opportunities which may arise to sail in oceanographical research ships. It is also hoped that students will be enabled to visit and work at oceanographical institutions and research stations abroad. A standing committee advises on the use of the fund, together with the Browne and Hill funds. (See p. 395.)

NAPIER

The trustees of the late Mr Montague Napier offered, in 1965, a capital sum of the order of £275000 to set up a trust fund, the income from which is to be used for the advancement of knowledge and the benefit of mankind by research, with the object of ascertaining the cause of cancer including any corresponding or allied disease and the means of its prevention, cure and alleviation. In accordance with the wishes of the trustees of the late Mr Napier, the income from the fund for the first seven years was transferred to the Institute of Cancer Research, and now supports a professorship. (See pp. 263, 395.)

PATTERSON

Under the will of H. S. Patterson, who died in 1970, the Society was bequeathed the residue of his estate to be accumulated for twenty years, the income then to be applied as far as possible for the endowment of a studentship or prize for research work on atomic physics, sub-atomic physics or similar problems. (See p. 395.)

PEDLER

Sir Alexander Pedler bequeathed to the Society in 1925 one-sixteenth of the residue of his estate to be used at the discretion of the Society for the advancement of science, and, as far as possible, for the advancement of chemical science. (See p. 395.)

PICKERING

Subject to the life interest of his widow, Mr P. S. U. Pickering, F.R.S., bequeathed the residue of his estate to the Society for the furtherance of scientific research especially those branches of science in which he had been interested. In the first instance research fellowships have been established to enable young graduates to undertake research either in chemistry (especially physical and inorganic) or in horticultural science. (See p. 395.)

Albert Reckitt
In 1949 the trustees of the Albert Reckitt Fund handed to the Society securities valued at £48 199 to be used for the promotion of learning and education in the field of science. (See p. 395.)

Rosenheim
Mrs M. C. Rosenheim bequeathed to the Society her residuary estate subject to two life interests for the purposes of research in Great Britain on the biochemistry of plants and of the simpler forms of animal life. In June 1968 Council decided to establish a Rosenheim Research Fellowship for research in these subjects, with preference being given to research on the biochemistry of higher plants. (See p. 395.)

Rosse
The fund, raised by Lord Rosse, F.R.S., for the maintenance of magnetic observations at Valencia Observatory, was transferred to the Society in 1910. The income is paid to the Department of Industry and Commerce of Eire. (See p. 395.)

Rutherford Memorial
This fund was raised by subscription in 1950–51 to commemorate Lord Rutherford, O.M., F.R.S. The income is to be used for Rutherford scholarships as well as a memorial lecture and the collection and copying of Lord Rutherford's correspondence. The following are the general regulations governing the Rutherford scholarships:

1. The Rutherford Scholarships are intended to encourage young graduates of exceptional promise and ability. They will be awarded for experimental research in any branch of the natural sciences. If there are candidates of similar merit, preference will be given to experimental physics. The Scholarships will not normally be awarded to graduates who have already held a senior research award. Candidates must have taken their first university degree at a university within the British Commonwealth.

2. A Rutherford Scholar will normally be required to carry out his research in some part of the British Commonwealth other than that in which he graduated, but in special circumstances he may be allowed to hold the award in a foreign country.

3. Each applicant must be under twenty-six years of age on 1 May in the year in which his application is received.

4. The value of the Scholarships will be determined from time to time and will be adjusted to meet the circumstances of each appointment. Additional allowances will be granted for travel, university fees, research expenses, etc.

5. The Scholarships will normally be tenable for three years but may, in very exceptional circumstances, be extended.

6. Appointments to the Scholarship shall be made by the President and Council of the Royal Society; in the selection of candidates from outside the United Kingdom use will be made of the machinery of the Royal Commission for the Exhibition of 1851 by kind permission of the Commissioners.

7. A Scholar shall normally devote his whole time to research and he may not hold or accept any other appointment or emolument without the consent of the President and Council of the Royal Society.

8. Scholars will be required to report on the progress of the work at the end of each year's tenure of the Scholarship. The continuation of the Scholarship will depend upon the satisfactory nature of the Scholar's work during the preceding year.

9. If, in the opinion of the President and Council, it should be desirable to do so from the point of view of the general distribution of the Scholarships throughout the Commonwealth, any one appointment may be limited to candidates resident in one or more specified parts of the British Commonwealth. (See p. 396.)

SADGROVE

Mr W. A. Sadgrove bequeathed his residuary estate, subject to the life interest of his widow and certain legacies, to the Society for general purposes or such special purposes as Council may determine. (See p. 396.)

SAINSBURY

In 1974 the Trustees of the J. Sainsbury Centenary Grant offered £16 000 over five years to support research fellowships in human nutrition. (See p. 396.)

SCOTT

In 1927 Professor A. W. Scott bequeathed to the Society the sum of £1 000 in aid of physical research. (See p. 396.)

SMITHSON

In 1928 Edward Walter Smithson bequeathed to the Society stock worth approximately £26 000, the income to be devoted to the establishment of a Fellowship for the carrying on of original scientific research with a view to the discovery of new laws or principles rather than the exploitation of what is known. The founder expressed a desire to associate the Fellowship with the University of Cambridge. The fund is administered under the following rules:

1. The capital of the fund shall be held in trust by the Royal Society. The income of the fund shall be received in the first instance by the Treasurer of the

Royal Society and shall be administered by a Committee consisting of four persons appointed by the Royal Society and three persons appointed by the University of Cambridge. The Treasurer of the Royal Society shall pay over such sums from the income of the fund and to such persons as the Committee may appoint on receipt of a requisition certifying that the Committee have so appointed, signed by the Chairman of the meeting at which they so appointed.

2. The Committee shall be appointed annually, and in each year one member shall retire and be ineligible for immediate re-election, such retirements being made from the members appointed by each of the appointing bodies alternately. No member of the Committee shall, in any case, serve for more than ten consecutive years.

3. Four Members of the Committee shall form a quorum. The Committee shall choose one of their number to be their Chairman. Meetings of the Committee shall be summoned by the Chairman when he shall deem it necessary, and he shall also summon a meeting of the Committee whenever requested to do so, in writing, by three Members of the Committee. The Chairman shall fix the time and place of the meeting. Except as hereinafter expressly provided, every question which comes before the Committee shall be decided by the vote of the majority of the Members present and voting. In case of an equality of votes, the Chairman shall have a casting vote in addition to his vote as a member of the Committee.

4. The Committee shall devote the income of the fund, or such part of it as may be necessary, to the establishment and support of a Fellowship for research in natural science, with a view to the discovery of new laws and principles, to be called the Smithson Research Fellowship.

5. The research by the holder of the Fellowship shall be carried out in the University of Cambridge, provided that an appropriate laboratory of that University is prepared to offer him the accommodation needed for his research, and to supply him with the ordinary laboratory facilities without charge. When the appropriate accommodation cannot be offered in Cambridge, or when the nature of the investigation so requires, the Committee may authorize the carrying out of the research in some other place.

6. The Fellowship shall normally be restricted to British subjects without distinction of sex, including citizens of the British Commonwealth. The Committee shall have the power, however, in special circumstances, to invite a foreigner of scientific distinction to become an applicant for appointment. In making an appointment the Committee shall give preference to candidates not more than thirty-five years of age.

7. It shall be the duty of the Fellow to devote his time and attention primarily to the research for which he has been appointed, and he may not undertake any work outside this research without the written permission of the Committee. The conditions governing the tenure of the Fellowship shall be such as the Committee may determine in each case.

8. The appointment shall be made for four years, but in exceptional circumstances may be renewed by the Committee for further periods of one year each.

9. The Fellow shall receive a salary from the income of the Smithson Research Fund.

10. Provision shall be made for a superannuation allowance to the Fellow, by a contributory scheme on the lines of the Federated Universities scheme, the fund contributing during the tenure of the Fellowship at the rate of 10 per cent of the salary and the Fellow contributing at the rate of 5 per cent of his salary.

11. From the balance of the fund the Committee shall have power to authorize

the payment of expenses incurred in the administration of the fund, and to make grants to meet the expenses of technical assistance or of special apparatus or materials required by the Fellow in his researches, or of special expenses in connexion with the publication of the results thereof.

12. From any balance of income remaining, after such grants have been made, the Committee shall create a Reserve Fund. The Council of the Royal Society shall have power at any time to order the transfer of any part of such reserve to the capital of the fund, or to use it for any other purpose consistent with the terms of the bequest.

13. The Fellow, if not already a member of the University of Cambridge, shall, unless the Committee should for special reasons otherwise decide, become a member, his matriculation fee being in that case paid from the income of the fund.

14. An annual report of the work done by the Fellow shall be presented to the Committee.

15. The Committee may decide to remove the Fellow from his Fellowship if it finds that he has not given attention to his duty of research; but such a decision shall not be made merely on the ground that the research has not produced definite results. The Committee may also decide to remove the Fellow from his Fellowship if it finds that he has been guilty of an act which is detrimental to the interests or the honour of the University of Cambridge or of the Royal Society.

16. Before making a decision to remove a Fellow, the Committee shall give him at least fourteen days' notice in writing of their intention to consider his removal, and shall fix a day, subsequent to the expiration of such notice, on which it will meet and hear the Fellow in his own defence.

17. A decision to remove a Fellow from his Fellowship shall only be made by the unanimous vote of the Members of the Committee present at the Meeting at which the matter is considered. Any such decision shall forthwith be notified to the Council of the Royal Society, and shall not take effect unless and until it receives the approval of the Council.

18. These rules may be revoked or amended by the Council of the Royal Society at any time after giving the University and the Committee an opportunity of stating their views on the proposed changes. (See p. 396.)

SORBY

In 1908 H. C. Sorby, F.R.S., bequeathed £15000 to be vested in the President, Council and Fellows of the Royal Society to the intent that the income thereof may be devoted to the establishment of a Fellowship for the carrying on of original scientific research, the object being to promote the discovery of new facts rather than the teaching of what is known.

The Founder expressed a desire to associate the Fellowship with his own city of Sheffield, so long as, in the opinion of the Council of the Society, the proposed researches can be properly carried out in connexion with the University of Sheffield.

The President and Council of the Royal Society, after consultation with the University of Sheffield, and with the approval of such

University, made the following rules with regard to the administration of the income of the fund, which said rules shall remain in force until revoked or amended by the said President and Council:

1. The income of the fund shall be administered by a Committee consisting of:
    (1) Four persons appointed by the Council of the Royal Society;
    (2) one person appointed by the Council of the University of Sheffield and
    (3) two persons appointed by the Senate of the University of Sheffield.

Such appointments shall be made in the month of December in each year; and the first meeting of the Committee thus appointed shall be summoned by the President of the Royal Society, who shall fix the time and place of meeting.

2. The members of the Committee shall be appointed for one year only, but shall be eligible for reappointment in each successive year.

3. The Committee shall choose one of their number to be their Chairman, who shall certify his appointment to the Secretaries of the Royal Society.

4. Meetings of the Committee shall be held in London or Sheffield, as determined by the Committee.

5. Meetings of the Committee shall be summoned by the Chairman when he shall deem it necessary, and he shall also summon a meeting of the Committee whenever required, in writing, to do so by three members of the Committee. The Chairman shall fix the time and place of the meeting.

6. In case the Chairman shall be unable to attend a meeting, the members present shall elect one of their number as Chairman for the time being.

7. Four members of the Committee shall form a quorum.

8. Except as hereinafter expressly provided, every question which comes before the Committee shall be decided by the vote of the majority of the members present and voting. In case of an equality of votes, the Chairman shall have a casting vote in addition to his vote as a member of the Committee.

9. The income of the fund shall be received in the first instance by the Treasurer of the Royal Society on behalf of the Society, but he shall pay over the same to the Chairman of the Committee, or such other person or persons as the Committee may appoint, on receipt of a requisition certifying that the Committee have so appointed, signed by the Chairman of the meeting at which they so appointed.

10. The Committee shall devote the income of the fund to the establishment of a fellowship for the carrying on of original scientific research.

11. The Committee may from time to time set apart sums to form a fund from which grants may be made for the purchase of special apparatus and material, or for publications, or for any other purpose consistent with the provisions of the bequest. Any apparatus and material purchased in accordance with this regulation shall remain the property of the University of Sheffield.

12. The Committee may also set apart from the yearly income of the fund a sum not exceeding five pounds to form a fund to meet the necessary expenses of the Committee; in addition, the travelling expenses of members attending meetings of the Committee may be charged to the fund.

13. The balance of the income, after deducting the said sums, shall be paid as a stipend to the Fellow. Any moneys falling in through vacancies or otherwise shall be placed to the account of the fund referred to in paragraph 11. But if

the Committee think it advisable they may, after obtaining the consent of the Council of the Royal Society, add such balance or any portion of such accumulated balances to increase the endowment of the fellowship.

14. In making an appointment the Committee shall pay special attention to the capacity for original work of a candidate, as shown by the work already done by him, and to the likelihood that he will continue to do reliable work. The Committee is to bear in mind that the object of the fellowship is not to train men for original research, but to obtain advances in natural knowledge by enabling men of approved ability to devote themselves to research.

15. Each appointment shall be in the first instance for five years, but may in special circumstances be prolonged for further periods if the Committee are satisfied with the Fellow's work.

16. An annual report of the work done by the Fellow shall be presented to the Committee. Should the Committee find that the Fellow does not give attention to his duties, it shall have the power to remove him from his fellowship, but it shall not do so merely because his work has produced no definite results.

17. A Fellow may be removed from his Fellowship if he shall do any act which may, in the unanimous opinion of the members of the Committee present at the meeting at which such act is considered, be detrimental to the interests of the University of Sheffield. Provided always that such removal shall forthwith be notified to the Council of the Royal Society, and shall not take effect unless and until it receives the approval of the Council.

18. No Fellow shall be removed except after at least fourteen days' notice in writing has been given to him of the intention to remove him, which notice shall specify the cause of the proposed removal, and shall fix a day, subsequent to the expiration of the fourteen days, on which the Committee will meet and hear the Fellow in his own defence.

19. A new appointment shall preferably be in a subject different from the previous one.

20. No Fellow shall be permitted to undertake any permanent duties outside his research work without the consent of the Committee, which shall not normally be withheld, when application is made to hold a paid teaching appointment in the University of Sheffield, provided that this does not involve a total of more than 48 hours of actual teaching in any one academic year.

21. The research shall be carried out in one of the laboratories of the University of Sheffield. This condition may however, be dispensed with when the nature of the investigation requires that the work should be done elsewhere.

22. Persons of all nationalities and of both sexes shall be eligible for appointment and in these rules words importing the masculine gender only shall include the feminine gender.

23. These rules may be revoked or amended by the Council of the Royal Society at any time after giving the University and the Committee an opportunity of stating their views on the proposed changes. (See p 396).

STOTHERT

John Henry Stothert, a lecturer in pharmacology at University College London, who was drowned at the age of twenty-seven in a canoeing accident in Austria in 1937, left his residuary estate to the Society for the support of research in the field of medicine, including the sciences on which medical knowledge is based, but particularly

RESEARCH FUNDS

with the view to increasing knowledge useful to the investigation or treatment of disease and relief of suffering in human beings or animals. The income of the fund is at present used to endow two Stothert Research Fellowships, governed by the following rules:

1. The stipend of a Fellowship shall be determined by the President and Council and shall normally carry an appropriate superannuation allowance.

2. Appointments to a Fellowship shall be made by the President and Council of the Royal Society acting, if they think fit, upon the recommendation of an advisory committee.

3. Each appointment to a Fellowship shall be in the first instance for two years, but may be renewed for such periods as Council may determine The total length of tenure of each appointment shall not exceed four years.

4. Every applicant for a Fellowship is required to state the general nature and scope of the research which he proposes to undertake, and to forward with his application the names of not more than two references.

5. Every applicant for a Fellowship is required to state whether he holds any other scholarship, endowment, or paid appointment, and whether he proposes, if appointed, to undertake any other work or research concurrently with the Fellowship. A Fellow may only undertake such duties upon obtaining the consent of the President and Council.

6. Fellows will be required to report on the progress of their work at the end of each year's tenure of a Fellowship.

7. Should the President and Council at any time find that a Fellow neglects, or has neglected, the obligations of his appointment, they shall have power immediately to terminate his Fellowship. (See p. 396.)

GENERAL HERBERT STUDD

In 1951 the Society received from Mrs Alice Maude Studd a legacy of £10 000 to form a fund to be called the General Herbert Studd Fund, the income of which is to be applied in such charitable purposes as the President and Council shall direct. (See p. 396.)

TOMES

Lady Tomes, who died in 1935, bequeathed a sum of £2 000 to the Society for scientific research in biology, physiology or medicine in memory of her husband, Sir Charles Sissmore Tomes, F.R.S. (See p. 396.)

TYNDALL

In 1910 Mrs Tyndall, in pursuance of a wish expressed by her husband, the late Professor Tyndall, F.R.S., entrusted to the Society the sum of £1 000, to be administered at the discretion of the President and Council for the purpose of encouraging and furthering fundamental research in all matters pertaining to mining, including such questions as ventilation, temperature, diseases incident to miners, and any other lines of scientific inquiry conducive to the improvement of mining and the lot of miners. In 1924 Mrs Tyndall made a further donation of £500, the income to be used, at the discretion of the Committee solely as a fund to meet out-of-pocket expenses incurred by the recipients of Tyndall Research Awards in the carrying out of their investigations and in 1942 Mrs Tyndall bequeathed £500 for printing and circulating their reports.

The fund is administered by a Committee of the Society, upon which the Institution of Mining Engineers and the Institution of Mining and Metallurgy are represented. The Committee may make Awards to research workers for any of the aforementioned purposes. The Awards are intended to assist with out-of-pocket research expenses and the purchase of equipment but are not to be used for maintenance. Equipment purchased with an Award from the Tyndall Fund is to be regarded as the property of the Royal Society and is to be returned to the Society at the completion of the research or at such other time as the Council of the Royal Society may determine. Recipients of Tyndall Research Awards are required to submit to the Committee brief annual reports (not later than 30 September) showing the expenditure of the Award and the progress of the research. Application may be made to the Committee for additional grants toward the preparation, printing and circulation of reports. (See p. 396.)

WARREN

The fund was established in 1936 as the result of an agreement between the executors of the late Mr H. B. Gordon Warren and the Royal Society. The fund is administered under the following regulations:

A. *General regulations:*

1. The capital of the fund, which shall be kept intact, shall be held by Williams & Glyn's Bank Limited as Custodian Trustee.

2. The income of the fund shall be applied for all or any of the purposes enumerated in the Trust Deed relating to the fund in the following terms: (i) the promotion carrying on or assistance of scientific research in metallurgy engineering physics and chemistry or any of those subjects including in such assistance the provision of any equipment building facilities or financial or other aid which may be thought proper and (ii) the use or application of such research or its results in or for industry and industrial development. These conditions may be fulfilled by the award of research fellowships, in accordance with the Regulations governing the same.

3. The fund shall be administered by a committee of twelve members:
2 nominated (and removable at any time) by Williams & Glyn's Bank Limited
8 nominated (and removable at any time) by the Royal Society
The Treasurer of the Royal Society
The Physical Secretary of the Royal Society

Of the eight members nominated by the Royal Society at least two shall be changed by the Royal Society during each period of three years, and those ceasing to be members shall not be eligible for renomination until after the lapse of one year. A Chairman of the committee may from time to time be appointed by the Royal Society which may determine the period for which he is to hold office from among the eight members nominated by the Royal Society. If the Chairman is unable to attend a meeting the members present may elect one of their number as Chairman for that meeting.

4. Subject to Regulations 6 and 7 the committee of whom five members shall form a quorum, shall act by the vote of the majority of those present and voting at any meeting. In the case of any equality of votes, the Chairman shall have a casting vote in addition to his vote as a member of the committee. The committee may delegate any of its powers (other than its powers under Regulation 7) to sub-committees and make and impose upon such sub-committees such rules and regulations, and vary the same from time to time, as it thinks fit. The committee may appoint and pay any administrative officers and may pay for such administrative services as shall from time to time be necessary.

5. Investment of the Warren Research Fund, including any accumulated and unexpended income, shall be directed and controlled by the committee or any sub-committee appointed for that purpose.

6. The committee may be consulted by correspondence and a resolution, other than a resolution to revoke alter or add to these regulations, to which all the members of the committee for the time being have signified their assent in writing, shall be as valid and effectual as if it had been passed at a meeting of the committee duly convened and held, provided that any member of the committee, who is not within the United Kingdom at the date when a letter purporting to consult him and ask him whether he assents is posted to him, need not be consulted and it shall not be necessary for him to signify his assent and provided further that if no reply is received from any other member of the committee within fourteen days of a letter consulting him and asking whether he assents having been posted to him, then such resolution shall be valid and effectual as aforesaid, if assented to in writing by all the remaining members of the committee whose consent is required provided they are not fewer than three in number. This regulation shall, *mutatis mutandis*, also apply to any sub-committee appointed in accordance with Regulations 4 and 5 above.

7. These Regulations, or any other Regulations for the time being in force in respect of the Warren Research Fund or the income thereof, may be revoked altered or added to from time to time by a resolution passed by the unanimous vote of all the members present at a meeting of not less than three-quarters in number of the committee for the time being and approved by the Royal Society and also by William & Glyn's Bank Limited if and while remaining the Custodian Trustee of the said Fund. But nothing herein contained shall authorise any alteration of the trusts and provisions set forth in the Second Schedule to the Trust Deed relating to the fund or the introduction of any Regulation or matter contrary to or inconsistent with such trusts and provisions.

B. *Regulations governing the Warren Research Fellowships:*

1. A Warren Research Fellow shall be a British subject; and shall carry out research at such place or places as the committee may prescribe.

2. A Warren Research Fellow shall be paid such stipend as the committee may decide.

3. A Warren Research Fellow shall be appointed, in the first instance, for four years. The appointment shall be renewable for a further period of four years and, in exceptional circumstances, the committee shall have power to renew it for further successive periods of four years, provided that it is satisfied that the Fellow is competent to discharge the duties of the Fellowship, and is not neglecting those duties. When a Fellow is over the age of 55, no renewal shall exceed three years or the period until he or she attains the age of 65, whichever is the shorter.

4. A Warren Research Fellow shall devote his or her whole time to research, and shall not undertake any paid work or hold any paid office apart from his or her Fellowship without the consent of the committee. The committee, however, will regard favourably a request by a Fellow to be allowed to undertake a limited amount of teaching or other work.

5. A Warren Research Fellow shall annually, or oftener if required, present to the committee a report on his or her work. The copyright in all such reports shall be the property of the Royal Society.

6. If any Warren Research Fellow shall commit a breach of any terms or conditions of his or her appointment, or shall be or become in the opinion of the committee unfit or unable to pursue the research work for which he or she is appointed, the committee may determine the tenure of the appointment by not less than one month's notice in writing. (See p. 401)

WEIR

In 1969 the Trustees of the James Weir Foundation made a grant to support fellowships in radioastronomy for three years. Subsequently the Foundation has renewed financial support for a further three years to support the Weir Research Fellowship in radioastronomy. (See p. 396.)

WELLCOME

The Council of the Royal Society at its meeting on 18 May 1961 accepted a gift of £100000 from the Trustees of the late Sir Henry Wellcome to establish and endow a Royal Society Professorship in Medical Research to be known as The Henry Dale Research Professorship. The Wellcome Trustees made this gift to commemorate the unique services of Sir Henry Dale, O.M., G.B.E., F.R.S., to their Trust as its Chairman for twenty-two years as well as his outstanding contributions to science and medicine in a wider context. In 1975 the Trustees donated a further £75000 as additional capital.

Appointments to the Professorship, which are governed by the general regulations for Royal Society Research Professorships, are especially, but not necessarily exclusively, in relation to research in physiology and pharmacology. (See pp. 263, 396.)

WOLFSON

In 1959 the Trustees of the Isaac Wolfson Foundation agreed to endow a research professorship to be known as the Wolfson Research Professorship of the Royal Society, the endowment being calculated to provide an annual income of £10000 a year. The regulations governing the Professorship are the general regulations governing the Royal Society Research Professorships subject to the over-riding restriction that the person appointed must be a British subject. (See pp. 263, 396.)

YARROW

In February 1923 Sir Alfred Yarrow, Bt, F.R.S., made to the Society a gift of securities to the value of £100000 to be used as capital or income for the purpose of the Society as the Council may think fit. Without creating any trust or legal obligation the donor expressed his wish that the money should be used 'to aid scientific workers by adequate payment, and by the supply of apparatus or other facilities, rather than to erect costly buildings, because large sums of money are sometimes spent on buildings without adequate endowments, and the investigators are embarrassed by financial anxieties'. (See p. 394.)

SPECIAL FUNDS

The following Special Funds are administered by the Society for the special purpose laid down by the donor or testator.

ARUNDEL LIBRARY

In 1666–7 Henry Howard, later sixth Duke of Norfolk, gave to the Society 'the library of Arundel House, to dispose thereof as their property'. In 1925 the non-scientific books and manuscripts of this collection were sold by auction after the British Museum authorities had been invited to purchase the volumes they required. The sum of £6496 realized by the Arundel Collection was invested and funded as a separate account for the use of the Library. (See p. 397.)

BOTANICAL CONGRESS

In 1966 the Society accepted the surplus arising from the Xth International Botanical Congress (Edinburgh, 1964); the income from the resulting fund is to be applied to assist research and education for the advancement of botanical sciences in the United Kingdom. In 1975 the Organizing Committee of the Third International Congress of Plant Tissue and Cell Culture transferred £4450 to the Society to be added to this fund. (See p. 397.)

BRADY

In 1891 Henry Bowman Brady, F.R.S., bequeathed to the Society his books and papers relating to the Protozoa, and also a sum of £300, the interest of which, or the principal or both, may be applied to the purchase of works on the same or kindred subjects for the Library. (See p. 397.)

BROWN

Mr S. G. Brown, F.R.S., bequeathed to the Society 'the sum of £2000 to be applied in such manner as the governing body of the Society may think fit for the promotion and development of mechanical inventions'. Council has created a fund with this sum, received in 1963, to provide for the award annually (in rotation, on the recommendation of the Institutions of Civil, Mechanical and Electrical Engineers) of an 'S. G. Brown Award and Medal' to a person who has, in the opinion of the appropriate Institution, made a contribution to the promotion and development of mechanical inventions. The Company founded by the testator—S. G. Brown Limited—supplements the award by means of a second seven-year covenant entered into in 1975. (See p. 398.)

CHURCH

Sir Arthur Church, F.R.S., bequeathed to the Society in 1915 forty-three £20 shares in the Westminster Bank Limited, and expressed the wish that the income of the fund should be applied to any purpose or purposes connected with the preservation and utilization of the archives of the Society. (See p. 397.)

CURL BEQUEST

Dr S. M. Curl of New Zealand died in 1911 leaving bequests to certain learned societies, who renounced them. Following lengthy Court proceedings the Cy-pres doctrine was invoked and as a result the Society receives an annuity and interest on the trust fund. This fund is held by the New Zealand Public Trustee. The income is to be used primarily for payment for special lectures, preferably in New Zealand. (See p. 397.)

EMBOSSED SCIENTIFIC BOOKS

In November 1913 the Royal Society agreed to receive in trust a sum collected by the managers of a fund for granting assistance towards the cost of publication of scientific books for blind persons. (See p. 397.)

FEDERAL COUNCIL OF CHEMISTRY

In 1936, on the constitution of the British National Committee for Chemistry, the Federal Council of Chemistry handed over to the Society securities to the value of about £800. The income may be used to meet entertainment expenses incurred in connexion with meetings of the International Union of Pure and Applied Chemistry in this country. (See p. 397.)

FEE REDUCTION (PUBLICATION)

This fund originated in 1878 from subscriptions amounting to £10111; its object was to relieve Fellows of the Society of the admission fee and of part of their increased subscription. In 1920 the increased expenses of publication led to an increase of the admission fee to £20; half of this fee was paid from the fund and applied to such expenses. In 1923 the fund was renamed the Publication Fund, but in 1941 it became the Fee Reduction (Publication) Fund. The whole of the income of the Fund has, since 1 October 1954, been transferred annually to the General Purposes Income and Expenditure Account. (See p. 397.)

GEOGRAPHICAL CONGRESS

The outstanding surplus arising from the 20th International Geographical Congress, together with royalties receivable, was transferred to the Society to assist research and education for the advancement of geography in the United Kingdom. (See p. 397.)

KECK AND KNOWLES MEMORIAL

In 1719 Robert Keck, F.R.S., bequeathed £500, the income of which was 'to be bestowed on some one of the Fellows whom they shall appoint to carry on a foreign correspondence'. In 1959 a bequest of MacGregor Knowles of £177 was added and until 1969 the total income was paid annually to the Foreign Secretary; the income is transferred annually to the General Purposes Income and Expenditure Account as the expenses of the Foreign Secretary are now met from the General Purposes Account. (See p. 397.)

OPTICS

In 1970 the Royal Society agreed to receive in trust the sum of £315 from the Optics Conference Committee, the income from which is to be used to assist research and education for the advancement of optics in the United Kingdom. (See p. 397.)

PARSONS MEMORIAL

This is the residue of a fund raised by subscription in 1931–1935 to commemorate Sir Charles Parsons, F.R.S. The income is now used to meet the cost of the annual Parsons Lecture, Medal and gift. (See p. 397.)

PENSION

This fund was founded in 1919 by Sir Arthur Schuster's gift of £3000 to which further sums were added by Sir George Beilby, Sir Charles Parsons, Sir Robert Hadfield, Sir Dugald Clerk, Sir Joseph Thomson and Sir Maurice Fitzmaurice (all F.R.S.) and by Miss Florence L. May by way of a bequest. By the wish of the original donors the capital is to remain intact and the income to be applied to the payment of pensions for servants of the Society. (See p. 397.)

Petavel

In 1936 Sir Joseph Petavel, F.R.S., bequeathed his residuary estate to the Society for general purposes. He also expressed the wish that part of the income be applied to assist in meeting expenses incurred by the Director of the National Physical Laboratory. (See p. 397.)

Royal Society General Travel Fund
Royal Society Travel Fund for Non-Fellows, including the L. J. Mordell Travel Fund

These funds were created in 1957, to be built up over a period of years, one to be available for all persons whether Fellows or not; and the other to be available only for non-Fellows. In 1963, Professor L. J. Mordell, F.R.S., gave a sum of £500, the income from which is to be used to meet travelling expenses of mathematicians and this was added to the appropriate fund. The Travel Funds will be used to advance natural knowledge as the President and Council shall direct, but principally for the purpose of providing grants to cover, in whole or in part, the expenses of scientists making short visits in the United Kingdom or abroad, or to the United Kingdom from abroad, for the purpose of consultation or to learn new techniques or to attend scientific meetings directly related to their own research. The decision to have two funds rather than one was taken after obtaining Counsel's opinion on the proper use which could be made of certain available incomes and funds of the Society. (See p. 397.)

Scientific Radio

This fund was set up in 1963 when the surplus of funds raised for the 1960 General Assembly was transferred to the Society, to be suitably invested in order to help finance the next General Assembly to be held in this country. Notwithstanding this, the whole or any part of the fund or its income in the meantime may be used at the absolute discretion of the President and Council of the Society for any purpose which in their opinion would be for the general advancement of electronics science.

Council has agreed that income from the fund be used, until such time as the fund is applied to finance an U.R.S.I. General Assembly in the United Kingdom, to finance a prize of £100 to commemorate the work of Sir Edward Appleton, President of the International Union of Radio Science (U.R.S.I.) from 1934 to 1952 and Nobel

Prizewinner for Physics in 1947. The Appleton Prize is awarded on the occasion of the triennial Assemblies of U.R.S.I. for distinguished contributions to ionospheric physics and the Prizewinner is selected after consultation with the Board of Officers of U.R.S.I. (See p. 397.)

SCIENTIFIC RELIEF

This fund, to aid scientific men and their families in need of assistance, was originated in 1859 at the suggestion of J. P. Gassiot, F.R.S. The capital of £6052 raised by subscription has been increased by various bequests and gifts. The fund is administered under the following regulations:

1. There shall be a fund called The Scientific Relief Fund, and the object of it shall be to aid such scientific men, or their families, as may from time to time require assistance. Assistance may also be given to enable retired scientists to continue to advance natural knowledge.

2. All contributions to the fund shall be invested in the name of the Royal Society in such manner as to form an account separate from that of the Society's other funded property.

3. The capital of the fund shall remain entire, and the interest only shall be at the disposal of the Committee.

4. If the whole of the interest shall not be expended in one year, the surplus shall be carried to the next year's account; and, if at any time any surplus in excess of the ordinary income of the year last past shall thus accrue, the Council shall cause the whole, or part of it, to be added to the capital sum already invested; or, should they think fit, may cause any accumulated interest to be invested as unexpended income, the securities purchased being liable from time to time to be realized, and the proceeds expended as income.

5. The fund shall be administered by a committee consisting of the Officers and six other Fellows of the Royal Society appointed by the Council. The Chairman of the Committee shall be appointed by the Council.

6. It shall be the duty of the Committee to consider applications for relief and to recommend the appropriate grant, if any, in each instance. The Committee shall appoint a Fellow of the Society or some other appropriate person to act as administrator of each grant: the recommendation of the Committee shall be reported to the Council for confirmation.

7. Any member of a nationally recognized scientific society within the British Commonwealth or the Republic of Ireland, acting through one of its officers, may bring cases of need to the attention of the Committee.

8. On the authority of the Council, the Treasurer of the Royal Society shall make such payments as the Committee recommends.

9. Notwithstanding the foregoing regulation the Chairman, after consultation with the Treasurer or one of the Secretaries, shall have power to act immediately in urgent applications reporting such action to the Council at its next meeting.

Sponsors of applicants for relief are desired to obtain confidential information about the applicant's financial situation. A form may be obtained from the Executive Secretary of the Royal Society.

In 1886 Sir William (afterwards Lord) Armstrong gave a sum of £7800 to the Scientific Relief Fund, on the understanding that the said fund should be used for remission of fees in cases of urgent necessity. By a resolution of Council passed 10 December 1889, 'The question of the remission of fees to Fellows of the Society in impecunious circumstances is reserved for the sole consideration of the President and Council of the Society, the amount thus from time to time bestowed being communicated to the Scientific Relief Committee'. (See p. 397.)

SCIENTIFIC RESEARCH IN SCHOOLS

The Committee on Scientific Research in Schools was established by the Council in March 1957, its terms of reference being to assist school science masters or mistresses who wish to pursue research in such a way that senior pupils may be able to take an interest in any research being pursued at their schools. A yearly transfer from the Reckitt Fund is usually made for the Committee's use in providing grants in certain circumstances for the purchase of apparatus, chemicals, etc. (See p. 397.)

The Atomic Energy Authority provides up to £1000 annually for equipment to enable teachers to carry out research which will be of interest to the Authority. In addition five industrial companies are also supporting the scheme by way of seven-year covenants.

SIMONSEN

In 1958 Sir John Simonsen, F.R.S., bequeathed the residue of his estate to the Society. He expressed the hope that this would be used to augment the Society's Scientific Relief Fund and not for other general purposes—except so far as the income in any year which is not required for assistance under the said Relief Fund. (See p. 397.)

STEAD

In 1940 W. H. Stead bequeathed the residue of his estate to the Society. One half of the income is to augment the Scientific Relief Fund; the other half is to be used for the advancement of natural knowledge. (See p. 397.)

TRAVELLING EXPENSES

This fund was founded by Sir Arthur Schuster, F.R.S., in 1908 with a donation of £1 500, to which a sum of £2 000 was subsequently added. For some years the income was used in paying the annual contributions of the Society to the International Research Council and to assist in defraying the expenses of the delegates to meetings of that Council or its Executive Committee. In 1930 the Treasury agreed that these expenses should be met from the annual grant for international research subscriptions. The income of the fund is now used for defraying the expenses of travelling officially undertaken by officers and Fellows on the Society's behalf. (See p. 397.)

WINTRINGHAM

In 1794 the sum of £1 200 Consols was bequeathed by Sir Clifton Wintringham, F.R.S., subject to certain conditions. As the conditions of the bequest cannot be fulfilled by the Society the income is paid to the Thomas Coram Foundation for Children under an alternative provision in the will. (See p. 398.)

THE R. W. PAUL INSTRUMENT FUND

This fund was established by a trust created under the will of Mr R. W. Paul who died in March 1943. The income from the fund is to be applied for the following purposes:

> The design, construction and maintenance of novel, unusual or much improved types of physical instruments and apparatus for investigations in pure or applied physical science, particularly in cases where a relatively large expenditure may be justified on experimental apparatus.

The income is administered by a committee, composed of representatives of the Royal Society, the Institute of Physics and the Institution of Electrical Engineers, which may make grants for the purposes set out above in such manner as it may determine. Grants shall not be used to relieve expenditure in any establishment controlled by the Government or to relieve any university or other educational establishment of its normal financial obligations.

When an application is favourably regarded by the Committee, an assessor is appointed to advise in detail on the merits of the application, especially in relation to the terms of the trust. If a grant is made the assessor is to report not less than once every twelve months on the progress of the work. He may recommend extra grants for running costs and salaries for the time being of investigators and assistants engaged in a particular investigation, provided that no research fellowship or research scholarship is thus created.

Applications may be submitted by any worker or group of workers in Great Britain; they must be British subjects. Further particulars and application forms may be obtained from the Executive Secretary of the Royal Society, 6 Carlton House Terrace, London, SW1Y 5AG.

GRANTS FOR TRAVELLING EXPENSES AND ORGANIZING EXPENSES OF INTERNATIONAL CONFERENCES

The Royal Society is willing to consider applications from both Fellows and non-Fellows for grants for travelling expenses overseas. Grants are allocated four times a year and applications, on forms to be obtained from the Executive Secretary, should be submitted well in advance of the proposed visit. The closing dates are 1 March, 1 June, 1 October or 1 December. Applications are considered within six weeks of these dates, and it is particularly important that those wishing to travel between July and October should submit their applications by 1 June. Only in very exceptional circumstances will applications be considered retrospectively. Particulars required from the applicant include place, purpose and duration of proposed visit, proposed expenditure, whether the visit is on the invitation of a National Academy or scientific institution and whether financial assistance has been sought elsewhere. If the applicant is not a Fellow of the Royal Society the application must be supported by a Fellow, preferably of the appropriate discipline, who is asked to submit, on the form, a brief statement of the applicant's scientific attainments and give any special reason for the award of a grant.

The attention of applicants for grants for travelling expenses is also drawn to the following notes:

1. Grants are not ordinarily made for attendance at summer schools.

2. Applicants should not seek substantial grants for visits to distant countries unless they are proposing to spend a reasonable time there in relation to the fare. For example, a visit to Australia might be expected to be six weeks at least. Shorter visits might be justified by special circumstances or when the journey is broken for other visits *en route*.

3. Grants for subsistence will be considered only if the applicant proposes to pursue research investigations, as distinct from attending a conference or visiting institutions.

4. The demand for grants is such that Council is seldom able to provide the full amount. Applicants should endeavour to obtain part

of the required amount from other sources. Grants are not ordinarily made to persons who are in receipt of substantial stipends in the country overseas (e.g. appointments during sabbatical leave).

5. Grants for travelling expenses are made mainly from the Society's Parliamentary Grant-in-aid and are not ordinarily available to civil servants or employees of the Research Councils, the British Museum and other government bodies.

6. Grants are not ordinarily made to applicants below Ph.D. status.

7. Note is taken of previous travel awards made to an applicant and not more than one travel grant will ordinarily be authorized in a calendar year.

The Society is also willing to consider applications from the organizers of scientific meetings held in the United Kingdom as follows:

(a) *Scientific Societies*

Scientific societies holding special meetings or conferences, in the United Kingdom, may apply for grants to assist with the travelling expenses of principal overseas speakers, or towards the travelling expenses of United Kingdom scientists (especially young scientists) to attend such meetings.

(b) *Organizing Expenses for International Conferences*

For international conferences or congresses being held in the United Kingdom, application may be made for grants or loans to assist with general organizational expenses, especially those incurred at an early stage before conference fees are received, and for assistance with the expenses of key speakers who are unable to obtain funds from their own organization.

Applicants for grants under (a) and (b) above should note that the Society expects organizers to charge realistic conference fees.

Applications should be made on forms to be obtained from the Executive Secretary, and should state the date, place and scientific purpose of the meeting, the expected number of participants, purpose for which the grant is required, and give full details of financial arrangements. The closing dates for applications are 1 March, 1 June, 1 October and 1 December.

6 *November* 1975

EUROPEAN SCIENCE EXCHANGE PROGRAMME

This programme, introduced in January 1967, is intended to further relations between research scientists in the university laboratories and other scientific institutions of western Europe. The Royal Society administers a grant from the Department of Education and Science for long and short-term visits to and from western Europe where matching funds are set aside by other European countries taking part in the scheme. The complete list of countries in the programme is: Austria, Belgium, Denmark, Finland, France, German Federal Republic, Greece, Republic of Ireland, Italy, Netherlands, Norway, Portugal, Spain, Sweden, Switzerland, and the United Kingdom.

Assistance can be provided in the following categories:

1. *Fellowships (for post-doctoral candidates)*

(a) The amount of the award will vary with the location of the laboratory to be visited, the seniority of the applicant, etc. but it will include (i) a salary payment corresponding to similar university or Royal Society appointments at current United Kingdom rates of payment, adjusted if necessary to the cost of living in the country visited, and (ii) all necessary travelling expenses. Supplementary grants may also be made (iii) as a contribution towards additional overhead costs incurred by the host institution because of the visit and (iv) as modest grants for special apparatus, equipment or materials essential to the research programme if these cannot be provided by the host institution.

(b) Preference will be given, in awarding fellowships, to applications for a full academic year. This may be extended for a second year. Applications for periods of six months or more will, however, also be considered.

(c) A fellowship may be held in any western European country other than that of the applicant. Each application must provide evidence of acceptance by the host country. In the first instance support will be given only for travel to or from the United Kingdom.

(d) Forms of application must reach the Executive Secretary, The Royal Society, before 1 January each year for fellowships tenable after July of the same year, and before 30 June each year for fellowships beginning in January or later in the following year. In exceptional circumstances, shorter notice in making the applications may be allowed. (Note: should sufficient applications be received by 15 March, an additional selection meeting will be held in April each year.)

2. *Study Visits*

(a) The amount of the travel awards for study visits will be assessed on the cost of travel and a maintenance allowance for the period of the visit.

(b) The awards will be made to United Kingdom research scientists (senior and junior) for periods of one week to three months, to be spent in laboratories in western Europe, and may be used for acquiring new techniques, for consultations with scientific colleagues, or for carrying out research. In certain circumstances applications for awards for periods from three to six months can be considered.

(c) Applications will be considered by the Royal Society throughout the year, but at least one month's notice for a visit should be given wherever possible.

(d) Forms of application may be obtained from the Executive Secretary, The Royal Society.

3. *Research Conferences*

The purpose of this part of the programme is to encourage scientists from western European countries to meet as specialists in their particular fields, in a relaxed atmosphere, and without publication of the discussions. In order to maintain the highest scientific level, provision is made for inviting a few leading authorities as speakers from countries outside western Europe.

It is hoped that these research conferences may also lead to new contacts, and as a consequence to increased exchanges between the scientists concerned.

Applications should be made on a form obtainable from the Executive Secretary, The Royal Society.

AGREEMENTS ON COOPERATION BETWEEN THE ROYAL SOCIETY AND THE SCIENTIFIC ACADEMIES AND RESEARCH COUNCILS OF OTHER COUNTRIES

In addition to the European Science Exchange Programme (see p. 254), the Royal Society has formal agreements or less formal arrangements on cooperation with the senior scientific organizations of many foreign countries. In most cases the agreements or arrangements provide for exchange visits by scientists in two general categories—short visits from two weeks to several months' duration, usually when the scientist concerned is visiting a number of different laboratories in the host country, and research worker visits (fellowships) for longer periods of up to an academic year, normally to engage in research in one laboratory, but with the possibility of short subsidiary visits to others. The administrative and financial arrangements vary in each case and those interested should write to the Executive Secretary asking for further details.

Countries with which formal agreements have been signed include:

East Europe
*Bulgaria
*Czechoslovakia
*Hungary
*Poland
*Romania
*U.S.S.R.
Yugoslavia

The Far East
China
India
*Japan

Latin America
Argentina
Brazil
Chile
Mexico
Peru
Venezuela

The Middle East
Egypt
*Israel

Fuller details of the agreements marked * were printed in the *Year Book* for 1975 on pp. 269–299 and pp. 302–304.

Informal arrangements exist with many other countries.

COMMONWEALTH BURSARIES SCHEME

ROYAL SOCIETY AND NUFFIELD FOUNDATION COMMONWEALTH BURSARIES
ROYAL SOCIETY AND COMMONWEALTH FOUNDATION BURSARIES

1. The purpose of the scheme is to provide a means by which scientists of proven ability may increase their competence by working with scientists of a Commonwealth country other than their own where the physical or personal environment is peculiarly favourable. The bursaries are for enabling such scientists to pursue research, learn techniques, or follow other forms of study in the natural and applied sciences. In the latter, Royal Society and Commonwealth Foundation bursaries will be devoted especially to agriculture, fisheries, forestry, and the development of natural resources.

2. Funds are available for two categories of candidates:

Category A. Scientists working in universities or other institutions in a Commonwealth country in Asia, Africa, the West Indies, the Pacific, or the Mediterranean.

Category B. Scientists working in universities or other institutions in the United Kingdom, Australia, Canada, or New Zealand.

3. Applicants should normally be of post doctoral level with several years of research experience, hold permanent salaried posts to which they will return, and be assured of receipt of salary during absence. Exceptionally, consideration may also be given to applicants of great promise in research without a permanent post. Bursars will not be permitted to prepare specifically for, or to take examinations for higher degrees or diplomas nor will support be given for general liaison visits nor for projects and courses without a clearly defined aim in the terms of Regulation 1. Bursars will be required to submit a brief report at the end of the tenure of the bursaries.

4. Bursaries may provide for travel costs and a contribution towards maintenance averaging £150 per month but varying considerably with individual circumstances and the cost of living in the country to be visited. No specific provision is made for families. Bursaries will be tenable usually for periods of six to twelve months,

but in special cases consideration may be given to supporting shorter visits (though rarely for less than three months) and second visits. Retrospective applications (i.e. applications from those who have already succeeded in reaching the country they wish to visit) will not be accepted. Applicants should take care to ensure that they have applied for a period of sufficient length for the completion of the work proposed, a point which should be confirmed by the head of the department to be visited

5. Special attention is drawn to the necessity of sending with the form of application:

(a) A sponsoring statement from the applicant's head of department testifying to the benefit likely to be derived from the visit in the context of the aim of the scheme as set out in **Regulation 1**.

(b) Confirmation from the head of the department to be visited, in the light of these Regulations, confirming willingness to receive the applicant to carry out the proposed project over the period applied for.

(c) The names and addresses of two scientists other than those mentioned in (a) and (b) who are closely acquainted with the applicant's scientific attainments and who, having seen these Regulations, would be prepared to recommend the visit.

6. Forms of application must reach the Royal Society and be addressed to the Executive Secretary, The Royal Society, 6 Carlton House Terrace, London, SW1Y 5AG, before 15 March each year for proposed visits beginning in July of the same year or later, and before 15 September each year for proposed visits beginning in January of the following year or later. These closing dates cannot be varied and applicants are therefore advised to make their arrangements as much in advance as possible.

7. Normally the result of applications will be communicated to candidates in May and November respectively.

November 1976

OVERSEAS VISITING PROFESSORSHIPS

Since 1962 the Royal Society, using funds from the Leverhulme Trust or from the Inter-University Council for Higher Education Overseas, has made arrangements for British senior scientists to help in higher education overseas by appointing visiting professors to universities and other scientific institutions needing such assistance.

The Royal Society Overseas Visiting Professorships Sub-committee recommends countries and institutions to be offered professorships. As offers are accepted the institutions concerned are asked to nominate fields of science in which visitors would be particularly welcome, and appropriate persons are then sought from within the Fellowship, or, if no Fellows are available, from elsewhere. Professorships are for a minimum of four months, preferably over a full university session. The Society provides 1st class return air fares for the professor, and for his wife if he is to be accompanied, together with an honorarium of £1 000 payable in advance, an outfit allowance, where required, of up to £60, and defrays the cost of medical, personal and baggage insurance over the period of the professorship. While in post, board and lodging to an appropriate standard for the professor and his wife are the responsibility of the host institution, as also is travel within the country connected with the professor's work programme.

The work programme varies in each case but would probably include lecturing, taking seminars, helping with research, advising on organization, etc. The host institution might be expected to provide facilities for the professor to continue with his own interests. In every case the details of the work programme, and the timing of the visit are decided by direct correspondence between the professor and the host institution once the former's appointment has been approved—mutual satisfaction being the only criterion.

November 1976

(For the Royal Society-Israel Academy Visiting Research Professorship Scheme please see p. 260.)

ROYAL SOCIETY–ISRAEL ACADEMY VISITING RESEARCH PROFESSORSHIPS SCHEME

A grant for three years, commencing in 1968, renewed in 1970 for a further three years from 1 January 1971 and again for five years from 1 January 1974, has been provided through the generosity of a donor who wishes to remain anonymous, to make possible an award or awards to include the miscellaneous expenses and travel of the scientists. The visits of the scientists are to alternate between the United Kingdom and Israel. It is preferred to support scientists of professorial standing but this is not essential, and visits of between four and eight months are envisaged.

It is intended that scientists making these visits would lecture, give seminars and supervise students. Payments at the monthly rate of £846 would be made, the tourist return air fare for the Visiting Research Professor and his wife, if she accompanies him, would be provided, and a claim for reasonable excess baggage expenses could be considered.

Further information on the scheme will be provided on application to the Executive Secretary.

October 1968, 1970, 1973

ROYAL SOCIETY LEVERHULME STUDENTSHIPS

1. The intention of these studentships is to enable young graduates of high quality of universities in the United Kingdom and who intend to make a career in scientific research to gain practical experience of scientific problems outside Europe and North America and especially in the developing countries. These awards are made possible by an annual grant to the Royal Society by the Leverhulme Trustees.

2. The studentships are restricted to recent graduates who wish to make observational studies which can only be made abroad, and will thus be of particular interest to those studying the environmental sciences (such as geology, geophysics, meteorology, oceanography and ecology), and animals, plants and the organisms of disease, and certain aspects of astronomy.

3. The studentships are tenable for a period of 6 to 12 months and will not be extended beyond 12 months. They cover the cost of travel to and from the country of choice, as well as local travel within the country, a maintenance allowance at a rate based on the local cost of living, a small amount of equipment and, if essential, purchase of a motor vehicle (to be sold at the end of the award period).

4. It is expected that the student will work under the general direction of a senior scientist in the country to which he goes. Applications should be accompanied by a statement from the scientist accepting responsibility for this general supervision.

5. Application forms and further details are available from the Executive Secretary. The closing date for applications is 15 January each year for proposed visits beginning in May of the same year or later. The final selection of candidates will be by interview in the rooms of the Royal Society, normally in March.

July 1972

ROYAL SOCIETY RESEARCH PROFESSORSHIPS

In June 1962 an announcement was made by the Chief Secretary to the Treasury that Her Majesty's Government had agreed to provide further direct financial support to the Royal Society to enable it to establish, with the approval of the universities concerned, five research professorships in British universities. In February 1964 it was announced that H.M. Government had agreed to provide the Royal Society with additional funds to enable it to establish a further three research professorships, and in 1967 funds were provided for an additional two. In 1971 and 1976 a further four were established, two to start on 1 October 1972 or thereafter and the other two on 1 October 1976 or thereafter, making a total of fourteen in all.

The purpose of this scheme is to meet a need, not previously covered, to provide opportunities for research scientists who are worthy of appointment to chairs but for whom none is available; this may be because they work in borderline fields or ones in which scientific developments are exceptionally rapid or for similar reasons.

The professorships are subject to the general regulations governing Royal Society Research Professorships (see p. 263), and a grant-in-aid is made to the Royal Society to provide for the salaries of the professors and their immediately supporting staff and for an annual sum for research expenses for each professor.

June 1962, *February* 1964, *February* 1967, *October* 1971, *October* 1976.

ROYAL SOCIETY SCIENTIFIC INFORMATION RESEARCH FELLOWSHIPS

In recognition of the value of research in the field of scientific information, the Royal Society, on 1 October 1968, established two Scientific Information Research Fellowships, tenable in British universities or other institutions approved by the Council of the Royal Society. Financial support for these fellowships was provided by Her Majesty's Government.

The fellowships are subject to the general regulations governing Royal Society Research Appointments (see p. 265) and a grant-in-aid is made to the Royal Society to provide for the salaries of the Fellows.

October 1968

GENERAL REGULATIONS GOVERNING ROYAL SOCIETY RESEARCH PROFESSORSHIPS

1. The President and Council may appoint to Royal Society Research Professorships persons who have shown outstanding ability in scientific research.

2. A Royal Society Professor shall normally devote his whole time to research. Any appointment shall be made subject to its being found possible to make suitable arrangements for the research being carried out at a university or other place, to be approved by the President and Council of the Royal Society. A Royal Society Professor shall not accept or hold any appointment, paid or otherwise, other than his Royal Society Professorship, except with the knowledge and approval of the President and Council.

3. A Royal Society Professor shall be appointed for a period of five years, the appointment being renewable for further successive periods of five years provided that the President and Council are satisfied that the Professor is competently discharging the duties of his Professorship.

4. Every Royal Society Professor shall normally vacate his Professorship during the year in which he attains the age of 65; except that the President and Council shall have power, by the vote of two-thirds of the members present at a meeting of the Council held within six months before the date on which the Professorship would otherwise be vacated, to extend the appointment for a period not exceeding two years.

5. Regulations 3 and 4 notwithstanding, a special Royal Society Professor may be appointed for a limited period of years without the opportunity of renewal at the end of this period, but the level of ability demanded must not be lower than that demanded from other Royal Society Professors.

6. If at any time in the opinion of the President and Council a Royal Society Professor is found to neglect or to be unable to discharge the duties of his appointment or to be guilty of conduct or of continuing a course of conduct unbecoming in the holder of a

Royal Society Professorship, the President and Council shall have power at once to terminate his Professorship.

7. Unless the President and Council order to the contrary, provision shall be made for the superannuation of each Royal Society Professor under a contributory scheme to be approved by the President and Council.

8. A member of Council who becomes a candidate for a Royal Society Professorship shall not receive any of the papers relating to the appointment or attend any discussions of Council on it until after the appointment has been made. A member of the relevant advisory committee who becomes a candidate for a Royal Society Professorship shall, *ipso facto*, vacate his membership of the Committee.

A Royal Society Professor shall not be eligible for service on the relevant advisory committee during his tenure of a Professorship, except in his official capacity if he be one of the Officers, and a Royal Society Professor who is a member of Council shall not attend any of its meetings at which any question concerning his tenure of the Professorship is under discussion.

9. The President and Council may make grants to the holder of a Royal Society Research Professorship towards the various expenses incurred in his research.

10. Persons of all nationalities (except where it is specifically stated otherwise) and of both sexes shall be eligible for appointment to Royal Society Research Professorships, and in these Regulations words importing the masculine gender only shall include the feminine gender.

January 1960 and *October* 1962

The current research professorships are the Foulerton (see p. 224), the Henry Dale (see p. 242), the Napier (see p. 232), the Royal Society (see p. 262) and the Wolfson (see p. 243).

GENERAL REGULATIONS GOVERNING ROYAL SOCIETY RESEARCH APPOINTMENTS

1. The President and Council may appoint men of proved ability for independent research to research fellowships or studentships for the purpose of carrying out original work.

2. The stipends attached to such appointments shall be determined by the President and Council and shall normally carry an appropriate superannuation allowance.

3. Research appointments shall usually be for two years in the first instance, but may be renewed for such periods as Council may determine. The total length of tenure of each appointment shall not normally exceed five years, but may in exceptional circumstances be extended.

4. Every applicant for a research appointment shall be required to state the general nature and scope of the research which he proposes to undertake, and to forward with his application the names of not more than two referees.

5. A research Fellow or Student shall normally devote his whole time to research, and shall not undertake any paid work, or hold any paid office, apart from his Fellowship or Studentship, without the written consent of Council. The Council is prepared, however, to consider sympathetically a request to undertake university teaching that does not involve more than a limited claim on the time of a Fellow or Student.

6. A research Fellow or Student shall annually, or more often if required, present to Council a report on the progress of his work.

7. If any holder of a Royal Society research appointment shall commit a breach of any terms or conditions of his appointment, or shall become in the opinion of Council, unfit or unable to pursue the research work for which he is appointed, Council may determine the tenure of the appointment by not less than one month's notice in writing.

8. Grants towards research or other expenses may be authorized by Council.

9. Persons of all nationalities and of both sexes shall be eligible for benefits from the various funds, except where excluded by the terms of a trust, and in these Regulations words importing the masculine gender only shall include the feminine gender.

December 1951 and *March* 1953

ROYAL SOCIETY RESEARCH APPOINTMENTS

CURRENT HOLDERS

	Commencement of tenure
Foulerton Research Professorship	
Professor R. MILEDI, F.R.S.	1 Mar. 1975
Henry Dale Research Professorship	
Professor J. L. GOWANS, F.R.S.	1 Oct. 1962
Napier Research Professor	
Professor R. J. P. WILLIAMS, F.R.S.	1 Oct. 1974
Royal Society Research Professorships	
Professor M. F. ATIYAH, F.R.S.	1 Jan. 1973
Professor H. B. BARLOW, F.R.S.	1 Oct. 1973
Professor G. H. BEALE, F.R.S.	1 Apr. 1963
Professor J. H. BEYNON, F.R.S.	1 Oct. 1974
Sir JOHN CORNFORTH, F.R.S.	1 June 1975
Professor R. H. DALITZ, F.R.S.	16 Sept. 1963
Professor P. H. FOWLER, F.R.S.	1 Oct. 1964
Professor J. HESLOP-HARRISON, F.R.S.	1 Mar. 1977
Professor R. A. HINDE, F.R.S.	1 Oct. 1963
Sir ANDREW HUXLEY, F.R.S.	1 Oct. 1969
Professor G. W. KENNER, F.R.S.	1 Jan. 1977
Professor H. C. LONGUET-HIGGINS, F.R.S.	1 Apr. 1968
Professor M. S. LONGUET-HIGGINS, F.R.S.	1 July 1969
Professor F. SONDHEIMER, F.R.S.	15 Aug. 1964
Wolfson Research Professorship	
Professor DOROTHY M. C. HODGKIN, O.M., F.R.S.	1 Oct. 1960
Henry Head Research Fellowship	
Dr S. M. ZEKI	1 Oct. 1975
Mr and Mrs John Jaffé Donation Research Fellowships	
Dr G. S. BEDDARD	1 Oct. 1975
Dr CAROLYN M. L. KERR	1 Oct. 1973
Dr J. V. WALL	1 Oct. 1975
Dr S. H. WHITE	1 Oct. 1973
Beringer Research Fellowship	
(Vacant)	
Johnston, Lawrence and Moseley Research Fellowship	
Dr R. T. HUNT	1 Oct. 1976

Locke Research Fellowships — Commencement of tenure
Dr C. BLAKEMORE . . . . 1 Oct. 1976
Dr ELLEN E. E. JARRETT . . . . . 1 Oct. 1976

J. Sainsbury Research Fellowships
Dr M. W. J. DAVIE . . . . 1 Oct. 1974
Dr P. J. GARLICK . . . . 1 Oct. 1974

Ernest Cook Trust Research Fellowships
Dr M. B. BECK . . . . 1 Jan. 1975
Dr R. M. SIBLY . . . . 1 Oct. 1974

Foulerton Gift Research Fellowship
Miss M. H. ABEL . . . . 1 Jan. 1977

Horace Le Marquand and Dudley Bigg Research Fellowship
Dr I. W. CHUBB . . . . 1 Oct. 1975

Pickering Research Fellowships
Dr J. EVANS . . . . 1 Oct. 1975
Mr A. J. KINGSMAN . . . . . . 1 Oct. 1975
Dr R. A. LEIGH . . . . 1 Apr. 1976
Dr D. K. RUSSELL . . . . . . 1 Oct. 1975

Rosenheim Research Fellowship
Dr D. E. HANKE . . . . 1 Jan. 1976

Rutherford Scholarships
Mr S. K. BURKE . . . . 1 Oct. 1976
Mr K. A. HUNTER . . . . 1 Oct. 1974
Dr D. J. COOKSON . . . . . . 1 Oct. 1975

Scientific Information Research Fellowships
Dr C. J. VAN RIJSBERGEN . . . . . 1 Oct. 1975
Dr S. E. ROBERTSON . . . . . . 1 Oct. 1973

Stothert Research Fellowship
Dr G. B. WARREN . . . . 1 Jan. 1975

Weir Research Fellowship
Dr A. C. S. READHEAD . . . . . 1 Oct. 1972

Florey Fellowships
From Australia:
Dr J. G. McDOUGALL . . . . . . 1 Oct. 1976

From United Kingdom:
Dr D. B. ARCHER . . . . . . 24 Jan. 1977

Bruno Mendel Fellowship
(Vacant)

	Commencement of tenure
John Murray Travelling Studentship	
Mr G. H. BROWN	1 Sept. 1976
Radcliffe Trust Research Fellow	
Dr D. K. AITKEN	1 Oct. 1975

The following research appointments are made by Joint Committees:

Armourers and Brasiers' Research Fellowship (see p. 122)
    Vacant

Smithson Research Fellowship (see p. 234)
    Dr H. N. ARST . . . . 1 Oct. 1974

Sorby Research Fellowship (see p. 236)
    Vacant

The following research appointments are made by the Warren Committee:

Warren Research Fellowships (see p. 242)
    Professor B. BLEANEY, F.R.S. . . . . 1 Oct. 1977
    Dr D. V. EDMONDS . . . . . . 1 Oct. 1975
    Dr A. E. VARDY . . . . . . 1 Oct. 1975

(Lists of holders of research appointments until 1940 are printed in *The Record* pp. 131–133, and lists for the years 1940–1974 in the *Year Book* for 1975, pp. 319–323.)

SCALES OF STIPENDS*

(with effect from 1 October 1975)

B. *Senior Research Fellowships* £6687 rising by annual increments of £216 to a maximum of £7551 per annum.

C. *Research Fellowships* £5280 rising by annual increments of £207 to a maximum of £6108 per annum.

D. *Junior Research Fellowships* £3645 rising by annual increments of £207 to £4059 in three years and exceptionally to £4473 in five years.

* Further changes effective from 1 October, 1976 are expected.

REPORT OF COUNCIL

for the year ended 31 August 1976

The Council presents to the Fellows of the Royal Society the report on its work and on the various activities of the Society in its 316th year.

Research Appointments
During the year Her Majesty's Government agreed to make funds available to enable two additional Royal Society Research Professors to be appointed from 1 October 1976 or thereafter, making the number fourteen in all. Negotiations have been proceeding with the two candidates selected by Council, and it is hoped to announce the appointments in the near future.

The Warren Research Fund Committee advertised a third Warren Research Fellowship in Category C, and appointed Professor B. BLEANEY who will take up appointment on 1 October 1977 after resigning as Dr Lee's professor of experimental philosophy and head of the Clarendon Laboratory, Oxford. The third Florey Fellows were selected both in Australia and the United Kingdom; the Florey Fellowships Committee of the Australian National University appointed Dr J. G. McDOUGALL, senior research officer at the Howard Florey institute of experimental physiology and medicine, University of Melbourne, to work in the department of physics as applied to medicine, the Middlesex Hospital, London, for two years from 1 October 1976, on the control of aldosterone secretion, and Council appointed Dr D. B. ARCHER, M.R.C. postdoctoral research assistant in the subdepartment of chemical microbiology, department of biochemistry, University of Cambridge, to work in the C.S.I.R.O. animal health research laboratory, Parkville, Victoria, Australia, for two years from 27 January 1977 on the biochemistry of the prokaryotic micro-organisms, mycoplasmas. Since August 1975 the following other research appointments have been made to date from 1 October 1976, except where otherwise stated:

Dr R. T. HUNT (department of biochemistry, University of Cambridge) to be Alan Johnston, Lawrence and Moseley Research Fellow.

Dr C. B. BLAKEMORE (physiological laboratory, University of Cambridge) and Dr ELLEN E. E. JARRETT (department of veterinary pathology, Wellcome Laboratories for Experimental Parasitology, University of Glasgow) to be Locke Research Fellows.

Miss M. H. ABEL (physiological laboratory, University of Cambridge) to be Foulerton Gift Research Fellow, to work in the M.R.C. unit of reproductive biology, Edinburgh, from 1 January 1977.

Mr G. H. BROWN (S.R.C. research assistant, department of zoology, University of Bristol) to be John Murray Travelling Student, to work in the department of zoology, University of Dar es Salaam, Tanzania, from 15 September to 31 December 1976.

Mr S. K. BURKE (department of physics, Monash University) to be a Rutherford Scholar, to work in the department of physics, Imperial College of Science and Technology, London.

Royal Society Leverhulme Studentships were awarded to the following:

Miss HELEN R. COLES to work in Brazil from September 1976
Mr R. R. DANIEL to work in Bangladesh from August 1976
Mr N. W. GALWEY to work in Colombia from October 1976
Mr A. N. MCWILLIAM to work in Kenya from October 1976
Mr A. M. SUGDEN to work in Colombia from August 1976

Ten holders resigned or ended their appointments on 30 September 1975. Dr A. E. HILL and Dr RUTH M. LYNDEN-BELL (Mr and Mrs John Jaffé Donation Research Fellows) continued to work in Cambridge, Dr HILL as research associate in the physiological laboratory and Dr LYNDEN-BELL as a joint college lecturer at New Hall and St John's College. Dr B. J. HOWARD (Pickering Research Fellow) took up a demonstratorship with lecturing responsibilities in the physical chemistry laboratory and a fellowship at St John's College, Oxford, and Dr P. J. LEA (Pickering Research Fellow) a permanent post at Rothamsted Experimental Station. Dr J. W. FABRE (Foulerton Gift Research Fellow) was awarded a Wellcome senior research fellowship in clinical science at the Nuffield department of surgery, Radcliffe Infirmary, Oxford, and Mr R. A. COX (Ernest Cook Trust Research Fellow) began consultancy work in air pollution and energy conservation. Dr C. JANE WARD returned from her two years' tenure of a Florey Fellowship in the John

Curtin School of Medical Research, Canberra, Australia. Dr D. C. JOY (Warren Research Fellow) decided to accept a post at the Bell Laboratories, New Jersey, U.S.A., where he had been working during a year's leave of absence, and Dr BRIDGET I. BAKER (Sorby Research Fellow) took up a lectureship in the department of biology at the University of Bath. Dr D. A. SMITH (Armourers and Brasiers' Company Research Fellow) became a departmental research assistant in the department of metallurgy and science of materials at the University of Oxford.

Dr R. A. DWEK and Dr T. B. BOLTON (Locke Research Fellows) both resigned during the year, Dr DWEK on 31 December on appointment to a lectureship in biochemistry at the University of Oxford and a fellowship at Exeter College, and Dr BOLTON on 31 January on appointment to a senior lectureship in pharmacology at St George's Hospital Medical School, London. Dr M. J. CLEMENS (Mr and Mrs John Jaffé Donation Research Fellow) also resigned, on 31 August, to go to St George's, as a lecturer in biochemistry. Dr R. N. MCBURNEY (Florey Fellow) ended his appointment on 29 August, and went to the U.S.A. to take up a visiting scientist position at the National Institutes of Health.

The following appointments were renewed:

Dr M. B. BECK (Ernest Cook Trust Research Fellow)
Dr M. W. J. DAVIE (J. Sainsbury Research Fellow)
Dr P. J. GARLICK (J. Sainsbury Research Fellow)
Dr CAROLYN M. L. KERR (Mr and Mrs John Jaffé Donation Research Fellow)
Dr A. C. S. READHEAD (Weir Research Fellow)
Dr S. E. ROBERTSON (Scientific Information Research Fellow)
Dr R. M. SIBLY (Ernest Cook Trust Research Fellow)
Dr G. B. WARREN (Stothert Research Fellow)
Dr S. H. WHITE (Mr and Mrs John Jaffé Donation Research Fellow)

On 1 October 1975 Dr G. B. WARREN transferred the tenure of his appointment from the department of pharmacology to the department of biochemistry, University of Cambridge.

In January Council approved final revised salaries for research professors and revised salary scales for other holders of Royal Society research appointments (i.e., Categories B, C and D) with effect from 1 October 1975; these replaced the 'notional' scales mentioned last year which had added to them the £6 per week allowable under H.M. Government's pay policy and the threshold additions which had been paid separately. The final scales from 1 October 1975 were:

B. *Senior Research Fellowships* £6687 × £216 to £7551 per annum
C. *Research Fellowships* £5280 × £207 to £6108 per annum
D. *Junior Research Fellowships* £3645 × £207 to £4059 and exceptionally to £4473 per annum

Reports on research undertaken with the aid of Royal Society funds are printed in Appendix A. Expenditure on research from the Society's funds was £333 300 (£303 340 in the previous year). Expenditure from the Warren Research Fund was £9439 (£3192 in the previous year).

The Gassiot Committee, as in previous years, made recommendations, which were approved by Council and accepted by the Meteorological Office, for the award of grants totalling £7804 for support of work in specific areas of meteorological research with special reference to the physical and chemical processes of the atmosphere (*see* Appendix A). Increases totalling £2441 were authorized by the Meteorological Office to the previous grant (£5041) awarded in July 1975. Gassiot Committee

The Anniversary Meeting and twenty-three Ordinary Meetings were held, including fourteen which were discussion meetings. There were three discussion meetings, a review lecture and an evening technology lecture additional to the Ordinary Meetings. Meetings and Lectures

Four prize lectures were delivered as follows:

The Leeuwenhoek Lecture for 1975 on 'Bacterial sporulation: a problem in the biochemistry and genetics of a primitive developmental system' by Professor J. MANDELSTAM on 6 November.

The Croonian Lecture for 1976 on 'Egg cytoplasm and gene control in development' by Dr J. B. GURDON on 13 May.

The Leeuwenhoek Lecture for 1976 on 'The varied contributions of protozoa to genetical knowledge' by Professor G. H. BEALE on 3 June.

The Bakerian Lecture for 1976 on 'Towards synthesis of proteins' by Professor G. W. KENNER on 17 June.

There were five review lectures as follows:
'Metal recycling from scrap and waste materials' by Mr A. W. FLETCHER on 5 February.
'Applications of DNA modification and restriction enzymes in biochemistry and genetics' by Dr K. MURRAY on 12 February.
'Compartments in insect development' by Dr P. A. LAWRENCE on 4 March.
'The early components of complement and their activation by antibodies' by Professor R. R. PORTER on 25 March.
'Rocket studies of atmospheric tides' by Professor G. V. GROVES on 29 April.

The review lecture held on an occasion other than an Ordinary Meeting was as follows:
'Relevance of physiological and biochemical research to problems in animal fertility' by Professor T. R. R. MANN on 23 October.

An evening technology lecture on 'Dams and their interfaces' was delivered by Sir ANGUS PATON on 28 April.

The discussion meetings held on the occasion of Ordinary Meetings were as follows:
'Water structure and transport in biology' on 13 and 14 November organized by Dr R. E. RICHARDS and Dr F. FRANKS.
'Rubber elasticity' on 20 November organized by Professor G. GEE, Professor G. ALLEN and Dr C. PRICE.
'Structural and functional aspects of plasticity in the nervous system' on 4 and 5 December organized by Professor H. B. BARLOW and Dr. R. M. GAZE.
'The meiotic process' on 10 and 11 December organized by Professor R. RILEY, Dr M. D. BENNETT and Dr R. B. FLAVELL.
'The northern Great Barrier Reef' on 28 and 29 January organized by Dr D. R. STODDART and Sir MAURICE YONGE.
'Contraceptives of the future' on 18 and 19 February organized by Professor R. V. SHORT and Dr D. T. BAIRD.
'Methods and applications of ranging to artificial satellites and the Moon' on 26 and 27 February organized by Professor ALAN H. COOK, Mr D. G. KING-HELE, Professor S. A. RAMSDEN and Dr A. R. ROBBINS.
'New particles and new quantum numbers' on 11 March organized by Professor R. H. DALITZ, Professor B. RICHTER, Mr W. T. TONER and Dr B. WIIK.
'Resource developments in semi-arid lands' on 17 and 18 March

organized by Sir JOSEPH HUTCHINSON, Professor A. H. BUNTING, Professor A. R. JOLLY and Dr H. C. PEREIRA.

'The changing environmental conditions in Great Britain and Ireland during the Devensian (Last) Cold Stage' on 1 and 2 April organized jointly for the Royal Society and the Royal Irish Academy by Professor G. F. MITCHELL and Professor R. G. WEST.

'Mineralogy: towards the twenty-first century' on 7 and 8 April organized jointly for the Royal Society and the Mineralogical Society by Mr J. E. T. HORNE and Sir KINGSLEY DUNHAM as part of the Mineralogical Society's centenary celebrations.

'Scientific research in Antarctica' on 19 and 20 May organized by Sir VIVIAN FUCHS and Dr R. M. LAWS.

'The biology of chemical carcinogenesis' on 27 and 28 May organized by Dr R. DULBECCO.

'The scientific aspects of nature conservation in Great Britain' on 10 June organized by Dr J. E. SMITH, Professor A. R. CLAPHAM and Dr D. A. RATCLIFFE.

The discussion meetings held on occasions other than the Ordinary Meetings were as follows:

'Scientific results from the Ariel-5 satellite' on 14 October arranged by the British National Committee on Space Research under the leadership of Sir HARRIE MASSEY, Professor K. A. POUNDS and Professor A. P. WILLMORE.

'High-power lasers' on 17 October organized by Sir GEORGE PORTER in cooperation with the Science Research Council.

'Anglo-American intellectual relations' on 29 and 30 June organized jointly by the Royal Society and the British Academy to mark the bicentenary of American independence.

A conference of editors was held on 21 October on 'Quality and economics of scientific journals' organized by the Scientific Information Committee of the Royal Society.

The number of papers published in the *Philosophical Transactions* and *Proceedings* during the year ended 31 August 1976 and the number for the previous year were:

Publications

	Series A		Series B	
	1975–76	1974–75	1975–76	1974–75
Papers received	257	229	149	139
Papers rejected	41	36	11	12
Discussions received	8	5	12	11

	Series A		Series B	
	1975–76	1974–75	1975–76	1974–75
Philosophical Transactions				
Parts published:				
Papers	18	21	26	17
Discussions	4	3	6	3
Pages published	1937	1581	2078	1833
Plates published	90	49	123	88
*Time from receipt to publication (weeks):				
average	49.3	44.6	41.3	44.4
best	29	29	25	29
worst	122	78	102	64
Proceedings:				
Parts published	20	22	14	14
Papers published	161	153	89	91
Discussions published	1	4	3	3
*Time from receipt to publication (weeks):				
average	37.1	36.1	31.1	33.4
best	9	23	12	10
worst	113	84	139	75

*including time taken by authors in the revision of their manuscripts

Two issues of *Notes and Records* were published: volume 30, number 2, in January and volume 31, number 1, in July 1976.

Volume V of *The correspondence of Isaac Newton* was published in October 1975 and volume VI in July 1976.

The numbers of subscribers to the Society's regular publications at the dates shown were:

	31 *August* 1976	1 *September* 1975
Philosophical Transactions, Series A	1002	1023
Philosophical Transactions, Series B	729	756
Proceedings, Series A	2191	2323
Proceedings, Series B	1620	1688

In addition to the subscriptions there were casual sales of separate parts and volumes, distribution to Fellows, gifts and exchanges. The standing orders for some other publications at the dates shown were:

	31 August 1976	1 September 1975
Year Book	412	407
Notes and Records	363	370
Biographical Memoirs	529	539

To help meet higher production costs, Council decided to increase the selling prices of *Philosophical Transactions* and *Proceedings* by 10% and that this take effect from the beginning of 1977.

Aldabra Research Station

On 29 June, Aldabra became part of the new Republic of the Seychelles and ceased to be one of the islands of the British Indian Ocean Territory, created in 1966 for the defence purposes of the United Kingdom and the United States of America, into which it had been transferred from the Seychelles Crown Colony. In preparation for the new status of Aldabra, talks were held in London by the Officers of the Society with Mr J. R. MANCHAM, now President of the Seychelles, and Mr F. A. RENÉ, now Prime Minister, and these talks were followed up by further discussions in the Seychelles by the Chairman of the Aldabra Research Committee, Professor T. S. WESTOLL, and the Scientific Coordinator of the Royal Society Aldabra research programme, Dr D. R. STODDART. Assurances were given by Seychelles ministers that there would be no immediate change in the status of Aldabra as a Strict Nature Reserve, formally declared on 17 February 1976, nor in the terms of the lease of Aldabra to the Society to 30 June 1985. During the year Council initiated a review of the Society's commitments to Aldabra with a view to establishing the future of Aldabra so far as the involvement of the Society was concerned.

Mr J. GALLSWORTHY took over as director of the research station from October 1975 and Mr J. WALKER was the new engineer. Despite increasing shipping problems, the research programme expanded to include long-term studies of the seabirds, the goats and the reef fishes, while the studies of the tortoises and landbirds were continued.

Expeditions

The two Argentine/Chilean/United Kingdom expeditions, referred to in last year's report, successfully completed their field work in the southern parts of Argentina and Chile during the austral summer 1975–76. The excellent collaboration established in the field between scientists of the three countries continued into the subsequent phase of working up the botanical and geological results.

Study Groups

The Study Group on Pollution in the Atmosphere held seven meetings and submitted a report on its first year of working. Among other matters it considered a report by the United States National Academy of Sciences on *Environmental Impact of Stratospheric Flight*.

The Study Group on Long Term Toxic Effects met five times and submitted a report on its first year of working. One of its meetings was arranged jointly with the Medical Research Council to consider possible hazards of various sources of lead.

British Academy

Officers of the Royal Society and of the British Academy met in May to review matters of mutual concern. A major joint activity during the year was the discussion meeting on 'Anglo-American intellectual relations' held on 29 and 30 June and reported above under Meetings and Lectures.

Mr J. F. EMBLING, under the guidance of the joint Royal Society/British Academy *ad hoc* committee, completed his survey of the problems of learned societies. The Councils of the Society and the Academy are considering this survey with a view to making recommendations for action to provide assistance to those learned societies which require it.

Following consideration by the Advisory Board for the Research Councils of the memorandum on the support of archaeological sciences, which had been prepared by the British Academy with advice from the Royal Society, the Science Research Council established a science-based archaeology committee to which Sir KINGSLEY DUNHAM was appointed as the Society's assessor.

The Society responded to the Academy's invitation to appoint three representatives on its newly established Technical Committee for the Study of the Conservation of Medieval Stained Glass (Professor N. KURTI, Dr D. S. OLIVER and Sir GORDON SUTHERLAND).

Engineering and Technology *ad hoc* Committee

The Engineering and Technology *ad hoc* committee, to study the place of engineering and technology in the Royal Society and the Society's relation to these matters generally both in the country and internationally, the appointment of which was reported last year, met several times and prepared a final report to Council, to be considered after the year covered by this report.

Council's Industrial Activities Committee set up a working party (Chairman, Professor D. W. HOLDER) on the organization of applied research in the United Kingdom to consider measures that would encourage the exploitation of science and technology in British industry, including contributions that might be made by the Royal Society towards this objective. It held two meetings during the year and in May arranged the first of a proposed series of seminars on aspects of government policies towards technological innovation in industry.

Industrial Activities Committee

In January Council learnt with satisfaction of the proposal by the Council of Engineering Institutions to form a Fellowship. Council expressed willingness to cooperate with the Fellowship but made it clear, in a letter to Fellows of the Royal Society, that the Society would not cease to elect Fellows in engineering.

Council of Engineering Institutions

The BIOLOGICAL SECRETARY and the DEPUTY EXECUTIVE SECRETARY gave oral evidence to the Biology Research Committee of the Advisory Board for the Research Councils, in amplification of the written statement submitted last year.

Advisory Board for the Research Councils' Biology Research Committee

Council responded to an invitation by H.M. Government to submit views to the Working Party on the Practice of Genetic Manipulation, set up by the SECRETARY OF STATE FOR EDUCATION AND SCIENCE, with Professor R. E. O. (subsequently Sir ROBERT) WILLIAMS as chairman.

Genetic manipulation and dangerous pathogens

The PHYSICAL SECRETARY and Dr T. M. SUGDEN represented the Society at the Energy Conference, held in June, convened by the SECRETARY OF STATE FOR ENERGY. Council accepted an invitation by the Department of Energy to comment on two documents, namely *Energy R & D in the United Kingdom*, and a *Strategy for Research and Development* issued by the Offshore Energy Technology Board. Two *ad hoc* committees were appointed to examine the documents and to report to Council.

Department of Energy

In February, representations were made to H.M. Government with a view to ensuring that civil interests were fully taken into account before decisions on the future of the Hydrographic Department of the Ministry of Defence were taken. This action followed expressions of concern by a number of committees of Council at

Hydrographic services

the possible loss of support for civil science which had been envisaged as a result of a Government study group report.

Library

Council records with particular satisfaction the gift from Lady BAWDEN of the general and scientific correspondence of Sir Frederick Bawden and also the deposit on permanent loan by Mr R. E. F. GREEN of original letters written to Cromwell Mortimer, F.R.S. (1699–1752), a former Secretary.

Material of historical, biographical and scientific interest in the library and archives was again extensively consulted. Enquiries by correspondence, a large proportion from overseas, continued at a high level. The number of loans from the library, as well as requests satisfied by the provision of photocopies, showed a marked increase. Microfilm copies of manuscripts were provided, on demand, for research in the history of science.

The subject classification of books published between 1950 and 1974 was completed and re-cataloguing of the whole collection continued. Two lists of additions to the library were circulated to Fellows in the United Kingdom and to library readers. Additional space was provided for books, periodicals and manuscripts by the replacement of some of the fixed shelving in the library by moveable stacks.

An exhibition to mark the bicentenary of American independence was arranged in the library. Further exhibits of manuscripts and books during the year commemorated the centenaries of Sir William Stanier, Sir Charles Wheatstone and others.

Council records the Society's thanks to those Fellows who presented copies of their works to the library, photographs of themselves and recordings of their voices; also to others who presented books.

Education

The response to the latest questionnaire sent by the Education Committee to initial teacher training establishments suggested a continuing fall in the number of those qualifying to teach the sciences and mathematics. A letter was sent to the Department of Education and Science urging that opportunities for employment be made available to those qualifying as teachers of mathematics.

Arising from its deep concern for the maintenance of high standards in science and mathematics in schools, the Education Committee organized three discussion meetings on 'Teaching of science and mathematics in secondary schools'. These meetings, which were attended by practising teachers and officials of the Schools Council, the Department of Education and Science and the Examination Boards, covered 'Current problems', 'Science and mathematics up to age 16+' including a review of the Schools Council's plans for a common system at 16+, and 'Science and mathematics in the 16–19 age range' including a review of the trial examinations that had been exploring the possibilities for a Certificate of Extended Education and the proposals for the introduction of Normal and Further examinations in place of the present General Certificate of Education 'A' level. As a result of these discussion meetings a working party under the chairmanship of Sir NEVILL MOTT was formed. A major area of concern noted in the discussion meetings had been the teaching of science and mathematics at primary school level and the working party would concentrate on this area and possibly later on extend itself to a study of the effects of mixed ability teaching in the sciences and mathematics. Several Colleges of Education were visited by the working party and a preliminary report made. The Education Committee also forwarded to the Schools Council a statement on the Schools Council's 'Examinations at 16+: proposals for the future'.

At a time when major proposals for increasing the provision of in-service training appeared to have been postponed as a result of financial stringency, the Education Committee decided that it would be appropriate to offer to review with the Department of Education and Science the role of the Science Centres in the in-service training of teachers. The Education Committee wished to encourage the provision of in-service training on a continuing basis and felt that the effectiveness of science teachers could be increased if they were offered opportunities to broaden their initial training experiences.

A meeting between representatives of the Royal Society and the Schools Council took place in June to discuss the Schools Council Industry Project.

The Physics Education Committee produced a Working Party report on 'The relationship between mathematics and physics at the pre-"O" level stage in secondary education'. The Royal Society/ Council of Engineering Institutions Education Committee produced reports on 'Some aspects of "O" level papers in physics and mathematics' and 'Ways in which a greater awareness of engineering might be fostered in schools'; the former was circulated to Examination Boards for comment. The Chemical Education Committee produced its final report of the Working Party on Mathematics and Chemistry. The Mathematical Education Committee produced its survey report on ' "A" level mathematics syllabuses' to assist planners of tertiary courses which have a substantial mathematical content, which was circulated to mathematics, physics and engineering departments of universities and polytechnics.

An *ad hoc* committee, with the PHYSICAL SECRETARY as chairman, prepared comments on reports on postgraduate education by the Committee of Vice-Chancellors and Principals, the Select Committee on Science and Technology and the Science Research Council. These comments were later sent by Council to the bodies concerned.

Scientific Research in Schools

In an effort to counter the falling number of participating teachers, all honorary advisers, together with the Science Advisers' Group of the Association for Science Education, were asked for their advice on ways to encourage science teachers to use the Scientific Research in Schools Scheme. At 31 August 1976, 45 projects were in progress, including two groups of British Association Young Scientists engaged in environmental studies in Yorkshire.

Council endorses the thanks of the Committee to Fellows and others who have acted as honorary advisers.

International Relations

The International Relations Committee met once during the year and reviewed the whole range of the Society's many international relations. The Officers submitted evidence to the Central Policy Review Staff in connexion with its review of overseas representation.

European Science Foundation

The PHYSICAL SECRETARY represented the Society at the Assembly of the European Science Foundation, held at Strasbourg on 7 and 8 October 1975, when Sir BRIAN FLOWERS, President of the Foundation, presented its first annual report which was later well received by the Society's International Relations Committee and Council. The existing European Medical Research Councils group and European Science Research Councils group (of which the Natural Environment Research Council and the Science Research Council are the British members) were accepted by the Assembly as Standing Committees of the Foundation.

Several European Science Foundation committees have been active during the year, reviewing the possibilities for further European cooperation in their subject areas. Of special interest to the Society have been the Standing Committee on Astronomy (which has reviewed the various proposals for the development of astrophysical research in the Canary Islands) and the *ad hoc* Committees on Mathematics (of which Professor M. F. ATIYAH is chairman), Recombinant DNA, and Space Science (of which Sir HARRIE MASSEY is chairman). Sir HARRIE MASSEY and other members of the last-named committee attended an international conference in January at Williamsburg, Virginia, to discuss with representatives of the United States National Academy of Sciences the scientific importance and use of space observatories with particular reference to the Space Telescope Project.

The European Science Research Councils group held a meeting at the Royal Society in April to consider what might be done on a European basis in studies in biological systematics, taxonomy and recording.

During the year the United Kingdom committee for the Foundation met on five occasions; Dr N. J. WILLIAMS, secretary of the British Academy, succeeded Sir WILLIAM HENDERSON as chairman on 1 January.

Unesco

In April, Sir JOHN KENDREW succeeded Sir HAROLD THOMPSON as chairman of the joint Royal Society/Ministry of Overseas Development Unesco Committee. The new assistant director-general of Unesco, Dr A. R. KADDOURA, formerly rector of the University of Damascus, visited the United Kingdom in June as a guest of the Society and H.M. Government: he discussed with the committee the development of the Unesco science programme. The Society continued to maintain close contact with the main scientific programmes of Unesco, especially the International Geological Correlation Programme, Man and the Biosphere, the International Hydrological Programme and Unisist.

International Council of Scientific Unions

The British National Committee for the International Council of Scientific Unions met twice during the year, firstly to consider agenda for a meeting of the General Committee of I.C.S.U. held in September and secondly to consider agenda for the 16th General Assembly to be held in October 1976. Special consideration was given to the desirability of the People's Republic of China becoming a member of I.C.S.U. and its constituent Unions and Scientific

Committees, and the difficulties arising from the membership of Taiwan. On the recommendation of the committee, Council expressed to I.C.S.U. its support for the admission of the International Union of Immunological Societies. Following initiatives of the National Committees for I.C.S.U. and for Biology, a paper on 'I.C.S.U. and the Agricultural Sciences' was submitted by the Society to I.C.S.U. and to the International Union of Biological Sciences.

General assemblies or similar meetings of eight unions, four scientific or special committees and three associations, all within the International Council of Scientific Unions' family, were held during the year. The names of delegates to these meetings, appointed by Council, are listed in Appendix B. Council's national committees associated with these unions, committees and associations all met to consider, among other things, agenda for the assemblies and to select and brief the United Kingdom delegates. Several of the committees produced statements of United Kingdom interests and activities for presentation at the international assemblies.

A meeting of the I.C.S.U. Committee on the Teaching of Science was held in London in May and members were entertained by the Officers to luncheon at the Royal Society.

Council agreed to the administration by the Society of a grant offered by the Wates Foundation of £3000 per annum for three years for an experimental scheme to enable younger scientists from the United Kingdom to be made aware of the affairs of the International Union of Pure and Applied Chemistry (I.U.P.A.C.) by attending business meetings of I.U.P.A.C. bodies. Sir DEREK BARTON was elected a member of the Bureau of I.U.P.A.C.

Coordination of the visual satellite observing programme was continued by the Subcommittee on Optical Tracking of Council's National Committee on Space Research which was also acting as the coordinating body for a major optical tracking project being undertaken by the Universities of Aston in Birmingham and Leicester.

Council's National Committee on Antarctic Research devoted much attention to the scientific aspects of the potentially exploitable resources of the Antarctic. A substantial contribution was made to a preliminary assessment by I.C.S.U.'s Scientific Committee on Antarctic Research (S.C.A.R.), undertaken at the request of the Eighth Antarctic Treaty Consultative Meeting, of the possible effects on the environment if mineral exploration or exploitation should occur in the Antarctic. A meeting of a group of specialists on marine living resources of the southern oceans, jointly sponsored by S.C.A.R. and I.C.S.U.'s Scientific Committee on Oceanic Research (S.C.O.R.) was held in Cambridge in October from which emerged plans for an international conference of experts held at Woods Hole, Massachusetts, U.S.A., from 16 to 21 August 1976. A number of British scientists took part in this conference at which proposals for long-term international programmes in biological oceanography were formulated.

Council's National Committee on Oceanic Research and a local organizing committee established in collaboration with other interested organizations were active in preparing for the fourth major international marine science congress, the Joint Oceanographic Assembly 1976, to be held in Edinburgh in September. The Committee has set up a subcommittee on marine pollution which is considering areas of importance where further research is needed.

In collaboration with the Natural Environment Research Council a British entry was compiled for a new International Directory of Marine Scientists to be published by the Food and Agricultural Organization of the United Nations.

Council's National Committee on Problems of the Environment maintained close contact with I.C.S.U.'s Scientific Committee on Problems of the Environment, especially in its preparation of a report to I.C.S.U. on *Environmental Issues 1976* and in the activities of the Monitoring Assessment Research Centre at Chelsea College. At the General Assembly in May, Dr R. W. J. KEAY was elected Treasurer. The National Committee also maintained close liaison with the United Kingdom Department of the Environment, the Royal Commission on Environmental Pollution and the Research Councils.

The National Committee for the International Centre of Insect Physiology and Ecology, meeting twice during the year, received reports from Professor J. W. S. PRINGLE on the progress of the Centre and its long-term funding. Sir ALAN HODGKIN visited the Centre in December and reported to the Society. Sir VINCENT WIGGLESWORTH represented the Society at a meeting of the International Committee, held in Washington, D.C., in August. At this meeting it was agreed that the International Committee be ultimately replaced by an I.C.I.P.E. Foundation, registered in Sweden, the aim of which is to provide an international channel for financial

Insect Physiology and Ecology Centre

support and scientific advice to the Centre. Sir VINCENT, on behalf of the Society, signed the agreement establishing the Foundation.

International Nature Conservation
Council accepted an invitation from the Nature Conservancy Council to be represented on a new United Kingdom committee on International Nature Conservation and appointed Professor W. H. THORPE and the DEPUTY EXECUTIVE SECRETARY as its representatives. The Society also joined, as a Category B (non-governmental) member, the International Union for the Conservation of Nature and Natural Resources, whose activities are of increasing concern to several of the unions and scientific committees within the International Council of Scientific Unions.

Convention on International Trade in Endangered Species
The Society made representations to the Department of the Environment about the proposed legislation to implement in the United Kingdom the Convention on International Trade in Endangered Species of Wild Fauna and Flora. One outcome was the strengthening of scientific interests on the Scientific Authority for Animals.

International Institute for Applied Systems Analysis
Sir KINGSLEY DUNHAM, as the United Kingdom member, attended the annual meeting of the Council of the International Institute for Applied Systems Analysis in November and was supported by Mr P. C. ROBERTS and the DEPUTY EXECUTIVE SECRETARY. This Council appointed Dr R. LEVIEN as the new Director, and raised membership dues for 1976 by 20%. Considerable concern was expressed over the financial situation for subsequent years. Membership of the various subcommittees of the Council was reviewed, and Sir KINGSLEY DUNHAM was elected Chairman of the new Membership Committee to investigate procedure and potential applicants for membership of the Institute. This committee met in February and outlined plans and priorities for admission.

The first I.I.A.S.A. Conference, as required by the Charter, was held in May and was attended by Sir KINGSLEY DUNHAM, Professor H. H. ROSENBROCK, Mr R. C. TOMLINSON, Mr P. C. ROBERTS and the DEPUTY EXECUTIVE SECRETARY. Following this conference, Mr P. C. ROBERTS deputized for Sir KINGSLEY DUNHAM at a short meeting of the Council at which the Swedish Committee for I.I.A.S.A. was admitted as a member.

The Institute held 15 research conferences in the year, at 12 of which the United Kingdom was represented. Five British scientists stayed at the Institute for periods of research, and many others visited for shorter times to discuss work and to attend seminars. Collaboration by United Kingdom groups with project teams at I.I.A.S.A. has increased considerably. Members of the Institute's management and technology research group toured the United Kingdom, especially to study the Scottish development plans. Three scientists from the Institute addressed small meetings in the Royal Society on computer systems, futures research and water resources.

The Institute published over 100 research reports. These were brought to the attention of about 200 individuals and institutes in the United Kingdom.

Interest continued in the European Science Exchange Programme and the total contributions provided by partner organizations to the scheme reached a total of £381 413, balanced by a similar amount contributed by the Royal Society. This sum included a special extra allocation by the Centre National de la Recherche Scientifique of 200 000 Fr. frs for this year only. Although the amount of the contributions continued to rise, due to inflation the number of awards possible remained at the same level as in past years.

A list of the 98 fellowships awarded to British scientists and 87 fellowships granted by partner organizations for visits to the United Kingdom since the last Report of Council is given in Appendix C. In addition, 9 candidates selected by the Fellowships Selection Subcommittee were offered fellowships under the Science Research Council and Nato schemes. There were 95 study visitors from, and 65 to, the United Kingdom.

European Science Exchange Programme

Visits were made under the various agreements between the Society and the academies of sciences of East European countries and brief details are given in Appendix D. A delegation from the Council of Academies of Sciences and Arts of Yugoslavia visited the United Kingdom at the invitation of the Royal Society from 7 to 14 April. The delegation consisted of Professor B. PAVIĆEVIĆ, Professor M. HERAK, Professor D. KANAZIR, Professor A. KUHELJ, Professor G. FILIPOVSKI, Dr D. VUKOTIĆ and Professor M. SULEJ-MANPAŠIĆ. Besides visiting scientific institutions in London and the

East Europe

provinces the delegation signed an agreement with the Society on the same pattern as those with other East European countries, providing for general collaboration and exchange visits.

Commonwealth Bursaries

There were 135 applications for Commonwealth Bursaries during the year with 31 awards made (as against 144 applicants and 37 awards in 1974–75). Awards are listed in Appendix E. The Commonwealth Foundation generously renewed its contribution to the Scheme for three years from 1976–77 at £10 000 per annum, 25% more than for the previous three-year period. Ghana, India and Singapore also increased their contributions.

Exchanges between older Commonwealth Countries

A further annual contribution of £10 000 (the fifth) was received from the same anonymous donor for the Society to use to support graduate exchanges between the older members of the Commonwealth. Visits supported are listed in Appendix F.

Overseas Visiting Professorships

In the year under review no Royal Society Leverhulme Visiting Professorships were taken up, partly because a number of senior scientists are able to make visits abroad as study visitors under the Society's various agreements with foreign academies and research councils. However, these agreements seldom cover developing countries of the Commonwealth and in this respect the continued financial support of the Inter-University Council enabled Royal Society and Inter-University Council Visiting Professorships to be arranged as follows:

Guyana	zoology	Dr G. C. L. BERTRAM
Kenya	animal physiology	Professor E. C. AMOROSO
Nigeria	applied biology	Dr ALICE EVANS
West Indies	zoology	Dr J. A. ALLEN

With the assistance of the Inter-University Council, all universities in developing Commonwealth countries were approached about their preferences for Visiting Professorships in future years and there was a most encouraging response.

Israel Academy Programme

Since the last Report of Council, 5 fellowships for visits to Israel and 3 for visits to the United Kingdom have been awarded. These are shown in Appendix D. There have been 19 study visit awards to United Kingdom scientists and 2 to Israeli scientists. There has been a very marked increase in the number of applications from British scientists for these awards and the total amount available was quickly allocated. The funds available in the United Kingdom were £14 200 from the Parliamentary Grant-in-aid and a contribution of £8900 in Israel. Private donors kindly agreed to continue contributions for a further three-year period and an additional £3000 for the period under review became available in this way.

The Israel Academy of Sciences and Humanities nominated Professor F. BERGMANN, Member of the Academy and head of the department of pharmacology, Hebrew University-Hadassah Medical School, Jerusalem, and Professor W. RESNICK, professor of chemical engineering, Technion, Haifa, for Royal Society-Israel Academy Visiting Research Professorships in the United Kingdom for four months, to be held at the National Institute for Medical Research, London, starting in April or October 1977, and the department of chemical engineering, Cambridge, starting in March 1977, respectively. Awards of professorships in this scheme have been made to Professor C. DOMB for an eight-month visit to Bar-Ilan University starting in January 1977, and to Professor R. L. WAIN for four months from September 1978 at the Hebrew University of Jerusalem.

A delegation from the Academy of Scientific Research and Technology of the Arab Republic of Egypt visited the United Kingdom at the invitation of the Society from 11 to 20 January. The delegation consisted of H.E. Professor M. A. ABOU-EL-AZM (President of the Academy), Professor M. FAHIM, Professor M. FAYEZ, and Dr Y. H. MORSI. In addition to making visits to laboratories in various parts of Britain, the delegation signed an agreed minute modifying the formal agreement on exchange visits concluded between the Society and the Academy in November 1974. Visits under the agreement are listed in Appendix D.

Following a number of visits by individual Iranian scientists to Britain and Fellows to Iran in connexion with the establishment there of a Science Research Council and an Academy, there was a meeting on 8 April at Marlborough House between the FOREIGN SECRETARY and Sir ALAN HODGKIN with the EMPRESS (the chairman designate of the Academy). Subsequently, the PRESIDENT and Sir ALAN HODGKIN visited Teheran from 15 to 19 May at the invitation of Dr BAHMAN PARSA, Deputy Minister of Scientific Research at the Ministry of Science and Higher Education, to sit as members of a committee to advise on the selection of charter members of the new Academy.

China
A party of Chinese scientists in the field of high-speed photography visited Britain as guests of the Society from 28 October to 26 November. The party consisted of Mr YUAN CHI, Mr LI YU-LIN, Mr WANG JEN-CHUAN, Mr KAO CHIH-MING, Mr YANG FENG-HE, Mr LI KUANG-CHUNG and Mr HSU SHE-CHUAN.

Professor R. A. GREGORY visited China in June under arrangements made with the Academia Sinica. Dr F. R. PARRINGTON visited Peking at the same time as a result of a private invitation from Professor YANG CHUNG-CHIEN, transferred at the request of the Academia Sinica to the arrangements made by the Society.

Exchanges with and visits to other countries
Exchanges with India and Japan under the agreements with the relevant bodies in these countries are listed in Appendix D. Sir HARRIE MASSEY visited India from 21 April to 5 May and gave the first Blackett Memorial Lecture. Under arrangements with the Japan Academy, Professor J. S. FORREST and Dr V. E. COSSLETT visited Japan as a delegation from 2 to 16 March. Under arrangements with the Korean Institute for Science and Technology, Dr A. L. MACKAY (crystallography, Birkbeck College) visited Korea from 18 to 25 July, immediately before his visit to Japan noted in Appendix D.

Latin America
Formal agreements for exchanges with the Comision Nacional de Investigacion Cientifica y Tecnologica of Chile and the Consejo Nacional de la Universidad Peruana of Peru were signed on 14 January 1976 and 15 September 1975 respectively, both agreements coming into force on 1 April 1976. Following a visit to the Royal Society on 7 November by Dr A. AYALA CASTANARES, President of the Mexican Academy of Sciences, a new and more formal agreement between the Royal Society and the Academy was signed during the FOREIGN SECRETARY's visit to Mexico from 24 to 29 January and came into force on 1 April 1976.

The Unilever Brazil Programme came into operation on 1 April as the result of an initiative by Unilever Ltd whereby it is to contribute £4000 per annum for four years for ordinary exchange visits with Brazil and £3500 per annum for a Visiting Professorship to Brazil. Corresponding amounts are to be given by Gessy Lever in Brazil to the Conselho Nacional de Desenvolvimento Cientifico e Tecnologico. The first scientist to go to Brazil under this new Programme was Dr J. R. FORREST (electrical engineering).

Exchanges with Argentina, Brazil, Mexico and Venezuela continued. A total of 19 study visits (14 from the United Kingdom and 5 to the United Kingdom) and 10 fellowships (2 from the United Kingdom and 8 to the United Kingdom) were completed or in progress since the last report (see Appendix G).

Lord ASHBY delivered the first Sir Isaac Newton Lecture to the Venezuelan Academy of Sciences in January.

The Society continued to have informal but frequent contacts with the United States National Academy of Sciences. Lord TODD visited the PRESIDENT of the Academy in October, and the FOREIGN SECRETARY had informal talks with the PRESIDENT and FOREIGN SECRETARY on several occasions. Reference has been made to the Royal Society-British Academy discussion meeting on Anglo-American Intellectual Relations in June: the United States National Academy of Sciences and the American Philosophical Society were formally represented at this meeting. In April, Professor R. E. DAVIES and the DEPUTY EXECUTIVE SECRETARY represented the Society at a Bicentennial meeting of the Academy of Natural Sciences of Philadelphia; the latter also attended the Annual Meetings of the United States National Academy of Sciences.

United States of America

On 27 July, the PRESIDENT wrote to all Fellows of the Royal Society enclosing a letter addressed to the FOREIGN SECRETARY by the FOREIGN SECRETARY of the National Academy of Sciences about a resolution taken by members of the Academy at its annual meeting on 26 April: they had resolved to support 'An affirmation of freedom of inquiry and expression' and invited others to join with them in doing so, offering the offices of the Academy as a repository for such individual statements of affirmation. The PRESIDENT also enclosed a copy of a letter he had sent to the PRESIDENT of the Academy saying, *inter alia*, that he proposed to make a public statement at the Anniversary Meeting on 30 November 1976.

Amongst the visitors to the Royal Society during the year, besides those mentioned elsewhere in this report, were the following:

Visitors

1975

10 October	Dr J. DION DE MELO TELLES, President of the Conselho Nacional de Desenvolvimento Cientifico e Tecnologico, Brazil, with Dr L. A. LOWNDES BRASIL, Superintendent for International Cooperation, and Dr A. C. DO REGO GIL, director.
22 October	Dr U. UYSAL and Mrs R. KANSU, of the Scientific and Technical Research Council of Turkey.
24 October	Dr J. M. LECLAIR, Permanent Secretary of the Ministry of Science and Technology, Canada.
27 October	Mr S. V. CHITTIBABU, Vice-Chancellor of Madurai University, India.
11 November	Professor P. DUVIGNEAUD, Chairman of the Belgian National Committee for Problems of the Environment.

1976

14 January	Officers of the Council of Engineering Institutions.
11 February	Professor G. BRUCKMANN, of the University of Vienna.
3 March	The Rt Hon. C. A. R. CROSLAND, Secretary of State for the Environment.
11 March	Dr F. ALA, of the National Scientific and Technical Research Council, Iran.
12 March	Dr A. KWAPONG, Vice-Rector of the United Nations University.
17 March	The Rt Hon. F. W. MULLEY, Secretary of State for Education and Science.
1 April	Academician A. N. NESMEYANOV.
12 May	Academician V. A. KOTEL'NIKOV, Vice-President of the U.S.S.R. Academy of Sciences, and Mr I. A. TIMOFEEV of the Foreign Relations Department of the Academy.
17 May	Dr COURTLAND D. PERKINS, President of the United States National Academy of Engineering.
20 May	Dr S. D. CLARK, President, and Dr G. D. HURST, Executive Officer, of the Royal Society of Canada.
3 June	Professor A. L. TAKHTAJAN, of the U.S.S.R. Academy of Sciences.

REPORT OF COUNCIL

21 June	Dr BAHMAN PARSA, Deputy Minister of Scientific Research at the Ministry of Science and Higher Education, Iran.
9 July	Professor Z. KACZMAREK, leader of the Water Resources Project at the International Institute for Applied Systems Analysis.
12 July	Mr S. DILLON RIPLEY, Secretary of the Smithsonian Institution.
22 July	Mr J. A. HAMILTON, Permanent Secretary of the Department of Education and Science.

Details of the Parliamentary Grant-in-aid being administered by the Society for the fiscal year 1976–77 are given below, together with the corresponding details for 1975–76:

	1976–77 £	1975–76 £
Research appointments		
Research professorships	249 200	191 400
Scientific information fellowships	14 020	8 400
Exchange fellowships, travel grants etc.		
Western Europe	452 680	404 170
Eastern Europe	14 200	14 500
Israel	14 200	13 750
Japan	36 070	37 100
Latin America	28 420	27 000
Middle East	3 280	—
Relations with overseas academies	13 120	15 590
Commonwealth bursaries	16 400	14 710
Travel grants	180 350	175 500
Grants for research, scientific societies, etc.		
Scientific investigations	313 480	289 740
Aldabra research station	66 550	49 000
Scientific publications	8 740	4 000
Libraries assistance	5 470	4 000
Rating assistance	50 280	46 000
History of science	21 860	12 000
Science/technology relations and education	29 510†	25 000*

*including grant of £20 000 for the British Association
†including grant of £22 000 for the British Association

	1976–77 £	1975–76 £
Study groups	4150	3500
International meetings in the United Kingdom	43720	38000

International subscriptions and national committees

	1976–77	1975–76
Subscriptions to unions, etc. . .	92910	84000
International Seismological Centre .	23500	21500
Scott Polar Research Institute . .	12020	11000
Committee travel	12020	10350
Reports and international relations library	6560	5750
Delegates	26230	27290

Administration and general expenses

	1976–77	1975–76
Rent and part-maintenance, 6–9 Carlton House Terrace . . .	51000	51000
S.C.I.B.P. office	500	1000
Contribution to operating costs . .	189560	147750
	£1980000	£1733000

The limit on applications for grants for Scientific Investigations was raised from £10000 to £12500 on 1 August. Commencing with 1977 the closing dates for receipt of applications will become 15 March, 15 July and 15 November. A number of other minor amendments were made to the conditions.

Travelling Expenses

Grants amounting to £131796 were made from the Parliamentary Grant-in-aid in response to individual applications for travel grants to attend scientific meetings and/or visits to scientific establishments outside the United Kingdom. In addition, block grants totalling £58272 were authorized to assist participants to attend large congresses and conferences; these were allocated by sub-committees of the relevant National Committees or groups of scientists nominated by the Travelling Expenses Committee. Grants to outside bodies were made from the Parliamentary Grant-in-aid totalling £17 809 in respect of organizing expenses of international meetings in the United Kingdom, or for the travelling expenses of invited overseas lecturers at meetings of scientific societies.

Although most of the contributions and deeds of covenant in response to the Appeal were initiated in the previous year, several additions were received and the total sum promised at 31 August 1976, representing gross value of covenanted deeds and donations, was £784 600. The following should be added to the corporate donors' list in Appendix A to last year's report: *Appeal*

British Schools and Universities Foundation, Inc.
Booker McConnell Ltd
Chloride Group Ltd
Christ Church, Oxford
The Wellcome Foundation Ltd

Income from the new Appeal fund is materially helping to offset some of the Society's increased costs but again the Finance Committee has reported on the need to maintain close control of expenditure. As reported above, Council decided to increase the selling prices of *Philosophical Transactions* and *Proceedings* by 10% to help meet higher production costs.

A bequest of £252 was received, the residue of the estate of the late F. G. Morris, for the general purposes of the Royal Society. *Bequest*

Council has acknowledged with gratitude the following gifts and grants: *Gifts*

By the TRUSTEES of the Wellcome Trust: £75 000 to provide additional capital for the Wellcome Research Fund which supports the Henry Dale Research Professorship.

By the TRUSTEES of the Leverhulme Trust Fund: £58 300 over three years for Studentships (see above under Research Appointments), Visiting Professorships (see under Overseas Visiting Professorships) and Visiting Fellowships to China.

By Marks and Spencer Limited: £1000 as the first of three annual contributions to the Royal Society-Israel Academy Programme.

By the Weizmann Institute Foundation: £2000 as the first of three annual contributions to the Royal Society-Israel Academy Programme.

Mention has already been made in this report of the gifts by Lady BAWDEN (under Library), Wates Foundation (International Council of Scientific Unions), Commonwealth Foundation (Commonwealth Bursaries), anonymously (exchanges between older Commonwealth countries) and Unilever Ltd (Latin America).

Representation by the Society

Professor T. S. WESTOLL represented the Society at a banquet held on 11 September at Newcastle upon Tyne on the occasion of the meeting there of the 4th World Congress on the Theory of Machines and Mechanisms.

The PRESIDENT, the BIOLOGICAL SECRETARY, LORD TODD and the EXECUTIVE SECRETARY represented the Society at a reception held in Cambridge on 18 September on the occasion of the symposium held there to mark the centenary of the birth of Sir Henry Dale.

The PRESIDENT attended the presentation of the 1975 S. G. Brown Award and Medal to Mr G. AUTON at the Institution of Electrical Engineers on 2 October.

The FOREIGN SECRETARY attended the celebrations of the 250th anniversary of the U.S.S.R. Academy of Sciences, which had been postponed in 1974, and were held from 5 to 15 October 1975.

The PRESIDENT represented the Society at the Parsons Memorial Lecture delivered by Dr E. R. PIKE before the Institute of Physics on 29 October.

The PRESIDENT sent messages of greetings and congratulations from the Royal Society to the Commonwealth Scientific and Industrial Research Organization, Australia, and the Department of Scientific and Industrial Research, New Zealand, on the occasion of the celebrations of the jubilee of their foundation.

Mention has been made elsewhere in this report of other attendance by representatives of the Society at meetings or anniversaries (for example, Energy Conference, European Science Foundation, United States bicentenary and, in Appendix B, at international meetings).

Representation on Outside Bodies

New responsibilities accepted during the year were the appointment of representatives on the following bodies (the names of the first representatives being shown in parentheses):

Birmingham University Court (Dr D. W. PASHLEY).
United Kingdom Coordinating Committee for the International

Phase of Ocean Drilling (of the Deep Sea Drilling Project) (Dr D. H. MATTHEWS).

Consiglio Nazionale delle Ricerche, Italy—international group to advise on the construction of a new volcanological observatory on Mount Etna and the scientific research to be undertaken at and from it (Dr J. E. GUEST).

The British Council disbanded its Science Advisory Committee and Science and Engineering Panel in a reorganization of its system of advisory panels and committees in science and technology and set up restructured panels as follows:

Science Advisory Panel (Professor J. HESLOP-HARRISON and Professor A. W. JOHNSON).

Agricultural Advisory Panel (Dr L. FOWDEN).

Reference has been made earlier in this report to other new responsibilities accepted (British Academy's Technical Committee for the Study of the Conservation of Medieval Stained Glass, Science Research Council's Archaeology Committee, United Kingdom Committee on International Nature Conservation).

The Queen's Lecture in Germany selection committee on which the representative was the PRESIDENT, *ex officio*, and Cambridge University Committee for Meteorology on which the most recent representative was Professor P. A. SHEPPARD were dissolved and the Society ceased to be represented on the Advisory Committee on Meteorology for Scotland.

Grants from the Scientific Relief Fund amounted to £11 931 (£5471 in the previous year). The Scientific Relief Committee has been able to make use of the extension of the Fund's regulations under which assistance may be given to retired scientists to enable them to advance natural knowledge; three grants were made for the continuation of personal research projects and fifteen for travelling expenses, nine of which were to retired Fellows. Grants for the traditional purposes of the 'relief of distress' of scientists and their families have, of course, continued to be made. Scientific Relief Fund

Council dissolved the Mathematical Tables Committee, the National Committee for the International Biological Programme and, with effect from 31 December 1976, the Coelacanth Research Committee and, jointly with the Royal Commission on Historical Manuscripts, the Scientific and Technological Records Committee. Committees

These decisions resulted, in the main, from the annual reviews by Council of its committees when those regarded as having served their purpose or whose work can be carried out by other means are dissolved.

Social Functions

The Anniversary Dinner was held at The Dorchester on 1 December when the principal guest was Professor R. Lüst, President of the Max-Planck-Gesellschaft, who proposed the toast of the Society. Mr G. RICHARDSON, Governor of the Bank of England, replied for the guests.

The Conversaziones were held on 6 May and 24 June. At the first there were twenty-nine exhibits and the film 'The Atlantic Tropical Experiment of the Global Atmospheric Research Programme' was shown. On the following morning senior pupils from selected schools were invited to inspect the exhibits and see the film; they were welcomed by the PRESIDENT. At the second Conversazione there were twenty-eight exhibits and the same film was shown. The attendance on the first occasion was about 650 Fellows and guests and on the second occasion about 800.

Receptions, etc.

Receptions, etc., were held in the Society's rooms to entertain guests of the Society, mainly from overseas, on the following occasions:

1975

15 September	International Cartographic Association
22 September	Provisional Space Science Advisory Board for Europe

1976

6 February	Bureau of the Scientific Committee on Problems of the Environment
1 March	European Science Foundation's *ad hoc* Space Science Committee
5 April	Council of the International Union of Nutritional Sciences
8 April	Royal Society/Mineralogical Society discussion meeting—as part of the Mineralogical Society's centenary celebrations

20 May	Holders of Royal Society research appointments
15 July	Members of the Association of British Science Writers with members of Council.

TODD
President

APPENDIX A

REPORTS ON RESEARCHES

		Page
R. MILEDI, F.R.S.	Foulerton Research Professor	302
J. L. GOWANS, F.R.S.	Henry Dale Research Professor	303
R. J. P. WILLIAMS, F.R.S.	Napier Research Professor	305
M. F. ATIYAH, F.R.S.	Royal Society Research Professor	306
H. B. BARLOW, F.R.S.	Royal Society Research Professor	307
G. H. BEALE, F.R.S.	Royal Society Research Professor	308
J. H. BEYNON, F.R.S.	Royal Society Research Professor	309
J. W. CORNFORTH, F.R.S.	Royal Society Research Professor	310
R. H. DALITZ, F.R.S.	Royal Society Research Professor	311
P. H. FOWLER, F.R.S.	Royal Society Research Professor	312
R. A. HINDE, F.R.S.	Royal Society Research Professor	314
A. F. HUXLEY, F.R.S.	Royal Society Research Professor	315
H. C. LONGUET-HIGGINS, F.R.S.	Royal Society Research Professor	316
M. S. LONGUET-HIGGINS, F.R.S.	Royal Society Research Professor	318
F. SONDHEIMER, F.R.S.	Royal Society Research Professor	319
DOROTHY CROWFOOT HODGKIN, O.M., F.R.S.	Wolfson Research Professor	321
S. M. ZEKI	Henry Head Research Fellow	322
G. S. BEDDARD	Mr and Mrs John Jaffé Donation Research Fellow	323
M. J. CLEMENS	Mr and Mrs John Jaffé Donation Research Fellow	324
CAROLYN M. L. KERR	Mr and Mrs John Jaffé Donation Research Fellow	326
J. V. WALL	Mr and Mrs John Jaffé Donation Research Fellow	327
S. H. WHITE	Mr and Mrs John Jaffé Donation Research Fellow	328
T. B. BOLTON	Locke Research Fellow	329
R. A. DWEK	Locke Research Fellow	330
M. W. J. DAVIE	J. Sainsbury Research Fellow	332
P. J. GARLICK	J. Sainsbury Research Fellow	334
M. B. BECK	Ernest Cook Trust Research Fellow	335
J. N. GALLAGHER	Ernest Cook Trust Research Fellow	336
R. M. SIBLY	Ernest Cook Trust Research Fellow	337
G. D. WIGHAM	Ernest Cook Trust Research Fellow	338
J. M. WILSON	Ernest Cook Trust Research Fellow	339
I. W. CHUBB	Horace Le Marquand and Dudley Bigg Research Fellow	340
J. EVANS	Pickering Research Fellow	342
A. J. KINGSMAN	Pickering Research Fellow	343
D. K. RUSSELL	Pickering Research Fellow	344
D. E. HANKE	Rosenheim Research Fellow	345
CHEW SING HOOI	Rutherford Scholar	346

D. J. Cookson	Rutherford Scholar	346
K. A. Hunter	Rutherford Scholar	347
C. J. van Rijsbergen	Scientific Information Research Fellow	349
S. E. Robertson	Scientific Information Research Fellow	350
G. B. Warren	Stothert Research Fellow	351
A. C. S. Readhead	Weir Research Fellow	352
W. M. Stobbs	Armourers and Brasiers' Research Fellow	353
H. N. Arst	Smithson Research Fellow	354
D. V. Edmonds	Warren Research Fellow	356
A. E. Vardy	Warren Research Fellow	357
R. N. McBurney	Florey Fellow	359
D. T. Spira	Bruno Mendel Travelling Fellow	360
G. Ziv	Bruno Mendel Travelling Fellow	360
G. A. B. Shelton	John Murray Travelling Student	362
D. K. Aitken	Radcliffe Trust Research Fellow	363
Gassiot Committee		364

R. MILEDI, F.R.S., Foulerton Research Professor

Last year, my work developed along two main lines: (a) noise analysis of drug action on membranes, and (b) neuromuscular effects of immunization against acetylcholine (ACh) receptors.

(a) After the cholinesterase is blocked at the nerve-muscle junction, a short train of nerve impulses is followed by a muscle membrane depolarization lasting several seconds. It had been suggested that this depolarization was the result of a 'freezing', in the open state, of the channels activated by ACh. An alternative explanation was that the channels opened and closed normally, and the depolarization was caused by the action of ACh molecules lingering about the membrane. Using the noise analysis that we introduced several years ago, Sir Bernard Katz and I found (9) that the depolarization was due to the continued presence of ACh. The question remains whether this is caused by trapping, and slow diffusion of some of the ACh released by the nerve impulses; or by molecular leakage of ACh from the nerve endings. Noise analysis was also used to study the action of procaine at the neuromuscular junction (6), and that of glutamate on squid nerve cells (7) and locust muscle (12).

(b) ACh-receptor protein was purified from membranes of the electric organ of *Torpedo* (4). The protein was injected into rabbits, and after a few weeks they developed a paralysis which was sometimes fatal (3). Anti-ACh-receptor antibodies were found in the blood of immunized animals. A study of their diaphragm muscle revealed that neuromuscular transmission was blocked at some endplates. The amplitude of miniature endplate potentials caused by the action of single quanta of ACh was greatly reduced, as was also the binding of α-bungarotoxin (which combines specifically with ACh-receptors). These effects of immunization are caused by a decrease in the number of ACh-receptors available for combination with ACh, presumably because the receptors in the muscle membrane are blocked by anti-receptor antibodies. This hypothesis was strengthened by the observation that the serum from immunized rabbits reduced the amplitude of miniature potentials in frog muscle (3).

Approximately three years ago, my colleagues and I began to study the human neuromuscular junction, particularly that from patients affected by Myasthenia gravis. Elmqvist *et al.* (*J. Physiol. Lond.* **174**, 417–434, 1964) had previously found that in myasthenic muscle miniature endplate potentials were abnormally small, and concluded that their small size was due to a decrease in the amount of ACh. We have confirmed that miniature potentials in myasthenic muscle have a small size, and have found that the content of ACh in myasthenic muscle was not reduced, but was, in fact, about twice that of control muscle (10). Using α-bungarotoxin as a marker, we found that in control muscle there are about 2×10^7 receptors per endplate, while in myasthenic musle this number is reduced to about one third (4). Thus, the endplates in myasthenic muscle resemble, in many respects, those of rabbits immunized against ACh-receptors.

Publications

1. Microinjection of calcium into droplets of aequorin. *Proc. R. Soc. Lond.* B **189**, 39–47 (1975). (With K. Kusano & J. Stinnakre.)
2. Postsynaptic entry of calcium induced by transmitter action. *Proc. R. Soc. Lond.* B **189**, 49–56 (1975). (With K. Kusano & J. Stinnakre.)
3. Neuromuscular transmission after immunization against acetylcholine receptors. *Proc. R. Soc. Lond.* B **189**, 57–68 (1975). (With D. P. L. Green & A. Vincent.)

4. Acetylcholine receptors. *Phil. Trans. R. Soc. Lond.* B **270**, 551–559 (1975). (With D. P. L. Green, M. Perez de la Mora & A. Vincent.)
5. Effect of Dendroaspis neurotoxins on synaptic transmission in the spinal cord of the frog. *Proc. R. Soc.* B **190**, 267–274 (1975). (With A. Szczepaniak.)
6. The effect of procaine on the action of acetylcholine at the neuromuscular junction. *J. Physiol. Lond.* **249**, 269–284 (1975). (With B. Katz.)
7. Membrane potential fluctuations produced by glutamate in nerve cells of the squid. *Proc. R. Soc. Lond.* B **191**, 561–565 (1975). (With S. J. Bevan & B. Katz.)
8. Neuronal characteristics of the Schwann cell. *J. Evol. Biochem. Physiol.* **11**, 561–566 (1975).
9. The nature of the prolonged endplate depolarization in anti-esterase treated muscle. *Proc. R. Soc. Lond.* B **192**, 27–38 (1975). (With B. Katz.)
10. Acetylcholine in human muscle. *Proc. R. Soc. Lond.* B **192**, 475–480 (1976). (With Y. Ito, P. C. Molenaar, A. Vincent, R. L. Polak, M. van Gelder & J. Newsom Davis.)
11. Light and electron-microscopic localization of ^{125}I-α-bungarotoxin binding in a sympathetic ganglion. 10*th Int. Cong. Anat.*, Tokyo, 1975, p. 221. (With M. R. Matthews & A. Vincent.)
12. Glutamate and quisqualate noise in voltage-clamped locust muscle fibres. *Nature, Lond.* **261**, 151–153 (1976). (With C. R. Anderson & S. G. Cull-Candy.)

Place of Research: Department of Biophysics, University College London.

J. L. GOWANS, F.R.S., Henry Dale Research Professor

We have made further progress on the three topics outlined in last year's report. Dr A. J. Husband and I have continued to study the origin and fate of the circulating large lymphocytes which migrate into the lamina propria of the small intestine and secrete IgA antibodies. Dr Husband has prepared Thiry-Vella loops of small intestine in immunized rats and has shown that the greatest density of specific antibody-producing cells always occurs in the loop which is challenged with antigen. This appears to show that antigen plays an important part in determining the region of the intestine into which the large lymphocytes migrate. We are now analysing the way in which antigen exerts its effect. Dr Husband has confirmed that the large lymphocytes which migrate into the gut originate in Peyer's patches. This was established by measuring the output of large lymphocytes in lymph from Thiry-Vella loops from which the Peyer's patches had been removed surgically. Thus, there is now general agreement that the Peyer's patches have the peculiar property of accumulating or generating B lymphocytes which are committed to IgA synthesis and of ejecting them into the lymph in response to antigenic challenge. However, the factors which determine the migration of these cells from the blood into the lamina propria of the intestine are still uncertain, although antigen in the gut plays some, as yet undefined part.

We reported last year that work had begun on the origin and function of cells which secrete IgE in rats infested with the intestinal parasite *Nippostrongylus brasiliensis*. Dr G. Mayrhofer had shown that large numbers of cells containing

IgE accumulated in the lamina propria of the intestine of infested rats. This raised the possibility that IgE, like IgA, was a secretory immunoglobulin and was synthesized by plasma cells in the lamina propria. Dr Mayrhofer has analysed further the nature of the cells in the lamina propria which contain IgE and has established by histochemical methods that they are mast cells and not plasma cells. The IgE in these animals was synthesized in an orthodox manner in the lymph nodes draining the sites of parasitic infestation and the mast cells must have acquired their IgE passively. IgE is known to absorb to the surface of mast cells in other sites but its intracellular location in intestinal mast cells is a new findings. These studies make it clear that IgE is not a secretory immunoglobulin but its function in defence against intestinal parasites remains to be determined.

The third topic on which we reported last year concerns the identity of the B lymphocytes which give rise to plasma cells secreting IgG antibody in secondary responses (see references). Dr D. W. Mason has now established that the large IgG response which can be generated in X-irradiated recipients after an injection of lymphocytes from primed donors arises from a very small subpopulation of lymphocytes ($\leq 3\%$ of all B cells) which carry IgG on their surface. We had suspected that the precursors were present among the B lymphocytes which carry surface IgM but by employing the Fluorescence Activated Cell Sorter (FACS) Mason has now established unequivocally that the large response is derived from the minority population. The results of these experiments maintain the orthodoxy that the class of immunoglobulin on the surface of a lymphocyte is the same as that secreted by the plasma cells into which it differentiates; they also illustrate the power of the FACS to separate subpopulations of cells for biological testing. The FACS should have wide applications in cell biology and we look forward to exploiting the machine which has recently been installed in our own Unit.

References

Mason, D. W. 1976. The requirement for C3 receptors on the precursors of 19S and 7S antibody-forming cells. *J. Exp. Med.* **143**, 1111–1121.

Mason, D. W. 1976. The class of surface immunoglobulin on cells carrying IgG memory in rat thoracic duct lymph: the size of the subpopulation mediating IgG memory. *J. Exp. Med.* **143**, 1122–1130.

Publications

Cellular kinetics of the intestinal immune response to cholera toxoid in rats. *J. Exp. Med.* **142**, 1550–1563 (1975). (With N. F. Pierce.)

Nature of cells binding anti-IgE in rats immunized with *Nippostrongylus brasiliensis*: IgE synthesis in regional nodes and concentration in mucosal mast cells. *Eur. J. Immunol.* **6**, 537-545 (1976). (With G. Mayrhofer & H. Bazin.)

The natural history of the cells producing IgA in the gut. In *Ciba Foundation Symposium on The Immunology of the Gut* (in the press). (With A. J. Husband & H. J. Monié.)

Subpopulations of B lymphocytes and the carriage of immunological memory. *Ann. Immunol. (Inst. Pasteur)* **6**, 537–545 (1976). (With D. W. Mason.)

Place of Research: Sir William Dunn School of Pathology, University of Oxford.

R. J. P. WILLIAMS, F.R.S., Napier Research Professor

The major experimental work of my group has continued to be in the area of the application of nuclear magnetic resonance spectroscopy to problems of biological interest. Detailed studies of the structure of cytochrome c in the iron (II), iron (III) and cobalt (III) forms by proton magnetic resonance supported by the solid state structural work of Professor R. E. Dickerson (California) are sufficiently advanced to show that the *internal* conformation of the protein is not altered significantly on change of charge from the two plus to the three plus state (Dr G. Moore). The two differently charged states bind with different strengths to various complex anions and cations and to certain proteins and it has been known for some time that they have rather different physical properties. As the metal ion is in the centre of the protein there would appear to be no other explanation for these two sets of facts than that the change of metal ion charge alters the *surface* conformation and energy of the protein. This mechanism of relaying information through a protein, simply using the influence of electrostatic charge, is very different from the commonly described allosteric conformation changes which involve covalently linked residues. This possibility will now be examined in detail. Other proteins which are under detailed study are lysozymes (Dr C. M. Dobson) peroxidases (Dr P. E. Wright) and certain calcium binding proteins (Dr B. Levine in cooperation with members of the Molecular Biophysics Laboratory).

Further work has been carried out in the application of n.m.r. methods to the examination of whole organs such as the adrenal cortex. Somewhat surprisingly it is possible to detect readily stored fatty acid compounds in this organ, as well as in various plant seeds and even in zoo-plankton. In view of these observations the possibility of using proton n.m.r. spectroscopy as a general analytical method for intact biological systems is being pursued. The limits imposed by the insensitivity of the method (concentrations must be $\geq$ 1 mM with present-day instruments) and the requirement for fast molecular tumbling times mean that only a few components of the total system can be studied as yet. (Parallel work on phosphorus resonances is under way in Oxford by Dr R. E. Richards and his collaborators.)

At the more general level I have been concerned with the analysis of two problems in bioenergetics: the nature and stability of 'phases' in living systems and the transduction of energy, from an initial source such as light, through charge (proton/electron) gradients to chemical energy, e.g. as adenosine triphosphate.

During the year I gave lectures at meetings in Bari (where there was further discussion of methods by which protons drive oxidative phosphorylation), in Prague (Heyrovsky Meeting on Electron Transfer Mechanisms), and in Namur (Conference of the Belgium Chemical Society on Drug/Receptor Interactions).

Publications

Phases and phase structure in biological systems. *Biochem. Biophys. Acta.* **416**, 237–286 (1975).

Protein connections between protons, electrons and ATP, in *Electron transfer chains and oxidative phosphorylation*, (ed. E. Quagliariello et al.), pp. 417–422 (1975).

Proton magnetic resonance studies of peroxidases from turnip and horseradish. *Biochim. Biophys. Acta.* **412**, 127–147 (1975). (With P. E. Wright, G. Mazza & J. R. Ricard.)

Chemical nature and sequence of alamethicin. *Biochem. J.* **153**, 181–190 (1976). (With D. R. Martin.)

The structures of some cobalamins in solution. *Phil. Trans. R. Soc. Lond.* B **273**, 365–357 (1976). (With O. D. Hensens, H. A. O. Hill, J. Thornton & A. M. Turner.)

Nuclear magnetic resonance studies of the adrenal gland and some other organs. *Nature, Lond.* **261**, 321–323 (1976). (With A. Daniels & P. E. Wright.)

Nuclear magnetic resonance study of the active-site structure of yeast phosphoglycerate kinase. *Eur. J. Biochem.* **63**, 249–262 (1976). (With P. Tanswell & E. W. Westhead.)

A study of redox reactions of biological importance between Fe(III) complexes and aromatic moieties. *Biochem. Biophys. Acta* **428**, 261–268 (1976). (With P. S. Burns, J. F. Harrod & P. E. Wright.)

The study of enzymes. *Chemistry in Britain*, vol. 12, no. 4, (1976). (With G. K. Radda.)

Conformation of peptides in water in *Environmental Effects on Molecular Structure and Properties* (ed. B. Pullman), pp. 95–108 (1976). (With B. A. Levine.)

Place of Research: Inorganic Chemistry Laboratory, University of Oxford.

M. F. ATIYAH, F.R.S., Royal Society Research Professor

I spent the first term at the Institute for Advanced Study in Princeton. During this time I worked closely with Professor W. Schmid of Columbia University on problems in the representation theory of semi-simple Lie groups. The main outcome was a new and simpler proof of Harish-Chandra's basic result on the local summability of the irreducible characters. In addition we worked on the construction of the discrete series of representations, using the results reported on last year as a starting point.

Back in Oxford I gave a series of lectures developing some aspects of this work. Professor Schmid visited Oxford for a week in May and this enabled us to clear up a number of technical points.

In a different direction I have become involved with the work of Professor R. Penrose and his group on problems in general relativity. It has turned out that many aspects of the Penrose twistor programme find their most natural formulation within the modern global theory of complex manifolds. In particular, sheaf cohomology groups provide very useful tools, and a basic theorem of Kodaira plays a key rôle. This is a most promising development and I intend to pursue it further.

My interest in solitons continues and I have helped to organize a three-day conference on this topic to be held in Newcastle in September. Great interest now centres on the use of solitons in quantum field theory.

While in the U.S.A. I visited a large number of Universities on the East Coast, including Harvard, Yale, Columbia and Johns Hopkins. I also spent a few days in Mexico delivering the Solomon Lefschetz lectures. In June I lectured at the Hodge Memorial meeting of the London Mathematical Society and in July I took part in a conference on partial differential equations at Durham. Visitors to Oxford included Professor G. W. Mackey and Professor P. A. Griffiths both from Harvard and Professor I. M. Singer (M.I.T.).

Publications

Spectral asymmetry and Riemannian geometry II. *Math. Proc. Camb. Phil. Soc.* **78**, 405–432 (1975) (With V. K. Patodi & I. M. Singer.)

Spectral asymmetry and Riemannian geometry III. *Math. Proc. Camb. Phil. Soc.* **79**, 71–99, (1976). (With V. K. Patodi & I. M. Singer.)

Global geometry. Bakerian Lecture 1975, *Proc. R. Soc. Lond.* A **347**, 291–299 (1976).

Elliptic operators, discrete groups and von Neumann algebras. *Soc. Math. de France, Asterisque* **32–33**, 43–72, (1976).

Classical groups and classical differential operators on manifolds. In: *Differential operators on manifolds*. Centro Internazionale Matematico Estivo, Varenna (1975).

Place of Research: The Mathematical Institute, University of Oxford.

H. B. BARLOW, F.R.S., Royal Society Research Professor

The retinal image is thought to be transmitted to the brain by nerve impulses from retinal ganglion cells, each of which signals the light-induced activity of a local group of receptor cells. It has recently been suggested that ganglion cells can also be excited vigorously from remote retinal regions; Fischer and Krüger shifted a grating of coarse period through half a cycle, and showed that ganglion cells responded with discharges reaching 250 impulses/second even when the receptive field and a region 20° around it were totally prevented from receiving the image of the grating. With Dr P. Lennie I have investigated this 'shift effect', as it is called, since it seemed to invalidate the notion that the ganglion cells each transmit information about a local point of the image.

We initially thought the effect was caused by intraocular scattered light, but this explanation was completely ruled out by experiments in which the receptive field or remote retinal regions were separately light adapted; the response is genuinely elicited by stimulation of remote retina. We find, however, that only those ganglion cells known as 'transient' or 'Y-type', forming about 5% of the total, show vigorous shift effects; in the remaining 'sustained', or 'X-type', the effect is small and sluggish. The shift response also differs from responses elicited from the proper receptive field in having a distinct threshold, and there are reasons for believing that it may be mediated by amacrine cells. The functional role of shift responses is somewhat mysterious, but it may be part of a mechanism ensuring that the retinal image seen when the eye settles into a new fixation position is not contaminated by the after-effects of the pattern of illumination received in the previous fixation position. Certainly the main cause of shift responses in the ordinary use of the eyes must be a saccadic eye movement.

Following last year's experiments in which the statistical efficiency was measured for perceiving sinusoidal modulations of the density of randomly placed dots I have started looking at performance in detecting other forms of regularity introduced into a random array. If about 20% of the dots are accompanied by a paired dot displaced through a certain distance and angle, this is detectable as a hard to define streakiness or regularity in the pattern. A random element can be introduced into the distance and direction of the displacement without destroying the distinguishing feature, and this enables one to estimate how accurately placed a pair must be to contribute to the illusion. Knowing this, one can calculate how many illusion-producing pairs occur unintentionally within a random dot pattern, and hence find what is the background noise of oriented pairs against which the additional pairs are seen. From this in turn one finds the statistical efficiency for the perception of the distinguishing feature. Efficiencies of about 25% are obtained; this is lower than for detecting variations in dot density, but the task being performed is much more complex since it involves looking at the properties of pairs of dots (of which there are about n^2) instead of simple counts of dots over a small number of discrete areas (of which there are less than n, since each discrete area usually contains several dots).

In December a Discussion Meeting was organized (with Dr R. M. Gaze) on Neural Plasticity, and in September a meeting on Photoreceptors (with Dr P. Fatt). In April we moved into additional space in the Craik-Marshall Laboratory.

Publications

Visual experience and cortical development. *Nature, Lond.* **258**, 199–204 (1975).

Adaptation to gratings: no compensatory advantages found. *Vision Res.* **16**, 1043–1045 (1976). (With D. I. A. MacLeod & A. van Meeteren).

Threshold setting by the surround of cat retinal ganglion cells. *J. Physiol.* **259**, 737–757 (1976). (With W. R. Levick).

Place of Research: Physiological Laboratory, University of Cambridge.

G. H. BEALE, F.R.S., Royal Society Research Professor

As in previous years, my research group studying *Paramecium* concentrated on mitochondrial genetics. Dr A. Tait, using immunological methods, compared the proteins in various interspecific 'hybrids', obtained by micro-injection of mitochondria from one species (syngen) to another. He found clear evidence that some differences in mitochondrial ribosomal proteins were under the control of the mitochondrial genome. L. Cockburn continued his work on mutation of mitochondrial genes controlling erythromycin resistance, and found that while acriflavine and manganese were effective mutagens in this system, ultraviolet light was not.

The genetic basis of some differences between mitochondria from species 1 and 7, of *P. aurelia*, in regard to the ability of the mitochondria to grow after transfer to other species, was shown by Dr J. K. C. Knowles and myself to be mainly controlled by the nuclear genome.

Dr Tait supplemented some earlier work on enzyme differences between different species of *P. aurelia*, and showed that species 1 and 5, which are otherwise very similar, could be clearly distinguished by examination of electrophoretic variants of glucose phosphate isomerase. We are thus now able to identify all 14 species of *P. aurelia* by enzyme comparisons.

My malaria group (Dr D. Walliker, Dr A. Brown and Dr V. do Rosario) demonstrated that chloroquine-resistance in *Plasmodium chabaudii* is a Mendelian character. Recombination between genes for chloroquine-resistance and three other genetic markers was demonstrated. Competition experiments involving mixtures of drug-resistant and sensitive parasites showed the rather alarming result that the resistant parasites were selectively favoured, even in the absence of chloroquine. A similar experiment involving mixtures of pyrimethamine-resistant and sensitive organisms, showed that in this case it was the sensitive strain which was selected.

Dr Walliker studied two independently obtained virulent strains of *Pl. yoelli*, and showed that each was due to a separate gene mutation. Other, i.e. nongenetic, mechanisms which have been thought to produce increased virulence were shown not be be important.

Publication

Interspecies transfer of mitochondria in *Paramecium aurelia*. *Molec. gen. Genet.* **143**, 197–201 (1976). (With J. K. C. Knowles.)

Place of Research: Institute of Animal Genetics, University of Edinburgh.

J. H. BEYNON, F.R.S., Royal Society Research Professor

The ion kinetic energy spectrometer being manufactured for my research laboratory is almost completed and is undergoing preliminary tests. Some additional novel features have been incorporated in it including some special scanning modes and an electrically insulated collision cell. The latter feature enables reactions to be induced in ions moving with high translational energy while at the same time the velocities of the products can be reduced to facilitate accurate measurements of velocity spread. I have visited the manufacturer on several occasions and am currently involved in the testing programme. Delivery to Swansea is expected in October.

The University College of Swansea has given me money to purchase parts for a second instrument and work is under way to construct this. It is hoped to obtain an ion beam later this year and then to use this instrument for the development of new high intensity ion sources so as to extend the applications of ion kinetic energy spectrometry in chemistry.

Dr R. K. Boyd of the University of Guelph, Ontario, spent more than six months in my laboratory and we collaborated in a study of the applications of ion enthalpy measurements to structure determination. We also determined all the possible ways of linked scanning of the fields of a mass spectrometer. We were able to predict that scanning the electric sector voltage, E, and the sector magnetic field, B, in such a way that E/B^2 remained constant during the scan would give a plot of all the daughter ion peaks arising from a single parent ion species without the discrimination effects against ions formed with conversion of internal into translational energy that are inherent in all other linked scans. Publications are being prepared.

I am currently collaborating with Professor K. R. Jennings of the University of Warwick in a study of the fine structure of 'metastable peaks' formed from fragmenting negatively charged ions. I am also working in collaboration with Professor Jože Marsel of the Institut Jožef Stefan, Ljubljana, on the properties of organic ions carrying two positive charges, especially as regards the influence on these properties of charge localization.

During the year, in addition to giving my inaugural lecture at Swansea, I lectured to the Royal Institute of Chemistry at Aberystwyth, to the American Society for Mass Spectrometry in San Diego, California, at the Texas, Oklahoma State, N. Carolina and Rockefeller Universities and at the University of Mons, Belgium. I took part in a Course on Mass Spectrometry at the Instituto Venezolano de Investigaciones Cientificas, Caracas, Venezuela, sponsored by the Organisation of American States, and also gave a short course of lectures at the University of Essex.

Publications

Ion kinetic energy spectrometry. In '*Mass Spectrometry*', *MTP International Review of Science, Physical Chemistry, Series II* (ed. A. Maccoll) **5**, 159–206 (1975). (With R. G. Cooks.)

Ion structure determination through collisions of ions at high kinetic energies. *Org. Mass Spectr.* **10**, 503–506 (1975). (With R. G. Cooks & J. F. Litton.)

Collision induced dissociation of the lower alcohols: a thermochemical study. *Org. Mass Spectr.* **10**, 625–638 (1975). (With R. G. Cooks & L. Hendricks.)

An imaging detector for mass spectrometry. *Anal. Chem.* **47**, 1734–1738 (1975). (With D. O. Jones & R. G. Cooks.)

Kinetic energy distributions in the fragmentation of metastable H_2S, HDS and D_2S ions. *Int. J. Mass Spectr. Ion Phys.* **18**, 43–56 (1975). (With D. T. Terwilliger & R. G. Cooks.)

$C^{+\cdot}$ and CH^+ from doubly-charged ions from malononitrile. *Org. Mass. Spectr.* **10**, 824–830 (1975). (With R. M. Caprioli, R. G. Cooks, N. M. M. Nibbering & T. A. Molenaar-Langeveld.)

The measurement of appearance potentials of gaseous ions. *Int. J. Mass Spectr. Ion Phys.* **18**, 87–99 (1975). (With R. G. Cooks, K. R. Jennings & A. J. Ferrer-Correia.)

Dissociative double-electron capture. Dynamics of fragmentation of the water and hydrogen sulfide negative ions. *Chem. Phys.* **12**, 191–196 (1976). (With T. Keough & R. G. Cooks.)

Attitudes and innovation in research. *Inaugural Lecture, University College of Swansea*, 20 pages (1976).

The concept and rôle of charge localization in mass spectrometry. *Org. Mass Spectr.* **11**, 103–116 (1976). (With D. H. Williams.)

Ion kinetic energy spectrometry. *Int. J. Mass Spectr. Ion Phys.* **19**, 107–137 (1976). (With R. G. Cooks.)

Place of Research: Department of Chemistry, University College of Swansea.

J. W. CORNFORTH, F.R.S., Royal Society Research Professor

After taking up my appointment and before moving to Sussex I deduced a quantitative relation between loss of chirality and loss of isotope in methylene groups made chiral by substitution with hydrogen isotopes and subsequently subjected to hydrogen exchange. This theory was used to analyse experimental findings on the enzymic sythesis of fatty acids from chiral acetates and from chirally labelled malonyl thiolesters. Two papers (with B. Sedgwick and others) have been prepared for publication. It was also shown that the theory can be used to determine the substrate stereochemistry of enzymic reactions in which methyl groups are converted into methylene groups irrespective of whether normal, inverse or null isotope effects are associated with the reactions.

At Sussex, while recruiting a small team and training a technician, I attacked and solved two long-standing problems of isatin chemistry: the structure of isamic acid (1842) and methylisatoid (1882). Physical methods are of limited use with these two compounds and the correct structures were proved chemically. A paper is in press.

Dr A. Sierakowski and Dr T. Wallace joined the team in February and May 1976 respectively. We are working on the catalysis of olefin hydration, with the objective of synthesizing catalysts of known structure which will show enzyme-like catalysis of this reaction. It has been necessary to study the stereochemistry of acid-catalysed olefin hydration and methods have been worked out for determining the relative amounts of *cis* and *trans* 2-deuteriocyclopentanols in mixtures with each other and with cyclopentanol. A method has also been found to discriminate between *threo* and *erythro* 3-deuterio-2-butanols and this will be developed into a quantitative analysis of mixtures. We expect soon to have determined the stereochemistry of addition of deuterium oxide, and of deuterium sulphate, to cyclopentene.

At the same time we are developing methods for synthesis of one class of catalysts that are considered promising. The work is too complex to summarize but the aim is to insert a chosen acidic group (in this case a suitably substituted phosphinic acid) into a hydrophobic cavity shaped to receive the olefin 'substrate'. Progress is being made in this direction.

Publications

Structure of isamic acid and of methylisatoid. *J. Chem. Soc.* (Perkin I) (in the press).

Asymmetry and enzyme action (Nobel lecture). *Les Prix Nobel en 1975*, in press; *J. Mol. Catal.* **1**, 145 (1976); *Science* **193**, 123–125 (1976); *Angew. Chem.* **88**, 550 (1976).

Place of Research: School of Molecular Sciences, University of Sussex.

R. H. DALITZ, F.R.S., Royal Society Research Professor

Much of our work during the past year has been concerned with a new aspect of hypernuclear physics, arising from recent experiments which give an accurate measurement for the spectrum of Λ hypernuclear states excited by the $K^- \to \pi^-$ strangeness-exchange process on a target nucleus. With A. Gal, we developed a quantitative explanation of the two-peak structure seen in the excitation spectrum for $^9_\Lambda Be^*$ in these experiments, as being due to three strangeness-analogue states (s.a.s.), an $I=1$ state, an $I=0$ state almost degenerate with it, and another $I=0$ state about 10 MeV below them (1). When further data became available for heavier nuclear targets, such as ^{40}Ca, we recognized that their interpretation required the existence of a different mechanism, that of quasi-free $Kn \to \Lambda\pi$ scattering (q.f.s.). This is possible for quite low momentum transfer since the Pauli principle places no constraints on the final states available for the recoiling Λ particle and calculations made on a rather intuitive basis gave us a good quantitative fit to the data available for nuclei ^{16}O to ^{40}Ca (2). We believe that generally both mechanisms exist. They represent extreme situations, one being s.a.s. excitation dominant, and the other being q.f.s. dominant. For nuclear targets with mass numbers between ^9Be and ^{40}Ca the two mechanisms interfere, and we are now making quantitative calculations appropriate to this intermediate regime.

At the Few Body Conference held at Delhi over the New Year, I gave an overall account of the ideas and developments in quark physics today (3). After the Conference, I delivered the B.B. Roy Memorial Lecture at the University of Calcutta, and I visited and spoke at the Tata Institute for Fundamental Research, Bombay.

Following the Workshop on 'New directions in baryon spectroscopy', held at the Argonne National Laboratory in July (1975), I gave an assessment (4) of the most immediate steps we can see ahead in this field of work, discussing especially our expectations concerning charmed baryonic systems. About the latter, there is no firm evidence available yet, but we now believe that they must exist, their relationship to the non-charmed baryonic states being parallel to that between the charmed mesons recently discovered and the well-known non-charmed mesons.

During the year, I participated in two meetings at the 'Ettore Majorana' School of Scientific Culture at Erice (Sicily), presenting a survey of hadronic spectroscopy for non-charmed states at one meeting, and an analysis of the origins of the spectrum calculated for baryonic states according to the three-quark harmonic shell model at the other meeting. Both of these contributions are now in course of publication.

In March, we held a well-attended Royal Society Discussion Meeting on the topic 'New particles and new quantum numbers', which I organized with the assistance of Mr W. Toner, and of Dr B. Richter and Dr B. Wiik, and to which I contributed a paper on 'Charm and the ψ-meson family'. In May, I attended the '4 × 50 Symposium' held at Nordita (Copenhagen) and contributed an invited paper on the excitation of Λ hypernuclear states in strangeness exchange reactions.

Since my last report, besides speaking at the institutions mentioned above, I have also given seminar talks at University College London, the Universities of Durham, Southampton and Virginia (Charlottesville, U.S.A.), and at the Rutherford Laboratory. I have also continued to organize our elementary particle seminars at Oxford.

Publications

1. Supersymmetric and strangeness analogue states in p-shell Λ hypernuclei. *Phys. Rev. Lett.* **36** pp. 326–366 (1976).
2. Quasi-free interactions in (K^-, π^-) strangeness-exchange nuclear reactions at 0°. *Phys. Lett.* **64B**, 154–158 (1976).
3. Quark physics, in *Few body dynamics* (Proc. VII Intl. Conf. on Few Body Problems in Nuclear and Particle Physics) (ed. A. Mitra), pp. 632–658. Amsterdam: North-Holland (1976).
4. Baryonic spectroscopy and its immediate future. In *New directions in hadron spectroscopy* (eds S. L. Kramer & E. L. Berger, Argonne National Laboratory, 1975), document ANL-HEP-CP-75-58, pp. 383–406.
5. The three-quark shell model and the spectrum of baryonic states. In *Hadron interactions at low energies*, Proceedings of the Triangle Meeting: Physics and Applications, Vol. 1 (eds. D. Krupa & J. Pisut), pp. 145–206. Bratislava: VEDA, Slovak Acad. Sci. (1975).

Place of Research: Department of Theoretical Physics, University of Oxford.

P. H. FOWLER, F.R.S., Royal Society Research Professor

During the past year a major part of my time has once again been concerned with our cosmic ray experiment on the forthcoming British satellite, UK 6. The satellite is now scheduled to be launched in April 1978. Production of important parts of the detector in the Physics Department workshops is proceeding well and is nearing completion.

In August and September I led our team at Palestine, Texas, for the balloon flight of our large spherical gas scintillation detector for heavy cosmic rays, BUGS 2. This was launched on 28 September from Palestine and gave us about 40 hours of good data at ceiling. The flight was terminated over Alabama about 60 hours after launch and the detector was recovered in good condition. The weather forecasts of the winds at flight altitude had indicated drift to the northwest where a down wind tracking station was sited to receive the data stream for the period when the balloon was expected to be below the horizon from Palestine. Unfortunately the balloon drifted irregularly, first to the southeast and then to the northeast, and finally went out of range about 48 hours after launch, never getting into range of our down wind station. The last few hours of data therefore were unfortunately lost.

The analysis of the flight data received and recorded on magnetic tape is essentially complete and we have an excellent charge spectrum for cosmic rays of charge $Z>14$ containing about 250 000 nuclei. The charge spectrum extends up to $Z\sim78$ where other work on track detectors indicates that there should be a small abundance peak of about 10^{-5}Fe. This is the first time that an electronic detector with sufficient collecting power has been flown for a sufficient duration to collect these rare heavy cosmic rays. Improved detectors in the future should enable one to achieve good charge resolution up to the highest charges which can be expected. One is confident that transuranic charges with charge $Z\sim96$ will be found, since there are indications of these in track analysis experiments, and since there are isotopes of Cm with sufficient lifetime against radioactive decay to survive the flight time. It is, however, possible that still heavier elements are present in the cosmic rays, and both our balloon-borne detectors and UK 6 satellite may detect such particles.

In October, Dr R. M. Redfern joined me, and is engaged in the development of our new generation of electronic detectors for ultra heavy cosmic rays. The new generation has as its heart a large spherical scintillating drift chamber. In the chamber the electrons released by the cosmic rays drift in a radial electric field to the central electrode and there produce a second scintillation which is carefully timed to yield the impact parameter for the track.

Our track analysis experiments on the ultra heavy components of the cosmic rays have also proceeded well. As reported last year, our payload was flown on the first Transatlantic Balloon Flight that was launched from Trapani, Sicily, on 5 August and recovered in Kentucky three days later. The material was recovered in good condition and has now been processed and preliminary analysis has been made. At the same time analyses of the data from the record-breaking flight of the previous year is nearing completion.

A further flight of very long duration is planned for 1977 for which a small scale proving flight is scheduled for September 1976, from Palestine. This will use a balloon system proposed by J. H. Davies and me at Bristol which is specially designed to carry heavy loads for long duration without the need for excessive quantities of ballast to preserve the float altitude during the nights. Long duration flights with heavy apparatus are highly desirable for a wide variety of scientific experiments, which include all our cosmic ray experiments to which I refer above.

The experiments described are mainly supported by grants from the Science Research Council for which I am very grateful.

Publication

Have we seen the track of a magnetic monopole? *Proc. 14th International Cosmic Ray Conference, Munich*, 4049–4064 (1975).

Place of Research: H. H. Wills Physics Laboratory, University of Bristol.

R. A. HINDE, F.R.S., Royal Society Research Professor

(1) *The development of social behaviour in rhesus monkeys*

(a) Dr M. J. A. Simpson (with Mrs A. E. Simpson and Miss D. Anderson) has concluded data collection for a longitudinal study of 20 rhesus infants over their first 6 months of life, using a computer-compatible keyboard method of recording. Analyses, aimed primarily at specifying dimensions of difference between mother-infant relationships, are in progress. Using eight multiparous mothers, he is also assessing consistencies in mother-infant relationships with successive infants. He is also studying the way in which mother-infant relationships are affected by the nexus of other relationships in which they are embedded.

(b) Dr Joan Stevenson-Hinde (with Miss M. Zunz) is using a variety of techniques to assess individual differences between juvenile and adult rhesus monkeys. She is exploring the values of different levels of analysis, her methods including both operant techniques and ratings of behavioural characteristics by observers familiar with the monkeys.

(c) Miss L. E. White is studying the development of social interactions and play in young rhesus monkeys.

(d) Miss A. Weisler is developing film and video techniques for recording the earliest mother-infant relationships, and is applying a method of movement notation for analysing her data.

(e) Two students have been concerned with social relationships in free living rhesus monkeys on Cayo Santiago, Puerto Rico. Miss C. Berman has been studying the social behaviour of infants in their first 30 weeks, and Miss S. Datta has been investigating the mechanisms of rank reversal whereby adolescent females rise above their elder sisters.

(f) I have been concerned with a comparison of the properties of various measures of mother-infant interactions in monkeys, and with developing a method for assigning responsibility for changes in triadic relationships.

2. *Social behaviour and behavioural ecology of other mammals*

(a) Dr Dian Fossey and Mr A. H. Harcourt have completed theses on aspects of the social behaviour of mountain gorilla in Rwanda. Miss K. Stewart is working on the development of social relationships in young gorilla.

(b) Two students, Dr R. Seyfarth and Mrs D. Cheney Seyfarth, have made an intensive study of one troop of baboons in South Africa. They have been able to account for many aspects of their social behaviour in terms of relatively few principles.

(c) Miss J. Oliver has completed a field study of the behavioural ecology of baboons and is at present analysing her data.

(d) Mr R. W. F. Barnes is engaged in field work on the behavioural ecology of elephants.

3. *Development of social behaviour in nursery school children* (with Mrs R. Roper and Dr Joan Stevenson-Hinde). We have started a study on the nature, stability and dynamics of the inter-individual relationships between nursery school children. Techniques have been developed for recording relevant behaviour in the classroom, and the resultant data compared with the factors emerging from a principal components analysis of the teacher's answers to a questionnaire.

4. *Integration in reproductive behaviour in female canaries and budgerigars*
   (a) (With Miss E. A. Steel). Studies of the gonad-independent mechanism(s) whereby photoperiod affects oestrogen-induced nest-building in canaries has continued along the lines indicated in the previous report. Recordings of male song have been found to have a similar effect. Comparable results have been obtained in budgerigars.
   (b) D. Croft has completed a thesis on the time budgets of canaries kept under different photoperiods.
5. *Conference Volume.* In collaboration with Dr P. Bateson I have helped organize and edit the proceedings of a conference on *Growing Points in Ethology*, held on the occasion of the 25th Anniversary of this laboratory.

Publications

The role of short days in the termination of photorefractoriness in female canaries (Serinus canarius). *J. Endocr.* **64**, 451–464 (1975). (With E. Steel & B. K. Follett.)

An oestrogen-mediated effect of photoperiod on the reproductive behaviour of the budgerigar. *J. Reprod Fert.*, **45**, 547–548 (1975). (With S. Gosney.)

Mothers' and infants' roles: distinguishing the questions to be asked. In *Parent-Infant Interaction—Ciba Foundation Symposium* 33. Elsevier (1975).

Qualities of mother-infant relationships in monkeys. In *Parent-Infant Interaction: Ciba Foundation Symposium 33*. Elsevier (1975). (With M. J. A. Simpson.)

Some factors affecting mother-infant relations in rhesus monkeys. *Anim. Behav.*, **23**, 527–542 (1975). (With L. E. White.)

Instinct and intelligence: Oxford Biology Reader no. 63 (ed. J. J. Head). Oxford University Press, 1976. (With J. Stevenson-Hinde.)

Interactions, relationships and social structure in non-human primates. *5th Cong. Int. Primat. Soc.* pp. 13–34 (1974). Japan Science Press (1975).

The concept of function. In *Function and evolution of behaviour*. Essays in Honour of Professor Niko Tinbergen (eds. G. Baerends, C. Beer & A. Manning.) Oxford: Clarendon Press (1975).

On describing relationships. *J. Child Psychol. Psychiat.* **17**, 1–19 (1976).

The use of differences and similarities in comparative psychopathology. In *Animal models in human psychobiology* (eds. G. Serban & A. Kling), pp. 187–202. New York and London: Plenum (1976).

Interactions, relationships and social structure. *Man*, **11**, 1–17 (1976).

Place of Research: M.R.C. Unit on the Development and Integration of Behaviour, Madingley, Cambridge.

A. F. HUXLEY, F.R.S., Royal Society Research Professor

I am still primarily engaged in analysing and writing up the series of experiments on mechanical transient responses in stimulated muscle fibres that were performed by Dr L. E. Ford, Dr R. M. Simmons and me in 1973–74. The first (and longest) of the papers is now practically ready for submission; it describes the equipment and the general features of the responses to single step changes of length applied to fibres at the length where there is maximum overlap of thick and thin filaments.

By applying corrections for (*a*) response of the tension transducer, (*b*) inertia of the fibre and (*c*) resistance due to the surrounding fluid, we have been able to plot tension change against length change during the first 100 microseconds of an imposed length change. During this period the 'early tension recovery' is almost negligible and the results show that the 'rapid elasticity', which almost certainly is a property of the crossbridges between thick and thin filaments, obeys Hooke's law, is practically undamped, and is considerably stiffer than had previously been supposed.

Dr R. M. Simmons, together with Dr Y. E. Goldman (supported by the Muscular Dystrophy Association of America), is recording the analogous transient responses in muscle fibres from which the surface membrane has been removed so that the chemical composition of the solution to which the contractile material is exposed can be altered at will. The chief result so far is that the rapid elasticity appears to be about the same in rigor as in the actively contracting state, while the early tension recovery is almost completely absent in rigor. The technique is working well, and is likely to produce very important results.

Dr J. Lännergren has returned for a short period with the hope of clearing up the uncertainties about the ultraviolet-absorbing material in the I bands of muscle fibres that he was studying during his stay in 1973-74.

Dr Lydia Hill (formerly Brocklehurst) is leaving at the end of August to take up a post at the Charing Cross Hospital Medical School. Her first attempts at fixing muscle fibres rapidly after a sudden stretch were unsuccessful because the action of the fixative (glutaraldehyde) was not rapid enough. Trials with other fixatives, however, have been very promising. She proposes to continue this work after leaving my laboratory.

I have written a historical article on studies of muscle by light microscopy for a volume to be produced by the Physiological Society in connection with its centenary.

I attended the International Conference on Muscle Disease held in June 1976 by the Muscular Dystrophy Association (of America), and visited laboratories at Harvard and at the University of Pennsylvania during the same journey.

On the nomination of the Royal Society, I was appointed a member of the Scientific Authority for Animals, set up in connection with the Convention on International Trade in Endangered Species. This occupied a substantial amount of time during the first six months of its existence, but is not likely to be so onerous in future.

Publications

The instantaneous elasticity of frog skeletal muscle fibres. *Proc. Physiol. Soc.*, 5 June 1976. (With L. E. Ford & R. M. Simmons.)

T. H. Huxley and the development of physiology in Britain. *Proc. Physiol. Soc.*, 2-3 July 1976.

Place of Research: Department of Physiology, University College London.

H. C. LONGUET-HIGGINS, F.R.S., Royal Society Research Professor

For some time I have been trying to understand the perception of Western music in terms sufficiently precise to allow the computer simulation of a common musical skill, namely a musician's ability to write down, in standard musical notation, a melody which is played to him on the keyboard. Two problems in particular have no obvious solution. First, standard notation distinguishes certain musical intervals (such as the major sixth and the diminished seventh) which are represented on the keyboard by the same number of semitones, the corresponding perceptual distinctions depending apparently on the context in which the interval occurs; and secondly, the time values (crotchet, quaver, etc.) which standard notation assigns to individual notes are more an indication of the metrical grouping of the individual notes than a literal representation of their actual durations, which will vary considerably in a musically interesting performance.

Early versions of the present theory were able to account for the perception of simple tunes of unvarying metre, but were insufficiently general to account for the perception of melodies as complex as those which are common in late nineteenth century European music. The theory has now been developed to the point at which a computer program based upon it can transcribe even quite sophisticated melodies, played on an organ console, into the equivalent of standard musical notation. The program embodies the following basic hypotheses:
(i) that the intervals between the notes of a melody are perceived independently of the rhythmic relations between them;
(ii) that the identity of any musical interval cannot in general be established without reference to both the preceding and the succeeding interval—with interesting implications for the theory of modulation;
(iii) that we conceptualize rhythms as hierarchical structures, created from the top downwards by perceiving whether a projected interval of time is or is not interrupted by the onset of a note; this decision requires the introduction of a maximum allowed discrepancy between the observed and anticipated times of onset of any note; the magnitude of this discrepancy is a parameter of the program, but its optimum value seems to be about 0.1 second.

The output of the program, when faced with syncopated, ornamented or metrical variable melodies, is not unduly sensitive to the rhythmic precision of the performance.

A related problem of current interest in this Laboratory is the rôle of rhythm and intonation in the perception of speech. In order to isolate the effects of intonation from those of other phonetic variables I have written a suite of programs for altering the intonation of recorded utterances in any desired manner. These programs are based on the linear prediction model of speech developed by Atal and his colleagues at the Bell Telephone Laboratories, and should provide useful material for the testing of hypotheses as to how the intonation contour of a given utterance is constrained by the distribution of stresses among its syllables.

During the year two other pieces of linguistic work have been accepted for publication, one dealing with the deictic significance of anomalous word order in English, and the other describing Dr A. C. Davey's computational model of discourse production (to which preliminary reference was made in an earlier Report). Davey's program complements, in a sense, the speech understanding program of T. Winograd, but breaks new ground in suggesting how, in the production of connected speech, a speaker may allocate his semantic material to separate sentences and contrive to say no more and no less than he need in order to be fully understood by the person he is addressing.

Publications

'... and out walked the cat.' *Pragmatics Microfiche 1*, f. 7 (1976).
The perception of melodies. *Nature, Lond.* **263**, 646–653 (1976).
A computational model of discourse production. *Stirling Psychology of Language Conference. New York: Plenum Press* (in the press). (With A. C. Davey.)

Place of Research: Centre for Research in Perception and Cognition, Laboratory of Experimental Psychology, University of Sussex.

M. S. LONGUET-HIGGINS, F.R.S., Royal Society Research Professor

Because of its relevance to air-sea interaction and to many aspects of coastal and offshore engineering I have again concentrated on the development of methods for computing steep gravity waves and plunging breakers.

Previous estimates of the speed of solitary waves in shallow water had unexpectedly showed that the highest wave was not the fastest or the most energetic. These calculations were based on the novel technique of Padé approximants, and an independent check seemed desirable. Now Byatt-Smith and I have carried out a quite independent calculation based on his integral equation for solitary waves, but modified so that the speed occurs as a dependent variable, not an independent parameter. We found remarkably good agreement with the previous method, and the existence of a maximum speed and energy was confirmed. The physical reason, which had previously been conjectured, is also verified, namely that the surface profile of the steepest waves intersects that of the less steep waves near to the wave crest, so the steepest wave actually lies below the less steep waves over most of the profile.

My student M. J. H. Fox and I have investigated the asymptotic form of the surface profile near the crest of any steep gravity wave and have succeeded in calculating its form, by two different methods. Assuming that the flow tends to the Sokes 120° corner flow at large distances, we find that the free surface crosses its asymptote and tends towards it very slowly, in an oscillatory manner. Hence the slope of a symmetric gravity wave can sometimes exceed 30°, in agreement with a conjecture of Sasaki and Murakami. We find the maximum slope to be 30.37°, and the downwards acceleration of a particle at the crest to be $0.39g$ (not $\frac{1}{2}g$).

Our first results from the new method of computing unsteady surface flows have been published (Longuet-Higgins & Cokelet 1976) and further computations are in progress at I.O.S. Wormley, where Dr Cokelet has a post-doctoral appointment. The paper by Longuet-Higgins (1976) discusses a class of time-dependent flows which may be relevant to the asymptotic form of plunging breakers after overturning takes place.

I have taken a close interest in recent proposals for extracting power from sea waves, particularly with regard to the mean horizontal force exerted on a wave power device, which may pose practical problems. The mean force is related to the momentum flux, hence the radiation stress, and by simple experiments I have shown that it is closely in accord with theory, provided the waves are not breaking. If the waves break, the mean force is reduced or even reversed, an effect that can be explained in terms of wave 'set-up'. A similar discussion applies to the forces exerted on off-shore sand bars, and helps to explain their observed migration shorewaves in long, low-wave conditions, and migration seawards under short, steep waves.

At the invitation of Sir George Deacon I gave nine lectures in the Autumn Course on Physics of Oceans and Atmospheres, held at the International Centre for Theoretical Physics, Trieste, in October 1975, and I also gave a series of lectures on water waves at the N.P.L. Ship Division, Feltham, this spring. During the Lent Term I gave a 16-lecture course for Part III of the Mathematical Tripos at Cambridge. I served on the Scientific Committee for an I.U.T.A.M. Symposium on Water Waves held in Canberra during July 1976.

Publications

On the nonlinear transfer of energy in the peak of a gravity-wave spectrum: a simplified model. *Proc. R. Soc. Lond.* A **347**, 311–328 (1975). For part II, see M. J. H. Fox, *ibid* **348**, 467–483 (1976).

Self-similar, time-dependent flows with a free surface. *J. Fluid Mech.* **73**, 603–620 (1976).

The deformation of steep surface waves: I A numerical method of computation. *Proc. Roy. Soc. Lond.* A **350**, 1–26 (1976). (With E. D. Cokelet.)

On the speed and profile of steep solitary waves. *Proc. R. Soc. Lond.* A **350**, 175–189 (1976). (With J. G. B. Byatt-Smith).

Inversive properties of the plane n-line, and a symmetric figure of 2×5 points on a quadric. *J. Lond. Math. Soc.* **12**, 206–212 (1976).

(Reflections)[3]. *Mathl. Gaz.* **59**, 181–183 (1975). (With C. F. Parry.)

In the press

The mean forces on floating or submerged bodies, with applications to sand bars and wave power machines. *Proc. R. Soc. Lond.* A.

The mean forces on wave power machines. *J. Soc. Underwater Tech.*

Some effects of finite steepness on the generation of waves by wind. *Deep-Sea Res.*

Places of Research: Department of Applied Mathematics and Theoretical Physics, University of Cambridge, and the Institute of Oceanographic Sciences, Wormley, Godalming, Surrey.

F. SONDHEIMER, F.R.S., Royal Society Research Professor

(1) *The synthesis of fused macrocyclic conjugated systems* (with T. M. Cresp & R. H. Wightman)

The synthesis of the first analogue of naphthalene in which both rings are macrocyclic was described in last year's Report. The compound prepared contained two *o*-fused dimethylbisdehydro[14]annulene rings, this being an example of an annuleno-annulene made up of two identical $(4n+2)$-membered rings. This work has now been extended through the synthesis of related [14]annuleno-[16]annulene and [14]annuleno[18]annulene derivatives. The first is an example of the fusion of a $(4n+2)$- and a $(4n)$-membered ring, and the second of the fusion of two different $(4n+2)$-membered rings. These compounds are of interest, since the effect of each π-electron system on the other can be studied.

Syntheses of a bisdehydro[16]annuleno[*c*]furan and a bisdehydro[18]annuleno-[*c*]furan have been carried out. The Diels-Alder reaction of the 16-membered ring compound with dienophiles was slower than that of a suitable model, whereas the 18-membered ring compound was faster. This extends the previously found 'reactivity' criterion of anti-aromaticity in macrocyclic $(4n)$ π-systems and aromaticity in macrocyclic $(4n+2)\pi$-systems.

(2) *The synthesis of conjugated cyclic diketones* (with L. Lombardo & H. N. C. Wong)

A remarkably simple synthesis of a trisdehydro[16]annulene-1,4-dione has been developed. This is the first example of a macrocyclic benzoquinone analogue containing a $(4n)$-membered ring. As expected, the electrochemical reduction of this substance (joint investigation with Professor R. Breslow, Columbia University) proceeded at a slower rate than that of the corresponding 18-membered ring diketone. Another interesting observation was the formation of a strongly diatropic ('aromatic') 14π-electron dication on treatment with concentrated sulphuric acid.

We have prepared 2,3,6,7-dibenzobicyclo[6.2.0]deca-2,6,8-trien-4-yne-9,10-dione, a substance containing a cyclobutene-1,2-dione fused to a planar conjugated eight-membered ring. The electrochemical reduction of this diketone proved to be relatively fast, and this may be due to the fact that fusion of two antiaromatic ($4n$)-membered rings results in an aromatic $(4n+2)\pi$-system.

(3) *The synthesis of dehydro[8]annulenes* (with H. N. C. Wong)

The only dehydro[8]annulenes to be isolated previously contained two fused benzene rings. It has now been possible to obtain 5,6,9,10-tetradehydrobenzocyclooctene, a bisdehydro[8]annulene containing only one fused benzene ring. This is the simplest known planar neutral conjugated eight-membered carbocycle. As expected, the eight-membered ring was found to be paratropic ('anti-aromatic'). The substance proved to be very unstable, but could be converted to stable products by Diels-Alder reaction of the strained acetylenes with suitable dienes.

(4) *The structure of the 'complex dimer' of 2,3-naphthoquinodimethane* (with T. W. Bell)

A problem we have been studying for some time concerns the structure of the main product obtained by the spontaneous dimerization of *o*-dipropadienylbenzene. This substance, named the 'complex dimer', has now been established to be 3,4-(2,3-naphtho)-9,10-benzo-11-methylenebicyclo[5.3.1]undeca-3,7,9-triene, formed by dimerization of the intermediate 2,3-naphthoquinodimethane. The problem proved to be unusually difficult, since the 'complex dimer' exists as a mixture of two conformers in solution, although it is a single entity in the crystalline state. The interconversion of the conformers in solution was studied, as well as various chemical transformations of the substance.

Publications

4,9,16,21-Tetramethyl-5,7,17,19-tetrakisdehydro[14]annuleno[14]annulene, a macrocyclic analog of naphthalene, *J. Am. Chem. Soc.* **97**, 4412–4413 (1975). (With T. M. Cresp.)

Annelated 12π-electron systems. The synthesis of a dimethylbenzomonodehydro-[12]annulene, dimethylmonodehydro[12]annuleno[*c*]thiophene, –[*c*]furan, and –[*b*]furan. *Tetrahedron Lett.*, pp. 4179–4182 (1975). (With R. H. Wightman.)

Annelated 14π-electron systems. The synthesis of a dimethylbisdehydro[14]-annuleno[*c*]thiophene, -[*b*]thiophene, and -[*b*]furan. *Tetrahedron Lett.*, pp. 4183–4186 (1975). (With R. R. Jones & J. M. Brown.)

The radical ions of benzo[*b*]biphenylene, a test for HMO models of biphenylene and its derivatives. *Helv. Chim. Acta* **58**, 2431–2437 (1975). (With F. Gerson, W. B. Martin & H. N. C. Wong.)

5,6,9,10-Tetradehydrobenzocyclooctene, the simplest known planar neutral conjugated eight-membered carbocycle. *Angew. Chem. internat. Edit.* **15**, 117–118 (1976). (With H. N. C. Wong.)

The synthesis of 2,3,6,7-dibenzobicyclo[6.2.0]deca-2,6,8-trien-4-yne-9,10-dione and 2,3,6,7-dibenzobicyclo[6.2.0]deca-2,4,6,8-tetraene-9,10-dione. The electrochemistry of cyclobutenediones ('cyclobutadienoquinones'). *Tetrahedron Lett.*, pp. 2715–2718 (1976). (With H. N. C. Wong, R. Goodin & R. Breslow.)

Place of Research: Department of Chemistry, University College London.

DOROTHY CROWFOOT HODGKIN, O.M., F.R.S.,
Wolfson Research Professor

The refinement of the crystal structure of 2-zinc insulin on data extending to 0.15 nm (1.5 Å) has continued throughout this year, carried out chiefly by G. G. Dodson and Eleanor J. Dodson. The reliability index, R, now stands at 19.1 % on structure factor calculations in which all the atoms of both the insulin molecules (a total of 806) have been placed at regularised positions together with 208 water molecules. In the case of 10 residues evidence was obtained that the atoms were disordered, the side chains having two, and in one case, three, alternative conformations. The solution of the crystal structure as a whole has been cross-checked by a series of difference electron density calculations carried out in January in which one-eighth of the unit cell contents was examined at a time, the phases being provided by calculation on the remaining seven-eighths of the structure (plus some very well-defined atoms). The eight difference maps covering the whole cell provided reasonably clear representations of most of the individual atomic positions, and enabled many improvements in atom placing to be carried out.

The experience of the refinement of 2-zinc insulin at 0.15 nm (1.5 Å) encouraged the extension of the data collection on 4-zinc insulin to 0.15 nm (1.5 Å) (G. Bentley). However the refinement of the 4-zinc insulin structure is presenting difficulties. R, by the procedures first applied, appeared to be converging at a rather high value. Difference density calculations in which several residues were removed from the phasing calculation were therefore carried out. These suggest considerable shifts, 0.1 nm (1 Å) or more, in the atomic positions from the starting coordinates. Refinement continues.

The crystal structure of cubic insulin has been essentially solved at 0.45 nm (4.5 Å) by rotation and translation calculations based on molecule II,2-zinc insulin coordinates (Anita Lewitova). One rather poor heavy atom derivative only could be obtained which provided some cross-checking of the solution. The data have been extended to 0.17 nm (1.7 Å) and it is hoped that these will permit the refinement of the structure which is comparatively simple. The asymmetric unit contains only one insulin molecule, part of a dimer with exact crystallographic two-fold symmetry, which should be worth further detailed study.

Very interesting experiments have been carried out by G. Bentley and Anita Lewitova on the interrelation of the 2-zinc and 4-zinc crystal structures. They have verified old observations of G. G. Dodson that structural change between the two forms can be effected within the crystals, though with considerable deterioration of crystal perfection in the process. Other negative ions than chloride can effect the changes and other transition metals than zinc. In some experiments, and particularly in the presence of cresol, a new rhombohedral crystal form appeared, having a cell volume of the order of twice the usual varieties. Clearly it will not be easy to unravel the stages involved in the crystal and molecular transformations.

Publications

1. Kathleen Lonsdale 1903–1971. *Biogr. Mem. Fellows R. Soc. Lond.* **21**, 447 (1975).
2. Dorothy Wrinch, an obituary notice. *Nature, Lond.* **260**, 564 (1976).
3. Fascination for discovery: review of 'The development of X-ray analysis' by Sir Lawrence Bragg (eds D. C. Phillips & H. Lipson). *Nature, Lond.* **260**, 733 (1976).
4. Structure of insulin in 4-zinc insulin. *Nature, Lond.* **261**, 166 (1976).

Place of Research· Laboratory of Molecular Biophysics, University of Oxford.

S. M. Zeki, Henry Head Research Fellow

Continuing my work on the anatomical and functional organization of the prestriate cortex in the rhesus monkey, I have been especially anxious to demonstrate the anatomical identity, in terms of both location and nervous connections, of the separate functional zones that lie within the cyto-architectonically uniform prestriate cortex. To do this anatomical and electrophysiological techniques were used simultaneously in the same preparation. During the past year, I have studied two areas using this approach:

(a) *The superior temporal sulcus*

In the rhesus monkey, the posterior bank of this sulcus has two regions, a medial one and a lateral one, which have their own, separate callosal connections (Zeki 1970). To learn whether these two regions of the sulcus correspond to different areas, the afferent input to them was studied in experiments where the corpus callosum was sectioned and labelled amino acids were injected into other visual areas, thus using double tracer anatomical techniques in the same hemisphere. By this method, it was found that area 17 (V1) projects to that part of the superior temporal sulcus occupied by the more medial of the two callosal inputs. By contrast, the part of the sulcus occupied by the more lateral callosal input was found to receive a projection from the fourth visual complex, an area rich in colour coded cells.

Recordings were made from cells in the superior temporal sulcus in animals in which the corpus callosum had been sectioned previously. The degeneration produced by this procedure was used to provide anatomical landmarks enabling one to assign cells to the lateral or medial regions of the sulcus. Such recordings revealed that receptive fields were topographically organized in the lateral part of the sulcus which had heavy concentrations of colour coded cells, often with very narrow action spectra. By contrast, cells recorded from in the region of the more medial callosal patch within this sulcus were directionally selective, without any obvious colour coding. It was concluded from these combined anatomico-electrophysiological experiments that there are at least two distinct regions in the superior temporal sulcus which have different afferent connections and functional properties.

I also recorded from this sulcus in intact animals. No obvious differences in the properties of the cells between such animals and animals with a sectioned corpus callosum could be detected. It was concluded that the effects of sectioning the corpus callosum are mild enough not to interfere with the more obvious properties of the cells, and yet severe enough to produce degeneration which could be used as a powerful anatomical marker in studies whose aim is to demarcate different cortical zones within the prestriate visual cortex.

(b) *Area V3 and its boundary with Area V2*

By recording from Areas V2 and V3 of rhesus monkeys in which the corpus callosum had been sectioned, and correlating the degeneration so produced with the electrical recordings, Mr D. R. Sandeman and I were able to show that as one records from the posterior bank of the lunate sulcus, at points increasingly more medial to the V1–V2 boundary, so receptive fields move out towards the horizontal meridian. This marks the boundary between Areas V2 and V3, as already suggested (Zeki 1969). Movement further anteriorly along V3 leads more and more towards the vertical meridian until, at the region of V3 which is callosally connected, cells have receptive fields extending to, or at, the midline.

These studies also showed that V2 is larger than V3 and that the receptive fields of cells in V3 are larger than those in V2.

In addition to the experiment described above, I undertook an experiment to show, anatomically, the boundaries of V2 and V3 in the same hemisphere. In this experiment, the corpus callosum which connects regions of vertical meridian representation was sectioned and [^{3}H]proline was injected into the region of horizontal meridian representation in V1. When the sections were stained for degeneration and autoradiographic label, two small patches of label, separated by a 500 μm gap, were found between two bands of callosal degeneration. The centre of the 500 μm gap was taken to be the boundary between V2 and V3 and this experiment showed that not only are V2 and V3 topographically organized but that they both receive a direct input from V1.

In another, separate experiment using a double tracer procedure, a lesion was made in Area V2 and [^{3}H]proline was injected in V1. It was found that these two areas project, in an overlapping manner, to the movement area in the posterior bank of the superior temporal sulcus.

In addition to the work described above, Dr D. Van Essen joined me in a more detailed study of the topographic organization of different prestriate visual areas, using the combined anatomical-electrophysiological approach outlined above.

The work reported was supported by the Science Research Council.

Reference

Zeki, S. M. *Brain Res.* **14**, 271–291 (1969); **19**, 63–75, (1970).

Publications

The projections to the superior temporal sulcus from areas 17 and 18 in the rhesus monkey. *Proc. R. Soc. Lond.* B **193**, 199–207 (1976).

Colour coding in the superior temporal sulcus of rhesus monkey visual cortex. *Proc. R. Soc. Lond.* B (in the press).

Combined anatomical and electro-physiological studies on the boundary between the second and third visual areas of rhesus monkey cortex. *Proc. R. Soc. Lond.* B (in the press). (With D. R. Sandeman.)

Simultaneous anatomical demonstration of the representation of the vertical and horizontal meridia in areas V2 and V3 of rhesus monkey visual cortex. *Proc. R. Soc. Lond.* B (in the press).

Place of Research: Department of Anatomy and Embryology, University College London.

G. S. BEDDARD, Mr and Mrs John Jaffé Donation Research Fellow

In photosynthesizing organisms a light harvesting antenna of chlorophyll molecules transports the absorbed light energy *via* energy migration to the photochemical traps. In model systems of this antenna at the concentration of chlorophylls in the chloroplast (~ 0.1 molal) we observed that, unlike the chloroplast, the fluorescence and energy migration is quenched, this occurs by the phenomenon known as concentration quenching.

A mechanism of concentration quenching has been proposed in which excitation energy migrates among the fluorophores, each step according to the well known Förster type transfer, until a pair of molecules is encountered that are close enough to collapse to form a quenching site. Because of the random distribution of the fluorophores an algebraic solution to this problem appears to be very difficult. I have therefore performed a detailed Monte Carlo calculation of the migration among a random three dimensional distribution of points, the pairwise transfer time is proportional to the sixth power of the distance between the molecules, as is appropriate for Förster transfer. The migration is considered as a multistep process without restriction on the number of times any site is visited. By repeating many random walks and averaging the results, a good account of the experimental concentration quenching curves for chlorophyll is obtained.[1] The migration is ended when a pair of molecules, called a statistical pair, closer than 1 nm (10 Å) is encountered. The migration also ends with fluorescence or intersystem crossing from any molecule.

This method has been generalized to calculate the rate of quenching and the mean square deviation of the random walk, both as a function of time. The quenching rate is found by counting the number of distinct sites visited/second at a given time. It is found that the quenching rate is time dependent because some of the excitations encounter more than the statistical average of molecules that are not quenchers, and hence the probability of quenching decreases in any specific time interval. Using this generalized approach has made it possible to match the calculated concentration quenching curve with the experimental curve.

Experimental work, in collaboration with Miss S. Carlin, has aimed at preventing concentration quenching of chlorophyll in lipid vesicles and liposomes. Lipid and lipoprotein membranes have been used. Some of these may have specific interactions with the chlorophyll and prevent the close approach of these molecules to inhibit quenching. With chlorophyll-b we are able to reproduce the concentration in the chloroplast with only slight quenching. With chlorophyll-a, using a mixture of galactolipids, we observed a half quenching concentration of 0.07 mol l^{-1} within a factor of 2 of the chloroplast value.[2] Preliminary results using β carotene and lutein indicate even higher half quenching concentrations may be achieved. With each lipid system studied we have measured fluorescence yields and lifetimes. These lifetimes were measured by single photon counting for decays greater than 1 ns and by the picosecond laser and streak camera for shorter decays. From the decays we extract a time dependent quenching rate as described earlier.

The kinetics of the energy migration is also studied by forming vesicles of diphenylanthracene as donor and small amounts of perylene as acceptor. In this system perylene is the only quencher and migration among diphenylanthracene is studied by fluorescence yield and lifetime measurements, at a fixed perylene concentration.

Publications

1. 'Concentration Quenching in Chlorophyll'. *Nature, Lond.* **260**, 366–367 (1976). (With G. Porter.)
2. Concentration quenching of chlorophyll fluorescence in bilayer lipid vesicles and liposomes. *Chem. Phys. Lett.* (in the press). (With S. Carlin & G. Porter.)

Place of Research: Davy Research Laboratory of the Royal Institution, London.

M. J. CLEMENS, Mr and Mrs John Jaffé Donation Research Fellow

(a) *The mechanism of action of interferon*

During the past year I have continued my investigations on the mechanism of the inhibition of protein synthesis observed in cell-free extracts of interferon-treated mouse L cells. In collaboration with Dr W. K. Roberts and Dr I. M. Kerr

I have been examining the nature of the process by which an inhibitor of protein synthesis forms when interferon-treated cell extracts are incubated with double-stranded RNA (ds RNA). Our evidence now indicates that ds RNA activates a pre-inhibitor by an ATP-dependent mechanism which may involve protein kinases. Following this activation the ds RNA is no longer required for the action of the inhibitor on the protein synthetic machinery. The chemical nature and mode of formation of the inhibitor are currently under investigation. It is not yet clear whether interferon treatment induces formation of the pre-inhibitor itself or an enzyme such as a protein kinase which converts it to the active inhibitor.

The identification of the activated inhibitor, from which ds RNA can be removed, now enables me to analyse its mechanism of action in the rabbit reticulocyte lysate cell-free system. This highly active system is itself very sensitive to the inhibitory effects of ds RNA and I am thus in a position to compare the characteristics of the ds RNA induced lesion in protein synthesis with those of the interferon induced lesion. The question of the relevance of ds RNA to the regulation of protein synthesis *in vivo* still remains open. It is known that at least some viruses produce ds RNA during the course of their replication in host cells. On a broader front, however, it is likely that there will prove to be a variety of specific intracellular signals capable of regulating transcription and/or translation in animal cells, of which ds RNA would be an example. The regulatory mechanisms involved in the anti-viral and other effects of interferon could thus be amplifications of normal cellular control processes.

Parts of this work were reported at a workshop held in the University of Wurzburg, Federal Republic of Germany, in September 1975 entitled 'Interferon: mechanism of action and application'.

(b) *Purification of a translational inhibitor from ascites cells*

Part of my time has been devoted to the isolation and characterization of an inhibitor of polypeptide chain initiation that may be involved in the regulation of protein synthesis in Ehrlich ascites tumour cells. In February 1976 I visited the laboratories of Professor I. London and Dr E. Henshaw in the U.S.A. in order to continue this work. The relation of this inhibitor to the interferon-specific inhibitor described above awaits further investigation.

Publications

Amino acid supply and protein synthesis in animal cells. *First International Symposium on Protein metabolism and Nutrition*, pp. 19-33. London: Butterworths (1976). (With V. M. Pain.)

Functional relationships between a reticulocyte polypeptide chain initiation factor (IF-MP) and the translational inhibitor involved in regulation of protein synthesis by haemin. *Eur. J. Biochem.* **66**, 413-422 (1976).

The molecular biology of interferon action. *Chemoprophylaxis and viral infections of the respiratory tract* (ed. Oxford, J.S.). Cleveland: CRC Press (in the press).

Interferon-induced inhibition of protein synthesis in L-cell extracts: an ATP-dependent step in the activation of an inhibitor by double-stranded RNA. *Proc. Nat. Acad. Sci., U.S.A.* (in the press). (With W. K. Roberts & I. M. Kerr.)

Place of Research: National Institute for Medical Research, Mill Hill, London.

CAROLYN M. L. KERR, Mr and Mrs John Jaffé Donation Research Fellow

Dye lasers can be used in a variety of ways to yield information on the structure of small molecules in the gas phase. I am concentrating on two of these: determination of ground state molecular geometry through excitation of individual fluorescent rotational levels in an upper electronic state; and saturation spectroscopy in which selective observation of molecules moving perpendicularly to two counterpropagating beams eliminates Doppler broadening, enabling one to obtain details of the electron distribution when the transitions show hyperfine structure.

I am interested in transient species, and am working with two experimental systems. The first, on which I am collaborating with Dr J. M. Brown, Dr F. D. Wayne and Mr S. W. Chalkley, incorporates a commercial c.w. dye laser with bandwidth 60 MHz and operating range 550–640 nm. We have looked for fluorescence of several free radicals using room-temperature atom-molecule reactions as the method of generation, but have seen only the relatively stable BO_2 and NH_2. There was, however, a strong background of scattered laser light in these experiments which could have rendered low intensity fluorescence signals undetectable. A long metal cell designed to minimize scattered light near the detector has been constructed, but not yet fully tested. We are also investigating alternative methods of producing transient molecules, in particular, high temperature reactions.

The second system is a pulsed dye laser pumped by a nitrogen laser, which offers the advantages of greater operating range (360–1100 nm) and higher power. I have built an intermediate bandwidth dye laser which can be tuned over 8 cm^{-1} by changing the gas pressure in a chamber containing the two wavelength selective elements of the laser. However, the power is lower than expected and the bandwidth and frequency jitter unacceptably large. The problem appears to lie in the pump laser, and a replacement laser channel is nearing completion. I hope that the dye laser will be ready for use in spectroscopic experiments in the autumn.

I am most grateful to the Council of the Royal Society for an equipment grant which has been used to improve the laser detection system.

Publications

Electron spin resonance studies of γ-irradiated phosphite and phosphate esters. Identification of phosphinyl, phosphonyl, phosphoranyl and phosphine dimer cation radicals. *J. Phys. Chem.* **79**, 2650–2662 (1975). (With K. Webster & F. Williams.)

Electron spin resonance studies of γ-irradiated phosphorus compounds containing phosphorus-chlorine bonds. *J. Phys. Chem.* **79**, 2663–2668 (1975). (With K. Webster & F. Williams.)

Mercury-201 quadrupole interaction in the electron spin resonance of the CH_2HgCl radical. *J. Chem. Soc. Faraday II* **72**, 552–556 (1976). (With J. A. Wargon & F. Williams.)

Intensity sum rules in molecular spectroscopy. *J. Mol. Spectr.* **60**, 433–436 (1976). (With J. M. Brown & B. J. Howard.)

Place of Research: Department of Chemistry, University of Southampton.

J. V. WALL, Mr and Mrs John Jaffé Donation Research Fellow

The number-flux density relations for extragalactic radio sources ('source counts') contain vital information on the cosmic history of radio source populations. My research is concerned principally with observation, compilation, and analysis of accurate counts over the widest possible frequency range, with the ultimate aim of delineating the relations between the different classes of source. The following aspects of the problem were pursued over the past year.

(1) *An improved number-flux density relation at* 2.7 GHz. In collaboration with J. G. Bolton and A. J. Shimmins (Australian National Radio Astronomy Observatory, Parkes, Australia) the source count from some 7 sr of sky covered in the Parkes 2.7 GHz survey—the first extensive search for extragalactic sources to be started at centimetre wavelengths—has now been compiled. Furthermore, the estimated extrapolation of this count to very faint sources by the analysis of background deflections, first carried out by D. J. Cooke and me last year, has been greatly improved with the reduction of an additional set of observations. The complete 2.7 GHz source count shows the same general features as the low frequency relations, but there are some differences of detail which clearly reflect the different types of sources selected by virtue of the relatively high survey frequency.

(2) *Isotropy on the sky.* Because the 'flat spectrum' sources are so well represented in the 2.7 GHz catalogues it is now possible to test suggestions of anisotropies in their distribution. Extensive analyses, carried out in collaboration with A. S. Webster and T. J. Pearson, indicate that *all* source types represented in the 2.7 GHz survey are remarkably isotropic in their distribution on the sky, as might be expected (a) if the sources are at the large cosmological distances implied by their red shifts and (b) if there are no serious instrumental effects in the survey.

(3) *Source count interpretation.* A major reanalysis of number-flux density relations at all frequencies has been undertaken in collaboration with M. S. Longair and T. J. Pearson. We have achieved the following: (a) the development of a procedure to compute source counts making near-optimum use of the identification and red shift data for sources constituting the counts, together with an appropriate way of comparing calculated counts with observed; (b) the demonstration with this procedure that all simple evolution models currently in the literature are wrong; (c) the discovery of two forms of evolution which satisfy the observations to within statistical uncertainty; and (d) the delineation of the critical observations to test these models. The programme has been confined to a reappraisal of low frequency counts only; we shall now move on to consider source counts at higher frequencies.

(4) *The spatial distribution of quasars.* In a related investigation, C. M. Masson and I have demonstrated that a complete sample of flat spectrum quasars selected from the Parkes 2.7 GHz survey has a spatial distribution not significantly different from uniform. This suggests that such objects do not partake in the strong cosmological evolution which similar analyses reveal for 'steep spectrum' quasars, and there is thus some indication that the different populations of radio sources show distinctive cosmic histories.

Publications

The Parkes 2700 MHz survey (eleventh part): catalogue for declinations $-4°$ to $-30°$, right ascensions 22h to 05h. *Aust. J. Phys. Astrophys. Suppl.* 39 (1976). (With A. E. Wright and J. G. Bolton.)

New optical identifications from the eleventh part of the Parkes 2700 MHz survey. *Aust. J. Phys. Astrophys. Suppl.* 39 (1976). (With Ann Savage.)
The distribution of radio sources found in 2.7 GHz surveys. *Proc. IAU Symp.* 74 *Radio astronomy and cosmology* (in the press).
Interpretation of source counts and red shift data in evolutionary universes. *Proc. IAU Symp.* 74 *Radio astronomy and cosmology* (in the press).

Place of Research: Mullard Radio Astronomy Observatory, Cavendish Laboratory, University of Cambridge.

S. H. WHITE, Mr and Mrs John Jaffé Donation Research Fellow

Research has continued on a high voltage electron miscroscope study of naturally deformed rocks and minerals.

Quartz studies have concentrated on the role of dislocation climb as a deformation mechanism. I spent two months working with Dr A. Ball of the Metallurgy Department at Cape Town University. We were able to demonstrate that the mechanical behaviour of quartz during deformation tests is similar to that of metals which only exhibit marked ductility at temperatures above which dislocation climb can occur. The microstructures of quartzites deformed in Nature to high strains all show evidence of climb, or alternatively the quartz has fractured. Simple calculations show that climb could be an important deformation mechanism in the Earth's crust.

Dr Ball and I perfected an etching technique to show up the dislocation substructures in quartz. This technique should greatly benefit geologists as it offers a quick, simple and cheap way to show up sub-grains in quartz. These sub-grains can be used to estimate paleo-stresses in the crust.

Work has continued on the study of texture and fabric evolution in naturally deformed quartzites. Dr J. Carreras (Barcelona) and I have established that stable quartz c-axis fabric develops at relatively low shear strains in the Cap de Creus mylonites. This is accompanied by the development of a constant microstructure and the onset of strain softening. The strain softening gives rise to characteristic elongate folds normally associated with very ductile rocks. The folds in turn affect the fabric in two distinct processes. The first is by passive rotation of the existing fabric, and the second is by the development of an identical second fabric, symmetrical about the axial plane of the fold. The second process is marked by grain elongation parallel to the axial planes. Cross girdles form when elements of the initial stable fabric and the second fabric coexist. The final stage in both processes is the regeneration of the initial stable fabric. It is hoped that a better understanding of folding mechanisms will result from this work.

Slate studies in association with Mr R. Knipe have progressed well and have been extended to cover variations of cleavage around folds. We have been able to establish that the relative rôles of the processes, namely mechanical rotation, crystallization and metamorphic mineral generation, vary around folds. We have given particular attention to the relationships between cleavage and the finite strain ellipsoid. The accepted relationship first proposed by Sorby in 1853 is that the cleavage is parallel to the x-y plane of the strain ellipsoid. However, we have been able to show that this relation is only apparent because the fine grain size of most slates precludes detailed microstructural studies. Our studies with the electron microscope have shown that the cleavage has no unique relation with the finite strain ellipsoid and may be initially controlled by crenulations.

Publications

1. Determination of deformation parameters from dislocation substructures in quartz. *Developments in electron microscopy and analysis* (ed. J. A. Venables), pp. 505–508. London: Academic Press. (1976).
2. Microstructural development of slaty cleavage. *ibid.*, pp. 513–516 (1976). (With R. J. Knipe.)
3. Fold development in a carbonate vein. *Ibid.*, 521–524 (1976). (With N. Shaw.)
4. Defects in naturally deformed quartz. *Proc. E. M. Soc. Southern Africa*, (1975). (With A. Ball.)
5. Geological significance of recovery and recrystallization processes in quartz. *Tectonophysics* (in the press).
6. Effects of folding on the c-axis fabric of quartz. *Tectonophysics* (in press). (With J. Carreras & A. Estrada.)
7. Slaty cleavage development around a fold. *Tectonophysics* (in the press). (With R. J. Knipe.)

Place of Research: Department of Geology, Royal School of Mines, Imperial College.

T. B. BOLTON, Locke Research Fellow

When the nerves to a muscle are stimulated there is a brief 'silent' period before any response of the cell membrane of the muscle can be detected. This silent period, or latency, is about 0.1 second or more when the parasympathetic nerves are involved and this is about 100 times longer than the latency seen when the somatic nerves supplying skeletal muscle are stimulated. The response of the muscle membrane evoked by parasympathetic nerve stimulation also has a much slower time course. One explanation for this has been that the distance between somatic nerve and skeletal muscle over which transmitter must diffuse, is less than between parasympathetic nerve and involuntary muscle. This is true, but parasympathetic nerve–muscle separation is still small, around 1 μm according to electron microscopists, and this is insufficient to explain the observed latency and time course unless an unusually slow diffusion of transmitter between nerve and muscle membrane is postulated.

For this reason I decided to examine the response to the direct application of the transmitter (acetylcholine) by means of a micropipette in order to discover if the unusual slowness of response to parasympathetic nerve stimulation was due to events at the nerve, or elsewhere. Release of transmitter from the micropipette was controlled electrically. The responses obtained had a similar latency and time course to those evoked by nerve stimulation, immediately suggesting that the time course was not determined by any special property of parasympathetic nerves.

The molecular entity with which the transmitter acetylcholine first reacts to produce its effects in the muscle cell is called the acetylcholine 'receptor'. This receptor in involuntary muscle is further designated 'muscarinic', and can be distinguished from the acetylcholine receptor of skeletal muscle, designated 'nicotinic', by its pharmacological properties. To this well-known pharmacological distinction we can now add a physiological difference in the time course of response. It is not only the muscarinic receptors of involuntary muscle, at which acetylcholine is generally excitant, which are slow to respond: those of cardiac muscle (where acetylcholine is inhibitory) salivary gland and some neurons of the central nervous system react similarly, so that there seems to be genuine difference in the speed of response of the muscarinic and nicotinic varieties of acetylcholine receptor. The muscarinic receptors of involuntary muscle are at present being investigated further in the hope of finding some clue to their slowness of response.

Another line along which I have been working with Dr R. D. Vaughan-Jones is to measure directly the concentrations of ions within cells by means of a micropipette, containing an ion selective resin, which is inserted into the cell. We have been studying chloride which is interesting in involuntary muscle because other methods of estimating its intracellular concentration suggest that the cell must expend energy to maintain a high level of internal chloride. It is not known why it does this, or how it does it. I hope eventually that we can obtain an accurate, direct and continuous measurement of internal chloride levels in involuntary muscle and begin to understand the importance to the cell of maintaining high internal chloride. So far, to obtain experience with the technique and improve its accuracy, we have been working mainly on the larger cells of skeletal muscle. Here, our results confirm what is well known—that these cells do not need to expend energy to maintain the level of internal chloride. This contrasts with the supposed situation in involuntary muscle.

This has been the last year of my Locke Research Fellowship. I am grateful to the Council of the Royal Society for making it possible for me to investigate the physiology and pharmacology of involuntary muscle during the last few years.

Publications

Effects of stimulating the acetylcholine receptor on the current-voltage relationships of the smooth muscle membrane studied by voltage-clamp of potential recorded by microelectrode. *J. Physiol.* **250,** 175–202 (1975).

Is the latency of parasympathetic nerve effects due to a slow activation of muscarinic receptors? An iontophoretic study. *Br. J. Pharmac.* **55,** 304*p* (1975).

Voltage-dependent behaviour of drug-operated ion channels. In 'Smooth Muscle Pharmacology and Physiology'. Colloque d'INSERM, Paris, **50,** 153–164 (1975).

On the latency and form of the membrane responses of smooth muscle to the iontophoretic application of acetylcholine or carbachol. *Proc. R Soc. Lond.* B **194,** 99–119 (1976).

Nervous system. In *Avian Physiology* (ed. Sturkie, P. D.), 1–27. New York: Springer-Verlag (1976).

The use of electrodes containing liquid ion-sensitive resin to measure the intracellular chloride activity of skeletal muscle. *J. Physiol.* **260,** 6-7 (1976). (With R. D. Vaughan Jones.)

Place of Research: Department of Pharmacology, University of Oxford.

R. A. DWEK, Locke Research Fellow

During this year my research team and I have succeeded in producing a structural picture of the combining site of the mouse myeloma IgA protein MOPC 315 (protein 315). This allows detailed conclusions to be made on the specificity of this myeloma protein for dinitrophenyl haptens (1). The method of attack on this problem has been fourfold. (i) On the basis of framework invariance in immunoglobulins a model of the combining site of protein 315 was built from the crystal data of other immunoglobulins but using the sequence of protein 315. This was considered as a first approximation to the structure which was then refined by using the data from physical studies as described below.

(ii) The general architecture of the combining site was found by the use of electron spin resonance (e.s.r.) from analysis of the e.s.r. spectra of a series of dinitrophenyl (Dnp) nitroxide spin labels. The method (2) involves comparison of the observed e.s.r. hyperfine splittings with these expected as a result of different possible motions for the spin label. It emerges that the Dnp ring of the hapten is rigidly held, that the depth of the site is 1.1 nm and that the lateral dimensions at the entrance to the site are 0.8 nm × 1.0 nm, although the site is asymmetric with respect to the plane of the Dnp ring.

(iii) The highly aromatic nature of the combining site is revealed by the use of nuclear magnetic resonance (n.m.r.) proton difference spectroscopy involving the Fv fragment and a variety of haptens. The hapten resonances experience extremely large upfield ring current shifts. An analysis of these leads to the concept of an 'aromatic box' surrounding the hapten ring. In conjunction with the model building studies it is then clear that the specificity of this antibody for Dnp ligands arises from a close stacking interaction between the Dnp ring and a tryptophan, carried out in an 'aromatic box' of Phe and Tyr residues (3). The ring current shifts on the side chain -CH_2 groups of certain haptens fix the orientation of the hapten within the site. This is such that the two -NO_2 groups on the hapten ring can H-bond to amino acid side chains on the antibody (Asn and Tyr). The full analysis of ring current effects has involved theoretical extensions of main theories on this topic and the method should now be of general use for proteins (9).

(iv) The specificity of side chain interactions has been assessed by measuring the pK_a values of the histidine in the combining site and a series of bound haptens containing ^{31}P groupings. It appears that the side chain interactions can contribute about 50% to the total binding affinity of the hapten

In the course of this study we have also confirmed that the antibody-hapten interaction may be visualized as a single encounter step. The main problem is now to put concepts in immunology such as multispecificity on a firmer structural basis, by extending these studies to other haptens.

The recognition of antibody for antigen can activate the complement sequence of proteins which controls many secondary immunological functions. Many of the approaches and techniques developed for structural studies described above can be extended to attempt the problem of how the trigger for the complement system is transmitted, and this is now a major part of the group's research effort (7).

On 1 January 1976 I resigned the Locke Research Fellowship to take up an appointment as lecturer in the department of biochemistry, Oxford. I am most grateful for the opportunity of the tenure of a Locke Research Fellowship which I believe has enabled me to make a significant advance in an important field. I should like to record my debt to Professor R. R. Porter, Professor D. C. Phillips, Professor R. J. P. Williams and Miss E. Press for all their help and encouragement in this work. The collaborative efforts with Professor D. Givol of the Weizmann Institute have been very successful—but none of this progress, involving several disciplines, would have been possible without my research students to whom the final thanks must inevitably belong.

Publications

1. Structural studies in solution on the combining site of the myeloma protein MOPC 315. *Contemporary topics in immunology*, vol. 6 (in the press).
2. The gross architecture of an antibody combining site as determined by spin label mapping. *Biochem. J.* (submitted). (With P. Gettins, D. Marsh, B. Sutton & S. Wain-Hobson.)
3. Comparison of the dimensions of the combining sites of the Dnp binding IgA myeloma proteins, MOPC 315, MOPC 460 and XRPC 25 using spin label mapping. *Biochem. J.* (submitted). (With D. Marsh, C. A. Sunderland, B. Sutton, S. Wain-Hobson, K. Willan, I. Pecht & D. Givol).
4. Difficulties in obtaining molecular motion parameters from water-proton relaxation data illustrated by the Gd(III) antibody complex. *Eur. J. Biochem.* (in the press). (With D. Burton, S. Forsén, G. Karlstrom, A. C. McLaughlin & S. Wain-Hobson.)
5. The mechanism of water-proton relaxation in a number of Gd(III)-antibody fragment complexes. A comparative study. *Eur. J. Biochem.* (submitted). (With D. Burton, S. Forsén, G. Karlstrom, A. C. McLaughlin & S. Wain-Hobson.)
6. A novel approach to water-proton relaxation in paramagnetic-ion macromolecule complexes. *Biochemistry* (1976) (in the press). (With D. R. Burton, S. Forsén & G. Karlstrom.)
7. The use of Gadolinium as a probe in the Fc-region of a homogeneous antitype III pneumococcal polysaccharide antibody. *Biochem. J.* (in the press). (With K. J. Willan, J. C. Jaton & K. H. Wallace).
8. The combining site of the Dnp binding mouse IgA myeloma protein MOPC 315. *Biochem. J.* (submitted). (With S. K. Dower, P. Gettins, D. Givol, C. A. Sunderland, B. Sutton, S. Wain-Hobson & Carolyn Wright).
9. Calculations of ring current interactions for the aromatic amino acids. *Biochem. J.* (1976) (submitted). (With S. J. Perkins, S. K. Dower, P. Gettins & S. Wain-Hobson.)
10. Lanthanides as probes in immunological systems. *Proc. 12th Rare Earth Research Conference* (1976). (With D. R. Burton, S. K. Dower, P. Gettins, D. Givol, W. R. C. Jackson, J. C. Jaton, A. C. McLaughlin, K. B. M. Reid, C. A. Sunderland, B. J. Sutton, S. Wain-Hobson, K. Wallace, K. Willan & Carolyn Wright.)
11. *Principles and problems in physical chemistry for biochemists.* Clarendon Press, Oxford (1974). (With N. C. Price.)

Place of Research: Department of Biochemistry, University of Oxford.

M. W. J. Davie, J. Sainsbury Research Fellow

I have carried out work this year on the characterization of calcium binding proteins in cytosol preparations of human intestinal mucosa. It has become evident that several calcium binding proteins exist in human intestinal mucosa which on gel chromatography separate into high and low molecular mass fractions. I find that over 60% of the total calcium binding activity of crude intestinal homogenate resides in the high molecular mass fraction and I have preliminary data suggesting that calcium binding activity in human intestinal mucosa declines with age.

The high molecular mass fraction shows a typical protein ultraviolet absorbance curve. The molecular mass is 900 000 by gel filtration and 700 000 by sedimentation equilibrium analysis. When analysed on gel electrophoresis there are two major bands which have molecular masses of 70 000 and 80 000 when estimated by SDS gel electrophoresis.

A further calcium binding fraction is found in the molecular mass range 11 000–15 000 on gel filtration. Whereas in animals one calcium binding protein is claimed to exist in this fraction, it has become apparent that this fraction in man contains more than one calcium binding protein. Human intestinal calcium binding proteins have not been extensively investigated and there is no uniform agreement about how many proteins are present. I have therefore spent some time this year in obtaining these proteins in a pure state so that their properties can be defined. The yield of these proteins is low, being about 0.1 % of total intestinal cytosolic proteins. I have been able to identify three calcium binding proteins in the low molecular mass fraction of intestinal mucosal homogenates. These three proteins are distinct on polyacrylamide gel electrophoresis (p.a.g.e.). Although three proteins are detectable in this way, gel filtration indicates the presence of two proteins with molecular masses 15 000 and 11 000. I have been able to establish that the protein eluting at molecular mass 11 000 on gel filtration can exist in two forms and represents two of the proteins found on p.a.g.e. Analysis with SDS gel electrophoresis shows that both forms exist as one peptide with a molecular mass of 2500. The protein eluting at molecular mass 15 000 on gel filtration runs as two peptides with molecular masses 8800 and 5500 on SDS gel electrophoresis.

Progress has also been made in establishing an immunoassay for these proteins. Antiserum has been raised and has been of considerable value in detecting calcium binding proteins prepared by different techniques. Work is currently in progress preparing antisera of high specificity.

Last year I reported work that I had carried out using the synthetic analogue of 1,25(OH)$_2$ cholecalciferol, 1 α hydroxycholecalciferol in chronic renal failure. This has shown that 1 α-hydroxycholecalciferol was successful in lowering elevated levels of PTH, possibly by a direct effect, but was not so valuable in improving osteomalacia. An improvement in intestinal calcium absorption was also demonstrated, but the mechanism by which this is achieved is not clear. The recent demonstration in the chick of intestinal calcium absorption preceding intestinal CaBP production has necessitated a reappraisal of the role of Vitamin D in calcium absorption. With the antisera mentioned above I am in a position to investigate more fully the role of calcium binding proteins in calcium absorption from human intestine.

During the year I attended the second International Workshop on calcified tissues and the XII European Symposium on calcified tissues At the latter meeting I presented part of my work on the purification and properties of human intestinal calcium binding proteins.

Publication

1 α-hydroxycholecalciferol in chronic renal failure. Studies of the effect of oral doses. *Ann. Int. Med.* **84,** 281–285 (1976). (With T. M. Chalmers, J. O. Hunter & E. Kodicek.)

Place of Research: Dunn Nutritional Laboratory, Cambridge.

P. J. GARLICK, J. Sainsbury Research Fellow

In the past year most of my attention has been spent on studies of whole body protein turnover in human subjects Using the technique of constant intravenous infusion of 1-^{14}C leucine we have studied the effects of different low-energy diets on obese subjects. In a previous study in this laboratory we were able to show that after 3 weeks on a diet providing 300 k cal (1255 kJ) daily (entirely in the form of glucose) the rates of protein synthesis and breakdown were depressed by about 50%. Recently, with Dr G. A. Clugston, we have studied the effects of a similar low energy diet, but also containing 50 grams of protein.

With Dr C. P. Swain (M.R.C. Clinical Research Centre) I have started a study of protein turnover in burned patients. Severe trauma results in the loss of body protein, the so-called catabolic response to trauma. This is commonly believed, although without direct evidence, to result from an increase in the rate of breakdown of body protein. Our experience in this laboratory with rats and with a few patients suffering from post-operative trauma suggests that at least a part of the protein loss may result from a depression in protein synthesis. A number of burned patients have now been infused with 1-^{14}C leucine but we have not yet obtained enough results to answer this question definitively.

In rats I have been focusing my attention on the liver because there is evidence that in this tissue protein breakdown is an important site of regulation. This contrasts with muscle in which we have demonstrated that regulation of protein synthesis appears to be the more important. In addition there are problems with the measurement of protein turnover in liver by constant amino acid infusion (the method I have used previously) which do not affect measurements in other tissues such as muscle. I have recently been able to complete and publish a study started three years ago with Professor J. C. Waterlow and Dr R. W. Swick of an independent method of measuring turnover in liver by following the decay of label in prelabelled protein. This method has been used previously by other workers but gave much slower rates of liver protein turnover than our own results from continuous infusion. I have been able to demonstrate that when allowance is made for the heterogeneity of turnover rates of liver proteins, the two methods give very similar results. I am now more confident that I can obtain valid results with the continuous infusion method. This method, however, does not include the synthesis of plasma proteins, many of which are also synthesized in the liver. With Dr Virginia M. Pain I am investigating methods of assessing plasma protein and fixed liver protein synthesis separately so that differences in their regulation may be studied.

Publications

The effect of protein deprivation and starvation on the rate of protein synthesis in the rat. *Biochim. Biophys. Acta.* **414**, 71–84 (1975). (With D. J. Millward, W. P. T. James & J. C. Waterlow.)

Skeletal-muscle growth and protein turnover. *Biochem. J.* **150**, 235–243 (1975). (With D. J. Millward, R. J. C. Stewart, D. O. Nnanyelugo & J. C. Waterlow.)

Measurement of protein turnover in rat liver. Analysis of the complex curve for decay of label in a mixture of proteins. *Biochem. J.* **156**, 657–663 (1976). (With J. C. Waterlow & R. W. Swick.)

Compartmentation of albumin and ferritin synthesis in rat liver *in vivo*. *Biochem. J.* **156**, 189–192 (1976). (With E. B. Fern.)

The relative importance of muscle protein synthesis and breakdown in the regulation of muscle mass. *Biochem. J.* **156**, 185–188 (1976). (With D. J. Millward, D. O. Nnanyelugo & J. C. Waterlow.)

Studies of amino acid and protein metabolism in normal man with ($U^{14}C$) L-tyrosine. *Clin. Sci. & Mol. Med.* **50**, 525–532 (1976). (With W. P. T. James, P. M. Sender & J. C. Waterlow.)

Place of Research: Department of Human Nutrition, London School of Hygiene and Tropical Medicine.

M. B. BECK, Ernest Cook Trust Research Fellow

This year I have worked on a broad spectrum of topics concerned with water and wastewater engineering. These topics include the identification of dynamic mathematical models for the anaerobic digestion and activated sludge processes of wastewater treatment, and for various aspects of river water quality, together with consideration of problems of reservoir regulation. Problems of a more theoretical nature have hampered the derivation of models from the typically poor quality data available in this subject area. While techniques such as 'heuristic self-organization' and pattern recognition algorithms have seemed attractive, it may well be that the only real solution to the problem will be better instrumentation and permission to implement specially designed experiments on full-scale process plant.

Much of the year's work has been spent on an analysis of daily data from the normal operating records of an anaerobic digestion unit at Norwich Sewage Works. The aim of the analysis has been to establish the form of basic cause and effect mechanisms within the process dynamics. Such information on the magnitude and speed of the output responses to input disturbances would eventually determine the type of automatic control required for process operation. The fact that the analysis began at such a simple level is indicative of the volume of previous investigation of the subject. A remarkable result of the study has been the identification of what is believed to be volatile acids (substrate) inhibition of the methanogenic bacterial species. It is not normally anticipated that substrate inhibition would be effective at the low levels of volatile acids concentrations observed; the results suggest, however, that process operation under such conditions is rather undesirable.

Two sets of field data, from the Bedford-Ouse River (spring 1974) and the River Cam (summer and autumn 1975) have been used for the continuing examination of river water quality dynamics. A particularly interesting feature of the Bedford-Ouse data is the predominant effect of an algal bloom. In view of the (assumed) strong interaction between algal growth and nitrogen-bearing nutrients, and the undesirability of algae, nitrates, and ammonia in public supply water, it had been hoped that a comprehensive d.o./b.o.d.-algae/nitrogen cycle model could be identified. This has so far proved largely unsuccessful; variations in nitrate levels in the river are found to be independent of the time-variations in the other water quality variables. The Cam data have not yet been analysed extensively, although it is thought that process dynamic behaviour here will be markedly different from the results of earlier work on the same river in 1972.

During the year I have supervised the work of a World Health Organization visiting fellow, Dr A. Salamin from the National Water Authority, Budapest. Jointly we have investigated the application of techniques of system identification and control to a telemetry network for flood/water quality control in Hungary. We have considered, in particular, the development of an adaptive controller and predictor for the purposes of reservoir regulation.

Finally, a collaborative project with the Anglian Water Authority has been initiated which will look at the dynamic behaviour of the activated sludge wastewater treatment process.

Publications

Identification and parameter estimation of biological process models. In *System simulation in water resources* (ed. G. C. Vansteenkiste), 19–43. Amsterdam: North-Holland (1976).

Dynamic modelling and control applications in water quality maintenance. *Water Res.* 10, 575–595 (1976).

The identification of biological process models in a water quality system. *Preprints IVth IFAC Symp. on Identification and System Parameter Estimation*; Tbilisi, U.S.S.R. part II, 112–123 (1976).

The identification and adaptive prediction of urban sewer flows. *Int. J. Control* (in the press).

Modelling of dissolved oxygen in a non-tidal stream. In *The use of mathematical models in water pollution control* (ed. A. James). London: John Wiley and Sons (in the press).

Place of Research: Control and Management Systems Division, University Engineering Department, Cambridge.

J. N. GALLAGHER, Ernest Cook Trust Research Fellow

This year I have concentrated on improving the equipment for measuring leaf extension and analysing environmental and growth measurements made in 1974 and 1975. Field measurements on a winter wheat crop were made this year, but on a smaller scale than in 1975.

With Mr R. A. Saffell and Dr P. V. Biscoe an electronic differentiator has been developed for use with the auxanometers. The differentiator measures the change in auxanometer output signal over periods of 0.25 or 1 h and leaf extension rate over that time is displayed digitally in units of mm h^{-1}. An analogue signal is also produced which is directly proportional to average leaf extension rate (R_e) over the time interval and can be monitored on a chart recorder. Analysis of dissection measurements made on the 1975 crop showed that 90% of leaf laminar extension occurs in an approximately linear phase, the duration of which is governed by temperature. High temperatures, which cause shorter growth durations, are largely compensated for by increases in R_e. Auxanometer measurements show that in the absence of water stress, R_e is directly related to tissue temperature between 0 and 20°C. During periods of bright sunshine, when transpiration is fast, R_e slows markedly and this is associated with a decline in leaf water potential and turgor. If cloud then obscures the sun, water potential rises again and R_e quickens. The results from the leaf growth work suggest that transient slowing of R_e, caused by water stress on bright days, results in shorter leaves of a smaller photosynthetic area.

The 1976 growing season was the driest at Sutton Bonington since records began but measurements on the wheat crop showed that the drought had no detectable effects on either tillering or ear development. In 1974 and 1975, when drought was not severe, after reaching a mass of about 6 mg the mean mass per grain ($\bar{M}_g$) increased at a constant rate (R_g) of 1.4 and 1.8 mg day^{-1} respectively.

This constant rate of grain growth continued for 33 days in 1974 and 25 days in 1975 resulting in a final $\overline{M}_g$ of about 50 mg in both seasons. In 1976 the drought was associated with unusually high temperatures and a fast R_g of 2.1 mg day^{-1}. However, the duration of this phase of grain growth was only 14.5 days, resulting in a small final $\overline{M}_g$ of 37 mg. Preliminary analysis indicates that grain growth stopped because of acute assimilate shortage which occurred despite considerable translocation of material stored temporarily in the stem to the grain. These results suggests that in regions where severe drought during grain growth is common, cereal varieties which can maintain a long grain growth duration, possibily by translocating material from the stem, are desirable.

In this final report I should like to thank the Ernest Cook Trust and the Council of the Royal Society for their generous financial support during the last three years.

Publications

Barley and its environment VI. Growth and development in relation to yield. *J. appl. Ecol.* **13**, (2) 563–584 (1976). (With P. V. Biscoe and R. K. Scott.)

A sensitive auxanometer for field use. *J. exp. Bot.* **27**, 704–716 (1976). (With P. V. Biscoe & R. A. Saffell.)

Weather, dry matter production and yield. *Proc. 5th Long Symposium on Environmental Effects on Crop Physiology.* (in the press). (With P. V. Biscoe.)

Place of Research: Department of Physiology and Environmental Studies, Faculty of Agricultural Science, University of Nottingham.

R. M. SIBLY, Ernest Cook Trust Research Fellow

I have been attempting cost-benefit analyses, of which examples are given below, of the behavioural strategies of individual animals using the theoretical framework developed last year. In each case consideration has been given to six points:

1. Can adequate estimates be made of the animal's internal state, and the state of the environment as seen by the animal?
2. What options are open to the animal and what courses of action is it able to perform?
3. What risks, to personal survivorship or to the survival of kin, and what benefits in terms of the potential production of offspring, are entailed by each course of action?
4. Is it feasible to measure these risks and benefits?
5. Can a mathematical model of the individual's situation be constructed, and if so what optimal strategy does it suggest?
6. How does this optimal strategy compare with the animal's actual behaviour?

In conjunction with Dr D. J. McFarland and R. H. McCleery I am engaged in a study of herring gull incubation behaviour using the techniques described last year. An incubating bird whose mate is absent has the option of temporarily leaving its nest to feed or drink, but though it may increase its personal survivorship by so doing it runs the risk of losing its eggs. A series of experiments were performed to establish the effect of desertion on the behaviour of the remaining parent. We suspect, for example, that as fat reserves are consumed feeding is given a higher priority, so a study is being made of the contribution to bodyweight of fat reserves in birds of a given skeletal size. Observations were continued on the natural course of incubation behaviour by following both parents of two incubating pairs continuously for over a week (by means of radio-tracking equipment) until natural accidents destroyed their nests. Although the risk of such accidents is an important aspect of the birds' situation, we had hoped not to find examples at our study nests! Less direct observations were made of an additional 11 nests, which were placed on spring balances set in the ground and weighed automatically every 5 minutes for periods up to 6 weeks.

I am also investigating the various risks incurred by woodpigeon eating Brassicae in mid-winter. Last year's work with Dr R. E. Kenward showed that wild woodpigeon are probably unable to maintain bodyweight on this diet, and analysis of data kindly made available by Dr R. K. Murton suggests that long-term individual survivorship increases linearly with bodyweight in mid-winter. Thus there is a (quantifiable) increase in long-term survivorship to be gained from crop-filling at dusk, for example. However, as it fills its crop a bird becomes less air-worthy and therefore more vulnerable to predation, as suggested by Kenward on the basis of his field data. The short-term risk has to be weighed against the long-term advantage that ensues if the short-term risk is survived, and the optimal amount of crop-filling for birds of different bodyweights can be calculated from a simple mathematical model.

Thirdly in conjunction with Dr N. G. Blurton Jones I have begun a case study of the situation of !Kung Bushman mothers, who decrease birth spacing of their children principally at the cost of increased loads (made up of their children under 4 years old and mongongo nuts to feed their families for 3 days) carried up to 6 miles/day in the hot dry spring. The difficulties here are in estimating the risks (e.g. of physical injury and dehydration) undertaken in carrying different loads.

I spoke about my theoretical framework at the XIVth International Ethological Conference at Parma last September, and about woodpigeon feeding strategies at Reading in July.

Place of Research: Animal Behaviour Research Group, Department of Zoology, University of Oxford.

G. D. WIGHAM, Ernest Cook Trust Research Fellow

During the past year I have continued my investigations into the levels of heavy metals in the marine environment, as determined by analysis of a number of marine organisms. Samples were collected from shores in North and South Wales and in Northumberland, and analysed with respect to copper, cadmium and zinc by atomic absorption spectrophotometry. The highest concentration factors were found in the molluscs and crustaceans and also in the alga *Fucus serratus*. In the mollusca the level of uptake of these metals varies considerably between species. The highest levels are to be found in the predatory gastropod *Nucella lapillus* L., though with respect to cadmium there are instances in which the highest levels at a given shore are to be found in the grazing *Patella vulgata* L. Perhaps the most striking difference is to be seen by comparing *Patella* with another grazing gastropod *Littorina littorea* L., where zinc and cadmium levels in the former are consistently (2 to 5 fold) higher than those of the latter, while copper levels in *Littorina* are greater (up to 8 fold) than those of *Patella*. This is extremely interesting in view of the fact that both species occupy similar shore and trophic levels and investigations into the reasons for such an anomaly would be rewarding.

The process of accumulation of heavy metals through trophic levels has been shown to be far from straightforward. Individuals of *Nucella lapillus*, at the sites examined, feed largely upon the barnacle *Balanus balanoides* (L), concentrating cadmium (up to 6 fold) and copper (up to 10 fold) as they do so. Concentrations of zinc, however, are on average five times greater in *Balanus* than in *Nucella* which suggests that some mechanism is in operation to prevent the predator inheriting the full complement of zinc from the prey. Zinc in barnacles is deposited as zinc phosphate granules in cells surrounding the gut lumen and I am at present exploring the possibility that an incomplete dissolution of these granules as they pass through the digestive cycle of the predator may account for the observed anomaly.

Feeding experiments, in which individuals of *N. lapillus* obtained from a comparatively 'clean' area in Pembrokeshire have been kept in an aquarium of local 'contaminated' seawater and fed locally collected *Patella, Mytilus* or *Balanus*, have revealed a number of interesting points. (i) No significant difference was to be found in the levels of copper, cadmium and zinc in groups of *Nucella* fed on these different food sources for 34 weeks. (ii) Levels were significantly higher in all three groups, after 18 weeks, as compared with Pembrokeshire controls. (iii) Cadmium levels, after 18 weeks, were not significantly different from local controls whereas copper and zinc levels, with the exception of animals fed upon barnacles, were still significantly less than local levels. (iv) The ratio of the two metals copper and cadmium in *Nucella* tissues is in the order of 1.99 (Cu/Cd), whereas locally the ratio is 6.00, and this ratio was more or less maintained (1.64–1.89) during the 34 weeks of the experiment despite overall increases in metal levels.

Work is still under way to evaluate the usefulness of certain species as indicators of environmental changes in heavy metal levels. At present the mollusc *N. lapillus* and the alga *F. serratus* appear to be worthy of consideration for the metals copper, cadmium and zinc, though strict standardization in sampling must be practised. Other areas of research include an investigation of heavy metal levels in locally exploited sea foods and how various stages in processing before consumption may effect these levels.

Place of Research: Department of Zoology, University College of Swansea.

J. M. WILSON, Ernest Cook Trust Research Fellow

Broadly speaking, chill-sensitive (tropical) plants can be divided into two categories based on their sensitivity to chilling-injury and their ability to harden or acclimatize to withstand chilling-injury at 5 °C, 85 % r.h.

Category I

Species in this category include *Phaseolus vulgaris, Cucumis sativus* and *Gossypium hirsutum*. Chilling at 5 °C, 85 % r.h. for 24 hours results in approximately 50 % leaf injury. However, chilling-injury to these species can be prevented for up to 9 days on direct transfer from 25 to 5°C by maintaining a saturated (100% r.h.) atmosphere. In addition it is possible to chill-harden these plants to withstand chilling at 5°C, 85% r.h. by a day 4 acclimatization period at 12°C, 85% r.h. Drought-hardening at 25°C, 40% r.h. is also effective in preventing injury at 5°C, 85% r.h. and it has been possible to demonstrate that the primary factor inducing hardening against chilling-injury is a water stress and not low temperature *per se*. The primary cause of chilling-injury to these species is leaf dehydration due to the rapid opening of the stomata on transfer to 5°C at a time when the permeability of the roots to water is low.

Category II

Species in this category include *Episcia reptans* and *Nautilocalyx lynchii*. These plants are extremely chill-sensitive and show injured spots after 2 hours at 5°C. Chilling for 4 hours can result in the complete death of the whole plant. In contrast to category I species, chilling-injury to *Episcia reptans* can not be prevented by maintaining a 100% r.h. atmosphere at 5°C. In addition it is not possible to chill or drought-harden these species to withstand chilling—even prolonged periods of acclimatization of several months in a cool greenhouse at 12–15°C results in very little increase in chill tolerance.

At the present time I am investigating the cause of the very rapid rise in the respiration rate of *Episcia reptans* leaves at 5°C. Preliminary results indicate that the primary cause of chilling-injury to this species is a rapid peroxidation of the membrane lipids by a free radical chain reaction resulting in damage to amino acid residues and eventually cell death.

In April 1976 I delivered a paper on my research at the Nottingham meeting of the Society for Experimental Biology.

At the conclusion of my fellowship I wish to thank the Ernest Cook Trust and the Council of the Royal Society for their support over the past two years.

Publications

The mechanism of chill and drought-hardening of *Phaseolus vulgaris* leaves. *New Phytol.* **76**, 257–270 (1976).

Leaf respiration and ATP supply in relation to chilling-injury in *Phaseolus vulgaris* and *Episcia reptans*. *New Phytol.* (in preparation).

Place of Research: Department of Botany, University of St Andrews, Scotland.

I. W. CHUBB, Horace Le Marquand and Dudley Bigg Research Fellow

Until recently nerves were not considered to be true secretory cells but rather cells able to release one specific molecule, the neurotransmitter, whose role was to transfer the nervous activity to the innervated cell. Now, however, it is known that nerves can secrete a whole variety of molecules ranging from the small neurotransmitters to high molecular weight proteins. My research during the past year has been concerned with the most recently discovered of these macro molecules, the acetylcholine hydrolyzing enzyme acetylcholinesterase.

The basis of this research comes from observations I made last year with Dr A. D. Smith. These were that an isolated and perfused adrenal gland could be induced to secrete acetylcholinesterase if various cell depolarizing agents were applied to the tissue. We also found that the released activity consisted of one single species of acetylcholinesterase whereas there were five multiple molecular forms in homogenates of the adrenal medulla.

We were concerned as to the origin of the enzyme; it could have been derived from the innervating, cholinergic, splanchnic nerve or it could have been from the innervated, adrenergic, chromaffin cells. Electrophoretic analysis of the nerve axons indicated that they were a likely source of the acetylcholinesterase. They had only a single soluble form of the enzyme and this was identical to the one which was released. Evidence against this suggestion, however, was the finding that depolarizing agents specific for the nicotinic receptors of the postsynaptic cells also evoked the release of the enzyme. A subsequent cytochemical study (with Dr P. Somogyi and Dr A. D. Smith) confirmed that both the splanchnic nerve axons and the chromaffin cells were potential sites of release of the enzyme: each contained some acetylcholinesterase activity within membranous structures in their cytoplasm. Our hypothesis, therefore, was that acetylcholinesterase is secreted largely from the chromaffin cells of the adrenal medulla and that it is secreted directly from the endoplasmic reticulum. Further support for this hypothesis was obtained when I found (with Dr R. Comline and Dr Marian Silver, The Physiological Laboratory, Cambridge) that denervated adrenal glands release as much acetylcholinesterase as their innervated contralateral controls.

The denervation experiments revealed another interesting property of acetylcholinesterase. When the splanchnic nerves were cut, and the glands examined at times ranging from 4 hours to 6 months later, it was found that there was neither a change in the acetylcholinesterase content of the gland nor any change in the electrophoretically distinguishable forms of the enzyme. This was a surprising result in view of previous information which suggested that when preganglionic nerves are cut then there is a decrease in the acetylcholinesterase activity in the organ corresponding to the amount lost from the degenerating nerve trunk. Our result implies that the amount in the nerve trunk must be insignificant compared with the amount in the chromaffin cells.

With Dr Somogyi, I now have evidence that preganglionic nerves contribute very little to the acetylcholinesterase content of a tissue. Instead, they seem to influence the amount of the enzyme within the innervated cells; in the presence of the nerve the cells can synthesize more of the protein than in its absence. The synthesis and release of acetylcholinesterase are, therefore, probably directly related.

In March 1976 I participated in a meeting on 'The Synapse' in St Andrews. During the year I was appointed to the editorial board of *Neuroscience*.

Publications

Isoenzymes of soluble and membrane-bound acetylcholinesterase in bovine splanchnic nerve and adrenal medulla. *Proc. R. Soc. Lond.* B **191**, 245–261 (1975). (With A. D. Smith.)

Release of acetylcholinesterase into the perfusate from the ox adrenal gland. *Proc. R. Soc. Lond.* B **191**, 263–269 (1975). (With A. D. Smith.)

A possible structural basis for the extracellular release of acetylcholinesterase. *Proc. R. Soc. Lond.* B **191**, 271–283 (1975). (With P. Somogyi & A. D. Smith.)

Is acetylcholinesterase secreted from central neurons into the cerebrospinal fluid? *Neuroscience* **1**, 57–62 (1976). (With S. Goodman & A. D. Smith.)

Panacea for injured nerves. *Nature, Lond.* **261**, 96–97 (1976).

Place of Research: Department of Pharmacology, University of Oxford.

J. Evans, Pickering Research Fellow

I have been writing a general semi-empirical molecular orbital program which involves most of the first 86 elements and is to be used in conjunction with experimental work. I have begun to examine the electronic structures of metal cluster compounds by this m.o. approach, using boranes as relatively simple models, particularly for metal carbonyl clusters. Three lines have been followed:

(1) Changes in the electronic structure have been followed as idealised borane polyhedra have been synthesised from each other by the capping of faces with single BH units, or by the mutual approach of two faces.

(2) For a particular cluster size, the stabilities of different structures were compared for differing overall charges.

(3) For five and six vertexed polyhedra, the effects of adding extra protons was investigated.

Although the results are still being analysed, some conclusions are evident.

(1) Structures derived from a polygon by the capping of a face maintain the basic electronic structure of the polygon. For example, a B_3H_3 triangle has 3 σ bonding and 3π bonding plus weakly antibonding framework orbitals. Capping faces to produce a bicapped tetrahedral structure does not alter the number of likely accessible orbitals. However, the effect of bringing two polygons together is dependent upon their relative orientations. Bringing two triangles together in an eclipsed manner, forming a trigonal prism, yields nine skeletal bonding orbitals, while a staggered approach to form a trigonal antiprism (octahedron) gives rise only to seven. The difference lies in the behaviour of the in-phase combination of the triangles' π^* orbitals.

(2) Energies of alternative structures were calculated for six, seven and eight vertexed structures. A different structure was favoured for $(B_6H_6)^{n+}$ when n was 0, -2, -4 and -6 (bicapped tetrahedral, octahedral, pentagonal pyramidal and trigonal prismatic respectively). All the stable forms had all their bonding orbitals occupied and, on that basis, were the structures one might expect from the first approach. However, the $(B_8H_8)^{n+}$ ($n=2, 0, -2, -4, -6$ and -8) system was dominated by the dodecahedral form. Only in the last hypothetical example of $(B_8H_8)^{8-}$ (isoelectronic with cubane) was another form, cubic, favoured. This dominance was also apparent in the $(B_7H_7)^{n+}$ ($n=2, 0, -2,$ and -4) series. In all cases a nido-dodecahedral structure (similar to a capped octahedral one) was favoured.

(3) Comparatively few metal clusters are pure polyhedra. Distortions must occur when the number of ligands is not a mutiple of the framework atoms. This third line probed where extra ligands would be accommodated. An extra terminal ligand in the B_5 system was represented by positioning one BH_2 group in trigonal bipyramidal and square pyramidal $(B_5H_6)^-$. The former geometry was prefered, with the odd group in the apical position. Within the pyramidal structure, the preferred orientation of the BH_2 group was in the square with the HBH plane normal to that square. Also investigated was the effect of placing one and two bridging hydrogens between boron atoms, in the B_5 and B_6 systems. For polyhedra consisting entirely of triangular faces, little site preference was evident. But when a square face was present, a marked preference for an edge bridging position below that square plane was observed. The effect was so marked that the presence of these extra hydrogens could alter the preferred framework of the

boron atoms from that predicted for the parent polyhedral anion into one with a square face.
This work will shortly be extended to small metal carbonyl polynuclear units.

Place of Research: University Chemical Laboratory, Cambridge.

A. J. KINGSMAN, Pickering Research Fellow

During the last year I have started a project aimed at elucidating the plasmid DNA metabolism involved in F*lac* conjugational transfer. There are eleven genes whose products are directly required for conjugational DNA transfer and of these I am interested in the three not involved in sex-pilus formation. The products of these genes, *tra*G, *tra*D and *tra*I may be required for DNA metabolism during transfer (Willetts 1972a). The generally held mechanism of F*lac* transfer in *Escherichia coli* involves an initiation event probably by an F-coded single strand specific DNA endonuclease which 'nicks' the plasmid DNA at a specific site, the origin of transfer (*ori*T) (Willetts, 1972b). The nicked single strand is then transferred to the recipient with its 5' end leading and replaced by new DNA synthesis probably by a rolling-circle type of mechanism (Vapnek and Rupp, 1971). The complementary strand of the transferred single-stranded plasmid DNA is synthesised in the recipient and the molecule is then re-circularized to form a covalently, closed circular (CCC) molecule.

In conjunction with Dr N. S. Willetts I have been developing an assay system for the initiating endonuclease. This has involved finding a suitable substrate for the nicking reaction. The substrate is required to be a CCC DNA molecule that contains an *ori*T site and it must be stable in the CCC-form. Experiments using F-DNA showed that, while obviously fulfilling the first two requirements, the molecule was extremely unstable. CCC F-DNA decays to 100% open-circular (OC) within a few days of isolation. I therefore turned my attention to possible lower molecular weight molecules which should be more resistant to breakage. I have now found a suitable substrate in a plasmid produced by Dr R. Skurray, University of California, Berkeley. The plasmid, pRS30, is a chimeric molecule composed of the 5.8Md, tetracycline-resistance carrying vector, pSC101 and *Eco*RI fragments f1, f3, f6 and f15 of F. It has a molecular weight of 30Md and I have shown that it is completely stable in CCC form for several weeks. I have also shown that pRS30 contains the *ori*T site since it is readily transferred to recipients by an F*lac* plasmid in the same cell. I am now developing a system for the essay of the conversion of pRS30 from CCC-form to OC-form. This will enable us to assay the initiating endonuclease.

I am also looking at conjugational DNA metabolism *in vivo*. Using as donors and recipients temperature sensitive *dna*B mutants I am able specifically to monitor conjugational DNA synthesis by mating at 42°. Under these conditions chromosomal and plasmid vegetative replication is switched off, but conjugational DNA synthesis is unaffected and easily measured by incorporation of ^{3}H-thymidine into plasmid DNA. I am now engaged in identifying plasmid-coded functions required for this synthesis.

In June I attended a workshop on Plasmids and Genetic Exchange between bacteria in Berlin and the Third International Symposium on Antibiotic Resistance in Bratislava. I am grateful to the Council of the Royal Society for providing support for these visits.

References

Willetts, N. S. 1972a. *Ann. Rev. Genet.* **6,** 257.
Willetts, N. S. 1972b. *J. Bacteriol.* **172,** 773.
Vapnek, D. and Rupp, W. D. 1971. *J. Mol. Biol.* **60,** 413.

Place of Research: Department of Molecular Biology, University of Edinburgh.

D. K. RUSSELL, Pickering Research Fellow

The study of small, short-lived, free radicals by the technique of laser magnetic resonance (l.m.r.) spectroscopy has continued during the past year. A large amount of data on the l.m.r. spectra of the NH_2 free radical has been collected and analysed. The majority of these spectra were measured using far infrared lasers in which the lasing gas was pumped by a CO_2 laser. The analysis yields rotational, distortional and spin-rotational parameters of considerably greater precision than those obtained from optical spectroscopy, and hyperfine and magnetic parameters of precision comparable to those obtained from other high-resolution techniques. This work represents the most complete study of the rotational spectrum of a triatomic hydride to date.

The free radicals PH_2 and PH were detected when H atoms were passed over red phosphorus within the laser cavity of a d.c. discharge H_2O vapour laser oscillating at a wavelength of 118.6 μm. The former species was also detected in the reaction of F atoms with PH_3. The PH radical was detected in two electronic states arising from the same electronic configuration, namely the ground $^3\Sigma^-$ state and the low-lying $a^1\Delta$ state. A preliminary account of these spectra has been given: further investigations currently being undertaken will yield precise values for rotational, fine-structure, hyperfine and magnetic parameters.

During the past year, we have been constructing in our laboratory a pumped far infrared laser similar to that described above. This laser will yield many more usable laser frequencies than the d.c. discharge lasers used previously, greatly increasing the range of molecules which can be studied using l.m.r.

Other projects undertaken during the year include the analysis of some l.m.r. spectra of the highly interesting and important species CH_3O, detected in the reaction of F atoms with CH_3OH or the pyrolysis of CH_3OOCH_3 in the laboratory of Dr H. E. Radford. The earlier study of the laser-excited fluorescence spectra of BO_2 has also been completed.

Publications

Laser magnetic resonance spectra of the PH radical. *Chem. Phys. Letters* **36,** 280–283 (1975). (With P. B. Davies & B. A. Thrush.)

Laser magnetic resonance spectrum of the PH_2 radical. *Chem. Phys. Letters* **37,** 43–46 (1976). (With P. B. Davies & B. A. Thrush.)

Analysis of the laser-excited fluorescence spectra of BO_2 *J. Chem. Phys.* (in the press). (With R. A. Beaudet & M. Kroll.)

Rotational and hyperfine parameters of $NH_2(X^2B_1)$ from l.m.r. spectra. *Chem. Phys. Letters* **42,** 35–38 (1976). (With P. B. Davies, H. E. Radford & B. A. Thrush.)

Analysis of the l.m.r. spectra of NH_2 (X^2B_1). *Proc. R. Soc. Lond.* A (in the press). (With P. B. Davies, H. E. Radford & B. A. Thrush.)

Place of Research: Department of Physical Chemistry, University of Cambridge.

D. E. HANKE, Rosenheim Research Fellow

I have been looking at the changes in pectin synthesis in a soybean suspension culture when the cells are induced to divide by kinetin. The work was initiated by the discovery that, in this tissue, much of the pectin is derived from endogenous substrate via *myo*-inositol oxidation, in preference to exogenously supplied glucose. A preliminary study of the pattern of labelling of pectins by [^{3}H]-*myo*-inositol and [^{14}C]-glucose showed:

(1) though the incorporation of [^{14}C]-glucose into pectins remained constant when kinetin was added, incorporation from [^{3}H]-*myo*-inositol increased twelve-fold, and

(2) a methyl-esterified pectin with a low content of neutral sugars (mostly arabinose residues) incorporated radioactivity from these precursors only when kinetin was present.

Since these alterations in the labelling pattern of pectin could be the result of changes in either rates of synthesis or the effective size of precursor pools, I have repeated the feeding experiments in a growth analysis to determine how much of each pectin type is made in dividing and non-dividing cells. Soybean cells grown without *myo*-inositol for 17 months were included in the comparison to detect any contribution from endogenous stores. Also, the effects of high (0.5 mM) and low (0.1 μM) concentrations of *myo*-inositol in the medium were examined.

Analysis of the radioactive material is now completed and it appears from the results that

(1) In the absence of kinetin, endogenous stores of *myo*-inositol are used for pectin synthesis. If this supply is inadequate, exogenously supplied *myo*-inositol can be used for 'topping up'.

(2) In the presence of kinetin, exogenous *myo*-inositol is the preferred source of substrate and any inadequacy is made good by synthesis.

(3) Incorporation of ^{3}H into the methyl-esterified pectin increases with increasing availability of unlabelled *myo*-inositol, suggesting that the cyclitol promotes the synthesis of this pectin type.

A chemical analysis of bulk, non-radioactive replicates of these samples is now in progress.

Myo-inositol oxygenase, the enzyme catalysing the first irreversible reaction of the oxidation sequence, was detected in soybean cells, but only when prepared entirely under nitrogen and by a method which drastically reduced the preparation time. The level of activity was very low and I am currently trying to concentrate the enzyme from a large bulk of tissue using affinity and covalent chromatography.

In collaboration with Dr Dianna J. Bowles I have been looking at the interaction of protoplasts of cultured soybean cells with the soybean lectin, SBA. We found lectin activity in the cultured cells. All of it was firmly membrane bound and had the same sugar specificity (N-acetylgalactosamine) as SBA. At 1 mg/ml, SBA caused soybean protoplasts to bind tightly together into large aggregates. Protoplast aggregation was reversed specifically by N-acetylgalactosamine, and in any case by 30 min after washing away cellulase. At this time the protoplasts began to form small clumps in response to concanavalin A, a result of the formation of a coat of glucan over the protoplast surface. Evidently the plasmalemma contains receptors for soybean lectin and it seems likely that the lectin and its receptor interact in the membrane.

I should like to thank the Council for permission to give a total of 13 lectures in the Departments of Botany and Biochemistry, and at the Cambridge Institute of Education.

Place of Research: Botany School, University of Cambridge.

CHEW SING HOOI, Rutherford Scholar

During the past year I have continued the detailed analysis of $^{15}N(p,\gamma_2)^{16}O$ in the excitation region between $E_x = 22-31$ MeV. The almost constant angular distribution both on and off-resonance in this region has led to the inference that the structure here arises from a giant dipole resonance based on the 3^- second excited state of ^{16}O at 6.13 MeV. This result has been reported in a paper submitted to *Physical Review Letters*.

In September last year I submitted my Ph.D. thesis and was subsequently awarded the degree.

In the analysis of the $^{15}N(p, \gamma)^{16}O$ data, a recurring problem was the lack of experimental data on the proton widths of the resonances observed. To determine this, measurements of $^{15}N(p, n)^{15}O$ were taken using time-of-flight techniques with a pulsed proton beam. The excitations functions for this reaction were measured at seven different angles between $E_p = 8.5-19$ MeV. Angular distributions were also taken at five different beam energies in this energy region. Various resonances were observed in $^{15}N(p, n)^{15}O$ which coincided in excitation energy with resonances seen in $^{15}N(p, \gamma)^{16}O$ and could well correspond to these. Further analysis of this (p, n) data is currently in progress.

Preliminary measurements have been made in $^{39}K(p, \gamma)^{40}Ca$ to look for a giant dipole resonance based on one of the first few excited states of ^{40}Ca at $E_x = 3.3-4.5$ MeV. The γ_0 transition was clearly observed over a range of beam energies. At some energies, γ transitions to the 5^- state at 4.49 MeV and to the 2^+ and 3^- states (unresolved) at about 3.8 MeV were also seen. However, the ^{39}K target oxidized rapidly and the contaminants gave rise to a large background yield. To achieve a better spectrum, a vacuum target transfer system will have to be built to enable pure ^{39}K targets to be used.

As this is the final year of my Rutherford Scholarship, I would like to thank the Council of the Royal Society and the Rutherford Memorial Committee for their support over the past three years.

Publication

Radiative width for the 10.35−6.92 MeV transition in ^{16}O. *Nuclear Physics* **A 252**, 8 (1975). (With J. Lowe.)

Place of Research: Department of Physics, University of Birmingham.

D. J. COOKSON, Rutherford Scholar

The use of high resolution nuclear magnetic resonance (n.m.r.) spectroscopy to study the solution conformation of biologically important molecules has reached a high degree of precision, and this year I have been using this technique to study the electron storage and transport protein, cytochrome c_3, as well as the oxygen storage protein, myoglobin. Both proteins contain iron (four atoms of iron per molecule in cytochrome c_3) which is coordinated to the four pyrolle nitrogens of a prophyrin molecule. In the case of cytochrome c_3, the fifth and sixth coordinating positions are occupied by imidazole nitrogens of the histidine residues of the polypeptide chain, whereas, in myoglobin, only the fifth position is coordinated in this way. Oxygen and other small molecules can coordinate with iron at the sixth site. The role of the metal ion in metallo-proteins has been the subject of numerous investigations, and it has been found that many proteins will function quite adequately if the physiological metal ion is replaced by another metal ion. In particular, the iron atom in myoglobin may be readily replaced by a cobalt atom, although the resultant protein has a lower affinity for oxygen than myoglobin. The metal ions in these proteins may exist in variable oxidation and spin states and it is the aim of my present work to determine the extent of the conformation change upon oxidation/reduction of cytochrome c_3, and to compare the solution properties of myoglobin with its cobalt analogue.

One of the inherent advantages of n.m.r. as a technique for studying proteins is the ability to resolve single atoms of individual amino acid residues within a protein molecule. However, in practice, this is true only for certain functional groups, particularly those which have unusual chemical environments in a protein. The assignment of proton resonances to particular types of amino acids has been made based upon the observed multiplet structure and upon spin decoupling experiments. The aromatic amino acids in particular lend themselves to this analysis due to the linewidths of their resonances.

In addition, I am also engaged in an electron spin resonance (e.s.r.) study of the glycoprotein, horse radish peroxidase (HRP). This protein contains one iron atom associated with a protoporphyrinIX prosthetic group and of special interest in this investigation is the effect of substrate and inhibitor binding upon the spin state of the metal ion. N.m.r. data suggest that substrate binding affects the heme electronic structure. E.s.r. evidence has shown that changes from high spin to mixed spin state species occur with increasing substrate concentration although n.m.r. data show no evidence of such a change. I am repeating some of the previous e.s.r. experiments on HRP and hope to obtain results which are consistent with those obtained from n.m.r. studies. The room temperature e.s.r. spectra of HRP and its substrate complexes are also being examined and, from the linewidths, a lower limit for the electron spin relaxation time can be calculated.

Place of Research: Inorganic Chemistry Laboratory, University of Oxford.

K. A. HUNTER, Rutherford Scholar

My work in the past year has been concerned with two aspects of the investigation of metal complexes with naturally occurring surface-active organic material (SOM) in seawater: the nature of the SOM itself and the extent of metal-SOM binding at the air-sea interface.

Because of the small concentrations and great complexity of the SOM mixture, classical organic chemical analysis has been largely fruitless in deciding the nature of this material. Recent work using surface chemical techniques, however, suggests that it consists of highly hydroxylated and carboxylated polymers, possibly degradation products of marine cellular material. I am attempting to assess the conclusions of this work by a different method. The natural SOM is absorbed on to micrometre-size carrier particles of various types (such as silica) whose modified electrophoretic properties are examined by the microscope electrophoresis method. Particles of widely different electrophoretic mobility in general approach a common mobility after adsorption of seawater SOM, indicating that more similar particle surfaces dominated by the ionisable groups of SOM molecules are produced by adsorption. The electrical double layer is within the plane of shear of the moving particles, so that the differences between untreated and SOM treated particles is more marked in solutions containing cations with multiple charge. In fact, with ions of high charge, such as Th^{4+} occupation of the diffuse double layer by this ion will reverse the charge on the particles at a metal concentration of only about $10^{-5}-10^{-6}$ mol l^{-1}. The relative charge reversal concentrations for a number of metals, the so-called charge reversal spectrum, can be used to identify surface ionizable groups. These experiments are currently being performed.

Curves of mobility against pH for SOM treated particles are consistent with the major acidic group of SOM being carboxyl, a conclusion in agreement with other work. This is significant, for the chemical models of heavy metal binding in sea surface layers use the assumption that carboxyl is the major group taking part in metal binding. No evidence for surface basic groups was found, so that amine and similar nitrogen coordination centres, among others, are apparently ruled out.

One of the expected consequences of the presence of natural acidic surfactants in a water column is a process identical in principle to ion flotation used in chemical engineering. Rising air bubbles with their surfaces covered with anionic surfactant strip heavy metal ions from the column giving rise to a surface layer enriched in heavy metals. The chemical model based on the binding of metal ions to carboxylic acid dispersions indicates for which metal ions this process is likely to be important. On this basis, analytical techniques for determining Cu, Zn, Cd, Pb, Fe and Ni in seawater have been developed. The first four metals are measured by differential pulse anodic stripping voltammetry with a hanging mercury drop electrode, iron by solvent extraction with bathophenanthroline in pentanol and subsequent colorimetry, while nickel is determined using solvent extraction of the nickel dimethyl-glyoxime complex in chloroform and flameless AAS.

Surface microlayer samples have been collected by the use of a fine mesh screen, the liquid surface film being trapped in the gaps between the mesh filaments and subsequently drained into a vessel. Consistently higher surface layer metal concentrations are observed, with the extra metal ions often associated with stable organic complexes (destroyed by photo-oxidative degradation).

In March 1976 I had the good fortune to attend the American Meteorological Society's annual conference in Seattle, and delivered a paper at the session on Air-Sea Interactions. During the visit I was also able to meet and talk with most of the major workers in the field and obtained a valuable insight into the current state of the subject. I should like to express my thanks to the Rutherford Memorial Committee for its support of this valuable visit.

Publications

Measurement of the solubility products of various metal ion carboxylates. *J. Electroanal. Chem. & Interface Electrochem.* (in the press). (With P. S. Liss.)
Chemical models of metal binding in the sea surface microlayer (abstract). *Bull. Amer. Met. Soc.* **57**, 143 (1976). (With P. S. Liss.)

Place of Research: School of Environmental Sciences, University of East Anglia.

C. J. VAN RIJSBERGEN, Scientific Information Research Fellow

Most of my time this year has been devoted to constructing a probabilistic model for information retrieval within which statistical dependence of index terms can be exploited. In recent work it has been shown that an assumption of statistical independence leads to a linear function for weighting index terms during retrieval. From an assumption of dependence one can derive a simple nonlinear weighting function the form of which is dictated by the approximation used for the underlying joint probability distributions. Through an optimisation procedure involving the generation of a maximum spanning tree I have shown that the use of a nonlinear weighting function is feasible. Extensive testing of the model on experimental document collections still remains to be done.

Almost all weighting functions involve several parameters which during retrieval can only be estimated from small samples. In the context of information retrieval it is possible to use relevance feedback techniques to build up good estimates. With Mr D. Harper I have been trying to derive appropriate optimisation procedures for doing this.

With Mr B. Croft I have continued working on document clustering. We are mainly concerned with establishing the viability of document clustering for large document collections. If the classification of documents is represented by a tree structure then one of our major problems has been to find a good starting point in the tree for any search of the clustered collection. We have also been doing further research on ways of characterising clusters of documents.

One of the major stumbling blocks to research in information retrieval is the unavailability of large, well-defined experimental test collections of documents, requests, and relevance assessments. During the year I have given some thought to the creation of such a test collection. Together with Dr Karen Sparck Jones I worked on the exact specification of such a collection.

I have also devoted some time to acquiring the experimental document collection used by Miss E. Barraclough at the University of Newcastle upon Tyne. I hope to use this test collection for some of my experiments when it has been implemented on the Cambridge University computer.

During the year I participated in two workshops, one on data compression organized by the Department of Librarianship and Information Science at Sheffield University, the other on associative memories organized by the Department of Electrical Engineering at Brunel University. I also gave some lectures on my current research to graduates in the Cambridge Computer Laboratory.

Publications

Information retrieval, London: Butterworths (1975).
Information retrieval test collections. *J. Docum.* **32**, 59–75 (1976). (With K. Sparck Jones.)
An evaluation of Goffman's indirect retrieval method. *Information Processing & Management* (in the press). (With B. Croft.)

Place of Research: Computer Laboratory, Corn Exchange Street, Cambridge.

S. E. ROBERTSON, Scientific Information Research Fellow

Last year's discovery of an optimal weighting function for weighting index terms in information retrieval has proved most rewarding. With Dr Karen Sparck Jones, I eventually succeeded in incorporating the weighting function into a working retrieval programme. Tests run by Dr Sparck Jones on a variety of test collections have consistently demonstrated the superiority of the weighting function suggested by the theory, as compared with a range of alternative functions. The tests have covered both the retrospective use of the weighting function (defining the best possible retrieval performance on a test collection with known relevant and non-relevant documents), and the predictive use (using relevance-feedback information from one search to improve the next). Further work is required on the predictive use, identifying various possible predictors of the value of the weighting function.

On a more theoretical note, the theory of the weighting function has raised questions about the status of the probability ranking principle (the principle that, for optimum performance, documents should be ranked in order of their probability of relevance). This seemingly obvious principle turns out not to be generally valid: problems arise where there is any kind of interaction between documents. It seems difficult to formulate an alternative principle with more general validity, but some progress has been made on identifying the situations in which the probability ranking principle can be applied with impunity.

A related problem is the nature of relevance itself. For some purposes, it seems to be necessary to regard relevance as a random variable. But an adequate model of relevance must include a continuous underlying variable, broken into two or more fairly arbitrary segments by the categories of relevance chosen. The locations of the boundaries must be user-dependent: that is, they must be subject to 'random' variations between users. The assessment of each document in terms of the underlying scale is also subject to variation. Experiments on relevance give some indication of the relative importance of these two types of variation, and of various predictors of them.

Work continues, with Miss J.-M. Griffiths, on a simulation model of a generalized retrieval system. The model involves representing the subject area of a collection in map form, with documents, index terms, and requests all represented as points or neighbourhoods or probability distributions in this space. A number of algorithms based on these ideas are being investigated, with a view to reproducing some of the observed statistical characteristics of retrieval systems. In March 1976, a joint paper was presented by Miss Griffiths at the European Conference on Research into Information Management (Eurim) in Amsterdam.

Publications

Journal acquisition by libraries: scatter and cost-effectiveness. *J. Document* **31**, 273–282 (1975). (With Miss S. Hensman.)

A theoretical model of the retrieval characteristics of information retrieval systems. Ph.D. Thesis, University of London (1976).

Relevance weighting of search terms. *J. Am. Soc. Information Sci.* **27**, 129–146 (1976). (With K. Sparck Jones.)

The simulation of IR systems. In: Eurim 2 (proceedings of a conference held in Amsterdam, March 1976). London: Aslib (in the press). (With J-M. Griffiths.)

Place of Research: School of Library, Archive and Information Studies, University College, London.

G. B. WARREN, Stothert Research Fellow

The wide variety of lipids in biological membranes is needed in part to satisfy the different lipid requirements of the many membrane proteins. The differences in specificity are often extreme. Dioleoylphosphatidic acid will support maximal ATPase activity of the Na^+, K^+ ATPase but abolishes the activity of the Ca^{2+}, Mg^{2+}-ATPase. Since many membrane proteins are embedded in the same heterogeneous lipid bilayer it might be a necessary feature of membrane structure that any penetrant protein can selectively bind those lipids that support activity and can exclude those that do not.

To test this hypothesis, I have been studying complexes of the purified calcium transport protein from sarcoplasmic reticulum with defined synthetic phospholipids. The penetrant part of the protein is surrounded by an immobilized annulus of about 30 lipid molecules which determine the ATPase activity of the protein (1,2). In my previous report I described the rigorous exclusion of cholesterol from this annulus, an exclusion necessitated by the potent inhibitory effect of cholesterol when forced to bind to the protein. I have now extended this work to determine whether the protein can select a particular species of phospholipid when presented with a mixture of two species of synthetic phospholipid.

When presented with two species of phosphatidylcholine which differ in their fatty acid chain composition, the protein is unable to select the phospholipid which best supports ATPase activity. The evidence suggests that the degree to which the fatty acid chains are bound to the protein depends on their chain length. The bulk of lipids in biological membranes have 16–18 carbon atoms in their fatty acid chains so that we would not expect the protein to be able to select lipids *in vivo* on the basis of their chain composition. The same is not true for the phospholipid headgroup structure. In collaboration with Mr J. P. Bennett I have determined the response of the ATPase activity of the protein to a mixture of dioleoylphosphatidylcholine and dioleoylphosphatidic acid. The latter potently inhibits the ATPase activity of the protein by virtue of its negatively-charged headgroup. As the proportion of dioleoylphosphatidic acid in the mixture is raised, the protein maintains its ATPase activity because it is able to exclude dioleoylphosphatidic acid from its annulus of dioleoylphosphatidylcholine molecules.

One recent discovery concerns the interaction of the protein with two phospholipid species which differ in both their headgroup and fatty acid chain structures (3). Dimyristoylphosphatidylcholine inhibits the ATPase activity of the protein because it has fairly rigid fatty acid chains. Dioleoylphosphatidic acid has fluid fatty acid chains but an inhibitory headgroup. However, a mixture of these two phospholipids supports an ATPase and calcium uptake activity in reconstituted vesicles which is as good as if dioleoylphosphatidylcholine had been used. It is as if the protein is selecting those *parts* of the phospholipid structure that best support activity and ignoring those parts that do not. The calcium transport protein can select both between and within lipid molecules for that structure which best supports activity.

In collaboration with Dr M. D. Houslay (4,5) I have studied the effect of lipid environment on the F^- and glucagon-stimulated activity of adenyl cyclase. Although the F^- response is unaffected by changes in lipid environment, sensitivity can be conferred by agents such as des-His-glucagon, which bind to the hormone receptor and structurally couple the receptor to the adenyl cyclase protein.

I would like to thank the Council of the Royal Society for a Scientific Investigations Grant to enable me to carry out the above work. Invited lectures were given in London and Hamburg.

Publications

1. The lipids surrounding a calcium transport protein: their role in calcium transport and accumulation. *Proc. of the Tenth FEBS Meeting* 3-15 (1975). (With J. P. Bennett, M. D. Houslay, T. R. Hesketh, G. A. Smith & J. C. Metcalfe.)
2. Annular lipids determine the ATPase activity of a calcium transport protein complexed with dipalmitoyllecithin. *Biochemistry* in press (1976). (With T. R. Hesketh, G. A. Smith, M. D. Houslay, K. A. McGill, N. J. M. Birdsall & J. C. Metcalfe.)
3. Phospholipid synergism in a reconstituted calcium pump. *Proc. Nat. Acad. Sci. U.S.A.* (submitted for publication).
4. The lipid environment of the glucagon receptor regulates adenylate cyclase activity. *Biochim. Biophys. Acta* **436**, 495-504 (1976). (With M. D. Houslay, T. R. Hesketh, G. A. Smith & J. C. Metcalfe.)
5. The glucagon receptor can couple to adenylate cyclase without activating it. *Biochim. Biophys. Acta* **436**, 489-494 (1976). (With M. D. Houslay, J. C. Metcalfe, T. R. Hesketh & G. A. Smith.)

Place of Research: Department of Biochemistry, University of Cambridge.

A. C. S. READHEAD, Weir Research Fellow

(1) *Hot spots in extragalactic radio sources*

The 81.5 MHz scintillation survey provides information on the compact structure in the complete sample of 200 3CR radio sources. Professor A. Hewish and I have made a detailed study of the compact regions, or 'hot spots' in these sources. We find that they are nearly always located in the outer components of the sources, and are therefore not to be confused with the very compact central components which are often prominent at high frequencies. The most successful theory of the formation of extragalactic radio sources involves a beam of high energy radiation and/or particles which is emitted by the central object; thus it may be that the hot spots which we see are formed by a highly collimated beam ploughing outwards into the intergalactic medium.

The hot spots range in size from a few kiloparsecs to 10 kpc. The fact that we see few hot spots smaller than about 1 kpc is very interesting, since this is the range in which our detection technique is most sensitive. We find that the most powerful extragalactic sources have hot spots about 7 kpc in size in two major components about 100 kpc apart.

(2) *Very long baseline interferometry (v.l.b.i.)*

The analysis of our v.l.b.i. observations at 610 MHz is now complete. Dr P. N. Wilkinson and I have developed a method for incorporating the 'phase closure' data with the amplitude data which works well provided one has long tracks of sources on at least six baselines, as was the case in the present series of observations. The use of the closure phase enables us to rule out the 180° ambiguities which are always present when one has only amplitude data and therefore leads to a much more realistic modelling of the source. We have tested our procedure by generating the amplitude and closure phase data (with noise added) which we would have seen for different brightness distributions, and then analysing this 'data' by our method. A series of 'blind' tests carried out in this way show that for all but the most complicated sources the method works well.

Eight of the sources which we observed in March 1975 had been observed on three baselines in December 1973 by Dr G. H. Purcell. A comparison of the results from these two epochs shows excellent agreement at the 5% level in both the total flux and the visibility curves. This is of particular interest since three of these sources 3C 454.3, CTA 21 and CTA 102 have been reported to vary by about 50% at these frequencies.

In May 1976 we made another large series of v.l.b.i. observations at 1666 MHz, on six baselines. We observed the same group of sources for which we have low frequency v.l.b.i. data, and in addition we searched for fringes in thirty 3C sources which are known to have compact structure in outer components from the synthesis maps and which scintillate strongly. We have not yet analysed this data, but we do know that the experiment was successful since interference fringes have been found on all six baselines.

Publications

The angular broadening of radio sources by scattering in the interstellar medium. *Mon. Not. R. Astr. Soc.* **174**, 7 (1976). (With P. J. Duffett-Smith.)

Compact features in a complete sample of radio sources. *Mon. Not. R. Astr. Soc.* **176**, 571 (1976). (With A. Hewish.)

Hot spots in radio sources as cosmological probes. *Astron. and Astrophys.* (in the press). (With A. Hewish.)

Places of Research: Mullard Radio Astronomy Observatory, University of Cambridge, and Owens Valley Radio Astronomy Observatory, California Institute of Technology.

W. M. STOBBS, Armourers and Brasiers' Research Fellow

The apparently 'plastic' deformation of a metal specimen can often leave it with some memory of its original shape. For example in dispersion strengthened metals, when no stress relaxation occurs at the elastically deformed inclusions, this 'memory' is perfect in the sense that it is only when the specimen has been returned to its original shape that the mean elastic strain in the matrix, with no applied load, is reduced to zero.

The title of my research is 'The shape memory effect' and over the past few months I have initiated a number of projects aimed first at gaining an understanding both of the way in which various modes of deformation help in assessing the effect and in relating it to the variety of defect structures with which it is associated. Secondly, I am also working on the fundamental question of what it is that makes a metal undergo a thermoelastic martensitic transformation, this transformation being fundamental in alloys which show the more spectacular 'Marmem' and 'pseudo-elastic' effects.

In the former area I have recently reviewed the ways in which elastic continuum theory and plasticity can be combined with a dislocation model for plastic relaxation to give an understanding of the degree of importance of shape memory in dispersion strengthened alloys and am currently working on the Bauschinger effect in single phase crystals (with Dr O. Pedersen). In the high strain, high strain rate area exemplified by metal cutting, I have (with Dr J. S. Kallend and Dr J. A. Williams) analysed the deformation behaviour of copper in ultramicrotomy and with this understanding am now engaged on determining the way in which the environment at the rake face of a tool in the cutting process can change the mode of deformation in the chip and thus change the remnant elastic strain distribution within it and thus its 'memory' of the process it has undergone.

In the second area I am at present engaged in an electron microscopical study of the structure of martensites in a number of different Marmem materials. In particular in Cu-Zn-Al I have found an imperfect superlattice of twins within the martensites which is certainly associated with the accommodation of the different martensite variants and, at least in this alloy, with its high damping properties. I expect this area of research to develop in an attempt to see the extent to which second order transformations are often associated with the first order martensitic transformation. In this connection I am continuing my work on both periodic lattice distortions and ordering effects (with Mr J.-P. A. A. Chevalier).

Publications

Deformation behaviour of copper in ultramicrotomy. *Acta Met.* **24**, (in the press). (With J. S. Kallend & J. A. Williams.)

The work hardening of copper-silica. V. Equilibrium plastic relaxation by secondary dislocations. *Phil. Mag.* **34**, 351 (1976). (With L. M. Brown.)

Dispersion strengthening. To be published by A.S.M. and A.I.M.E. in a book on their Fall 1975 meeting in Cincinnati.

Place of Research: The Cavendish Laboratory, University of Cambridge.

H. N. ARST, Smithson Research Fellow

I have continued work in the following areas using the ascomycete fungus *Aspergillus nidulans:*

(1) *An integrator gene* (with H. A. Penfold and C. R. Bailey)

One of the most intriguing questions in biology today is how the regulation of a particular structural gene can be programmed so that it can function in a variety of different contexts. To put it in another way, how can the concomitant expression of two or more structural genes whose expression can also occur independently be achieved. Britten and Davidson (1969, 1971, 1973) have proposed a model for gene regulation in development in which positively acting regulatory genes, designated integrator genes, effect such concomitant expression. Although the Britten–Davidson model was developed to account for differentiation in higher eukaryotes, there is no reason why a similar, although possibly less elaborate, form of regulatory machinery might not exist in lower eukaryotes such as *A. nidulans*. Indeed, given the considerable metabolic versatility of *A. nidulans*, the most obvious systems in which to seek mutations in integrator genes would be those in which a single enzyme participates in more than one metabolic pathway. I have shown (Arst 1976) that the *int*A gene in linkage group II fulfils the criteria for an integrator gene and controls at least three structural genes: *amdS* in linkage group III, coding for an acetamidase; *gab*A in linkage group VI, coding for a permease for 4-amino-*n*-butyric acid (GABA); and *gat*A in linkage group VII, coding for α transaminase for GABA, β-alanine, N^α-acetyl-L-ornithine, and certain other ω-amino acids. The acetamidase structural gene, at least, is also subject to a parallel positive control by the product of a specific regulatory gene, *amd*A. GABA and β-alanine induce acetamidase synthesis via the *int*A gene product whereas amide induction of acetamidase probably involves the *amd*A product. The two forms of induction are competitive, probably indicating partial or complete overlap of *int*A and *amd*A product receptor sites. The receptor sites for the *int*A product adjacent to the three structural genes definitely differ in structure, and it is possible that the *int*A product is able to alter the relative efficiencies of expression of the three structural genes according to which effector (β-alanine or GABA) is bound to it. This is probably the first convincing evidence for the existence of integrator genes.

(2) *Control of proline degradation* (with Dr D. W. MacDonald and K. N. Rand)

Proline degradation in *A. nidulans* is determined by a gene cluster (Arst and MacDonald, 1975). I have now shown this cluster to have the structure *prn*A–*prn*D –control region–*prn*B–*prn*C. Mutations in *prn*B eliminate a proline permease. Mutations in *prn*A and *prn*D eliminate proline oxidase. Mutations in *prn*A and *prn*C eliminate pyrroline-5-carboxylate dehydrogenase. *Cis*-acting regulatory mutations occur in the control region. We have isolated conditional *prn*A⁻ and *prn*C⁻ mutations to see whether the *prn*A and *prn*C products are structural components of the enzymes the mutations affect or whether the growth defects are regulatory in nature. Very preliminary results indicate that the *prn*C product probably plays a structural role but have thus far failed to indicate any structural involvement for the *prn*A product. I have developed a system for obtaining and characterising spontaneous *prn*⁻ mutants. This system should enable deletion mutations to be obtained so that deletion mapping can facilitate determination of the genetic fine structure of the *prn* cluster.

(3) *Carbon catabolite repression* (with C. R. Bailey)

We have shown that the non-hierarchical herogeneity of alleles in the *cre*A gene (Bailey and Arst, 1975) is sufficient to establish that the *cre*A gene product is directly involved in the regulation of carbon catabolite-repressible activities. This supports our proposal (Arst and MacDonald, 1975) that carbon catabolite repression is mediated by a negative control system in *A.nidulans*. We have also shown that in order to exert catabolite repression, a carbon source must be not only taken up but must undergo some intracellular metabolic transformations as well.

(4) *Nitrogen metabolite repression* (with K. N. Rand)

By using a mutation from which a translocation break-point is inseparable, we have established the phenotype of a complete loss of function mutation in the *are*A gene. This supports our proposal (Arts & Cove, 1973; Arst & Scazzocchio, 1975) that the *are*A product is a positively acting regulatory molecule required for the expression of ammonium-repressible genes.

(5) *Promoter/initiator mutations* (with C. R. Bailey and H. A. Penfold)

A *cis*-dominant regulatory mutation tightly linked to the structural gene for the GABA permease, *gab*A (Arts 1976) has been obtained. Since this gene occurs in a well-mapped region, good flanking markers are available to facilitate fine structure mapping.

(6) *Nitrate assimilation* (with K. N. Rand)

We have obtained a number of new regulatory mutations affecting nitrate assimilation. These should help to sort out the rather complicated regulation of this pathway.

References

Arst, H. N., Jr. 1976 Integrator Gene in *Aspergillus nidulans*. *Nature, Lond.* **262**, 231–234.

Arst, H. N., Jr. & Cove, D. J. 1973 Nitrogen metabolite repression in *Aspergillus nidulans*. *Molec. gen. Genet.* **126**, 111–141.

Arst, H. N., Jr. & MacDonald, D. W. 1975 A gene cluster in *Aspergillus nidulans* with an internally located *cis*-acting regulatory region. *Nature, Lond.* **254**, 26–31.

Arst, H. N., Jr. & Scazzocchio, C. 1975 Initiator constitutive mutation with an 'up-promoter' effect in *Aspergillus nidulans*. *Nature, Lond.* **254**, 31–34.

Bailey, C. & Arst, H. N., Jr. 1975 Carbon catabolite repression in *Aspergillus nidulans*. *Europ. J. Biochem.* **51**, 573–577.

Britten, R. J. & Davidson, E. H. 1969 Gene regulation for higher cells: a theory. *Science* **165**, 349–357.

Britten, R. J. & Davidson, E. H. 1971 Repetitive and non-repetitive DNA sequences and a speculation on the origins of evolutionary novelty. *Quart. Rev. Biol.* **46**, 111–138.

Davidson, E. H. & Britten, R. J. 1973 Organisation, transcription, and regulation in the animal genome. *Quart. Rev. Biol.* **48**, 565–613.

Publications

Three genes determine the carboxin sensitivity of mitochondrial succinate oxidation in *Aspergillus nidulans*. *Genet. Res., Camb.* **26**, 297–305 (1975). (With I.A.U.N. Gunatilleke and C. Scazzocchio.)

Integrator gene in *Aspergillus nidulans*. *Nature, Lond.* **262**, 231–234 (1976).

Place of Research: Department of Genetics, University of Cambridge.

D. V. EDMONDS, Warren Research Fellow

Work has continued on the examination of an alloy carbide precipitation reaction which occurs at the transformation interface during austenite decomposition in Fe-C-X alloys, where X is a strong carbide forming element. A study of the reaction by high-temperature photoemission electron microscopy, initiated in previous years at the University of Neuchâtel, Switzerland (with Dr C. J. Middleton) has been continued in Cambridge by carrying out comparative studies using conventional optical and electron microscopy. It has been possible to demonstrate that the surface reactions observed using photoemission electron microscopy are representative of the bulk behaviour of the alloys investigated. A number of microstructural features of the phase transformation were also observed by emission microscopy which would have been impossible to examine by other techniques.

This interface precipitation reaction creates a fine uniform alloy carbide dispersion in an equiaxed ferrite matrix, and in previous experiments the creep resistance of this microstructure was examined in simple ternary alloys. I have recently carried out a more detailed electron microscope examination of the microstructure following high temperature ageing and creep testing, and found evidence of microstructural instability caused by the migration of the ferrite grain boundaries to give a discontinuous coarsening reaction. Such discontinuous reactions have not previously been recorded for ferritic steels, which coupled with the fact that this behaviour was not found in a commercial steel studied in the same microstructural condition (Dunlop, Edmonds & Honeycombe 1973) points to its dependence on impurity content. I am at present attempting to establish the mechanism and crystallography of the reaction by further electron metallography.

The reaustenitisation process and grain size control during heat treatment, and the resistance to fatigue and brittle fracture of the non-random precipitate dispersions resulting from the phase transformation, are also being studied (with N. C. Law and J. P. Benson). An optical and electron metallographic study has shown the importance of the prior microstructure (ferrite, bainite or martensite) to the nucleation and growth kinetics of the austenite, and to its morphology in the early stages. Particular attention is now being given to the influence of the carbide dispersion usually present in these starting microstructures, and in future the importance of retained austenite will also be investigated. Preliminary work has shown the possibility of producing very fine ferritic grain structures (about 5 µm diameter) strengthened by the interface precipitation reaction, by rapid reaustenitization or cyclic reaustenitization treatments.

In order to study the influence of the fine-scale precipitate dispersion on fracture behaviour a technique has been developed for carrying out transmission electron microscopy on specimens prepared from material adjacent to the fracture surface. The main conclusion emerging from this study is that the fracture process in low-alloy steels will not be seriously modified by the alignment of precipitates by the phase transformation. Such an aligned precipitate dispersion does not seem to change the ferrite cleavage plane, but it is possible that the anisotropy of the deformation process due to the non-random nature of the precipitate dispersion could influence the plastic relaxation of cleavage microcracks.

Reference

Dunlop, G. L., Edmonds, D. V. & Honeycombe, R. W. K. Proceedings of a Conference on Creep Strength in Steel and High Temperature Alloys, Sheffield, *Iron St. Inst. Spec. Rep. no.* **153**, 222–229 (1973).

Publications

The creep properties of a low-alloy ferritic steel containing an intermetallic precipitate dispersion. *Proceedings of the Fourth International Conference on Strength of Metals and Alloys, Nancy*, **2**, 864–869 (1976). (With A. D. Batte & M. C. Murphy.)

The application of photoemission electron microscopy to the study of diffusional phase transformations in steels. *Metallography* **10** (in the press). (With C. J. Middleton.)

Place of Research: Department of Metallurgy and Materials Science, University of Cambridge.

A. E. VARDY, Warren Research Fellow

Aerodynamic problems have become increasingly important in the design and operation of railway systems in recent years. Some problems are associated with trains travelling over open ground, but many are related to air flows developed in tunnels. For example, high air velocities can occur in underground systems where other problems include long term ambient temperature increases. In main-line systems, large pressure waves can be generated when the nose or tail of a train enters or leaves a tunnel. Also, sudden pressure changes are caused when two trains pass one another. Both these effects lead to the possibility of passengers and maintenance personnel suffering aural discomfort.

During the early part of this year, I considered particularly British Rail's High Speed Train, already in use, and their Advanced Passenger Train, due to come into service in a few years' time. The latter vehicle will be sealed in order to protect passengers from pressure disturbances, but the former is not and neither is conventional rolling stock which must coexist with the high speed traffic. This is especially unfortunate because when two trains cross, the higher speed train exerts a greater pressure on the lower speed vehicle than does the latter on the former.

The sealing of trains may be an effective long term solution, but in the short term, tunnels rather than trains must be modified. I have previously dealt with shaped and porous tunnel entrance regions and I have this year concluded an investigation into the use of airshafts for pressure transient alleviation. A surprising result is that one well positioned small-bore airshaft is almost as effective as several such shafts for the most common case of a single train in a tunnel. For the more important but less usual event of two trains passing within the tunnel, several large-bore shafts are required in order to keep the pressure fluctuations within acceptable limits.

Work is currently being done on the use of cross-ventilation between two parallel tunnels in an attempt to reduce air velocities in underground systems. Ventilation may be provided either by means of a slightly porous wall or by several large, discrete holes. At present, the latter configuration appears to offer the greater promise, but both methods require a trade-off between reduced velocities and increased pressure wave transmission.

I have continued to collaborate with Mr J. A. Fox and our research student, Miss C. A. Woodhead, both of Leeds University, in the design of a water curtain which could be used as the basis of an actively controlled pressure alleviation device. Its feasibility from an aerodynamic point of view has been verified experimentally and its possible use for the containment of explosive waves in mines is also being considered.

In the latter part of the year, a start was made on the building of an experimental rig in which a train fastened on to the circumference of a large rotating disk will pass once per revolution through a tunnel pressed on to the edge of the disk. The design is such as to permit rapid and economical changes to the geometry of both the train and the tunnel so that a wide range of previously untried hypotheses can be experimentally evaluated.

Publications

Ventilated approach regions for railway tunnels. *Transp. Engng J. Am. Soc. civ. Engrs*, **101**, 609–619 (1975).

The use of airshafts for the alleviation of pressure transients in railway tunnels. *Proc. 2nd int. Symp. on the Aerodynamics and Ventilation of Vehicle Tunnels*, Cambridge (in the press).

The reduction of pressure transients in railway tunnels. *Proc. 6th Thermodynamics and Fluid Mechanics Conv., Inst. mech. Engrs*, Durham (in the press).

Place of Research: University Engineering Department, Cambridge.

R. N. McBurney, Florey Fellow

In the second year of my fellowship I have continued to investigate features of the postsynaptic response at excitatory neuromuscular junctions on giant muscle fibres from the Spider Crab, *Maia squinado*. This work has been carried out in collaboration with Dr A. C. Crawford.

Our main interest during this year has been in the process which inactivates the neuromuscular transmitter substance, L-glutamate, once it has been released from the presynaptic nerve terminal into the synaptic cleft. The need for such a process was indicated in our experiments which have compared the average duration of a single postsynaptic ionic channel activated by L-glutamate with the postsynaptic response to a quantum of transmitter. We have found that the time course of a quantum of transmitter in the synaptic cleft is too brief to be accounted for by simple diffusion of the transmitter away from the receptor area.

A similar situation exists at vertebrate cholinergic neuromuscular junctions where it has been known for some time that inactivation of the transmitter, acetylcholine, is accomplished through enzymatic breakdown by acetylcholinesterase. Attempts by other workers to demonstrate an equivalent enzyme system at invertebrate neuromuscular junctions have proved uniformly unsuccessful. We have therefore turned our attention to the possibility that an uptake system for glutamate performs the function of transmitter inactivation.

It is known that L-aspartate is a potent blocker of a glutamate uptake system in *Maia* nerve. We have examined the action of L-aspartate on the postsynaptic response to externally applied glutamate and to quanta of transmitter released from the nerve terminal. Our main findings are that L-aspartate, at concentrations known to be effective in blocking glutamate uptake, causes marked potentiation of the postsynaptic response to applied glutamate and an increase in the duration of the postsynaptic action of released transmitter. We feel that these results provide strong evidence for the involvement of an uptake system in transmitter inactivation at a glutamate synapse.

As this is my final report I should like to thank the Council of the Royal Society and the Florey Fellowships Committee for the opportunity to live and work in the United Kingdom and for their support during the past two years.

Publications

The time course of action of L-glutamate at the excitatory neuromuscular junction in *Maia squinado*. *J. Physiol*. **254**, 47–48P (1967). (With A. C. Crawford.)

The post-synaptic action of some putative excitatory transmitter substances. *Proc. R. Soc. Lond.* B **192**, 481–489 (1976). (With A. C. Crawford.)

On the elementary conductance event produced by L-glutamate and quanta of the natural transmitter at the neuromuscular junctions of *Maia squinado*. *J. Physiol.* **258**, 205–225 (1976). (With A. C. Crawford.)

The synergistic action of L-glutamate and L-aspartate at crustacean excitatory neuromuscular junctions. *J. Physiol.* (in the press). (With A. C. Crawford.)

The termination of transmitter action at the crustacean excitatory neuromuscular junction. *J. Physiol.* (in the press). (With A. C. Crawford.)

Place of Research: The Physiological Laboratory, University of Cambridge.

D. T. Spira, Bruno Mendel Travelling Fellow

Previous *in vitro* studies showed that the responses of spleen cells from rats infected with *Plasmodium berghei* markedly differ from responses of normal rat spleen cells (Golenser, Spira & Zuckerman 1975; Spira, Golenser & Gery 1976). During the tenure of this fellowship my interest focused on the functional and structural changes occurring in the intact spleen *in vivo* during the course of experimental murine malaria.

Histological changes in the spleen of inbred rats during the course of infection with *P. berghei* KSP II have been observed. The most prominent feature was the massive accumulation of haemopoietic tissue in early stages of the disease. Erythroblasts in all stages of development, megakaryocytes, but few myeloblasts invade the area between lymphatic follicles. The lymphatic tissue undergoes a certain degree of disorganization. First, the perivascular area increases in size; then, during the peak of infection, the distinction between the periarterial sheet and the mantle layer disappears. The large numbers of mitotic figures and other measures of increased cell activity correlate in time and quantity with the increased DNA synthesis observed *in vitro*. Large numbers of plasma cells appear in the mantle layer of lymphoid follicles. The germinal centres are very active during the course of infection. Although the proportion of lymphoid tissue in the spleen diminishes as the spleen size increases, the virtual non-reactivity of certain populations of spleen lymphocytes and the general immunosuppression can not be explained by the lack of lymphocytes.

Two known spleen functions are investigated in the malarious rat: increased trapping of syngeneic lymphocytes after antigenic stimulation and distribution of labelled macromolecules in the spleen. Both systems are measuring the *in vivo* activity of spleen macrophages, the cells most profoundly affected by the disease, yet apparently capable of normal performance during the disease. It seems that the increased antigen dependent trapping in malarious spleens is identical to the increase induced by antigen in normal rat spleens. The total number of cells trapped in the malarious spleen is equal to the number trapped in a normal rat spleen, despite a ten fold increase in size of the malarious spleen.

The discreet accumulation of labelled starch in circumfollicular macrophages observed in normal rats disappeared at peak parasitaemia. Labelled material was found in phagocytic cells throughout the red pulp, at apparently lower concentration per unit volume than in the normal spleen.

Additional work along the lines initiated during the tenure of the fellowship is needed to understand the functional changes in the spleen during malaria.

References

Golenser, J., Spira, D. T. & Zuckerman, A. 1975 *Clin. exp. Immunol.* **22**, 364–371.
Spita, D. T., Golenser, J. & Gery, I. 1976 *Clin. exp. Immunol.* **24**, 139–145.

Place of Research: National Institute for Medical Research, Mill Hill, London.

G. Ziv, Bruno Mendel Travelling Fellow

During the past year I have been concerned with two problems associated with the kinetic behaviour of chemotherapeutic agents in farm animals;

(a) The comparative pharmacokinetics of [^{35}S]-dapsone and [^{35}S]-sulphadiazine in the lactating goat.

(b) The effect of milk and experimentally induced fever on the oral absorption and kinetic disposition of ampicillin derivatives in young calves.

(c) By the use of several computer model programs, data on the absorption, distribution, elimination and metabolism of the drugs, obtained with radiochemical and chemical assay methods, were analysed with the objective of examining the likelihood that milk can kinetically represent the extracellular body compartment. In addition, the use of the mammary gland as a model organ for drug absorption was studied.

Several interesting observations were made:

(i) After equal doses of labelled sulphadiazine were administered i.v., i.m., orally, and by the intramammary route, serum radioactivity levels followed a two compartment open model system pattern whereas drug concentrations declined monoexponentially.

(ii) The opposite pattern of serum drug elimination was found with the labelled dapsone, i.e. radioactivity data could best be analysed in terms of a single compartment open system model whereas drug concentrations declined in a biexponential fashion.

(iii) The specific kinetic behaviour of each drug was due to a different rate and extent of drug metabolism.

(iv) The milk parent drug/metabolites ratio was consistently different from the ratio found in serum and was characteristic of the ratio for the other biological fluids and body organs, excluding the main organs of drug metabolism.

(v) The rate and extent of drug absorption after intramammary treatment were greater than after oral dosing.

Work on the physico-chemical properties of dapsone metabolites is still under way.

(b) The comparative oral absorption of ampicillin, amoxycillin, pivampicillin and hetacillin was studied in a multiple cross over trial involving a group of 2–4 weeks old starved and milk-fed dairy calves. Drug bioavailability was compared in terms of the area under the concentration-time curve (AUC) in serum after i.v. and oral dosing. The effect of experimentally induced pyrexia (i.v. injection of purified *Escherichia coli* endotoxin) on the pharmacokinetics of ampicillin following i.v. and oral drug administration, was investigated in another group of calves.

The following observations were made:

(i) Milk exhibited a profound inhibitory effect on the rate and extent of oral drug absorption. The effect was ranked as highest for ampicillin > hetacillin > amoxycillin > pivampicillin.

(ii) Pivacmicillin and amoxycillin were absorbed at the fastest rate and to the greatest extent; both drugs showed the highest peak concentrations in serum and had the greatest AUC.

(iii) Intravenous injection of ampicillin during a course of experimental pyrexia resulted in higher serum drug levels, a slower drug elimination rate and a smaller calculated volume of distribution compared to control.

(iv) Definite conclusions could not be reached concerning the effect of experimental pyrexia on the oral absorption of ampicillin.

Publications

Kinetics of absorption, distribution and elimination of [^{35}S]-dapsone in the lactating goat. *Res. Vet. Sci.* (in the press). (With A. Dekker & R. Hageman.)

Metabolism of dapsone in the goat. *Zbl. Vet. Med. (A)* (in the press). (With A. Dekker.)

Pharmacokinetics of [^{35}S]-sulphadiazine in the lactating goat. *Res. Vet. Sci.* (in the press). (With A. Dekker & R. Hageman.)

The effect of milk on the oral absorption of ampicillin derivatives in calves. *Am. J. Vet. Res.* (in the press). (With J. F. M. Nouws, A. S. J. P. A. M. van Miert & D. Groothuis.)

Disposition kinetics of ampicillin in calves under experimentally induced pyrexia. *Am. J. Vet. Res.* (in the press). (With J. F. M. Nouws, A. S. J. P. A. M. van Miert & D. Groothuis.)

Place of Research: Department of Pharmacology, University of Nijmegen, The Netherlands.

G. A. B. SHELTON, John Murray Travelling Student

The work reported here was carried out in 1975 in collaboration with Dr I. D. McFarlane. A follow-up to studies undertaken at the Lerner Marine Laboratory, Bimini, Bahamas, it concerned the investigation of nervous and non-nervous mechanisms co-ordinating behaviour in the Cnidaria. The bulk of the work was carried out on the hermatypic madreporarian corals *Dendrogyra cylindrus* (Ehrenberg), *Meandrina meandrites* (L), *Mussa angulosa* (Pallas) and *Eusmilia fastigiata* (Pallas). The main technique employed was electrophysiology, extracellular suction electrodes being used to monitor the small electrical potentials produced by these animals.

A colonial conduction system, believed to be the nerve net, was present in all species investigated. It conducted without decrement between all polyps. A second colonial system was found in *Meandrina*, *Mussa* and *Eusmilia*. Pulses could only be recorded from tentacles and oral disks but the system could be excited by electrical or mechanical stimuli to any part of the outside of the colony. In the tentacles and oral disks, this conduction system had a refractory period of about 60 ms while in the column and inter-polyp regions, the refractory period was much longer (several seconds). This had the effect of limiting the frequency at which pulses in this system could be conducted between polyps. Polyps thus seem to have some independence of action but the colony still receives a low level of information concerning their activities.

The second conduction system is a 'slow conduction system' similar to those found in sea anemones. In sea anemones, two slow conduction systems are present in addition to the nerve net and further investigation may well reveal a second slow conduction system in corals. The nerve net is involved in the excitatory control of muscle contraction. The slow system in corals may have a role during feeding by promoting expansion of tentacles and the production of mucus. The presence of e.g. crushed mollusc in the water increases the rate of 'spontaneous' firing in the slow system. The discovery of multiple conduction systems in these animals necessitates a thorough reappraisal of the mechanisms of behavioural control in corals.

Some preliminary observations were also made on the hydrozoan *Physalia*. Recordings made from the inner sac (pneumatosaccus) of the float revealed a conduction system which produced large, easily recordable pulses. Refractory period was long (2–3 s). There was a reduction in pulse amplitude and conduction velocity with repetitive stimulation. The system is almost certainly neuroid, electron microscopical study failing to reveal the presence of any nerves in the pneumatosaccus ectoderm. If so, this preparation is ideal for further studies of the propagation of spiking activity in simple epithelia, being robust, simple to prepare and easy to record from.

Invited talks have been given at the Durham Meeting of the Systematics Association, the Department of Zoology, Oxford, and the Third International Cnidaria Symposium, Victoria, British Columbia.

Publications

Electrophysiology of two parallel conducting systems in the colonial Hexacorallia. *Proc. R. Soc. Lond.* B **193**, 77–87 (1976). (With I. D. McFarlane.)

Slow conduction in solitary and colonial Anthozoa. In *'Coelenterate Ecology and Behavior'* (ed. G. O. Mackie) 599–607 (1976). New York: Plenum Publishing Corp.

Coordination of behaviour in cnidarian colonies. *Spec. Vol. Syst. Ass.* (*'Biology and Systematics of Colonial Organisms'*) (ed. G. P. Larwood) (in the press). London: Academic Press.

Place of Research: Bellairs Research Institute of McGill University, St James, Barbados.

D. K. AITKEN, Radcliffe Trust Research Fellow

My activities since 1 October 1975 have been in three main directions:

(1) To continue the analysis of observations obtained using an infrared spectrometer mounted at the cassegrain focus of the Anglo-Australian Telescope in July 1975. These observations gave spatial maps of the radiation from ionized neon and also of the thermal continuum radiation due to warm dust grains in a very bright compact southern H$_{II}$ region. The analysis invloved constructing models of the ionization structure and dust heating mechanisms which fit the observed spatial distributions of line and continuum radiation and which indicate that the region is very depleted in dust compared with the interstellar medium and that a significant amount of dust heating is due to nebular rather than direct stellar radiation. These results have recently been submitted for publication.

(2) The design and construction of a new grating spectrometer in which the components are cooled to liquid helium temperature was begun last autumn and is now almost completed. This spectrometer replaces the warm (room temperature) spectrometer developed at U.C.L. about 4 years ago and which has been used successfully on a number of telescopes including the A.A.T. in July 1975. The new spectrometer will have a sensitivity of nearly two orders of magnitude better than its predecessor and will first be used in September on the 60 in flux collector in Tenerife.

(3) During June 1976 I collaborated with Dr D. Rank of the University of California Santa Cruz in using the A.A.T. in further observations of southern compact H$_{II}$ regions in the radiation from a number of ionic species. These observations proved highly successful and have more than doubled the number of infrared line observations made to date. It is hoped that analysis of the results will be completed during the next few months.

The Royal Society Radcliffe Lecturer, Mrs B. Jones, appointed as my *locum tenens*, has, after fulfilling her teaching obligations, been of great assistance in considering the problems of interfacing the new spectrometer to a mini-computer and also took part in the collaboration in the use of the A.A.T. in June.

Future plans for the coming year involve using the spectrometer in collaboration with Professor G. Neugebauer on the Mount Wilson telescopes during an extended period of up to 6 months at the California Institute of Technology, and it is also hoped to make use again of the A.A.T. and the 88 in telescope on Hawaii. The observations will primarily be concerned with spatial studies of infrared line and continuum radiation from H$_{II}$ regions, planetary nebulae and some extragalactic objects.

Publications

On the abundance of heavy elements in the galactic centre. *Mon. Not. R. Astro. Soc.* **176**, 73 (1976). (With B. Jones & J. Griffiths.)

Infrared line and continuum spatial studies of the southern H$_{II}$ region G 333.6–0.2 in. *Mon. Not. R. Astr. Soc.* (in the press). (With B. Jones & J. Griffiths.)

Place of Research: Department of Physics and Astronomy, University College London.

GASSIOT COMMITTEE

Grants for support of research assistance and provision of equipment were recommended by the Gassiot Committee and approved by the Meteorological Office for award to the following for expenditure in the financial year 1976 to 1977:

Professor T. R. Kaiser
(Upper atmosphere meteor wind studies: University of Sheffield)

Dr J. A. Kerr
(Kinetic studies of gas phase reactions relevant to the chemistry of air pollution in the lower atmosphere: University of Birmingham)

Dr B. A. Thrush
(Study of reactions of hydroperoxyl radicals: University of Cambridge)

Professor W. R. S. Garton
(Study of the absorption spectra of atomic oxygen in the region 1.0 to 60 nm: Imperial College, London)

Dr W. D. McGrath
(Study of the influences of vibrational excitation on gas-phase reaction rates: The Queen's University of Belfast)

Professor W. C. Price
(High temperature photoelectron studies: King's College, London)

Professor J. B. Hasted
(Study of ion molecules reaction rates: Birkbeck College *and* University College London).

APPENDIX B

REPRESENTATION AT INTERNATIONAL MEETINGS

The following Royal Society delegates attended international meetings, mainly in connexion with scientific unions and committees, during the period September 1975 to August 1976:

XL *session of the International Statistical Institute* (*Warsaw, 1-9 September 1975*)
  Professor D. G. Kendall
XVIII *Council Meeting of the International Union of Pure and Applied Chemistry* (*I.U.P.A.C.*) (*Madrid, 9 and 11 September*)
  Dr T. M. Sugden (leader), Dr P. J. Agius, Dr J. W. Barrett, Sir Derek Barton, Professor N. N. Greenwood, Sir David Martin (secretary)
III *General Assembly of the International Federation for the Theory of Machines and Mechanisms* (*Iftomm*) (*Newcastle upon Tyne, 12 September*)
  Dr J. M. Prentis (chief delegate), Professor L. Maunder, Professor J. D. Robson, Mr T. H. Davies, Professor A. D. S. Barr
XV *General Assembly of the International Union of Pure and Applied Physics* (*I.U.P.A.P.*) (*Munich, 23-27 September*)
  Professor S. F. Edwards (leader), Professor M. Blackman, Professor D. J. Bradley, Professor B. L. Clarkson, Professor P. H. Fowler
I *International Congress of Historical Metrology* (*Zagreb, Yugoslavia, 28-30 October*)
  Dr D Vaughan
A *meeting organized by the Royal Swedish Academy of Sciences in conjunction with the Scientific Committee on Problems of the Environment* (*Sweden, 14-18 December*)
  Dr A. C. Chamberlain
I *International Institute for Applied Systems Analysis Conference* (*Laxenburg, Austria, 11-13 May* 1976)
  Sir Kingsley Dunham, Dr R. W. J. Keay, Mr P. C. Roberts, Professor H. H. Rosenbrock, Mr R. C. Tomlinson
III *General Assembly of the Scientific Committee on Problems of the Environment* (*S.C.O.P.E.*) (*Paris, 17-19 May*)
  Professor V. C. Wynne-Edwards (leader), Dr M. W. Holdgate, Dr R. W. J. Keay, Sir Frederick Warner
General Meeting of the Special Committee for Solar-Terrestrial Physics (*Scostep*) (*Boulder, Colorado, 2-5 June*)
  Professor W. J. G. Beynon (leader), Professor T. R. Kaiser, Dr J. W. King
XIX *Plenary Meeting of the Committee on Space Research* (*Cospar*) (*Philadelphia, U.S.A., 8-18 June*)
  Sir Harrie Massey (chief delegate), Professor R. L. F. Boyd, Mr P. Wigley (secretary)
X *General Assembly of the Committee on Data for Science and Technology* (*Boulder, Colorado, 2 and 3 July*)
  Sir Gordon Sutherland (voting delegate), Mr N. H. Robinson

XIV *General Assembly of the International Geographical Union (I.G.U.)* (*Moscow, 29 and 31 July and 3 August*)
　　Professor H. C. Darby (leader), Professor W. R. Mead, Mr D. J. H. Griffin (secretary)

IX *General Assembly of the International Union of Biochemistry (I.U.B.)* (*Hamburg, 28 July*)
　　Professor T. W. Goodwin (leader), Professor P. N. Campbell, Dr T. S. Work

V *General Assembly of the International Cartographic Association (I.C.A.)* (*Moscow, 3–10 August*)
　　Brigadier R. A. Gardiner (leader), Professor W. G. V. Balchin, Mr D. J. H. Griffin (secretary)

III *General Assembly of the International Commission for Mathematical Instruction (I.C.M.I.)* (*of the International Mathematical Union*) (*Karlsruhe, Federal Republic of Germany, 16–21 August*)
　　Sir James Lighthill (leader), Professor H. B. Griffiths, Dr E. A. Maxwell, Miss H. B. Shuard

Council Meeting of the International Union of Geological Sciences (I.U.G.S.) (*Sydney, Australia, 19 and 23 August*)
　　Professor J. Sutton

Council Meeting of the XXV International Geological Congress (*Sydney, Australia, 16–25 August*)
　　Dr S. H. U. Bowie

Meeting of the International Committee of the International Centre of Insect Physiology and Ecology (I.C.I.P.E.) (*Washington, D.C., 18–19 August*)
　　Sir Vincent Wigglesworth

VII *General Assembly of the International Organization for Biological Control of Noxious Animals and Plants (I.O.B.C.)* (*Washington, D.C., 24 August*)
　　Professor J. S. Kennedy

XVI *General Assembly of the International Astronomical Union (I.A.U.)* (*Grenoble, 24 August–2 September*)
　　Professor M. J. Seaton (chief delegate), Professor D. W. N. Stibbs, Professor R. J. Tayler

XIV *General Assembly of the International Union of Theoretical and Applied Mechanics (I.U.T.A.M.)* (*Delft, The Netherlands, 30 August–4 September*)
　　Professor P. R. Owen (leader), Professor G. K. Batchelor, Sir James Lighthill, Dr E. H. Mansfield, Professor L. Maunder

APPENDIX C

FELLOWSHIPS AWARDED IN THE EUROPEAN SCIENCE EXCHANGE PROGRAMME

From the United Kingdom

Dr M. Aitken—microbiology (France)
Miss M. S. Banks—genetics (Italy)
Dr A. W. H. Bartram—palaeontology (France)
Mr C. M. Bate—biological sciences (Germany)
Dr S. J. Bayne—chemistry (Denmark)
Dr R. W. Beales—geology (Sweden)
Dr I. A. Beattie—neurobiology (France)
Mr N. R. A. Beeley—chemistry (Switzerland)
Mr P. D. Bloch—physics (France)
Mr F. R. Booy—physics (France)
Dr A. G. W. Bradbury—chemistry (Germany)
Mr C. R. Bridges—physiology (Denmark)
Mr R. A. Brown—zoology (Sweden)
Mr D. J. Bruce—mathematics (Denmark)
Mr T. P. Burchette—geology (Germany)
Dr Jennifer C. Burt—chemistry (Germany)
Dr Gillian S. Butler-Browne—biophysics (France)
Dr D. McK. Caird—neurophysiology (France)
Dr C. M. Campbell—physiology (France)
Mr M. S. N. Carpenter—geology (France)
Dr J. C. Carter—chemistry (France)
Mr R. P. Casey—biochemistry (Netherlands)
Dr G. H. Cheetham—geography (Sweden)
Miss L. Cherns—geology (Sweden)
Dr R. M. Clay—chemistry (Italy)
Mr P. S. Collecott—physics (Germany)
Mr T. E. Conlon—mathematics (Germany)
Mr C. T. J. Dodson—mathematics (Italy)
Mr D. H. Edgar—biochemistry (Switzerland)
Mrs B. Fagg—physiology (Germany)
Mr G. E. Fagg—pharmacology (Germany)
Mr S. A. E. G. Falle—astronomy (Germany)
Miss B. Gledhill—physiology (France)
Dr S. R. F. Godwin—neurobiology (France)
Dr D. J. Griffiths—physics (Netherlands)
Mr P. J. Griffiths—physiology (Germany)
Dr D. C. Gubb—molecular biology (Spain)
Dr L. Hall—biochemistry (Switzerland)
Mr S. K. Hanmer—geology (France)
Dr G. P. Haywood—zoology (France)
Mr J. E. Hesketh—biochemistry (France)
Mr A. A. Holder—physiology (Denmark)

Dr C. J. Holloway—chemistry (Germany)
Dr N. G. Holmes—biophysics (Netherlands)
Mr D. G. Hughes—biochemistry (Switzerland)
Dr R. G. Humphreys—physics (Germany)
Mr B. Huntley—biological sciences (Ireland)
Mr G. B. Irvine—biochemistry (Denmark)
Dr R. I. Jones—botany (Finland)
Mr B. S. Kay—physics (Italy)
Dr P. D. Keane—neuropharmacology (France)
Mr J. R. Kinghorn—genetics (Switzerland)
Miss A. R. Kinsella—biology (Belgium)
Dr J. K. C. Knowles—genetics (France)
Mr I. D. Lawrie—physics (France)
Mr P. M. Leckstein—entomology (Netherlands)
Dr P. W. Ledger—biological sciences (France)
Dr R. W. Lennox—molecular biology (Germany)
Miss M. Lewandowska—plant physiology (Sweden)
Mr P. E. Long—plant biology (Netherlands)
Mr G. McElhiney—chemistry (Germany)
Mr M. Maier—chemistry (Germany)
Mr D. A. Mathers—physiology (Sweden)
Dr D. F. Mayhew—geology (Netherlands)
Mr N. D. Mitchell—animal physiology (Netherlands)
Mr C. J. Moody—chemistry (Switzerland)
Dr L. E. Morris—mathematics (France)
Dr H. Mykura—physics (Germany)
Mrs C. M. R. Nisbet—geophysics (Switzerland)
Mr E. G. Nisbet—geology (Switzerland)
Mr J. C. Osborn—biological sciences (Belgium)
Mr C. J. Pearce—biochemistry (France)
Mrs H. C. Prentice—botany (Norway)
Mr I. C. Prentice—botany (Norway)
Dr Janet A. Pryke—plant biochemistry (Belgium)
Mr N. Quirke—physics (Denmark)
Mr M. J. Roberts—physics (France)
Mr A. J. Samuel—chemistry (France)
Mr P. D. Say—hydrobiology (France)
Mr J. H. Shea—physics (Germany)
Dr A. Shenkin—biochemistry (Sweden)
Mrs E. Sim—biochemistry (Germany)
Dr M. S. Skolnick—physics (France)
Mr E. A. Smith—astronomy (France)
Mr D. McN. Summers—geophysics (Germany)
Dr G. C. L. Tait—genetics (France)
Mr A. J. Taylor—biochemistry (Germany)
Mr J. V. Tucker—mathematics (Norway)
Mr I. F. Tulloch—psychology (Germany)
Mr M. J. Tully—biochemistry (Portugal)
Dr J. Walker—physics (France)
Mr P. C. West—physics (France)
Dr Susan Whitehouse—biochemistry (Germany)
Mr J. P. Williams—zoology (Switzerland)
Dr C. Workman—zoology (Finland)

Mr L. I. Wright—geology (France)
Dr M. J. York —physics (Italy)
Mr P. F. Zagalsky—biochemistry (France)

To the United Kingdom

Dr U. Arnason—biological sciences (Sweden)
Mr S. Balibar—physics (France)
Mr D. Barbotin—engineering (France)
Mr J. F. Bergeretti—computer science (France)
Dr H. Berndt—biological sciences (Germany)
Dr M. Bouchy—chemistry (France)
Dr J. M. Bregeault—chemistry (France)
Mr Y. Brocard—engineering (France)
Dr N. Buran—engineering (Italy)
Mr P. G. Burkhardt—engineering (Switzerland)
Dr A. Busch—chemistry (Germany)
Dr E. F. Buschmann—chemistry (Germany)
Dr M. Champion—engineering (France)
Mr B. Chaudret—coordination chemistry (France)
Miss M. Chauveau—agronomy (France)
Dr W. Curati—physiological and medical sciences (Switzertand)
Dr H. H. Dahl—biological sciences (Denmark)
Dr J. Deitmer: physiological and medical sciences (Germany)
Dr A. De Santis—electrophysiology (Italy)
Mr R. Diaz Orejas—biollogical sciences (Spain)
Dr A. Dworkin—chemical engineering (France)
Miss K. Erdmann—mathematics (Germany)
Dr F. Flores—physics (Spain)
Mr J. L. Forget—chemistry (France)
Professor J. J. Frausto da Silva—chemistry (Portugal)
Dr H. Friedrich—physics (Germany)
Dr J. L. Gacougnolle—metallurgy (France)
Dr F. Gianni—chemistry (Italy)
Dr K. O. Grape—astronomy (Sweden)
Dr S. Grego—biological sciences (Italy)
Mr J. Y. Gregoire—engineering (France)
Dr J. Grosse—chemistry (Germany)
Dr W. Haecki—medical sciences (Switzerland)
Dr J. Hausler—chemistry (Austria)
Dr J. M. Hermoso Nunez—biochemistry (Spain)
Mr F. Hernandez Sanchez—biochemistry (Spain)
Mr R. Hollenstein—chemistry (Switzerland)
Mr R. Hummervoll—geophysics (Norway)
Mr A. Jablon—computer science (France)
Dr J. Jensen—theoretical physics (Denmark)
Dr K. Kleemann—natural sciences (Austria)
Mr R. Koreman—control systems (Belgium)
Dr H. Korhonen—dairy science (Finland)
Dr J. J. Lazaro Paniagua—biochemistry (Spain)
Mr P. Le Roux—engineering in medicine (France)
Dr R. Levy—physics (France)

Mr C. Lillocci—chemistry (Italy)
Mr S. Loukas—biochemistry (Greece)
Miss N. T. Luong-Thi—chemistry (France)
Dr P. Marino—cardiology (Italy)
Mr F. Meca—physics (France)
Dr S. Metafora—biochemistry (Italy)
Dr M. A. J. Michels—chemical technology (Netherlands)
Mrs I. Morgenstern—chemistry (France)
Mr J. Mulqueen—engineering (Ireland)
Dr O. Parriaux—engineering (Switzerland)
Mr M. Pettini—astronomy (Italy)
Dr P. Pittet—physiological and medical sciences (Switzerland)
Dr M. Pfeffer—chemistry (France)
Mr B. Plau—chemistry (France)
Dr O. Pongs—biological sciences (Germany)
Mr J. P. Prunier—plant pathology (France)
Dr P. Rabette—chemistry (France)
Dr C. Reina—astronomy (Italy)
Dr L. J. Reinders—theoretical physics (Netherlands)
Mr J. Reymond—electronics (France)
Dr M. Roques—chemical engineering (France)
Dr Luciana Rosa—biological sciences (Italy)
Mr J. M. Roure—materials science (France)
Dr H. Rupp—biological sciences (Germany)
Dr G. Schalow—physiological and medical sciences (Germany)
Mr A. Seiler—biology (brewing) (Switzerland)
Dr G. Serra Errante—chemistry (Italy)
Mrs K. M. Silvennoinen—mathematics (Finland)
Mr F. Soria Gallego—physics (Spain)
Mr J. N. Spaltenstein—mathematics (Switzerland)
Mr B. Stroustrup—computer sciences (Denmark)
Dr H. M. Textor—chemistry (Switzerland)
Mr P. Toint—mathematics (Belgium)
Mr M. Tremeau—chemical engineering (France)
Mr R. Triponel—electronic engineering (France)
Dr J. C. Trombe—chemistry (France)
Dr J. P. Van Dijken—biochemistry (Netherlands)
Dr F. Verhulst—mathematics (Netherlands)
Dr J. Vicente Soler—chemistry (Spain)
Mr S. Vire—metallurgy (France)
Mr R. Westgaard—neurophysiology (Norway)

APPENDIX D

FORMAL EXCHANGES WITH FOREIGN ACADEMIES

The following visits were made or begun in the year ended 31 August 1976 under the arrangements for scientific exchanges between the Royal Society and the Academies of Sciences in the countries named:

Bulgaria
Senior scientists (2 weeks)
To U.K.: Professor T. S. Stoichev (toxicology)
Professor I. Kostov (crystal morphology)

Czechoslovakia
Senior scientists (2 weeks)
From U.K.: Professor J. G. Buchanan (carbohydrate and nucleoside chemistry)
To U.K.: Dr A. G. Curev (hydromechanics)
Dr L. Vyklický (physiology)

Research workers (18 man-months)
To U.K.: Dr Vlasta Sovová (experimental biology)
Dr J. Závada (virology)

Egypt (*Academy of Scientific Research and Technology*)
Study visits (minimum of 3 weeks)
From U.K.: Dr T. W. Tinsley (insect virology)
Dr K. A. G. Mendelssohn
Dr J. W. Humberston (physics)
Professor J. T. Davies (chemical engineering)
To U.K.: Dr Gamila M. O. Wassel (pharmacognosy)
Professor M. Abd El-Salam (dairy chemistry)
Professor M. A. Kassem (pharmacology)

Fellowships (minimum of 4 months)
To U.K.: Dr A. B. Moustafa (polymers)
Dr A. F. Abdel-Fattah (microbiology)

Hungary
Senior scientists (3 weeks)
To U.K.: Dr I. Tamassy (plant breeding)
Dr M. Arato (mathematical statistics)

Research workers (10 man-months)
To U.K.: Dr P. Szepesvary (chemistry)

India (*Indian National Science Academy*)

From U.K.: Dr B. Chadwick (geology)
Dr T. L. Blundell (protein crystallography)
Professor F. T. Barwell (mechanical engineering)
Professor N. W. Pirie
Dr F. G. H. Lupton (plant breeding)
Professor R. A. Cawson (oral medicine)
Dr J. McLelland (veterinary anatomy)
Dr M. V. Berry (physics)

To U.K.: Professor S. Ranganathan (metallurgy)
Professor P. Mukhopadhyay (electrical engineering)
Dr V. D. Gupta (nitrogen fixation)
Dr P. S. Rao (physiology)

Israel (*Academy of Sciences and Humanities*)

Fellowships
From U.K.: Miss K. E. Koller (pharmacology)
Dr L. Lyons (physics)
Dr J. E. Paton (physics)
Mr M. Tabor (chemistry)

To U.K.: Dr D. Durban (aeronautical engineering)
Dr B. Goldman (genetics)
Dr D. Wool (animal and plant genetics)

Japan (*Japan Academy, the Science Council of Japan, and the Japan Society for the Promotion of Science*)

Study visits (2 weeks to 3 months)
From U.K.: Professor J. G. Feinberg (physiology)
Dr M. C. Flowers (chemistry)
Professor R. W. Fearnhead (dental anatomy)
Dr G. Parry Jones (physical sciences)
Professor K. J. Ives (civil engineering)
Dr R. Hinchcliffe (otology)
Dr J. Watson (electrical engineering)
Professor M. P. Haggard (perception of speech sounds)
Dr J. Farrant (cryobiology)
Professor W. Johnson (engineering)
Dr P. B. C. Matthews
Dr Ilse Lasnitzki-Glücksmann (steroid hormones)
Professor A. M. Neville (civil engineering)
Dr Pauline M. Harrison (biochemistry)
Dr R. B. Kemp (cell biology)
Professor F. T. Barwell (mechanical engineering)
Professor J. W. S. Cassels
Professor A. Fröhlich
Professor A. Jeffrey (enginering mathematics)
Dr J. H. Coates (statistics)
Dr B. J. Birch
Dr R. C. W. Berkeley (bacteriology)
Dr O. L. Krivanek (solid state physics)
Professor J. W. Christian

REPORT OF COUNCIL

Dr D. Hodgetts (combustion engines)
Dr A. L. Mackay (crystallography)
Professor R. D. Peacock (inorganic chemistry of fluorine)
Dr J. M. Hancock (cretaceous stratigraphy)
Dr W. J. Kennedy (cretaceous biogeography)
Dr J. H. Holloway (inorganic fluorine chemistry)

To U.K.: Professor M. Kawaguchi (high energy physics)
Professor K. Tamaru (heterogeneous catalysis)
Professor A. Morimoto (differential geometry)
Professor T. Nakane (entomology)

Fellowships (6 to 12 months)
From U.K.: Dr J. D. Bassett (electrical engineering)
To U.K.: Dr K. Ishii (mathematical biology)
Dr I. Hirota (atmospheric sciences)
Dr M. Hayakawa (radio physics)
Dr M. Tanaka (mechanical engineering)
Dr N. Wakasugi (animal breeding)
Dr M. Sakata (diffraction crystallography)
Dr M. Kono (geophysics)
Dr T. Fukumura (applied microbiology)
Dr T. Iseki (ceramics and nuclear materials)

Poland

Senior scientists (2 weeks)
From U.K.: Professor G. W. Series
Professor A. B. Foster (cancer research)
Professor R. L. Wain

To U.K.: Prrfessor W. Gajewski (genetics)
Professor M. Mordarski (microbiology)
Professor A. Urbanek (palaeozoology)

Study visits (1–6 months)
From U.K.: Dr R. Goldring (palaeontology)
Mr P. G. Hall (mathematics)
Dr C. Brown (organophosphorus chemistry)

To U.K.: Dr W. Stec (stereochemistry)
Dr J. Ziolkowski (theoretical astrophysics)
Dr J. Golka (theoretical solid state physics)

Fellowships (6–12 months)
To U.K.: Mr J. Ciborowski (physics)
Dr G. Kozlowski (superconductors)

Romania

Senior scientists (3 for 2 weeks)
From U.K.: Dr T. E. Allibone
Dr T. R. G. Williams (mechanical engineering)
Dr R. Butterfield (civil engineering)
Professor Edith Bülbring

To U.K.: Professor I. Fagarasanu (surgery)
Professor G. Buzdugan (strength of materials)

Research workers (18 *man-months*)
To U.K.:   Mr E. Rusu (metallurgy)
           Dr C. Dumitru (radioactivity)

U.S.S.R.

Senior scientists (3–8 *weeks*)
From U.K.: Dr J. B. Richardson (geology)
           Professor R. Penrose
           Dr J. A. Hudson (geophysics)
           Dr A. Thorpe (zoology)
           Professor J. M. Alexander (mechanical engineering)
           Dr R. B. Rickards (geology)
           Professor G. Kreisel
           Dr Lesley S. Dent Glasser (crystallography)
           Professor F. Llewellyn-Jones (electrical discharges in gases)
To U.K.:   Dr B. S. Tsybakov (communication)
           Professor A. I. Shapovalov (evolutionary physiology)
           Professor M. I. Aliev (semiconductor physics)
           Professor V. G. Lazarev (computer networks)
           Professor K. P. Ivanov (thermoregulation and bioenergetics)

Research workers (4 *for up to* 10 *months each*)
From U.K.: Dr G. K. Eagleson (mathematical statistics)
To U.K.:   Dr V. I. Tanyashin (molecular biology)
           Dr B. A. Kolovandin (engineering)
           Dr S. D. Shutov (applied physics)

Yugoslavia (*Council of Academies of Sciences and Arts*)
Research workers (10 *man-months*)
To U.K.:   Mr J. Jovoćević (electrochemistry)

APPENDIX E

COMMONWEALTH BURSARIES SCHEME

Awards made in the two categories, Royal Society and Commonwealth Foundation Bursaries and Royal Society and Nuffield Foundation Commonwealth Bursaries, in November 1975 and May 1976 were as follows:

Royal Society and Commonwealth Foundation Bursars

Dr P. K. Bitakaramire—veterinary medicine (Kampala to Glasgow)
Dr N. Chandra—botany (Rajasthan to Leicester)
Dr O. O. Dipeolu—veterinary pathology (Ibadan to Pirbright)
Professor D. Nasipuri—chemistry (Kharagpur to Oxford)
Dr E. K. Obiakor—food science (Benin to London)
Professor A. S. H. Ong—chemistry (Penang to Oxford)
Dr P. Satyanarayana—geology (Sagar to London)
Dr K. L. Yau—physics (Cape Coast to Hamilton)

Royal Society and Nuffield Foundation Commonwealth Bursars

Dr G. B. Allison—soil science (Glen Osmond to Waterloo)
Dr R. M. Case—physiology (Newcastle upon Tyne to Sydney)
Dr H. T. A. Cheung—chemistry (Sydney to London)
Dr E. A. Colhoun—geology (Tasmania to Cambridge)
Dr A. Falconer—geography (Guelph to Canberra)
Dr T. G. A. Green—botany (Waikato to Bristol)
Dr S. K. Kar—molecular biology (Pilani to Cambridge)
Dr R. J. Le Roy—chemistry (Waterloo to Oxford)
Dr Jennifer A. McComb—botany (Perth to Leicester)
Dr R. A. McIntosh—plant breeding (Sydney to Cambridge)
Professor J. W. McConkey—physics (Windsor to Manchester)
Dr J. M. Oades—soil science (Glen Osmond to Reading)
Professor A. R. Poletti—nuclear physics (Auckland to Oxford)
Dr M. D. Rickard—veterinary science (Melbourne to London)
Dr S. K. Roy—botany (Varanasi to Sydney)
Dr B. J. Selman—agricultural biology (Newcastle upon Tyne to Canberra)
Dr L. C. Schmidt—civil engineering (Melbourne to Cambridge)
Dr P. D. Sharma—botany (Meerut to Exeter)
Dr P. J. Shipton—plant pathology (Aberdeen to Sydney and Glen Osmond)
Dr N. J. Stone—physics (Oxford to Vancouver)
Dr D. R. Taylor—physics (Ontario to Oxford)
Dr I. F. Wardlaw—botany (Canberra to Aberdeen)
Dr A. R. Wellburn—biochemistry (Lancaster to Canberra)

APPENDIX F

EXCHANGES WITH THE OLDER COMMONWEALTH COUNTRIES SUPPORTED FROM THE SCIENTIFIC EXCHANGES (ANONYMOUS) FUND

U.K. to Bangladesh
Professor C. Andrew (mechanical engineering) 26–29 January 1976

Bangladesh to U.K.
Dr M. S. Khan (botany)　　　　　　　　　　2 September 1975–29 June 1976

Canada to U.K.
Dr D. Smith (physical chemistry)　　　　　October 1975–12 months

U.K. to India
Dr P. J. W. Olive (zoology)　　　　　　　　September 1975–2 weeks
Dr D. J. Chivers (primates)　　　　　　　　2–9 November 1975
Dr T. J. Pedley (fluid dynamics)　　　　　　8–19 December 1975
Dr R. Horgan (theoretical physics)　　　　29 December 1975–20 January 1976
Dr G. Martelli (equatorial ionosphere)　　　February 1976

India to U.K.
Professor K. N. Saxena (insect physiology)　3–7 November 1975

New Zealand to U.K.
Dr D. G. Jenkins (geology)　　　　　　　　1 September 1975–August 1976

APPENDIX G

AWARDS MADE IN THE ROYAL SOCIETY LATIN AMERICAN PROGRAMME

Study visits to U.K.
Dr H. Bonadeo—atomic physics (Argentina)
Professor L. de Meis—muscle biophysics (Brazil)
Dr O. H. H. Mielke—entomology (Brazil)
Professor R. Soares—physiology (Brazil)
Dr E. Stefani—physiology (Mexico)

Study visits from U.K.
Dr C. J. Bradish—virology (Venezuela)
Professor B. Capon—chemistry (Chile)
Professor C. N. Hales—medical biochemistry (Argentina)
Dr W. D. Hamilton—genetics (Colombia)
Dr J. R. Hubbuck—mathematics (Mexico)
Dr R. Hughes—chemical engineering (Brazil)
Mr W. J. Lockyer—blood transfusion (Brazil)
Professor A. M. Neville—civil engineering (Argentina)
Professor R. M. Shackleton—earth sciences (Brazil)
Dr D. W. Snow—ornithology (Venezuela)
Dr E. M. Vaughan Williams—pharmacology (Mexico)
Mrs E. Williams—mathematics education (Argentina)
Dr P. G. Withrington—physiology (Brazil)
Dr M. G. Yates—nitrogen fixation (Brazil)

Fellowships to U.K.
Dr A. Brunner—experimental biology (Mexico)
Dr E. Chicurel—mechanical engineering (Mexico)
Dr J. M. F. Gonzalez—chemistry (Mexico)
Mrs M. A. D. P. Martinez—botany (Argentina)
Dra C. Matteri—bryophyte ecology (Argentina)
Dr M. Peimbert ⎫
Dr Silvia Peimbert ⎬—astronomy (Mexico)
Dr M. J. Yacaman—metallurgy (Mexico)

Fellowships from U.K.
Dr R. M. E. Parkhouse—immunology (Mexico)
Mr W. A. A. Robertson—marine botany (Peru)

APPENDIX H

PARLIAMENTARY GRANT FOR SCIENTIFIC INVESTIGATIONS

The third allocation of the Parliamentary Grant for Scientific Investigations during the year 1975 was as follows:

	£
D. J. GOODMAN, Installation of three continuously recording strain-meters on a large ice mass	2395
D. W. SCIAMA, Resonant-like features in heavy ion transfer reactions of importance inexplosive nucleosynthesis	6588
A. THOM, Astronomy of Megalithic man	1008
K. J. ROSS, Computer processing of spectra from electron spectrometers	1674
J. F. ALDER, Analytical spectroscopic studies using a radio-frequency inductively coupled plasma	2065
R. J. BUTCHER and W. J. JONES, Stark-tuned spectroscopy in the infrared	1537
M. A. A. CLYNE, Spectroscopic studies of diatomic molecules with a tunable ultraviolet laser	1340
A. J. MCCAFFERY, Laser-induced emission and Raman spectroscopy	1296
A. D. PETHYBRIDGE, Kinetic and equilibrium studies of aqueous solutions of calcium carbonate	1557
A. B. TRENWITH, A re-examination of the dissociation of ethane	1148
D S. URCH, X-ray emission spectroscopy: sample temperature control	1600
T. E. ALLIBONE, Impulse breakdown of long gaps in air	80
P. W. FRANCIS, Preliminary visit to volcanic areas of Ecuador and Colombia	320
I. G. GASS, Oman Ophiolite project	9526
A. S. GOUDIE, Late Quaternary cultural and climatic changes in Pakistan	610
I. J. SMALLEY, Mineralogy, sources and distribution of loess in the Danube Basin	420
J. B. THORNES, Weathering-leaching balance in relation to hillslope processes in tropical catchments	3180
A. D. Q. AGNEW, Expedition to Kenya to study upland vegetation ecotones	1240
H. G. DICKINSON, Cytophysiological investigations in plant reproductive tissue	up to 3800
R. E. KENDRICK, Phytochrome and photomorphogenesis	1000
C. LEGG, Study of foliage density distribution in tropical rain forests	815
T. D. V. SWINSCOW, Taxonomy and distribution of lichens in East Africa	400
G. TURNOCK, Control of RNA synthesis in *Physarum polycephalum*	723
C. E. RIDSDALE, Botanical expedition to Travancore, South India	1058

	£
BRIDGET I. BAKER, Investigation of the pars intermedia peptides of fishes and lampreys	1906
J. A. BISHOP, Pleiotropic effects of the gene for Warfarin resistance in rats	551
SIR CYRIL CLARKE and P. M. SHEPPARD, Mimicry in butterflies, sex ratios and climatic changes	3409
E. R. CREED, Breeding programme relating to melanism in insects	2016
GILLIAN D. SALES, Sound reception and ultrasonic behaviour in small mammals	up to 7185
M. A. SLEIGH, Patterns of ciliary and flagellar movement	4289
I. F. SPELLERBERG, The ecology and active management of Britain's reptiles	810
G. W. STOREY, Production biology of soil and litter nematodes	1284
M. J. BAZIN, Growth of *Escherichia coli* under transient conditions	1135
J. A. BUSWELL, The enzymology of aromatic metabolism in thermophilic micro-organisms	2397
R. Y. CALNE, Experimental organ grafting, immunological analysis and study of organ preservation	3000
A. C. CRAWFORD, Post-synaptic mechanisms at a glutamate synapse	4302
J. K. GRANT, An investigation of zinc and steroid hormone binding in human tissues involved in reproduction	1598
ELSIE M. WIDDOWSON, Are large amounts of linoleic acid harmful to infants and young animals?	4353
G. B. WARREN, Selected lipids seal membrane proteins in biological membranes	4614
D. J. CHIVERS and F. P. G. ALDRICH-BLAKE, Ecology and behaviour of Malayan forest primates	782
	£89 011

The first allocation of the Parliamentary Grant for Scientific Investigations during the year 1976 was as follows:

	£
J. F. JAMES, Passage of an eclipse shadow through the upper atmosphere	1300
D. H. MARTIN, Submillimetre-wave solar and atmospheric measurements from Gornergrat	533
B. W. DELF, Micro-structural studies of certain polymeric systems	2669.66
E. R. WOODING, Study of high density plasmas	8316
B. CLEAVER, Adiabatic thermal pressure coefficients of molten salts	1892
P. B. DAVIES, Far infrared laser paramagnetic resonance spectroscopy	5087
M. C. HOLMES, The rheological properties of lyotropic liquid crystals	270
P. JOHN, Study of the reactions of SiH_2 in the gas phase.	2260
J. MACMILLAN, Tailor-made gibberellins and analogues by microbiological transformation of appropriate substrates	4502
J. PANNELL, Polymerisation on macromolecular template and the preparation of new polymeric materials	up to 1500
B. RIDGE, Synthesis of model chromopeptides related to cytochrome *c*	288
K. SCHOFIELD and R. B. MOUDIE, Mechanisms of electrophilic aromatic substitutions and mechanisms of acyl transfers	2732

	£
M. L. SINNOTT, Mechanisms of action of glycosidases	4119
A. WILLIAMS, A study of elimination-addition mechanism of acyl transfer	1398
J. O. WILLIAMS, Photochemical and photophysical investigations on molecular crystals	3653
J. R. JORDAN, A comparative study of methods of implementing a correlation function	2310
R. D. WING, Undersea application of diesel engines	5000
G. S. BOULTON, P. N. CHROSTON and J. JARVIS, Sedimentation and late Quaternary history of a Western Scottish sea-loch	400
M. A. BUSSELL, Structure and petrology of the coastal batholith of Peru	1370
H. C. JENKYNS, Diatomite-evaporite relations in the Miocene of Sicily	245
H. G. READING, Geological fieldwork in Finnmark, north Norway, 1976	590
R. S. J. SPARKS and L. WILSON, Historic Plinian eruptions in Iceland	1420
F. C. STINTON, A study of recent and fossil fish otoliths	2550
B. G. J. UPTON, The petrology of Rodriguez Island, Western Indian Ocean	1650
W. B. WHALLEY, Investigation of quartz grain surface textures by scanning electron microscopy	1300
J. A. BRYANT, Properties and metabolism of reiterated DNA in *Pisum sativum L*	2666
SHEILA M. FRANCIS, The microfungi of palm and certain other hosts	1922
D. READ, Mycorrhiza and the nitrogen nutrition of plants	3160
P. F. WAREING and R. HORGAN, High performance liquid chromatography	2500
J. R. WITCOMBE, Genecology and genetic conservation in northern India	2000
EVA SANSOME, Cytological investigations in *Phytophthora*	900
N. P. ASHMOLE, Studies of terrestrial invertebrates in Los Tayos caves, Ecuador	475
P. J. S. BOADEN, Investigations of Northern Ireland's coastal water	3123
L. DAVIES, Entomological and botanical expedition to Iles Crozet (French sub-Antarctic)	2540
D. B. LEWIS, Oxygen requirements of burrowing lesser weever fish (*Trachinus vipera* cuv.)	794
J. G. PHILLIPS, The assessment of environmental stresses on homeostatic mechanisms in birds	3450
SARAH E. SOLOMON, A study of the histophysiology of the reproductive tract of *Chelonia mydas L*	1531
B. W. STADDON, Epidermal glands of Heteroptera	2749
C. H. CLARKE, Frameshift mutagenesis in bacteria and fission yeast	1125
R. B. CUNDALL, Fluorescence polarisation of cell membrane associated fluorochromes	5475
G. H. DODD, A photoaffinity method for studying the olfactory code	2710
B. J. EVERITT, Monoaminergic mechanisms in the sexual behaviour of primates	6750
J. O. FORFAR and N. R. BELTON, Vitamin D metabolism in pregnant women and newborn infants	3849
P. B. GARLAND and B. A. HADDOCK, Bacterial proton-translocating respiratory chains studied by dye laser photolysis	8348

C. F. PHELPS, Comparative biochemistry, physiology and evolution of Amazon fish haemoglobins	635
J. Z. YOUNG, 1. The statocysts of cephalopods 2. Regeneration of colour patterns in octopus 3. The memory system of octopus	2814
M. W. FOWLER and W. FERDINAND, Assimilation of inorganic nitrogen in plant cells	622
J. D. PYE, Comparative acoustic behaviour and auditory anatomy of bats	163
R. MILEDI, The analysis of 'noise' in nerve and muscle membranes, the averaging of signals, the measuring of various parameters of synaptic events, etc.	14 663
	£132 318.66

The second allocation of the Parliamentary Grant for Scientific Investigations during the year 1976 was as follows:

H. MCKERRELL, Archaeometric studies of ancient Greek and Cretan kilns	1530
S. K. RUNCORN, Pre-Cambrian palaeomagnetism and polar wandering	3000
J. B. HASTED, Ion-molecule reactions in the injected ion drift tube	4212
D. M. ADAMS, Raman spectroscopy at very high pressures	4369
P. CADMAN, (a) Reactions of highly energetic species; (b) Unimolecular reactions at high temperatures	4036
A. M. NORTH and R. A. PETHRICK, Molecular origins of sub-millimetre dielectric loss in polymeric materials	732
D. S. URCH, Soft X-ray excitation	6102
T. S. WEST and B. L. SHARP, Tunable dye lasers: their application in analytical atomic spectrometry	4957
T. E. ALLIBONE, Impulse breakdown of long gaps in air	100
P. E. BAKER, Rare earth element geochemistry in recent and Archaean volcanics	2500
W. W. BISHOP, Geological and palaeoenvironmental studies, lower Suguta valley, Kenya	4950
R. M. C. EAGER, North European Namurian and late Carboniferous-Permian non-marine Bivalvia	814
P. W. FRANCIS, Reconnaissance expedition to Sangay, Reventador and Sumaco volcanoes, Ecuador	2128
K. J. MILLER, Radio echo sounding of temperate glaciers	991
W. E. STEPHENS, Palaeomagnetism and geochemistry of igneous rocks forming the Seychelles Bank	895
A. J. COLVILL, Investigation into surging characteristics of Roslin Glacier	850
P D. COKER, The distribution of cryptogam communities on Höyrokampen, Böverdal, Norway	418
E. A. DREW, St Andrews University underwater research expedition to Malta, 1976	300
J. N. HEDGER, Padi straw mushroom (*Volvariella volvacea*) cultivation in Java	419
P. G. JARVIS, Photosynthesis and stomatal conductance of leaves in canopies	2608

	£
A. PENTECOST, Light intensity and epiphyte distribution in the tropical rain forest	115
F. ROSE, Study of lichen epiphyte vegetation in Norwegian hardwood forests	280
E. V. J. TANNER, Reproduction and regeneration in tropical montane forest, Jamaica	2125
S. R. J. WOODELL, Experimental ecology of a dioecious flowering plant.	2608
W. R. BRANCH, Karyosystematic studies on southern African reptiles	100
MARY J. BURGIS, A quantitative, seasonal study of the zooplankton in Lake Tanganyika	830
M. BURROWS, Neural integration by non-spiking interneurons in locust motor systems	5452
M. F. CLARIDGE, The ecology and behaviour of some European cicadas and grasshoppers	552
T. H. CLUTTON-BROCK, Contest strategies in red deer	793
M. J. DANIEL, Diurnal and tidal variations in the distribution and behaviour of littoral animals	470
C. H. FRY, Palaearctic-African bird migration through the eastern Mediterranean	1070
H. E. HINTON, Subsocial behaviour of bugs of the family Membracidae	577
R. D. MARTIN, Behaviour and ecology of the lesser bushbaby, *Galago senegalensis*	1715
J. RILEY, The taxonomy and systematics of the Pentastomida	350
K. E. L. SIMMONS, Biology of Brown Booby and sea-bird conservation at Ascension Island	1297
B. H. ANDERTON, Structural and functional studies on neurofilaments.	1000
R. B. BARLOW, Measurement of enthalpies of adsorption.	2000
D. H. BOXER, Radio-iodination to study orientation of respiratory enzymes in *E. coli*	6804
P. COHEN and PATRICIA T. W. COHEN, Molecular basis of phosphorylase kinase deficiency	1309
R. L. GARDNER, Analysis of early mammalian development by micro-surgical methods	3345
I. A. JOHNSTON, Compensatory adaptations in myofibrillar proteins for function at different temperatures	2412
C. T. JONES, The effect of blood supply on foetal metabolism and growth	4309
G. K RADDA, Positron annihilation in biological membranes	4875
M. SCRUTTON, Hypoxanthine production in normal and diseased human blood platelets	5753
R. N. P. SUTTON, Culture of brain cells from elderly human subjects.	1945
N. TUDBALL, The significance of L-cystathionine in mammalian brain.	3510
H. N. A. WILLCOX, The induction and differentiation of bone-marrow derived (B) lymphocytes	6789
	£108 296

APPENDIX I

PARLIAMENTARY GRANT FOR SCIENTIFIC PUBLICATIONS

The following grants and/or loans were authorized from the Parliamentary Grant for Scientific Publications (*from the Libraries Assistance Grant):

	£
Association of Natural History Societies in Cumbria	50
*British Lichen Society	120
*British Psychological Society	1000
British Society for the History of Science	200
Edinburgh Mathematical Society	500
Geological Society of Glasgow	1500
*Geological Society of London	1500
Palaeontological Association	1500
*Royal Entomological Society of London	750
*Royal Institution	2811
Wiltshire Archaeological and Natural History Society (Natural History Section)	200
	£10 131

APPENDIX J

PARLIAMENTARY GRANT FOR HISTORY OF SCIENCE

The following grants were authorized from the Parliamentary Grant for Research in the History of Science:

	£
S. BENNETT, The development of control engineering, 1920–1945	150
E. BOOTH, A history of the British seaweed industry (in six parts)	150
FRANCESCA BRAY, A comparative study of *padi*-cultivation techniques in Malaysia	600
S. T. BUCZACKI, The life and work of the Reverend M. J. Berkeley, F.R.S.	200
D. S. L. CARDWELL, The life and work of James Prescott Joule	200
A. C. CROMBIE, Galileo's scientific thought and its contemporary influence	150
JENNIFER A. DRAKE-BROCKMAN, The *perpetuum mobile* of Cornelius Drebbel	40
E. G. FORBES, Editing the correspondence of John Flamsteed, F.R.S., first Astronomer Royal	700
D. M. GAVINE, Astronomical activity in Scotland, c. 1745–1900	55
R. J. HARRISON, History of scientific research (significance, value, conclusions) on small cetaceans	300
N. LINGARD, Life and work of Sir Henry Enfield Roscoe, F.R.S.	150
D. M. A. MERCER, Friction, temperature and escapement errors in weight-driven regulator timepieces	400
J. B. MORRELL, The early British Association for the Advancement of Science	200
J. G. O'HARA, An historical survey of classical physics (research in libraries at Dublin, Cambridge and Leiden)	150
R. S. PORTER, The growth of geology in British universities	200
MAGDA WHITROW, *ISIS* Cumulative Bibliography, Volume 4	1000
	£4645

ORGANIZATION OF THE ROYAL SOCIETY OFFICE

The Executive Secretary is responsible to Council for conducting the Society's administrative business and is in charge of the office (see Statutes 52–58). He is assisted by the Deputy Executive Secretary and other members of the staff who number about 100. Dr R. W. J. Keay was appointed as Executive Secretary on 13 January 1977 following the death of Sir David Martin.

The office is divided into a number of sections headed by senior members of the staff (see p. 12). The main activities and the names of those members of the staff who deal with them are given below; their room numbers and telephone extensions are given at the end.

1. COUNCIL AND OFFICERS' BUSINESS
(a) COUNCIL BUSINESS

Agenda and minutes of Council, Council procedure, report of Council, appointment of representatives (other than delegates to international meetings), medals (other than S. G. Brown, Esso and Parsons), named lectures and prizes (Mr W. M. Malcolm).

S. G. Brown Award and Medal, Parsons Memorial Medal (Miss U. M. A. Maunsell).

Royal Society Esso Award (Mr P. Wigley).

Committee: Royal Society Mullard Award (Mr Malcolm), Royal Society Esso Award (Mr Wigley).

(b) OFFICERS' BUSINESS

Officers' meetings and other matters (Dr R. W. J. Keay).

Secretary to the President and the Executive Secretary: Miss D. P. Chapman
Secretary to the Deputy Executive Secretary: Miss C. A. Johnson.

(c) MEMBERSHIP OF COMMITTEES

Changes in membership of all committees (Miss Maunsell).

2. FELLOWS AND CANDIDATES

Personal records and photographs of Fellows, candidates for the Fellowship and Foreign Membership (Mr N. H. Robinson, Miss V. G. Hammill).

Committees: Sectional, General Candidates, Applied Sciences Candidates (Mr Robinson, Miss Hammill).

3. MEETINGS OF THE SOCIETY
(a) SCIENTIFIC MEETINGS

Arrangements for scientific meetings in the Society's regular programme (Mrs P. B. Carter, Mr W. G. Evans).

Committee: Hooke (Mrs Carter).

(b) BUSINESS MEETINGS
Ordinary Meetings, Special General Meetings, Anniversary Meetings (Mr W. M. Malcolm).

4. PUBLICATIONS
(a) EDITORIAL
Proceedings, Philosophical Transactions (Mr W. G. Evans).
Notes and Records (Mr N. H. Robinson).
Biographical Memoirs (Mr Evans, Mrs J. R. Lamb).
Year Book (Miss Maunsell).
Mathematical Tables (Mr Evans).
The Correspondence of Isaac Newton (Mr Robinson).
Non-serial publications (Mr C. R. Argent).
Committees: Newton Letters (Mr Robinson), Symbols (Mr Evans).

(b) DISTRIBUTION
Distribution, sales, stock (Mr J. H. Boreham, Mr R. G. Theobald).

(c) OTHER MATTERS
Scientific information services, Conference of Editors (Mr Robinson).
Committee: Scientific Information (Mr Robinson).

5. LIBRARY
Library, archives, portraits, antiquities, repository for standard weights and measures (Mr N. H. Robinson).
Committee: Library (Mr Robinson).

6. HOUSE MANAGEMENT
Upkeep of rooms, booking of rooms (including bedrooms), office routine services, printing and reproduction services, soirées, Anniversary Dinner (Mr J. H. Boreham), catering (Mrs J. Hutchinson).
Committee: Soirée (Mr Boreham).

7. ACCOUNTS
Accounts, trust funds, investments, audit, appeal, staff appointments, salaries and superannuation, estimates, rating grants (Mr N. A. W. Le Grand).
Committees: Audit, Investment Advisory, Finance (Mr Le Grand).

8. RESEARCH APPOINTMENTS
(a) SALARIED APPOINTMENTS
Rutherford Scholarships (Mr W. M. Malcolm).
Scientific Information Research Fellowships (Mr N. H. Robinson).
All research professors and other research fellows (Miss U. M. A. Maunsell).

Committees: Rutherford Memorial (Mr Malcolm), Scientific Information (Mr Robinson), Head Bequest, Medical Sciences Research, Bruno Mendel Fellowship, Armourers and Brasiers' Company Research Fellowship, Smithson Research Fund, Sorby Research Fund, Warren Research Fund (Miss Maunsell).

(b) BURSARIES AND SHORT TERM APPOINTMENTS

Rutherford Memorial Lecturer (Mr Malcolm).
Overseas Visiting Professors, Commonwealth Bursaries (Mr J. J. P. Deverill).
Leverhulme Studentships (Mr D. J. H. Griffin).
John Murray Studentships (Miss Maunsell).

Committees: Rutherford Memorial (Mr Malcolm), Overseas Visiting Professorships Subcommittee of the International Relations Committee, Royal Society Commonwealth Bursaries (Mr Deverill), Royal Society Leverhulme Studentships (Mr Griffin), Browne, Hill and Murray (Miss Maunsell).

9. GRANTS

(a) RESEARCH PROJECTS

Parliamentary Grant-in-aid (Scientific Investigations) and other funds.

Committees: Government Grant Boards, Expeditions, Paul Instrument Fund (Mr W. M. Malcolm), Browne, Hill and Murray, Tyndall Mining Bequest (Miss U. M. A. Maunsell), Gassiot (Mr P. Wigley), History of Science (Mr N. H. Robinson).

(b) PUBLICATIONS AND LIBRARIES

Parliamentary Grant-in-aid (Scientific Publications and also Libraries) (Mr Malcolm).

Committee: Scientific Publications Board (Mr Malcolm).

(c) TRAVEL AND MEETINGS

Parliamentary Grant-in-aid for travel and other funds (Miss B. M. de Vere).

Committee: Travelling Expenses (Miss de Vere).

10. INTERNATIONAL RELATIONS

(a) GENERAL

General policy, relations with overseas academies, relations with I.C.S.U., Unesco, and other international organizations and research stations, including the European Science Foundation (Dr R. W. J. Keay).

Committees: International Relations, British National Committee for I.C.S.U., Royal Society Unesco (Dr Keay), Naples Zoological Station (Miss U. M. A. Maunsell).

(b) BRITISH NATIONAL COMMITTEES (and related national activities)

Antarctic Research (Mr G. E. Hemmen)
Astronomy (Mr P. Wigley)
Biochemistry (Mrs R. Z. Bulsara)
Biology (Miss B. M. de Vere)
Biophysics (Mrs Bulsara)
Chemistry (Mrs Bulsara)
Crystallography (Mrs Bulsara)

Data for Science and Technology (Mr N. H. Robinson)
Geodesy and Geophysics (Mr C. R. Argent)
Geodynamics (Mr Argent)
Geography (Mr D. J. H. Griffin)
Geology (Mr Argent)
Global Atmospheric Research Programme (Mr Argent)
History of Science, Medicine and Technology (Mr Robinson)
Hydrological Sciences (Mr Argent)
International Centre of Insect Physiology and Ecology (Dr R. W. J. Keay)
International Geological Correlation Programme (Mr Argent)
International Institute for Applied Systems Analysis (Dr Keay, Mr P. R. Cooper)
Mathematics (Mr D. W. Harlow)
Nutritional Sciences (Miss de Vere)
Oceanic Research (Mr Hemmen)
Pharmacology (Miss de Vere)
Physics (Mr Harlow)
Physiological Sciences (Miss de Vere)
Problems of the Environment (Mrs Bulsara)
Radio Science (Mr Argent)
Solar-Terrestrial Physics (Mr Argent)
Space Research (Mr Wigley)
Theoretical and Applied Mechanics (Mr Harlow)

(c) WESTERN EUROPE AND ISRAEL

Fellowships, study visits and research conferences in the European Science Exchange Programme and the Royal Society–Israel Academy Programme (Miss N. Slow).

Committees: Fellowships Selection Subcommittee of the International Relations Committee (Miss Slow), *ad hoc* Space Science Committee of the European Science Foundation (Mr P. Wigley).

(d) EASTERN EUROPE

Exchange of lecturers and research workers under agreements with academies in Bulgaria, Czechoslovakia, Hungary, Poland, Romania, U.S.S.R. and Yugoslavia (Mr J. J. P. Deverill).

Incoming research workers from U.S.S.R. (Miss Slow).

(e) LATIN AMERICA

Fellowships, study visits, etc., in the Royal Society Latin American Programme (Mr Deverill).

(f) CHINA, INDIA, JAPAN AND MIDDLE EAST (EXCEPT ISRAEL)

Fellowships, study visits, etc. (Mr Deverill).

(g) EXPEDITIONS AND THE ROYAL SOCIETY ALDABRA RESEARCH STATION

Expeditions mounted by the Royal Society (Mr Hemmen).

(Note that applications for grants towards other expeditions are considered under Grants for Research Projects (q.v.).

Committees: Aldabra Research, (Mr Griffin), Southern Zone Research (including Pacific Science), Volcanological and Seismological Research (Mr Hemmen), Etna Research (Mr Argent).

11. **EDUCATIONAL ACTIVITIES**

Scientific Research in Schools (Mr N. A. W. Le Grand). Other educational matters, including metrication in schools (Mr D. W. Harlow).

ORGANIZATION OF THE ROYAL SOCIETY OFFICE 389

Committees: Education (Standing), Biological Education, Chemical Education, Engineering Education, Mathematical Education, Physics Education (Mr Harlow), Scientific Research in Schools (Mr Le Grand).

12. STUDY GROUPS
Long Term Toxic Effects (Mrs R. Z. Bulsara).
Pollution in the Atmosphere (Mrs Bulsara).

13. OTHER ACTIVITIES
Industrial Activities Committee (Mr P. Wigley).
Scientific Relief Committee (Miss U. M. A. Maunsell).
Ordnance Survey Committee (Mr D. J. H. Griffin).
Space Ranging Research Committee (Mr C. R. Argent).
Coordination of information about Royal Society activities and press relations (Mr P. R. Cooper).

Room numbers and telephone extensions of staff mentioned on pages 385–389:

Room Number	Name	Telephone extension
319	Argent, Mr C. R.	249
213	Boreham, Mr J. H.	226
316	Bulsara, Mrs R. Z.	288
326	Carter, Mrs P. B.	278
112	Chapman, Miss D. P.	279
	President's business	201
	Executive Secretary's business	200
306	Cooper, P. R.	242
206	de Vere, Miss B. M.	222
228	Deverill, Mr J. J. P.	262
218	Evans, Mr W. G.	276
314	Griffin, Mr D. J. H.	286
120	Hammill, Miss V. G.	215
325	Harlow, Mr D. W.	266
313	Hemmen, Mr G. E.	245
B30	Hutchinson, Mrs J.	213
103	Johnson, Miss C. A.	202
113	Keay, Dr R. W. J.	200
216	Lamb, Mrs J. R.	229
215	Le Grand, Mr N. A. W.	228
202	Malcolm, Mr W. M.	219
204	Maunsell, Miss U. M. A.	221
117	Robinson, Mr N. H.	261
201a	Slow, Miss N.	218
304a	Theobald, Mr R. G.	240
322	Wigley, Mr P.	205

December 1976

ACCOUNTS OF THE ROYAL SOCIETY

	PAGE
GENERAL PURPOSES ACCOUNTS	392
RESEARCH FUNDS	394
SPECIAL FUNDS	397
PARLIAMENTARY GRANT	399
WARREN RESEARCH FUND	401

NOTE BY THE TREASURER ON 1975-76 ACCOUNTS

Summarized accounts for the year to 31 August 1976 are set out in the following pages. The General Purposes accounts on the first two pages are followed by research and special trust funds, Parliamentary grant and Warren Research Fund. It should be noted that the closing balances on certain trust funds include commitments made in the year 1975-76 but not paid by 31 August.

The General Purposes account has been balanced by the transfer of accumulated income from trust funds which may be utilized in this manner, together with the income arising from the new Appeal Fund. Contributions to the Appeal Fund continue to be added to the capital of the fund and it is my hope that this practice can be continued in order to create the income required to help balance the Society's accounts. Detailed scrutiny of running costs continues in order to contain the impact of inflation.

It proved necessary to increase the subscription rates of the Society's publications during the year to offset the rapid escalation of costs. There has been some loss of subscribers, due no doubt to the general pressure on library budgets, particularly in academic institutions.

The increased cost of fellowships and studentships has outstripped the growth of income of many trust funds and fewer appointments can be funded from these sources. The decline in numbers of research workers in post at a given time due to this problem has been offset to some extent by limited term funds from a number of Companies and Foundations. The Society is indebted to these bodies for their interest and support.

ACCOUNTS OF THE ROYAL SOCIETY
For the year ended 31 August 1976
GENERAL PURPOSES ACCOUNTS 1975–76
STATEMENT OF BALANCES—31 AUGUST 1976

1975		1975	
	General Purposes Account:		Investments at Market Value—
			General Purposes Account—
755 180	Capital Fund	£755 500	£754 525
306 783	General Reserve Fund	311 027	311 044
257 233	Appeal Fund	496 360	27 649
28 644	Library Fund	28 278	495 801
33 672	Repairs and Maintenance Account	48 392	87 695
13 592	General Reserve Income Account	32 472	12 605
163 740	Sundry Creditors	191 502	222 083
184 654	Appeal Account	50 655	2 113
2 608	Library Account		2 146
554	Euchem Conferences	1 475	
			752 347
			306 764
			28 016
			267 799
			81 778
			13 627
			301 871
			1 544
			7 086 (dr) Robert Fleming and Co. Ltd
1 746 660		1 915 661	1 746 660
2 707	British National Committee for Chemistry	2 916	11 333 Balances at Bank
8 626	Florey Fund	3 340	1 915 661
			6 256
£1 757 993		£1 921 917	£1 757 993	£1 921 917

GENERAL PURPOSES CAPITAL ACCOUNT

	RECEIPTS			PAYMENTS	
1 718	Balance, 1 September 1975	£2 832	284 130	Purchase of investments	£235 427
375	Composition fees	1 078	2 832	Balance, 31 August 1976	975
281 169	Sale of investments	232 492			
3 700	T. A. Common: part bequest	—			
£286 962		£286 402	£286 962		£236 402

APPEAL CAPITAL ACCOUNT

249 000	Transfer from Appeal Account	£200 000	259 566	Balance, 1 September 1975	£10 566
10 566	Sale of investments	394 407		Purchase of investments	583 282
	Balance, 31 August 1975	—		Balance, 31 August 1976	559
£259 566		£594 407	£259 566		£594 407

393

APPEAL ACCOUNT

1975				1975	
40 702	Balance, 1 September 1975	£184 654			Fleming's advisory fee	£87
382 704	Donations	49 124			Transfers to:	
10 248	Income tax recovered, deeds of covenant	16 964		249 000	Appeal Capital Account	200 000
17 029	Dividends/Interest	46 832		17 029	Income and Expenditure Account	46 832
				184 654	Balance, 31 August 1976	50 655
£450 683		£297 574		£450 683		£297 574

REPAIRS AND MAINTENANCE ACCOUNT

1975				1975		
22 642	Balance, 1 September 1975	£33 672		1 970	Repairs	£1 280
3 000	Transfer from General Purposes Account	6 000		33 672	Balance, 31 August 1976	48 392
10 000	Contribution from H.M.G.	10 000				
£35 642		£49 672		£35 642		£49 672

INCOME AND EXPENDITURE
(including Publications and Library)
GENERAL PURPOSES

	INCOME				EXPENDITURE	
14 040	Fees	£14 630		172 221	Establishment charges	£177 024
117 009	Dividends, etc.	102 851		347 680	Stipends and pensions, etc.	446 506
189 931	Contribution to administration from sundry funds	223 300			Publications:	
41 000	Contribution from H.M.G. for rent	41 000		260 809	Printing, paper and distribution, etc.	331 506
329 789	Publications sales	438 940			Library:	
38 946	Catering sales	42 778		6 630	Binding, books, periodicals, etc.	3 857
6 744	Other receipts	8 549		24 927	Catering purchases	23 211
77 808	Transfers	116 056		3 000	Transfer	6 000
£815 267		£988 104		£815 267		£988 104

GENERAL RESERVE FUND INCOME ACCOUNT

	RECEIPTS				PAYMENTS	
31 736	Balance, 1 September 1975	£13 592		263	Fleming's advisory fee	310
21 231	Dividends, etc.	18 651		—	Corporation tax on Underwriting Commission	226
599	Underwriting Commission	765			Transfers to:	
				30 000	General Reserve Capital account	—
				9 711	Income and Expenditure account	—
				13 592	Balance, 31 August 1976	32 472
£53 566		£33 008		£53 566		£33 008

RESEARCH FUNDS 1975-76

With the exception of those marked (S), which are specifically invested, and (P2)—Consolidated Investment Pool No. 2—the investments and invested income of the funds form part of Consolidated Investment Pool No. 1.

FUNDS	Balances in hand 1 Sept. 1975	RECEIPTS Dividends and Income Tax Recovered	RECEIPTS Other	RECEIPTS Transfers	PAYMENTS Administration Contribution	PAYMENTS Grants etc.	PAYMENTS Purchase of Investments	PAYMENTS Transfers	Balances in hand 31 Aug. 1976	INVESTMENTS AND CAPITAL CASH Market Value 31 Aug. 1975	INVESTMENTS AND CAPITAL CASH Additions and Sales during year	INVESTMENTS AND CAPITAL CASH Market Value 31 Aug. 1976	RESERVE FUNDS (INVESTED INCOME) Market Value 31 Aug. 1975	RESERVE FUNDS (INVESTED INCOME) Additions and Sales during year	RESERVE FUNDS (INVESTED INCOME) Market Value 31 Aug. 1976
£	£	£	£	£	£	£	£	£	£	£	£	£	£	£	£
General															
Forsyth (P2)	11 192	3 139			28	8 108			14 303	51 051		51 878			
Locke (P2)	14 662	7 938			100			13 949	14 492	140 469		142 747	11 179		11 361
Messel (P2)	12 288									201 740		205 011			
Yarrow (P2)	1 761	4 520						4 520		87 116		88 529			
Specific															
Beringer	1 193*	1 449				2 009			256	17 232		17 670	6 279		6 439
Browne	534*	2 665	45			308			167	39 848		40 861	3 377		3 463
Conway	4 433	308	28 959		2 557	24 178			6 657	4 991		5 119			
Ernest Cook															
Courtauld's Educational Trust	9 849				183	1 830			7 836						
Cumulative Research (Anon.) (S)	230	2 441				258	2 595		76	45 349	2 595	48 032	2 186		2 242
Darwin	179	255							176	4 138		4 243			
Dewrance, Donation and Jodrell	343*	968				642			150	13 524		13 868			
Fleck	628	554	167		68	154			960						
Florey (P2)	673	3 419	7 501			3 545	5 048		3 000	56 753	2 305	59 234	10 183	3 432	13 687
Folley (P2)	280	114	9 750			280	9 750		114		9 750	9 750			
Forsyth Annuity (S)	38	163				163			38	1 850		1 800			
Foulerton Gift	37 322	10 158				13 018			34 462	117 712		120 707	20 311		20 828
Gassiot	5 203	2 241				1 502			5 942	23 951		24 560	8 672		8 893
General Research (Pool 1 and (S)		688				688				11 161		11 444			
George (S)	769	846			21	165		12 985	1 594	12 720		13 518	897		920
	(P2) 8 662	4 352	3 194		29	100	3 194		139	75 227	3 194	79 404			
Gore	126	178							57	2 883		2 957			
Gunning	89	68						103		1 104		1 132			
Handley	1 271	402				250			1 320	5 550		5 691			
Carried forward	£95 297	£59 154	£49 616		£2 986	£57 198	£20 587	£31 557	£91 739	£914 369	£17 844	£948 155	£63 084	£3 432	£67 833

*Overdrawn

RESEARCH FUNDS 1975-76

With the exception of those marked (S), which are specifically invested, and (P2)—Consolidated Investment Pool No. 2—the investments and invested income of the funds form part of Consolidated Investment Pool No. 1.

Funds	Balances in hand 1 Sept 1975	Receipts			Payments				Balances in hand 31 Aug 1976	Investments and Capital Cash			Reserve Funds (Invested Income)		
		Dividends and Income Tax Recovered	Other	Transfers	Administration Contribution	Grants etc.	Purchase of Investments	Transfers		Market Value 31 Aug. 1975	Additions and *Sales* during year	Market Value 31 Aug. 1976	Market Value 31 Aug. 1975	Additions and *Sales* during year	Market Value 31 Aug. 1976
	£	£	£	£	£	£	£	£	£	£	£	£	£	£	£
Brought forward	95 297	59 154	49 616		2 986	57 198	20 587	31 557	91 739	914 369	17 844	948 155	63 184	3 432	67 833
Specific (continued)															
Head	10 156	5 019				5 159			10 016	67 896		69 623	6 148		6 305
Maurice Hill (P2)	5 276	1 606	616		7	297	568		6 626	30 826	568	31 848			
Jaffé (S)	22 974	21 193			2 372	26 130			15 665	304 782		314 173	15 418		16 417
E. Alan Johnston		715						715		10 105		10 362	1 503		1 541
Joule		174						174		2 816		2 887			
Lawrence		383						383		4 384		4 496	1 828		1 874
R.S./Leverhulme Studentships	400		16 549		1 500	10 325			5 124						
Leverhulme/China Academy															
Mackinnon	190	887	3 300		300	895			2 295						
Le Marquand and Bigg (S)	2 351			216		1 000			2 454	12 707		13 030			
Medical Research (P2)	8 509	5 444			472	3 600			9 881	47 924		49 143			
Mendel	8 949	3 359							12 308	78 104		79 370			
Mond	7 171	4 357				5 006			6 522			58 725	6 169		6 326
Moseley	1 335	3 911		1 098		1 080			37	57 268		18 517	6 423		6 587
John Murray	5 724	1 769				940			8 591	18 058		21 084	1 677		1 719
Napier	1 317	1 431				17 641			1 808	20 561		295 199			
Naples Zoological Station	36 395	19 371	4 235	1 316		4 375			38 125	287 876					
									1 176						
Patterson (P2)	3 305	732				13 755			4 037	14 084		14 312			
Pedler	928	308				4 913			1 236	5 011		5 139			
Pickering (P2)	27 668	13 319	6 913		691	1 379			27 232	233 127		236 908			
Radcliffe Trust			1 000		917	2 286		19 986	1 309						
Reckitt (S)	12 216	10 181	2 200		446	15	2 200		1 115	237 777	2 200	250 673			
Rosenheim (P2)	8 487	3 552							9 307	54 910		58 286			
Rosse		15								245		251			
Carried forward	£258 648	£156 880	£84 429	£2 630	£9 691	£155 994	£23 355	£56 944	£256 603	£2402 830	£20 612	£2482 181	£102 250	£3 432	£108 602

* Overdrawn

RESEARCH FUNDS 1975-76

With the exception of those marked (S), which are specifically invested, and (P2)—Consolidated Investment Pool No. 2—the investments and invested income of the funds form part of Consolidated Investment Pool No. 1.

FUNDS	Balances in hand 1 Sept. 1975	RECEIPTS			PAYMENTS				Balances in hand 31 Aug. 1976	INVESTMENTS AND CAPITAL CASH			RESERVE FUNDS (INVESTED INCOME)		
		Dividends and Income Tax Recovered	Other	Transfers	Administration Contribution	Grants etc.	Purchase of Investments	Transfers		Market Value 31 Aug. 1975	Additions and *Sales* during year	Market Value 31 Aug. 1976	Market Value 31 Aug. 1975	Additions and *Sales* during year	Market Value 31 Aug. 1976
	£	£	£	£	£	£	£	£	£	£	£	£	£	£	£
Brought forward															
Rutherford Memorial	258 648	156 880	84 429	2 630	9 691	155 994	23 355	56 944	256 603	2 402 830	20 612	2 482 181	102 250	3 432	108 602
Sadgrove . . . (P2)	4 769	5 899	550		45	8 149			3 024	92 199		94 545			
J. Sainsbury . . .	3 225	1 598			67	16 017		4 756	1 452	30 655		31 152			
Scientific Exchanges (Anon.)	2 323		16 818		1 672	19 232			3 531						
Scott	14 686		10 000		1 923			42	9 767	678		696			
Smithson	12 683	2 807				5 723			1 439*	29 944		30 706	6 594		6 762
Sorby	1 959*	1 382				862			5 155	16 866		17 295	5 552		5 693
Stothert . . . (S)	4 638	5 255	560		475	4 263	560		2 122	55 213		60 916	6 077		6 561
Studd	1 497	1 125						500	573	18 250		81 714			
Tomes	417	156							119	2 521		2 585			
Tyndall	1 627	118				1 626				1 901		1 949			
R.S. and Commonwealth Foundation Bursaries Scheme	5 218		8 000			11 092			2 126						
R.S. and Nuffield Foundation Commonwealth Bursaries Scheme	10 845		19 135	15 555		28 640			16 895						
R.S./Israel Academy Scientific Exchanges	1 485		8 800		210	7 650			2 425						
R.S./Leverhulme Visiting Professorships	989		10 491		500	13			10 967						
R.S./Inter-University Council Visiting Professorships	11 100				1 041	10 412			353*						
Unilever/Brazilian Programme			4 000		750	675			2 575						
Wates Foundation (Egypt)	2 571		5 000		244	2 442			4 885						
Wates IUPAC			3 000		500	1 035			1 465						
James Weir Foundation	1 299		4 320		432	3 395			1 792						
Wellcome	373*	11 663	75 000			9 867	75 000		1 423	102 484	75 000	172 542			
Wolfson	2 213	16 044			1 710	14 075			2 472						
Totals	£337 901	£202 969	£250 103	£18 185	£19 260	£301 162	£98 915	£62 242	£327 579	£2 753 541	£95 612	£2 913 281	£120 473	£3 432	£127 618

* Overdrawn

SPECIAL FUNDS 1975-76

With the exception of those marked (S), which are specifically invested, and (P2)—Consolidated Investment Pool No. 2—the investments and invested income of the funds form part of Consolidated Investment Pool No. 1.

Funds	Balances in hand 1 Sept. 1975	Receipts			Payments				Balances in hand 31 Aug. 1976	Investments and Capital Cash			Reserve Funds (Invested Income)		
		Dividends and Income Tax Recovered	Other	Transfers	Administration Contribution	Grants etc.	Purchase of Investments	Transfers		Market Value 31 Aug 1975	Additions and *Sales* during year	Market Value 31 Aug. 1976	Market Value 31 Aug. 1975	Additions and *Sales* during year	Market Value 31 Aug. 1976
	£	£	£	£	£	£	£	£	£	£	£	£	£	£	£
Specific															
Arundel	7 812	571				989	4 450	571	3 727	9 258	4 450	9 493			
Botanical Congress	104	1 354				25			102	12 339		17 216			
Brady	368	23							404	366		375			
Church	1 329	719				1 639			409	581		596			
Curl	7	117				130			6*						
Embossed Scientific Books										1 898		1 946			
Federal Council of Chemistry	276	60							336						
Fee Reduction (Publication)		947						947		971		996			
Gassiot Committee:										15 358		15 749			
Ministry of Defence	89		6 028		252	6 512			647*						
Geographical Congress	2 310	1 08.	371		23	2 926			815						
International Institute for Applied Systems Analysis	3 668		102 558		2 984	103 151			91	15 862		16 266			
Keck and Knowles (P2)	288	52			2	65		52	355	850		872			
Optics		69								1 333		1 354			
Parsons Memorial	7	60							2	973		998			
Pension		1 159						1 159		18 793		19 271			
Petavel		1 918				1 275		643		31 106		31 897			
Royal Society:															
General Travel	1 804	1 114				807			2 111	15 150		15 535	2 310		2 985
Travel for Non-Fellows and L. J. Mordell Travel (P2)	2 276	1 597				1 180			2 693	28 965		29 435	1 827		1 856
Scientific Radio (S)	1 248	459							1 666	6 166		6 345			
Scientific Relief	1 998	7 735		2 439	41	11 931	5 000		4 759*	62 092		63 671	61 080	5 000	67 130
Scientific Research in Schools	4 853		1 680			1 355			5 178						
Simonsen	321	3 178	77				321	3 255		15 541	32 321	49 080			
Stead		4 879						4 879		79 021		81 031			
Travel Expenses Schuster		261						261		4 238		4 346			
Carried forward	£28 758	£27 391	£10 714	£2 439	£3 302	£131 985	£9 771	£11 767	£12 477	£320 861	£36 771	£366 472	£65 817	£5 000	£71 971

*Overdrawn

SPECIAL FUNDS 1975-76

With the exception of those marked (S), which are specifically invested, and (P2)—Consolidated Investment Pool No. 2—the investments and invested income of the funds form part of Consolidated Investment Pool No. 1.

Funds	Balances in hand 1 Sept. 1975	Receipts			Payments			Balances in hand 31 Aug. 1976	Investments and Capital Cash			Reserve Funds (Invested Income)		
		Dividends and Income Tax Recovered	Other	Transfers	Administration Contribution	Grants etc.	Purchase of Investments	Transfers		Market Value 31 Aug. 1975	Additions and *Sales* during year	Market Value 31 Aug. 1976	Market Value 31 Aug. 1975	Additions and *Sales* during year	Market Value 31 Aug. 1976
	£	£	£	£	£	£	£	£	£	£	£	£	£	£	£
Brought forward	28 758	27 391	110 714	2 439	3 302	131 985	9 771	11 767	12 477	320 861	36 771	366 472	65 817	5 000	71 971
Specific (continued)															
Wintringham		39				39				633		649			
Medal															
S. G. Brown	407	108	98		5	199			409	1 752		1 796			
Buchanan	26	12		209					38	190		194			
Davy		35				244				567		581			
Esso			1 680		680	1 000									
Hughes (P2)		183				239			536	2 973		3 049			
Mullard	1 348*	829	2 450	56	243	1 152			78	15 961		16 220			
Rumford		78								1 266		1 298			
Sylvester	32	30							62	485		497			
Lecture															
Bakerian and Copley	276	68		103		171			384	1 098		2 116			
Bernal (P2)	19	108							3	2 082		2 116			
Croonian (S)	187	51			7	60			240	793		956			
Ferrier		53								863		885			
George Gabb		35				200				574		589			
Clifford Paterson (P2)	1 675	81	2 450	165			1 675		2 531		1 675	1 702			
Wilkins	56	32							88	527		541			
Totals	£30 088	£29 133	£117 392	£2 972	£4 237	£135 289	£11 446	£11 767	£16 846	£350 625	£38 446	£398 672	£65 817	£5 000	£71 971

* Overdrawn

SUMMARY OF MARKET VALUES AT 31 AUGUST 1976

	Pool No. 1	Pool No. 2	Specific	Cash	Total
	£	£	£	£	£
Research funds	1 283 963	1 040 393	710 033	6 510	3 040 899
Special funds	410 659	52 683	7 301	—	470 643
	£1 694 622	£1 093 076	£717 334	£6 510	£3 511 542

PARLIAMENTARY GRANT 1975-76

Grants	Balances in hand 1 Sept. 1975	Receipts: Grants received	Receipts: Other	Payments: Grants Paid	Payments: Transfers	Balances in hand 31 Aug. 1976
	£	£	£	£	£	£
Aldabra Research Station		61 775		61 775		
Committee travel		11 185		11 185		
Delegates' travel	484*	15 355	574	15 353		92
History of science		18 000	366	18 345		21
International Fellowships: Europe	3 947*	363 973	4 156	366 802	1 000	2 620*
East Europe	471	11 906	7 287	18 835		171*
Israel	323	12 300		11 390		1 233
Japan	531*	42 765		42 912		49
Latin America	1 515	26 105	727	27 290		330
Commonwealth bursaries		15 555			15 555	
International meetings in U.K.	8 763	28 285	4 524	41 157		415
International Seismological Centre		23 500		23 500		
Libraries assistance		8 225		8 206		19
Rating assistance		46 000		46 000		
Relations with overseas academies	257*	14 700		11 361		3 082
Rent and repairs, 6-9 Carlton House Terrace		51 000			51 000	
Reports and international relations library		6 155			6 155	
Royal Society Research Professorships		164 660		164 546		71
S.C.I.B.P. office rent	43*	1 000		900		179
Science/technology/education	79	26 950	100	28 259		67
Scientific Information Fellowships	1 276	9 550		9 440		115
Scientific investigations	5	318 740	4 391	319 265		2 762
Scientific publications	1 104*	1 350	1 667	2 450		1 367
Scott Polar Research Institute	800	12 000		12 000		
Study groups	312	2 400		2 418		294
Subscriptions to International Unions	4	103 259		103 230		33
Travel grants	4 487	183 810	2 781	191 598		520*
Contribution towards operating costs		165 172			165 172	
Deposit interest	1 232		1 849		810	2 271
Totals	£12 901	£1 745 675	£28 422	£1 538 217	£239 692	£9 089

* Overdrawn

The detailed accounts of the Society, of which the foregoing is a summary, are available for inspection by Fellows. Such accounts were duly audited and the reports of the Auditors thereon are as follows:

We have audited the above accounts and have found them to be in accordance with the Society's books and vouchers and with the explanations given to us by the Society's officers and we accordingly certify that, to the best of our knowledge and belief, they are correct. The bank balances have been certified to us by the Society's bankers and we have received verifications from the appropriate banks that the securities were held by them in the name of the Society or their nominees at 31 August 1976.

KNIGHTWAY HOUSE,
20 SOHO SQUARE,
LONDON, W1V 6QJ.

Signed
NORTON KEEN & CO., *Chartered Accountants*
PROFESSIONAL AUDITORS

We, the undersigned, being members of the Committee duly appointed under Chapter VIII, Statute 46, of the Statutes of the Royal Society, to audit the accounts of the Treasurer for the year ended 31 August 1976, hereby report that we have examined the accounts relating to:

(*a*) General Purposes; (*b*) Research Funds; (*c*) Special Funds; (*d*) Parliamentary Grant

and have obtained all the information and explanations we have required. The accounts have been audited in detail by Messrs Norton Keen & Co., Chartered Accountants, the professional auditors, who have also verified the securities and bank balances and have certified accordingly.

Signed

B. KATZ
J. H. WILKINSON
J. SUTTON
} *On the part of Council* HONORARY AUDITORS.

Signed

J. S. KENNEDY
W. C. PRICE
E. S. ANDERSON
} *On the part of the Society.* HONORARY AUDITORS.

26 November 1976

WARREN RESEARCH FUND 1975-76

Balance in hand 1 Sept. 1975	Receipts		Payments		Balance in hand 31 Aug. 1976	Investments and Capital Cash			Reserve Funds (Invested Income)		
	Dividends and Income Tax Recovered	Other	Administration Contribution	Grants etc.		Market Value 31 Aug. 1975	Additions and *Sales* during year	Market Value 31 Aug. 1976	Market Value 31 Aug. 1975	Additions and *Sales* during year	Market Value 31 Aug. 1976
£ 22 714	£ 18 685	£	£ 1 984	£ 9 439	£ 29 976	£ 250 468	£	£ 267 327	£ 5 320	£	£ 5 226

We have audited the accounts of the Warren Research Fund and certify them to be in accordance with the books and vouchers of the Fund. We have verified the investments and the bank balances.

KNIGHTWAY HOUSE,
20 SOHO SQUARE,
LONDON, W1V 6QJ
26 *November* 1976

Signed:
NORTON KEEN & CO.,
Chartered Accountants.

INDEX

	PAGE
Abstracts, Length of (S.O. 33)	193
Abstracts, Publication of (S.O. 45)	195
Accounts (Royal Society office)	386
Accounts of the Society	391
Accounts of the Society, Statutes	170
Address, postal	8
Admission Money, Statutes	170
Admission of Fellows, Statutes	160
Advisory Board for the Research Councils, Biology Research Committee (Council Report)	279
Agreements on cooperation with other scientific academies and research councils	256
Agricultural Research Council, Assessor	157
Aldabra (Council Report)	277
Aldabra Research Committee	114
Aldabra Research Station Account	399
Algae and Protozoa Culture Centre Steering Committee, representative	157
Anniversary Dinner (Council Report)	298
Anniversary Dinner (Royal Society office)	386
Anniversary Meeting, Quorum	185
Anniversary Meeting, Statutes	178
Annual Contribution, Consequences of non-payment, Statutes	170
Annual Contribution of Fellows, Statutes	170
Anonymous Fund (*see* Medical Research Fund)	
Antarctic Research, National Committee	150
Appeal (Council Report)	295
Appeal Account	393
Applied Sciences Candidates Committee	113
Archives of the Society, Statutes	182
Argentina, Agreement on exchanges	256
Armourers and Brasiers' Company Fellowship Committee	122
Armourers and Brasiers' Research Fellow	269
Arundel Library Fund	244
Arundel Library Fund Account	397
Aslib Council, representative	157
Aslib, International Relations Committee, representative	157
Associate Editors	107
Associate Editors, appointment of (Standing Orders)	192
Aston University Convocation, representative	157
Astronomy, National Committee	137
Astronomy, Space and Radio Board, representatives	162
Auditors, Statutes	174
Auditors' Report	400
Bakerian Fund Account	398
Bakerian Lecture	213
Balances, Summary of, General Purposes Account	392
Bath University Court, representative	157
Bedford Fund (*see* General Research Fund)	
Benefactions to the Society, Memorandum	10
Bequests and Gifts (Council Report)	295

	PAGE
Beringer Research Fellow	267
Beringer Research Fund	281, 394
Bernal Lecture	215
Bernal Lecture Fund Account	398
Biochemistry, National Committee	137
Biological Council, observer	157
Biological Council's Coordinating Committee for Symposia on Drug Action, representative	157
Biological Education Committee	122
Biological Information: Joint Institute of Biology/Biological Council/ Aslib Committee, representative	157
Biology, National Committee	138
Biophysics, National Committee	140
Bird Preservation, International Council, representatives	160
Birmingham University Court, representative	157
Booking of rooms (Royal Society office)	386
Books and Papers, Statutes	181
Botanical Congress Fund	244
Botanical Congress Fund Account	397
Bradford University Court, representative	157
Brady Fund	244
Brady Fund Account	397
Bragg Lecture Fund Committee, representative	157
Brazil, Agreement on exchanges	256
Bristol University Court, representative	157
British Academy (Council Report)	278
British Academy, Committee for the study of the conservation of medieval stained glass, representatives	157
British Academy, Committee on cheaper methods of book production, representative	158
British Academy, National Committee for the Philosophy of Science, representatives	158
British Association, General Committee, representatives	158
British Broadcasting Corporation (consultative group), representative	158
British Council committees, representatives	158
British Heart Foundation, Science Committee, representative	158
British Library Board, Advisory Council, representatives	158
British Museum: National Reference Library for Science and Invention Committee, representative	158
British Museum, Trustee	158
British Museum (Natural History), Trustee	158
British National Bibliography, representative on Council	158
British National Committees	136
British Nutrition Foundation, representatives	158
British Standards Institution, Committee, representative	158
Brown Fund	244
Brown Fund Account	398
Browne Fund	221
Browne Fund Account	394
Browne, Hill and Murray Committee	114
Bruno Mendel Fellow	268
Bruno Mendel Fellowship Committee	118

	PAGE
Bruno Mendel Fellowship Fund	228
Bruno Mendel Fellowship Fund Account	395
Buchanan Fund Account	398
Buchanan Medal, Conditions of Award	208
Bulgarian Academy of Sciences, Agreement	256
Bureau of Hygiene and Tropical Diseases, representative	158
Caird and Scott Fund (*see* Scott Fund)	
Calendar for 1977	11
Cambridge University Committee for Geodesy and Geophysics, representative	158
Cancer Research Campaign, representatives	158

CANDIDATES FOR FELLOWSHIP—

Certificates, Renewal of, Statutes	166
Certificates, Statutes	164
Council to select	165
Date for receiving proposals	165
Date of Election, Statutes	166
Elected	106
Election Procedure	166
List to be printed	165
Proposers and Seconders, Statutes	165
Quorum of Council for Selection	185
Renewal of Candidature	166
Royal Society office	385
Selected names to be announced	167
Charities Aid Foundation, Council, representatives	159
Charles Darwin Foundation, representative	159
Charter Book, Statutes	181
Charterhouse (School), Governor	159
Chelsea Physic Garden, representative	159
Chemical Education Committee	123
Chemistry National Committee	140
China, Agreement on exchanges	256
China (Council Report)	290
China, exchanges (Royal Society office)	388
Christ's Hospital, Governor	159
Church Fund	245
Church Fund Account	397
City and Guilds of London Institute, President, a Governor	157
City and Guilds of London Institute, representatives	159
City University Court, representative	159
Clifford Paterson Lecture	215
Committees, Royal Society office organization	385–389
Committees, standing orders	108

COMMITTEES—

Aldabra Research	114
Antarctic Research, National	156
Applied Sciences Candidates	113
Armourers and Brasiers' Company Research Fellowship	122
Astronomy, National	137

COMMITTEES—continued

	PAGE
Biochemistry, National	137
Biological Education	122
Biology, National	138
Biophysics, National	140
British National	136
Browne, Hill and Murray	114
Bruno Mendel Fellowship	118
Chemical Education	123
Chemistry, National	140
Commonwealth Bursaries	125
Crystallography, National	141
Data for Science and Technology, National	150
Education	115
Esso Award	119
Expeditions	115
Finance	115
Gassiot	115
General Candidates	113
Geodesy and Geophysics, National	142
Geodynamics, National	151
Geography, National	144
Geology, National	145
Global Atmospheric Research Programme, National	154
Government Grant Boards	129
Head Bequest	116
History of Science, National	146
Hooke	116
Hydrological Sciences, National	154
Industrial Activities	116
International Centre of Insect Physiology and Ecology, National	154
International Council of Scientific Unions, National	136
International Geological Correlation Programme, National	155
International Institute for Applied Systems Analysis, National	155
International Relations	116
Investment Advisory	117
Joint Committees	122
Library	117
Mathematical Education	123
Mathematics, National	146
Medical Sciences Research	119
Mendel Fellowship	118
Naples Zoological Station	124
National Committees	136
Newton Letters	118
Nutritional Sciences, National	147
Oceanic Research, National	151
Ordnance Survey	118
Papers	179, 196
Paul Instrument Fund	124
Pharmacology, National	147
Physics Education	125
Physics, National	148

INDEX 407

COMMITTEES—*continued*   PAGE
    Physiological Sciences, National 148
    Problems of the Environment, National 152
    Radio Science, National 149
    Royal Society Commonwealth Bursaries 125
    Royal Society Leverhulme Studentships 119
    Royal Society Mullard Award 119
    Royal Society Unesco 126
    Rutherford Memorial 119
    Scientific Information 120
    Scientific Publications Board 130
    Scientific Relief 120
    Scientific Research in Schools 126
    Sectional 110
    Sectional, Quorum 190
    Sectional, Standing Orders 188
    Smithson Research Fund 127
    Soirée 120
    Solar-Terrestrial Physics, National 152
    Sorby Research Fund 127
    Southern Zone Research 120
    Space Ranging Research 121
    Space Research, National 153
    Symbols 127
    Theoretical and Applied Mechanics, National . . . 149
    Travelling Expenses 121
    Tyndall Mining Bequest 127
    Unesco 126
    Volcanological and Seismological Research 121
    Warren Research Fund 128

Common Seal and Deeds, Statute 182
Commonwealth Bursaries Committee 125
Commonwealth Bursaries Scheme 257, 288, 375
Congresses, Royal Society representatives (Council Report) . . . 365
Contributions, Annual, of Fellows, Statutes 170
Contributions, Annual, Consequences of non-payment, Statutes . . 170
Conway Evans Trust, President, a Trustee 157
Conway Fund 221
Conway Fund Account 394
Cook Trust, Ernest, Fund 222, 394
Cook Trust, Ernest, Research Fellows 268
Copley Medal, Conditions of Award 207
Copley Medal Fund Account (*see* Bakerian Fund)
Council and Officers 12
Council and Officers' Business (Royal Society office) . . . 385
Council and Officers, Election of, Quorum for 185
Council and Officers, Election of, Statutes 172
Council and Officers, Election to fill casual vacancies, Statutes . . 173
Council of Engineering Institutions (Council Report) . . . 279
Council of Engineering Institutions, representative 159
Council, Procedure in nomination of 198
Council Quorum 185

INDEX

	PAGE
Council Report	270
Council, Standing Orders of	186
Courtauld's Fund	222
Courtauld's Fund Account	394
Cranfield Institute of Technology: Court, representative	159
Croonian Fund Account	398
Croonian Lecture	213
Cruelty to Animals Act, Advisory Committee, representative	159
Crystallography, National Committee	141
Cumulative Research Fund	222, 394
Curl Bequest	245
Curl Bequest Account	397
Czechoslovak Academy of Sciences, Agreement	256
Dale, Henry, Research Professor	264, 267
Dale, Henry, Research Professorship	242
Darwin Fund	222
Darwin Fund Account	394
Darwin Medal, Conditions of Award	208
Data for Science and Technology, National Committee	150
Davy Medal, Conditions of Award	208
Davy Medal Fund Account	398
Deaths	105
Deaths, Statutes	171
Deeds and Common Seal, Statutes	182
Department of Education and Science, representatives on committees	159
Department of Energy (Council Report)	279
Department of Trade and Industry, Fundamental Standards Requirements Board, representative	159
Deposit Interest Account	399
Dewrance, Donation and Jodrell Fund	222
Dewrance, Donation and Jodrell Fund Account	394
Discussion Meetings, Standing Orders 6–9, 26	187, 192
Donation Fund (*see* Dewrance, Donation and Jodrell Fund)	
Dulwich College, Governor	159
East Europe (Council Report)	287
East Malling Research Station, Governor	159
Eddington Memorial Lectureship Fund, Trustee	159
Education Committee	115
Education (Council Report)	280
Educational Activities (Royal Society office)	388
Egypt, Agreement on exchanges	256
Egypt (Council Report)	289
Ejection of Fellows, Statutes	171
Embossed Scientific Books Fund	245
Embossed Scientific Books Fund Account	397
Endangered Species (Council Report)	286
Engineering and Technology, *ad hoc* Committee on (Council Report)	278
Essex University, Court, representative	159
Esso Award Committee	119
Esso Fund Account	398
Esso Medal, Conditions of Award	210

INDEX

	PAGE
Eton College, Governor	160
European Programme	254, 367
European Programme (Council Report)	287
European Programme Fellowships awarded (Council Report)	367
European Science Foundation (Council Report)	282
Exchange with Foreign Academies (Council Report)	288, 376
Executive Secretary, Statutes	176
Exeter University, representative	160
Expeditions Committee	115
Expeditions (Council Report)	277
Federal Council of Chemistry Fund	245
Federal Council of Chemistry Fund Account	397
Fee Reduction Fund	245
Fee Reduction Fund Account	397

FELLOWS (*see also under* Candidates)—

	PAGE
Admission of, Statutes	168
Date of Election of, Statutes	166
Death or Recess of, Statutes	171
Deceased	105
Ejection, Causes and Form of, Statutes	171
Elected	106
Election of, Quorum for Meeting	185
Election of, Statutes	162
List of	13
Number of	106
Obligation to be Subscribed, Statutes	169
Payments, Statutes	170
Register of, Statutes	171
Restraint of Dividends to, Statutes	183
Royal Society office	385
Special Election of, Statutes	167
Fellowship (Research) Appointments	267
Ferrier Fund Account	398
Ferrier Lecture	213
Field Studies Council, representative	160
Finance Committee	115
Fisher, Sir Ronald, Memorial Committee of Great Britain, representative	160
Fleck Fund	223
Fleck Fund Account	394
Florey Fellow	268
Florey Fund	223, 394
Folley Fund	224, 394
Foreign Academies, Exchanges with (Council Report)	288, 376

FOREIGN MEMBERS—

	PAGE
List of	100
Statutes	168, 169
Foreign Secretary, Statutes	176
Forsyth Funds	224
Forsyth Funds Accounts	394
Foulerton Funds	224

INDEX

	PAGE
Foulerton Funds Accounts	394
Foulerton Gift Research Fellow	268
Foulerton Research Professor	267
Freshwater Biological Association, representative	160
Gabb (George) Lecture Fund	214
Gabb Fund Account	398
Gassiot Committee	115
Gassiot Committee (Council Report)	273, 364
Gassiot Committee: Ministry of Defence Account	397
Gassiot Fund	225
Gassiot Fund Account	394
General Candidates Committee	113
General Purposes Accounts	392
General Research Fund	225
General Research Fund Account	394
General Reserve Fund Account	393
General Travel Fund (*see* Royal Society General Travel Fund)	
Genetic manipulation (Council Report)	279
Geodesy and Geophysics National Committee	142
Geodynamics National Committee	151
Geographical Congress Fund	246
Geographical Congress Fund Account	397
Geography National Committee	144
Geology National Committee	145
George Fund	225
George Fund Account	394
Gifts and Bequests, Memorandum	10
Gifts to the Society (Council Report)	295
Global Atmospheric Research Programme, National Committee	154
Goodall Lecture Committee, President, representative	157
Gore Fund	225
Gore Fund Account	394
Government Grants (*see* Parliamentary Grant)	
Grants for Travelling Expenses, regulations	252
Great Britain/China Committee, representative	160
Gunning Fund	225
Gunning Fund Account	394
Handley Fund	226, 394
Harrow School, Governor	160
Hartley, Sir Harold, Lecture Committee, representatives	160
Hatfield Memorial Lectureship Committee, representatives	160
Head Bequest Committee	116
Head Fund	226
Head Fund Account	395
Head Research Fellow	267
Henry Dale Research Professorship (*see* Dale, Henry)	
Henry Head Research Fellow (*see* Head Research Fellow)	
Heriot-Watt University: General Convocation, representative	160
Hill, Maurice, Fund	226
Hill, Maurice, Fund Account	395
History of Science Account	399

INDEX

	PAGE
History of Science (Council Report)	384
History of Science, National Committee	146
Hooke Committee	116
Horace Le Marquand and Dudley Bigg Research Fellow	268
Horace Le Marquand and Dudley Bigg Trust	227
Horace Le Marquand and Dudley Bigg Trust Account	395
House Management (Royal Society office)	386
Hughes Medal, Conditions of Award	208
Hughes Medal Fund Account	398
Hull University, representative	160
Hungarian Academy of Sciences, Agreement	256
Hunterian Museum, President, a Trustee	157
Hydrological Sciences, National Committee	154
Hydrographic services (Council Report)	279
Imperial Cancer Research Fund, representatives	160
Imperial College of Science and Technology, representative	160
India, Agreement on exchanges	256
India (Council Report)	290
India, exchanges (Royal Society office)	388
Industrial Activities Committee	116
Industrial Activities Committee (Council Report)	279
Institute of Cancer Research, Royal Cancer Hospital, representative	160
Institutions on which the Society is represented	157
International Associations, etc. (*see* Parliamentary Grant)	
International Biological Programme Account	399
International Centre of Insect Physiology and Ecology, National Committee	154
International Centre of Insect Physiology and Ecology (International Committee), representative	160
International Centre of Insect Physiology and Ecology (Council Report)	285
International Congresses (Council Report)	365
International Council for Bird Preservation, representatives	160
International Council of Scientific Unions	131
International Council of Scientific Unions (Council Report)	283
International Council of Scientific Unions National Committee	136
International Fellowship Scheme, Account	399
International Geological Correlation Programme, National Committee	155
International Institute for Applied Systems Analysis Account	397
International Institute for Applied Systems Analysis (Council Report)	286
International Institute for Applied Systems Analysis, National Committee	155
International Institute for Applied Systems Analysis, representative	160
International Nature Conservation (Council Report)	286
International Relations Account	399
International Relations (Council Report)	282
International Relations (Royal Society office)	387
International Relations Committee	116
International Seismological Centre (Governing Council), representative	160
International Seismological Centre Account	399
International Unions	131
International Wildfowl Research Institute, representative	160
Investment Advisory Committee	117

	PAGE
Investment of Moneys, Statutes	174
Iran (Council Report)	289
Israel Academy of Sciences and Humanities, Programme	256
Israel Academy of Sciences and Humanities Scientific Exchanges Account	396
Israel Academy Programme (Council Report)	288
Israel Academy, Visiting Research Professorships	260
Jaffé Donation Fellows	267
Jaffé Fund	226
Jaffé Fund Account	395
Japan, Agreement on exchange visits	256
Japan exchanges (Council Report)	290
Japan exchanges (Royal Society office)	388
Jenner Museum Trust, representative	161
Jodrell Fund (*see* Dewrance, Donation and Jodrell Fund)	
Johnston (E. Alan), Fund	227
Johnston (E. Alan), Fund Account	395
Johnston (E. Alan), Lawrence and Moseley Fellow	267
Joint Mathematical Council of the United Kingdom, representative	161
Joule Fund	227
Joule Fund Account	395
Journal Books, Statutes	181
Jungfraujoch Research Station, representatives	161
Keck and Knowles Fund	246
Keck and Knowles Fund Account	397
King's School, Grantham, Governor	161
Knowles Memorial Fund (*see* Keck and Knowles Fund)	
Lanchester Polytechnic (Board of Governors), representative	161
Latin America (Council Report)	290, 377
Latin American Programme	256
Lawes Agricultural Trust Committee, representatives	161
Lawrence Fund	227
Lawrence Fund Account	395
Lawrence Research Fellow (*see* Johnston, E. Alan)	
Learned and Professional Society Publishers Association, representative	161
Leathem Fund (*see* General Research Fund)	
Le Bel Fund (*see* General Research Fund)	
Lecture Funds	213, 398
Lecturers, Procedure of appointment	201, 213
Lectures (Council Report)	273
Lectures, 1976	216
Leeuwenhoek Lecture	214
Legacies (*see* Gifts)	
Le Marquand and Dudley Bigg Research Fellow	268
Le Marquand and Dudley Bigg Trust	227
Le Marquand and Dudley Bigg Trust Account	395
Leverhulme Visiting Professorships	259
Leverhulme Studentships	261
Leverhulme Studentships Committee	119
Leverhulme Medal, Conditions of Award	209
Libraries Assistance Account	399

	PAGE
Library Committee	117
Library (Council Report)	280
Library, Regulations	217
Library (Royal Society office)	386
Library, Statutes	182
Life Compositions, Statutes	170
Lindemann Fellowships Selection Committee, representatives	161
Lister Institute, representative	161
Liverpool University Court, representative	161
Locke Research Fellows	268
Locke Research Fund	228
Locke Research Fund Account	394
London School of Hygiene and Tropical Medicine, representatives	161
Loughborough University of Technology, Court, representative	161
Mackinnon Fund	228
Mackinnon Fund Account	395
MacRobert Award, Selection Committee, representatives	161
Marine Biological Association, representative	161
Mathematical Education Committee	123
Mathematics, National Committee	146
Mechanics, Theoretical and Applied, National Committee	149

MEDALS—
Adjudication of, Procedure of Council	200
Awarded in 1976	211
Conditions of Award	208
Funds	208
Funds Accounts	398
Medical Research Council, Assessor	161
Medical Research Fund Account	395
Medical Research Fund (Anonymous)	228
Medical Sciences Research Committee	119

MEETINGS—
Admission of Strangers, Statute	176
Anniversary, Quorum	185
Anniversary, Statutes	178
Conduct of, Statutes	178
Conduct of (S.O. 1)	186
(Council Report)	273
Days, Statutes	177
Discussion, Standing Orders 6–9 and 26	187, 192
Ordinary, Business of, Statutes	177
Ordinary, Cancellation of (S.O. 5)	187
Ordinary, Duration of Session, Statutes	177
Ordinary, Procedure at, Statutes	178
Ordinary, Procedure at (S.O. 2)	186
Ordinary, Quorum	185
Ordinary, Standing Orders	186
Ordinary, Statutes	177
Royal Society office	385

INDEX

	PAGE
MEETINGS—*continued*	
Special General, Statutes	178
Special General, proceedings, confidential (S.O. 9)	187
Mendel Fellow	268
Mendel Fellowship Committee	118
Mendel Fellowship Fund	228
Mendel Fellowship Fund Account	395
Messel Fund	230
Messel Fund Account	394
Mexico, Agreement on exchanges	256
Mond Fund	230
Mond Fund Account	395
Moseley Fund	231
Moseley Fund Account	395
Mullard Award Committee	119
Mullard Medal, Conditions of Award	209
Mullard Medal Fund Account	398
Murray (John) Research Fund	231
Murray (John) Research Fund Account	395
Murray (John) Travelling Studentship	269
Napier Fund	232
Napier Fund Account	395
Napier Research Professor	232, 264, 267
Naples Zoological Station Account	395
Naples Zoological Station Committee	124
National Committees	136
National Committee for Photogrammetry, representative	161
National Electronics Council, representative	162
National Physical Laboratory, Advisory Board, representatives	162
National Vegetable Research Station, Governing Body, representative	162
Natural Environment Research Council, Assessor	162
Newton Letters Committee	118
Nutritional Sciences, National Committee	147
Obligation to be Subscribed by Fellows, Statutes	169
Oceanic Research, National Committee	151
Office staff	12, 385
Officers and Council, Election of, Quorum for	185
Officers and Council, Election of, Statutes	172
Officers and Council, Election to fill casual vacancies, Statutes	173
Officers and Council for 1976–1977	12
Officers, Past	7
Open University, Advisory Committee on Studies in Education, representative	162
Open University, Council, representative	162
Optics Fund	246
Optics Fund Account	397
Ordnance Survey Committee	118
Organization of Royal Society office	385
Origin of the Royal Society	9
Overseas Academies, relations with, Account	399
Overseas Visiting Professorships	259

INDEX 415

	PAGE
Overseas Visiting Professorships (Council Report)	288
Overseas Visiting Professorships Account	396
Papers and Books of Society, Statutes	181

PAPERS (*see also* Philosophical Transactions *and* Proceedings)—

Abstracts (S.O. 33, 48)	193, 195
Associate Editors	107, 193
Committee of, Quorum, Statutes	179
Committee of, Standing Orders	196
Committee of, Statutes	179
Communication of	178
(Council Report)	275
Length of, for *Proceedings* (S.O. 25, 39)	192, 194
Original, the property of the Society	178
Publication of, Standing Orders	193
Publication of, Statutes	179
Reading of (S.O. 2, 49)	186, 196
Referees (S.O. 40–47)	194, 195
Register of, Statutes	181
Suitable for *Transactions* or *Proceedings* (S.O. 25, 26)	192
Summary to be furnished (S.O. 33)	193
Summary to be published (S.O. 48)	195
Parliamentary Grant (Council Report)	293
Parliamentary Grant (Royal Society office)	387

PARLIAMENTARY GRANT-IN-AID—

General Description	156
Account	399
Regulations (History of Science)	205
Regulations (Scientific Investigations)	202
Regulations (Scientific Publications)	204
Regulations (International Relations)	206
Scientific Investigations, Allocation 1975, 1976	378
Scientific Investigations, Government Grant Boards	129
Scientific Publications, Allocation 1975, 1976	383
Scientific Publications Board	130
Parsons Memorial Fund	246
Parsons Memorial Fund, Account	397
Past Officers	7
Paterson, Clifford, Fund Account	398
Paterson, Clifford, Lecture	215
Patterson Fund	232
Patterson Fund Account	395
Paul Fund Regulations	251
Paul Instrument Fund Committee	124
Payments out of Society's Fund, Statutes	174
Payments to be made by Fellows, Statutes	170
Pedler Fund	232
Pedler Fund Account	395
Pension Fund	246
Pension Fund Account	397
Percy Sladen Memorial Fund, representative	162

	PAGE
Petavel Fund	247
Petavel Fund Account	397
Pharmacology, National Committee	147

Philosophical Transactions (see also PAPERS)—
- Abstracts (S.O. 33, 48) 193, 195
- Associate Editors 107, 193
- Council Report 278
- Delivery of, to Fellows 181
- Fellows entitled to free copies 180
- Papers suitable for (S.O. 26, 28, 39) 192, 194
- Separate Papers (S.O. 30) 192
- Series A and B (S.O. 30) 192
- Standing Orders 192
- Statutes 180
- Time-limit for ordering 181

Physics Education Committee	125
Physics National Committee	148
Physiological Sciences National Committee	148
Pickering Fund	232
Pickering Fund Account	395
Pickering Research Fellows	268
Poland, Agreement	256
Postal address	8
President, Statutes	173
Press, Communications to (S.O. 9)	187
Primary Communication Research Centre, University of Leicester, representative	162
Problems of the Environment, National Committee	152

Proceedings (see also PAPERS)—
- Abstracts (S.O. 33, 48) 193, 195
- Associate Editors 107, 193
- Council Report 278
- Delivery of, to Fellows 181
- Fellows entitled to free copies 180
- Length of Papers (S.O. 25, 39) 192, 194
- Papers suitable for (S.O. 25, 28, 29) 192
- Series A and B (S.O. 27) 192
- Standing Orders 192
- Statutes 180

Professorships, Appointments	267
Professorships, Overseas Visiting	259
Publication Fund (see Fee Reduction Fund)	
Publications (Council Report)	275
Publications of the Royal Society	219
Publications (Royal Society office)	386, 387
Publications Grant (see Parliamentary Grant)	
Quorum of Council	185
Quorum of Government Grant Boards	203
Quorum of Meetings of the Society	185
Quorum of Sectional Committees (S.O. 14)	190

INDEX

	PAGE
Radcliffe Trust Account	395
Radio Science National Committee	149
Rating Assistance Account	399
Reading of Papers (S.O. 2, 49)	186, 196
Recent Past Officers	7
Receptions (Council Report)	298
Reckitt (Albert) Research Fund	233
Reckitt (Albert) Research Fund Account	395
Rent and Repairs Account	399
Referees for Papers (S.O. 40–47)	194, 195
Register of Fellows, Statutes	181
Register of Papers, Statutes	181
Repairs and Maintenance account	393
Representation by the Society (Council Report)	296
Representation on outside bodies (S.O. 61)	198
Representatives appointed to institutions	157
Research Appointments	267
Research Appointments (Council Report)	270
Research Appointments, regulations	265
Research Appointments (Royal Society office)	386
Research Funds	221
Research Funds Accounts	394–396
Research Funds Balances	394–396
Research Professorships, Parliamentary Grant-in-aid	156, 262
Research Professors, regulations	263
Research reports (Council Report)	300
Romania, Agreement	256
Rosenheim Fund	233, 395
Rosenheim Research Fellow	268
Rosse Fund	233
Rosse Fund Account	395
Royal Anthropological Institute: Blood Group Committee, representative	162
Royal Family, Election of Members of, Statute	167
Royal Geographical Society Expeditions Committee, representative	162
Royal Medals, Conditions of Award	208
Royal Society Commonwealth Bursaries Committee	125
Royal Society Commonwealth Bursaries Scheme	257, 288, 375
Royal Society and Commonwealth Foundation Commonwealth Bursaries Scheme Account	396
Royal Society and Nuffield Foundation Commonwealth Bursaries Scheme Account	396
Royal Society/Council of Engineering Institutions Education Committee	126
Royal Society European Programme	254
Royal Society General Travel Fund	247
Royal Society General Travel Fund Account	397
Royal Society—Inter-University Council Visiting Professorships Account	396
Royal Society—Israel Academy Programme	256
Royal Society—Israel Academy Scientific Exchanges Account	396
Royal Society—Israel Academy Visiting Research Professorships Scheme	260
Royal Society Latin American Programme	256
Royal Society Leverhulme Visiting Professorships	259

INDEX

	PAGE
Royal Society Leverhulme Studentships	261
Royal Society Leverhulme Studentships Account	395
Royal Society Leverhulme Studentships Committee	119
Royal Society Leverhulme Visiting Professorships Account	396
Royal Society Research Appointments, regulations	265
Royal Society Research Fellows	267
Royal Society Research Professors	262, 263, 267
Royal Society Research Professorships Account	399
Royal Society Research Professorships, regulations	263
Royal Society Scientific Information Research Fellowships	262
Royal Society Travel Fund for Non-Fellows	247
Royal Society Travel Fund for Non-Fellows and L. J. Mordell Travel Fund Account	397
Royal Society Unesco Committee	126
Royal Society Visiting Professorships	259
Royal Veterinary College, representative	162
Rugby School, Governor	162
Rumford Medal, Conditions of Award	207
Rumford Medal Fund Account	398
Rutherford Memorial Committee	119
Rutherford Memorial Fund	233
Rutherford Memorial Fund Account	396
Rutherford Memorial Lecture	214
Rutherford Scholars	268
Sadgrove Fund	234, 396
Sainsbury Fund	234, 396
Sainsbury, J., Research Fellows	268
Salford University: Council, representative	162
Schools, Colleges and Universities, representatives	157
Science Research Council, assessor and representatives on boards and committees	162
Science/Technology Education Account	399
Scientific Exchanges (anon.) Account	396
Scientific Information Committee	120
Scientific Information Fellowships Account	399
Scientific Information Research Fellows	262, 268
Scientific Investigations Grant (*see* Parliamentary Grant)	
Scientific Publications Board	130
Scientific Publications Grant (*see* Parliamentary Grant)	
Scientific Radio Fund	247
Scientific Radio Fund Account	397
Scientific Relief Fund	248
Scientific Relief Fund (Council Report)	297
Scientific Relief Fund Account	397
Scientific Relief Committee	120
Scientific Relief Fund Regulations	248
Scientific Research in Schools Account	397
Scientific Research in Schools (Council Report)	282
Scientific Research in Schools Committee	126
Scientific Research in Schools Fund	249
Scott Fund	234

INDEX

	PAGE
Scott Fund Account.	396
Scott Polar Research Institute Account	399
Scott Polar Research Institute Committee, representative	162
Seal of the Society, Statutes	182
Secretaries, Statutes	175
Secretary, Executive, Statutes	176
Secretary, Foreign, Statutes	176
Sectional Committees	110
Sectional Committees, Appointment of (S.O. 10–14)	188–191
Sectional Committees, Business of (S.O. 11)	188
Sectional Committees, Dates of Meetings (S.O. 20)	191
Sectional Committees, Elections to fill casual vacancies (S.O. 18)	191
Sectional Committees, Members of Council (S.O. 15)	190
Sectional Committees, Membership (S.O. 14)	190
Sectional Committees, Minutes (S.O. 23)	191
Sectional Committees, Procedure at (S.O. 22)	191
Sectional Committees, Quorum (S.O. 14)	190
Sectional Committees, Quorum, Procedure without (S.O. 21)	191
Sectional Committees, Retirement of Members (S.O. 16, 17)	191
Sectional Committees, Standing Committee (S.O. 24)	191
Sectional Committees, Standing Orders	188
Session, Duration of, Statutes	177
Shrewsbury School, Governor	163
Simonsen Fund	249
Simonsen Fund Account	397
Smithson Fund	234
Smithson Fund Account	396
Smithson Research Fund Committee	127
Smithson Research Fellow	269
Smithson Research Fellowship Regulations	234
Soane Museum, representative	163
Social Functions (Council Report)	298
Social Science Research Council, Assessor	163
Soirée Committee	120
Soirées (Royal Society office)	386
Solar-Terrestrial Physics National Committee	152
Sorby Fund	236
Sorby Fund Account	396
Sorby Research Fund Committee	127
Sorby Research Fellow	269
Sorby Research Fellowship Regulations	236
Southern Zone Research Committee	120
Space Ranging Research Committee	121
Space Research, National Committee	153
Special Election of Fellows, Statutes	167
Special Funds	244
Special Funds Accounts	397–8
Special Funds Balances	397–8
Special General Meetings, Statutes	178
Staff	12
Standing Conference on Schools' Science and Technology, representatives	163
Standard Weights and Measures, Custodians	156

	PAGE
Standing Orders of Council	186
Standing Orders, Statutes	183
Statute Book, Statutes	181
Statutes, Interpretation of	184
Statutes, Making, Amending or Repealing	183
Statutes of the Society	164
Stead Fund	250
Stead Fund Account	397
Stothert Research Fellows	268
Stothert Research Fund	238
Stothert Research Fund Account	396
Strangers, Admission to Meetings, Statutes	177
Strathclyde University (General Convocation), representatives	163
Studd Fund	239
Studd Fund Account	396
Study Groups Account	399
Study Groups, Royal Society (Council Report)	278
Study Groups (Royal Society office)	389
Surrey, University of: Court, representative	163
Sylvester Medal, Conditions of Award	208
Sylvester Medal Fund Account	398
Symbols Committee	127
Telephone and Telex	8
Tercentenary Lectures	214
Theoretical and Applied Mechanics, National Committee	149
Title deeds, charge of, Statutes	175
Tomes Fund	239
Tomes Fund Account	396
Trans-Antarctic Association (U.K. Advisory Committee), representative	163
Travel Fund for Non-Fellows (*see* Royal Society Travel Fund)	
Travel grants (Parliamentary Grant) Account	399
Travelling Expenses Committee	121
Travelling Expenses (Council Report)	294
Travelling Expenses Fund	250
Travelling Expenses Fund Account	397
Travelling Expenses Grants, regulations	252
Travelling Expenses (Royal Society office)	387
Treasurer, Statutes	174
Trevelyan Fund (*see* General Research Fund)	
Tyndall Fund	239
Tyndall Fund Account	396
Tyndall Mining Bequest Committee	127
Unesco Committee	126
Unesco (Council Report)	283
Unilever—Brazilian Account	396
United Kingdom Committee for International Nature Conservation, representative	163
United Kingdom Coordinating Committee for the International Phase of Ocean Drilling, representative	163

INDEX

	PAGE
United States National Academy of Sciences (Council Report)	291
Uppingham School, Trustee	163
U.S.S.R. Academy of Sciences, agreement on cooperation	256
Venezuela, Agreement on exchanges	256
Vice-Presidents, Statute	174
Victor Horsley Memorial Fund, President, representative	157
Visiting Professorships, Overseas	259
Volcanological and Seismological Research Committee	121
Walcott Fund, representative	163
Wales, University of: Court, representative	163
Warren Research Fellows	269
Warren Research Fund	240
Warren Research Fund Account	401
Warren Research Fund Committee	128
Warren Research Fund (Council Report)	270, 273
Warren Research Fund Regulations	240
Warwick University (Court), representative	163
Wates Foundation Account	393
Wates IUPAC Account	396
Weights and Measures, Custodianship	156
Weir Foundation Account	396
Weir Fund	242
Weir Research Fellow	268
Wellcome Research Fund	242
Wellcome Research Fund Account	396
Westminster School, Governor	163
Wilkins Lecture	214
Wilkins Lecture Fund Account	398
Winchester College, Governor	163
Wintringham Fund	250
Wintringham Fund Account	398
Wolfson Research Professor	243, 264, 267
Wolfson Research Professorship Fund	243
Wolfson Research Professorship Fund Account	396
Wolfson Research Professorship Fund, Trustees	163
Woolsthorpe Manor Committee of Management, representatives	163
World Energy Conference, representative	163
Yarrow Research Fund	243
Yarrow Research Fund Account	394
Year Book (S.O. 31)	193
York University (Court), representative	163
Yugoslavia, Agreement on Exchanges	256